How Cooking Works

For Erik, Noah, and Stephen, hearty trenchermen and fine cooks

How Cooking Works

The Indispensable Kitchen Handbook

Sylvia Rosenthal
and Fran Shinagel
Illustrated by Cal Sacks and Ray Skibinski

Macmillan Publishing Co. Inc.
New York

Collier Macmillan Publishers
London

A Tree Communications Edition

Macmillan Publishing Co., Inc.
866 Third Avenue, New York, N.Y. 10022
Collier Macmillan Canada, Ltd.

Library of Congress Number LC 81-3685
ISBN 0-02-605090-0

CREATED AND PRODUCED BY
Tree Communications, Inc.
250 Park Avenue South
New York, New York 10003

Carol Hamoy, Art Director
Sara Bowman, Format Designer
Amy Gateff, Picture Editor
Yaron Fidler, Production Artist

Printed in the United States of America

10   9   8   7   6   5   4   3   2   1

Contents

Foreword

This book was prompted by the questions that beset virtually everyone who cooks. Why are some vegetables cooked covered and others uncovered? Why must some meats be cooked slowly in a liquid, tightly covered, while others are given a quick turn under the broiler? And how do we know which method to use? Why do we cream butter and sugar for a cake batter? Why is it so important to beat egg whites until "stiff but not dry"? What happens if we overbeat them? Why did the mayonnaise separate? Can we rescue it? Why do bone-in roasts need less time to cook than boneless ones? Why are some meats rubbery and tough even after long immersion in boiling water? Why must we brown or sear meats? Why does fish need such careful timing? The list of whys stretches on and on, a puzzle to even experienced cooks.

The answers in the pages that follow will help you to understand not only what you are doing but, more important, why you are doing it. There is no doubt that great chefs, like the great artists in every field, are born inspired and touched by genius, but cooking is an acquired skill for most of us. Good cooking is the sum of many simple operations, and the more we know about them (and the more we cook), the easier it becomes, making the time we spend in the kitchen enjoyable and relaxing, crowned with the pride and satisfaction of preparing fine food for appreciative friends and family.

The same cooking processes are used over and over. The ingredients vary, but the basic techniques remain the same. Once you have mastered them, you will find that you are less dependent upon recipes for many food preparations, except as a reminder of ingredients you may have forgotten. We hope that ultimately, you will cook not by rote, according to a printed direction, but out of your understanding of the ingredients and how they should be handled to bring them to the peak of their flavor. The recipe will then become an incentive and general guide, rather than a rigid formula to be followed to the last detail. Precise measurements are critical in pastries, soufflés, and some sauces, but in soups or stews or roasts, it doesn't really make much difference whether you use a large onion when the recipe calls for a medium-size one (the bigger one may be even better), or whether you double the amount of garlic or omit it because of the way your family feels about garlic.

As you learn, you will develop a sense of what can be modified or changed; which ingredients are essential and which optional. The cook who understands the function of each ingredient feels free to make substitutions and uses judgment in varying the amounts. An ingredient may enhance a dish, but its omission won't necessarily damage it. If you don't have a crunchy green pepper, how about another vegetable with crunch—celery, zucchini, carrot? You don't have quite enough port wine for the dessert sauce? Fill in with some orange juice. Some fine discoveries have been made when a clever cook ran out of an ingredient. No recipe is ever really final; each person who makes it brings a bit of individuality and spontaneity to its creation. You have only to consider some great recipes that, like folksongs, have traveled around the world, absorbing local tastes and traditions, to appreciate that there is indeed more than one way to prepare a dish.

You will notice that we do not include specific amounts of salt and pepper in most of our recipes, except those in which the amount of salt is important to the chemistry of the recipe. With the growing awareness of the possible adverse effect of excessive salt in a hypertension-prone society, we chose to leave the amount of salt up to you. Season to taste.

Fashions in foods are as trendy and changeable as those governing skirt lengths and home furnishings. In the late fifties and sixties, all manner of convenience foods flooded the market and were eagerly snapped up by a not too discriminating or well-informed public. Tastes gradually grew more sophisticated as ever-growing numbers of world travelers returned home with a new appreciation of foreign cuisines and ethnic foods. By the mid-seventies, exotic spiced foods from all over the world captured the interest and imagination of the public. Dijon and Düsseldorf mustard replaced the yellow ball-park variety and the wok became as ubiquitous as the barbecue. The culinary world became more concerned with nutrition and ways of coping with rising food costs.

Today we are in the midst of a revival of freshly made foods, free of chemical additives and artificial colors and flavors. Fussy, pretentious food is out. Food that is disarmingly simple and honest, in which the taste of each ingredient is highlighted, is in. True elegance stems from first-rate ingredients, carefully and simply prepared. This kind of cooking will never go out of style.

There are more men and young people involved in the preparation of food than ever before, and they bring a new viewpoint and enthusiasm to it. The days of the old-fashioned English squire, swollen with food and sitting over his walnuts and wine, are no more. These days he is more likely to be found in the kitchen tossing the salad.

We have assembled in this book a great variety of recipes that range from basic dishes, such as a perfect omelet, to hearty family fare, buffet and company dishes, and a generous sprinkling of ethnic foods to add interest to your daily meal planning.

Since good cooking begins at the market with careful selection of ingredients, we have devoted considerable space to guides for marketing: what to look for, how to judge freshness, how to store foods at home. The vegetable and fruit chapters include descriptions of just about everything you are likely to find at a well-stocked green-grocer's, with suggestions for basic ways to prepare the produce.

It is always best to set off on your shopping expeditions with as few preconceived ideas as possible and let your menu planning take shape according to whatever is freshest, best, in season, and perhaps even on sale. Take a marketing list with you if you like, but do as the professional chefs do—let the ingredients dictate the menu rather than the other way around. Don't rush your shopping; the time needed to carve radish roses or flute mushrooms might be better spent selecting the radishes and the mushrooms.

Do look over the introductory text in each chapter before you begin a recipe so that you will be familiar with the techniques that are called for. There are some general rules that would be space-consuming and tiresome if repeated in each recipe.

Don't be discouraged if each meal doesn't turn out dazzling in its perfection. Rockets and shooting stars don't go off with stopwatch precision in every situation, and a failure here and there has occurred in every cook's life. Occasionally you can blame it on the weather, as when a damp day affects the flour and your usual towering fluff of a cake just sits on your best cake plate like a heavy lump. It goes without saying that the more experienced you are, the fewer chances there are for failure, but bear in mind that even four-star restaurants have their off days.

Cooking can really be fun, and to make the most of it, get involved with your materials, just as gardeners and painters do. Smell, feel, and taste the ingredients. You cannot get involved from a distance. Think of your kitchen as a kind of fortress—a warm, aroma-filled place where you can flush out anxieties and beat vexations into oblivion in a flurry of kneading, mixing, chopping, and stirring.

We hope that you find this book a basic tool and a means to make an important daily task simpler, more efficient, and more enjoyable.

We are deeply grateful to Joan Whitman, our editor, for her guidance, wisdom, good taste, and never-failing patience and good humor while this work was in progress. We also wish to express warmest thanks to Amy Gateff, Louise Gikow, Valerie Marchant, Dennis Southers, and Barnet Friedman for their most important contributions.

Sylvia Rosenthal
Fran Shinagel

1
Cooking Techniques and Tools

Cooking is a mixture of common sense, experience, knowledge of basic cooking techniques, and a touch of imagination. It is more illusion than reality that the variety of dishes that comes out of creatively managed kitchens is infinite. The fact is that, however different they appear to be, many dishes are variations on a theme and are based on identical cooking methods. Irish stew, Hungarian goulash, *blanquette de veau*, and chili have more in common than their diverse names would suggest.

Once you understand the basic cooking techniques, you will have the freedom to improvise, substitute ingredients, and create your own personal style of cooking. For example, some cuts of meat can be made juicy and tender only if they are cooked long and slowly in a liquid—a process known as braising. With an understanding of braising, you know that you will want some flavoring vegetables such as onion, carrots, and celery; and for the liquid, either stock or broth, wine, beer, cider, tomato purée, or perhaps a combination of some of these. The final flavor will depend on the vegetables and liquids you have chosen to use. As long as you have employed the proper cooking technique, the meat will be tasty, succulent, and tender, without your having slavishly followed a written recipe.

For cooking to be the effortless, fulfilling, and creative activity that it can be, you also need to understand the tools at your disposal. Good equipment can't guarantee spectacular food, but the business of cooking is surely pleasanter,

more efficient, and easier with the right tools. However, don't overlook the best tool of all—your hands. Get into the habit of using your hands freely in preparing food. A well-known cook who learned her skills from her grandmother tells of the elderly lady's admonition: "If you're afraid to get your fingers in the food, then go make lace." Few utensils can do a better job than your hands in assembling a meat loaf, folding beaten egg white into a cake batter or a soufflé mixture, or mixing a pastry dough. Hands are versatile and sensitive. With experience, you will be able to tell just by the feel of the food when it has had enough manipulation or exposure to heat. Experienced cooks can judge how well done a piece of meat or poultry is by touching it. And then there are some foods, such as onions, that are better when they are chopped by hand than when subjected to the speed and vigor of a machine. Food processors quickly reduce onions to an almost liquid state, which means they will not brown properly. Mechanical devices are not likely to completely replace skillful, experienced hands.

Another important part of a good cook's stock in trade is an easy familiarity with the aromatics and seasonings that can turn pedestrian ingredients into a mouth-watering dish. In this chapter you will find descriptions of the flavoring vegetables, spices, and other bits of kitchen magic that can bring an extra dimension of taste and interest to the simplest preparation.

Heat

If we were to list in order of importance all the essentials needed for the process of cooking, heat would surely be number one. It performs minor miracles on food, changing its

appearance and affecting its texture, flavor, and color. It softens and tenderizes, making food digestible and releasing its aromas. Heat thickens foods; it turns solids into liquids and transforms liquids into solids. It can convert thick balls of paste into golden puffs of crisp, airy lightness. But, used improperly, it can make a mess of the most beautiful ingredients—a fact not unknown to even the most experienced cook.

The effect of heat on food has been recognized since earliest times. Anthropologists tell us that our club-toting ancestors were familiar with the process. We could speculate endlessly on how these early people first discovered the difference heat made on their usual fare of meat, grains, and the tough shoots of plants. Perhaps a group of hunters, dragging their day's haul of animal carcasses, stopped to warm themselves over a blaze set off by a bolt of lightning and a carcass slipped into the fire by accident. Or they might have come across the burned bodies of animals after a forest fire. Impelled by curiosity or hunger, they tasted the flesh and decided that roasted meat was easier to chew than raw meat. And even though they were not aware of it, the cooked meat made them healthier, because the fire destroyed some of the parasites in the food.

However, these early barbecues had nothing to do with cooking for palatability. Foods to titillate the palate and please the eye were many millenniums away. It took a long time for people to realize that food could be pleasurable as well as life-sustaining.

If the use of fire was man's first great chemical discovery, making cooking utensils of baked clay was the second and a step forward from the earlier practices of cooking strips of meat on a hot rock or using a hollowed-out stone for a pot. But the clay pots, however useful, were fragile and porous and in time were replaced by metal ones. The discovery of metal, which became part of every aspect of man's civilized life from enduring works of art to weapons for warfare, was a boon for the cook. Metal pots, unlike those made of clay, neither leaked nor

shattered. Finally, burning began to give way to cooking.

The sources of heat progressed from stacks of rocks surrounding a fire to open fireplaces equipped with hooks or wooden bars on which pots of food could be suspended. It was a slow business, and impatient and resourceful cooks would often drop a heated rock into the stew—the equivalent of our increasing the heat in automatic ranges to speed things up.

Stoves made of clay, tile, and earthenware were in use in parts of Europe as early as Roman times, but it was not until late in the fifteenth century that cast-iron stoves were first made in Europe. They were used primarily for heating and few people regarded them as a cooking device. The fireplace was supreme in that department and the stove, which was positioned near it, was merely a supplement. The stovepipe was connected to the fireplace chimney and provided the channel through which the smoke could escape.

The fireplace remained the primary heat source until about the middle of the nineteenth century, when coal-burning ranges with removable lids came into general use. Top-of-the-stove cooking was thus possible and the back-breaking tasks of feeding open fires and manipulating heavy cooking vessels were at an end. Heat could be channeled from the fire to the food inside the pot with comparative ease. This development was the one that set the scene for a major revolution in food preparation.

Today, of course, the wood-burning or coal-burning range has been largely superseded by a variety of cooking apparatuses using natural or manufactured gas, electricity, gasoline, or other fuels. Automatic devices set and control temperatures and cooking time with the precision of a perfectly programmed robot.

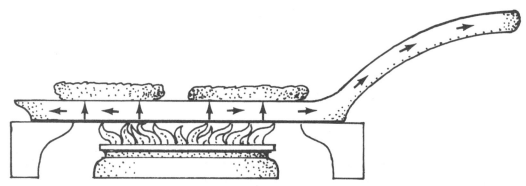

Heat flows, or is conducted, from a warmer area to a cooler one. It moves from the bottom of the pan, which is in direct contact with the heat source, to the sides, then to the end of the handle.

How Heat Works

Heat produces a chemical reaction in food. It has the effect of setting the food molecules in motion, and this agitation of the molecules causes the food to become tender and soft. Besides tenderizing, it thickens foods containing starch, such as sauces and puddings; it browns foods; and it leavens and firms baked products and egg mixtures. However, unless heat is carefully meted out and controlled, it can scorch or burn and rob the finest preparation of its optimum taste and texture.

Like other natural forces, heat has its own immutable pattern of behavior. It always moves from a warmer spot to a cooler one, and there are three different methods by which it moves— conduction, convection, and radiation.

Conduction
The metal handle of a saucepan that becomes too hot to hold even though the handle was not near the heat unit illustrates the process of

conduction. Heat flows—or is conducted—from a warmer area to a colder one when there is some substance through which it can travel. The heat is transferred to the handle through the pot itself. When you boil a vegetable in water, or fry a chicken in deep fat, or bake a pancake on a metal griddle, the heat is being transferred through conduction.

Convection
All the food in a covered pot will become cooked, even if only a small portion of it is immersed in liquid. This phenomenon is due to the process called convection. Steam or vapor forms and circulates in the covered pot, cooking the entire contents. Convection depends upon the fact that a liquid or gas becomes lighter when it is warmed and heavier when it is cooled. As the portion of the liquid nearest the source of heat becomes warm, it rises and pushes through the colder material. The colder portion then sinks, becomes heated, and rises, creating a flow called a convection current. Heated fat in a frying pan or heated air in an

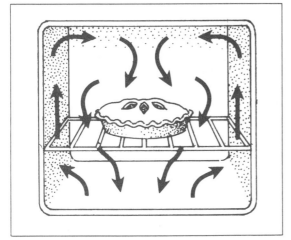

Circulating currents of hot air flow around the food in a heated oven. Hot gases rise and colder ones flow downward, giving center of oven the most uniform temperature.

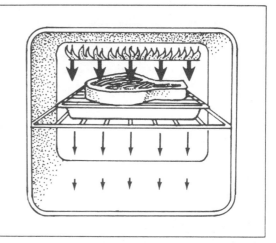

Broiling is cooking by radiant energy. The heat is at its most intense near the source. Foods should be broiled 2 to 5 inches from heat source; shorter distance for thin cuts, longer for thick.

oven are other examples of heat carried to food by convection.

Radiation

When we broil or toast food, or cook over hot coals on an outdoor grill, we are using the process called radiation. Unlike heat that travels through conduction or convection, radiated heat does not have to travel through material. The movement of heat in radiation is similar to the way in which light travels. The farther an object is from the source of radiant heat, the fewer rays it receives and the less it is heated. This is why food placed too close to the broiler flame will scorch; it will brown and cook through when it is a few inches away.

Cooking Methods

We can penetrate much of the mystique of what seems like a dizzying assortment of different cooking terms—broil, roast, simmer, sauté, fry,

poach, to mention just a few—if we understand that there are actually only two basic cooking methods. They are the dry- and moist-heat methods, and each of the various cooking terms can be pigeonholed under one or the other.

In dry-heat cooking, no water is added and the food is cooked uncovered so that evaporating moisture from the food itself can escape. Dry-heat cooking can be done on top of the stove or in the oven. Roasting, broiling, baking, pan-frying, and sautéeing are all classed as dry-heat cooking, as is deep-fat frying. This last may seem curious, but in deep-fat frying the food is in contact with hot oil, not hot water. The steam that is created from the food juices is forced into the fat and then out into the atmosphere.

In moist-heat cooking, the food cooks in liquid or by steam in a covered utensil. The steam may be created by the liquid in the food itself. Boiling, poaching, braising, pot roasting, stewing, and fricasseeing are moist-heat cookery methods. Many of these methods, such as braising and pot roasting, or stewing and fric-asseeing, differ only in the amount of liquid and vegetables used.

Many foods are adaptable and may be cooked by either dry heat or moist heat. You can bake a potato or boil it; sauté a young chicken or braise it; broil a fish or poach it. But there are others, principally cereals, grains, some root vegetables and fruits, and certain types of poultry and cuts of meat that dictate their own firm rules for how they shall be cooked. These are discussed in the appropriate chapters.

Following are brief descriptions of dry- and moist-heat cooking methods:

Dry-Heat Cooking Methods

Bake. To cook uncovered in an oven. The terms baking and roasting are the same: a baked ham is a roasted one and a roasted chicken is baked. Poultry, game birds, and tender cuts of meat may be cooked by this process. Vegetables and fruits that are high in moisture and contain sufficient cellulose (a carbohydrate that helps to make plant structures more rigid, and which we know as roughage) to hold their shape during cooking may also be baked successfully.

Barbecue. To grill over coals, or on a rotisserie. The term is also used to describe meat, fish, or poultry that is basted with a spicy sauce while it is cooking.

Broil. To expose foods, one side at a time, to a direct source of heat, such as an oven broiler, a campfire, or a gas, charcoal, or electric grill. The terms broiling and grilling are synonymous. Only the tenderest cuts of meat may be broiled, but it is highly successful with young chickens, fish, shellfish, and some vegetables and fruits.

Deep-Fat Frying. To cook food by

immersing it completely in hot fat. Any deep heavy kettle can serve for deep-fat frying. A wire basket in which foods can be lowered and raised is helpful, as are a slotted metal spoon and long-handled metal tongs. The kettle should be about half full of fat, enough to cover the food and allow it to move freely in the kettle and still leave ample room for the quick bubbling of the fat that takes place when food is added.

The temperature of the fat is important, for if the fat isn't hot enough to crust the food immediately, the food will be soaked with the fat. A frying thermometer is the best way to test the temperature of the fat. But you can test with a 1-inch cube of bread. When you think the fat has reached the proper temperature, drop in the bread cube and count slowly to 60, or use a timer for 60 seconds. If the cube browns in this time, the temperature will be about 375 degrees, which is satisfactory for most frying. If food requires higher or lower temperatures, it will be noted in the recipe. Butter and margarine are not suitable for deep-frying because of their low smoking points. Liquid oils or solid vegetable shortenings are recommended. (For more information about frying oils, see page 261.)

Foods for frying should be of uniform size so they will all take the same cooking time. They should be dry and at room temperature, not chilled. A light coating of flour or batter is used for most foods except potatoes. Doughnuts, fritters, and other batter foods will brown by themselves when placed in the hot fat bath, because of their egg and starch mixture.

Fry. To cook in fat over direct heat. See Deep-Fat Frying, Pan-Broil, Pan-Fry, Sauté, Stir-Fry.

Pan-Broil. To cook in a lightly greased and slightly preheated pan on top of the stove. This is a quick method suitable for lean or thin pieces of meat or fish that might be too dry if cooked under the broiler.

Pan-Fry. Synonymous with Pan-Broil.

Roast. See Bake.

Sauté. To cook in a skillet on top of the stove in a small amount of fat. The food is thin or minced and it is cooked rapidly over sufficient heat to sear it and prevent the loss of juices. Food to be sautéed should be at room temperature and dry on the surface. If it is too cold, it will lower the heat; if it is wet, it will not brown properly. Foods to be sautéed are frequently lightly floured or breaded. For most successful sautés, use clarified butter or a combination of butter and oil. The butter is for flavor; the oil to raise the smoking point so that the food will brown well without burning.

Stir-Fry. To fry foods quickly over high heat, stirring and tossing continuously. This method, basic in Chinese cooking, uses very little fat and is very fast. Foods must be shredded or thinly sliced. It is suitable for preparing vegetables, meat, poultry, and fish, alone or in combinations.

Moist-Heat Cooking Methods

Blanch. To pour boiling water over food as an aid to removing outer covering; to boil rapidly, uncovered, for a brief period as a preliminary cooking process in order to set color, to help preserve nutrients, or to retard enzyme action preparatory to canning and freezing. Precooking for a short time in boiling water is also called parboiling.

Boil. To heat a liquid until large bubbles rise to the surface in rapid succession and break. At sea level, water and other liquids boil at 212 degrees. Once the liquid has reached that

temperature, it won't get any hotter, regardless of how vigorously it is boiling. The potatoes won't soften any faster in water that surges like an erupting volcano than they will in liquid that forms into slow easy bubbles. (Cutting the potatoes in small pieces is the only way to shorten the cooking time.) The fast, furious boil known as a rolling boil is desirable only when you want to encourage evaporation, as in thickening and reducing sauces, or in making preserves. A rolling boil can actually toughen meats, discolor eggs, and do other unpleasant things to food. Watch your cooking directions carefully and never boil when they call for a simmer.

Braise. To cook slowly in a covered pot, using a small amount of liquid or fat. Braising is similar to pot roasting or stewing, except for the amount of liquid used. Meat, fish, poultry, and many root vegetables lend themselves to this method.

Fricassee. To cook gently and slowly in liquid seasoned with aromatic vegetables. A fricassee is a white stew, also known as a *blanquette*, for which the meat or poultry is not browned first. A cream sauce is made from the water or stock in which the meat or poultry was simmered.

Parboil. See Blanch.

Poach. To cook in a liquid just under the boiling point. The liquid simmers gently throughout. Eggs, poultry, and fish may be cooked by this method.

Simmer. To boil very gently, between 135 and 160 degrees. The bubbles rise to the surface slowly and break as softly as a dust speck settling into a corner. This is one of the most important moist heats; it will protect delicate foods and tenderize tough ones. It is the recommended heat for soups, uncovered, and for stews and all braised foods, covered.

Steam. To cook food over (not in) water that is boiling and creating steam, which is free to circulate around the food. Steaming also takes place when foods are baked in airtight foil or cooking parchment packages. Steaming is a popular cooking method for fish and vegetables.

Stew. To cook slowly in a seasoned liquid. For brown stews, cubes of beef or veal or pieces of poultry are first browned and then simmered in liquid. (For white stews, see Fricassee.)

Gas Versus Electricity

Gas stoves tend to be better insulated than electric stoves and will generally outlast them. Gas surface burners are easier to control and allow more precise and instantaneous adjustments than electric.

On the other hand, electric ovens preheat more quickly than gas. Because electric elements generally cover more of the oven than a gas flame, electric ovens also tend to heat more evenly and hold the temperature more steadily. If you have to open the door of an electric oven during baking, the temperature will climb back more quickly to the preset level than it does in a gas oven.

In broiling, the intense heat of the electric coils does a superb job of sealing in meat juices, but it does not char the food as readily as a gas flame.

The ideal arrangement would be a gas range for stovetop cooking and a separate electric wall oven, but a competent cook can make do with an all-gas or electric range.

Microwave Ovens

Among the recent innovations that have enlivened the kitchen scene is the process of cooking without direct heat. This kind of space-age magic has been made possible by the electronic (microwave) range that converts electric power to microwaves. The microwaves cause the liquid molecules within the food to vibrate at a furious rate; the friction created by this rapid vibration produces heat that is then conducted through the food. Thus the food cooks not by means of heated air, but by the action of its own molecules. The result is hot food in a cold oven.

Cooking time is shorter than in a conventional oven; most foods, but not all, take only one-fourth to one-half as much cooking time. Four medium-size potatoes that would require from 45 minutes to 1 hour in a conventional oven will cook in 8 to 12 minutes in a microwave oven. A roast that might need 3 hours in a conventional oven will cook in less than 30 minutes in a microwave oven. Microwave ovens are used widely in the food-vending business where speedy warming is desirable.

But in spite of their many virtues, microwaves present some drawbacks for home use. One is the multiplier effect. As an example, one strip of bacon is usually ready in about 1 minute, but four strips require 4 minutes or more of cooking time. Large amounts of food may need almost as much cooking time as in a conventional oven. In addition, food does not brown in a microwave oven. Poultry or roasts have to be browned first using conventional heat, although some manufacturers have tried to overcome this problem by including built-in browning elements in their units. Actually, the microwave oven is not ideal for roasts (if you like them pink inside) because the interior of the meat cooks first.

It should be noted that in spite of the initial

apprehension about the dangers of this appliance, the type of wave given off in microwave cooking has not been identified as harmful and should not be confused with nuclear radiation.

Microwave cooking requires special utensils—glass, paper, ceramics, and certain plastics. Metal deflects the microwaves and interferes with the cooking. Foods must be carefully watched or they can burn. The microwave oven is fast and convenient, but it must be considered as an auxiliary to your oven and stove, and not as a substitute for either.

Convection Ovens

Another technological advance in equipment is the recently introduced convection oven. Convection ovens are new for American home kitchens, although they have been in use in Europe and in American restaurants for years. The distinguishing feature of the convection oven is a built-in blower that bombards food with constantly recirculating hot air. The food cooks more evenly, at a lower temperature, and 25 to 35 percent faster than in regular ovens. Unlike regular ovens, the convection oven will cook dishes of foods that are placed directly over each other on two racks because they are being brushed with a never-ending stream of hot air.

A few American firms now manufacture standard kitchen stoves with convection ovens. They are powered by gas or by electricity. More common is a wide assortment of electrically powered countertop convection ovens, large enough to hold a 14- to 16-pound bird. They perform extremely well and can be most useful as an extra oven.

Know Your Oven

It might be considered pretentious to equate a cook's kitchen range with a concert performer's grand piano, but the stove *is* the instrument that most often brings our cooking efforts to fruition, and it should not be out of tune. Which is to say the oven heat should be accurate. A variance of 25 degrees can affect the quality of your baking or roasting. If you are not sure of the accuracy of your oven, buy an oven thermometer. They are inexpensive and will tell you quickly whether the oven temperature agrees with the setting. If not, the adjustment is generally a simple one to make. The appliance dealer or someone from your utility company will be able to take care of it.

But even in the most perfectly calibrated oven, temperatures are never completely uniform throughout and you have to be aware of the areas of greater or less heat. If you will recall the movement of heat by convection current, hot gases and liquids rise and cold ones flow downward. (This is why the heating unit of an oven is placed at the bottom.) Consequently, oven temperatures tend to be hotter near the top and bottom and close to the back and sides. The most stable temperature is to be found in the center of the oven; this is generally the best position for a cake or roast.

Always place the oven racks in the correct position before heating, not after. When baking something that would benefit from being browned on top, such as a fish, a quiche, or a preparation with a cheese topping, place it in the top third of the oven where the convection current is strongest. A soufflé can benefit from a gentle nudge from the bottom to help it rise, so place it in the lower third of the oven. Recipes often include directions for positioning the oven racks—top third, center, or lower third. You'll do well to heed them.

Never overcrowd your oven. Ideally, the baking sheets or pans should have a two-inch space between them and the oven walls. You get better circulation of hot air in regular ovens if you do not bake more than one thing at a time. But if you have no choice and are obliged to place more than one baking dish in the oven, adjust the racks and stagger the baking pans so there is room for circulation of hot air in and around them. Inadequate space for the circulation of hot air can cause the baking to burn at the bottom. If you must use baking sheets on two shelves, quickly switch their positions at least once so they will bake uniformly. Do it late in the baking period and quickly, so as to keep the temperature as even as possible. When using two cake pans, place them on the same rack, if possible, leaving a space between. This allows for more uniform exposure to the heat. Watch and shift them if they seem to be baking at different speeds.

Don't try to shorten your cooking time by setting the heat control higher than the recipe calls for. The stated temperature will give you the best results. And bear in mind that a clean oven will reflect heat and maintain temperature more satisfactorily than a messy one.

Preheating

Always follow recipe directions for preheating the oven. You can ruin a cake with a slow start in a cool oven because the cake can rise too quickly and then fall when the oven heat takes a spurt upward. Even in these energy-conscious days, little saving of energy is accomplished by

Oven Temperatures

225 degrees	Very slow
300 degrees	Slow
350 degrees	Moderate
375 degrees	Moderately hot
400 degrees	Hot
475 degrees	Very hot

putting foods into a cold oven, for the cooking time will have to be extended to give the foods the full heating they require.

In baking, set the oven control for the temperature indicated in the recipe and preheat for at least 5 minutes. Don't interrupt the baking process by opening the oven door and peeking. For broiling, it is essential to preheat the broiler at the highest setting until it is good and hot. Otherwise, the food will not be properly seared or charred. Familiarize yourself with the characteristics and idiosyncrasies of your broiler. With experience, you can determine the correct timing and distances from the heat unit that are needed for various cuts of meat, poultry, or fish. When broiling in some electric stoves, the oven door must be left ajar, or the thermostat will switch off the broiler when a certain temperature is reached.

Cooking at High Altitudes

Cooking and baking in mountainous country is a bit different from cooking at sea level. Roasting procedures do not differ greatly from those at sea level, but high altitudes do have an effect on boiling. At sea level, water boils at 212°F (100°C). For each 960-foot increase above sea level, the boiling point is lowered by 1°C. At 5,000 feet above sea level, the boiling point is 203°F (95°C). Consequently, food at high altitudes needs more time to cook. It takes longer to boil a potato or cook a 3-minute egg in mile-high Denver, Colorado, than it does in New York City.

Baking, particularly at altitudes above 3,000 feet, requires changes to be made in cooking time, temperature, and balance of ingredients. Not only do water and liquids evaporate faster and boil at lower temperatures at high altitudes, but leavening gases expand more. Baked products rise too quickly and textures can be coarse and crumbly if the proper balance of ingredients is not achieved. Many recipes, especially those for cakes, soufflés, and yeast doughs, need some adjustment—less baking powder and sugar, and an increase in liquid. Unfortunately, there is no exact conversion table that will adjust recipes into exact formulas for high-altitude cooking. Ingredients and proportions will vary with each recipe, and the cook will have to experiment to find the appropriate balance.

The Cooperative Extension Service for Colorado State University (Fort Collins, Colorado 80523) offers a helpful pamphlet on high-altitude cooking, which is available on request.

Basic Kitchen Equipment

While first-rate cooks have produced some dazzling culinary triumphs using improvised and inadequate equipment, no dedicated cook will dispute the joys of a well-equipped kitchen. Proper pots and an array of utensils and gadgets can simplify and enhance almost any kitchen task and add greatly to the attractive presentation of food.

Early cooking utensils were made of pottery, which explains the origin of the word *pots*. With that word, all resemblance to the early products ends. Today we are given an enormous choice of materials, sizes, and shapes. Every material has its good points and its drawbacks, and often final choice comes down to individual preferences. Of major importance is that the pots be heavy duty, with bottoms that distribute heat evenly and tight-fitting covers. Poor heat distribution translates into scorched foods and ruined sauces. Carefully designed hand tools made of stainless steel or other nonrusting materials can also make a cook's life easier.

Be highly selective and discriminating when you buy your kitchen equipment. It can give you a lifetime of use, outlasting your living room chairs. Consider carefully before you invest in "sets" of matching pots. They are generally most attractive in price and appearance but too often they include one or two pieces that are all wrong for your family. For the most part, you are better off choosing your sauté pan, roaster, saucepans, etc., individually, with your own cooking habits in mind.

Plan your equipment list in terms of the kind of cooking you do. If you rarely cook a huge quantity of soup or pasta, and your needs for chicken broth can be met by the purchase of a few cans, you won't have much use for a large stockpot. Will you have many large parties or will most of your cooking be limited to four or six? Your lifestyle will determine the kind of cooking equipment you need, and you should reserve the largest portion of your kitchen budget for the items that will get the greatest use.

It is so easy to be seduced by the beguiling displays in the ubiquitous "kitchen boutiques" that feature an endless variety of appliances and gadgets guaranteed to bring unending joy to cooks. Resist them unless you are sure they fill a genuine need, and that—most important—you have room for them. The items that lie buried in a drawer or tucked away on a high, inaccessible shelf will not get much use.

Cooking Pot Materials

There is no one perfect metal or material for cooking pots and pans. Each has its advantages and drawbacks, but modern technology has learned to compensate for some of the difficulties.

Copper. Without peer as a conductor of heat, which makes it the preferred metal for professional chefs. It corrodes and interacts chemically with foods containing acidic substances, such as lemon juice, vinegar, and wine, and can form compounds that could make you ill. Consequently, copper pots must be given a protective lining—usually tin. Stainless steel and, for true elegance, silver, are also used for lining. Copper vessels are very expensive and require constant polishing.

Stainless Steel. This splendid metal is an alloy made with nickel and chromium and is the easiest material of all to keep clean, although "stainless" is a slight exaggeration. It is also a poor conductor of heat, but manufacturers have gotten around this drawback by sandwiching the pot bottom with a layer of aluminum, copper, or iron. For all-around durability, ease of cleaning, and good heat conduction, the best choice of material is stainless steel with an aluminum bottom or core. Stainless steel never interacts with food—you can make a hollandaise or a wine sauce without a worry.

Aluminum. Light in weight, strong, tough, and an excellent conductor of heat. It has a tendency to pit, but it is often combined with other metals such as chromium, nickel, and magnesium to give it added strength. Unlined aluminum pots should not be used for preparations containing wine or other acid foods, such as vinegar or tomatoes, because of the chemical reaction that takes place between the acid foods and the metal, which can cause discoloration. This is not harmful in any way; it's simply unattractive. Heavy, cast aluminum pots with a shiny polished finish are a good choice in cooking ware.

Some of the drawbacks connected with aluminum—pitting and interaction with acid foods—have been eliminated in a number of recently introduced products. Among them are Calphalon, which has a dull, charcoal-gray finish that is not a coating but is integral with the metal. When properly seasoned, it forms a "low-stick" surface and can't be damaged by stirring or scraping.

Enamel over Cast Iron. Heavy, handsome cooking utensils, rustproof and resistant to acids, and the first choice of many who don't object to their weight. However, this material will not brown food as well as bare metal. It is excellent for slow simmering and can be used for oven-to-table serving. It needs special handling because it can chip or develop hot spots unless the pan contains sufficient liquid.

Cast Iron. Heavy, absorbs heat slowly and evenly and retains it. It is also brittle, and it rusts, stains, and can become pitted on exposure to air and dampness. The rust can be prevented if the pan is dried over a stove burner after being washed and is then oiled. In spite of the drawbacks, many cooks are as sentimental about their iron skillets (called spiders in New England) as they are about the lock of hair saved from their first-born. There are many uses for an iron skillet with a metal handle that can go into the oven. Its slow, steady heat makes it excellent for pan-broiling and baking.

Glass. Attractive but fragile and a poor conductor of heat. Glass transmits heat directly, but the heat does not spread or diffuse and thus food cooks faster. When you use a glass pan in baking, lower the heat by 25 degrees or shorten the baking time by about 10 minutes. Flameproof glass can be used over low heat on top of the range as well as in the oven.

Sturdier than conventional glass is opaque white Pyroceram, a line of bakeware developed by the Corning Glass Works. It can go directly from freezer to hot oven without cracking. As with glass, the oven temperature should be 25 degrees lower than for a metal pan.

Earthenware (Clay). A poor conductor of heat but, glazed or unglazed, it holds heat well. When used according to directions, the covered casseroles made of porous clay are especially effective for tough cuts of meat and for roasting chickens. Roasts do not need to be turned or basted. Clay pots are heavy and can break easily with sudden temperature change. A hot pot will shatter if placed on a cool surface, as will a cold pot if placed in a preheated oven.

Tin. Too soft and not strong enough to be used by itself for pots. It is an excellent coating material, however, especially for copper. Tin develops a surface tarnish from exposure to acid foods, but this darkening is a protective coating and should not be removed.

Nonstick Surfaces. These are easy to clean, and you can cook without fat—two big advantages. As with porcelain enamels, food does not brown satisfactorily in pans with nonstick surfaces, and you cannot deglaze the pans. Deglazing is the process of dissolving in a liquid browned bits of food that stick to the pan, forming a rich sauce. Wooden, plastic, or rubber utensils must be used for stirring or turning to avoid marring even the most resistant finishes. However, the newer nonsticking surfaces, such as T-Fal and Silverstone, are superior to the earlier versions and of excellent quality. A nonstick omelet pan is a most useful

bit of kitchen equipment and makes omelet-making a breeze.

Care of Pots and Pans

Good cooking habits not only prolong the life and looks of your cookware and make it easier to clean, but they can also save fuel and improve the quality of your food. Always use the lowest heat setting possible. Even the best pots will suffer from constant assaults by very high heat and, if pots are not very heavy, keeping the heat low will minimize the hot spots. Low heat also lengthens the life of nonstick surfaces. You may use brisk heat to bring liquid to a boil, but then reduce the heat to the lowest point at which the boil can be maintained. An obvious but important word of caution is never to allow an empty pan to stand over high heat.

Pay attention to the manufacturers' recommendations for seasoning and caring for pots. Some pots must be seasoned with a coating of vegetable oil followed by heating either on the stove or in the oven before using for the first time. This results in a low-stick surface that makes cleaning easier. For the most part, avoid harsh abrasives or steel wool that can scratch the finish on a pot and detract from its appearance. The scouring pads made of metallic ribbons of copper alloy or stainless steel are less abrasive than steel wool. Use wooden or plastic utensils for stirring in enamel-lined or coated pots; metal spoons will leave scratches.

To clean copper, use a commercial copper cleaner or a mixture of coarse salt and either vinegar or lemon juice. The tin lining should be washed with hot water and a detergent, never scoured. The dark surface that forms on the tin increases the absorption of heat and improves the cooking quality of the pot.

Wash stainless steel with hot water and a detergent. Do not use steel wool on a stainless steel pot because it will scratch the surface. There are various commercial stainless steel cleaning products that will remove stains.

Aluminum tends to pit and discolor but, since it is a fairly soft metal, a vigorous scouring will renew its surface. It can be brightened by cooking a liquid in it that contains an acidic substance, such as lemon juice or vinegar.

Wash enameled cast iron in warm water with mild soap or detergent. If you must scour it, use baking soda, which will not damage the glaze as will a harsh abrasive. If the pan becomes caked with food, soak it overnight in warm water with some baking soda or a mild detergent. For stains, use household bleach, followed by a thorough rinsing.

Unlined cast iron will put up with any kind of abuse except dampness, which causes it to rust and lose its seasoning. Wash the pot after using it and dry it thoroughly, perhaps even turning it over a low flame to dry. Wipe it with oil to prevent rusting, and store it in an airy place.

Nonstick finishes should be washed in warm soapy water with nothing tougher than a sponge—never abrasive powders or scouring pads.

Pot Handles

Considering how much we manipulate pots during the course of a cooking session—taking them on and off the heat, tilting them, tossing the food in them, placing them in the oven or under the broiler—their handles become a worthy subject for our attention. Take a moment to see how the handle feels. Do you find it comfortable and manageable? Also, consider the important business of heat transfer. Heat slows down when it moves from one metal to another, which is why handles are often made from a metal other than that used in the basic pot. Metal handles are not harmed by fire, but they will get hot and require the use of a pot holder. Wood and plastic, on the other hand, remain comfortable and cool to the touch, but either one can scorch during a cook's careless moment or if placed under the broiler for even a second. Some recipes call for placing a pan in the oven, and the material of the handle can be a factor in this situation. Most handles should be safe at warming temperatures—200 degrees and below. Some manufacturers state that their plastic or wood handles are unaffected by oven temperatures up to 350 or 375 degrees. But there is no doubt that metal handles are the most versatile.

Vegetables, Herbs, and Spices for Seasonings

Aromatics

Aromatics are the flavorful leafy and root vegetables that, properly blended, bring character and interest to what might otherwise be a pallid, banal dish. They are indeed the cook's tools. The list of essential fresh aromatics is short—carrots, celery, various members of the onion family, parsley, garlic, and lemons. They are inexpensive, easily accessible, and keep well. There are other aromatics, such as turnips, even tomatoes, but the following can be considered basic and you should try not to be without them:

Carrots. They take on the flavors of the roast they are cooked with, returning their own sweetness. Grated over a pot roast, they melt into the gravy and thicken it.

Celery. The greener the celery, the more flavor it has. Save the leaves and use them in soups.

Onion family. *Yellow onions* are a staple, and it would be difficult to cook without them. They are full of flavor and moisture, which they impart to all foods. *Shallots* have a fresh, pungent, scallionlike flavor, milder than onion. Chopped and added to the quota of onions in a dish, they bring additional character to the taste. Snipped fresh *chives* will perk up a salad, a sauce, or a soup. *Green onions*, or *scallions*, as they are also known, lend a subtle, fresh oniony flavor to cooked or uncooked dishes. *Leeks*, tightly rolled green and white cylinders, are the sweetest and mildest member of the onion family.

Parsley. Add sprigs of parsley to soups and pot roasts as they are cooking. Chopped and sprinkled over meat, fish, vegetables, salads, and soups, parsley enhances flavor, and its bright green color makes the food look more appetizing. Don't bother with the dried parsley flakes on your grocer's shelves. They are completely without flavor and add nothing but a dingy green color.

Garlic. Use only the fresh, never the powdered, flaked, or salt form. You can use a garlic press to crush the garlic, but you will find that you get better garlic flavor if you mince or chop it finely, particularly if you are going to sauté it. Pushing the garlic through the press releases too much of the flavor oils, which then quickly evaporate. Cook garlic gently, only until golden. It develops a bitter taste when browned or scorched. Garlic keeps well in a covered jar in the refrigerator.

Lemons. Although not a vegetable, the lemon has a tart, flavor-enhancing quality that earns it a place in a listing of essential aromatics. Whole volumes have been devoted to the splendors of the lemon in food preparation. Lemon juice and lemon zest (the thin peel) may play a part in every course of a dinner, beginning with the pre-dinner drink, continuing on to the fish appetizer, the sauce for the meat, the vegetables, the salad dressings, and ending with the fresh fruits that bring the meal to a close. A teaspoon or two of lemon juice can brighten a dull dish or sauce. Avoid the reconstituted or bottled lemon juice. It tastes less like lemons and more like the laboratory that dreamed it up. The frozen lemon juice is better, but again, fresh is the best.

The zest is the yellow part of the rind that gives a concentrated, bright lemony taste to dishes. There are special little gadgets that remove zest without the pith (the bitter white covering of the lemon under the skin): a stripper for narrow strips of peel, and a zester for tiny shavings of peel. You may also use a grater or a vegetable peeler. The supermarket jars of dried lemon peel are tasteless and best ignored.

Cutting Techniques

We frequently use a combination of chopped aromatics to provide a juicy, flavorful bed for meat, poultry, or fish. While there are all sorts of machines and mechanical devices for the cutting-up procedures, it is often quicker, easier, and in some cases better to do it by hand. Use a sharp chef's knife and a wooden chopping board. The cutting techniques described below are simple, and with practice you will develop speed and dexterity.

Chop

Hold the handle of the knife in one hand, using the other to guide the thin end. Bring the blade up and down in a rocking motion. Gather the pieces together in a heap as you go along so sizes will be uniform.

Dice

If the object is round, cut a thin slice from the bottom. Make horizontal cuts ¼ inch apart. Repeat with same size vertical cuts. Slice straight down at intervals of ¼ inch and pieces will fall into even dice.

Julienne

Cut the food into ⅛-inch slices. Stack the slices and cut into strips ⅛ inch wide. The strips may then be cut into whatever lengths you wish.

Chop. To cut into small, irregularly shaped pieces about the size of a pea. *Finely* chop implies smaller pieces. Hold the handle of the knife in one hand and use the other to guide the thin point. Get a firm grasp on the knife. With a rocking motion, bring the large blade up and down over the material you are chopping. You don't need to move the knife about; the tapering of the blade does the work.

Dice. To cut into uniform cubes. If you are cutting something that is round, cut a thin slice from the bottom so it will lie flat and not roll. Use one hand to hold the vegetable steady and make horizontal cuts about ¼ inch apart. Repeat with vertical cuts about ¼ inch apart. Hold the vegetable firmly, bending your fingers so that the tips rest on the vegetable and the bent fingers serve as a guide for the knife blade. Slice straight down at intervals of ¼ inch and move the fingers back with each slice. The pieces will fall into even cubes. Dice foods

when you need small uniform pieces that will cook quickly.

Slice. If you are slicing a round object, cut a slice from the bottom to make it lie firmly. Use the pointed end of a chef's knife to puncture the skin and make the first cut. Hold the object being sliced with your fingers bent (as in Dice) and cut vertical slices to the desired thickness. With each slice, move your fingers back to the width of the next slice.

Julienne. To cut foods into thin, matchlike strips. First cut into ⅛-inch-thick slices, then into strips the same width.

Mince. To cut or chop into very fine pieces. To mince a shallot or a garlic clove, use a sharp paring knife and cut very thin horizontal, then vertical, then up and down slices.

Shred. To cut into long, narrow strips or to

Slice

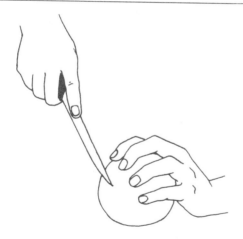

1 *If the object is round, cut a thin slice from the bottom so it will lie firmly and not roll. With the pointed end of a knife, puncture the skin and make the first cut.*

2 *Grip the object to be sliced firmly and cut vertical slices to the desired thickness. Keep fingers bent, just behind each cut, to guide the knife.*

Shred

To shred cabbage or lettuce, cut the head in quarters and remove the hard white core. Place flat side down and cut in thin slices parallel to the core.

grate coarsely. To shred cabbage or lettuce, cut the head into quarters and, with the cut side down, cut slices as thin as possible. Use a coarse grater for other vegetables and for cheeses.

Snip. To cut with a knife or scissors into small pieces. You snip (or chop) parsley, chives, and dill.

Herbs, Spices, Seeds, and Seasonings

We often use the word *spice* as a blanket term to mean any aromatic flavoring substance of vegetable origin, and in this broad sense, spice includes herbs, seeds, and other seasonings. It is a word filled with delicious overtones, conjuring up exotic flavors and mouth-watering aromas. In a horticultural sense, spice is an aromatic substance obtained from the bark, root, berry, or fruit bud of, more often than not, a tropical plant. Cinnamon, nutmeg, and cloves are examples. The word *herbs* is applied to plants of which the leaves, or the stems and leaves, are used for their scent and flavor as seasoning in foods.

Until comparatively recently, American cooks relied chiefly on the simplest seasonings to flavor their food. Although their colonial ancestors had planted herb gardens outside their kitchen doors, many modern Americans approached herbs with reservations, if not with downright suspicion. Now, however, the American palate, perhaps inspired by interesting fare sampled in distant lands, has become more appreciative of the nuances of flavor that a pinch of an herb or spice can bring to a traditional dish.

Fresh herbs are infinitely superior in flavor to the dried ones. If you are able to grow them in a garden or on a windowsill, or buy them in your market, you are in luck. Parsley, dill, and, in season, chives and basil, are not strangers to even big city dwellers. But if you must use the dried, as most of us must, make sure it is still flavorful. You will know if an herb or spice is fresh if it has an aroma when you open the jar. If you find yourself having to make an effort to sniff out the aroma, it is probably too stale to use. Taste a pinch. If the flavor doesn't come through to you immediately, it can't do much for the dish you are cooking.

Whole spices keep fresher longer than the ground ones, so it is advisable to buy them whole, if you can, and grind or grate them as you need them. Date your spices when you buy them. This will help you keep track of their freshness. Buy your ground spices in small quantities, since they do not generally retain their full flavor for more than about six months.

Store all herbs and spices in a cool dry place out of direct sunlight. Sunlight will fade them.

An array of herbs and spices may make an attractive wall treatment over the range or sink, but heat and moisture rob them of flavor. Be sure that you keep them in tightly sealed containers and that you screw the tops on firmly after you use them.

The possibilities of herb cooking are infinite and there are no rigid rules except those dictated by taste and judgment. If you are unfamiliar with cooking with herbs, start with a trustworthy recipe, or experiment with simple combinations. Don't use too many kinds at once, or too much of any kind. It is impossible to be specific about amounts because so much depends on the pervasiveness of the herb and what it is being used with. In cooking with fresh herbs, you will need two or three times the quantity of the dried. Amounts can range from ¼ to 1 teaspoon of a dried herb for four servings and 2 to 3 tablespoons or more of the fresh for the same number of servings. Delicately flavored herbs should be added to sauces or soups toward the end of the cooking, and left just long enough to lose their volatile oils. With familiarity, you'll develop the "feel" of how much dill or mint to snip into your carrots, or how much sage and thyme to use in the poultry stuffing.

An herb butter is a lovely thing to make when fresh herbs are in abundance. You can freeze it in small quantities and have it on hand to be used with broiled meat and fish, as a spread for bread, or to be swirled into a sauce. Cream together a cup or more of finely chopped parsley, tarragon, basil, or herbs of your choice, 1 teaspoon of lemon juice, and ¼ pound (1 stick) of softened sweet butter. The lemon juice heightens the herb flavor. This may also be prepared in a food processor or a blender. Let it stand at room temperature for at least an hour to give the flavor time to develop.

Allspice. In spite of its name, this is not a blend of spices but a separate berry. It is reminiscent in flavor of a mixture of cinnamon, nutmeg, and cloves. It is most commonly used ground, although it also comes whole. Used in baking and spiced fruit compotes.

Anise. With its subtle licorice flavor, anise is available as seeds, an oil, or the Chinese star anise used in pickling. The seeds are used in cookies, cakes, and sweet rolls. Crush the seeds between plastic with a rolling pin to release their full flavor.

Basil. An easily grown herb, useful both dried and fresh. It has a robust flavor and a distinctive aroma. Basil has a special affinity for tomatoes and is the leading ingredient of a popular uncooked pasta sauce called *pesto*. It is also used with many other foods—soups, basting butter for fish, salad greens, green vegetables, and roasted meat.

Bay Leaf. The distinctively flavored leaf of the laurel plant, to which the ancient Greeks attributed great magical powers. It is difficult to grow and is generally available only dried. We still value it highly for the flavor it imparts to soups, stews, roasts, and chowders. It should be used sparingly; one leaf, fresh or dry, will flavor 6 cups of liquid adequately. Bay leaf is usually added whole at the beginning of the cooking and discarded before the dish is served. It is a must for a bouquet garni.

Bouquet Garni. A combination of herbs and spices, tied together in a faggot or in a square of cheesecloth fastened with a string, or in a stainless metal tea ball, that is added to soups and stews during cooking and discarded before serving. Basic herbs for a bouquet garni are parsley, thyme, and bay leaf, to which may be added a large variety of other herbs, such as chervil, basil, marjoram, or savory.

Capers. Small, bulletlike buds of the caper

bush grown in the Mediterranean. They are usually pickled in vinegar and add a piquancy to fish preparations, sauces, and salads.

Caraway Seeds. Pungent seeds best known in rye bread. They also form a happy combination with sauerkraut and cabbage, beef stews, veal roasts, and noodles.

Cardamom. A sweet seed with a lovely fragrance, available whole and ground. Ground cardamom is good in coffee cakes and Danish pastry.

Cayenne (Ground Red Pepper). A golden red member of the pepper family. Always ground, it must be used with care. The smallest pinch will do—it's hot.

Celery Seed. The seeds of the wild celery plant (smallage). It is used in soups, sauces, vegetables, potato salad, and coleslaw. It has strong flavor and should be used sparingly— ½ teaspoon to a quart of salad.

Chervil. A delicate herb similar to parsley in its fresh state. It is available fresh and dried. The fresh leaf is markedly more flavorful than the dried. This is a mild herb and can be used lavishly—1 teaspoon to 2 cups of sauce or soup.

Chili Powder. A blend of ingredients including several varieties of ground chili peppers, cumin seeds, garlic, oregano, and herbs. Brands vary in their degree of hotness, so it's judicious to add it slowly, tasting as you go.

Chives. The tender, tubular leaves of a plant belonging to the onion family. Best when fresh, but also available dried, freeze-dried, and frozen. The freeze-dried are better than the dried or frozen; chives tend to get slimy when frozen. Chives bring a subtle onion flavor to

soft cheese, meat, vegetable or fish salads, egg dishes, cream sauces, and soups.

Cinnamon. The fragrant bark of the cinnamon tree, available ground and in stick form. Ground cinnamon is used in baking, cooked fruit desserts, and in Middle East meat dishes. Mixed with sugar, it is a delicious topping for toast or pancakes. Stick cinnamon is used in mulled drinks and as a flavorful stirrer for hot chocolate or hot toddies.

Cloves. Flower buds of the clove tree, available ground or whole. Ground cloves are used in cooking and baking pies and spice cakes. A few whole cloves, either stuck in an onion or tied in a cheesecloth bag for easy removal, lend flavor to soups and stews. And, of course, the traditional baked ham is studded with cloves.

Coriander or Cilantro. Sometimes called Chinese parsley or Mexican parsley. Available fresh, in seeds, and ground. Ground coriander is an ingredient of curry powder and is sometimes used in fruit pies. Whole coriander seeds are used in pickling. Cilantro is the fresh leaf of the coriander plant. It is more tender than parsley and may be used the same way, but in smaller quantities than parsley because the taste is zestier. Use leaves only—no stems. The flavors of the leaf and of the seeds differ greatly and one cannot be substituted for the other to duplicate flavor.

Cumin Seed. Available whole and ground. Although related to the caraway seed, it is quite different in flavor. Cumin is an ingredient in both curry and chili powders. Versatile, it can be used with eggs, meat, fish, or poultry. Try it over scrambled eggs or rice.

Curry Powder. A blend of many spices, varying with the manufacturer. Usually coriander, cumin, fenugreek, cayenne pepper, and turmeric are used. You might want to sample a few brands until you find one that pleases you. Curry enthusiasts may want to concoct their own blend. The use of curry powder need not be limited to curries; a few pinches of the powder adds interesting flavor to cream soups, salads, mayonnaise sauces, and bland vegetables.

Dill. Available fresh, dried (dillweed), and in seeds (dillseed). The flavor of this feathery plant is best in the fresh form, except for dill pickles. With its pungent, provocative flavor, it adds interest to fish, cucumber and cabbage dishes, sour cream sauces, soups, potatoes and potato salad, and many other food preparations. You can snip the dill fronds by hand, but a food processor will do it faster.

Fennel Seed. Although a member of the parsley family, fennel has a licorice flavor, similar to anise. It must be used lightly or it will impart a bitter flavor. Try it in bread and rolls, in spaghetti sauce, with vegetables, and , for wonderful flavor, sprinkled over fish and shellfish before broiling. The seeds are also used in Indian curries and for pickling. The seeds are generally sold whole, but occasionally they are ground. There is also the celerylike vegetable called fennel, or finocchio, with a distinctive licorice flavor.

Garlic. A pungent root with a characteristic odor and taste that are either revered or vilified, depending on how the diner feels about them. Garlic is used to flavor a wide variety of dishes—meats, shellfish, vegetables, stews, poultry, soups, salads, sauces, dressings, and in the preparation of pickles and sausages. Garlic should always be used with care—an innuendo rather than an overwhelming statement—unless you are sure your guests are pro-garlic. How aggressive it is depends upon how you use it. Raw minced garlic added to foods or chopped

garlic cooked in hot fat will give the most pronounced flavor; minced garlic sprinkled over foods that are being baked or broiled will also make its presence known; whole garlic cloves cooked slowly in a soup or stew will add a subtle flavor, and you can remove the garlic before serving; whole unpeeled cloves of garlic braised for a long time with poultry or meat become delicate and mild, buttery in texture.

A garlic bulb is made up of a number of individual cloves. To peel a clove of garlic easily, smash it lightly with the flat side of a cleaver and the skin will separate from the clove. Never brown or scorch garlic or it will give off a bitter taste. Always use fresh garlic. The powdered garlic and garlic salt tend to have a rancid quality that leaves an unpleasant aftertaste.

Ginger. The hot and spicy root of a tropical perennial, available fresh or ground. Ground ginger is used in baking as well as in poultry and vegetable dishes. Fresh ginger root has now become widely available. The fresh root will keep indefinitely stored in the refrigerator in a covered jar of dry sherry, or it can be frozen and grated in its frozen state as needed. It is used to enliven the taste of a variety of fish, shellfish, meat, poultry, and dessert dishes. Thin slices of candied ginger can do nice things for meat, fish, and chicken dishes, and in sweet and sour sauces. Slices of the chunky stem ginger preserved in heavy syrup are a wonderful addition to a fresh fruit salad.

Horseradish. A pungent root prized for use in meat or cocktail sauces. Available fresh or prepared in jars. Grate the fresh root and cover with white vinegar or lemon juice.

Juniper Berries. The berries of a species of shrub or low tree that grows wild in the northern hemisphere. They are used in the distillation of gin and bring their characteristic flavor to meat marinades, game, and other dishes including sauerkraut and beans.

Mace. From the same fruit as the nutmeg, and similar to the nutmeg in flavor. The nutmeg is the central stone, and the outer flesh is the mace. Available in dry flakes or ground. It is the traditional pound cake spice, and is also used in chocolate dishes and fruit pies.

Mint. Refreshing, tangy flavor, available fresh and dried. Choose the fresh when possible, but the dried will also make a contribution to flavor. Besides its popular uses in tea, juleps, fruit punches, and jellies, it is good in salads, with peas, and in cold yogurt-cucumber soup.

Mustard. A classic condiment ranging from mild to fiery hot. Available in two forms: mustard powder or dry mustard, and prepared mustards of different flavors, strengths, and textures. The American mustards are the mildest; German mustards and French Dijon mustards give foods added flavor. Become acquainted with the various types of mustards. Use dry or prepared mustard to flavor dressings and mayonnaise sauces, in addition to meat, fish, and poultry preparations.

Nutmeg. The inner kernel of the nutmeg fruit, available whole and ground. For the true flavor, buy the nutmeg whole and grate it fresh. The ground tinned nutmeg is greatly inferior because the oils in the ground nutmeg disappear within a few weeks and you are left with a flavorless brown powder. There are special small nutmeg graters but you can do equally well with the finest side of your kitchen grater. Add freshly grated nutmeg to baked goods, spinach, veal, French toast, and always to eggnog and mint juleps.

Oregano. A dominant flavor to be used sparingly, seldom available fresh. Buy it in small quantities; it stales quickly, losing quality.

Originally called wild marjoram, it is stronger and more assertive than marjoram. It owes its fame to the popularity of pizzas. Oregano is good in tomato dishes, cheese and egg preparations, and in stuffings for fish.

Paprika. The ground pod of a variety of capsicum peppers, ranging from sweet to hot. Sweet paprika is what is called for in most recipes, unless otherwise specified. Try to buy a good quality of imported Hungarian paprika; the commercially packaged supermarket varieties do not have the flavor of those sold in specialty shops, usually in bulk. Stored in a covered container in the refrigerator, it will keep for a long time. Paprika is sensitive to heat and should be added toward the end of the cooking period. It is used in meat and poultry stews, salad dressings, and sauces, adding color and flavor.

Parsley. One of the few fresh herbs in full supply the year round. Delicious and nutritious, it deserves more attention than limited use as a garnish. There is virtually no meat, fish, poultry, soup, vegetable, or salad preparation that would not benefit from the addition of parsley. Besides being flavorful in itself, it blends in with dried herbs and increases their flavor. It is effective as a breath sweetener when garlic or raw onions have been on the menu.

In addition to the familiar curly parsley, we have the Italian flat-leaf variety, which has a more pronounced flavor. It should be used for cooking rather than as a garnish, for it wilts easily. Regular parsley can be substituted for Italian parsley in any recipe.

Pepper. A basic spice, available whole and ground. Use only the best quality of whole *black peppercorns* and grind them fresh in a pepper mill with every use. In all forms of ready-ground pepper, the flavor oils fade and evaporate within a few weeks, dissipating their value as a seasoning. Fresh pepper has a way of strengthening food flavors without masking them as much as other spices do. If you are using whole peppercorns in a recipe, crush them lightly first to release their flavor. Pepper can be used in almost any food except sweets—and even here we have an exception in the German Christmas cookie, *pfeffernusse* (peppernuts).

White pepper, available whole and ground, is merely black pepper with the outer black skins removed, which also eliminates most of the flavor. White pepper was developed to please the aesthetic sense of diners who can't bear to see a few black specks in their white sauces. Not everyone agrees that a few black specks that taste good are a matter of moment.

Green peppercorns, a relatively new product that has attracted a great deal of interest because of its pungency and fine flavor. The green peppercorns are fresh, soft, immature berries, preserved in vinegar brine, or water, or freeze-dried. The freeze-dried have almost no taste. Green peppercorns can be used as a replacement for crushed black peppercorns in sauces, meat, and poultry preparations.

Crushed red pepper (hot dried red pepper flakes). A seasoning for people who like their food incendiary. Use with restraint. Just a dash will spark a pasta sauce, a chili, soups, or eggs.

Hot pepper pods, red and green. Seed and chop. Use cautiously.

Pimientos are a type of sweet red pepper preserved in oil. They are mild in flavor and used primarily for color and garnish.

Poppy Seeds. Available only in whole seed form. Sprinkle them on breads or rolls before baking or combine them with cooked noodles. Crushed poppy seeds are a popular filling for many Middle European holiday pastries and breads.

Rosemary. A strong, distinctive herb, available fresh or dried. It has a delightful flavor but it must be used cautiously or it can overpower the natural food flavors. Good in sauces, with chicken, stews, soups, and pork and lamb roasts. Lightly crush the leaves with mortar and pestle to release the full flavor.

Saffron. A golden, pungent (and very expensive) spice made from the stigmas of special crocus blossoms, available ground and in threads. It is intense in color and flavor and must be used with great caution or it can produce a medicinal taste. The threads generally have a fresher flavor and, before using, should be steeped in hot water or white wine to develop flavor. It is used to flavor cakes, breads, and dressings and is a classic in rice dishes and the French fish stew, bouillabaisse.

Sage. A strong, fragrant herb that comes in dried leaf form as well as ground, crushed, or rubbed. It is a popular American seasoning for fatty meat like pork, sausages, duck, goose, and rabbit, and is often used in bread stuffings for poultry, meat, and fish.

Salt. Salt is a unique substance that brings its own flavor to foods and also heightens the flavors of other foods. It is probably the world's oldest preservative and seasoning. Since taste and personal preference vary so widely, it would be impossible for any recipe to state unequivocally the exact amount of salt needed. What would be undersalted to one palate would be excessively salted to another. Taste and salt as you go along, except in situations such as in some baking where the amount of salt used is critical to the success of the result. If you are cooking for someone on a salt-restricted diet, you will naturally omit adding additional salt and concentrate instead on enriching flavors with wine, herbs, spices, and aromatic vegetables.

Industrial salt companies produce more than 300 types of specialized salts for various uses, but we will concern ourselves only with those used for cooking.

Cooking or table salt, a finely ground free-flowing type, is the most commonly used salt. It is often mixed with tiny amounts of chemical dehydrators to make it flow easily. It is available plain and iodized, the latter recommended for the parts of the country where the water and soils are lacking in iodine.

Kosher salt, a squarish-grained sea salt. Coarser in texture and less salty than common table salt, it is the choice of many cooks who prefer it for cooking and table use because of its flavor and purity. It is pure salt with no additives. Sprinkled over rolls, pretzels, and breads before baking, it adds sparkle.

Sea salt, rough salt, crystallized out from sea water. This salt must be ground in a salt mill. It is expensive and used mainly as a table salt by people who find its taste fresher than regular salt.

Rock salt, a nonedible, unrefined variety used in freezing ice cream.

Vegetable salts, a combination of sodium chloride with added vegetable extracts, such as celery and onion. If you use them, decrease the amount of additional salt.

Seasoned salts, a combination of vegetable salts, spices, and monosodium glutamate (MSG). Read the list of ingredients on the label before you buy; MSG causes an allergic reaction in some people. Some seasoned salts contain inordinately large amounts of sugar. If you use seasoned salts, don't add regular salt without first tasting.

Savory. A popular herb with a slightly peppery flavor. There are two varieties: summer savory, the type we usually find dried on spice shelves, and winter savory, slightly more pungent. The leaves of the summer savory are more delicately flavored and have many more uses. They are a classic with green beans and green bean salad, in lentil soup, horseradish sauce, fish, meats, and in poultry stuffings. If the Pilgrims stuffed their game birds on the first Thanksgiving, they probably seasoned the dressing with the savory they brought from England. This attractive plant was a staple in Colonial gardens along the East Coast.

Sesame Seed (Benne Seed). Tiny white seeds that have an almond flavor when browned in butter or toasted. Sprinkle them on any food that is to be broiled or baked. If you plan to add them to a salad, stuffing, or cooked vegetable, first bake them in a 350-degree oven for 15 to 20 minutes, stirring frequently.

Soy Sauce. A dark-colored flavoring sauce made from fermenting soybeans, roasted wheat, and salt. Used in Oriental cooking, it has found its way into Western kitchens and is frequently used in meat marinades. It is very salty, so taste before adding additional salt.

Tabasco Sauce. A sauce made from hot tabasco peppers. Easy does it with Tabasco—a drop or two may be all you need. Add to soups, cocktail or piquant sauces, fish stews, and creamed dishes that could do with a bit of pepping up. If added to a cooked sauce, wait until the last few minutes of cooking or immediately after you remove the dish from the heat to add it. Long cooking destroys the essence.

Tarragon. An interesting herb with a sweet flavor with anise overtones. Available fresh and dried. It must be used with discretion because it can overpower other flavors. Salad dressings made with tarragon-flavored vinegar can perk up the most ordinary salad greens. It is too pungent for soups, but it works well with practically everything else—eggs, mushrooms, tomatoes, fish, chicken, and sauces such as béarnaise, tartar, and mustard.

Thyme. Versatile herb in leaf form and ground, moderately potent. It is traditional in New England fish chowders, in a bouquet garni, with creole and gumbo dishes, stews, stuffings, and many vegetables.

Turmeric. An Indian spice made from the root of a plant in the ginger family, to be used sparingly. It is a deep yellow color with a flavor more reminiscent of saffron than ginger. Its golden color tints curry powders and it is usually one of the spices in prepared mustard and in mustard pickles. It can be used as an alternative to saffron as a coloring agent.

Vanilla. An aromatic flavoring used in cakes, puddings and dessert sauces. It is available in its original bean form or, more commonly, as an extract. The bean itself gives the best flavor. Slit the vanilla bean lengthwise and scrape the tiny black seeds into the liquid of a recipe or use a part of the pod if you are heating a preparation. However, vanilla beans are not easy to locate and they are very expensive. Pure vanilla extract is satisfactory, but avoid the imitation or synthetic vanilla extract. Add the vanilla when the food is cooling; heating diminishes its flavor.

Vinegar. Sour liquid, the product of the fermentation of wine under the action of certain bacteria. It is an everyday condiment, useful as a seasoning, as a preservative, and in marinades to break down tough connective tissues in meats. Vinegars have a corrosive action on metals; when marinating or pickling use glass, enamel, or stainless steel bowls or pans. The common vinegars are the white, all-purpose vinegar; which is the sharpest; the full-bodied cider vinegar; and the blander white and red wine vinegars, popularly used in salad dressings. Herb vinegars, the fourth type, can be made with any of the other three by steeping an herb of your choice in the vinegar until the flavor is well absorbed. Garlic and tarragon are favorites. You can blend your own wine vinegars by diluting sharp vinegars with a little red or white wine until you reach the degree of mellowness you wish.

Worcestershire Sauce. A spicy bottled sauce for meats and general cooking. A few drops can zip up a bland sauce or dressing, but be careful about the amount or it can overwhelm other flavors.

Correct the Seasoning

"Taste and correct the seasoning," reads the tag line of many recipes. It is a direction that can inspire a gifted cook or frighten an insecure one. But it's sound advice based on the fact that you cannot dispute personal preferences. Tastes are variable: A curry that verges on the incendiary may be sheer bliss to one person and anathema to another. Ingredients, too, are not always the same. Some lemons are more sour than others; not all salts are equally salty nor are all sugars equally sweet. No recipe can be all things to all people. In the end, you must trust your own taste and intuition and be the final judge of whether it shall or shall not pass. Sound judgment comes with successive sampling and experience.

Tasting is a highly complex physiological process, not all of which is completely understood even by scientists working in the field. The taste buds of adults are located in the bright-pink spots on the tongue; young children have taste buds on the hard and soft palates and the pharynx as well as on the tongue. It is estimated that humans have nine to ten thousand taste buds. (Antelopes and other animals are reported to have more, and one can only wonder who took the time to count them.) After we reach the age of 45, the number of taste buds begins to decline. Perhaps that is why we recall with longing some of the soul-filling goodies we ate as children and wonder why today's foods don't taste as good. While no one would deny that commercialism in the food processing and farming industries has caused a diminution in quality of many of the things we eat, part of our problem may also come from the process of attrition that has overtaken some of our taste buds.

The taste sensations that the taste buds register are sweet, salt, sour, and bitter, but the taste buds in different areas of the tongue are not equally sensitive to each. The taste buds near the tip of the tongue are finely attuned to sweet and salt, those on the sides to sour, and those near the back to bitter. The central surface of the tongue contains no taste buds. When we take food into our mouths, the taste sensations blend together like a musical chord formed by individual notes. Some individuals, approximately one-fourth of the population, are said to be "taste-blind." They are unable to taste a group of specific chemical compounds that produce an unpleasant, bitter sensation. These people may never make it to the front line in the fine-cooking department.

But the tongue and its response to sweet, sour, salt, and bitter are only one part of the process of tasting. Of equal importance is the ability to detect odors—or aromas, since we are talking about food. We have all complained on the occasion of suffering through a head cold that food had no taste. But our taste buds were not impaired by our indisposition; it was our ability to detect aromas that suffered. The pleasant sensations in eating food come as much from the aromas as from the taste.

The flavor of food is also influenced by the temperature at which it is served. Extreme cold and extreme heat, like a local anesthetic, affect the ability of our taste buds to pick up taste sensations. As an example, ice cream that tastes perfect in its frozen state is cloyingly sweet when melted. Really hot coffee tastes less bitter than it does after it has cooled in the cup. Chilled foods taste less salty than hot and require more seasoning. The lesson to be learned from this observation is simply to try, as far as possible, to judge the seasoning of a food at the temperature at which it will be served.

With experience, you will learn how different types of seasonings affect each other. Salt can make sugar less intense, for example, and reduce acidity. A pinch of sugar or a dollop of vinegar can sometimes modify saltiness. Many an oversalted vegetable soup or chili has been saved by a sprinkle of sugar. Salt, pepper, and parsley can often act as catalysts for other flavors. Get to know the various flavor properties of the herbs, spices, and seasonings. Use them discreetly, for seasonings should enhance the natural flavors of foods but never overpower them.

About Bread Crumbs

There is doubt among some cooks about exactly what is meant by "fresh bread crumbs" versus "dry bread crumbs." Both fresh and dry crumbs are made by processing or blending bread in a food processor or blender until fine. Fresh bread crumbs are made from fresh bread that is slightly dried out. If the bread is too fresh, the crumbs may be gummy. Bread that is two to four days old is generally satisfactory. Don't use stale bread, for stale bread will give you stale-tasting crumbs. For dry bread crumbs, crisp the bread on a baking sheet in a 250-degree oven. Some or all of the crusts may be used for either the fresh or the dry crumbs. Cut the bread into cubes before processing or blending.

Store the crumbs in a tightly closed plastic bag or covered container in the refrigerator. If you must keep them for more than a short period of time, store them in the freezer to prevent mold. An average slice of white bread will yield about ½ cup of fresh bread crumbs; a slice of dry bread will yield ¼ to ⅓ cup dry bread crumbs.

Finely crushed cracker crumbs, crushed cornflakes, or potato chips are sometimes used in place of bread crumbs.

Buttered bread crumbs are used as a garnish for game and gratin dishes. Melt 3 tablespoons butter in a skillet, add 2 cups fresh white bread crumbs and sauté over moderate heat until the crumbs are evenly browned and golden. For vegetables *Polonaise*, sauté 1 cup dry bread crumbs in 3 tablespoons melted butter and sprinkle over cauliflower, broccoli, or asparagus.

About Nuts

Store shelled nuts in the freezer or the refrigerator. Always taste them before using; stale, rancid nuts can ruin the most beautiful preparation. Bring them to room temperature before using.

To Blanch Almonds. Cover almonds with boiling water and let stand. When they become cool enough to handle comfortably, remove them one at a time and pinch off the skins, using thumb and forefinger. Allow to dry on absorbent paper towels. Place them in a single layer in a shallow baking pan in a 200-degree oven for 20 to 30 minutes, until they are completely dry, but don't let them brown. If they are to be slivered (cut into long, thin pieces) cut them immediately after you remove the skins, while they are still soft and moist.

To Blanch Hazelnuts (Filberts). Place the hazelnuts in a single layer in a shallow baking pan in a 350-degree oven for about 15 minutes, or until the skins dry and begin to flake off. Rub them, a few at a time, in a coarse Turkish towel. Most of the skin will come off and can be discarded. The few bits and pieces of skin that remain can be ignored.

To Blanch Pistachio Nuts. These lovely little green nuts are difficult to skin after they have cooled, so don't try to do more than about one-third cup at a time. Drop them in a few inches of boiling water and let them boil for just a few seconds. Prolonged boiling will fade them. Test a nut by pinching off the skin. If it comes off easily, drain the nuts, and spread them out on absorbent paper towels. Pinch off the skins while they are still warm. They are used whole for their decorative effect, or chopped or slivered.

To Grind. Ground nuts are nuts that have been reduced to a coarse, flour like powder. Hand grinders are preferable to food processors or blenders, which tend to crush the nuts (except for almonds) and release their oils, causing them to form lumps. If you do use an electric machine, don't overblend, do only one-half cup of nuts at a time, and turn the

machine on and off quickly. If in spite of this, they have clumped together, with your fingertips push them through a strainer set over a bowl to aerate them and make them powdery.

To Chop. Chopped or broken nuts are nuts reduced to small, identifiable pieces. You can break nuts like pecans or walnuts with your fingers, if rather larger pieces are needed. For finer pieces, use a knife and chopping board, or a chopping bowl and chopper.

Wine in Cooking

Both people and food can be refreshed by an infusion of wine or spirits. But their effect on food has nothing to do with alcoholic content. The alcohol evaporates in the cooking and only the flavor is left, which enhances the finished dish.

There are two main categories of wine: table wine and fortified wine. The fortified wines—port, vermouth, sherry, Madeira, Marsala—are those to which a spirit such as brandy has been added. They serve as a predinner drink and a dessert wine. They are used in cooking principally as final flavorings, whereas the table wines are most generally used for long cooking with meat, poultry, or fish. Wines range in taste from dry to sweet. A dry wine is one in which the sugar has been fermented out. The label on the bottle indicates which it is, and your wine dealer may also be counted on for guidance.

Don't cook with a wine that you would not drink. Always taste it first. If it is pleasing, it will add to the taste and if it is too sweet or too vinegary or flat, it will detract. The taste of wine is always heightened because cooking reduces volume and emphasizes flavor. The so-called cooking wines on your supermarket shelves are unsuitable. Many are salted and seasoned and are best avoided.

Use wine in your cooking with restraint. Too

much will overbalance and drown out the characteristic flavor of the food. When adding wine, figure the amount as part of the liquid called for, not as an extra. Wine is used in all sorts of moist-cooking, from braising to poaching.

You may find in making a wine sauce that you must increase the amount of flour or what-ever thickening agent you have used. This is because wine is an acid and acids tend to reduce the thickening power of starches. Wine evaporates very quickly and ten minutes of rapid boiling will reduce a cup of wine to about a quarter of a cup. The reduction is only in volume and not in taste. Never let the food cook above a simmer when cooking with wine. To prevent curdling or separating, add wine to a dish before you put in the dairy products. Then mix in the dairy products off the heat and keep the sauce warm in the top of a double boiler. Wine makes a splendid sauce without any thickening if you add three or four tablespoons of it to a pan in which meat or poultry has been cooking and swirl it around to dissolve all the crusty bits on the bottom of the pan (de-glazing). When you want a pronounced wine flavor, add it to the food at the very last minute and keep the pot on the heat only until its contents are warmed through.

2
Stocks and Soups

No one should overlook the virtues of soup in these nutrition-conscious, budget-conscious, flavor-conscious times, for it has something to offer in each of these departments. It is one of the most versatile of kitchen preparations, allowing a free-wheeling cook full range for improvisation and creativity. A soup can be hearty or delicate, thick or thin, steaming or chilled; it can serve as a first course of a formal banquet or provide the main course of a satisfying meal with good friends. Some soups need hours of long cooking, others can be done in well under an hour, and there are still others that need no cooking at all. Anyone with a full repertoire of soups, or who is adventurous enough to experiment with new ones, can add a great deal of variety and interest, as well as nutrients, to mealtimes.

Soup making can also be a thrifty habit. The bits and pieces of lean meat, jelled gravies, and leftover vegetables that have been taking up space in your refrigerator can be put to good use in the soup kettle. Puréed through a food mill, blender, or food processor and combined with chicken or beef stock, they will produce a most satisfactory soup. Because ingredients for soup do not have to be precisely measured, you have considerable latitude in assembling them. You will only want to be sure that the ingredients are fresh and that their flavors blend well together. A cream of carrot soup, for example, is enhanced by the addition of cooked celery, mashed squash, or mushroom stems. But be careful with vegetables like cabbage and yellow turnip whose strong flavors can overpower the soup.

There is an endless variety of canned, dehydrated, powdered, and frozen soups on supermarket shelves, but they are likely to come off second best to what you can produce in your own kitchen at a lower cost per serving. It might be noted, also, that most canned soups are extremely high in sodium, which makes them off limits for people whose salt intake must be restricted.

Stocks

Most fine soups and sauces are based on a stock that is made from the bones and flesh of meat, poultry, or fish, and flavored with vegetables and herbs. The word *stock* has an intimidating sound for noncooks because it denotes hours of laborious preparation with perhaps a bit of alchemy thrown in. Actually, it is simply the liquid, or broth, obtained from simmering together the above-mentioned ingredients. A full-bodied stock has a depth and richness of flavor that is not easily duplicated.

It isn't necessary to keep a stockpot simmering at the back of the stove, adding to it daily, in order to keep a supply of homemade broth on hand. Few of us have the time or inclination for such projects. If you have sufficient freezer space, a few stock-making sessions a year can take care of most of your needs. The stock will keep well in the freezer for up to three months.

Kinds of Stock

The stockpot has four elements: the *stock base*, which might be meat, bones, fish, poultry, game, or vegetables; the *seasonings*, salt and pepper; the *aromatics*, such as onions, carrots, and herbs; and the *liquid*, water. The basic stocks are white, brown, fish, and vegetable. White stock is made from white meats—chicken or veal, or a combination of both; brown stock is made from bones and meat that have been browned in a hot oven before being consigned to the soup pot; fish stock is made from fish heads, bones, and trimmings; and vegetable stock is the water in which the vegetables were cooked. Vegetable stock should get last priority in your plans for storing because it is easily replaced and there is no point in giving it valuable freezer space.

What Goes into the Stockpot?

Treasures for the stockpot are standard equipment in most kitchens—celery and its tender leaves, mushroom stems, onions, carrots, peppercorns, scallion and leek tops, white turnips, poultry carcasses, meat bones, and vegetable juices. In addition, see what your refrigerator yields in the way of leftover meats, gravies, and vegetables that are still fresh. The tidy little packages of meat and vegetables that we buy at our supermarkets also give us an increasing amount of trimmings. And be sure to ask the butcher for the bones that are left when he has boned your meat.

Set aside a bone and scrap bag for stocks in your freezer and keep accumulating meat and poultry bones until you have enough for a stock-cooking session. If you have chicken often, you can easily build up a spare parts supply that can be turned into a quart of good chicken stock. Save the backbones, wing tips, necks, and giblets in your freezer. Do not include the livers; they muddy the color of the stock.

Stockpot ingredients are the exception to the rule about the advantages of young, tender foodstuffs. Meat from mature animals has the most flavor. A mature hen well past its egg-laying prime will yield a richer broth than a young thing. The animal parts best suited to stock-making are marrow bones, shin bones,

knee bones, and neck bones, which are rich in a gelatin-producing substance. Shanks of beef and veal are excellent for soup because they contain both the shin bone and the strip of meat surrounding it. Stock can be made from bones alone, but it will have less body and be less nutritious than that made with meat and bones. Equal amounts of meat and bone are the ideal proportion. You may combine both cooked and uncooked meat and bones in the same stock, but a darker, cloudier stock will result than if you use just uncooked bones.

Lamb is a strong-tasting meat and is less adaptable than beef, veal, or chicken for an all-purpose stock. Ham bones should also not be used in an all-purpose stock, but they are wonderful in preparations made with dried legumes. Vegetables with pronounced flavors, such as yellow turnips and those in the cabbage–cauliflower family, are not recommended in a general-purpose stock.

Basic Cooking Methods

The same basic cooking rules apply to all meat and poultry stocks. To get the maximum flavor from the meat and bones, always start the stock with cold water. Place the meat and bones in the pot and add water to about two inches above the level of the ingredients. Ideally, the soup pot should be large enough to allow three or four inches between the level of the water and the top of the pot. Cover the pot, but tilt the cover so that there is an inch or so of open space to allow for evaporation. This helps to reduce the stock and strengthen the flavor.

Bring the liquid slowly to the boiling point. As the liquid heats, a scum forms and rises to the surface. The scum is a layer of slightly coagulated albumen released by the meat and bones. It is not harmful—in fact, it contains some nutrients—but if it is not removed, it clouds the liquid and looks unattractive. Skim the surface carefully at frequent intervals. You can use a slotted spoon or, better still, one of the special long-handled skimming devices shaped like a shallow ladle. Eventually, the scum will change to a white foam, at which point you can forget about it. After the last skimming, wipe off the ridge of scum on the sides of the pot at the level of the stock.

When the liquid in the pot reaches the boiling point, add the vegetables and herbs and adjust the heat so that the liquid simmers very slowly, a lazy bubble or two of motion. Unless you can adjust the heat source precisely, use a flame control device under the pot to insure slow, even cooking. Slow cooking is essential to give the gelatin-rich substance in the bones and meat time to melt and be released from the connective tissues. The substance is called collagen, which disintegrates in hot water and converts to gelatin. When meats are submerged in water, various products are released in increasing amounts as the water becomes hotter—vitamins, fats, mineral salts, the gelatin produced by the melting collagen—to form the stock. At the same time, the vegetables and herbs release their starches, acids, and pectins, which flavor the stock and give it a distinctive, pleasant aroma.

A meat stock should cook from four to six hours, or until you are sure that you have extracted every bit of flavor and nutrients from the meat and bones. If the level of the liquid evaporates below the ingredients, add boiling water. Should you be interrupted in the course of your soup making, you can stop the cooking and resume later. A fowl will take three to four hours, and a roasting chicken about an hour.

Pour or ladle the finished stock into a large bowl through a strainer lined with two or three thicknesses of cheesecloth that have been wrung out in water. Let the stock cool in a cool place, uncovered, as quickly as possible. Never cover hot stock; covering it may cause it to turn sour. When cool, cover and refrigerate.

Seasonings

It is advisable to season stock toward the end of its cooking instead of at the beginning because, as it cooks down, it becomes more concentrated. Flavors intensify, and what might have started out as the proper amount of salt could end up as too much. Storing the soup will also intensify saltiness. Be moderate, too, in the amount of herbs and spices that you use; you do not want to overbalance the natural flavors of the ingredients. About 6 crushed peppercorns and ½ bay leaf are safe amounts. A bouquet garni (bay leaf, thyme, and parsley tied together) adds flavor to all stocks.

Removing Fat

The best way to degrease a stock is to chill it in the refrigerator, preferably overnight. The fat will congeal into a firm layer that can be lifted off easily, or, in the case of chicken fat that never gets quite firm, spooned off. Leave the layer of fat in place until you are ready to use the stock; it preserves it and keeps it fresh. Remove fat before you freeze stock. If you are in a hurry and need only a small amount of stock for a sauce, put a cup or two in a small metal bowl and place it in the freezing compartment until the fat congeals.

If you do not have time for a lengthy chilling process and must skim the stock at once, use a spoon to remove the clear fat that rests on the surface as completely as you can, then float a paper towel on the surface until it has absorbed as much fat as it will hold. Repeat with a second paper towel if necessary.

Clarifying Stock

After stock has been degreased, it is clear enough for most uses. But if you are planning to use it as a consommé, an aspic, or a jellied soup, it will have to be clarified, a process that makes it clear and sparkling.

Start with a stock that has been thoroughly skimmed of fat and is completely cold. You will need one egg white and one eggshell, crumbled, to each quart of stock. Beat a cup or so of cold stock in a large mixing bowl with the egg white and eggshell. Bring the rest of the stock to a boil in a soup pot. Slowly pour the hot stock in a thin stream over the egg white mixture, stirring well with a wire whisk or a rotary beater. Pour the mixture back into the soup pot and, over moderate heat, whisk constantly until a simmer is reached. The constant stirring is essential to keep the egg white circulating throughout the liquid. Otherwise, it could fall to the bottom of the pot, burn, and ruin the taste. As soon as the simmer is reached, stop stirring and keep the heat low to maintain the barest simmer. The egg white and shell act as a magnet, attracting all the particles that would have made the soup cloudy, and then rise to the surface, bringing with them a heavy, foamy crust. Do not skim this crust, but push it gently away from the side of the pan so you can observe the movement of the simmering—no true boil must take place. Simmer for 15 minutes, turn off the heat, and let the soup settle for 10 minutes.

Line a colander with a napkin or kitchen towel that has been wrung out in hot water and place it above a large pot or deep bowl. Carefully ladle or pour the stock and egg white through the colander, agitating it as little as

possible. The clear liquid will drain through the cloth, leaving the egg white particles behind. Give it enough time to drain, undisturbed. Cool the clarified stock, uncovered, and refrigerate, covered tightly, when cooled.

Storing and Freezing

Stock can be safely kept in the refrigerator up to three days. Reheating and boiling for about two minutes every three days will keep it from spoiling. Always boil refrigerated stock before using it or adding to it.

Stock freezes very well. Store it in containers that are a useful size for your family or company needs, such as 1-cup, 1-pint, or larger containers of heavy duty plastic that can be taken directly from the freezer and quickly heated. Stick a strip of freezer tape on each container and mark the name of the stock and the date of preparation. For the occasions when you need a small quantity of stock for a sauce, freeze it in ice cube trays and store the cubes in plastic bags in the freezer compartment. Be sure to boil stock that has been frozen before you use it, to insure safety.

For a space-saving freezer practice, reduce stock so that it is strongly concentrated. It can be brought back later to its original volume by adding water. Use stock that has been well degreased. To reduce it, boil it slowly in an uncovered pan until it boils down to half its original amount. Cool, uncovered, transfer to freezer containers, and store in freezer.

Meat Glaze

A meat glaze is the ultimate reduction of a brown stock; a quart of brown stock is cooked down until it is reduced to about four ounces of a thick, shiny brown jelly. It is so concentrated that it must be used discreetly, or it will over-balance other flavors. It is used to enhance the flavor of sauces, or it can be reconstituted with water in the proportion of 4 ounces of glaze to 3½ cups of water to again become brown stock. In this concentrated form it is a fine space saver, but the cooking time may be ten to twelve hours or even longer before the glaze reaches the proper consistency.

Start with a rich homemade stock that is completely degreased. It can be boiled quickly at the beginning and skimmed often, but the heat must be reduced at the end when the glaze thickens, or it will scorch. Cook un-covered until the sauce becomes jellylike and makes a thick coating on the back of a spoon.

Meat glaze does not need to be frozen; it will last for months in a covered jar in the refrigera-tor. If any mold develops, scrape it off and reboil the glaze for five minutes. It will be as good as ever.

Simple Beef Stock

This is a basic recipe made from meat, bones, and vegetables. It can be used for braising meats and vegetables, as a base for soups, or in meat sauces. If you use beef shin or neck, you can remove it from the pot after it is tender, about 2½ hours, and put the meat to good use as boiled beef or hash or a stuffing ingredient.

1 veal knuckle, cut into 4 pieces
5 to 6 pounds beef bones, or bones and meat, chopped into 2- or 3-inch pieces
3 quarts cold water
2 scraped carrots, cut into thick wedges
2 onions, sliced
1 celery stalk, sliced, with leaves
1 teaspoon dried thyme
1 bay leaf
6 parsley sprigs
2 unpeeled garlic cloves (optional)
6 crushed peppercorns
1 teaspoon salt

Blanch the veal knuckle by boiling it for 5 minutes and rinsing it well under cold water. This lessens the large amount of scum given off by veal. Place the meat and bones in a large soup kettle and cover them with cold water. Cover the pot, tilting the lid so that there is an inch of open space. Bring slowly to a boil and skim off the scum as it rises. Add the rest of the ingredients except the salt, and add more water if needed to cover. Reduce the heat to keep the liquid at a slow simmer, never letting it rise above a quiet, lazy breaking of a bubble or two at the surface. Continue to skim until the foam turns white. Cook for 3 or 4 hours more, until you are sure you have extracted all the flavor possible from the ingredients. Add salt during the last hour of cooking. Taste and correct seasoning. Strain and cool, uncovered. (See directions for removing fat, storing, and freezing, page 32.)

Yield: About 10 cups.

Brown Stock

Brown stock is the base for brown sauces, consommé, and braising liquids for vegetables and red meats. It gets its characteristic brown color from roasting the meats, bones, and vegetables in the oven before they are put into the soup kettle.

1 veal knuckle, sawed into 4 pieces

5 to 6 pounds beef shin or marrow bones, *or* same weight of equal amounts of beef bones and stew meat

3 scraped carrots, cut into quarters

3 peeled onions, cut into halves

4 quarts cold water

1 celery stalk, sliced, with leaves

1 small white turnip

1 teaspoon dried thyme

1 bay leaf

6 sprigs parsley

2 unpeeled garlic cloves (optional)

6 crushed peppercorns

1 teaspoon salt

Heat oven to 450 degrees. Blanch the veal knuckle by boiling it for 5 minutes and rinsing it well under cold water. Arrange the meat and bones in a shallow baking pan and place it on the center rack in the oven for about 10 minutes. Turn the meat and bones a few times. Add the carrots and onions and roast for another 35 or 40 minutes, or until they are well browned. If the finished stock does not have a rich, dark color, it will be because you did not brown the ingredients sufficiently. Turn them from time to time so they will brown evenly and not scorch.

Remove from the oven and transfer the browned ingredients to a large soup kettle. Discard any fat in the roasting pan and add a cup or two of boiling water to the pan. Place over heat and scrape up all the browned bits on the bottom of the pan. These little crusty things are flavorful meat juices that have caramelized in the pan and they will add taste and color to the stock. Add to the soup kettle along with the 4 quarts cold water and slowly bring to a boil. Skim off all the scum that forms. Add the rest of the ingredients except the salt and cover the pot, leaving about an inch of space open. Simmer very slowly for 4 or 5 hours. Continue to skim until the foam turns white. Add more boiling water if the level of the liquid evaporates below the ingredients. Add salt during the last hour of cooking and taste shortly before the stock is finished, adding more salt if needed. Strain and cool, uncovered. (See directions for removing fat, storing, and freezing, page 32.)

Yield: 12 to 16 cups.

Chicken Stock

Chicken stock is a basic ingredient for many soups and sauces, and any recipe that calls for a white stock. A simple stock can be made in an hour or two, but it will need more time if you wish to reduce it to make it richer and more concentrated.

3 pounds chicken parts (wings, backs, gizzards, necks, bones), *or* 4 pounds of stewing hen or roasting chicken

3 quarts cold water

1 peeled onion, stuck with 2 cloves

2 carrots, scraped and cut in two

2 celery stalks and leaves, cut in two

1 bay leaf

6 crushed peppercorns

2 sprigs parsley

1 teaspoon dried thyme

1 teaspoon salt

Wash the chicken parts thoroughly, drain, and place in a large soup kettle. Add the water and remaining ingredients except the salt. Cover the pot, leaving an inch of open space, and bring slowly to a boil. Lower the heat at once and simmer slowly, partly covered, for 2½ to 3 hours, or longer if it is convenient. Skim as necessary.

If you have included a stewing hen, remove it when it is tender, 2 to 2½ hours. A roasting chicken will be tender in about an hour. Turn off the heat, unless you have extra chicken bones in the pot. When the chicken is cool enough to handle, remove the skin and bones and return the bones to the pot for more cooking. (The cooked chicken can be used in salad, chicken pie, hash, sandwiches, crêpe fillings, or any one of the dozens of uses you can think of for tender cooked chicken.)

Add salt to the stock during the last hour of cooking and, after 10 minutes or so, taste for seasoning and add more salt if necessary. Strain and cool, uncovered. (See directions for removing fat, storing, and freezing, page 32.)

Yield: About 10 cups.

Note: Chicken stock is chicken soup. You can intensify the flavor by a rapid boil to reduce it. Taste and correct seasoning. It may be enriched with fine cooked noodles or rice, or some julienned strips of vegetables.

Veal Stock

Veal stock, also called white stock, has a delicate, distinctive flavor and is used in fine cream sauces and soups. Its chief drawback is the astronomical cost of veal. Howevever, you can fashion a veal stock from less expensive parts, such as neck of veal, the bony parts of the shoulder, and a veal knuckle. Lean shank meat is an excellent cut and occasionally supermarkets have veal shanks on sale. A calf's foot, if available, can be added to the stockpot. Chilled veal stock generally makes a strong gel because of the high gelatin content of the bones.

Veal releases an enormous amount of gray scum that requires a lot of skimming, but you can reduce both the scum and the effort required to remove it by first blanching the veal. It will not affect the flavor. Place the veal and veal bones in a kettle and cover with cold water. Bring to a boil and boil slowly for 5 minutes. Rinse the meat and bones under cold running water and clean the kettle thoroughly. Replace the bones and meat in the kettle and you're ready to go.

5 to 6 pounds cracked, raw veal bones and lean meat, blanched

1 peeled onion, stuck with 2 cloves

2 carrots, scraped and cut in two

2 celery stalks and leaves, cut in two

1 bay leaf

1 sprig parsley

6 crushed peppercorns

3 quarts cold water

1 teaspoon salt

Put all the ingredients except the salt in a large kettle. Bring slowly to a boil and skim off all the scum that forms on the surface. Reduce the heat so that the stock simmers gently and cook, partly covered, for 4 to 5 hours. Skim as needed. After about 2½ hours, test the meat to see if it is tender. If it is, remove it from the pot and, when cool enough to handle, strip the meat from the bones and return the bones to the stock. You can use the meat for stuffing vegetables or in a cold meat salad. Add the salt toward the end of the cooking.

When you have gotten everything out of the bones that they have to give, taste and correct seasoning. Strain and cool, uncovered. (See directions for removing fat, storing, and freezing, page 32.)

Yield: 10 cups.

Fish Stock

Fish stock is the base for fish soups or is used in aspics or sauces to be served with fish. It can be kept frozen for several weeks or refrigerated for a day or two, but not longer. Any white fish, fresh or frozen, such as halibut, whiting, flounder, fluke, or sole, is suitable, but avoid strong-flavored fish like mackerel or bluefish. Salmon stock should be used only with salmon dishes. Shells from shrimp, crab, and lobster, cooked or uncooked, make splendid additions to the fish stock. Fish heads are particularly flavorful and your fish purveyor may oblige with some extras, if asked.

1½ to 2 pounds washed fish bones, heads, tails, and trimmings

1 celery stalk, thinly sliced

1 onion, thinly sliced

1 carrot, thinly sliced

1 teaspoon lemon juice

3 cloves

2 or 3 tablespoons sliced mushroom stems (optional)

½ bay leaf

6 crushed peppercorns

1 cup dry white wine

6 cups cold water

¼ teaspoon salt

Combine all the ingredients in a stainless steel or enamel-lined saucepan. Do not use aluminum because the acid in the wine combines with the aluminum to produce a dark-colored stock. Bring to a boil, skim, reduce heat, and simmer uncovered for 25 to 30 minutes. A fish stock does not need long cooking because the gelatin-producing substance in fish bones dissolves very quickly. If it cooks longer than 30 minutes, the stock may become bitter. Skim as necessary during cooking. Strain the stock through a fine sieve and correct the seasoning. If the stock is too thin, further boiling will reduce it. Cool, uncovered, and refrigerate covered. Stock stored in the refrigerator should be brought to the boil every two days.

If you wish to use the stock for aspic, it must be clarified. (See directions for clarifying stock, page 33 .)

Yield: About 6 cups.

Vegetable Stock

Vegetable stock is the liquid in which vegetables have been cooked. It contains valuable nutrients that have leached out of the vegetables during the cooking and should be put to use whenever possible. Use it in place of water to enrich a soup stock. But to be safe, taste the vegetable stocks you reserve. Stocks from highly flavored vegetables such as cauliflower, cabbage, broccoli, or yellow turnips (rutabagas) must be used with discretion. They could be an asset in a hearty meat and cabbage soup but a disaster in a delicate chicken broth. Carrots and parsnips tend to sweeten the pot and must be

used with care. Vegetable juices such as those from watercress, asparagus, leeks, and mushrooms blend with almost everything.

Canned Broths and Other Substitutes

If you have run out of time or ingredients for a homemade chicken or beef stock, canned bouillon or canned chicken broth can be used, particularly if it is for a cream soup or one in which the stock plays a supporting role to another ingredient. Experiment with a few brands of chicken and beef broth until you find one that is not too highly seasoned or too concentrated. Canned consommé is strong in flavor, rather sweet, and less suitable than either canned bouillon or beef broth.

Always refrigerate canned chicken broth before using it. You will then have no difficulty in skimming off the ever-present blob of fat found in canned chicken soups.

To improve the quality of canned chicken broth, add to each 2 cups of broth ¼ cup each of sliced carrots, onions, and celery; 2 sprigs of parsley; ½ bay leaf; a pinch of thyme; and ⅓ cup dry white wine. If you happen to have any chicken gizzards, necks, or bones, add them to the pot. Cover and simmer over low heat for 30 minutes. Strain the stock and cool, uncovered. When cool, cover and refrigerate.

There are also various types of packaged products that can be used to substitute for chicken or beef broths or to reinforce flavors, but watch your own seasonings because most of these products tend to be salty. However, if you taste as you go, the chicken and beef bouillon cubes and dehydrated broth powders can be most useful in an emergency, as can the commercially prepared meat glazes, such as Bovril.

A fish stock can be made with bottled clam juice, which is an invaluable product in areas of the country where fish bones are hard to come by. Combine 1½ cups bottled clam juice; 1 cup water; ½ cup dry white wine; 1 thinly sliced onion; and 3 tablespoons fresh mushroom stems (optional). Use a stainless steel or enamel-lined saucepan, in order not to darken the stock. Simmer for 25 to 30 minutes, uncovered, until the liquid has reduced to two cups. Strain and taste. Clam juice is salty and the saltiness increases as it is reduced. Hold salt until the end; you may not need it. If you find the stock too salty, dilute it further.

Types of Soup

Despite the infinite variety of ingredients that can be blended into soups, all soups can be divided into half a dozen categories: clear, vegetable, cream, puréed, fish, and gumbo. The preparation and ingredients vary for the different categories of soups, but all of them are combinations of basic sauces and stocks with meat, seafood, or vegetables.

A supply of homemade soups can be a source of comfort to a busy homemaker. Consider doubling a recipe the next time you make soup and freezing what you don't need. However, do not add thickeners before freezing or storing. Soups that have been held in the refrigerator or freezer tend to thicken and may need to be diluted before being served. Additional seasoning may also be needed. Always bring a soup that has been frozen to a full boil immediately after defrosting.

Soups can always be made a day or two in advance and most are even better after a short storage period, which gives their flavors a chance to mellow and blend. Soups stored in the refrigerator should be brought to a boil every three days to keep them fresh.

Clear Soup

Broth, bouillon, consommé, and jellied soups are all clear soups made from the stocks described on the preceding pages. Bouillon was originally a French term for stock or broth, but it is now identified with a rich, concentrated brown stock. Consommé represents the high point in the evolution of a stock that has been enriched, concentrated, and clarified until it becomes a sparkling clear liquid. Jellied soups are made from rich, homemade stocks that contained meat and bones rich in collagen, a gelatin-producing substance. Unflavored gelatin can also turn any broth into a shimmering jellied soup.

In spite of the mystique that has surrounded soup, particularly chicken soup, and imbued it with the powers of a cure-all for bodily ills, clear soups have little nutritive value unless they are enriched by other products such as grains, pasta, eggs, milk, and the like. However, clear soup does have an effect as a stimulant, similar to coffee, tea, or chocolate. And in some curious way, it imparts a sense of well-being.

Vegetable Soup

Vegetable soup can be made of all vegetables or be based on meat and poultry stocks and contain chunks of meat and potatoes. It can be austerely studded with just a few floating vegetables or be thick enough to support a spoon, which is how some trenchermen prefer it. Every country in the world has its own regional vegetable soup, based on ingredients in best supply in the area and the cook's inclination, which is probably based on what the cook's mother used to make. To make vegetable soup, you assemble your vegetables in a pot; add water or, better still, stock; season; and "cook until done." A hearty vegetable soup can serve as a family dinner main course, accompanied by hot breads, a fresh salad, and an interesting dessert.

Cream Soup

Cream soups, which include bisques, are the glamorous members of the soup family. When properly made, their velvety texture and full flavor can get any meal off to a fine start, from a simple lunch to a special dinner party. Cream soups are based on a purée of vegetables, fish or meat, or a clear broth, thickened and enriched. The thickening agents, which give the soup its body, texture, and soft creamy color, can be anything from a starch, such as flour, to a mixture of egg yolk and cream, according to your choice. They must be added to the liquid in proper proportion or the soup can become too thick and starchy.

Flour Thickening. The basic proportions are 1 tablespoon of flour mixed with 2 tablespoons of cold stock, milk, or water to 2 cups of soup. Shake the flour and liquid together vigorously in a small covered jar. Add this mixture, called a *slurry*, to the soup over medium heat. Stir constantly until the soup reaches a boil. Reduce heat and simmer, stirring, until smooth and thickened.

Flour and Butter. The basic proportions are 1 tablespoon of flour and 1 tablespoon of butter to 2 cups of soup. Melt the butter in a small pan, stir in the flour and cook for 2 or 3 minutes, until bubbly, but not brown. Add some hot soup to the flour and butter mixture and cook over low heat, stirring, until it is smooth and thickened. Return the mixture to the remaining soup. Heat and stir until smooth.

Egg Yolk and Cream Thickening. Thickening with egg yolks gives soup a lavish richness. It takes just a few minutes and should be done immediately before serving. The thickening takes place through the action of the hot soup on the egg yolk, coagulating it. Use 1 tablespoon of cream to 1 egg yolk for each cup of soup. Mix the egg yolk and cream in a small bowl and whisk in a cup or so of hot soup, little by little, to heat the egg yolk slowly. Return the mixture to the remaining soup, reheat slowly, and stir until it thickens. Make sure that you do not allow it to come to a boil or the eggs will curdle.

Puréed Soup

Since blenders and food processors have entered the kitchen scene, the ranks of puréed soups have swelled considerably. Puréed soups made from leafy vegetables or those low in starch may require further thickening with one of the thickening agents mentioned above, or with the addition of 2 or 3 tablespoons of uncooked rice or grated raw potato added during the cooking. A purée made from starchy products, such as dried legumes—peas, beans, split peas, lentils, and the like—will produce a thick soup that needs little or no additional starch. A soup that is too thick can be thinned with stock, water, or milk.

Blenders and food processors do an acceptable job of puréeing most soups and certainly make life simpler for those of us who operate one-person kitchens. There are a few situations, however, when the mechanical action of those wonderful machines is less desirable than processing by hand. Very starchy vegetables, particularly potatoes, are lighter and more delicate when pushed through a strainer than when exposed to the speed of the metal blades. It causes the formation of gluten, which makes the soup gummy. Purées of dried beans should also be strained to eliminate the skins, which are sometimes difficult to digest. Use a food mill, which is a hand-operated strainer with a circular lever arrangement that forces the beans through a perforated bottom disk and purées the beans but holds back the skins. The strain-

ing will be easier if you break the bean skins first by giving the beans a couple of whirls in the blender at low speed.

Chowder and Fish Soups

A chowder is a special type of substantial soup containing large pieces of seafood and vegetables. It is a meal in itself and great informal party fare. The genesis of the word *chowder* is to be found in *la chaudière*, the enormous copper pot of early French coastal villages. The fishermen returning from their expeditions would toss part of their catch into *la chaudière*, whereupon the villagers cooked up a soup to celebrate the safe return of their men from the sea. The word *chaudière* became corrupted into *chowder* on its way to New England via French Canada, but clam chowder has continued to be a cause for celebration.

A chowder always contains potatoes. Salt pork and cream or milk are also added. Clam chowder may or may not include tomatoes, depending on whether the cook comes from New England or elsewhere. The matter of clams and tomatoes is viewed with considerable passion in some areas, as evidenced by the fact that the Maine legislature once considered a bill that would have made mixing clams and tomatoes illegal.

Timing is the essential factor in preparing a fish soup or chowder. Because fish cooks very quickly, it must be added at the last minute or it will fall apart and lose its identity. Shellfish is equally temperamental and will repay you for overcooking by getting tough. Mussels and clams are interchangeable in almost all chowder recipes.

Gumbo

Gumbo is a regional dish, halfway between a soup and a stew, that originated in the South. It is generally served with rice and contains okra, green pepper, tomatoes, onions, and all manner of shellfish, meat, or poultry. A characteristic gelatinous quality is produced by the thick sap that exudes from the sliced okra pods as they cook.

The Louisiana or Creole gumbo is always made with a powder made of ground sassafras leaf, called *filé*, which thickens and darkens the gumbo. The Creole cooks learned about the filé powder from the early French and Spanish settlers, who in turn had learned the trick from the Choctaw Indians of Louisiana. Filé powder is sprinkled over the gumbo at the last minute; it becomes stringy if boiled.

Bouillon

Boil degreased brown stock, uncovered, until it is reduced by about one-third, in order to concentrate the flavor. Taste and correct seasoning. The bouillon may be garnished with lemon slices or thinly sliced avocado; sprinkled with minced parsley or chives; or enriched with pasta such as fine noodles or spaetzle.

Consommé

Consommé is a clear full-bodied soup, the end product of a rich stock that has been clarified. A flavorful consommé makes a delicious low-calorie appetizer course that is appropriate for even a formal dinner. It may be garnished with a few julienned vegetables or some sliced, sautéed mushrooms.

Beef consommé is made with brown stock (page 35) and beef meat; white consommé is made with chicken stock (page 36) and/or veal stock (page 37) and veal or chicken. The same procedure is followed for both beef and white consommé.

1 pound ground lean beef (for beef consommé), *or*

1 to 2 pounds chicken backs, wings, necks and veal bones (for white consommé)

1 or 2 leeks, white part only, finely chopped

2 small carrots, grated

1 onion, minced

4 peppercorns, crushed

6 cups cold, degreased stock

Combine all the ingredients and slowly bring to a boil. Reduce heat, cover, and simmer gently for 1 hour. Strain and cool. When completely cold, clarify stock. (See directions on page 33 .)

Yield: 5 servings.

Cold Jellied Soup

Any broth can be made into a jellied soup with the addition of unflavored gelatin. However, some stocks contain more collagen, a gelatin-producing substance, than others. To get an idea of how much, if any, additional gelatin is needed to produce a jellied soup, pour one half inch of homemade broth into a chilled saucer and refrigerate for at least 30 minutes. Then break it up with a fork and leave it at room temperature for 10 minutes. For jellied soup, it should keep its shape softly. If the lumps are firm enough to stand alone, it is an aspic.

One envelope unflavored gelatin to a quart of stock that has thickened a little will provide the additional body need for a jellied soup. Sprinkle the gelatin over ½ cup of the cold stock to soften. Heat 1 cup of stock to the simmering point. Add the softened gelatin and stir until dissolved. Add the remaining stock and chill in the refrigerator for 4 hours.

Break up the soup into cubes with a fork and serve in individual chilled bowls. Top with a dollop of sour cream, crème fraîche, or plain yogurt, a sprinkling of chopped chives, or some thin slices of lemon.

Fresh Vegetable Soup

The day after a party when your refrigerator is overflowing with leftover crudités *is the moment for fresh vegetable soup. Almost any vegetable can go into it, from asparagus to zucchini. Not beets, though. They color the soup too much. Cauliflower, peas, beans, mushrooms, pepper, squash, cabbage, tomatoes, and more—they're all grist for your vegetable soup mill. The ones listed below are only a general guide. Use what you have, but do include the aromatic vegetables—onions, carrots, and celery. Any small pasta may be substituted for the barley. Add it for the last ten minutes of cooking. You may use chicken broth, beef broth, or, as in this recipe, water, which will make it a vegetarian soup, and very good it is.*

2 tablespoons butter
2 onions, coarsely chopped
2 carrots, diced
3 celery stalks, sliced
2 to 2½ quarts water
½ cup barley, washed
1 turnip, diced
1 cup green beans
1 medium-size zucchini
1 cup cauliflowerets
2 ripe tomatoes, peeled, seeded,
    and cut into small pieces, *or*
    a 1-pound can of tomatoes
1 cup green peas
Salt and freshly ground pepper

Heat the butter in a large, heavy pot. Add the onion, carrots, and celery and stir and cook until soft, 5 to 8 minutes. Add the water and bring to a boil. Add the barley and the rest of the vegetables, except the peas, and simmer, covered, until the vegetables and barley are tender, 45 to 50 minutes. Add the peas for the last 10 minutes of cooking. Add salt and pepper to taste. Serve with grated cheese if you wish.

Yield: 12 servings.

Hot Borscht (Beet and Cabbage Soup)

2 quarts beef stock, preferably
  homemade
5 young beets, cut julienne, *or*
  a 1-pound can julienne beets
3 cups finely shredded cabbage
2 onions, sliced
1 1-pound can tomatoes, chopped
3 carrots, cut julienne
¼ cup lemon juice
1 teaspoon sugar
2 tablespoons Worcestershire
  sauce
Salt
Sour cream (optional)

If are you making your own beef stock, prepare it the day before so that you can refrigerate it and skim the fat completely. Trim off the cooked meat from the bones, cut it into small dice, and add it to the soup before serving.

Bring the stock to a boil. Add the raw beets and cook for 15 minutes. If you are using canned beets, strain them, set the beets aside, and add the liquid to the soup. Reduce heat and add cabbage, onions, pulp and juice of tomatoes, carrots, lemon juice, sugar and Worcestershire sauce. Simmer, covered, for 40 minutes longer, or until vegetables are soft. Stir in reserved beets, if using canned ones, and diced meat. Taste for seasoning; the soup should be sweet-sour, and you may want a bit more lemon juice, sugar, or both. Add salt as needed. Serve in large heated soup bowls topped with a dollop of sour cream, if you wish.

A whole boiled potato may be added to each portion before serving.

Yield: 8 servings.

Escarole Soup With Meatballs

1 egg
½ small onion, roughly chopped
1 tablespoon chopped parsley
½ pound lean ground beef
2 tablespoons freshly grated
  Parmesan or Romano cheese
8 cups chicken broth, preferably
  homemade
1 head escarole (1½ to 2 pounds)
Additional grated cheese
  (optional)
Salt and freshly ground pepper

In a blender, purée the egg, onion, and parsley. Scrape into a bowl and mix with the meat and cheese. Use your hands to blend the mixture well. Make small balls, about ½ to ¾ inch in diameter, rolling them between your palms. Set aside.

In a large kettle, slowly bring the broth to a boil. Wash the escarole, shake off the water, and shred or chop it roughly. Be sure that you buy escarole and not chicory. Escarole is the green with a bushy head made up of broad leaves that do *not* curl at the tips.

When the soup has reached a boil, add the escarole and meatballs. Cover and simmer for 20 to 30 minutes, or until the escarole is very tender and the meatballs float to the top. Taste and correct seasoning. If you are serving additional cheese, you may not need salt. Serve hot in heated bowls.

Yield: 6 servings.

Mushroom and Barley Soup

Nutritious and filling enough to serve as a whole meal. It stores well in the refrigerator or freezer.

1 ounce dried mushrooms
1 cup barley
1 cup dried baby lima beans
4 quarts water
2 whole celery stalks and leaves
1 bay leaf
1 peeled onion, studded with 3 cloves
3 whole, unpeeled garlic cloves, tied in cheesecloth
3 parsley sprigs
3 whole carrots, scraped
Salt and freshly ground pepper
3 tablespoons minced fresh parsley or dill

Dried mushrooms are sometimes gritty. Wash them in several changes of water, lifting them out of the bowl so that the grit is left behind. Soak them in 2 cups of water for an hour or so and use the water as part of the soup liquid. Chop the mushrooms if they are large.

Wash and drain the barley; wash and pick over the lima beans. Put the barley and lima beans in a large kettle with 4 quarts of water (including the liquid from the mushrooms), and add the celery, bay leaf, onion, garlic cloves, and parsley sprigs. Cover the kettle and bring to a boil. Tilt the cover so that about an inch of space is left open and simmer the soup slowly for 1 hour, stirring from time to time. Add the carrots, salt, and pepper and simmer for 1 hour longer, or until the lima beans and barley are tender. Continue to stir from time to time to prevent sticking. Discard bay leaf before serving.

Yield: 12 servings.

Chinese Egg Drop Soup

A fine idea for your freshly made beef or chicken broth.

4 cups clear chicken or beef broth
3 water chestnuts, chopped
1 tablespoon cornstarch
3 tablespoons water
2 scallions, sliced
1 egg, well beaten
Salt and freshly ground pepper

Bring the broth and water chestnuts to a boil. Dissolve the cornstarch in the water and add it slowly to the soup, stirring until it thickens. Stir in the scallions and mix well. Gently stir in the beaten egg and turn off the heat at once, as soon as all the egg has been stirred in. The egg will float to the surface. Taste for seasoning and add salt and pepper if needed.

Yield: 4 servings.

Black Bean Soup

Served with its satellite of garnishes and accompanied by a spinach and mushroom salad and some hot breads, this thick, hearty soup makes a fine main course for a supper for family or friends.

1 pound dried black beans
8 to 9 cups water
¼ pound salt pork (in one piece)
3 tablespoons vegetable oil
1 large onion, coarsely chopped
1 or 2 bell peppers, coarsely
  chopped (about 1½ cups)
4 garlic cloves, mashed or minced
2½ tablespoons ground cumin
2 tablespoons dried oregano
2 tablespoons dry mustard
Juice of 1 lemon
Salt and freshly ground pepper

Garnishes:

1 lemon, thinly sliced
3 hard cooked eggs, white and
  yolks chopped separately
Hot cooked rice
Spanish onion, finely chopped
Bell pepper, finely chopped
Sour cream

Combine beans and water in a large kettle. Cover, bring to a boil and boil for 5 minutes. Turn off heat and let stand for 1 hour. You may also soak the beans in water overnight and omit the 5-minute boil. Discard the soaking water.

Wash the chunk of salt pork and add it to the kettle. Add fresh water to cover. Bring to a boil, cover, and simmer for 2 hours. Skim and stir often.

Heat the oil in a medium-size skillet and sauté the onion and pepper over high heat, stirring constantly, for 7 minutes. Add the onion and bell pepper to the beans.

In a small bowl, combine the mashed garlic, cumin, oregano, dry mustard, and half the lemon juice. Mix well with a fork. Add this to the beans and cook an additional hour, skimming from time to time until no foam appears on the surface. Remove from the heat.

Ladle the bean mixture in batches into a food mill set over a large clean pot. Purée the soup and return purée to the soup pot. Discard the bean residue left in the food mill. (Bean soup is infinitely more digestible when it is put through a food mill; puréeing it in a processor or blender is not a substitute and will not give the same result.) Add salt and pepper to taste and the remaining lemon juice. If the soup is too thick, add up to 1 cup of water. The soup may be made in advance and reheated at serving time. Serve in warmed bowls.

Serve the garnishes in individual bowls and let the guests serve themselves with whatever combination they choose.

Yield: 6 servings.

Split Pea Soup

A simple soup for a cold day. If you have a ham hock or a meaty ham bone, use it. If not, you will still have a splendid soup. You may use either green or yellow split peas. Split peas no longer need a prolonged soaking period and they cook relatively quickly.

2 carrots, scraped and sliced
1 onion, coarsely chopped
1 celery stalk, cut in two
1 pound quick-cooking dried split
   peas
1 garlic clove
Ham hock or ham bone (optional)
2 quarts water
2 tablespoons butter
Salt and freshly ground pepper
2 cooked frankfurters (optional)

Combine everything except the salt, pepper, and frankfurters in a large soup kettle. Cover and simmer for about 1½ hours, or until the peas are soft, stirring occasionally.

Remove the ham hock or bone, if used, and celery and put the soup through a food mill. Return to the pot. Cut off any little bits of meat clinging to the ham bone and add them to the soup. Add salt and pepper to taste. If the soup is too thick, dilute it with cream, milk, or broth. Serve hot with some cooked frankfurter or thinly sliced sausages floating on top, if desired.

Yield: 10 servings.

Lentil Soup

Follow the above directions, substituting lentils for the split peas. You can purée the lentils or leave them whole, or purée half, for a variety of textures. You may also add some tomato purée or a large ripe tomato, peeled, seeded, and chopped into small chunks. A tablespoon or two of dry sherry mixed through just before serving will do it nothing but good.

Zucchini Soup

With the addition of some diced, cooked chicken, this can serve as a pleasant summer lunch dish. It is rich in flavor and low in calories.

2 to 2½ pounds zucchini, *or a combination of zucchini and yellow summer squash*

1 onion, thinly sliced

1 cup water

1 chicken bouillon cube or broth powder

1½ to 2 cups chicken broth, preferably homemade

Salt and freshly ground pepper

1 cup diced cooked chicken (optional)

Plain yogurt (optional)

Scrub the squash well, leaving the skins on, and removing the stem ends. Slice about 12 paper-thin slices from a zucchini and set aside for garnish. Slice the remaining squash into ¼-inch-thick slices and cook, covered, in a saucepan with the onion, water, and bouillon cube or broth powder. Simmer until soft, about 20 minutes, and blend the vegetables and liquid until liquefied. You will have to do it in two or three batches.

Transfer to a soup pot or a bowl, depending on whether you will heat or chill the soup. Add enough chicken broth to give you the consistency you want; the soup should be on the thick side, like heavy cream. Taste and correct the seasoning. The amount of salt will depend upon the saltiness of the broth.

To serve, either chilled or heated, add some of the diced chicken to each portion and top with a dollop of yogurt and a sprinkle of chopped zucchini slices.

Yield: 6 servings.

Variation: For a spicy flavor, add the following to the squash when cooking it: 1 teaspoon curry powder or more, according to taste, ½ teaspoon dry mustard, or ½ teaspoon ground ginger.

Basic Recipe For Vegetable Cream Soups

Here is a simple formula for creamy fresh vegetable soups. The base of the soup is a purée of leek and onion plus any vegetable of your choice—asparagus, broccoli, beans, cucumber, carrot, celery, peas, pumpkin, squash, zucchini, spinach, sorrel, watercress, even lettuce—whatever is fresh in the market or your garden. To the base, you will add chicken stock, a light cream sauce, salt, pepper, and a sprinkling of chopped chives or fresh parsley to finish it off. The cream sauce may be made with heavy or light cream, whole milk or skim milk. Any of them will produce a velvety smooth soup. The soup can be served chilled in the summer and hot in the winter.

2 leeks

1 medium- to large-size onion

1 pound or more of any vegetable of your choice

Wash leeks and cut down to within a couple of inches of the root end to rinse out any sand. If your base vegetable is green, use both the white and green parts of the leeks; if the vegetable is pale or golden, use only the white. Slice leeks and onion. Wash

4 tablespoons butter
3 cups chicken stock
2 tablespoons flour
3½ cups milk, heated
Freshly grated nutmeg
Salt and freshly ground pepper
Chopped chives or parsley for
  garnish

and pare or scrape the vegetable and cut into chunks, slices, flowerets, or whatever shape is needed to achieve small pieces that will cook quickly.

Heat 2 tablespoons of the butter in a heavy, 3-quart saucepan. Cook the leeks and onion until they are limp and transparent. Add the chicken stock and the cut vegetables. (Tender green vegetables like broccoli flowerets, spinach, and watercress may be added during the last 10 minutes of cooking so that their color will be preserved, but the stems of broccoli and asparagus need longer cooking. Discard the coarse watercress stems; use only the leaves and the thin, tender parts of the stems.) Cover the pot and simmer, slowly, until the vegetables are soft, 25 to 30 minutes. Put in a blender in batches until all are liquefied; set purée aside.

Using the same pot, heat the remaining 2 tablespoons of butter. Whisk in 2 tablespoons flour and, over medium-low heat, stir constantly until bubbly without coloring, about 2 minutes. Remove from the heat, add the heated milk (heating prevents lumps), whisk well, and cook over medium heat, stirring, until the sauce comes to a boil and is smooth and thickened. Add a few gratings of fresh nutmeg. Add the vegetable purée to the cream sauce, mix together, and taste for seasoning. The amount of salt you need will depend on the saltiness of the chicken stock.

If the soup is to be served cold, cool it, then cover and refrigerate. If it is too thick, thin it with chicken broth, milk, or cream. Garnish with a sprinkle of chopped chives or parsley.

Yield: 8 servings.

Cream of Mushroom Soup

1 pound fresh white mushrooms
2 tablespoons butter
1 small onion, coarsely chopped
1½ cups chicken broth
2 tablespoons flour
½ cup cold water
1½ cups light cream or half-and-half
¼ teaspoon dried thyme
Salt and freshly ground pepper

Wipe the mushrooms and set aside four large caps to use as garnish. Slice the remainder.

Heat the butter in a heavy saucepan. Add the chopped onion and sliced mushrooms and cook, covered, over low heat for 10 minutes. Add the chicken broth and bring to a boil. Reduce heat and simmer for 15 minutes. During this time, drop in the four mushroom caps and poach for 2 or 3 minutes. Remove with a slotted spoon. When cooled, slice thinly and reserve.

Purée the soup in a blender or food processor but do not liquefy—some texture from the mushrooms and onion should remain. Return the puréed soup to the pot. Combine the flour and water in a small jar with a tight lid and shake well to blend. Add the mixture to the simmering soup, beating it with a wire whisk. Add the cream and thyme and continue to stir until the soup is smooth and thickened. Season with salt and pepper and simmer slowly for 5 minutes longer, but do not boil. Taste and correct seasoning. Ladle soup into bowls and garnish each portion with some sliced mushrooms.

Yield: 4 servings.

Cream of Pea and Watercress Soup

1 bunch watercress
1 large celery stalk, chopped
1 medium onion, chopped
1 tablespoon freshly grated Parmesan cheese
2 cups chicken broth, preferably homemade
1 tablespoon fresh snipped dill, or 1 teaspoon dried dillweed
1 10-ounce package frozen green peas
Salt and freshly ground pepper
2 tablespoons butter
2 tablespoons flour
2½ cups milk, warmed

Strip the leaves from the watercress, discarding the coarse stems. In a saucepan, combine the watercress, celery, onion, Parmesan cheese, chicken broth, and dill and bring to a boil. Lower the heat and simmer, covered, for 10 minutes. Thaw the green peas under hot running water and add them to the soup for the last 3 or 4 minutes of cooking. Add salt and pepper to taste. Purée in batches in a blender or food processor, and reserve the purée.

Using the same saucepan, heat the butter until foamy, blend in the flour, and stir until bubbly, about 3 minutes. Remove from the heat, add the heated milk, whisk well, and cook over medium heat, stirring, until it comes to a boil and is smooth and thickened. Add the vegetable purée to the cream sauce, blend well, and taste and correct the seasoning. Serve hot.

Yield: 6 servings.

Vichyssoise

Thanks to the knowledgeable Craig Claiborne, food editor of The New York Times, *and his incredibly efficient filing system, here is what is believed to be the original recipe for the cold leek-and-potato soup created by Louis Diat of the Ritz-Carlton Hotel. Practically overnight, this soup transformed the once-lowly leek, known in France as "poor man's asparagus," into a stylish (and expensive) vegetable.*

4 leeks, white part
1 medium-size onion
2 ounces (½ stick) sweet butter
5 medium-size potatoes
1 quart water or chicken broth
1 tablespoon salt
2 cups milk
2 cups light cream
1 cup heavy cream

Finely slice the white part of the leeks and the onion and brown very slightly in the sweet butter, then add the potatoes, also sliced finely. Add water or broth and salt. Boil from 35 to 40 minutes. Crush and rub through a fine strainer. Return to the heat and add the milk and light cream. Season to taste and bring to a boil. Cool and then rub through a very fine strainer. When the soup is cold, add the heavy cream. Chill thoroughly before serving. Finely chopped chives may be added when serving.

Yield: 10 servings.

Note: We have no wish to criticize M. Diat, who was indeed an inspired master chef, but if you make this vichyssoise with water instead of a strong, well-flavored chicken broth, you will end up with a pallid, rather uninteresting brew.

Yogurt Soup

3 tablespoons butter
1 onion, finely chopped (about 1 cup)
7 cups chicken broth, preferably homemade
¼ cup barley, washed
4 cups plain yogurt
1 tablespoon finely minced fresh parsley
1 tablespoon finely minced fresh mint, *or* 1 teaspoon dried mint

Melt the butter in a 3-quart kettle, add the onion, and cook until limp and transparent, stirring often, 3 or 4 minutes.

Add the broth and bring to a boil. Skim off any fat globules that rise to the surface. Stir in the washed barley. Cover pot and simmer over low heat for 45 minutes, or until the barley is tender.

Remove from the heat and with a wire whisk or wooden spoon, whisk in the yogurt until well blended. Cool and chill, or keep warm, but do not boil. Just before serving, stir in the parsley and mint.

Yield: 10 servings.

Fish Chowder

The aroma and taste of this chowder are wonderful. A homemade fish stock is recommended; bottled clam juice just won't work as well.

1½ ounces salt pork, cut into small cubes

3 large onions (about ¾ pound), thinly sliced

3 tablespoons flour

8 cups fish stock

5 medium-size potatoes (about 1½ pounds), peeled and thinly sliced

2½ pounds cod, haddock, or fluke fillets, cut into 1½-inch squares

½ teaspoon dried thyme

Pinch of dried sage

Salt and freshly ground pepper

In a heavy kettle over a medium flame, heat the small cubes of salt pork until the fat is melted and the pieces are lightly browned. Remove the browned bits and reserve. Add the onion to the fat and cook until softened and lightly colored, stirring often. Sprinkle with flour and stir to mix well. Add the fish stock and blend well with a wooden spoon.

Bring to a boil and add the potato slices. Simmer, partly covered, until the potatoes are a bit tender, about 10 minutes. Skim the surface to remove excess fat.

Add the fish and simmer until the fish becomes opaque. This will take very little time, 5 to 7 minutes, depending on the size of the fish cubes. Do not overcook. Add the thyme, sage, and salt and pepper to taste.

Quick Fish Soup

This can be assembled quickly from ingredients stashed in your freezer and on your pantry shelves. It is substantial enough to serve as a main course.

2 tablespoons butter

1 large onion, chopped

½ green pepper, diced

1 large garlic clove, minced

1 1-pound, 12-ounce can tomatoes in tomato purée

1 13¾-ounce can chicken broth

1 10½-ounce can minced clams, drained (reserve the juice)

1 1-pound package frozen cod or perch fillets, partly thawed, *or* equivalent of fresh fish fillets

⅓ cup pasta (elbow macaroni or small shells)

Salt and freshly ground pepper

⅓ cup dry sherry

Melt the butter in a medium-size pot, and cook the onion, green pepper, and garlic until soft but not brown. Add the tomatoes and purée, chicken broth, and reserved clam juice. Cook over low heat for 15 minutes, stirring from time to time and breaking up the tomatoes with a wooden spoon.

Cut the fish fillets into 1-inch squares and add to the soup. Add the clams and pasta, and simmer, covered, for 10 minutes, or until the fish is cooked and the pasta is tender. Add salt and pepper to taste. Clams are generally salty, so you'll need very little. Add sherry and heat through.

Yield: 6 servings.

Cream of Mussel Soup

2 quarts mussels

8 shallots, peeled and coarsely chopped

1 onion, peeled and quartered

3 parsley sprigs

Freshly ground pepper

Pinch of ground red pepper

1 cup dry white wine

5 tablespoons butter

1 small bay leaf

1 teaspoon dried thyme

1½ cups cream

2 tablespoons finely minced fresh parsley

Scrub the mussels with a stiff plastic pot scrubber under cold running water. Pull or cut off the beards. Discard any mussels that are broken or opened. Place them in a large kettle with the shallots, onion, parsley, pepper, ground red pepper, wine, butter, bay leaf, and thyme. You may not need any salt because mussels are quite salty. Cover the pot tightly, bring to a boil, reduce the heat, and steam for about 10 minutes. Shake the steamer after the steaming begins to redistribute the shellfish by holding the steamer pot by the handles while keeping the cover tightly shut with your thumbs. After 10 to 12 minutes, remove the opened mussels. Allow another 4 or 5 minutes for any with shells that remain shut. If they still do not open after the additional time, discard them.

Remove the mussels from the opened shells and place them in a blender or food processor, keeping out a few to use as garnish for the soup. Strain the broth through a colander lined with three thicknesses of cheesecloth to strain out any sand that may have been in the mussel shells. Add the shallots and onions from the mussel broth to a cup of the broth and place in the blender or food processor. Blend until smooth. Combine the mussel purée with the remaining mussel broth, stir in cream, and reheat, but do not boil. Taste and correct seasoning. Garnish each portion with a few mussels and a sprinkling of parsley. This may also be served chilled.

Yield: 6 servings.

Spinach and Clam Soup

1 medium onion, finely chopped

3 strips of bacon, chopped

4 anchovy fillets, minced

1 large garlic clove, finely minced

1 10-ounce package frozen leaf
    spinach

1 cup chopped fresh clams, *or* 2
    6½-ounce cans chopped clams

¼ pound (1 stick) butter

2 tablespoons flour

4 cups chicken broth, preferably
    homemade

1 cup heavy or light cream

Freshly ground pepper

Heat a small skillet over medium heat. Add onion, bacon, anchovies, and garlic and sauté lightly, stirring often, until onion is limp and transparent. Do not let it brown. Remove from the heat.

In a small saucepan, cook the spinach quickly until thawed. Drain and, when cool enough to handle, squeeze as dry as possible between the palms of your hands. Spread out on a wooden chopping board and chop coarsely. Set aside.

If you are using canned clams, drain them and reserve the liquid.

In a large saucepan, melt the butter over medium-high heat. Add the flour and stir constantly until the liquid bubbles, about 3 minutes. Remove from the heat, whisk in the chicken broth and reserved clam liquid, beating vigorously, and return to the heat. Cook and stir until the sauce becomes thickened and smooth. Add the onion mixture and spinach and bring to a boil, stirring occasionally. Pour in cream and chopped clams and bring to a boil again. Reduce the heat. Add a few grinds of pepper and taste for seasoning—you may not need any additional salt. Serve in heated bowls.

Yield: 6 servings.

Oyster Stew

Fresh everything—milk, cream, butter, oysters—and speedy cooking make this perfection.

2 cups milk

2 cups light cream

3 cups shucked oysters and juice

6 tablespoons butter

Salt and freshly ground pepper

Dash of ground red pepper *or*
    Tabasco sauce (optional)

Heat together the milk, cream, and juice from the oysters to the boiling point, but do not boil. While this is heating, melt the butter in a skillet until bubbling, and toss in the oysters. Shake the pan vigorously until the oysters have plumped and barely curled at the edges, about 3 minutes. Combine the oysters with the hot milk and cream mixture, and season with salt, pepper, and ground red pepper, if you wish. Cook for a minute or two, just until very hot. Oysters, like other shellfish, get tough if overcooked, their sweet tenderness forever gone. Serve the stew in heated bowls with crackers or hot buttered toast.

Yield: 6 servings.

Gulf Coast Gumbo

A memorable main course for lunch or brunch.

3 tablespoons oil

3 tablespoons butter

2 medium onions, coarsely chopped

1 green pepper, coarsely chopped

1 pound boiled ham, cut into ½-inch cubes

1 pound chicken breasts, cut into ½-inch cubes

Salt and freshly ground pepper

1 pound okra, cut into ¼-inch-thick slices

4 cups chicken broth, preferably homemade

4 cups water

2 cups cooked fresh or canned tomatoes

½ teaspoon dried thyme

1 bay leaf

¼ teaspoon ground red pepper *or* a few dashes of Tabasco

2 tablespoons minced fresh parsley

2 cloves garlic, minced

2 pounds raw shrimp, shelled and deveined

1 pound crabmeat

Boiled rice

In a large kettle, heat the oil and butter and lightly sauté the onion and green pepper. Remove with a slotted spoon and place on paper towels to drain. Add the ham and chicken cubes and brown, tossing often. Sprinkle with salt and pepper. Remove and drain on paper towels. Pour off any fat remaining in the pan. Return the meat and vegetables to the pot and add the okra, broth, water, tomatoes, thyme, bay leaf, red pepper, parsley, and garlic. Cover and simmer slowly for 1½ to 2 hours. Add the shrimp and crabmeat and cook 5 to 6 minutes, just until the shrimp turn pink. Mix gently so that all is distributed. Remove the bay leaf. Taste and correct seasoning. Serve in soup plates over hot boiled rice.

Yield: 10 servings.

3
Meat

Americans' passion for meat has propelled the business of producing it into one of the nation's leading industries. Meat is usually the first thing we think of when planning a menu, and most of us lavish a good deal of time and effort (not to mention money) on it. The various cuts of meat and the cooking processes best suited to preparing them are described on the following pages. We hope that there are some you have overlooked before that will bring variety and new interest to your daily meals.

Most of the commercial beef we eat comes from desexed young male animals called steers, some from heifers, which are young cows that have not produced a calf, and a limited quantity of inferior quality from cows, or mature females. Veal is the meat of a young calf, lamb the meat of a young sheep from six to eight months old. Older than that, the sheep gives us mutton. Pork remains pork, regardless of the age and sex of the pig.

Nutritional Values

The composition of meat varies from one cut to another, but meat is an excellent source of high-quality protein, which accounts for 15 to 20 percent of its total calories. A 3½ ounce serving of meat can contain fewer than 150 calories or more than 500, depending on the type of animal, its breed, feed, and age. Animals, like humans, tend to get fatter as they get older, so it follows that veal, the meat from a young calf, will be leaner than that from a fully grown and well-nourished steer.

The edible portions of meat, aside from the fat, consist of one or more muscles, each of which is made up of many bundles of muscle fibers. This edible portion is low in calcium, because most of the calcium is to be found in the bones of the animals. Lean muscle meats are excellent sources of phosphorus, iron, and

the B vitamins, particularly niacin and riboflavin. Pork is richer in thiamine, another of the B vitamins, than is beef.

The organ meats, such as liver, kidney, brains, sweetbreads, and heart, are lower in fat and, consequently, in calories, than the muscle meat from the same animal. But they are also higher in cholesterol. Liver is an especially rich source of iron and a concentrated source of vitamin A.

Cooking does not appreciably lower the nutritive value of the proteins in meat, which means that a cooked hamburger has as much protein as steak tartare. But there is some loss of the B vitamins—thiamine, riboflavin, and niacin—in cooking, although the loss of thiamine tends to be greater than the other two. And, just as the long cooking of vegetables diminishes vitamins, there is greater vitamin loss in meat that is cooked for a long time; rare meat contains more of the B vitamins than well-done. When meat is braised or stewed, a considerable amount of each vitamin is captured in the cooking liquid, which is an important reason to use natural gravies.

Buying Meat

As all food shoppers know, meat is generally the most expensive item in the family food budget and a source of concern to anyone attempting to keep the cost of feeding a family from being prohibitive. One way to reduce meat bills is to concentrate on less expensive cuts. Few people have a problem identifying luxury cuts such as rib roasts, porterhouse steaks, shells of beef, legs of lamb, and the like, but they may find themselves at a loss in the presence of a supermarket tumult of precut, prepackaged meats, many of them seductively and fancifully labeled. The uninitiated shopper who thinks that anything called "steak" can be broiled may be in for an unpleasant surprise.

However, the meat shopper with even a superficial knowledge of the anatomy of the meat-producing animals will have a good idea of how tender or how tough a cut from a particular part of the animal is likely to be. Words like *blade, loin, shoulder,* and *neck* will signal whether you should heat the broiler or get out the braising pot.

The drawings of the four meat-producing animals that give us beef (see page 73), lamb (see page 96), pork (see page 106), and veal (see page 118) illustrate the positions of the various cuts. You will notice that the skeletal structure of all four animals is basically the same. Bone and muscle from corresponding parts of different animals are similar in shape and the meat is also likely to be comparable in tenderness.

What Makes Meat Tender?

Meat is muscle, and the less work the muscle does the more tender the meat will be. The long muscles in humans that extend from our shoulder blades to our lower back have a job to do in keeping us erect. But in four-legged animals, these same muscles have little to do. Consequently, from this section in all of the animals come the most tender cuts—the rib, the loin, and the sirloin. The tougher cuts are from the neck, shoulder, and shanks. A great deal also depends on the conditions under which the animal was raised, its breed, and its age. It is logical that young animals are more tender than older ones, and that pampered herds that grow up in a feedlot where their only mission in life is to loll around and eat are going to be much less tough than those that are raised on the range, where they have to forage for their food.

Connective tissues surround and hold together the muscle fibers of which meat is composed. In these connective tissues are embedded protein fibers called collagen and elastin. There are more collagen fibers than elastin, which is fortunate because the collagen melts in the cooking and is slowly released from the tissues, while the rubberlike elastin is scarcely affected. As collagen disintegrates, it converts into gelatin and the meat becomes soft and tender. However, this process takes long hours of cooking. It is possible to tenderize meat by adding an enzyme to it, but this has disadvantages. The most commonly used enzyme is papain, which is obtained from an unripe papaya and is spread on the meat. However, it is almost impossible to do this uniformly; some parts end up being too mushy, others remain too chewy. Piercing the meat to get the tenderizer into the center releases juices and you can very well end up with tender meat that has been robbed of its flavor.

Some meat packers have developed a procedure of injecting the enzyme preparation into the live animal shortly before slaughter. The enzyme is carried by the blood to all parts of the animal and when the meat is cooked, it is reactivated and acts as a tenderizer. However, this procedure has not met with universal approval, one of the criticisms being that enzymes alter the taste and texture of meat significantly. Without question, the best solution for tenderizing meat is to cook it properly, using the method best suited to the cut and grade.

Thin cuts of meat can be tenderized by scoring the surface with a sharp knife or pounding the meat with a mallet. Both procedures weaken the muscle fibers.

Another procedure directed toward increasing the tenderness of meat is aging it. The meat is hung for three to six weeks. To control the growth of microorganisms, the temperature is kept between 34 and 38 degrees and the humidity held to approximately 70 percent. During this time, the exterior surfaces of the meat become hard and have to be trimmed off, and there is further loss from evaporation. This is an expensive procedure and most of the loins and ribs of beef that are aged in this manner go to top-grade restaurants and hotels. However, there is also a fast-aged meat that is sold in retail outlets. The fast-aged meat is held at a higher temperature for two days.

Food scientists cannot say with certainty why aging increases the tenderness of meat. Some believe that it is due to the action of the enzymes present in the meat on the muscle fiber proteins. Others attribute it to an increase in the water-holding capacity of the proteins of the muscle fibers. This means that less water is given up during cooking and the meat is thus more tender.

Immediately after an animal is slaughtered, the flesh is soft and flabby. Then rigor mortis sets in and the meat becomes firm and tough. This is followed by the muscles again becoming soft and flexible and the meat more tender. Beef is toughest from one to three days after slaughter. Normally, six to ten days elapse from the time the animal is slaughtered until it reaches your kitchen. The toughness of the meat caused by rigor has lessened appreciably during this period.

Veal, lamb, and pork are from young animals and are naturally tender, but some butchers feel that a short period of aging for pork and lamb improves texture. Veal is never aged, nor is kosher meat, because Jewish law requires that meat be eaten within seventy-two hours of slaughtering.

Inspection and Grading

All meat that crosses state lines must be federally inspected to ensure that the meat comes from healthy animals and sanitary packing plants. The small proportion of meat that stays within state borders receives equally careful state inspection. The state inspection stamp is usually in the shape of the state as it appears on the map, with the name of the state and *Department of Agriculture* on it.

The federal stamp is round and purple and says *U.S. Insp'd & P'S'D* (Inspected and Passed) together with the official number of the packing plant. The colored stamping fluid is a vegetable dye and harmless if eaten.

But this inspection tells us only that the meat is clean and free from disease. Quality is monitored by the grading service of the United States Department of Agriculture. The stamp denoting quality is a purple shield enclosing the letters *USDA* and the grade designation. Grading is voluntary and is requested and paid for by a large proportion of meat packers. Some packers do their own grading, using brand names instead of grades to represent the levels of quality of their products. Each brand name stands for a different quality level, which may or may not parallel the standards of the federal grading system.

The symbol indicating approval by the government inspection service and the grade symbol are both stamped so extensively on the animal carcass that you should have no trouble finding them. If you wish to know the grade and cannot see it on the meat that is displayed, ask the butcher to show it to you on a larger section of the carcass. Following are the government meat grades:

Beef	**Veal**	**Lamb**	**Pork**
Prime	Prime	Prime	U.S. No. 1
Choice	Choice	Choice	U.S. No. 2
Good	Good	Good	U.S. No. 3
Standard	Standard	Utility	Medium
Commercial	Utility	Cull	Cull

Beef also has Utility, Cutter, and Canner grades, and veal has Cull, but these grades never appear in retail markets. They are perfectly good in terms of safety in eating, but they may come from older animals or less choice ones and they are used in sausages and other processed meat products. Retailers rarely sell anything below Good. Grades for veal are not always used because veal must of necessity come from a young animal. Also, relatively little veal is marketed.

In evaluating the grade of a carcass, the inspector first considers the age of an animal. The character of the meat—its color, texture, and firmness—is next taken into account. In beef, marbling, or the amount and distribution of fat, is an important index to quality. Marbling was once thought to contribute to tenderness, but now there is a large body of opinion among food scientists that it is not an infallible indication of tenderness. However, there is no doubt that well-marbled meat tastes juicier from the fat melting into it as it cooks. Much of the distinctive flavor of meat is carried in the fat.

Choice, the most widely available grade of beef, has less marbling of fat than Prime. Government grading procedures were changed in 1976, requiring less marbling in Prime and Choice beef. As a result, some formerly Choice beef has been upgraded to Prime and some of the former Good grade, with proportionately less marbling, is now Choice. The consequence of this is an uneven range of quality in Choice meat. If you are buying this grade, look for lacy marbling and a fair amount of outside fat.

Selection. When you are shopping for meat, keep in mind the features that concern the professional meat graders. The appearance of the bones is a clue to the maturity of the animal. Dark-colored bones are less desirable than bright-colored ones. As the animal matures, the bones become less red and grow harder. The color of the bones is more revealing than the color of the fat, which can vary with the breed and feed of the animals and is not always an indication of quality. Look for meat that is fine-grained, firm looking, and with good color, characteristic of the type of meat. (Specific quality characteristics are discussed in the sections on beef, lamb, pork, and veal.) Look for a good ratio of usable meat to bone and fat.

If you are shopping in a supermarket, always look at a few packages of meat before making your selection. They are not all the same. The color of the meat and the amount of bone and fat vary from package to package, so take a few extra minutes to compare and judge.

How Much To Buy

No firm rule can be given for the number of servings per pound of meat. You have to consider the individual appetites of your family and the amount of fat and bone in a particular cut. A pound of veal scallops will serve three, and a pound of lean hamburger will serve three or four, because they are solid meats with no waste, but a pound of spareribs or breast of veal might be sufficient for only one. As a general guide, allow 8 to 12 ounces per person for bone-in steaks and roasts and 6 to 8 ounces per person for boneless meats. But this might be totally unrealistic for a male teen-ager with a healthy appetite.

Storage

Meat must be stored in a cold place and loosely wrapped to allow air to circulate around it. This will discourage the growth of bacteria, which thrive on warmth and moisture. The high percentage of water contained in fresh meat provides a friendly environment for microorganisms. It is the growth of bacteria that produces an off-taste and ultimately causes the meat to spoil. Spoiled meat does not keep its secret to itself; the unpleasant smell is unmistakable and the surface of the meat is rather slimy and slippery.

Remove the meat from the store wrappings as soon as you get it home. Pat it dry and rewrap it loosely in wax paper or plastic wrap. You do not need to wash meat because cooking it will destroy any bacteria.

Store the meat in the coldest part of the refrigerator. This is usually the top shelf, which gets some of the cold air from the freezer above it. If you have a side-by-side model, or one with the freezer on the bottom, use a thermometer to locate the coldest part. Do not crowd the meat or pile one piece on top of another; you want the air to circulate around each piece.

You can keep large pieces of meat such as roasts, steaks, and chops for up to four days. Ground meat, whether beef, lamb, or pork, should be used within a day because the many small surfaces provide inviting spaces for contamination by microorganisms. If you find it impossible to use ground meat at once, freeze it in portions suitable for cooking.

The variety meats, such as liver, kidney, sweetbreads, and brains, are highly perishable and should be used within twenty-four hours of purchase.

Freezing and Thawing Meat

There seems to be no consensus about whether freezing affects the taste and juiciness of meat. Many people with educated palates freely admit that they cannot tell the difference between frozen and unfrozen beef or lamb that has been well prepared. We are assuming, of course, that the meat was properly frozen and carefully thawed. We know that freezing raw meat alters the protein somewhat, but there are times when the advantages of frozen meat outweigh the real or imagined disadvantages. No one who has been faced with unexpected guests or a sudden blizzard needs to be reminded of the comfort of a meat and poultry supply in the freezer. It is safe to say that if meat has been properly frozen at a steady temperature of 0 degrees Fahrenheit, not held too long, and then thawed carefully, it will not change appreciably in either appearance or flavor.

The danger in keeping meat too long in the freezer is not that it might spoil. It will remain safe to eat, but it will lose flavor, juiciness, and nutritional value. Even when meat is perfectly wrapped, it undergoes some dehydration during a prolonged stay in the freezer.

The United States Department of Agriculture suggests up to twelve months storage for beef and lamb, eight months for fresh pork, four months for ground beef and lamb. These time periods, however, are suitable if you have a self-contained freezer that keeps a steady temperature of or under 0 degrees. If your freezer is a compartment in your refrigerator, cut the time in half.

Beef and lamb freeze more successfully than veal and pork. Veal is tender and perishable with little fat so it should not be held too long; veal scallops should be used within a month. Like veal, good pork is tender and freezing tends to harden it.

To prepare meat for freezing, double wrap it in a good grade of coated freezer paper, or in polyethylene bags sealed with twisters. Aluminum foil is not a good choice; it tends to become brittle when frozen. Make the package as airtight as possible and seal it securely. If you are freezing ground beef patties or chops, separate them with squares of wax paper or freezer paper. Mark each package with the name of the meat cut, weight, and date.

To defrost meat, place it in its wrappings in the refrigerator on a deep platter to catch the juices. Allow one to four days, depending on the size of the piece. Cook the meat as soon as possible after it is defrosted—certainly within a day. Because freezing has robbed it of some of its moisture, it will not keep as long as a piece of fresh meat without loss of flavor and juiciness. Do not refreeze meat after it has thawed. Aside from the danger of spoilage, flavor and nutrient values will be seriously impaired.

Frozen steaks can go directly under the broiler or into the skillet without thawing, but you will have to increase the cooking time to at least double the cooking time needed for unfrozen cuts. It is best to partly thaw the large tender cuts that are to be roasted to shorten the cooking time.

Marinating

Marinating in a seasoned mixture of oil and an acid is a process designed to add flavor and to tenderize meat. An acid, such as wine, vinegar, lemon, or orange juice, acts to break down the fibers of the meat, making at least the outer portions more tender; the oil carries the flavor and seasonings into the meat. It is unlikely that anyone these days uses a marinade for its original purpose, which was to keep meat from spoiling. Nevertheless, a marinade containing salt and acid will retard the growth of bacteria and suppress enzyme activity. Marinated meats can be stored longer under home conditions than meats not so treated.

Because of the acid, use a nonaluminum bowl or pan for the marinating; glass, pottery, stainless steel, or enamel-lined metal will do. The meat should be turned from time to time so that all sides get equal exposure to the marinade. Placing the meat and marinade in a heavy plastic bag, tightly closed, is a convenient way to marinate. Turn the bag from time to time so the meat stays well bathed on all surfaces with the marinade. Put the bag on a deep platter, in case it should leak. If you are going to marinate for more than a few hours, you will have to refrigerate the meat; otherwise keep it at room temperature.

If you are marinating for flavor, three or four hours will be sufficient; if it is for tenderizing, you will need one to two days. Generally, you should marinate only those cuts that are to be broiled, such as flank steak, London broil, or chunks of meat that are to be skewered for shish kebab, where both flavor and texture need some help. It is usually not necessary to marinate meats that are going to be braised, because the fibers will be softened by long cooking, and the meat will be seasoned and flavored by the liquid, spices, and vegetables that are cooked with it. Marinating duplicates what happens in the braising process. The exception to this is the classic German sauerbraten, which means sour-roasted. For this, a beef shoulder or similar cut is soaked in a mixture of vinegar, water, and seasonings for one day to one week. It is then cooked in the marinade.

The usual formula for a marinade is about three parts oil to one part acid. Salt, pepper, and a wide range of herbs, spices, and seasonings are added, along with flavoring vegetables such as onions, carrots, celery, and garlic.

Cooking Techniques for Meat

Dry Heat Procedures

Dry heat cooking methods—broiling, pan-broiling, roasting, and sautéeing—are suitable only for the most tender cuts of meat. Actually, dry heat cooking may make the meat slightly less tender than it was before it was cooked because the heat coagulates the muscle protein and toughens it a bit.

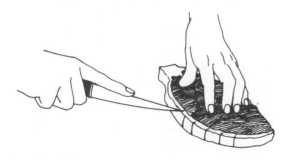

Make shallow cuts at 1-inch intervals in the outside rim of fat so that the steak will lie flat and cook evenly.

Broiling

Broiling, or grilling, is a cooking method that dates almost from the beginning of time. Broiling is fast and functional and, while it will not tenderize meat, it melts away fat and chars the surface, giving it eye and taste appeal. Beef and lamb lend themselves to broiling, but pork and veal tend to dry out.

To prepare meats for broiling, trim the outside rim of fat, leaving about one-quarter inch all around. This will reduce spattering. Score the outside edges of the border of fat by making shallow cuts at 1-inch intervals so that it will lie flat and cook evenly. When choosing a steak, bear in mind that thicker cuts yield plumper and juicier cooked results. You are better advised to choose one steak, 1½ to 2 inches thick, for two servings, than two steaks, each of which is ¾ to 1 inch thick.

The type of heat source you have makes a difference in the way you handle the broiling process. Gas broilers produce extremely high heat and foods can burn if placed too close to too high a flame. Electric broilers give concentrated heat without a flame and foods can be placed closer to the coils. It may be necessary when broiling with electricity to leave the oven door ajar to prevent the thermostat from turning off the current. With a gas range, the oven door is kept closed.

Foods are broiled at a distance of 2 to 5 inches from the source of the heat. The shorter distance is suitable for thin cuts, such as flank steaks. When thin cuts of meat are cooked for a short time close to the heat source, they will be crisp and browned on the outside and juicy in the center. Thicker cuts, 1½ to 2 inches or more, are placed farther away from the heat source. If placed too close, the outside will be charred before the inside loses its chill. The farther the meat is placed from the source of heat, the more uniformly cooked it will be, and with less spattering and smoking.

Try to have the meat at room temperature before broiling. It will cook faster and better if it has been out of the refrigerator for at least an hour.

Always remove the rack and broiler pan before preheating the broiler. They must be cold or the underside of the meat will be overdone. If the meat is very lean, grease the broiler rack with some of the fat from the meat or a little vegetable oil to prevent sticking. To make cleaning easier, line the broiler pan with aluminum foil.

With the broiler preheated to its highest setting, slide the meat into the broiler. When it is approximately half done and the top surface is brown, turn it with kitchen tongs, not a fork. A fork will pierce the meat and release some of the juices. Continue cooking until the desired doneness is reached. It is difficult to be specific about time because so much depends on the thickness of the steak. A ½-inch difference in the thickness of a cut makes a difference of about 5 minutes in broiling time.

You can test for doneness with an instant meat thermometer, which gives an immediate reading. Readings of 120 degrees for very rare, 125 to 130 degrees for rare, 140 to 145 degrees for medium, and 170 degrees and up for well-done are about right. Another way to test for doneness is to press the meat with your finger.

Rare meat will feel soft, but slightly firm on the surface. Well-done will feel firm. If it is not too soft and yielding, nor too hard and resistant, it is medium-rare. With experience, you will be able to sense the state of doneness by finger pressure. You can also make a little cut in the meat near the bone and have a look. The shade of pink, rosy red or, heaven forfend, no red at all, will tell you what you want to know. If the meat is not done to your liking, return it to the broiler for another minute. When done, remove to a serving platter, sprinkle with salt and pepper, and serve at once.

Broiling Frozen Steaks. Place frozen steak 2 inches below the heat source and sear well on both sides. Then lower the rack to about 4 inches below the heat and continue cooking until the proper doneness is reached. Allow about twice the length of time needed for an unfrozen cut.

Salting. There is no general agreement about whether meat should be salted before, during, or after broiling. Some cooking experts equate salting before broiling with disaster, citing the fact that salt melts in the heat, thereby producing unwanted moisture, shrinking some of the muscle fibers, and drawing the juices from the meat. No one can argue with the fact that salt does draw out meat juices, but the cooks who salt before broiling contend that the high heat in a preheated oven immediately seals the surface of the meat, salted or not, thereby preventing the escape of moisture. We prefer to salt after the broiling; it's a sound cooking practice for other techniques, such as sautéeing and pan-broiling.

Charcoal Grilling

Any meat that can be broiled can be grilled over charcoal. The charcoal should be heated until it is covered with a fine white ash. This may take 30 to 45 minutes. Trim excess fat off steaks and chops to reduce the risk of flare-up. Place the meat on a rack over the coals and cook until half-done; turn and cook the other side. No time schedule can be established, because heat, thickness, and quality of meat, as well as personal preferences, are variable. Test for doneness by any of the methods mentioned earlier.

Pan-Broiling (Pan-Frying)

Pan-broiling (or pan-frying) is done on top of the stove using a frying pan that heats evenly and is heavy enough to prevent scorching the meat. The pan is preheated and the meat cooked in its own fat. Grease the pan lightly if the meat is lean. A 1½-inch-thick cut of meat is the maximum for pan-broiling, because thick pieces will be seared on the outside before the interior is done. Pieces less than 1 inch thick are preferred.

Cook the meat over moderate heat and pour off any fat as it accumulates. If the fat smokes or spatters, the heat is too high and the meat could toughen. If this occurs, remove the pan from the stove for a minute to cool. As soon as the meat is brown on the underside, turn it with kitchen tongs, and continue cooking. When red juices appear on the surface of the meat, it will be at the rare stage. To test for doneness, make a small cut in the meat next to the bone, or in the center if it is boneless. Pork and well-done beef should not have any traces of pink showing; medium beef will be pink in the center, and rare beef will be pink to red. You can also use the touch test described earlier. Deglaze the pan by swirling in a bit of stock, cream, or wine and scraping up any of the browned bits remaining on the bottom of the pan. Thin, tender beef steaks, ham slices, ½-inch-thick pork chops, thin lamb chops, and bacon are suitable for pan-broiling.

Salt-broiling. This is a variation of pan-broiling. The bottom of the skillet is covered with a layer of coarse salt and heated. The meat is placed over the heated salt and cooked on each side for the required length of time. The meat does not become excessively salty, but this method would be a poor choice for anyone on a sodium-restricted diet. Salt-broiling has no advantages over pan-broiling and we can't think of any reason to recommend it.

Roasting

Roasting is a process in which meat is cooked, uncovered, in an oven. The oven heat seals the meat surfaces so that the juices are trapped and concentrated inside and cannot escape. Some of the confusion about the technique of roasting may have had its roots in the incorrectly labeled roasting pan, the large, oval-shaped pan with a domed cover. Foods cooked in this kind of pan will be steamed or braised, not roasted. The ideal roasting pan has shallow sides, allowing good circulation so that the moisture from the meat can evaporate instead of condensing to form steam that will bathe the roast and interfere with the sealing of the meat.

Meat will inevitably shrink and lose weight when it is cooked. The fat that marbled the meat is liquefied and squeezed from the fat storage cells, moisture is lost, and connective tissues and muscle fibers are shrunk by heat. The higher the internal temperature to which the meat is heated, the greater the shrinkage.

After the meat has been in the hot oven for a while, you will detect the delicious aroma of meat cooking. These lovely smells are caused by the heat-induced chemical changes in the protein and fat contained in the meat and their liberation into the air. Each type of meat has its own distinctive aroma.

There are several schools of thought about the proper temperature for oven roasting. Some cooks prefer a low temperature of 300 to 325 degrees. This results in less shrinkage and generous drippings for a gravy. Roasting at medium temperature, 400 degrees, causes more shrinkage; it gives a highly concentrated flavor and a juicy meat, but few drippings for gravy. Another popular method is to sear the roast in a 500-degree oven until well-browned, then reduce the heat to 325 degrees and cook until the desired doneness is reached. This gives the roast a pleasant crusty exterior. All of these methods give successful results and the only way to decide which works best for you is to experiment with each of them.

The roast will cook faster if you allow it to stand for 2 hours or more at room temperature before starting to cook it. Add salt and pepper when the cooking is more than half over. Little flavor change is accomplished by seasoning before roasting because the flavors will penetrate only a fraction of an inch. You might want to insert minced onions or garlic slivers into slits in the meat. These flavors are held well by the fat they contact in a roast.

Place the roast on a rack or trivet in the roasting pan. This will keep the roast free of the the pan's fat and juices and prevent the underside from getting soggy. You can skip the rack if you are cooking a rib roast; the rib bones will serve as a rack and keep the meat out of the drippings. The fat side of the roasts should be at the top so that the melting fat will baste the meat as it drains downward.

A meat thermometer is a must for successful roasting. You will not have to guess how rare or well-done the interior of the meat is. Timetables for roasting cannot be completely accurate, for heat penetration varies from one cut to another. Two roasts may be identical in weight but differ widely in shape and thickness, which will affect the cooking time required.

A thermometer should be inserted in the thickest part of the meat away from the bone. You will get an incorrect reading if the thermometer touches the bone, for bones conduct heat. This is why a roast with the bone in cooks more quickly than a boneless one.

It is important to remember that the heat in roasted meat will continue to cook the meat for 10 to 15 minutes after it is removed from the oven. Even though the roast is resting on the kitchen counter, it is cooking by its own stored-up heat. In a large roast, the temperature may rise as much as 10 to 15 degrees when the roast is cooked rare, and 25 degrees when cooked to well-done. Remove a large roast from the oven when the thermometer reaches within five degrees of the desired final temperature. Cover it loosely with aluminum foil and let it rest for 20 to 25 minutes. This gives the juices time to settle and the connective tissue time to become firm. You will also find it easier to carve the meat into attractive servings.

Roasted meat does not have to be watched carefully while it is cooking because the heat is not high enough to cause it to burn. An occasional peek is all that is needed to make sure that the bottom of the pan isn't dry and scorched.

Deglazing is adding liquid to dissolve pan juices and browned bits of solidified, flavorful juices that have accumulated in a cooking pan. After you remove the roast from the pan, pour off all but a tablespoon or two of fat. Add ¼ cup of water, wine, or an appropriate stock— beef stock for beef, or chicken or veal stock for veal, lamb, and pork. Scrape up all the browned bits on the bottom of the pan and stir and cook over medium heat for a few minutes until well blended. Or the meat-flavored glaze can be part of a more elaborate sauce enriched with cream and/or butter.

Sautéeing

Sautéeing is cooking food on top of the stove in a small amount of fat. The skillet or frying pan should be big enough to accommodate the food to be cooked in a single layer. There are also special sauté pans, which are thick-bottomed, straight-sided pans about two and one-half or three inches deep. If you are planning to prepare a sauce for the sauté that includes egg yolks, wine, or other acid foods such as vinegar and tomatoes, do not use an aluminum or iron pot, which will discolor the sauce.

Many meats are suitable for sautéeing—tender cuts such as veal scallops and thin steaks, or organ meats such as kidney, liver, and sweetbreads. Fats for sautéeing include butter, margarine, lard and hydrogenated shortenings, and vegetable oils. Because butter burns easily, it should be used in combination with vegetable oils, which have a higher burning point than butter. The butter is for flavor, the oil to prevent burning. Clarified butter (see page 260) is a good choice for delicate sautés, because it will not burn as readily as butter.

About an eighth of an inch of fat in the bottom of a skillet is sufficient for most sautéeing. Recipes cannot be completely accurate in specifying the amount of fat needed for a sauté, because so much depends on the diameter of the pan you are using. In general, there should be enough fat so that the food can slide easily but not be enveloped by it. We save that for deep frying. The food to be sautéed must be perfectly dry or it will steam and spatter and not brown properly.

To sauté meat, heat the amount of fat needed in a skillet and add as much of the meat as will fit in a single layer. Do not crowd the pieces or they will steam instead of sauté. If necessary, do them in batches and keep warm in a low oven until all are done. Deglaze the pan (see page 67) to make a sauce for the meat.

Stir-Frying

This is a technique used in Oriental cooking. The foods are cooked quickly in a small amount of oil over a high flame with continuous stirring. Flank steak sliced paper-thin, strips of liver, and shredded pork are among the likely candidates for stir-frying.

Moist Heat Procedures

Moist heat cooking can convert a tough, chewy cut of meat into one that is meltingly tender and delicious. The various procedures of moist heat cooking—boiling, braising, pot roasting, stewing or fricasseeing, and poaching—are all variations on the same theme. The food is cooked in a tightly covered pot with a little or a lot of liquid, or, in some cases, with only the steam that is released from the meat as it cooks and its proteins coagulate. Actually, since all foods contain water, the changes that take place in their interior are occurring in a watery medium, regardless of whether they are being roasted dry or immersed in hot liquid. However, cooking with moist heat gives us all the time we need to cook tougher cuts long enough to tenderize them without danger of cooking them dry and scorching them.

We have spoken earlier of how long exposure to heat affects the collagen in the connective tissue of the meat. The collagen disintegrates and changes into water-soluble gelatin, causing the fibers in the meat to separate, making the meat tender. The time required to convert collagen to gelatin varies with the cooking temperature. Not much happens to the connective tissue between 140 and 149 degrees, but the melting process picks up speed as the temperature rises and is faster at the boiling point, 212 degrees, than it was at 185 degrees.

This would seem to mean that boiling the meat at a vigorous boil will tenderize it more quickly. But such is not the case. Besides the fibers of the connective tissues, meat contains muscle fiber proteins that also influence tenderness, and muscle fiber proteins do not take kindly to too much heat. This fact was undoubtedly the inspiration for the old adage "A stew boiled is a stew spoiled." Too long a cooking period at too high a temperature causes excessive coagulation of the muscle fibers, which makes the meat rubbery and stringy.

The aim, then, in cooking less tender cuts of meat is to soften the connective tissue with a minimum toughening of the muscle fibers. This is not an impossible task and can be accomplished by slow, gentle cooking. The liquid should come to a boil that is scarcely a boil at all—some sluggish, feeble bubbles will barely move the surface of the liquid. At this slow, lazy boil, you will avoid the danger of toughening the muscle fibers.

Liquids for Moist Heat Cooking

There is a wide choice of liquids for moist heat cooking. Water is always a possibility, but, unless you season it well, it will not do as much for flavor as a good stock or broth. You may use all stock or a combination of stock with an acid, such as lemon juice, tomato juice, wine, cider, or beer. Stewed tomatoes may also be used for all or part of the broth to give different character to the dish. Acids have a direct effect on the connective tissue in the meat, softening it and thereby shortening the cooking time needed to make it tender. Wine and other acids should be added early in the cooking or they will have no effect on the texture of the meat.

Boiling

Boiling means cooking in covering liquid heated to a temperature of about 200 degrees. At this temperature, the liquid moves gently in the pot instead of breaking into seething bubbles and giving off clouds of steam. Simmering is a more precise term to describe the action; boiled beef is truly simmered beef. This process gives you both a stock and cooked meat.

Put the meat and flavoring vegetables and seasonings in a large pot with water to cover. You can use onion, carrot, leek, white turnip, garlic cloves, bay leaf, parsley, dried thyme,

and, of course, salt and freshly ground pepper. Bring the water to a boil over high heat and let boil briskly for 4 or 5 minutes. Skim off the scum that rises to the surface. Reduce the heat until the water just simmers, cover the pot, and cook for 2½ to 3 hours, or until the meat is tender, skimming away the scum as necessary. Remove the meat when done, strain the stock and skim the fat. If possible, cool and refrigerate for complete fat removal.

Beef brisket, corned or fresh, is a popular meat for boiling. You may also use bottom round, rump, and various cuts from the shoulder. Short ribs and flanken are good but excessively fatty and must be trimmed and reheated before serving. Tender cuts of meat that are suitable for roasting, such as a prime rump of beef, may also be boiled and served rare. As with roasts, allow the meat to stand for 15 minutes before being carved and served. Boiled meats are generally served with a spicy mustard or horseradish sauce.

Braising

Braising and pot roasting are the same process, in which well browned meat and aromatic vegetables are simmered slowly in liquid in a covered pot. Beef stew, Hungarian goulash, Yankee pot roast, boeuf bourguignon, and the like are all braised. It is the perfect method for the preparation of the less tender cuts of meat. It requires a heavy pot with a tight-fitting cover.

The first step is to brown the meat well in a few tablespoons of hot fat to sear all its surfaces. This concentrates the juices at the center of the roast and gives the drippings an appealing rich brown color. You can dip the meat in flour before browning, or sprinkle it with flour afterward, although browning the flour first will deepen the color of the gravy. If you do not flour the meat, be sure to wipe it very dry with paper towels. You can sear the meat on top of the stove or in a hot oven, turning it until all the surfaces are well browned. Searing the meat in the oven reduces the amount of fat and gives it a nice crusty coat. Searing is recommended for all large pieces of red meat and also for meat cubes, but it is not essential for white meats.

Celery, leeks, onions, carrots, turnips, minced garlic—almost any vegetable—can be added to the braising pot. Cut them into pieces or julienne strips. Classic French cookery recommends a mirepoix, a combination of carrots, onions, and celery cut into ¼-inch dice or into julienne strips and sautéed in butter until soft and tender. Mix in a pinch of thyme and half a bay leaf and spread the vegetable mixture over the bottom of the braising pot. After the meat has been browned, place it on the bed of vegetables in the braising pot and add the liquid. Be very light-handed with salt, particularly if you have used a canned stock, which tends to be salty. Often the concentration of pan juices will provide sufficient flavoring.

Try to use a pot that is just the right size for your ingredients. If the pot is much larger than the meat, leaving a lot of air space around it, the liquid in the ingredients will condense into steam. However, if your pot is overly large, you can compensate by covering the meat first with a large piece of aluminum foil that rests directly over the meat like a lid to catch the moisture that condenses on the inside of the pot cover. Make a tiny hole in the foil so that the moisture that forms under it can escape. Then cover with the pot lid. If at any time you need to lift the pot lid, do it quickly and invert it so that the moisture that has condensed on it will not drip back into the braising pot.

You can braise the meat on top of the stove or in the oven. The essential consideration is that the cooking liquid stay at a simmer, a state of activity described in *Larousse Gastronomique* as "the slight quivering of a liquid just before it comes to the boil." This can present a problem with stoves that have an unpredictable perform-

ance record. The liquid vacillates between bubbling and doing nothing at all and the tiniest increase in heat sets off a boil. You can deal with this uneven state of affairs by using an asbestos pad or a metal flame control device on top of the burner to produce the low heat needed for slow, even cooking, or you can use the oven. Temperatures vary from oven to oven and you will need to determine at what temperature your oven will maintain a simmer in the pot. The range is usually between 300 and 325 degrees.

Check from time to time to make sure that there is liquid in the pot. It may be necessary to add a small amount of liquid, since there is always some evaporation even in the best engineered pot, and this liquid must be replaced. If you hear a sizzling sound, you may be sure that the meat is being cooked without liquid. Although the meat is less likely to go dry when cooked in the oven, there is evaporation there, too, so keep an eye on it. After about 45 minutes, stir the vegetables so they will brown evenly, and continue with the cooking. Turn the meat often to keep it moistened by the pan juices.

Braised meat is always cooked until well-done—never rare. You do not need a thermometer for braised meats, just test with a skewer. If it goes in and out easily, the meat is done; if you encounter resistance, simmer it a little longer. Braising time for red meats can be relatively long, but it is difficult to be precise about time because so much depends on the grade, the type of meat, its size, and the kind of liquid in which it is cooked.

After the meat has become tender, the vegetables can be puréed to make a sauce, although it is very likely that they have turned into a thick purée because of the long cooking. If they have retained their shape, they may be served as a garnish for the meat.

Try to prepare the braised meat a day in advance so that you can refrigerate it overnight and let the fat solidify, which makes the fat removal simple and thorough. Braised meats and stews, like soups, improve in flavor when they are reheated. But if time does not permit, skim the fat with a spoon as completely as possible. Or strain the pan juices into a metal bowl and chill in the freezer. When the sauce has cooled, skim off the fat that has crusted the surface.

Some meats suitable for braising are beef brisket, chuck, bottom and top round, cross-rib, boiling beef or flanken, eye round, boned lamb shoulder, lamb shanks, neck of veal with or without bones, veal shoulder, rump, shanks with bones, fresh tongue, oxtails, and center loin of pork with bones, a lovely lean but expensive cut.

Stewing

Stewing is another version of braising, the chief differences being the amount of liquid used and that meat for stewing is cut into pieces. Vegetables, too, may be a visible ingredient in stews, in contrast to braising, where they are used mainly for flavoring. The cooking procedures are identical to those of braising with long, slow cooking of major importance.

Any kind of meat can be stewed. Of course it would be wildly extravagant to waste tender steaks or chops or ribs of beef in a stew, but you have a wide choice of other cuts that can serve well, even for company occasions. Stews can be made of beef, lamb, pork, veal, kidney, venison, oxtails, or rabbit.

The meat can be cut in any size you wish, from cubes to large pieces. Beef cubes, lightly floured, are first browned in a mixture of oil and butter to sear them. Don't crowd them in the pan; do them in small batches or they will steam and give up their juices. Transfer the meat to a heavy pot and add just enough liquid to cover the meat, not to submerge it. The liquid may be stock or a combination of wine and stock. Vegetables are added at the start or later, depending on what they are and how long they need to cook. You will probably need to thicken the sauce after the cooking is finished.

White stews are made of light-colored meats, usually veal or lamb. Irish stew and blanquette of veal are types of white stews. The meat is never browned first and only white vegetables are used—potatoes and onions in the Irish stew and small white onions and mushrooms in the blanquette.

Whenever possible, make stew a day in advance to give the flavors time to blend and mellow. All stews improve with reheating, with the possible exception of kidney stew, in which the kidney can toughen if exposed to too much heat.

Beef

More beef is eaten in the United States than any other meat and, because of its popularity, a good deal of research has been directed toward improving the breeding of good beef cattle. Today's animals, with compact bodies and short legs and necks, yield a higher proportion of meat to bone than did the long-legged, muscular cattle of a couple of centuries ago.

When you are familiar with the parts of the animal that the various cuts come from, you will know how they are best prepared. We'll start our bovine cooking tour at the head end of the animal and move clockwise, ending at the foreleg.

Chuck

The chuck or shoulder is at the working end of the animal. The closer to the neck, the tougher the meat, so meats from this portion are more suitable for braising, stewing, pot roasting, or grinding for hamburger. The individual chuck cuts are blade roast, arm cut, and cross-rib pot roast. Different butchers use different names and you may find some chuck steaks called chuck short ribs, blade steak, and arm pot roast or steak. Another cut found in some markets is the flat, thick California roast, which is an underblade pot roast. The bony cuts from this section can be used for stock. Trim away the meat and use it for hash or a casserole dish.

Rib

The rib section extends from the shoulder to the end of the ribs and is the source of the most expensive and desirable cuts for roasting. This is where our fine standing rib roasts and the French rib steaks called entrecôtes come from. The three ribs closest to the chuck are the least desirable and are generally used for boiled beef. The remaining seven ribs can be used for a single large rib roast or they can be divided into a four- and a three-rib roast, or into smaller sections. Butchers generally cut off the rib ends, trim them of fat, and sell them separately as short ribs. The short ribs can be braised, or marinated and barbecued. Any individual steak cut from the ribs can be broiled or pan-broiled.

Loin

Next to the rib is the short loin, from which we get top-grade roasts and steaks. Shell steaks and fillets, T-bones, and the splendid porterhouse steaks come from this section of the animal. The first cut nearest the rib portion provides club steaks. A few inches in, the cut has a small amount of the fillet and a different bone structure. This is butchered into T-bone steaks. Porterhouse steak comes next with a larger fillet. If the entire loin section is boned and the fillet removed, the remaining section is sold as a shell roast. Or it may be cut into steaks that are labeled shell steak, strip steak, top loin, sirloin strip, club steak, *contrefilet, faux filet*, New York, or Kansas cut, depending on the part of the country you are in. These steaks are broiled. The tender boneless fillet, or tenderloin, runs through the short loin. Shaped somewhat like a flattened oval, it can be roasted whole or cut into individual steaks that are quickly pan-broiled. The châteaubriand is cut from the thickest part of the fillet. Toward the tip and nearest the head of the animal come filets mignons. Smaller steaks from the tenderloin, never more than 1¼ inches thick, are called fillet steaks or tournedos. The fillet of beef can be cut into cubes for elegant kebabs to be skewered and broiled, or it can be thinly sliced for beef stroganoff. The fillet meat is soft and tender but it has a bland flavor and benefits from a seasoned sauce such as béarnaise or Bordelaise, or seasoned butter.

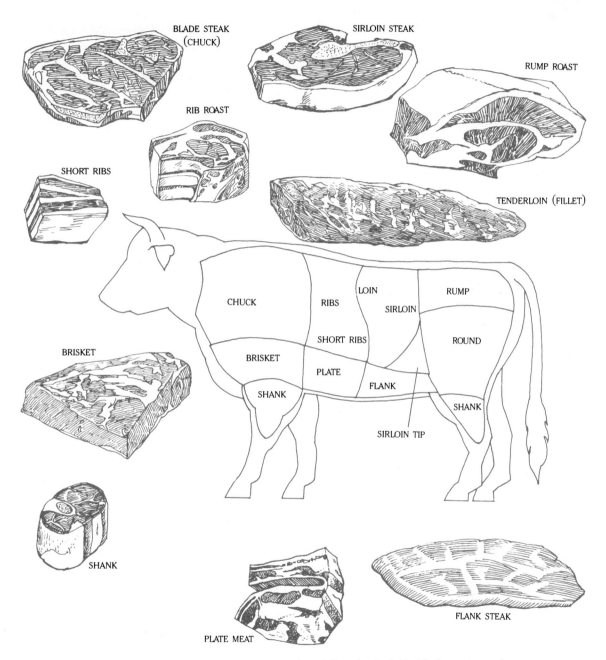

BLADE STEAK (CHUCK)

SIRLOIN STEAK

RUMP ROAST

RIB ROAST

SHORT RIBS

TENDERLOIN (FILLET)

BRISKET

CHUCK

RIBS

LOIN

RUMP

SIRLOIN

SHORT RIBS

ROUND

BRISKET

PLATE

FLANK

SHANK

SHANK

SIRLOIN TIP

SHANK

PLATE MEAT

FLANK STEAK

The butcher subdivides steer parts into various cuts of beef. The chuck yields blade steaks and roasts, arm and cross-rib pot roasts. Ribs (minus short ribs) are cut into steaks or roasted. The loin may be cut into steaks, or the tenderloin (fillet) may be separated and roasted or cut into steaks. The sirloin yields steaks. Below the rump, the round and shank form the hind leg. From the underside come the flank and plate.

Sirloin

Next to the loin lies the sirloin or hip. The latter word suggests quite correctly that this is a working muscle that will not be as tender as the meat in the loin section. However, it is an excellent cut that can be successfully broiled. Through this section runs the butt end of the tenderloin, a continuation of the tender fillet in the short loin. Sirloin steaks contain a variety of shapes and sizes of marrow bones. Nearest the porterhouse is the pin bone, which contains a lot of bone but is nevertheless the most tender. The flat bone has less waste than the pin bone, and the wedge bone, farthest from the loin, is the least tender.

Round

The beef round starts at the back of the hip-bone and extends down the leg to the ankle. From this part of the animal we get some fine cuts for broiling or roasting and others for braising. The beef round includes the top (or tip) sirloin, rump, top round, eye round, bottom round, and shin or shank.

Top sirloin steaks are cut from the largest part of the sirloin, a continuation of the top loin. The sirloin tip is a triangular boneless piece trimmed from the base of the sirloin. If top quality, this may be broiled, but it will not be as tender as the sirloin steak from the sirloin.

Above the back end of the hipbone is the rump, which is sold as a steak or roast. It has good flavor and a chewy quality that some people prefer to the tenderer cuts. If it is Prime grade and well-aged, it may be broiled or roasted, but braising is safer. The meat from the hind leg is divided into top round, eye round, and bottom round. The top round is the most tender and can be roasted if it is Prime. This is the cut that is sold in delicatessens as roast beef. The 2-inch-thick London broil that you

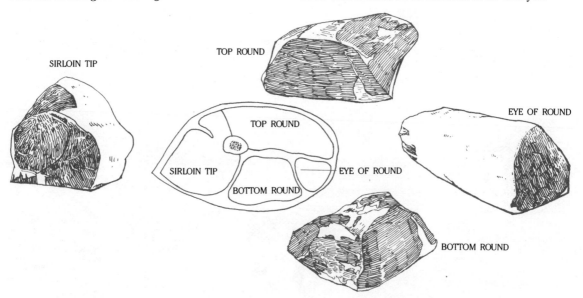

The round steak is a cross-section of the round, which is often separated into its muscle divisions. The sirloin tip, at the left, is the section of the round at the base of the sirloin. Next, reading clockwise, is top round, which, if prime, is tender enough to roast. At the right is the eye of round, or eye round, and finally, the bottom round. Eye and bottom round generally need to be braised. At the center is the little round bone.

find in supermarkets may be round, chuck, or even flank. Ground round steak makes a good lean hamburger. The eye of the round and bottom round are excellent for braising. Sometimes the eye round can be roasted, but for this you need Prime, well-aged meat and a dependable butcher who will advise you. The shin meat can be used for soups, for grinding, and for braising.

Flank

The flank lies just below the loin and the ribs. Flank steak is a flat, long-grained meat that is also used for London broil. This was once an inexpensive and not very highly regarded cut but it has risen greatly both in public esteem and in cost. If it is Prime quality, it is delicious when marinated first, quickly broiled to rare, and thinly sliced on the diagonal. It has the added virtue of being comparatively lean. Flank steak can be rolled around a stuffing, tied, and braised. It is also widely used in Chinese beef dishes.

Plate

Next to the flank just below the rib section is the plate. It includes the lower part of the rib bones. Plate short ribs, also called plate flanken, are near the brisket. They require extensive trimming and can be broiled or braised. The skirt steak is also in this section. It is similar to a flank steak in texture and can be ground, rolled, or braised, or, if it is of superior quality, marinated and quickly broiled. There is another piece of loose meat about ½ inch thick in this part of the animal called a hang tenderloin. There is only one to an animal so it is not commonly seen (the butcher usually gets to it first), but if you do happen on one, it can be pan-broiled since it is generally tender.

Brisket

Next we come to the brisket, a favorite cut for boiled beef, braised beef, or corned beef. An entire brisket makes a huge pot roast, but it is generally cut into halves or thirds for smaller roasts. The first cut, nearest the hindquarter, is sometimes known as thin cut. As you go toward the shoulder the meat has more fat and fibrous graining. The middle portion is well suited for boiled beef and corned beef. The outside surfaces of this cut are lavishly coated with fat, which can be trimmed away, but the meat is juicy and flavorful.

Shank

Our last stop is the shank or shin of beef, the lower part of the hind or forelegs. Shanks contain a good bit of gelatinous fiber and are excellent for soup or stock. They are also used for grinding or for long, slow braising.

Carving a Standing Rib Roast

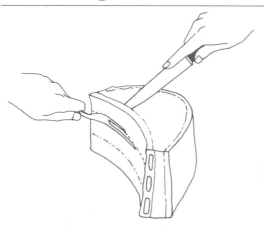

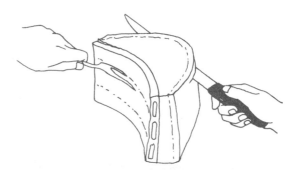

1 *Place the roast on its side, with the ribs to your left, if you are right-handed. Following the ribs with the knife, cut vertically along the bone. Anchor the roast by inserting a fork between the ribs.*

2 *Next, cut across the grain, horizontally, toward the bone. When a slice is cut, use the knife to carry it to the warmed platter, steadying it from above with the fork.*

Standing Rib Roast
(Moderate-Temperature Method)

4½- to 12-pound standing rib roast
  (2 to 4 ribs)
Garlic, peeled and crushed
Flour
¼ cup beef stock or water
Salt and freshly ground pepper

Preheat the oven to 450 degrees.

Rub meat with garlic and flour.

Place rib side down in a shallow roasting pan and roast for 15 minutes.

Reduce the heat to 325 degrees and roast for 1 to 2½ hours longer. Start checking with the instant thermometer before the hour for the small roast, and before 2 hours for the larger roast. For rare beef, remove roast from the oven when the thermometer reads 125 to 130 degrees. Cover lightly and let stand for 20 to 30 minutes before carving.

Drain off all but 1 or 2 tablespoons of fat from the roasting pan. Add about ¼ cup of beef stock or water and scrape off the browned bits from the bottom of the pan. Stir over low heat until well blended and add salt and pepper to taste.

Remove the bones in one piece and reserve for deviled beef bones. Thinly slice the beef and serve on warm plates with the pan juices. You may also carve the beef without removing the bones.

Yield: 4 to 8 servings.

Roast Ribs of Beef (High-Temperature Method)

This popular method of roasting beef produces a crunchy exterior and a rosy pink interior. Don't attempt it, however, unless your oven is well insulated or you have an efficient kitchen fan because it produces a lot of smoke.

8- to 12-pound rib roast of beef (3 to 4 ribs), short ribs removed
Flour
¼ cup beef broth or water
Salt and freshly ground pepper

Have the meat at room temperature for 3 to 4 hours before roasting.

Preheat the oven to 500 degrees. This may take 30 minutes, depending on your oven.

Rub the flour into the fat on the top and sides of beef. Place the meat in a shallow roasting pan (the ribs serve as their own rack) and roast for exactly 5 minutes per pound (weight without short ribs). Turn on the kitchen fan if you have one; there will be a lot of smoke if your oven isn't well insulated.

When the cooking time is up, turn off the oven and leave the roast undisturbed in the oven for at least 2 hours. Do not open the oven door during this time.

Remove the roast from the pan and drain off all but one or two tablespoons of fat.

Add beef broth or water and scrape off all the browned bits from the bottom of the pan. Stir over low heat until well blended and add salt and pepper to taste. Serve with the sliced beef.

Yield: 6 to 8 servings.

Deviled Beef Bones

If you saved the bones from the standing rib roast, this makes a crunchy and delicious snack.

Bones from a cooked rib roast
Wine or cider vinegar
1 to 2 tablespoons melted butter
Bread crumbs for dredging

Preheat the oven to 400 degrees.

Sprinkle the bones with vinegar and brush them with melted butter. Dredge in bread crumbs.

Place the bones on a wire rack in a shallow pan and roast until crunchy and brown, 15 to 20 minutes. Serve hot.

Short Ribs

This is a good dish to serve as part of a Chinese meal because it needs little attention while you prepare other dishes.

2½ to 3 pounds lean short ribs, cut into 2-inch lengths

Marinade I:
2 tablespoons sesame seeds (toasted in a dry skillet until golden)
1 clove garlic, finely chopped
⅓ cup soy sauce (Japanese preferred)
¼ cup coarsely chopped scallions
1 teaspoon freshly grated ginger
1 teaspoon sugar

Marinade II:
1 cup pineapple juice or apricot nectar
2 tablespoons honey
1 tablespoon cider vinegar
¼ cup soy sauce (Japanese preferred)
1 teaspoon freshly grated ginger
1 clove garlic, crushed

Choose Marinade I or II and combine the ingredients until well blended. Place the ribs in a plastic bag or nonaluminum container and pour the marinade over the meat. Cover and refrigerate for 24 hours.

Preheat the oven to 375 degrees. Remove the ribs and reserve the marinade for basting. Arrange the ribs on a wire rack set in a shallow roasting pan.

Add 1½ to 2 cups water to the pan, but do not let it touch the meat. The water will catch the fat as it drips from the ribs and keeps the kitchen from smoking up.

Bake for 1 to 1½ hours, or until the ribs are crisp and brown. Brush frequently with the marinade.

Serve hot.

Yield: 2 to 3 servings.

Roast Fillet of Beef

This cooking technique frees you from the worry of overdone beef and gives a perfect result even if dinner guests are late. The beef is cooked in two stages; the final one is brief and need not be started until everyone has arrived.

1 3- to 6-pound trimmed fillet of
  beef
1 garlic clove, peeled
4 tablespoons butter
Salt and freshly ground pepper
2 tablespoons Worcestershire
  sauce
Minced parsley

Remove the fillet from the refrigerator 2 hours before you start to cook it so that it is at room temperature. Trim away some of the excess fat and turn the thin end of the roast under. Rub it all over with the garlic clove and butter, season lightly with salt and pepper, and sprinkle with Worcestershire sauce.

An hour or even two before you are planning to serve the roast, preheat the broiler. Put the fillet in a shallow pan and place it about 3 inches from the broiler heat. Broil for 12 minutes on each side. Remove from the broiler and set aside.

About 40 minutes before serving time, preheat the oven to 375 degrees. Roast the fillet for 20 to 25 minutes, depending on size. Rare meat will register 125 degrees on an instant thermometer. Or you can make a little cut in the center of the fillet with a sharp-pointed knife to check on the amount of pinkness. When done as you like it, remove it from the oven, tent loosely with foil, and allow it to rest for 15 minutes. It will continue to cook by its own stored-up heat and its juices will settle. Cut into slices about ½ inch thick, sprinkle with parsley, and serve with béarnaise sauce (see page 463).

Yield: 6 to 12 servings.

Oven-Broiled Shell, Rib, T-Bone, or Sirloin Steaks

4 1½-inch-thick steaks (about 10 ounces each)
Vegetable oil (optional)
Salt and freshly ground pepper

Have the steaks at room temperature and remove the broiler pan from the oven.

Preheat the broiler to hot.

Arrange the steaks on a wire rack set in the broiler pan. Rub the steaks lightly with oil, if desired.

Broil 4 to 5 inches from the heat for 4 minutes on each side for rare, a minute or two longer for medium. To test for doneness, make a small cut near a center bone. Turn the steak with tongs.

Remove from the oven and season with salt and pepper. Serve immediately on warm plates.

Yield: 4 servings.

Pan-Broiled Shell, Rib, T-Bone, or Sirloin Steaks

2 to 4 tablespoons clarified butter (see page 260), or beef suet
4 1½-inch-thick steaks (about 10 ounces each)
Salt and freshly ground pepper

Melt the butter in a large heavy skillet over medium-high heat. Use just enough to prevent sticking.

Add the steaks (do not crowd the pan) and sear on both sides. Turn the steaks with tongs.

Reduce the heat to medium and cook for 3 to 4 minutes on each side for rare, 1 to 2 minutes longer for medium. Place on a carving board and sprinkle with salt and pepper. Slice and serve immediately with seasoned butter or béarnaise sauce (see page 463).

Yield: 4 servings.

Skewered Beef

2 pounds boneless sirloin, cut into 1½-inch cubes
1 cup dry red or white wine
3 tablespoons brandy
¼ cup olive or vegetable oil
1 large onion, peeled and thinly sliced
¼ teaspoon dried thyme
1 bay leaf, crumbled
½ teaspoon freshly ground pepper
2 cloves garlic, finely chopped
6 strips of bacon cut into 1½-inch pieces

Combine all ingredients except the bacon in a plastic bag or nonaluminum container. Seal or cover tightly and refrigerate for 6 to 24 hours.

Allow the meat to come to room temperature before cooking. Wipe the cubes with paper towels (reserve the marinade) and thread on 4 skewers alternately with bacon pieces. (You can put mushroom caps, blanched onions, and green pepper strips on separate skewers and broil with the beef.)

Place the skewers on a wire rack set in a broiler pan 4 inches from the heat. Broil for a total time of 10 to 20 minutes, depending on the desired degree of doneness. Turn the skewers often to brown well on all sides. Brush frequently with the marinade.

Sprinkle with salt before serving, if desired. Serve immediately.

Yield: 4 servings.

Skirt Steaks with Mustard Sauce

Skirt steaks make a delicious quick meal. They freeze well and can be cooked while still frozen if the cooking time is increased. You could also substitute thinly sliced loin, rib, or sirloin steaks for skirt steak.

3 tablespoons clarified butter (see page 260)
3 pounds skirt steak, trimmed of fat and cut into serving pieces
3 tablespoons finely chopped shallots
¼ cup dry vermouth
½ cup cream
1 teaspoon Dijon mustard
Chopped parsley

Melt the butter in a large heavy skillet. Cook the steaks 2½ to 3 minutes a side for the thicker pieces, less for the thinner. Do not crowd the pan. Cook them in batches, if necessary. Remove steaks to a platter and keep warm.

Discard all but a thin film of fat from the pan. Add the shallots and stir for 30 seconds. Return the steaks and accumulated juices to the skillet. Add the vermouth and carefully flame it. Add the cream and mustard and spoon over the steaks. Heat but do not boil the sauce. Sprinkle the steaks with parsley and serve hot.

Yield: 4 to 6 servings.

Beef Stroganoff

Chuck fillet can be substituted for tenderloin in any dish calling for beef strips.

4 to 6 tablespoons vegetable oil

1½ pounds sweet (Spanish) onions, thinly sliced

1 pound mushrooms, thinly sliced

2 pounds fillet of beef, well trimmed, cut into finger-size strips

Salt and freshly ground pepper

1 pint (2 cups) sour cream

1 tablespoon Dijon or Düsseldorf mustard

Heat 2 tablespoons oil in a large skillet. Add the onion and mushroom slices. Stir and cook until soft and all the liquid has evaporated. Transfer to a bowl and keep warm.

In the same skillet, heat 2 tablespoons oil and add the beef strips in batches. Do not crowd the pan. Stir-fry quickly until the meat is well-browned on the outside but rare on the inside. Transfer with a slotted spoon to the mushroom mixture. Proceed with the remaining meat, adding more oil if necessary.

Return the meat, mushrooms, and onions to the skillet. Add salt and pepper to taste. Stir in the sour cream and the mustard. Heat thoroughly but do not boil.

Serve immediately on warm plates with noodles, rice, or sautéed potatoes.

Yield: 4 to 6 servings.

Stir-Fry Beef and Noodles

½ pound egg noodles

3 tablespoons peanut or corn oil

1 pound lean ground beef

1 clove garlic, finely chopped

1 cup bean sprouts

1 tablespoon sugar

1 cup beef broth

2 teaspoons cornstarch

2 tablespoons water

1 10-ounce package frozen peas, defrosted

4 scallions, green part included, sliced into rings

Cook the noodles until just tender. Do not overcook. Drain and rinse under cold water and drain again. Toss with 1 tablespoon oil and reserve.

Heat a wok or skillet over high heat. Add the remaining oil and, when hot, add the meat. Stir-fry until the meat browns and separates. Remove the excess fat with a bulb baster or a large spoon.

Add the garlic, bean sprouts, sugar, and broth and bring to a boil. Make a well in the center of the mixture and add the cornstarch mixed with water.

Add the peas and noodles and stir until hot and thickened. Sprinkle with scallions and serve immediately.

Yield: 2 to 4 servings with other Chinese dishes.

Best Beef Stew

4 tablespoons vegetable oil

4 large onions

Salt and freshly ground pepper

1 cup flour

3 pounds chuck, trimmed of fat and cut into 1-inch cubes

2 cups beef broth, homemade or canned

1 white turnip, scraped and cut into dice

1 carrot, coarsely grated

3 celery stalks with leaves

1 bay leaf

10 to 12 small white onions, peeled and left whole

8 medium-size carrots, scraped and cut into quarters, lengthwise

10 to 12 small new potatoes, peeled, *or* 3 or 4 large ones, cut into 1-inch cubes

1 cup dry red wine (optional)

¼ cup chopped fresh parsley

Flour (if needed to thicken gravy)

Heat the oil in a large, heavy kettle. Peel two of the large onions, chop them coarsely, and brown them well in the oil. Remove them with a slotted spoon and reserve. Combine the salt, pepper, and flour in a brown paper bag. Add the meat cubes and shake well to coat. Brown the meat cubes in batches in the hot oil. Do not crowd them or they will not brown evenly. Add more oil if needed. When all the meat cubes have been browned, pour off and discard any oil remaining in the kettle.

Return the browned meat to the kettle with the cooked onion. Add the beef broth and enough boiling water almost to cover the meat. Slice the two remaining onions and add them to the kettle with the turnip, grated carrot, celery, and bay leaf. Simmer over low heat, partly covered, for 1 hour.

Add the small white onions, quartered carrots, and potatoes. Continue simmering for another 35 to 45 minutes, by which time both meat and vegetables should be completely tender. If there isn't enough liquid to come to the top of the stew, add additional broth, or 1 cup dry red wine. Taste for seasonings and correct. Discard the celery and bay leaf. Stir in the parsley. If the gravy seems too thin, make a paste of 1 tablespoon flour and 2 tablespoons cold water and add it to the stew, stirring until the gravy is smooth and thickened. Repeat if necessary.

The flavor of the stew improves on standing. If possible, chill and refrigerate overnight. When ready to serve, skim the fat and reheat slowly.

Yield: 6 to 8 servings.

Swiss Steak

1 2-pound round or chuck steak, 1½ inches thick
⅓ cup flour
Salt and freshly ground pepper
2 tablespoons butter
2 tablespoons vegetable oil
1 large onion, thinly sliced
2 cloves garlic, finely chopped
2 cups beef broth, approximately
1 small bay leaf
1 teaspoon dried marjoram, thyme, or savory

Dredge the steak in flour seasoned with salt and pepper. Use a meat pounder or the heel of your hand to get the flour to adhere. Allow to stand for 20 to 30 minutes.

Melt the butter and oil in a heavy skillet and add the steak. Brown well on both sides. Remove to a dish.

Add the onion and garlic and cook until softened and lightly colored. Return the steak to the skillet and add the remaining ingredients. The broth should come about halfway up the side of steak. Bring to a boil, cover tightly, and lower the heat. Simmer gently for 2 to 2½ hours, or until the meat is very tender. Use a flame-taming device, if necessary, to keep the sauce from boiling.

Remove the steak to a warm platter. Skim the fat from the sauce and strain, if desired. Pour over the meat and serve immediately.

Yield: 4 to 6 servings.

Beef and Beer Stew

4 ounces salt pork, cut in small cubes
3½ to 4 pounds lean, boneless chuck, cut into finger-size strips
1½ pounds onions, peeled and thinly sliced
1 clove garlic, finely chopped
2 tablespoons flour
2 12-ounce bottles light or dark beer
Salt and freshly ground pepper
1½ teaspoons dried thyme, crumbled
1½ to 2 tablespoons brown sugar
1 bay leaf
3 tablespoons cider or wine vinegar
1 teaspoon Dijon or Düsseldorf mustard

Preheat the oven to 325 degrees.

Cook the salt pork in large heavy casserole until golden and rendered of fat. With a slotted spoon, remove and reserve cubes.

Add the beef strips to the fat in the casserole. Do this in batches, so that the pan is not overcrowded. Brown the meat well and remove it as each batch is done.

Add the onions and garlic to the casserole and cook until soft and lightly colored. Sprinkle with flour and stir until the onions are evenly coated. Add the beer and mix well.

Return the meat and salt pork to the casserole. Add the remaining ingredients and bring to a boil. Stir well, cover tightly, and place in the oven.

Cook for 1½ hours, or until the meat is tender. Remove the meat with a slotted spoon and keep warm on a platter. Degrease the sauce and pour over the meat. Serve with crusty bread and cold beer.

Yield: 6 to 8 servings.

Pot Roast

1 4½- to 5-pound pot roast, (top, bottom round, chuck, rump, or brisket)

Flour for dredging

2 tablespoons vegetable oil, *or* 2 ounces salt pork cut into small dice

2 large onions, peeled and thinly sliced

1 clove garlic, crushed (optional)

2 cups beef broth or water

1 bay leaf

2 sprigs parsley

¼ teaspoon dried thyme, crumbled

3 carrots, peeled and cut into chunks

2 to 3 parsnips, peeled and cut into chunks

3 to 4 potatoes, peeled and cut into chunks

Salt and freshly ground pepper

Freshly chopped parsley for garnish

Dredge the beef in flour on all sides. In a deep heavy casserole just large enough for the meat and vegetables, heat the oil or cook the salt pork until the fat is rendered. Remove and reserve pork cubes. Brown the meat well on all sides, turning with tongs or wooden spoons.

Set meat aside and add the onions and garlic to the casserole. Cook, stirring, until soft and lightly colored. Return the meat (and reserved salt pork cubes, if used) to the casserole and add the broth, bay leaf, parsley, and thyme.

Bring to a boil, cover tightly, and simmer for 2½ to 3 hours, or until almost tender. Use a flame taming device, if necessary, to keep the meat at a very slow simmer.

Add vegetables and season to taste. Cover and continue to simmer for 30 to 45 minutes longer, or until vegetables are tender.

Remove meat and vegetables to a warm platter. Discard the bay leaf. Strain the sauce, pushing the solids through as much as possible, and degrease thoroughly. Return the sauce, meat, and vegetables to the casserole. Reheat. Sprinkle with chopped parsley, if desired.

Yield: 6 to 8 servings.

Variations: Add browned beef or veal bones to enrich the sauce.

Add dry red or white wine as part of the liquid, or tomato purée or crushed tomatoes. Sprinkle with oregano and basil instead of thyme.

A dollop of sour cream and a sprinkling of caraway seeds whisked into the sauce creates quite a different taste.

Cover and refrigerate any leftover pot roast. Several days or even a week later, reheat it gently and serve with pepper and tomato garnish (see following recipe).

Pepper and Tomato Garnish

2 tablespoons olive oil

4 red and/or green bell peppers
cut into 1-inch squares

1 medium onion, coarsely
chopped

1 clove garlic, finely chopped

3 to 4 tablespoons tomato paste

Freshly chopped parsley (optional)

In a large skillet, heat the oil and add the peppers, onion, and garlic. Cook, stirring, until lightly colored and soft.

Add the tomato paste and stir it gently through the peppers. Cook only long enough to heat through. It should not look like a tomato sauce, but peppers lightly bound by the tomato.

Arrange the hot, sliced meat on a warm platter. Spoon the sauce down the center. Sprinkle with chopped parsley, if desired.

Note: This sauce is also delicious over broiled or poached fish, stewed squid, or as a filling for omelets.

Beef Goulash

2 pounds boneless chuck or
round, cut into 1½-inch cubes

2 tablespoons butter

2 tablespoons vegetable oil

1 medium bell pepper, coarsely
chopped

2 pounds onions, peeled and
coarsely chopped

1 clove garlic, finely chopped

2 tablespoons sweet paprika
(Hungarian preferred)

2 tablespoons flour

2 cups beef broth

2 tablespoons tomato paste

1½ tablespoons caraway seeds

Salt and freshly ground pepper

1 cup sour cream (optional)

Dry the meat well with paper towels. Heat the butter and oil in a deep heavy casserole. Brown the cubes, a few at a time, on all sides. Remove with a slotted spoon and set aside. Do not crowd the pan, or the meat will steam and not brown.

If necessary, add more butter and oil to the casserole and add the pepper, onions, and garlic. Cook, stirring, until soft and lightly colored. Sprinkle with paprika and flour and stir until the onions are evenly coated.

Add the broth, tomato paste, caraway seeds, and the meat. Bring to a boil, lower the heat, cover tightly, and simmer gently for 1½ to 2 hours, or until the meat is tender.

Remove the meat with a slotted spoon to a warm platter. Skim fat from the sauce, correct the seasonings, and pour over the meat. Serve sour cream separately at the table. A dollop on each serving is delicious.

Yield: 4 to 6 servings.

Beef Birds in Brown Sauce

4 thin slices beef round (about 2 pounds total weight)

4 tablespoons butter or oil

1 medium onion, peeled and finely chopped

2 celery stalks, finely chopped

½ cup Madeira or Marsala wine

½ teaspoon dried oregano

½ cup bread crumbs

¼ cup pine nuts

Salt and freshly ground pepper

⅛ pound Canadian bacon or prosciutto, finely chopped

2 tablespoons flour

2 cups beef broth

Arrange the beef slices on a flat surface between sheets of wax paper. Pound with a mallet, or the bottom of a heavy cast-iron skillet, until thin.

Heat 2 tablespoons butter or oil in a skillet and add the onion and celery. Cook, stirring, until soft and lightly colored.

Add ¼ cup Madeira or Marsala and cook over high heat until reduced by half. Scrape the mixture into a bowl and add the oregano, bread crumbs, pine nuts, and salt and pepper to taste.

Spread equal amounts of the mixture over the beef slices and cover with bacon or prosciutto. Roll the meat tightly like a jelly roll and tie with kitchen string or skewer with toothpicks.

In a heavy, ovenproof casserole, heat the remaining butter or oil and brown the beef rolls on all sides. Turn with tongs. Remove the rolls and add the flour to the fat remaining in the casserole. Cook, stirring, until lightly colored. Add the beef broth, stirring constantly with a whisk until the sauce is smooth and slightly thickened.

Return the rolls to the casserole and bring to a boil. Cover, lower heat, and simmer slowly until beef is tender, 1 to 1½ hours.

Remove the rolls from the casserole and discard strings or skewers. Arrange the rolls on a platter and keep warm. Skim the fat from the sauce and add the remaining ¼ cup wine. Add additional broth if the sauce is very thick and cook 5 minutes longer. The consistency should be that of heavy cream. Pour the sauce over beef rolls.

Serve hot with noodles or rice. Garnish with parsley and lemon wedges, if desired.

Yield: 4 servings.

Sauerbraten

Most recipes for sauerbraten call for too much vinegar, which produces a sharply flavored dish. If this is your preference, increase the vinegar and reduce the amount of wine.

3 pounds bottom or top round roast
1 tablespoon black peppercorns
½ tablespoon mustard seeds
6 whole cloves
4 bay leaves
2 carrots, peeled and thinly sliced
3 large onions, peeled and thinly sliced
2 cups dry red wine
2 cups water
1 cup red wine vinegar
2 tablespoons butter
2 tablespoons vegetable oil
Flour for dredging
Beef broth
2 to 3 tablespoons heavy cream

Trim the excess fat from the meat, and cut the meat into 6 chunks. Place in a heavy plastic bag. Combine the peppercorns, mustard seeds, cloves, bay leaves, carrots, onions, wine, water, and vinegar and pour it over the beef. Seal the bag tightly and marinate for at least 3 days in the refrigerator. Turn the bag frequently.

When ready to cook, drain the meat and dry well. Strain and reserve the vegetables and marinade.

Preheat the oven to 325 degrees.

Heat the butter and oil in a deep heavy casserole. Dredge the meat in flour and brown well on all sides.

Remove the meat and all but a thin film of fat. Add the reserved vegetables. Cook, stirring, until soft and lightly colored. Add half the marinade (about 2½ cups), and bring to a boil. Return the meat to the casserole, cover, and place in the oven for about 2 hours, or until tender. Turn the meat two or three times.

Remove the meat to a warm platter. Strain the sauce, discard the vegetables and bay leaves, and skim the fat. Pour the sauce into a 4-cup measure and add beef broth to bring the level up to 4 cups. Reheat the sauce and stir in the cream. Serve hot with noodles, potatoes, or dumplings.

Yield: 6 servings.

Marinated Rump Roast

1 4½- to 5-pound rump roast
½ cup dry sherry
¼ cup vegetable oil
¼ cup soy sauce (Japanese preferred)
2 cloves garlic, crushed
1 small onion, coarsely chopped

Place meat in a plastic bag or nonaluminum bowl. Combine the remaining ingredients and pour over meat. Seal tightly and refrigerate for at least 24 hours. Turn meat as often as you think of it.

Bring the roast to room temperature before cooking. Preheat the oven to 400 degrees. Remove the meat from the marinade and dry well. Place it on a wire rack in a shallow pan. Roast 15 minutes a pound for rare, or until internal thermometer reading is 135 degrees. (Rump roast is a triangular shaped piece of meat. The thick end will be rarer than the thinner end.)

Allow to rest on a warm platter for 15 to 20 minutes, then slice very thin.

Yield: 6 to 8 servings.

Quick Brown Gravy

3 tablespoons flour
½ cup dry red wine (optional)
2½ cups beef broth
1 tablespoon tomato paste
1 teaspoon Bovril meat extract (optional)

Discard all but 3 tablespoons of fat from the roasting pan. Heat the pan on top of the stove and add the flour. Stir with a whisk until golden brown and bubbly.

Add the wine, if desired, and cook until it evaporates. Add the beef broth, tomato paste, beef extract, and any accumulated juices from the meat. Stir constantly with a whisk until the gravy is smooth and thick, about 7 minutes. It should be the consistency of heavy cream. Thin it with water or broth if it is too thick. Taste and adjust seasonings. Serve hot with the sliced rump roast.

Steak Tartare

In restaurants, the waiter usually mixes the ingredients at the table with a great deal of flourish. We prefer to mix them ahead and let the raw beef and seasonings mellow for 30 to 60 minutes.

½ pound very lean round steak
1 egg yolk
1 slice sweet (Spanish) onion, finely chopped
2 anchovy fillets, washed and mashed, *or* ¼ teaspoon anchovy paste
1 teaspoon capers
½ teaspoon Dijon or Düsseldorf mustard
Dash of Worcestershire sauce
½ teaspoon ketchup
Salt and freshly ground pepper

Grind the meat yourself if you have a food processor. Or have the butcher grind it while you wait. Do not buy the meat already ground because it must be absolutely fresh for this dish.

Mix all the ingredients together lightly with the fingers or a fork. Taste and adjust seasonings.

Pack into a small bowl and refrigerate, covered, until ready to serve (no more than 1 hour).

Unmold onto a small platter. Garnish with sour pickles, radishes, and parsley, if desired. Serve with thinly sliced rye or white toast.

Yield: 4 to 6 appetizer servings.

Hamburgers

The secret of a good hamburger is to handle the meat very lightly. Don't compress it when you form the patties, and don't press down with a spatula when you cook them.

1 tablespoon vegetable oil
2 pounds lean ground round or chuck

Film a heavy skillet lightly with oil. Form the meat into patties, each about 1 inch thick. Cook over medium heat for 3 to 4 minutes on each side for rare. Remove from the skillet and serve immediately. Or keep warm and serve with the following shallot sauce.

Yield: 4 servings.

Note: The hamburgers can also be broiled on a wire rack set in a shallow pan 3 inches from the heat. Cook for 2 to 3 minutes a side for rare.

Shallot Sauce

2 tablespoons butter
¼ cup finely chopped shallots
¼ cup wine vinegar
Freshly chopped parsley

Melt the butter in the skillet in which the hamburgers cooked and add the shallots. Stir to cook lightly. Add the vinegar and cook until reduced slightly.

Remove from the heat and pour over the hamburgers. Sprinkle with parsley.

Stuffed Flank Steak

3 tablespoons clarified butter

1 pound mushrooms, finely chopped

½ cup finely chopped shallots or onions

¼ cup dry vermouth

¼ cup dry bread crumbs

1¾- to 2-pound flank steak

1 to 2 tablespoons vegetable oil

1 medium onion, coarsely chopped

1 clove garlic, unpeeled

3 to 4 small, whole tomatoes, peeled, seeded, and coarsely chopped, *or* 1 tablespoon tomato paste

½ cup red wine (optional)

½ cup beef broth (increase to 1 cup if not using wine)

1 small bay leaf

¼ teaspoon dried thyme

2 to 3 sprigs fresh parsley

Heat the butter in a skillet and add the mushrooms. Cook, stirring, over high heat until all moisture evaporates.

Add the shallots and stir until soft, but not brown. Add vermouth and cook until it evaporates.

Remove from the heat, add the bread crumbs, and mix well. Cool while preparing the meat.

Hold a long sharp knife parallel to the cutting board and cut the steak lengthwise almost to the other side. Be careful not to cut all the way through. Put the palm of one hand on top of the steak while cutting. Open up the steak and pound it carefully so that it lies flat.

Spread the stuffing evenly over the surface of one side of the meat. Cover with the other side and roll it tightly, turning in the open side. Tie securely in several places with kitchen string.

Heat the oil in a heavy casserole and brown the meat well on all sides, turning with tongs. An oval casserole about 12½ inches in length is perfect. Remove the meat to a dish and wipe out the casserole. Add a little more oil and cook the onion and garlic, stirring, until soft and lightly colored. Add all remaining ingredients. Return the meat to the casserole.

Bring to a boil, cover, reduce the heat and simmer slowly for 2 to 2½ hours, or until the meat is tender. (The meat can also be cooked in a 325-degree oven for about 2 hours.) Turn several times during cooking.

Remove the meat to a warm platter, cover lightly with foil, and let stand for 15 to 20 minutes. Degrease the pan gravy and strain it, if desired. Remove the bay leaf.

Remove strings and slice the meat roll. Arrange on a warm platter and cover with some of the sauce. Serve remaining sauce in a gravy boat. Garnish with watercress, if desired.

Yield: 4 servings.

Chili con Carne

3 tablespoons vegetable oil

1 pound Italian sausage, thickly sliced

2 large bell peppers, coarsely chopped

2 large onions, peeled and coarsely chopped

3 to 4 celery stalks, coarsely chopped

3 cloves garlic, finely chopped

3 pounds ground chuck

1 1-pound, 12-ounce can whole tomatoes

1 cup beef broth or water

3 tablespoons ground cumin

3 tablespoons dried oregano, crumbled

3 tablespoons dried basil, crumbled

2 tablespoons chili powder, or to taste

1 small can jalapeño peppers, chopped (optional)

2 cups cooked kidney or pinto beans

Heat the oil in a deep, nonaluminum casserole and cook the sausage slices, stirring, until well browned.

Add peppers, onions, celery, and garlic. Cook, stirring, until soft but not brown.

Add the beef and cook, stirring, until it loses its red color.

Add the remaining ingredients except the beans. Break up the tomatoes and stir to mix well. Bring to a boil, lower the heat, cover, and simmer for 1 hour. Stir occasionally to prevent sticking. Add additional broth or water if the chili seems too thick. Skim and discard the fat as it rises to the surface.

Add the cooked beans to the chili 15 minutes before serving, or serve separately. Serve hot in bowls. Corn chips, sour cream, shredded Monterey Jack cheese, and hot rice can be passed separately for guests to add as they wish.

Yield: 6 to 8 servings.

Note: Commercial chili powders vary greatly in strength and should be added to taste. Jalapeño peppers are also hot and should be used judiciously.

Swedish Meatballs

3 tablespoons butter

¼ cup finely chopped onion

1 pound lean ground round (twice ground)

2 slices dry white bread, shredded

¾ cup cream

1 egg, lightly beaten

1 tablespoon finely chopped parsley

¼ teaspoon freshly grated nutmeg

Pinch of allspice

Melt 1 tablespoon butter in a small skillet. Add the onions and cook, stirring, until soft. Scrape into a large mixing bowl. Add the meat, bread, ¼ cup cream, egg, parsley, nutmeg, allspice, and salt and pepper.

Mix well with the hands. Form into walnut-size balls.

In a heavy skillet, heat the remaining butter and the oil. Add half the meat balls and shake the pan constantly until they start to brown and crust on the outside. This will keep them round. Cook until well browned. Transfer to a platter and keep warm. Continue with the second batch.

Salt and freshly ground pepper
2 tablespoons vegetable oil
1 tablespoon flour
½ cup beef broth

Pour off all but 1 or 2 tablespoons of fat from the pan. Add the flour and stir until lightly colored.

Whisk in the broth, scraping the bottom and sides of the skillet to dissolve any brown bits. Bring to a boil, lower the heat and add the remaining ½ cup cream, whisking to blend. Skim off any fat. Return the meatballs to the sauce and heat gently until warm, 3 to 5 minutes.

Spear with toothpicks and serve hot as a cocktail snack. Or they may be served as a main course with noodles or boiled potatoes.

Yield: 20 to 35 meatballs.

Meat Loaf

3 eggs
4 slices dry bread (white, rye, or whole wheat), shredded
1 large onion, coarsely chopped
1 teaspoon dried thyme
1 small green or red bell pepper, coarsely chopped
2 pounds lean ground round or chuck
1 pound ground pork, Italian or breakfast sausage, casings removed
Salt and freshly ground pepper
⅓ pound sliced bacon (optional)

Preheat the oven to 325 degrees.

Place the eggs, bread, onion, thyme, and bell pepper in the container of a blender or food processor. Process until puréed and somewhat liquid.

Scrape into a bowl and add the meats. Mix lightly with your hands, just enough to blend. Add salt and pepper to taste. Form into a loaf (about 14 inches long) and place in a baking pan. Pat gently into shape to remove any air pockets.

Arrange the bacon slices on top of the loaf without overlapping.

Bake for approximately 1½ hours, or until well browned. Skim fat with bulb baster as it accumulates. Remove and allow to stand for 15 to 20 minutes before slicing. Top each slice with a spoonful of tomato sauce, if desired (see following recipe).

Yield: 6 to 8 servings.

Tomato Sauce

¼ cup olive oil
1 medium onion, coarsely chopped
1 clove garlic, finely chopped
1 28-ounce can whole tomatoes
¼ teaspoon dried oregano
2 bouillon cubes (beef or chicken)
Pinch of red pepper flakes
1 to 2 tablespoons freshly chopped parsley

Heat the oil in a medium saucepan and cook the onion and garlic, stirring, until soft and lightly colored.

Add the tomatoes, breaking them up with a fork or your hands.

Add remaining ingredients except parsley and bring to a boil. Lower heat and simmer for 15 to 20 minutes, stirring occasionally. Add parsley before serving.

Corned Beef and Cabbage

1 4- to 5-pound corned beef brisket

1 large onion studded with 2 cloves

1 bay leaf

6 to 8 peppercorns

1 pound carrots, peeled and trimmed

6 to 8 small potatoes, peeled

1 small head cabbage, cut into 8 wedges

Rinse beef well in cold water and wipe with a damp towel.

Place in a deep kettle and cover with cold water. Add the onion studded with cloves, bay leaf, and peppercorns and bring to a boil. Cover, lower the heat, and simmer until the meat is almost tender, 2½ to 3 hours. Skim frequently.

Add whole carrots, potatoes, and cabbage wedges. Push carrots and potatoes down into the liquid. Arrange cabbage wedges on top of the meat so they are not covered by liquid.

Cover and continue to cook for 30 to 45 minutes longer, or until the vegetables are tender. Let the beef rest for 15 to 20 minutes before slicing it. Remove the bay leaf. Arrange meat and vegetables on a large platter and serve hot with a good mustard or horseradish.

Yield: 6 servings.

Lamb

There are more sheep than any other livestock in the world and the principal meat in many countries is lamb or mutton. But for some reason, Americans have never been a great lamb-eating people, which is a pity because lamb provides some of our most glamorous and delicious cuts of meat—racks and saddles, leg, crown roast, and Frenched rib chops. While these are all expensive cuts, there are other less costly ones that are lovely braised or in stews.

Much of the lamb we find in our markets is yearling lamb, slaughtered at about one year old. Older than that, it becomes mutton, which is seldom available here. Younger, choicer lamb, called spring lamb, is from sheep born in February and March and generally available from the beginning of April to the beginning of October of the same year. These animals were able to graze and their better feed is reflected in the quality of their meat.

Young lamb should have bright pink, well-marbled flesh, waxy, creamy white fat, and young bones that are moist and red at the joints. Size is a clue to age. A leg of spring lamb will weigh up to 7 pounds. Winter lamb will weigh up to 8 or 9, and any leg that weighs more than 9 has to be called mutton. There is nothing wrong with mutton, as long as it is marketed as such. Mutton is not only older, but stronger in taste and less tender than lamb. It is cooked the same as lamb but it generally needs 5 to 10 minutes longer per pound.

There was a time in American kitchens when lamb was invariably overcooked, but now people have discovered the juicy, delicious taste of lamb that is a little pink in the middle instead of being roasted until it becomes gray-brown and stringy. If you are not acquainted with lamb that is a little underdone, we suggest that you try it.

Neck and Shoulder

The neck is a bony cut that does nicely as a stew. It is sometimes included with the shoulder. The shoulder has a delicious flavor and, cut into chunks, makes an elegant stew or good shish kebab. But because of its many bones, it makes a good roast only when boned. It can be cooked flat, or rolled and tied for braising, poaching, or roasting. Shoulder lamb chops are bony but well flavored. They are best braised and are popular in Irish stew.

Rib

The section next to the shoulder is the rib, or rack. The whole rack is a popular roast, although there is not much meat on it and one rack will barely serve three people. Two racks can be tied together to make a crown roast. The ribs are also cut into single or double rib chops, which may be broiled or braised. For very special occasions, when all thought of cost is thrown to the winds, the eye section is removed from the rack and cut into thick slices, known as medallions. They are sautéed.

Loin

Next comes the loin, the laziest and most tender muscle and the choicest part of the lamb. Both loins in one piece are called the saddle. A single piece consisting of a saddle and the two legs is called a baron, and is as aristocratic as it sounds and not meant for a modest budget. The loin can be cut into single or double chops, which may be braised or broiled. Boned loin lamb chops trimmed of all fat and gristle and tied into small compact rounds are called noisettes of lamb, another extravagance. They are generally pan-broiled and served with a rich béarnaise sauce.

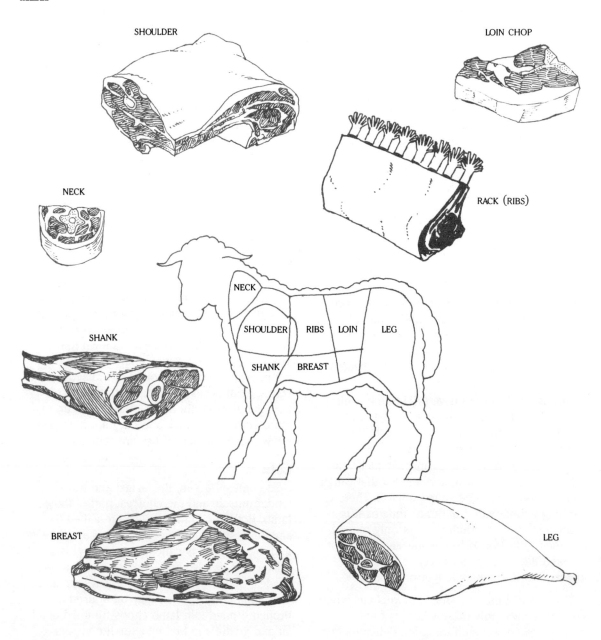

Lamb parts are subdivided into fewer cuts than those of beef and what would be steaks in beef are small chops in lamb. Neck pieces are stewed, and the shoulder stewed, cut into chops, or boned and roasted or braised. The rack may be cut into rib chops; a pair of racks forms a crown roast. The loin yields tender chops or a roast. The leg is sometimes cut in half. The breast can be left whole, boned, or cut into riblets.

Leg

The leg is the most familiar and commonly used cut of lamb. It can weigh from 4½ to 9 pounds, according to the size and age of the animal. Many markets sell half a leg, either the shank (leg) half or the sirloin or butt, the part that is next to the loin. The shank half costs more, but has more meat on it and looks better, showing the round end of the leg bone. The sirloin or butt half is bonier and harder to carve. Ask the butcher to crack the bones for you to make carving easier. It is also possible to buy the whole leg and have the sirloin end cut off as steaks.

The leg is covered by a tight parchment tissue called the fell. We prefer to cut it away, although there are those who maintain that keeping it makes for stronger flavor and holds the leg in shape. You could try it both ways and see which you prefer. If the leg is to be boned and rolled, the fell should definitely be removed.

Leg of lamb is versatile and lends itself to a variety of preparations. It may be roasted or braised. It may be boned and flattened (butterflied) and broiled in less than thirty minutes. It may be boned and rolled with a stuffing for a rolled roast. Boned and cubed leg of lamb is the preferred cut for shish kebab.

Breast and Shank

Beneath the rack are the remaining breast portion and the foreshank. This is sometimes cut off in one piece and divided into portions for stew. The breast can be cut into lamb spareribs, or into strips called riblets. Some markets sell large pieces of breast, which can be braised. They have good flavor but they are messy to eat. The breast can also be stuffed like a veal breast, but it is less meaty than veal. The front legs of the lamb are generally cut short and sold as shanks, which need long slow cooking and must be braised.

Ground Lamb

A word of caution about ground lamb: there is no way to tell what cut it comes from when you buy supermarket packages. It is most likely shank and neck meat and trimmings. There may be nothing wrong with it, but it may contain more fat than you want. You are better off buying shoulder, which has fine flavor, trimming away the fat, and grinding the meat yourself. Leave a little fat for juiciness. One pound of ground lamb makes three plump patties or four thin ones.

Carving a Leg of Lamb—American Style

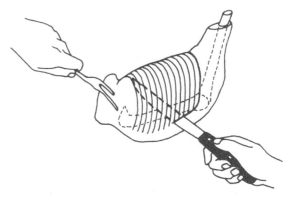

3 *When you have cut enough slices, release them by running the knife along the top of the leg bone.*

1 *With the roast on its side, cut a few slices from the thin cushion of meat underneath, parallel to the bone. This should form a base broad enough to rest the roast on.*

Carving a Leg of Lamb—French Style

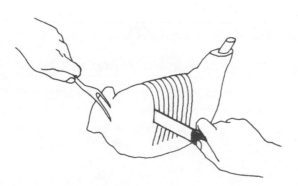

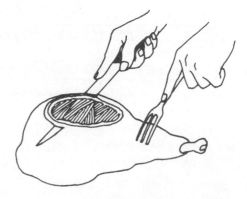

2 *Set the roast on its base. Beginning where the protruding shank bone joins the leg bone, make vertical cuts about ¼ inch apart. Hold the roast at the end with a fork. (A left leg is shown here.)*

The French carve their gigot much more simply. Holding the shank bone with your hand or a fork, cut slices parallel to the leg bone, turning the roast as necessary.

Roast Leg of Lamb

1 6-pound leg of lamb
2 cloves garlic, slivered
1 tablespoon dried rosemary or thyme
10 to 12 snips of fresh parsley
Juice of 1 lemon
Salt and freshly ground pepper

Preheat the oven to 350 degrees. Remove the fell and cut away the excess fat.

Make 10 to 12 slits in the meat and insert a sliver of garlic, a pinch of rosemary or thyme, and a snip of parsley into each slit. Rub lemon juice over all and sprinkle with salt and pepper.

Place on a rack in a shallow pan, fat side up. Roast for 15 to 20 minutes a pound for rare, or until a meat thermometer registers 130 to 135 degrees. Increase the time for medium, which will register 145 to 150 degrees.

Let stand, lightly covered, for 15 to 20 minutes before carving. Serve thinly sliced on warm plates.

Yield: 6 to 8 servings.

Roast Leg of Lamb (High-Temperature Method)

Use this method only if your oven is well insulated and you have a ventilating fan, because there will be a good deal of smoke.

1 6- to 7-pound leg of lamb
1 to 2 cloves garlic, slivered
Salt and freshly ground pepper
1 teaspoon dried thyme or rosemary

Have the meat at room temperature. Remove the fell and the excess fat.

Preheat the oven to 500 degrees. Make 6 to 8 slits in the meat and insert garlic slivers. Rub all over with salt and pepper.

Place on a rack in a shallow roasting pan and roast for 45 minutes. Remove from oven, sprinkle with herbs, cover loosely with foil, and let stand 10 to 20 minutes. Carve in thin slices and serve on warm plates.

Yield: 6 to 8 servings.

Broiled Leg of Lamb

This is a favorite way to cook lamb because of the short cooking time and because there is rare, medium, and even a bit of well-done meat—something for everyone.

1 6-pound leg of lamb
½ cup olive or vegetable oil
3 cups dry red wine
1 medium carrot, peeled and coarsely chopped
2 medium onions, peeled and coarsely chopped
2 cloves garlic, crushed
1 tablespoon dried thyme or rosemary
Several parsley sprigs
Freshly ground pepper

Have the butcher bone, trim, and flatten the lamb, a process known as butterflying. Trim away the excess fat.

Place the butterflied lamb fat side down in a large plastic bag or a nonaluminum pan. Combine the remaining ingredients and pour over the meat. Tie the bag tightly, or cover the pan tightly with plastic wrap. Marinate for 5 to 6 hours at room temperature or refrigerate overnight and bring back to room temperature before broiling.

Remove the meat, reserving the marinade, and place on a rack in a shallow pan 4 inches from the meat. Broil about 10 minutes on each side. Brush or baste occasionally with the marinade.

Remove from the broiler and turn the oven to 425 degrees. Roast for 10 to 15 minutes longer, or until the internal temperature is 130 to 135 degrees in the thickest part. Cover loosely with foil and let stand for 10 to 15 minutes. Carve at an angle into thin slices and serve on warm plates.

Yield: 6 to 8 servings.

Note: The butterflied leg will have two main sections, or lobes. You can freeze one lobe if the whole leg is more than you need.

Grilled Lamb Chops

2 rib chops per person, each 1¼ inches thick
Clove of garlic, cut (optional)
Pinch of dried thyme or rosemary

Rub the cut side of garlic over the chops, if desired. Place the chops on a wire rack in a shallow roasting pan and set the pan 4 inches from the heat. Broil for 4 minutes on each side for rare. Remove from the broiler, sprinkle with herbs, and serve immediately.

Roast Rack of Lamb

2 racks of lamb, trimmed of fat
(about 7 chops on each)
1 to 2 tablespoons oil
1 clove garlic, crushed
Salt and freshly ground pepper
⅔ cup bread crumbs
4 tablespoons butter, melted
⅓ cup finely chopped parsley
2 tablespoons dried rosemary,
crumbled
1 clove garlic, finely chopped
2 tablespoons Dijon or Düsseldorf
mustard

Preheat the oven to 500 degrees.

Rub a little oil and garlic over the racks. Place meat side down in a shallow roasting pan and roast for 15 minutes. Remove from the oven and sprinkle with salt and pepper. Lower the oven temperature to 400 degrees.

Combine the bread crumbs, butter, parsley, rosemary, chopped garlic, and mustard. With your fingers or a small spatula, press the crumb topping evenly on the meaty side of the rack.

Return to the oven and cook for 30 minutes, or until the internal temperature is 130 to 135 degrees for rare. Baste occasionally with the pan drippings. When done, remove from oven, cover lightly with foil, and let rest for 5 to 7 minutes.

Carve between the ribs and serve on warm plates.

Yield: 4 to 6 servings.

Shish Kebab

¼ cup vegetable oil
½ cup lemon juice
1 tablespoon soy sauce (Japanese
preferred) or Worcestershire
sauce
1 teaspoon dried thyme, crumbled
1 teaspoon dried rosemary,
crumbled
2 cloves garlic, crushed
2 pounds boneless leg of lamb,
cut into 1½-inch cubes
2 to 4 bell peppers, cut into
wedges
14 to 16 cherry tomatoes
1 medium Spanish onion, peeled,
separated, and cut into wedges
about the same size as the
peppers
½ pound small mushrooms

In a plastic bag or nonaluminum dish, combine the first six ingredients. Add the lamb cubes and refrigerate for at least 4 hours, or overnight.

Drain the meat, reserving the marinade, and thread the lamb loosely on metal or wooden skewers. (Wooden skewers must be soaked in water for several hours before using.) Thread the vegetables on separate skewers, because they need less cooking time.

Place meat on a wire rack in a shallow roasting pan 4 inches from the heat. Leave room between the skewers so the meat will cook evenly. Broil for 5 to 6 minutes. Turn the meat. Add the skewered vegetables to the broiler at this point. Brush both meat and vegetables with the marinade and cook for 5 to 6 minutes longer.

Remove the meat to a warm platter. Turn the vegetable skewers, brush with the marinade, and cook until soft and lightly colored. Do not char them. Remove vegetable skewers to a platter.

Yield: 4 to 6 servings.

Grilled Lamb Cubes with Yogurt Marinade

This preparation lends itself to outdoor grilling. The yogurt adds a delightful tang to the flavor of the lamb.

4 pounds boneless leg of lamb,
  cut into 1½-inch cubes
2 large onions, coarsely grated
1 cup yogurt

Combine the lamb, onions, and yogurt in a plastic bag or nonaluminum bowl. Mix well. Cover and refrigerate for 1 to 2 days.

Remove the lamb from the marinade and thread on skewers. Grill over charcoal or on a wire rack set in a broiler pan 4 inches from the heat. Cook for 10 to 12 minutes in all, turning the skewers frequently. Test for doneness with a small knife.

Yield: 6 to 8 servings.

Lamb Curry

4 pounds boneless lamb (shoulder
  or leg), cut into 1½-inch cubes
⅓ cup vegetable oil
4 medium carrots, peeled and
  thinly sliced
3 celery stalks, coarsely chopped
2 large onions, coarsely chopped
2 to 3 large greening or Granny
  Smith apples, peeled, cored, and
  cut into ½-inch cubes
⅓ cup shredded coconut
1 clove garlic, finely chopped
2 small bay leaves
2 teaspoons dried thyme
1½ tablespoons curry powder, or
  more according to taste
4 tablespoons flour
¼ cup tomato paste
4 cups chicken broth
1 10-ounce jar chutney
½ to ¾ cup heavy cream

Preheat the oven to 400 degrees.

Wipe the lamb cubes with paper towels to dry them. Heat the oil in a large skillet and add the lamb a few cubes at a time. Do not crowd the pan. Brown lamb on all sides and transfer to an ovenproof casserole. Continue until all the cubes are browned.

In the same skillet, cook the carrots, celery, and onion, stirring, until they are soft and lightly colored. Transfer to the casserole with the meat.

Add the apples, coconut, garlic, bay leaves, thyme, curry powder, and flour to the lamb. Stir with a wooden spoon to blend well. Stir in the tomato paste dissolved in the chicken broth and the chutney and bring to a boil. Cover tightly and cook in the oven for 1 to 1½ hours, or until tender.

Drain the sauce from the meat and skim off the fat. Remove the bay leaves. Purée the sauce in a food mill, food processor, or blender. Return the sauce to the meat. Add the cream (to taste) and stir to mix well. Heat through but do not boil. Serve hot with rice, chutney, coconut, diced apples, and yogurt, if desired.

Yield: 6 to 8 servings.

Note: If you do not wish to purée the sauce, you can eliminate that step. The sauce will taste the same but will have a different texture. Be sure to skim the fat, though.

Spring Lamb Stew

2 tablespoons bacon fat

4 pounds lean lamb, cut into 1½-inch cubes

Lamb bones, if possible

2 medium onions, quartered

2 cloves garlic, peeled and crushed

3 tablespoons flour

½ cup drained, chopped tomatoes

⅔ cup water, approximately

⅔ cup beef broth, approximately

⅔ cup dry white wine, approximately

2 sprigs parsley

1 teaspoon dried thyme

3 peppercorns

1 bay leaf

Salt and freshly ground pepper

Heat the bacon fat in a deep heavy casserole. Add the lamb cubes in batches. Do not crowd the pan. Brown well on all sides. Remove with a slotted spoon and set aside. If using bones, brown them well, also.

In the same casserole, cook the onions and garlic, stirring, until wilted and lightly colored. Return the lamb to the casserole and sprinkle with the flour. Stir to coat the meat well.

Add the tomatoes and enough water, broth, and wine to almost cover the meat. Tie the parsley, thyme, peppercorns, and bay leaf in a piece of cheesecloth and add to the casserole. Bring to a boil, skim well, lower the heat and simmer gently for 1½ hours, or until a fork pierces the meat easily.

Before serving, skim fat, remove the bones (if using) and the bouquet garni. Adjust seasoning and serve hot from the casserole. This is good with sautéed mushrooms, baby carrots, and green beans.

Yield: 6 to 8 servings.

Braised Lamb Shoulder with Vegetables

2 tablespoons vegetable oil

1 4½-pound boned and tied lamb shoulder, excess fat removed

2 medium onions, quartered

2 garlic cloves, crushed

1 cup dry white wine

1 cup beef broth

1 bay leaf

¼ teaspoon dried thyme

1 to 2 sprigs fresh parsley

4 peppercorns, crushed

1 pound turnips, peeled and quartered

1 pound carrots, peeled and cut into 3 or 4 pieces

Pinch of sugar

Salt and freshly ground pepper

Freshly chopped parsley

Preheat the oven to 325 degrees.

Heat oil in a large, heavy casserole and brown the meat on all sides. Remove to a plate. Pour off all but 1 tablespoon oil.

Add the onions and garlic. Stir and cook until soft and lightly colored. Return the meat to the casserole and add the wine. When it evaporates, add the broth, bay leaf, thyme, parsley, and peppercorns. Bring to a boil, cover tightly, and place in the oven for 1½ hours, or until the meat is almost tender when tested with a fork.

Add the turnips, carrots, sugar, and salt and pepper to taste. Continue to cook for 30 to 45 minutes longer, basting occasionally, until the vegetables are tender. Remove the lamb and slice it. Skim fat from the sauce and serve sauce with the lamb and vegetables. Sprinkle with parsley.

Yield: 4 servings.

Braised Lamb Shanks with Beans

2 cups precooked navy or white pea beans (see note)

1 tablespoon vegetable oil

4 lamb shanks 1¼ to 1½ pounds each, trimmed of all fat

1 medium onion, coarsely chopped

1 carrot, peeled and coarsely chopped

2 cloves garlic, finely minced

1 cup chopped tomatoes, drained

1 cup dry white wine or vermouth

½ cup beef broth

1 teaspoon dried thyme

1 small bay leaf, crumbled

Salt and freshly ground pepper

Freshly chopped parsley

Preheat the oven to 325 degrees.

Precook the beans and set aside (see below).

Heat the oil in a heavy casserole, add the shanks, and brown well on all sides. Drain and discard all but a thin film of fat.

Add the onion, carrot, and garlic. Stir until lightly colored, about 2 minutes. Add the tomatoes, wine, broth, thyme, and bay leaf. Bring to a boil, cover tightly, and place in the oven for 1 to 1½ hours, depending on the size of the shanks.

Add the hot, drained beans to the casserole. Sprinkle with salt and pepper to taste and stir to mix with juices in the casserole. Cover, and cook for 30 to 40 minutes, or until all is tender. Serve hot garnished with the parsley.

Yield: 6 to 8 servings.

Note: This dish is easy to prepare if the beans are cooked in advance. The time it takes to cook dried beans can vary considerably depending on their age.

Navy or White Pea Beans

1 cup dried navy or white pea beans

1 stalk celery

1 small onion, coarsely chopped

4 cups water

Presoak beans overnight, or use the quick-soaking method (see page 301).

Drain the beans and place in a medium-size saucepan. Add the celery, onion, and water. Bring to a boil, cover, lower the heat, and simmer until almost tender. Depending on the age of the beans, this could take from 1 to 1½ hours. When almost tender, remove from the heat and set aside. You will have 2 cups. Heat the beans before adding them to the lamb.

Pork

Ever since wild pigs were first domesticated by the Chinese more than 5,000 years ago, pigs have been among the most popular of the meat-yielding animals. Pork was always a favored meat of farmers and people who lived in rural areas, and understandably so, since it was the only meat that tasted better cured than fresh. But even today, with refrigeration and modern preservation methods, less than a third of the pork produced in the United States is sold as fresh pork; the rest is made into ham, bacon, sausages, lard, and other related products. From snout to tail, ears to feet, the pig offers a huge variety of eating. It has been noted that every part of the pig is edible except the "oink."

To buy the best fresh pork, look for pale, whitish-pink flesh, deep pink to red bones, and firm white fat. The pinker the flesh, the older the animal. The meat should look grainy, like beefsteak. Avoid any pork that looks soft and mushy.

For many years pork was overcooked because of the fear of trichinosis parasites that might lurk in undercooked pork meat. But now scientists have found that the bacteria are killed at 150 to 155 degrees, and pork may be considered safe if it is cooked to 165 degrees, which yields a much better, juicier result than the former 185-degree temperature that left the meat dried out and tasteless.

Even though pork is a tender, succulent meat, it is usually best to braise or roast it. It is generally too dry for broiling. The graining you see in pork is not fatty tissue but muscle.

We'll begin our porcine tour with the jowl butt back of the ear and move clockwise. The jowl butt, a square fatty piece at the end of the head is used mostly for flavoring meats. It is often smoked like bacon and is popular in southern cooking where it is boiled with greens, or sometimes sliced and fried. Next to the jowl is the shoulder butt, which makes a choice smoked cut and, when used fresh, is braised, roasted, or boiled.

Loin

The loin, extending from the shoulder to the ham, is one of the choicest cuts. It can be divided into the blade loin, which is the part next to the shoulder; center loin; and sirloin, the end next to the ham. These sections can be cut into single or double chops. Country-style spareribs cut from the shoulder end of the loin are not true spareribs but are actually meatier than those cut from the breast and not too fatty. They are good braised. Extra thick loin chops are often split and stuffed and braised. The center cut of the loin is the most desirable roast—also the most expensive. The loin cuts may be roasted with the bone or boned, rolled, and tied. Two loin racks may be tied together for a crown roast. Also in this section is the pork tenderloin, which weighs from ¾ to 1 pound and is tender and delicious. It may be roasted plain, stuffed and roasted, braised, or broiled if larded with strips of bacon.

Above the loin is the fatback, the plain white fat used for larding or to serve as a covering of fat on delicate meats to be roasted (barding) or for lining pâté molds. It is used fresh in these preparations, but it can also be found salted.

Leg

The hind legs are sold as fresh hams or smoked hams. The leg can be sold as a huge roast or separated into the butt end (closest to the loin) and the shank end (closest to the foot). The shank end is easier to slice. Fresh ham may be roasted or braised. Steaks from ½ to 2 inches may be cut from the leg and boiled, sautéed, or braised.

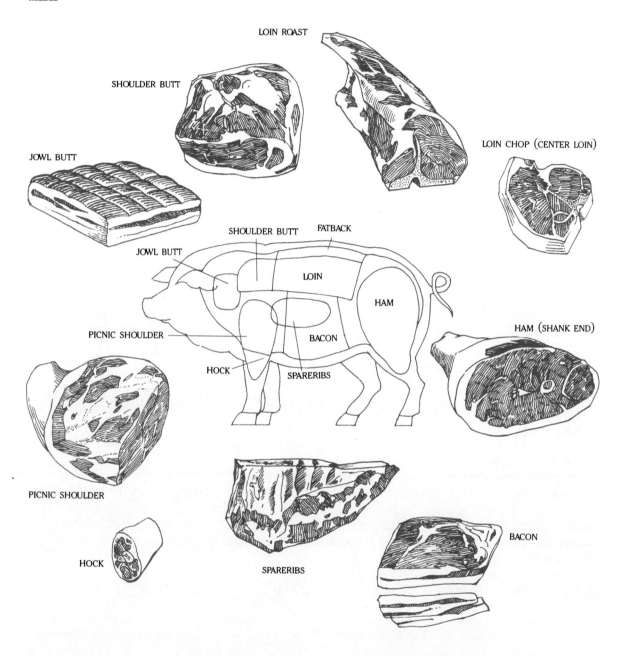

LOIN ROAST

SHOULDER BUTT

LOIN CHOP (CENTER LOIN)

JOWL BUTT

SHOULDER BUTT   FATBACK

JOWL BUTT

LOIN

HAM

HAM (SHANK END)

PICNIC SHOULDER

BACON

HOCK

SPARERIBS

PICNIC SHOULDER

BACON

HOCK

SPARERIBS

All of the pig may be eaten, from snout to tail, but these are the most popular cuts. The jowl butt, behind the ear, is often smoked, as may be the shoulder butt. The loin is cut into blade, center, and sirloin roasts or chops. The leg, or ham, is often smoked. From the underside come the flank—smoked as bacon or salted as side meat—and the breast, or spareribs. The picnic shoulder and hock come from the foreleg.

Salt Pork and Bacon

Almost in the center of the pig below the loin is the pork belly, the meat used for salt pork and for bacon. Salt pork is called side meat in the southern and midwestern parts of the United States. We rarely see these parts fresh at retail stores; they go directly to packers who salt or cure them.

Spareribs

The spareribs are the breastbones and have very little meat in proportion to bone. They may be bought in sheets or cut into sections and are roasted, braised, or broiled.

Shoulder and Hock

The upper arm and small end of the shoulder blade provide the picnic ham. The meat is well-flavored but not as tender as the leg nor as lean a cut as the loin and it is difficult to carve. It is often smoked, but it may also be fresh and it can be braised, boiled, or roasted.

Hams

Strictly speaking, the term "ham" refers only to a leg of pork, but current usage has extended its meaning to include a shoulder of pork or any other cut that has been put through a preserving process. However, an astute shopper should be able to tell from the label which cut was used for the piece under consideration.

Fresh pork becomes smoked ham through a process of curing with brine or with dry salt. The meat is soaked in the brine or injected with a solution of it. The dry-cured pork is rubbed all over with salt and then aged. The next step is smoking, although not all hams are smoked. Unlike in the past when smoking was needed for preservation, it is done today for flavor, although some people prefer the milder salt-curing.

Ham was one of the earliest preserved meats and the American-style country ham, first produced in Virginia, around the town of Smithfield, earned the enthusiastic approval of world gastronomy. The dry-cured Smithfield ham, with its dark color, nutty dry texture, and almost wine-like flavor, has never lost its magic and is still highly prized. Magnificent dark smoked hams are also produced by skilled farmers in other states, among which are Kentucky, Vermont, Georgia, and the Carolinas. Country-style hams are available from mail-order houses and specialty shops.

Supermarkets offer a wide variety of styles of ham, all of them blander than the heavily cured and smoked country hams. Hams with the bone in, weighing from 8 to 20 pounds, are available whole, cut in half as butt and shank ends, or as ham slices. The bone-in hams are generally the most flavorful of all the commercially processed hams. Then there are hams that have been skinned, boned, and shaped into rolls. You can buy regular picnic shoulder, or one that has been skinned, boned, rolled, and tied. It has good flavor, but it is fatty and will not cut into fine slices. The boneless shoulder butt is also very fatty. A whole skinless, boneless ham weighs up to 14 pounds. These hams have little waste and are easy to carve, which some people feel compensates for their lack of flavor. This is equally true of canned hams, which are convenient and serviceable, two qualities that can't be ignored by busy homemakers. Pork loins and other cuts are also cured as ham is.

Most of these hams are either partly or fully cooked and are labeled with information on how they should be prepared. Be sure to check the wrapper on the ham you buy, or, if the information is not available, ask your butcher for instructions. However, even the so-called ready-to-eat hams will benefit from cooking. They have been processed to an internal temperature of 150 degrees, which makes them safe to eat, but does nothing for palatability. Further cooking, 10 to 15 minutes per pound in a 350-degree oven, and basting with cider, dry white wine, or ginger ale will improve their flavor.

Country-style hams differ from most other American hams in that they require cooking. They must be vigorously scrubbed with a stiff-bristled brush to clean off the mold and salt accumulated over their long aging period. Then they need about twelve hours of soaking, fol-lowed by long, slow simmering, before they are ready to bake with their final garnish. Among other famous hams is the Italian Parma ham, usually called prosciutto, which is cured and dried, but not smoked as the country-style hams are. Both Smithfield and Parma are served in very thin slices. Prosciutto is frequently served raw as an accompaniment to fruits; it is also used in a variety of meat and poultry preparations, as is Smithfield ham.

Roast Pork Loin

1 4- to 5½-pound pork loin (bone in or out)
2 cloves garlic, crushed
1 tablespoon dried rosemary, crumbled
Salt and freshly ground pepper
⅓ cup apple jelly
1 tablespoon dry mustard
2 carrots, peeled and coarsely chopped
2 medium onions, coarsely chopped
½ cup dry white or red wine
1½ cups beef broth
1 tablespoon flour

Preheat the oven to 325 degrees.

Trim the excess fat from the loin.

Mix the garlic, rosemary, salt and pepper, jelly, and dry mustard until pastelike. Rub over the meat.

Spread the carrots and onions over the bottom of a shallow baking pan and place the meat on top. Pour the wine and ½ cup broth over all.

Roast for 2½ to 3 hours, basting occasionally, or until the internal temperature of the roast is 165 degrees.

Remove the meat to a carving board or warm platter, cover loosely with foil, and allow to rest for 15 to 20 minutes before carving.

Remove all but 1 tablespoon fat from the roasting pan. If the vegetables are scorched, discard them; otherwise mash them into the fat. Add flour and cook on top of the stove until golden.

Add the remaining broth and whisk until smooth and thickened. Taste and adjust the seasonings. Add any juices that have exuded from the roast and serve the sauce hot in a gravy boat. Slice the loin if it is boneless, or cut between the ribs.

Yield: 6 to 8 servings.

Pork Braised in Milk

1 3½-pound boneless loin of pork (with bones, if possible), *or* a 5½- to 6-pound loin, bone-in

2 tablespoons vegetable oil (or a small piece of fat removed from the loin)

1 medium onion, coarsely chopped

2 cloves garlic, unpeeled

1 carrot, peeled and coarsely chopped

3 cups milk

2 teaspoons dried rosemary, crumbled

¼ teaspoon dried sage, crumbled (do not use too much; it is a strong herb)

¼ teaspoon freshly grated nutmeg

Salt and freshly ground pepper

½ cup sour cream

1 tablespoon fresh lemon juice

Preheat the oven to 325 degrees.

Remove the excess fat from the loin and tie the roast into a compact shape.

Heat the oil in a heavy casserole and brown the pork well on all sides. Turn the pork with tongs or two spoons so as not to pierce the flesh. Set aside.

Brown the bones if you are using them. Add the onion, garlic, and carrot. Stir to prevent sticking, and cook until lightly colored. Return the meat to the casserole, pushing the bones to the side so that the loin rests on the bottom of the casserole.

Add the milk, herbs, nutmeg, and salt and pepper. The milk should come halfway up the sides of the meat.

Slowly bring to a boil, cover, and place in the oven. Bake for 2 to 2½ hours, or until tender. Turn the meat once or twice during this time. Don't worry if the sauce looks curdled; the end result will be a rich brown gravy.

Remove loin to a carving board and cover loosely with foil to keep warm. Remove the bones. Strain the sauce into a bowl, pressing the vegetables with the back of a spoon to extract all the liquid from them. Discard the pulp. Skim the fat and pour sauce back into the casserole. Whisk in the sour cream and heat gently, but do not boil. Adjust the seasonings, if necessary. Remove from the heat and add the lemon juice.

Remove the strings from the loin and slice or cut between the ribs. Serve with some of the sauce spooned over the slices and additional sauce in a gravy boat. Garnish the platter with watercress, if desired.

Yield: 6 to 8 servings.

Roast Fresh Ham

Leftover fresh ham makes delicious sandwiches and is good thinly sliced and served with potato salad and French bread.

1 5- to 6-pound fresh ham (leg or shoulder)
1 large onion, coarsely chopped
2 carrots, peeled and coarsely chopped
2 cups white wine
1 cup beef broth
1½ teaspoons cornstarch
¼ cup Madeira, port, or Marsala wine

Preheat the oven to 400 degrees.

With a sharp knife, remove the skin and all but ¼ inch of fat from the ham. Place in a shallow pan and spread the vegetables around the ham. Pour white wine over all. Roast for 30 minutes.

Lower the heat to 325 degrees and cook for 2 hours longer, basting often. Cook 20 to 25 minutes per pound, or until the internal temperature of the ham is 165 degrees.

Remove the ham to a warm platter, cover loosely with foil, and let stand for 15 to 20 minutes before carving.

Discard the vegetables if they are scorched. Most of the liquid will have evaporated. Discard all the fat from the pan and add the broth. Bring to a boil, scraping up any particles in the pan. Strain into a small saucepan, bring to a boil, and add the cornstarch mixed with the ¼ cup wine. Cook, stirring, for 5 minutes, or until thickened. Serve in a gravy boat with the thinly sliced ham.

Yield: 6 to 10 servings.

Braised Pork Shoulder with Cabbage

3 pounds fresh pork shoulder

1 carrot, peeled and coarsely chopped

1 large onion, coarsely chopped

2 cloves garlic, unpeeled, crushed

1 head red cabbage (about 1½ pounds), cut into 1-inch slices

2 tart apples, peeled, cored, and cubed

2 whole cloves

1 cup apple juice

1 cup dry red wine

Preheat the oven to 325 degrees.

Heat a heavy casserole and brown the ham fat side down. Then turn and brown on all sides. Remove and set aside.

Add the carrot, onion, and garlic. Cook, stirring, until soft and lightly colored. Add the cabbage and apples and cook for 5 to 6 minutes, or until reduced slightly in volume.

Return the meat to the casserole.

Add the cloves, juice, and wine and bring to a boil. Cover tightly and place in the oven for 2 hours, or until the meat is fork tender. Be sure that the liquid barely bubbles; otherwise the meat will be tough. Serve sliced with steamed or boiled potatoes.

Yield: 4 to 6 servings.

Breaded Pork Chops or Cutlets

8 to 10 thin pork chops or cutlets, approximately ½-inch thick
Salt and freshly ground pepper
Flour for dredging
2 eggs beaten with 3 tablespoons water
1½ to 2 cups fresh bread crumbs
⅓ cup vegetable oil
2 tablespoons butter
Freshly chopped parsley
Lemon wedges

Sprinkle the pork lightly with salt and pepper, if desired. Dredge in the flour and shake off the excess. Dip in the egg mixture and then in bread crumbs, using your fingers to press the crumbs onto the meat. Place the breaded chops in one layer on a rack and refrigerate for 20 to 30 minutes, which helps to set the coating.

Heat the oil and butter in a heavy skillet. Brown a few chops at a time until golden, about 4 minutes on each side. Remove with tongs to a warm platter and keep warm while proceeding with the remaining chops or cutlets.

Serve hot sprinkled with parsley and garnished with lemon.

Yield: 4 servings.

Baked Pork Chops and Potatoes

4 baking potatoes, peeled and thinly sliced
6 loin pork chops, 1¼ inches thick
3 tablespoons olive or vegetable oil
1 large onion, peeled and thinly sliced
2 cloves garlic, crushed
2 small bay leaves, crumbled
1 teaspoon dried rosemary, crumbled
¼ teaspoon dried leaf sage, crumbled
¼ teaspoon freshly grated nutmeg
Salt and freshly ground pepper
½ cup dry white wine
Freshly chopped parsley

Preheat the oven to 400 degrees.

Cover the sliced potatoes with cold water and set aside.

Arrange the pork chops in a baking dish in one layer. Rub them with 1 tablespoon oil. Arrange the onion slices over the chops. Sprinkle with the garlic, bay leaves, rosemary, sage, nutmeg, and salt and pepper. Bake for 30 minutes, basting with the pan juices several times.

Lower the oven temperature to 350 degrees. Drain and dry the potatoes, toss with 2 tablespoons oil, and arrange over the chops. Add the wine.

Return to the oven. Continue to cook for 30 to 40 minutes, or until the meat and potatoes are tender. Shake or stir the pan several times so that the potatoes cook evenly. Baste several times.

Sprinkle with freshly chopped parsley and serve hot from the baking dish.

Yield: 4 to 6 servings.

Pork Goulash

This is a good dish to prepare in advance. A few days in the refrigerator will heighten the rich flavor.

2 slices bacon, chopped
3 pounds boneless pork (shoulder or loin), cut into 1-inch cubes
2 large onions, coarsely chopped
2 tablespoons Hungarian sweet paprika
2 tablespoons flour
2 cups beef broth
2 tablespoons tomato paste
1 tablespoon caraway seeds
1 cup sour cream

Cook the bacon in a heavy casserole until crisp. Remove the bacon and set aside. Add the pork cubes to the bacon fat in batches, stirring to brown all sides. Do not crowd the casserole. With a slotted spoon, remove the cubes to a dish as they are browned. Continue until all meat is browned.

Add the onions and cook, stirring, until soft and lightly colored. Add the paprika and flour and cook, stirring, for 2 minutes. Return all the meat to the casserole.

Add the beef broth, tomato paste, caraway seeds, and reserved bacon. Stir to mix well and bring to a boil. Lower the heat, cover, and simmer until meat is very tender, 1½ to 2 hours.

Drain the cooking juices into a bowl and degrease. Return the sauce to the meat and serve from the casserole with sour cream on the side. This is good with dumplings or noodles.

Yield: 6 to 8 servings.

Note: If you plan to refrigerate the goulash, be sure to degrease the cooking juices first. Otherwise the fat will harden and cling to the meat.

Pork Patties with Tomatoes and Caraway

Pork patties make a pleasant change from beef. Pork has a naturally sweet flavor that complements the taste and texture of tomatoes.

1½ pounds ground pork

½ cup dry bread crumbs, *or* 2 slices rye or white bread, shredded

1 egg, beaten

1 tablespoon caraway seeds

Salt and freshly ground pepper

4 tablespoons vegetable or olive oil

1 medium onion, finely chopped

1 clove garlic, finely minced

1 1-pound, 12-ounce can whole tomatoes, crushed

1 teaspoon dried basil, crumbled

1 teaspoon dried thyme, crumbled

1 bay leaf

Freshly chopped parsley

Place the pork in a mixing bowl. Add the bread crumbs, egg, caraway seeds, salt, and pepper. Blend well with moistened fingers and form into 8 patties. Refrigerate for 30 minutes.

Heat 2 tablespoons oil in a nonaluminum saucepan and cook the onion and garlic until soft and lightly colored. Add the tomatoes, basil, thyme, and bay leaf. Bring to a boil, cover, lower the heat, and simmer for 20 to 25 minutes. Remove the bay leaf.

Heat the remaining oil in a large skillet and brown the patties for 3 to 4 minutes a side, or until no longer pink inside. Drain well and arrange on a platter. Spoon the hot tomato sauce over all. Sprinkle with freshly chopped parsley.

Yield: 4 servings.

Oven-Barbecued Spareribs

3 to 4 pounds spareribs

1 cup soy sauce (Japanese preferred)

1 cup orange, apricot, or peach preserves

3 cloves garlic, finely minced

1 tablespoon freshly grated ginger

¼ cup dry sherry

Place the ribs in a large plastic bag or a large shallow dish. Mix the remaining ingredients and pour over the ribs. Seal or cover tightly and refrigerate overnight.

Preheat the oven to 350 degrees. Remove the ribs from the marinade, reserving the marinade. Place them on a wire rack set in a shallow roasting pan. Add water to the pan to a depth of about 1 inch. Do not let it touch the meat. The water will catch the drippings and keep the kitchen from becoming filled with smoke.

Bake for 1½ hours, basting often with the marinade. Cut the ribs into serving pieces with a cleaver or knife and serve immediately.

Yield: 4 appetizer or 2 main course servings.

Note: This marinade can be reused within 5 to 7 days for other meats or chicken.

Glazed Ham

This and the following brine-cured ham, with shiny glazes, are a welcome addition to a buffet table. A selection of cheeses, salads, dark breads, and a variety of mustards would be good accompaniments.

1 12-pound tenderized ham
1 cup firmly packed brown sugar
1 tablespoon dry mustard
¼ teaspoon ground cloves
½ cup apricot, orange, or peach
   preserves
¼ cup bourbon or brandy

Preheat the oven to 350 degrees.

Remove most of the skin from the ham, and trim all but ¼ inch of fat. With a knife, score the remaining layer of fat in a diamond pattern.

Place the ham in a shallow baking pan. Mix the remaining ingredients to a pastelike consistency and spread evenly on the ham. Bake for 2 hours. Allow to stand for 20 to 30 minutes before carving. Serve hot or at room temperature.

Yield: 8 to 10 servings.

Brine-Cured Country Ham

1 10- to 12-pound brine-cured
   country ham
½ cup brown sugar, *or* ½ cup
   apricot, orange, or peach
   preserves
1 tablespoon dry mustard
1 tablespoon vinegar

Preheat the oven to 325 degrees.

Place the ham in shallow roasting pan and bake for 3½ to 4 hours, or 20 minutes a pound.

Thirty minutes before the end of the cooking time, remove the ham from the oven and cut off the rind with a sharp knife. Leave ¼ inch of fat. Score the fat in a diamond pattern.

Mix the sugar or preserves, mustard, and vinegar and spread evenly on the fat.

Return the ham to the oven and continue cooking until the glaze is well browned, about 30 minutes.

Serve hot or at room temperature thinly sliced.

Yield: 8 to 10 servings.

Dry-Cured Country Ham

1 10- to 12-pound dry-cured country ham
½ cup brown sugar
1 tablespoon dry mustard
1 tablespoon cider or wine vinegar

Soak the ham in cold water to cover for 24 to 36 hours. It is not necessary to refrigerate it. Change the water at least three times.

With a stiff brush, scrub the surface of the ham to remove any mold. Place in a deep kettle, cover with water, and bring to a boil. Lower the heat, cover, and simmer gently for 3½ to 4 hours, or 20 minutes a pound.

Remove the ham from the broth and allow it to cool until you can handle it. Cut off the rind, leaving ¼ inch of fat. Score the fat in a diamond pattern.

Preheat the oven to 400 degrees. Mix the sugar, mustard, and enough vinegar to form a paste and rub the mixture into the fat. Place the ham on a rack in a shallow roasting pan and roast for 20 to 30 minutes, or until the glaze is well browned.

Serve hot or at room temperature in thin slices.

Yield: 8 to 10 servings.

Note: The cooking liquid can be used as a base for soups or stocks. Taste it. If it is too salty or spicy, discard it. If not, refrigerate or freeze to use as a base for a bean or vegetable soup.

Veal

Top-quality veal is an elegant, delicate meat that is unfortunately expensive and in limited supply. The finest veal comes from baby calves eight to fifteen weeks old that have been fed only on milk. It is palest pink with white fat and soft red bones. Reddish pink meat and brown bones indicate that the animal left its youth behind and was really young beef, which is what we frequently find in supermarkets. Choice veal from genuine calves is most likely to be found in specialty meat markets, although from time to time supermarkets will have some acceptable veal.

Since veal comes from a young animal, it has little fat and no visible marbling. Consequently, with the exception of scaloppine (thin slices from the leg that are quickly sautéed), or the thinly pounded paillard that is briefly grilled, veal is better braised than roasted or broiled. You may roast a good leg or loin, but it must be basted frequently and perhaps have fat added. Veal is one of the most gelatinous of meats, and the bones and bony cuts are excellent for aspics and stocks.

Veal is notable, too, for its natural affinity for a large variety of other foods and flavors. It goes well with many spices and there are almost no herbs that will not complement it. Veal makes a harmonious combination with fish and has earned itself a permanent place in gastronomy in a preparation that teams cold sliced veal with a sauce made of tuna fish and anchovies (vitello tonnato).

The inflated price of veal has caused some homemakers to "think turkey" when they see a recipe calling for veal scallops. Thinly sliced breast of turkey or chicken can indeed be used in place of veal scallops, and although the distinguishing features of veal flavor and texture will not be present, the substitution is an agreeable and economical alternative.

Let's start at the head and move clockwise around the animal.

Neck and Shoulder

The bony neck makes a fine stock and can also be used ground or in stuffings.

The veal shoulder can be boned and braised for a lovely dish. It is also fine for stews. Shoulder chops, while not the most wonderful cut in the world, may also be braised, but don't try to sauté them.

Rack

The first eight ribs, or the rack, are cut into chops or left in one piece for a rib roast of veal, which is cooked like a beef roast. The chops can be single or double for broiling, or double with pockets for stuffing and baking. If the chops are broiled, they must be very well basted to prevent their drying out. Two racks may also be joined to make a crown roast. The rack can also be boned, rolled, and roasted, or the whole piece with the bones cracked can be braised.

Loin

The veal loin is the tenderest part of the animal. The two loins and part of the leg make up the saddle. It may be rolled and tied, with or without the bone, and is an extravagant and wonderful roast. The loin portion can be cut into regular loin chops or roasted whole with or without the bone.

Rump and Leg

The rump makes a good roast with or without the bones, but if it is boned and rolled, don't expect tidy slices when it is carved; it tends to fall apart.

The leg, or the round, can be roasted or braised. From the leg come the thin slices that

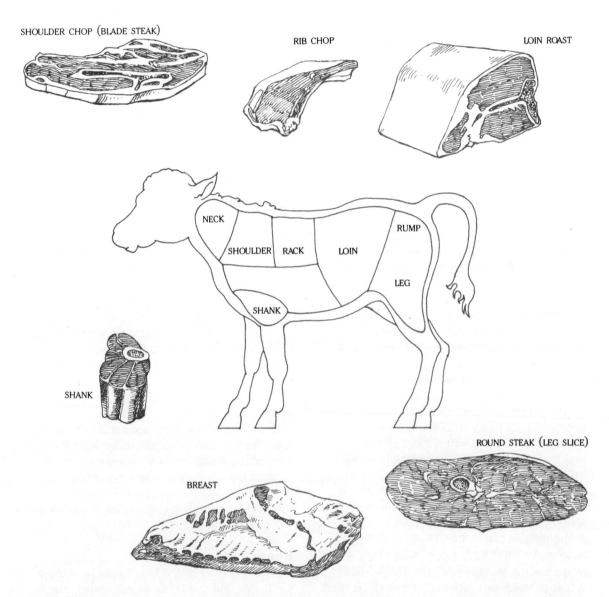

SHOULDER CHOP (BLADE STEAK)

RIB CHOP

LOIN ROAST

NECK

SHOULDER RACK LOIN

RUMP

LEG

SHANK

SHANK

ROUND STEAK (LEG SLICE)

BREAST

Because the best veal comes from a calf that has not yet begun to graze, it is lean, and many cuts need to be braised—neck and shoulder, for example, including the shoulder chop, or blade steak. The rack, or ribs, and loin may be roasted or cut into chops and broiled. Cutlets and scaloppine are slices from the separated leg muscles. The breast may be boned or cut into spareribs. The shank is prized for its gelatin.

are known as scaloppine, and the thicker cut-lets. Steaks are cut across the leg with the tiny round bone left in. Scallops are sautéed or rolled around a stuffing and braised.

The makings for the splendid veal shank dish, called osso buco, also come from the leg. The best shanks, which are the bone from the ankle up through the calf, are said to come from the hindquarters.

Breast and Shank

Breast of veal can be prepared boned or bone-in. Stuffed breast of veal, with a pocket cut in the half nearer the loin, is a popular dish. The breast may also be cut into strips and trimmed to serve as spareribs. The bones from the breast and leg, particularly the knucklebone, are rich in gelatin and make wonderful sauces and stocks.

Adjoining the breast is the foreshank. The juicy, delicious cut can be cross-cut through the bone into 2½- to 3-inch lengths and braised, or cut up for veal stew, or the meat may be ground.

Ground Veal

Some ground veal goes into sausages and it is important in pâtés. If you are using ground veal, you are best advised to buy the meat and grind it yourself, which will assure you of good quality and a minimum of gristle and trim-mings. You can use chunks of veal cut from the breast, neck, or shanks, or a package of stew meat, if available. Because of its lack of fat, veal makes a dry meat loaf unless it is com-bined with fattier meat such as beef and pork.

Veal Roast in Foil

1 3- to 4-pound boneless veal roast
1 tablespoon chopped parsley
2 whole scallions, finely chopped
1 small onion, finely chopped
1 teaspoon dried thyme, crumbled
1 bay leaf, crumbled
½ pound fresh mushrooms, thinly sliced
¼ cup olive oil
Salt and freshly ground pepper
½ cup chicken broth
Juice of ½ lemon

Put the veal in a plastic bag or nonaluminum container. Mix together all ingredients except chicken broth and lemon juice and add to the veal. Marinate at room temperature at least 3 hours, or refrigerate overnight.

Preheat the oven to 325 degrees.

Remove veal from the marinade and place it on a large square of heavy foil. Pour the marinade over. Wrap tightly and place in a shallow roasting pan. Place in the oven for 1½ to 2 hours, or until meat is tender when tested with a fork.

Unwrap carefully, transfer meat to a platter, and keep warm. Drain herbs and juices from the roast into a small saucepan. Skim the fat. Add chicken broth and lemon juice and heat. Taste for seasonings. Slice the veal and serve with the sauce.

Yield: 4 to 6 servings.

Veal Pot Roast with Baby Carrots

2 tablespoons flour

2 teaspoons dry mustard

Salt and freshly ground pepper

1 3½- to 4-pound veal roast, boned and tied

Veal bones (if possible)

2 tablespoons butter or vegetable oil

1 cup beef or chicken broth

¼ teaspoon dried thyme, crumbled

10 to 12 small baby carrots, peeled and trimmed

2 tablespoons cream

2 tablespoons lemon juice

Combine the flour, mustard, and salt and pepper and sprinkle over the veal. In a deep heavy casserole, heat the butter or oil and brown the veal and bones on all sides. Include as many veal bones as you can; they will enrich the sauce. Turn the meat with tongs.

Add the broth and thyme and bring to a boil. Cover, lower the heat, and simmer gently on top of the stove or in a 325 degree oven for about 2 hours. Turn the meat after 1 hour.

Add the carrots and cook for 30 minutes more.

Remove the meat and carrots to a serving dish and keep warm. Skim the fat from the sauce. Add the cream and lemon juice and heat gently, but do not boil. Serve hot with the sliced veal.

Yield: 6 to 8 servings.

Vitello Tonnato (Cold Veal with Tuna Sauce)

1 2- to 2½-pound boneless veal roast, cut from the leg and tied

2 carrots, peeled, trimmed, and thinly sliced

2 celery stalks

1 medium onion, thinly sliced

4 sprigs parsley

4 peppercorns

1 small bay leaf

Water to cover

Tuna Sauce:

2 whole eggs

Juice of 2 lemons (about 4 to 6 tablespoons)

2½ cups olive oil

1 7-ounce can Italian-style tuna in oil

5 flat anchovy fillets, rinsed

3 tablespoons capers

To determine the amount of water needed, place all the ingredients in a deep kettle. Cover with water. Remove the veal and set aside. Bring the water to a boil. Add the veal. Cover and simmer gently for 1 to 1½ hours. Remove from the heat and let the meat cool in the broth.

To the container of a blender add the eggs and the juice of 1 lemon. Turn the machine on and off several times. Very slowly, add 2 cups of oil, drop by drop at first until the mayonnaise thickens, then in a thin stream. Transfer to a bowl and reserve.

To the same blender add the tuna, anchovies, the remaining lemon juice, and capers. Process until well blended. Add the remaining ½ cup olive oil very slowly in a stream until well mixed and creamy.

Fold the tuna sauce into the mayonnaise.

When the veal is cold, slice into thin, uniform slices. Have ready a shallow serving platter.

Spread a generous layer of sauce on the bottom of the platter and arrange a layer of veal on top. Cover with a layer of sauce. Repeat. Cover top layer well. Be sure to use all the sauce.

Cover with plastic wrap and refrigerate for 24 hours so that the meat will absorb the flavors of the sauce. Before serving, garnish the platter with lemon slices, olives, capers, and finely chopped parsley. Serve with cold rice salad.

Yield: 6 to 8 servings.

Note: This is a classic veal dish, but you can substitute a boneless loin of pork or a turkey breast for the veal. Poach either one very slowly as you would the veal.

Braised Stuffed Breast of Veal

Breast of veal is one of the most economical cuts and is a superb dish stuffed with vegetables and ground meats. It's also good cold.

3 medium zucchini, about 1 pound, coarsely grated, *or* 1 10-ounce package frozen chopped spinach, cooked and squeezed dry

1 tablespoon coarse salt

2 to 3 tablespoons finely chopped shallots or onion

½ pound ground pork or sausage, casing removed

½ pound ground veal

1 cup fresh bread crumbs

3 eggs

1 teaspoon dried thyme, crumbled

1 teaspoon salt

Freshly ground pepper to taste

¼ teaspoon freshly grated nutmeg

2 to 3 tablespoons finely minced parsley

1 4½- to 5-pound veal breast, boned, with a pocket (reserve the bones)

2 tablespoons vegetable oil

1 carrot, peeled, trimmed, and thinly sliced

1 medium onion, coarsely chopped

1 clove garlic, crushed

3 tablespoons flour

1 cup dry white wine

1½ cups beef broth

1 bay leaf

½ teaspoon dried thyme

3 to 4 sprigs fresh parsley

Sprinkle zucchini with coarse salt and let stand in a colander to drain for about 30 minutes. Put the zucchini in a kitchen towel and squeeze out as much of the liquid as possible.

Put it in a large mixing bowl and add the shallots, pork, veal, bread crumbs, eggs, and seasonings. Mix well. Cook a tablespoon or two in a small skillet and taste for seasoning. Correct if necessary. Because of the raw pork, taste only after it is cooked.

Check to make sure the pocket in the veal is deep enough. If not, use a sharp knife to enlarge it, being careful not to cut holes in the meat. Fill the pocket with the stuffing mixture and sew or skewer the pocket closed.

Tie the veal at intervals with kitchen twine, just enough to coax it into a fat sausage shape. If you have made any holes in the meat, close them with a needle and thread. Leave the thread long so you will be able to remove it later.

Preheat the oven to 300 degrees.

Heat the oil in a large oval casserole and brown the veal on all sides. Remove and set aside. Add the bones, carrot, onion, and garlic. Cook until golden, stirring frequently. Add the flour and stir to coat the vegetables.

Return the veal to the casserole. Add the wine, broth, and the seasonings. The liquid should come a little more than halfway up the meat. Bring to a boil, cover, and transfer to the oven. Cook gently until veal is tender, 2 to 2¼ hours. Turn once or twice during cooking.

Remove the veal to a platter or carving board and keep warm.

Strain the sauce and skim the fat. Reheat the sauce if it has cooled. Remove the strings and any thread from the veal. Slice and arrange it on a platter. Cover with some of the sauce. Serve the remaining sauce in a gravy boat.

Yield: 6 to 8 servings.

Veal Scallops with Marsala

1½ pounds veal scallops (cut from the leg), pounded thin
Flour for dredging
3 tablespoons clarified butter (see page 260)
½ cup Marsala
Juice of 1 lemon
Salt and freshly ground pepper

When ready to cook the veal, dredge it lightly in flour and shake off excess.

Heat the clarified butter in a large heavy skillet until very hot. Add a few scallops at a time and brown well on both sides over medium-high heat. Do not overcrowd the pan. If the scallops touch, they will not brown properly. As each scallop browns, transfer it to a warm platter.

Return all the veal to the skillet, add the Marsala, and cover. Simmer for 5 minutes, or until the veal is tender.

Squeeze the lemon juice over the scallops. Sprinkle with salt and pepper and serve immediately.

Yield: 4 servings.

Vienna-Style Veal Scallops

1½ pounds veal scallops, pounded thin
Salt and freshly ground pepper
Flour for dredging
2 eggs beaten with 2 tablespoons water
1½ cups fresh bread crumbs
½ cup corn or peanut oil
8 tablespoons butter
1 lemon, thinly sliced

Season the veal with salt and pepper. Dredge first in flour, shaking off any excess, then in eggs, and then in bread crumbs. Use your fingers to get the bread crumbs to adhere.

Arrange the scallops on a baking sheet or rack as they are breaded. Refrigerate for 20 to 30 minutes to help the breading adhere.

Heat the oil and butter in a large skillet. When it is hot, add the veal scallops, a few at a time. Do not crowd the pan. Cook for 2 to 3 minutes on each side until crisp and golden. Remove with tongs and drain on paper towels. Keep warm in a 200-degree oven while preparing the remaining veal.

Arrange on a warm platter, garnish with lemon slices, and serve immediately.

Yield: 4 servings.

Note: Thinly pounded chicken breast can be substituted for the veal.

Veal Birds

2 tablespoons finely chopped
  parsley
2 tablespoons finely chopped
  scallions
Salt and freshly ground pepper
8 to 12 slices veal, pounded thin
  (1¾ to 2 pounds)
4 to 6 slices bacon, cut in half
2 tablespoons butter
1 small onion, finely chopped
2 celery stalks, finely chopped
⅓ cup beef broth

Combine the parsley, scallions, salt, and pepper. Sprinkle each slice of veal with the mixture and cover with a slice of bacon. Roll the meat tightly, like a jelly roll, and secure with a sturdy round toothpick.

Melt the butter in a heavy skillet. Add the onion and celery and cook over low heat until soft but not colored.

Add the veal rolls. Shake the pan from time to time so that they roll back and forth. Cook evenly on all sides but do not allow them to brown. Cover tightly and simmer very slowly for 1 hour, or until very tender.

Remove the rolls to a platter and keep warm. Add the broth to the skillet and bring to a boil. Cook over high heat for 3 minutes. Pour over the veal rolls and serve immediately with steamed rice.

Yield: 4 to 6 servings.

Veal Chops with Vinegar

4 loin veal chops, about ½ pound
  each
Salt and freshly ground pepper
2 tablespoons butter
4 cloves garlic, peeled and
  coarsely chopped
2 small bay leaves, crumbled
½ teaspoon dried thyme,
  crumbled
2 tablespoons wine vinegar
¾ cup chicken broth

Sprinkle the chops with salt and pepper. In a large heavy skillet, heat the butter and brown the chops on both sides. This will take about 10 minutes.

Add the garlic, bay leaves, and thyme. Cook for 3 minutes, shaking the pan often. Add the vinegar, which will create a cloud of steam, then the broth and bring to a boil. Cover, lower the heat, and simmer for 30 to 45 minutes or until chops are fork tender.

Yield: 4 servings.

Veal Stew

2 pounds veal breast, cut into 2-inch pieces

2 pounds boneless veal shoulder, cut into 1½-inch cubes

2 carrots, peeled, trimmed, and coarsely chopped

1 large onion studded with 2 cloves

1 bay leaf

¼ teaspoon dried thyme, crumbled

Salt and freshly ground pepper

12 small white onions

3 tablespoons butter

3 tablespoons flour

1 pound fresh mushrooms (leave whole if small)

2 tablespoons heavy cream (optional)

1 tablespoon lemon juice

1 tablespoon freshly chopped parsley

Place all the veal in a large heavy casserole, cover with water and bring to the boil. Drain and rinse the veal under cold running water. Return the veal to the casserole, add water to cover, carrots, onion studded with cloves, bay leaf, thyme, salt, and pepper. Bring to a boil. Skim foam as it rises. Cover, lower heat, and simmer very gently for 1½ to 2 hours, or until tender. Add the onions for the last half hour of cooking.

Drain the liquid from the casserole into a bowl, using the pot lid to hold back the solids. Skim fat from the sauce. Discard onion studded with cloves.

In a clean saucepan, melt the butter, add the flour and stir with a whisk until well blended. Add the veal cooking liquid and stir vigorously until it comes to a boil and is thickened and smooth.

Return the sauce to the casserole. Add the mushrooms and cook over low heat for 10 to 15 minutes, or until all is very hot and well blended.

Add the cream, lemon juice, and parsley and heat but do not boil.

Serve hot from the casserole with noodles or dumplings.

Yield: 4 to 8 servings.

Note: The veal breast adds a marvelous quality to this stew. There usually is not much meat on a breast, but the bones are delicious to chew and they enrich the sauce considerably.

Veal Paprika with Spätzle

2 tablespoons butter

1 medium onion, finely chopped

3 pounds boneless veal shoulder, cut into 1-inch cubes

2 tablespoons Hungarian sweet paprika

⅓ cup crushed tomatoes (approximately 3 whole canned tomatoes)

1 bell pepper, seeded and coarsely chopped

Salt and freshly ground pepper

⅓ cup beef broth, if necessary

1 cup sour cream

Melt the butter in a deep heavy casserole and add the onion. Cook, stirring, until soft and lightly colored. Add the veal cubes and toss and stir until the cubes lose their raw color.

Sprinkle with paprika and stir to coat well. Cook until paprika begins to give off a sweet pungent aroma, about 5 minutes.

Add the tomatoes, bell pepper, salt, and pepper and stir to mix well. Cover tightly and simmer gently for 1 to 1½ hours, stirring occasionally. The veal should not be swimming in liquid, but if it does not produce enough liquid of its own, add the beef broth.

Ladle out about 1 cup of the sauce into a small bowl and mix it with the sour cream. Return the sauce to the casserole, mixing well. Heat gently but do not boil because the sauce will curdle. Serve hot with spätzle (see following recipe).

Yield: 4 to 6 servings.

Spätzle (Flour Dumplings)

4 eggs

1 cup milk

½ teaspoon salt

Freshly grated nutmeg

3 cups all-purpose flour

4 to 8 tablespoons butter

Combine the eggs, milk, salt, and nutmeg in a blender, food processor, or mixing bowl. Mix well and slowly add the flour. Mix until the batter is thick and smooth. If using a blender, push mixture down as needed so that all is blended well. In a large kettle, bring 4 to 5 quarts of salted water to a boil.

Set a coarse colander over the pot. Press the batter through the holes, a little at a time. Stir gently and cook for 8 minutes. The dumplings will rise to the surface when they are cooked.

Lift the dumplings out with a slotted spoon and put into a bowl of cold water. Drain and spread on a towel to dry.

Melt the butter in a large skillet and add half the spätzle. Shake the pan until they are coated with butter and become golden. Repeat with the remaining dumplings, and add more butter, if needed.

Yield: 4 to 6 servings.

Poached Veal Balls in Dill Sauce

2 tablespoons butter
1 small onion, finely chopped
½ to ¾ cup dry bread crumbs
½ cup sour cream
1½ to 1¾ pounds finely ground veal
1½ teaspoons anchovy paste, *or* 4 anchovy fillets, mashed
¼ cup finely chopped parsley
¼ teaspoon freshly grated nutmeg
2 eggs
6 to 8 sprigs fresh dill, snipped
Salt and freshly ground pepper
1 small onion, thinly sliced
1 bay leaf

Sauce:
3 tablespoons butter
3 tablespoons flour
3 cups poaching liquid
¼ cup sour cream
2 to 3 tablespoons drained capers

Melt the butter in a small skillet and cook the onions until soft. Scrape into a large bowl and cool slightly. Add the bread crumbs, sour cream, veal, anchovy paste, parsley, nutmeg, eggs, half the dill, salt, and pepper and mix well with the hands. (If you have a blender or food processor, blend all the ingredients except the meat until puréed. Mix with the meat.)

Moisten your hands and form the mixture into 20 meatballs. The mixture will be soft and a little sticky.

Bring 1½ to 2 quarts of water to a boil in a casserole or deep skillet. Add the onion and bay leaf. Lower the heat to simmer and add the veal balls. Simmer for 15 to 20 minutes, or until they rise to the surface.

With a slotted spoon, transfer the veal balls to a warm platter and cover with foil or plastic wrap while you prepare the sauce. Strain the poaching liquid. Reserve 3 cups.

Make the sauce. In the same casserole or skillet, melt the butter, add the flour and stir with a wire whisk until bubbly. Add the 3 cups of poaching liquid and remaining dill and bring to a boil, whisking constantly. Lower the heat and simmer for 10 minutes, stirring occasionally, until thick and smooth. Whisk in the sour cream and add the capers. Return the veal balls to the sauce and heat but do not boil. Serve hot on a bed of noodles.

Yield: 4 to 6 servings.

Osso Buco Milanese (Braised Veal Shanks)

4 to 5 pounds meaty veal shanks, sawed into 2- to 3-inch pieces

Flour for dredging

2 to 3 tablespoons oil

2 to 3 tablespoons butter

1 small onion, finely chopped

1 clove garlic, crushed (optional)

1 cup dry white wine

1 1-pound can whole tomatoes, chopped or crushed

1½ to 2 cups beef broth

Salt and freshly ground pepper

Grated rind of ½ lemon

1 clove garlic, finely minced

2 tablespoons finely minced parsley

Dredge the shanks in the flour and shake off the excess. Heat the oil and butter in a heavy casserole. Brown the shanks on all sides. Don't crowd them. Transfer to a dish as they brown.

To the same pan, add the onion and garlic. Cook, stirring, until soft and lightly colored. Return the shanks to the casserole. Place them on their sides so that the marrow does not fall out. They can fit together tightly in one layer.

Add the wine, bring to a boil, and cook until reduced by half. Add the tomatoes, broth, salt, and pepper. The liquid should almost cover the veal. Return to a boil. Cover, lower the heat, and simmer gently for 2 hours. Skim occasionally.

Mix the lemon rind, garlic, and parsley. Sprinkle over the shanks just before serving (see note). Serve hot from the casserole with rice, if desired.

Yield: 4 to 6 servings.

Note: The garnish of lemon rind, garlic, and parsley, called gremolata, can be eliminated. We feel that the taste overpowers the taste of the veal, but it is traditional.

Variety Meats

Variety meats include organ meats, such as sweetbreads, brains, liver and kidney; muscle meats, such as heart, tongue and tripe; and bony structural meats, such as tails. We offer a figurative salute to the person who dreamed up the term *variety meats* to describe this food category; it surely has a more inviting sound than the previously used *innards* and *offal*. In spite of the unpleasant connotation of the word *offal*, it has an eminently respectable and logical origin. It comes from "off-fall," the name given to all parts of the animal that fell off the cutting block when the animal was being butchered after it was slaughtered. This included everything from the animal's insides to

its blood, as well as head, feet, and tail.

Variety meats offer an interesting change of pace for menu planning. Their textures range from the creamy softness of brains and sweetbreads to the fork-tender delicacy of calf's liver and the chewiness of tripe. Variety meats are high in protein, B vitamins, vitamin A, phosphorus, and iron. Liver is particularly high in iron. They are low in fat and generally lower in calories than the muscle meat from the same animal, but they contain a large amount of cholesterol. Brains are the highest in cholesterol of any food.

All organ meats except kidneys are removed from carcasses and sold separately. The reason for this is that organ meats are highly perishable and must be cooked promptly. Aging does nothing but spoil these meats. The most perishable are brains, fresh tongue, and sweetbreads. If you find you cannot cook them within a day of purchase, rinse them in fresh water, dry them well, and freeze them promptly. They will keep in a refrigerator freezer for four weeks.

All variety meats need some simple preparation before they can be cooked.

Brains

Brains are the most delicate in texture and taste of all organ meats. When buying, look for soft, plump, pinkish-gray brains. Avoid any that look dry and shriveled. Calves' brains are considered the best of all animal brains, but sheep, lamb, pork, and beef brains are also used. The average calf's brain weighs about ½ pound; beef brains are larger, weighing about ¾ pound each, and are somewhat coarser, because the animal is larger and older; lamb brains are very small, weighing less than ¼ pound, and are not commonly available for sale. The same techniques are used in preparing all animal brains.

Preparation. Soak the brains for 30 minutes in cold water seasoned with 1 teaspoon salt and 1 tablespoon lemon juice. Remove from the water and peel off as much of the covering membranes and dark thin veins as you can.

Unless otherwise specified in a particular recipe, place the brains in a saucepan with 4 cups of water, 1 teaspoon salt, and 1 tablespoon lemon juice or 1½ teaspoons vinegar. Simmer slowly, uncovered—do not allow to boil—for 15 minutes. Immediately drain and plunge into very cold water and allow to cool. Drain and dry. They are now ready to be used. They can be sliced or cut into chunks and sautéed, or breaded with egg and crumbs or batter and fried, served cold with a vinaigrette sauce, combined with other ingredients in a salad, or brushed with oil and broiled.

Heart

Beef and veal hearts are sold in markets, but pork and lamb are not commonly found. Heart meat is firm and rather dry and is best cooked by slow moist cooking, either braising or stewing. It can also be ground with other meats for hamburger, or stuffed and braised. Veal heart is more tender than beef heart, of course, because it comes from a younger animal.

A beef heart can weigh up to 5 pounds; a veal heart about 1 pound; lamb hearts 5 to 6 ounces; and pork hearts about 8 ounces.

Preparation. Wash hearts well in cold water and remove fat, arteries, veins, and blood and dry well. If you are going to stuff them, enlarge the cavity for stuffing.

Kidney

Veal and lamb kidneys are the most tender and can be prepared by any fast cooking method. They can be sautéed, broiled, or skewered; cooked whole or sliced. They should be cooked as quickly as possible over medium heat; the centers will still be slightly pink. Kidneys harden and toughen if they are overcooked.

Beef kidneys come from large, mature animals and have a more pronounced taste than veal or lamb kidneys. Only braising will make them tender.

A beef kidney weighs about 1 pound; a veal kidney from ½ pound or less to about ¾ pound; a pork kidney is about the same size as a veal kidney, but it has a strong taste and it is used most often in ground meat mixtures, such as a pâté or a meat loaf. Lamb kidneys weigh only about 3 ounces.

Do not buy any kidney that has a disagreeable odor. Unwrap them as soon as you get home to make sure they are fresh before storing them. If you are not going to use them within a day, trim and parboil them at once, then finish cooking later.

Preparation. Snip away the outside membrane from the kidney. For large beef and veal kidneys, cut into the center of the kidney along the fatty line. Cut them in half lengthwise and scoop out the hard core of tubes and fat with scissors or a sharp knife. For a lamb kidney, cut out a ½-inch circle and scoop out the hard little center as if you were coring an apple.

It is not necessary to soak veal or lamb kidneys before cooking. It is enough to rinse them and pat dry. Large beef kidneys and pork kidneys should be soaked for one hour in cold water to which you have added a couple of tablespoons of lemon juice or vinegar. After soaking, rinse and pat dry and plunge into boiling, salted water for a minute or two. This will do away with any off-flavor. Rinse again under cold running water and pat dry.

Liver

Liver is probably the most widely used variety meat. Calf's liver is the tenderest, with baby beef liver next in quality. Beef liver used to be avoided by most food shoppers because it was heavy and coarse in texture. But with today's improved breeding practices that produce smaller cattle and shorter grazing and fattening periods, beef liver has become more acceptable. It also costs less than calf's liver. Lamb liver has a pronounced taste, but it is very tender. Pork liver is popular in pâtés.

A whole beef liver weighs 7 to 14 pounds; a calf's liver 2½ to 5 pounds; a lamb liver ¾ to 1½ pounds, and a pork liver ¾ to 1¼ pounds.

Liver must never be overcooked or it will tighten and toughen. Calf's liver may be sliced and broiled or sautéed, or cut into strips and quickly stir-fried. It can also be left whole, marinated, and baked. Young beef liver may be quickly stir-fried. It can also be left whole, marinated and baked. Young beef liver may be prepared the same way but liver from an older animal is best braised or simmered in wine,

although it may be sautéed if it is very thinly sliced and cooked quickly.

Preparation. Scrape and peel off the outer skin and remove all cartilage and veins. Rinse well in cool water and pat dry with paper towels.

Sweetbreads

Sweetbreads are the thymus glands of young animals, which disappear when the animal matures, just as they do in humans. Veal sweetbreads are considered the best, and they are the most readily available. Sweetbreads are similar to brains except that they have a slightly nuttier taste; they are equally perishable and also interchangeable in recipes. Look for sweetbreads that are soft and plump, creamy white if they come from calves or lamb, and slightly gray if they come from young beef. The membrane in the young beef sweetbread is tougher than that of the veal.

Sweetbreads are often spoken of as "a pair." In each animal there are two lobes, a heart sweetbread, which is the larger, and a throat sweetbread. This pair is also called a cluster. It weighs between ¾ pound and 1¼ pounds. Sweetbreads that weigh under ¾ pound are pieces only; they are less desirable than a whole pair.

Preparation. Soak the sweetbreads in cold water for at least an hour or longer, changing the water a few times until all signs of blood are gone. If the sweetbreads were frozen, immerse them still frozen in the water and lengthen the soaking time. The soaking bleaches them and creates an attractive appearance.

The next step is blanching. Place them in a stainless steel or enamel pot (not aluminum) with cold water and lemon juice and bring them very slowly to a boil. If you bring them to the boil too quickly, the outside supporting membranes could burst from the sudden swelling of the tissues. As soon as the boiling point is reached, reduce the heat and let them poach for 3 or 4 minutes if you intend to braise them, and for 10 minutes if they are to be sliced and sautéed.

Drain the sweetbreads and rinse them thoroughly under cold running water to stop the cooking. With a sharp knife, remove sinews, blood vessels, connective tissue, and outer skin. Do not remove the delicate inner membranes that hold the sweetbreads together or they will fall apart. Pat dry. Some cooks weight the sweetbreads between two plates to firm them before cooking, but it is not necessary.

Tongue

There are beef, veal, lamb, and pork tongues. Beef is the most widely used and is to be found in our markets smoked, pickled, and fresh. Beef tongues weigh from 2 to 5 pounds, but for prime texture they should be about 3 pounds.

Pork tongues are usually ground for various canned products. Lamb tongues are ground or pickled or sold in jars. Fresh veal tongues are in short supply and must be ordered from the butcher. Veal tongues weigh from 1½ to 2 pounds; lamb tongues seldom weigh more than 4 ounces.

Fresh, pickled, and smoked tongues can be used interchangeably. The choice is merely a matter of taste and preference; the fresh tongue has the most delicate flavor. Use a fresh tongue within three days, smoked and pickled within eight.

Preparation. The preparation is the same for smoked, pickled, or fresh tongue. Scrub the tongue well with a vegetable brush. Soak it in cold water for at least one hour before poaching it. Drain and transfer to a cooking pot. Cover it with cold water that has been seasoned with a sliced onion, 2 bay leaves, 6 crushed peppercorns, 1 teaspoon thyme, 2 teaspoons salt, a few cloves, and some sprigs of dill, if you have it on hand. Bring to a boil, partly cover the pot, and simmer until tender, about one hour per pound.

Let the tongue cool in the broth. When cool enough to handle, remove from the broth, slit the underside of the tongue, and peel off the tough skin that encases it. If the tongue is fully cooked, most of the skin can be peeled off like a glove. Trim away all the small bones and gristle at the root end. Slice thin on a slight angle.

Tongue can be served hot with a variety of sauces, or cold with a vinaigrette. It is equally good hot or cold. It makes lovely leftovers for sandwiches or meat salads.

Tripe

Tripe is the muscular lining of beef stomachs. There are four kinds, but we are likely to find only two in our markets—the honeycomb and the smooth. Honeycomb tripe is easily recognizable by its thick ridges that do indeed resemble a honeycomb. This is the best known, the meatiest, and the most desirable. Smooth tripe is thinner, but the taste is the same. Tripe requires long, careful preparation at the meat-packing plant where it is processed to remove the stomach contents and the mucous surface. It is therefore partly cooked when you buy it, but it still needs a lot of cooking to make it edible. Before this processing became standard practice, cooking fresh tripe was a long, drawn out affair, sometimes taking as much as twenty-four hours of continuous cooking.

Once the tripe is cooked and cooled, it can be cut into strips and breaded for sautéeing, or brushed with melted butter and broiled, to be served with a well-seasoned sauce. There are a few world-famous dishes based on tripe, originally devised out of the need to use every part of meat animals. Tripe à la mode de Caen, a stew flavored with apple brandy baked in a dough-sealed baking pot, is a brilliant example.

Preparation. Trim the tripe, if necessary, and scrub it well with a vegetable brush. Blanch it by covering it with cold salted water, bring to the boil, and boil for a minute or two. Drain and plunge it into cold water. Place it back in the saucepan and cover it with cold salted water. Add 1 onion stuck with a few cloves, 1 bay leaf, some chopped celery leaves, 4 crushed peppercorns, and a little dry white wine.

Cover the pot and simmer gently until tender. This will take from one to three hours, depending on how much precooking was done in the processing plant. The only way you can tell if it is done is by tasting it. The texture should be like that of soft gristle; it should have a slight chewiness and not be completely soft.

Oxtails

There may have been a time when oxtails were actually used, but today oxtails are really beef tails. Buy fresh ones and use them fresh. They range from ¾ pound to 2 pounds. They make a hearty delicious stew or a fine stock. If you serve the oxtails as a stew, they will not be exactly elegant party fare; each vertebra contains small holes filled with marrow, which must be sucked out—good, but a bit messy. All oxtails should be cooked slowly, from three to five hours. It is advisable to cook the oxtail preparation a day in advance so that it can be refrigerated overnight and thoroughly degreased. For a stew, figure approximately a pound per person.

Sweet and Sour Fresh Tongue

2½ to 3 pounds fresh beef tongue
3 slices bacon
1 carrot, peeled
1 celery stalk, peeled
1 small onion, peeled
1 cup white wine
½ cup currants or raisins
1 tablespoon Dijon or Düsseldorf mustard
1 tablespoon cornstarch
1½ tablespoons port or Madeira

Prepare the tongue, simmering it for 1 hour (see page 131). Reserve 1½ cups of the broth in which the tongue cooked.

Chop the bacon, carrot, celery, and onion together until almost pastelike. Put in a heavy casserole and cook over low heat until softened and lightly colored.

Add the peeled tongue, wine, 1½ cups reserved broth, and currants or raisins. Bring to a boil, cover, lower the heat, and simmer gently for 1½ to 2 hours or until very tender.

Add the mustard and cornstarch mixed with port or Madeira and whisk until the sauce is thickened and smooth. Slice the tongue and arrange on a warm platter. Cover with some of the sauce; serve remaining sauce in a gravy boat.

Yield: 4 to 8 servings.

Note: This same method can be used with a smoked or pickled tongue.

Veal Kidneys with Mushrooms

3 veal kidneys, about 2¼ pounds
total weight
Flour for dredging
4 tablespoons butter
1 pound fresh mushrooms, thinly
sliced
2 tablespoons finely chopped
shallots
½ cup port or Madeira
1 cup beef broth
1 tablespoon Dijon or Düsseldorf
mustard
¼ cup cream
1 tablespoon cornstarch
1 tablespoon cold water
Freshly chopped parsley

Prepare the kidneys (see page 130).

Drain, dry well, and cut into ¼-inch slices. Dredge the slices in flour. Melt 2 tablespoons butter in a large heavy skillet. When hot, add the kidneys and cook and stir for 3 minutes. They will stiffen but still be quite pink inside. Do not overcook or they will toughen. Remove to a plate.

Melt the remaining butter in the same skillet and add the mushrooms. Cook, stirring, until golden brown and the liquid evaporates. Add the shallots and stir to coat with fat.

Add the port (it will sizzle) and cook until reduced by half. Add broth and bring to a boil. Lower the heat and add the mustard and cream. Blend the cornstarch and water and add to the sauce. Stir until the sauce is thickened.

Add the reserved kidney slices and any accumulated juices. Heat through, but do not boil. Serve immediately on warm plates in patty shells or with rice, garnished with parsley.

Yield: 6 servings.

Note: Pork, lamb, or beef kidneys may be substituted, although veal is the most delicate in flavor.

Calves' Brains with Eggs

2 calves' brains
2 to 3 tablespoons butter
1 medium onion, finely chopped
4 eggs, lightly beaten
1 teaspoon capers, optional
Freshly chopped parsley

Prepare and precook the calves' brains (see page 129). Place on a board and coarsely chop.

Melt the butter in a large skillet, and cook the onion, stirring, until soft. Add the brains and cook, stirring often, until heated through, 2 or 3 minutes.

Raise the heat, add the eggs, and stir until the eggs are set. Sprinkle with capers and parsley. Serve immediately on warm plates.

Yield: 4 to 6 servings.

Liver with Onions

1¾ pounds liver (calf or beef),
　thinly sliced
Milk to cover
1¾ pounds Spanish onions, thinly
　sliced
2 tablespoons butter
2 tablespoons oil
Flour for dredging
Salt and freshly ground pepper
Lemon wedges
Parsley sprigs

Place the calf's liver in a deep dish or bowl and cover with milk. Let stand for 30 minutes. If using beef liver, cover with milk and refrigerate overnight.

Put the onions in a heavy cast-iron skillet, cover, and place over low heat. Do not add fat. Stir occasionally and cook the onions until very soft, 30 to 45 minutes. Keep warm while preparing the liver.

Heat the butter and oil in a large skillet. Remove the liver from the milk and dredge in flour, a few slices at a time, shaking off any excess. Cook the slices quickly in the hot oil, 1 to 1½ minutes on each side. Remove the pieces to a platter and keep warm while cooking the remaining pieces. Season with salt and pepper.

Serve immediately on a bed of onions. Garnish with lemon wedges and sprigs of parsley.

Yield: 4 to 6 servings.

Note: Calf's liver should be thinly sliced and cooked quickly so that it remains pink inside. Beef liver can be cooked longer, but not too long or it will become tough. The milk acts as a tenderizer and enhances the flavor.

Broiled Liver

2 pounds liver (calf or beef),
　sliced ½ inch thick
Milk to cover
Flour for dredging
4 tablespoons butter, melted
Salt and freshly ground pepper
Lemon wedges

Soak the calf's liver in milk to cover for 30 minutes. Cover the beef liver with milk and refrigerate overnight.

Just before cooking, drain the liver, dredge in flour, and shake off any excess. Place on a wire rack set in a shallow pan 5 inches from the flame.

Broil for 3 to 4 minutes on each side, or until the liver is still pink inside. Baste with melted butter. Season with salt and pepper.

Garnish with lemon wedges and serve immediately. Onion or bacon are suitable accompaniments.

Yield: 6 servings.

Sautéed Sweetbreads

1½ to 2 pounds sweetbreads (2 pairs)
2 tablespoons Dijon or Düsseldorf mustard
1 cup bread crumbs
Salt and freshly ground pepper
¼ pound clarified butter (see page 260)
Lemon wedges
Freshly chopped parsley

Prepare the sweetbreads (see page 130), and refrigerate. Cut the sweetbreads into ½-inch-thick slices. Brush both sides of the slices with mustard and dip into crumbs. Season with salt and pepper.

Heat the butter in a large skillet and add the sweetbreads in batches. Do not crowd the pan. Cook until golden on both sides, shaking the pan gently.

Arrange on a large warm platter. Garnish with lemon wedges and sprinkle with parsley. Serve immediately on hot plates. Sautéed sweetbreads are good with boiled new potatoes and steamed asparagus.

Yield: 4 to 6 servings.

Braised Sweetbreads

1½ to 2 pounds sweetbreads (2 pairs)
4 tablespoons butter
1 carrot, peeled and thinly sliced
1 medium onion, finely chopped
½ cup dry white wine
1½ cups beef broth, plus additional broth for the sauce
1 teaspoon dried tarragon
2 to 3 sprigs fresh parsley
1 bay leaf
2 tablespoons flour
¼ cup cream
1 to 2 tablespoons lemon juice
Freshly chopped parsley

Prepare the sweetbreads (see page 130).

Preheat the oven to 350 degrees.

Melt 2 tablespoons butter in a heavy casserole just large enough for the sweetbreads. Add the carrot and onion and cook, stirring, until soft and lightly colored. Add the sweetbreads and the wine. Cook until the wine is reduced slightly. Add the broth, tarragon, parsley, and bay leaf and bring to a boil. Cover and transfer to the oven. Cook for 1 to 1¼ hours, basting occasionally. The sweetbreads are done when the edges begin to crack slightly.

Carefully remove the sweetbreads to a serving dish and keep warm. Handle them carefully because they are very fragile. Strain the liquid from the pan into a 2-cup measure. Skim the fat. Add additional beef broth to come to 2 cups.

Melt the remaining butter in a saucepan and add the flour. Stir with a whisk until lightly colored. Add the 2 cups reserved liquid and whisk constantly until blended and smooth. Bring to a boil, lower the heat, and simmer for 5 minutes. Add the cream and heat but do not boil. Taste and correct the seasonings. Discard the bay leaf and add lemon juice. Pour the sauce over the sweetbreads, sprinkle with parsley, and serve immediately on warm plates.

Yield: 4 to 6 servings.

Braised Tripe with Cheese

3 pounds tripe

¼ cup olive oil

2 pounds veal bones, cracked

1 carrot, peeled, trimmed, and sliced

1 celery stalk, sliced

1 medium onion, coarsely chopped

2 cloves garlic, crushed

1 cup dry white wine

1½ cups beef broth

1½ cups drained and crushed canned tomatoes

2 tablespoons chopped parsley

½ teaspoon dried rosemary, crumbled

Salt (if necessary; cheese may be salty) and freshly ground pepper

1 cup or more freshly grated Parmesan or Romano cheese

Scrub and blanch the tripe (see page 132) and cut it into finger-size pieces.

Preheat the oven to 300 degrees.

Heat the oil in a heavy casserole and brown the veal bones, carrot, celery, onion, and garlic. Add the tripe, wine, broth, and tomatoes. Sprinkle with parsley and rosemary and bring to a boil. Cover the pot and wrap it tightly in foil, pressing the foil around the casserole so it is completely sealed.

Place in the oven and cook for 6 to 8 hours. The tripe will be slightly chewy. Before serving, skim the fat and season. Serve hot in bowls with thick slices of French or Italian bread. Serve the grated cheese separately.

Yield: 6 to 8 servings.

Note: The veal bones add a special texture to this dish. Tripe is particularly gelatinous and the natural gelatin in the veal is complementary.

Oxtail Stew

This is a marrow-rich stew, a favorite of the bone lovers.

4 pounds oxtails, trimmed of all visible fat and cut into serving pieces

Flour for dredging

¼ cup vegetable oil

1 medium onion, coarsely chopped

2 celery stalks, coarsely chopped

1 medium carrot, coarsely chopped

2 white turnips, peeled and cubed

1 clove garlic, crushed

1 bay leaf

1 tablespoon dried rosemary, crumbled

Dredge oxtails in the flour, shaking off any excess. Heat the oil in a large heavy casserole and add about one-third of the oxtails. Brown them well and remove with a slotted spoon to drain. Proceed with remaining oxtails.

Add the onion, celery, carrot, turnips, and garlic. Cook, stirring, until soft and lightly colored. Return the meat to the casserole.

Add the bay leaf, rosemary, thyme, tomatoes, broth, salt, and pepper. The liquid should barely cover the oxtails. Add more broth, if necessary. Bring to a boil over high heat, skimming the fat as it rises to the surface. After 3 to 5 minutes, cover and lower the heat. Simmer for 3 to 5 hours, or until the oxtails are tender. Oxtails are fatty and it is best if you allow them to cool so that you can do a more complete job of skimming off the fat. Reheat

1 teaspoon dried thyme
1 1-pound can whole tomatoes
1½ to 2 cups beef broth
Salt and freshly ground pepper
Freshly chopped parsley

and sprinkle with parsley. Remove the bay leaf. Serve from the casserole into warm bowls.

Yield: 4 to 6 servings.

Rabbit

Rabbits are raised commercially throughout the United States and are available fresh or frozen. They have a delicate, flavorful meat, very like chicken, although a bit drier. Like chicken, rabbit can be fried, stewed, or roasted.

Fresh rabbits are generally sold skinned and cut up, but you can buy them whole and

disjoint them yourself. The packaged frozen ones are already cut up. Defrost the frozen rabbit slowly in the refrigerator and dry it well with paper towels before cooking. You can cook the giblets along with the rabbit for added flavor. Cook the liver separately and quickly.

Rabbit Stew

Rabbit can be used in almost any recipe calling for chicken. It has very much the same flavor.

1 2½- to 3½-pound rabbit, fresh or defrosted, cut into 8 pieces
1 cup dry red or white wine
2 cloves garlic, crushed
½ teaspoon dried rosemary, crumbled
½ teaspoon dried marjoram
Scant pinch of dried leaf sage, crumbled
⅓ cup olive or vegetable oil
Flour for dredging
1 large onion, coarsely chopped
1 1-pound can whole tomatoes, chopped or crushed
1 teaspoon dried basil
1 bay leaf, crumbled
Salt and freshly ground pepper

Combine the rabbit, wine, 1 clove garlic, rosemary, marjoram, and sage in a large heavy plastic bag or nonaluminum bowl. Seal tightly and refrigerate for 24 to 36 hours. Turn as often as you think of it.

Drain and dry the rabbit and reserve the marinade. Heat the oil in a large heavy nonaluminum skillet or shallow casserole. Just before cooking, dredge a few pieces of rabbit in flour, shaking off any excess. Add to the skillet and brown well on all sides. Do not crowd the pan. Transfer to a warm platter and continue to dredge and brown the rabbit pieces in batches. When all the rabbit is browned, add the onion and the remaining clove of garlic to the same skillet. Cook, stirring, until softened and lightly colored. Stir in the reserved marinade and bring to a boil. Lower the heat and simmer for 10 minutes, or until reduced slightly. Add the tomatoes, herbs, salt, and pepper and blend well. Return the rabbit to the skillet and bring to a boil. Cover, lower the heat, and simmer gently for 1 to 1½ hours, or until tender.

Remove the rabbit to a warm platter. Skim the fat from the sauce and pour the degreased sauce over the rabbit. Sprinkle with parsley and serve immediately.

Yield: 4 to 6 servings.

Venison

Deer are not raised commercially so all venison must be hunted, and it needs the game warden's seal to be sold. Today, venison has come to mean the flesh of deer, although originally it was a term used for any animal taken by hunting and used for food. Of all furred game, it is the meat most generally available even to nonhunters, because it is sometimes sold in retail markets and is available from specialty mail-order houses.

The age of the deer is the most important guide in choosing the proper method of cooking it, and the advice of the hunter or an experienced butcher can be most valuable. The best meat comes from the young buck (male) less than two years old. The anatomy is much like that of domestic animals and, like them, the tenderest cuts come from the less used muscles. The choice cuts of a young deer can be roasted or broiled like beef, but an old animal is best relegated to the stew pot or to the meat grinder. If you are not sure of the age, marinate the meat for 24 to 36 hours to tenderize it, then braise it. Venison is a lean meat and needs barding (covering the meat with strips of fat) if it is roasted.

The fat of venison quickly turns rancid and should be discarded.

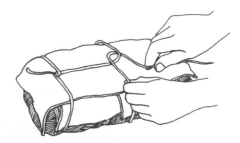

To bard venison or other lean meat, cover it with strips of fat and loop string around the meat, crosswise and lengthwise, as you would tie up a parcel.

Venison Pot Roast

1 6-pound venison roast, marinated (see following directions)

¼ cup olive oil, or rendered pork or bacon fat

1 medium onion, coarsely chopped

1 carrot, coarsely chopped

2 tablespoons flour

1½ to 2 cups strained marinade

2 cups beef broth (or more)

Salt and freshly ground pepper

2 to 3 tablespoons currant or apple jelly

½ cup heavy cream

Remove venison from the marinade and dry well with paper towels. Reserve the marinade.

Heat the oil in a deep heavy nonaluminum casserole and brown the venison well on all sides, turning with tongs. Remove to a plate.

Add the onion and carrot to the fat remaining in the pan. Cook and stir until softened and lightly colored. Sprinkle with flour and stir to coat the vegetables.

Return the venison to the casserole and add the marinade and beef broth. Bring to a boil, cover, and simmer slowly for 2 to 2½ hours, or until fork-tender. The time required depends on the quality and age of the meat. Season with salt and pepper halfway through the cooking.

Remove the venison to a platter or carving board and keep warm. Skim the fat from the pan juices. If they have evaporated, add additional beef broth. You should have about 3 cups. Whisk in the jelly and cream and stir until the sauce is well blended and heated through. Slice the venison and cover with some of the sauce. Serve remaining sauce in a gravy boat.

Yield: 6 to 8 servings.

Venison Marinade

1½ cups dry red wine

2 tablespoons olive oil

2 carrots, sliced

2 medium onions, thinly sliced

½ cup coarsely chopped shallots

3 to 4 juniper berries, crushed (or 2 tablespoons gin)

1 clove garlic, coarsely chopped

¼ teaspoon whole peppercorns, crushed

1 small bay leaf, crumbled

1 teaspoon dried thyme

1 to 2 sprigs fresh parsley

Combine all the ingredients in a small nonaluminum saucepan and bring to a boil. Remove from the heat and allow to cool.

Place the venison and marinade in a heavy plastic bag or deep, nonaluminum bowl. Cover or seal tightly and refrigerate for 24 to 36 hours. Turn the meat several times.

Venison Meat Loaf

1 to 2 tablespoons rendered pork
  or bacon fat
1 large onion, finely chopped
2 cloves garlic, finely chopped
1½ pounds ground venison
¾ pound ground pork
½ pound ground fresh pork fat
½ cup finely chopped parsley
1 egg, lightly beaten
¼ teaspoon thyme
¼ teaspoon marjoram
1 teaspoon soy or Worcestershire
  sauce
Freshly ground pepper

Preheat the oven to 350 degrees.

Heat the fat in a heavy skillet and add the onion and garlic. Cook, stirring, until soft and lightly colored. Scrape into a large bowl.

Add the remaining ingredients and mix with your hands until well blended.

Pat the mixture into a loaf shape and place in a shallow roasting pan.

Bake for 1½ hours, or until no pink appears in the juices. Serve hot or cold.

Yield: 6 to 8 servings.

Note: If you are unable to get fresh pork fat, blanch ½ pound bacon to remove the smoky taste.

4
Poultry and Game Birds

For hundreds of years, a cooked chicken has been a symbol of abundance and plenty. As long ago as the sixteenth century, Henri IV, King of France, is reputed to have said that he wished that there would be no peasant in all his kingdom who was too poor to have a chicken in his pot every Sunday. This wish has been realized to a degree, for poultry is now one of the most reasonably priced foods on our marketing list. Chicken takes honors as the least expensive source of high-quality protein available, costing very little more than it did twenty years ago. The industrialization of the poultry business has brought a heavier bird to market in a shorter period of time than ten years ago. The shorter time means less feed and fewer man-hours of work, which are reflected in lower cost to the consumer. In the past, young broilers and larger roasters were seasonal, but streamlined marketing gives us a steady supply of poultry all year.

Chicken lends itself to an infinite range of preparations. It can be cooked in a brown sauce, a white sauce, a red sauce, or no sauce at all; it can be served hot, cold, shiny with glaze, or highlighted in aspic. We can produce chicken dishes in never-ending variety with an accent that is French, Spanish, Italian, Hungarian, Russian, Indian, Chinese, or completely American.

Types of Poultry

The term poultry includes all the domestic fowl that are raised for food—chicken, turkey, duck, goose, Rock Cornish hens, squab, guinea hens, and pheasants.

Chicken

Broilers, or young chickens from six to eight weeks old, weigh from 1 to 2½ pounds, fryers from 2½ to 3½ pounds; and the broiler-fryer from 2 to 3½ pounds. But the lines of difference between these names are fuzzy. Each market has its own terminology, which is not to be taken literally. You can fry broilers and you can broil fryers and you can roast, fricassee, or braise either if you do it carefully and don't overcook them. The 1-pound squab chickens generally have to be special-ordered. They can be split and broiled or stuffed and roasted.

The roaster, sometimes called a pullet, is a little older and larger than the broiler. It is more fleshy and rounded than the younger birds and is bred for tenderness. It is upward of twelve weeks old and can weigh from 3½ to 6½ pounds. In addition to roasted, it can be jointed and braised or potted, and it is first-rate for barbecuing on an outdoor spit.

The capon is a desexed male bird under seven months old, weighing from 5 to 9 pounds. It has fine flavor and a generous proportion of white meat. It is generally roasted.

The stewing chicken, fowl, or hen is an older bird weighing up to 8 pounds. It makes wonderful stock and is good for leisurely stewing. October is often the month when egg farmers sell off their older hens that can no longer compete in the egg-laying race with their younger sisters. These mature birds need a few hours in the stewpot, but their meat is rich in flavor and makes splendid chicken salad, creamed chicken, or chicken hash.

Turkey

Improved breeding techniques have changed the turkey from a holiday-time bird to one that is available throughout the year. The birds range from the small 4- to 6-pounders to impressive specimens that can weigh up to 40 pounds. Some food experts prefer a tom turkey over a hen for tasty eating, but others—equally authoritatively—maintain that the broad-breasted hen is sweeter and juicier than the male. The hens rarely weigh more than 19 pounds, so if you buy a jumbo-size bird during the holidays, you can be sure it is a male. A large turkey offers more meat per pound than any other fowl and is the most economical buy for a large crowd. Figure about a pound per serving, which will leave you with ample leftovers.

Duck

A large proportion of the ducks in our markets are frozen. They generally weigh from 4 to 5½ pounds and contain a small proportion of meat to bone and fat. Restaurants usually serve half a 5-pound bird per person. However, duck is a rich bird, and if you serve it at home with wild rice, a favorite accompaniment, and a sweet sauce, such as orange or Bing cherries, a smaller portion could do. Ducks can be roasted, broiled, or braised. The Oriental Peking Duck, which is a popular dish in the West as well as in its homeland, is air-dried, marinated, and finally roasted. The crisp skin and meat are served separately, to be rolled up in paper-thin pancakes.

Goose

Geese are not readily available and must generally be ordered. A commercially grown goose is ready to eat at ten weeks, but no goose older than six months should be purchased because it tends to be tough. Figure 1 to 1½ pounds of ready-to-cook goose per serving. Oven-ready

fresh geese weigh from 4 to 14 pounds, the most popular size being in the 7- to 11-pound range. Slow roasting is the best method of preparation.

Rock Cornish Hen

Back in the 1800s, an enterprising American crossbred a Cornish game cock with a White Plymouth Rock chicken and the Rock Cornish hen came into existence. Except for squab chickens, it is the smallest of the chicken family, weighing only 1½ pounds or less at six weeks, just enough for one person. It is a tender, plump-breasted bird and may be stuffed and roasted, broiled, braised, or sautéed. It can now be bought fresh in many markets, as well as frozen.

Squab

Squabs are young pigeons, weighing about 1 pound each. They are available fresh all year but usually have to be ordered in advance. All squabs are raised domestically. They are most generally roasted, with frequent basting to keep them moist.

Nutritional Values

Poultry is brimful of protein—about one-fifth of the edible portion is protein—and is a rich source of B-vitamins. The fat content varies with the age of the bird, from under 5 percent in young chickens to nearly 25 percent in mature fowl. The amount of fat also varies with the type of poultry. Duck has more fat than chicken, and goose is the fattiest of all. The dark meat in all poultry is fattier and has more connective tissue than the white, which explains why the dark meat needs more cooking time than the white

and is also juicier. Chicken is the lowest in calories of all popular meats: there are 171 calories in 3½ ounces of a combination of white and dark meat. It is low in fat and the fat contains 64 percent polyunsaturated fatty acids, which is a plus for people on a low cholesterol or low-fat regimen. As an added bonus, chickens have short muscle fibers, which our digestive systems break down quickly.

Inspection and Grading

Poultry, like meat, is inspected for wholesomeness by the United States Department of Agriculture. The USDA's circular mark of inspection can be found on a paper tag attached to the wing or on the giblet wrap. All domestic poultry—chicken, turkey, goose, duck, or guinea hen—that is shipped across state lines will be inspected. The inspection generally takes place in the processing plant, where the inspector checks to make sure that the birds come from a healthy flock, that rigid sanitary conditions have been observed, that no chemicals or additives considered harmful by the Food and Drug Administration have been used in the feed, and that the bird has been properly packaged and truthfully labeled.

Grading, unlike USDA inspecting, which is mandatory, is provided only if requested and paid for by the poultry processor. Top-quality birds are awarded a Grade A shield to be found near the inspection tag. Grades B and C are given to lower quality birds, but often birds that rank in one of these classes will have no grading shield. The qualities on which the bird is judged are its conformation (how well

shaped it is); meatiness; amount of fat (it should have a layer of fat); whether it was well plucked; and discoloration and blemishes or cuts of the skin and flesh. A whole chicken with a blemish on the wing could have the wing cut off and be graded C, but if the rest of the bird is in top condition, it can be cut up and the separate parts sold with a Grade A shield.

There are no government rules regulating the period of time within which a slaughtered bird must be sold. Unlike milk and eggs, which usually have an expiration date stamped on their containers, poultry carry no expiration date. However, birds are usually transported quickly and reach markets within twenty-four hours of being slaughtered. If your past experience with your poultry purveyor has been satisfactory, you can assume that the poultry is fresh.

You may have noticed the disappearance from the scene of two items that were commonly found in butcher shops at one time—chicken feet, used to make soup, and cockscombs, used for garnishes. It had been discovered that the spongy texture of these parts can serve as a focal point for disease-producing cells. Since 1973, chicken feet can be legally processed for human food only under certain stringent conditions. This translates into a virtual embargo against transporting chicken feet across state lines for ordinary use (unless propelled by the chicken itself), and you will

not find either feet or combs for sale in general markets. However, here and there a market or a friendly farmer will have the chicken feet and, if you want to take advantage of their availability, they can be frozen most successfully. The cockscombs are no loss; you can always use parsley or watercress.

Selection

When buying a chicken, use the same criteria as the government inspectors when grading a bird: conformation, more breast than leg, no bruises or blood marks, and a fairly solid color. The color of the bird makes no difference in taste or nutritional value. Color simply reflects regional preferences based on nothing more than the consumer's visual response. The northeast part of the country prefers yellow chickens so, to meet this demand, poultry raisers add marigold petals and/or a yellowing chemical and corn gluten, the yellow part of the corn, to the chicken feed. Other parts of the country favor white-skinned chickens and no color-inducing matter is added to their feed. But it is not skin color that determines flavor in poultry; it is proper feed and care. There is as much substance to the notion that yellow chickens taste better than white—or vice versa—as there is to the brown egg/white egg myth.

Look for a plump, rounded breast area and unbruised skin. If a bird looks scrawny, pass it up. You can sometimes tell a bird's age and, presumably, its tenderness, by pressing against the tip of its breastbone. If it is bendable, it is a young bird; if not, it is a likely candidate for stewing, fricasseeing, or braising.

Sniff for fresh aroma. No fresh chicken or giblet package should have the slightest off-odor. If you detect one, return the bird at once. Cooking cannot save a bird once decomposi-

tion has set in. Regardless of what you do with it, it will never be right. Cooking can make it safe to eat, but it cannot rescue the flavor.

Figure on about ¾ pound of whole chicken per serving and slightly less if you are buying chicken in parts. The birds we buy today have an edible yield of 51.5 percent—not quite as generous as pork chops, rib roasts, or hamburger. On the other hand, chicken is considerably less expensive.

Whole chickens are generally a more economical buy than prepackaged parts, except for those families with such decided preferences for either white meat or dark meat that the remaining parts would be wasted. It is easy to prepare a cut-up chicken yourself (see page 147). Not only will your result probably be tidier than the supermarket operation that often splinters bones and commits other acts of mayhem on the birds, but you will also have some fine stockpot ingredients—backbone, neck, and giblets. Boneless and skinless chicken breasts are readily available in most supermarkets and are wonderfully convenient for emergency situations. But filleting them yourself is a simple procedure (see page 149) and will cost you much less.

If you are buying frozen chickens and find a good deal of frozen liquid in the package, you can be reasonably sure that the package was defrosted and refrozen. This does not mean that the chicken is spoiled, but it will not taste the way a good bird should. The juices that would have made the bird flavorful have seeped out.

When buying turkey, try to get a fresh rather than a frozen one, because it will have better flavor and be juicier. But if you must buy a frozen one, avoid self-basting turkeys. If you read the label, you may find that even those whose names suggest that they will self-baste with butter are in truth suffused with a highly saturated (and cheap) vegetable oil. The frozen, self-basting turkey breasts have suffered the same fate. You are better off to do your own self-basting by inserting slivers of butter between the skin and the flesh.

Storage

Fresh poultry is highly perishable. Don't buy it and stash it in the trunk of your car for a couple of hours while you do other errands. Get it home as quickly as possible and unwrap it immediately. Remove the package of giblets from inside the chicken's cavity and pull out all the loose fat from around the vent opening. Do not wash or rinse the bird until you are ready to prepare it. Bacteria like moisture as much as they like heat. Rewrap the bird loosely in wax paper so that the air can circulate freely around it, which slows bacterial growth. Refrigerate the bird and use it within two days. The chicken neck, gizzard, and heart can be frozen and kept for the stockpot until needed. Store the liver separately or freeze it until you collect enough for a pâté.

Preparing Poultry

Most poultry is sold ready-to-cook and needs little preparation. Before cooking, rinse it thoroughly inside and out under cold running water. Pat it dry inside and outside with paper towels. If you have not already done so, remove the fat from the rear cavity. If the neck protrudes beyond the point where the wings join the shoulders, cut it off and add to the giblets. The bird is now ready to be seasoned and trussed.

Chickens can be divided into halves; or quartered into two breast halves with wings attached and two legs and thighs; or disjointed into smaller pieces, with the wings separated from the breasts and the legs from the thighs. The wing tips are not very meaty and will make a more important contribution to your stockpot than as an inedible appendage to the wing, so cut them off.

To Split or Quarter a Bird

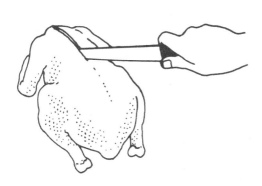

1 *Place bird breast side down and, with a very sharp knife, slit the bird from neck to tail on either side of the backbone and as close to it as possible. Remove the backbone.*

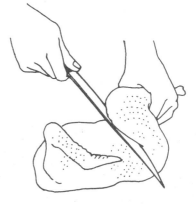

3 *To quarter the bird, place skin side up. With the knife at a 45-degree angle, place the blade of the knife underneath the leg joint and slice the leg away from the wing portion.*

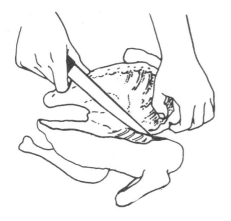

2 *Spread the bird open, skin side down, and cut through the breastbone, dividing the carcass in two.*

To Cut the Bird into Serving Pieces

Repeat Step 1 as under *To Split or Quarter a Bird*. Turn the bird skin side up and flatten it as much as you can by pressing down on the breastbone.

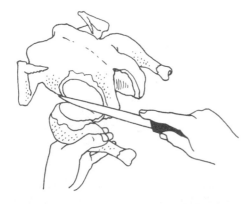

1 *Slit the skin around the drumstick. Pull the leg out at right angles to the body to break open the thigh joint at the small of the back. Cut the whole leg away.*

2 *Cut through the joint at the knee to separate the drumstick from the thigh portion. Repeat on the other side.*

3 *Slit the skin at the wing. Move the wing back and forth and feel for the joint that holds the wing to the shoulder. Cut through to detach the wing from the body. Repeat on the other side.*

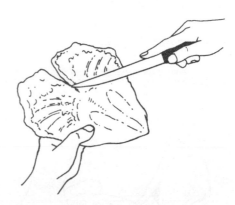

4 *With skin side down, cut the breast into two lengthwise pieces by cutting along the breastbone. Or you can chop the breast in two, crosswise.*

You now have eight pieces of chicken: two wings, two breasts, two legs, and two thighs, plus backbone, neck, and giblets that can be used for stock. Freeze the bones and giblets until you have accumulated enough. Livers should be used separately and not as part of stockpot ingredients; they make the stock dark and cloudy.

To Bone Chicken Breasts

Skinned, boned chicken breasts can be prepared in an endless variety of ways and, except for the dark-meat-only people, they are widely enjoyed. The whole breast is made of two half-breasts. Each half-breast has two fillets, a large one and one much smaller, joined at the shoulder. For a fancy presentation, leave a small piece of the wing bone attached to the breast; the bone will stick out like a handle and it can be trimmed and topped with a frill.

For most purposes, half a breast is an adequate portion.

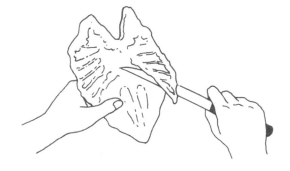

2 *Turn the breast bone side up. Use your fingers or a sharp knife to pull, tease, and scrape the rib cage away from the flesh.*

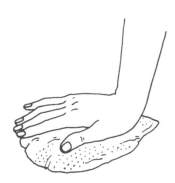

1 *With the skin side toward you, break the breastbone by pressing on it firmly. Pull the skin off the meat.*

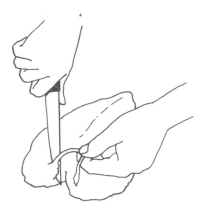

3 *With a sharp knife, gently scrape the meat away from the wishbone and the bone at the shoulder.*

149

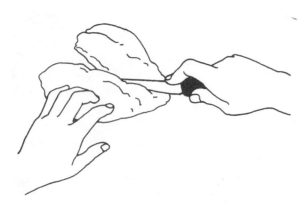

4 *Remove the tendon on the underside of the meat where it was attached to the shoulder. If the two fillets become detached, pat them together. Cooking will fuse them together.*

5 *Cut the breasts in half through the center. Pat the boned breasts into their original shape and trim away all fat. They are now ready for sautéeing, poaching, or stuffing.*

To Render Poultry Fat

Chicken fat and goose fat can be useful in cooking, but duck fat is too strong in flavor for general purposes and is not considered desirable as a cooking ingredient. Chicken fat can be used for basting chicken or for sauce-making. Goose fat is a favorite among Europeans for sautéeing potatoes, or for seasoning cabbage and other vegetables. Chicken fat and goose fat may be prepared the same way and will keep fresh for months in the refrigerator.

Pull off all excess fat from the bird, chop it up and simmer in a little water in a covered saucepan for 10 or 15 minutes, until the fat has melted and the residue has lightly browned. Pour it through a fine strainer. When it is cool, the fat will congeal and rise to the top. Transfer the solidified fat to a covered jar and refrigerate.

If strips of chicken, duck, or goose skin are added to the fat when you are rendering it, you will have cracklings—lovely browned crisp bits that are good for snacks, or for sprinkling over salads, stews, or chowders. Cut the skin into strips about 1 inch long and ¼ inch wide. As they cook, the bits of skin will give up their fat and turn crisp and brown. After you strain the fat, spread the browned bits on paper towels and sprinkle them lightly with salt and pepper.

Stuffing Poultry

You can prepare poultry stuffing in advance and keep it refrigerated, but do not put it into the bird until just before roasting. Inconvenient though it may be, it is the safest procedure because of the danger of contamination from salmonella or some other type of food-poisoning microorganism that can develop in a prestuffed fowl. Even though the bird may be refrigerated, the cold cannot fully penetrate the stuffing in the interior of the bird quickly enough to inactivate dangerous microorganisms.

Fill the bird only three-fourths full because any dressing containing bread or other dry ingredients will swell during cooking. If you have more dressing than the bird can comfortably hold, bake it separately in a greased baking dish for the last 1¼ hours that the bird is in the oven. Baste it two or three times with the drippings from the bird. Cover with foil if it gets too brown on top. Figure about ¾ to 1 cup of stuffing for each pound of bird. Keep in mind, too, that stuffed poultry needs 20 to 30 minutes more cooking time than unstuffed poultry.

Place a little stuffing into the neck cavity, pull the skin over to the back, and skewer closed. Trussing the bird will help to keep the skin in place. Lightly stuff the body cavity and either sew the body cavity closed or use skewers and wrap string around the skewers as you would lace shoes.

Do not stuff ducks; the stuffing would absorb too much fat to be palatable. Geese may be stuffed with fruits such as apples or prunes or other nonabsorbent stuffings that will not soak up fat.

Trussing

Stuffed or unstuffed, a bird should be trussed to keep its shape during cooking and present an attractive appearance when brought to the table. Trussing also helps to prevent the loss of juices from the cavity of the bird.

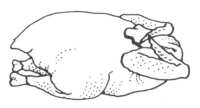

1 *With the breast side down, fold the neck skin over the vent and bend the wing tips over the shoulder to where they will hold the skin in place.*

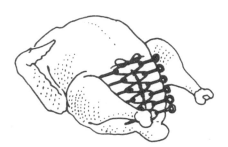

After stuffing the bird, place several skewers across the opening. Then lace by criss-crossing a piece of string around the skewers. Tighten the string to close the opening, and tie the ends.

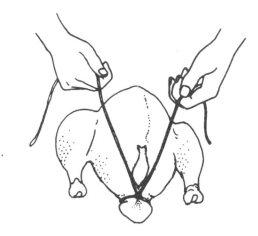

2 *Turn the bird breast side up. Measure one yard of string. Tie the middle of the string around the tail and knot.*

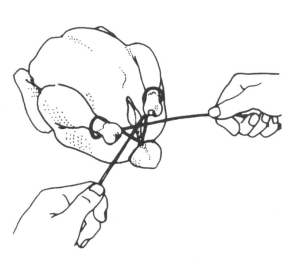

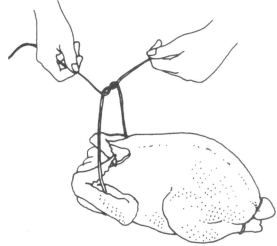

3 *Firmly push the legs back toward the chest close to the body to make the bird more compact. Cross the string over and around the ends of the drumsticks and knot.*

5 *Turn the bird breast side down and tie the ends of the string over the back. At serving time, there is only one string to cut.*

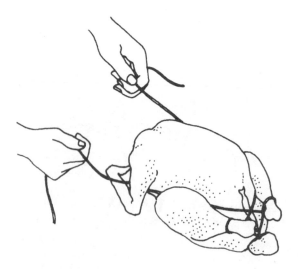

4 *Run the string tightly alongside the breast and on each side pull it through the holes made by the folded wings.*

Testing for Doneness

Poultry is always cooked to the well-done stage. However, an overcooked bird is as unwelcome as an underdone one. One way to test the state of doneness is to slit the flesh between the leg and the body. If the juices that run out are pink, more cooking is required. Clear juices tell us that the bird is done. Another sign of sufficient cooking is a thigh that moves easily in the socket. The only problem with this is that it can occur in an overcooked bird as well. A more accurate test is made with an instant meat thermometer. As you approach the end of the cooking time, insert the tip of the thermometer into the thickest part of the thigh, being careful not to touch the bone. A temperature of 185 degrees indicates that the bird is done. A 3-pound chicken will take 70 to 80 minutes in a 350-degree oven, but like so many imponderables in this uncertain world, we cannot be precise about timing because the skeletal structure and the amount of flesh and fat vary among birds and will affect cooking time. Try to feel the springiness of the breast and thigh when the desired state of doneness is reached and, with experience, you will be able to sense when the bird is done just by using finger pressure on the breast and thigh.

Safety First

In addition to the injunction against stuffing a bird long in advance of cooking it, you should never partly cook a bird with the idea of returning it to the refrigerator and finishing the cooking five or six hours later. There is a valid reason for this. Microorganisms, including the food-poisoning type, can multiply rapidly within the temperature range of 50 to 120 degrees, which generally represents the temperature of a half-cooked bird. This range is called the "dangerous incubation zone," and a bird should not be held within this temperature range for more than four hours. By cooking poultry all at once, you will not be giving unfriendly bacteria an opportunity to grow.

Leftover cooked poultry and stuffing should be cooled promptly and refrigerated. Remove any stuffing left inside the bird and refrigerate separately.

Cooking Methods for Poultry

Poultry may be roasted, broiled, sautéed, braised, or poached (boiled). When possible, have poultry at room temperature before cooking because it will need longer cooking if taken directly from the refrigerator.

Roasting

Roasting is the most popular method of cooking whole chicken or capon, turkey, duck, goose, guinea hen, Rock Cornish hen, and squab. All birds except duck and goose should be generously brushed with fat or oil. Guinea hen, squab, and game birds should be barded (covered with strips of fat) before roasting.

One of the secrets of juicy poultry is basting. After the first 20 minutes of cooking, it should be basted every 15 minutes, using melted butter, stock, wine, or pan drippings. Roasting chicken or turkey with the breast down during the first two-thirds of the cooking time will help to keep the white meat moist. The fat from the back filters down through the bird as it cooks and makes the breast juicy. For even browning, turn the bird breast side up during the last third of the cooking time. However, duck and goose, which have a good deal of fat in the breast area, should be cooked breast up. Prick the skin often to allow the fat to run out of the birds and siphon it off with a bulb baster.

Braising

Chickens of all sizes, from young broilers to large roasters, ducks, and wild birds like pheasant, can be braised with memorable results. Tough birds can be made tender, and tender birds can be bathed in delicious sauces. The same rules of braising—slow cooking in a covered pot with flavoring vegetables, herbs, and spices—that pertain to meats also apply to poultry. The main difference is that poultry generally requires much less cooking time than meat. Fricasseeing or stewing chicken is a form of braising.

Poaching

A boiled chicken is actually a poached chicken. It has been simmered in hot water until tender. Poaching is suitable for older fowl, although whole trussed roasting chickens are used for some preparations in which the soup also plays a leading role. Poaching is often used to prepare poultry for use in other dishes, such as salads, hashes, and creamed chicken dishes, or for special low-calorie or other restrictive diets.

Broiling

Young chickens from 1 to 3 pounds, squab, and duck may be broiled. One-pound chickens can make an attractive presentation when flattened and broiled whole. Cut through the backbone and open the bird out. Break the breastbone by pressing firmly on it to flatten it out. Poultry, except for duck, should be brushed with butter or oil before, during, and after broiling. Always preheat the broiler. Broil 4 to 6 inches from the heat source, starting with the bone side toward the heat. Allow 13 to 15 minutes per side, depending on the size of the bird. Move the bird closer to the heat source for the last 3 or 4

minutes of cooking to char the skin, but be careful to avoid scorching. For variety in flavors, you can season the basting butter with garlic, rosemary, tarragon, parsley, lemon juice, or any herb of your choice.

Sautéeing

You can sauté chicken or game birds such as young pheasant or quail. Chicken is usually cut into serving pieces, which may be dredged in flour or not, or given a thicker coating of first flour, then beaten egg, followed by fine bread crumbs. Since butter has a low smoking point, it is not ideal for sautéeing and should be combined with oil. For delicate sautés, clarified butter (page 260) is recommended. Sautéeing is the quickest of all cooking methods, needing only about ½ hour for larger birds and as little as 20 minutes for smaller ones. Chicken breasts can be done in 10 minutes. Food to be sautéed should be well dried in order to brown properly, and not crowded in the pan, or it will steam.

Carving Cooked Chicken or Turkey

Always let the bird rest at room temperature for 15 to 20 minutes after you have removed it from the oven to give the juices time to settle. Place bird breast side up on the carving board.

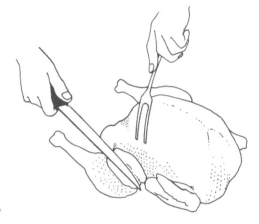

1 *Remove drumstick and thigh by pressing them away from the body. The joint connecting the leg to the backbone will often snap free, or you may cut it with a knife.*

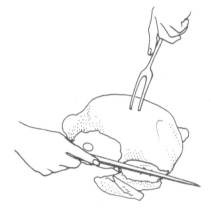

3 *Remove the wings.*

2 *Separate the drumstick and the thigh by slicing through the connecting joint. If it is a large bird, slice off the dark meat from the drumstick if you wish.*

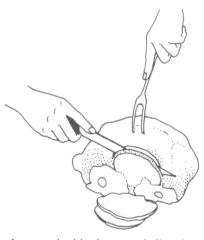

4 *Slice the meat in thin downward slices from either side of the breastbone.*

Lemon-Roasted Chickens

It doesn't take any longer to roast two chickens than one. Cook both; serve one hot and one another day, cold.

2 2- to 2½-pound chickens

1 carrot, peeled and cut into two

4 celery stalks, cut into pieces

2 cloves garlic, crushed, *or* 2 to 4 tablespoons chopped shallots

2 lemons, each cut into quarters

2 to 3 tablespoons olive oil

1 tablespoon chopped shallots or onion

3 tablespoons flour

¼ cup dry vermouth

2 cups chicken broth

Pinch of dried thyme

1 bay leaf

2 to 3 tablespoons light or heavy cream

¼ cup fresh lemon juice

Preheat the oven to 350 degrees.

Remove the giblets and chicken fat and reserve. Stuff each chicken with carrot, celery, garlic or shallots, and lemons. Skewer closed and truss. Rub all over with oil.

Place in a shallow pan, breast side down; leave room between the chickens so that all parts cook evenly.

Roast for 1 hour and 15 minutes; turn chickens breast side up for the last 15 to 20 minutes. Baste often with the pan drippings and move the chickens around occasionally so that the breasts do not stick to the pan. When done, the juices will run clear and the internal temperature in the thigh will be 185 degrees.

Remove to a platter and cover lightly with foil while preparing the sauce. Let stand for 15 to 20 minutes before carving if you are not serving with a sauce.

Place the roasting pan on top of the stove and remove all but 3 tablespoons of fat from the pan. Add the giblets and cook until brown and crusty. Add the shallots or onion and cook, stirring, until lightly colored. Add the flour and cook until lightly colored. Stir in the vermouth, scraping the bottom of the pan to dissolve any brown bits that may have adhered to the pan. Add the broth and herbs and bring to a boil. Transfer the sauce to a small saucepan. Cook, stirring, until smooth and thickened. Stir in the cream and lemon juice. Heat through but do not boil. Remove the bay leaf.

Cut each chicken into quarters and arrange on a platter. Nap with some of the sauce, if desired, and serve remaining sauce in a gravy boat.

Yield: 4 to 6 servings.

Roast Chicken

1 3- to 3½-pound fryer, broiler, or roasting chicken
2 cloves garlic, crushed
2 sprigs parsley
1 tablespoon olive or vegetable oil

Preheat the oven to 325 degrees.

Remove the excess fat and giblets from chicken and reserve the giblets for stock. Put the garlic and parsley into the cavity. Truss and rub the skin with about 1 tablespoon oil.

Place breast side down on a rack in a shallow pan. Roast 25 minutes per pound, basting often with the pan juices. Turn the bird breast side up after about 1 hour. The internal temperature of the thigh when done will be 185 degrees.

Remove to a warm platter, cover lightly, and let stand for 10 to 15 minutes before carving.

Yield: 4 servings.

Pan-Fry or Sauté of Chicken

Once you have mastered the technique of a pan-fry or sauté of chicken, experiment with various herbs and liquids. For example, add ½ teaspoon dried thyme, tarragon, or rosemary when you add the vermouth. Dry white or red wine can be substituted for the vermouth. And chopped tomatoes can be used in place of the broth.

1 3½- to 4-pound chicken, cut into 8 pieces
Salt and freshly ground pepper
2 tablespoons butter
2 tablespoons olive or vegetable oil
¼ cup chopped shallots, onions, or scallions (white part only)
¼ cup dry vermouth
¾ cup chicken broth

Dry chicken pieces well with paper towels. If they are damp, they will not brown well and the fat will spatter. Season with salt and pepper. Heat the butter and oil in a large heavy skillet. Add the chicken pieces skin side down. Cook until golden brown, 15 to 20 minutes. Turn with tongs and continue to cook for 15 to 20 minutes, or until done. Shake the skillet occasionally. Remove to a warm serving platter.

Discard the fat from the skillet. Add the shallots, onions, or scallions and cook, stirring, until soft and lightly colored. Add the vermouth and cook over high heat until evaporated. Add the broth, bring to a boil, and simmer for 1 minute. Pour over the chicken and serve immediately.

Yield: 4 servings.

Chicken in Wine Sauce

This dish can be made with red or white wine. Each gives it an entirely different taste.

1 2½- to 4-pound chicken, cut into 8 pieces

Salt and freshly ground pepper

2 tablespoons butter

2 tablespoons olive or vegetable oil

1 pound fresh mushrooms, left whole if small, quartered if large

¼ cup chopped shallots or scallions (white part only)

1 to 2 cloves garlic, finely chopped

3 tablespoons flour

2 cups dry red or white wine

¾ cup chicken broth

1 small bay leaf

2 to 4 sprigs parsley

½ teaspoon dried thyme or rosemary

Dry chicken pieces well with paper towels. Season with salt and pepper. Heat the butter and oil in a heavy skillet. Add the chicken pieces skin side down and cook until golden. Turn with tongs and cook until golden on the other side, a total of 12 to 14 minutes. Do not crowd pan. Cook in batches if necessary. Remove to a plate and set aside.

To the same skillet, add the mushrooms. Cook over medium heat, stirring, until moisture evaporates and mushrooms become golden. Add the shallots or scallions and garlic, and cook, stirring, until slightly softened. Sprinkle with flour, and cook until lightly colored. Add the wine, broth, and herbs. Stir to blend well. Return the chicken to the skillet. Bring to a boil, cover, and simmer gently for 25 to 30 minutes, or until tender.

Remove chicken and arrange on a platter. Discard the bay leaf. Skim the fat and pour sauce over the chicken.

Yield: 4 servings.

Baked Chicken with Parmesan

You will find a world of difference between the flavorless grated Parmesan that comes in jars and the cheese that you grate yourself. Keep a chunk of Parmesan in the refrigerator (it will keep well for weeks) and grate it as you need it.

3 tablespoons olive or vegetable oil

½ cup finely chopped parsley

1 teaspoon dried oregano or marjoram

Freshly ground pepper

2 to 4 cloves garlic, finely chopped

1 cup freshly grated Parmesan cheese

2 3- to 3½-pound chickens, quartered

1 cup dry white wine

Preheat the oven to 350 degrees.

Mix together the oil, parsley, oregano or marjoram, pepper, garlic, and cheese. (The cheese is salty so you do not need to add salt.) With your fingers or a spatula, spread some of the mixture on the skin side of the chicken pieces. Arrange in a shallow baking pan skin side up. Do not overlap the chicken pieces and do not crowd them. Use two pans if necessary. Pour the wine into the pan or pans. Bake for 1 hour, using a bulb baster to remove fat as it accumulates.

Yield: 4 to 6 servings.

Curried Chicken

Curry powder, a blend of herbs and spices, varies in strength. Experiment with several brands to find one that pleases your taste.

1 3½- to 4-pound chicken, cut into 8 pieces
Salt and freshly ground pepper
2 tablespoons butter
2 tablespoons olive or vegetable oil
1 medium onion, finely chopped
2 celery stalks, finely chopped
2 cloves garlic, finely chopped
3 tablespoons flour
1 to 2 tablespoons curry powder (or to taste)
2 greening or Granny Smith apples, peeled, cored, and cut into ½-inch cubes
1 tablespoon tomato paste
2 cups chicken broth
¼ cup raisins
¼ cup light cream

Dry chicken pieces well with paper towels. Sprinkle with salt and pepper.

Heat the butter and oil in a large heavy skillet and add the chicken pieces skin side down. Cook until golden brown on both sides, 6 to 7 minutes each side, turning with tongs. Remove the chicken to a platter and keep warm.

To the same skillet add the onion, celery, and garlic. Cook over medium heat until softened. Sprinkle with flour and stir until lightly colored. Add the curry powder, apples, tomato paste, chicken broth, and raisins. Stir until smooth and thickened.

Return the chicken to the skillet. Cover, bring to a boil, and simmer gently for 15 to 20 minutes, or until tender.

Remove chicken and arrange on a platter. Skim the fat from the sauce. Add the cream and heat gently but do not boil. Pour over the chicken. Serve hot with rice, yogurt, and chutney if desired.

Yield: 4 servings.

Fried Chicken

2 2½- to 3½-pound chickens, each
  cut into 8 pieces
1½ cups flour
1 tablespoon freshly ground black
  pepper
2 teaspoons salt
1½ cups peanut oil

Dry the chicken pieces well with paper towels. If they are damp, the oil will spatter. Combine flour, pepper, and salt in a large bag. Heat the oil slowly in a large skillet until it is 370 degrees (a 1-inch cube of stale bread should brown in 1 minute). When ready to cook, add the chicken to the flour mixture a few pieces at a time, and shake to coat evenly.

Add a few chicken pieces at a time, skin side down, to the fat. It should bubble briskly. After 10 to 15 minutes, turn the chicken with tongs and brown the other side for 10 to 15 minutes longer. Dark meat will take longer than white meat to cook. Remove to a wire rack and keep warm in a 170- to 200-degree oven until all the chicken is cooked. Arrange on a platter and serve immediately.

Yield: 4 to 6 servings.

Variations: Marinate the chicken in buttermilk to cover for 30 minutes before flouring. Or, just before frying, dredge chicken in flour, then dip into 2 eggs beaten with 2 tablespoons of water, then in flour again. Use your fingers to help the egg mixture adhere.

Oven-Fried Chicken

This method results in crunchy, brown-skinned chicken with very little work.

4 tablespoons sweet butter
1½ cups plain yogurt or buttermilk
1 egg, beaten
1½ cups flour
½ cup sesame seeds
Salt and freshly ground pepper
2 3- to 3½-pound chickens, each
  cut into 8 pieces
Lemon wedges
Parsley

Preheat the oven to 350 degrees.

Melt the butter in a small saucepan and set aside. Mix yogurt or buttermilk and egg together in one bowl. Blend the flour, sesame seeds, salt, and pepper in another bowl. Coat the chicken pieces with yogurt or buttermilk mixture, then dredge in the flour. Arrange skin side up in a shallow pan. If necessary, use two pans so that chicken pieces are not crowded.

Pour melted butter evenly over the chicken. Bake for 1 hour, basting often, until golden. Remove all the accumulated fat from the pan 15 to 20 minutes before the end of the cooking time. Arrange chicken on a platter and garnish with lemon and parsley.

Yield: 4 to 6 servings.

Baked Chicken in Wine

2 2- to 2½-pound broilers, cut into quarters
6 tablespoons butter
Salt and freshly ground pepper
½ teaspoon dried rosemary
4 or 5 shallots, finely chopped
2 cloves garlic, minced
Dry red wine

Preheat the broiler.

Wash the chicken pieces and pat them dry with paper towels. Place the chicken pieces skin side up in a shallow greased baking pan large enough to hold them in a single layer. Dot with half the butter and sprinkle lightly with salt and pepper. Broil them about 4 inches from the heat until the skin is nicely brown, about 10 minutes. Do not turn the chicken.

Remove the baking dish from the oven and reduce the heat to 350 degrees. Sprinkle the rosemary, shallots, and garlic over the chicken and dot with the remaining butter. Add wine to the depth of ½ inch. Return the pan to the oven and bake for 50 minutes, or until tender. Baste a few times and add more wine if the sauce seems to be drying out. Transfer the chicken to a heated platter and cover with sauce.

Yield: 4 to 6 servings.

Broiled Yogurt Chicken

1 cup plain yogurt or buttermilk
¼ cup brown sugar
4 garlic cloves, finely chopped
3 tablespoons cider vinegar
1 tablespoon soy sauce (Japanese preferred)
1 3½- to 4-pound chicken, cut into 6 or 8 pieces

Combine all the ingredients except the chicken in a food processor or blender and blend until smooth.

Place the chicken in a heavy plastic bag or nonaluminum bowl and pour the marinade over all. Seal tightly and refrigerate for 2 to 4 days. Turn as often as you think of it.

When ready to cook, preheat the broiler.

Remove the chicken from the marinade and wipe off most of the marinade. Arrange the chicken pieces skin side down on a wire rack set in a shallow pan. Place the pan as far from the heat as possible. Broil for 15 to 20 minutes; turn the chicken and broil for 20 to 25 minutes longer, or until golden and tender. Baste often with pan drippings.

Yield: 4 servings.

Soy Sauce Chicken

This is a classic method of poaching a chicken Chinese-style. It is called "red cooked."

1 3½ to 5 pound chicken

2 cups soy sauce (Japanese preferred)

6 cups water or chicken broth

½ teaspoon five spice powder, available in Oriental groceries, *or* ¼ teaspoon each ground cloves, fennel, and anise

¼ cup gin, vodka, or dry sherry

4 scallions, trimmed

2 slices fresh ginger (about the size of a quarter), *or* ½ teaspoon ground

2 tablespoons sugar

1 to 2 tablespoons sesame oil, available in Oriental groceries (optional)

Truss the chicken and set aside. Put all the ingredients except the sugar and sesame oil into a pot just large enough to hold the chicken and bring to a boil. Add the chicken breast side down (the liquid will not cover it). Adjust the heat to the lowest point (use a flame control device, if necessary), cover, and cook for 1 hour. Turn the chicken over with a wooden spoon, add the sugar, and continue to cook for 30 to 60 minutes longer, depending on size. The liquid should never boil.

Remove the trussing string and chop chicken with a cleaver into bite-size pieces. Sprinkle a little of the cooking liquid and sesame oil over the chicken. Serve warm or cool. Strain and refrigerate the cooking liquid. Cornish hens, pork shoulder, or fowl can be cooked in the same soy liquid; it will improve in flavor each time.

Yield: 4 to 6 servings.

(That Ol') Devil Chicken

For the best flavor, use a good-quality mustard rather than the bland, ball-park variety.

2 2- to 2½ pound chickens, split

4 tablespoons melted butter

2 tablespoons Dijon or Düsseldorf mustard

1 clove garlic, chopped

1 teaspoon dried tarragon or thyme, crumbled

Salt and freshly ground pepper

Freshly chopped parsley

Preheat the broiler to medium, 350 to 375 degrees, if possible.

Arrange the chickens skin side down on a wire rack in a shallow pan. Brush with butter and mustard on both sides. Sprinkle with garlic, tarragon or thyme, and salt and pepper.

Place the pan as far away from the heat as possible. Broil for 20 to 25 minutes, basting often. Turn the chicken with tongs and continue to broil for 15 to 20 minutes longer, or until golden brown. Baste often with the pan drippings.

Transfer to a warm platter and sprinkle with chopped parsley.

Yield: 4 servings.

Poached Chicken Breasts

Poaching chicken breasts gives you large, solid pieces of cooked white meat that are useful for such dishes as Hot Chicken Salad (page 403), or for times when you need a small amount of white meat chicken. Poaching them in the oven is the perfect method of cooking. They are done in a matter of minutes, but must be timed carefully. Overcooking will make them tough and stringy.

3 whole chicken breasts, boned, skinned, and trimmed of fat
2 tablespoons butter
2 tablespoons lemon juice
Salt and freshly ground pepper
2 tablespoons dry white wine
½ cup chicken stock

Preheat the oven to 450 degrees. Wash and dry the chicken breasts and cut in two. Use half the butter to grease a baking dish that will hold them snugly. Arrange the breasts in the dish and sprinkle with lemon juice, salt, and pepper. Pour in the wine and chicken stock and dot with the remaining butter. Cover the dish tightly with aluminum foil. Place in the oven for 8 to 10 minutes, depending on the size of the breasts. To test, press the center of a breast with your finger. If it is soft and spongy, it needs a few minutes more; if it is slightly resistant to the touch and springs back, it is done.

Yield: 6 servings.

Variations: Poached chicken breasts, known in classic French cooking as suprêmes de volaille, make splendid main courses. Serve on a bed of spinach purée and top with a rich cream sauce or cover with a fine homemade tomato sauce sprinkled with Parmesan cheese or a wine-flavored cream sauce topped with mushrooms that have been sautéed or poached.

Chicken Breasts Piquante

4 boneless and skinless chicken
  breasts (¾ to 1 pound each)
Salt and freshly ground pepper
Flour for dredging
4 to 6 tablespoons butter
2 to 4 tablespoons olive or
  vegetable oil
2 tablespoons flour
½ cup Madeira
1 cup chicken broth
¼ cup fresh lemon juice
Finely chopped fresh parsley

Cut each breast in half. Pound between pieces of wax paper or plastic wrap until very thin. Pat dry and season with salt and pepper. Dredge in flour, shaking off any excess. Heat 2 tablespoons butter and 2 tablespoons oil in a large nonaluminum skillet. Add as many chicken breasts as will fit in one layer without crowding. Cook for 2 to 3 minutes on each side, or until golden brown. Remove to a platter lined with paper towels and keep warm in a 170- to 200-degree oven while preparing the remaining breasts. Add more butter and oil to the skillet as needed.

When all the chicken has been cooked, wipe out the pan with a paper towel. Melt 2 tablespoons butter and add the flour. Stir with a whisk until golden. Add Madeira and broth, whisking constantly until thickened and smooth, about 5 minutes. Skim fat as it rises to the surface. Add lemon juice.

Return the chicken to the skillet. Heat very briefly in the sauce, no more than 1 to 2 minutes. Sprinkle with parsley.

Yield: 4 to 6 servings.

Chicken Rollups

2 whole large chicken breasts,
  skinned, boned, split, and
  pounded thin
Salt and freshly ground pepper
¼ pound (1 stick) sweet butter at
  room temperature
2 tablespoons finely chopped
  shallots or scallions (white part
  only)
¼ cup finely chopped parsley
½ teaspoon dried tarragon
Grated peel and juice of 1 lemon
1 tablespoon peanut or corn oil
Flour for dredging
½ cup dry white wine
¾ cup chicken broth
¼ cup heavy or light cream

Arrange the chicken on a flat surface and season with salt and pepper. Whisk 6 tablespoons butter until soft and fluffy. Add half the shallots or scallions, half the parsley, the tarragon, grated lemon rind, and 1 tablespoon lemon juice and mix well. Spread the mixture evenly over each breast. Roll up from the short side, jelly-roll style, into neat packages. Chill for 30 minutes.

Heat the remaining butter and oil in a heavy skillet. Dredge the chicken in flour, shaking off any excess. Brown in the skillet for 6 to 8 minutes, turning several times. Remove to a warm platter.

Add the remaining shallots or scallions to the skillet and stir until softened. Add the wine and broth. Cook over high heat until the liquid is reduced by half. Add the cream and heat gently; do not boil. Skim the fat if necessary. Return the chicken to the pan. Turn the rolls over in the sauce until all are hot and the sauce is slightly thickened, 1 to 2 minutes. Sprinkle with the remaining parsley and serve hot.

Yield: 4 servings.

Chicken Strips Sauté

2 pounds boneless, skinless chicken breasts, cut into finger-size strips
1 cup flour
1 tablespoon paprika (optional)
½ teaspoon salt
2 to 4 tablespoons butter
2 to 4 tablespoons oil
2 to 3 cloves garlic, finely chopped
¼ cup fresh lemon juice (about 1 large lemon)
2 to 3 tablespoons finely chopped fresh parsley

Just before cooking, dredge one-third of the chicken in flour mixed with paprika and salt. Shake and toss in a colander to remove any excess flour so that the pieces of chicken remain separate and do not stick together.

Heat 2 tablespoons butter and 2 tablespoons oil in a large nonaluminum skillet. When hot, add the chicken and stir-fry until lightly browned, about 3 minutes. Remove to a platter and keep warm in a 170- to 200-degree oven. Add more butter and oil to the skillet if necessary, and repeat the flouring and cooking process with all the chicken.

Return all the chicken strips to the skillet. Over high heat, add the garlic and stir to mix well. Add the lemon juice and parsley and stir to mix. Remove from the heat and serve with green noodles.

Yield: 4 servings.

Sesame Chicken

This is equally good hot or cold, and makes wonderful picnic fare.

2 pounds skinned and boned chicken breasts
½ cup flour
Salt and freshly ground pepper
2 eggs, beaten with 2 tablespoons water
2 cups fine, fresh bread crumbs
⅓ cup sesame seeds
1 cup corn or peanut oil (or enough oil in the skillet to measure ½ inch)
Lemon slices
Parsley sprigs

Cut each chicken breast in half and pound between sheets of wax paper or plastic wrap until thin. Dredge in flour mixed with salt and pepper, shaking off any excess. Dip the chicken into the egg mixture then into bread crumbs mixed with sesame seeds. Use your fingers to pat the crumbs so that they will adhere. Place on a baking sheet in one layer and refrigerate for 20 to 30 minutes.

Heat the oil slowly in a large skillet. When hot (370 degrees), slide a few pieces of chicken into the fat. Do not crowd the pan. Cook for 3 to 5 minutes on each side. Remove and drain on a wire rack or on paper towels. Keep warm in a 170- to 200-degree oven while cooking the remaining chicken.

Arrange on a warm platter and garnish with lemon slices and parsley sprigs.

Yield: 4 servings.

Chicken Patties

2 pounds skinless and boneless
  chicken breasts
¼ cup finely chopped scallions
  (white part only)
4 slices bread, finely shredded
½ cup sour cream
Salt and freshly ground pepper
2 tablespoons vegetable oil
2 tablespoons butter
Fine bread crumbs for dredging
Lemon wedges
Parsley sprigs

Remove fat and tendons from the chicken and cut the chicken into small cubes. Place in a food processor or blender and process until coarsely chopped. If using a blender, you will have to do this in several batches. Scrape down as necessary.

Spoon the chicken into a mixing bowl and add the scallions, bread, sour cream, salt, and pepper. Mix well with wet fingers because the mixture will be sticky.

Divide the mixture into 8 patties and place them on a baking sheet in one layer. Cover and refrigerate for 1 to 2 hours.

Heat the oil and butter in a large heavy skillet. Dredge the patties in bread crumbs and sauté for 3 minutes on each side, or until golden brown and cooked through. Do not crowd the pan. Transfer cooked patties to a platter and keep warm in a 170- to 200-degree oven while cooking remaining chicken.

Arrange on a platter and garnish with lemon wedges and parsley.

If you wish, serve with Mushroom Sauce (page 455), or Tomato Sauce (page 456).

Yield: 4 servings.

Variation: If fresh leeks are available, use them in place of the scallions for a subtly different flavor. Use only the white part of the leeks.

Chicken Pie

A perfect fall or winter meal.

1 3- to 3½-pound chicken, cut into
  8 pieces
Salt and freshly ground pepper
3 carrots, peeled, trimmed, and
  thinly sliced
2 celery stalks, thinly sliced
1 large onion, coarsely chopped
Chicken broth to cover
6 tablespoons sweet butter
6 tablespoons flour
½ cup light cream

Put the chicken in a large kettle and add salt, pepper, carrots, celery, onion, and chicken broth to cover. Bring slowly to a boil, which will take 45 minutes to 1 hour. Turn off the heat and let the chicken cool in the broth, about 1 hour.

Drain, reserving the broth and vegetables. Skin and bone the chicken and cut it into large chunks. Return skin and bones to the broth and continue to cook until reduced and concentrated in flavor.

Melt the butter in a large saucepan and add the flour. Cook, stirring, until golden. Add 3 cups reserved chicken broth, whisk-

1 package frozen artichoke hearts, each cut in half, *or* half a 10-ounce package frozen peas
2 tablespoons lemon juice
1 pie crust (see page 501)
1 egg beaten with 1 tablespoon water or milk

ing constantly. Simmer for 5 minutes or until sauce is thickened and smooth. Add the cream, artichoke hearts or peas, lemon juice, reserved vegetables, and chicken. Taste and correct seasoning.

Preheat the oven to 400 degrees.

Spoon the mixture into a shallow, 2-quart baking dish (round or rectangular). Arrange the pie crust over the filling and flute the edge. Cut several slits in top. Brush with the egg and water mixture. Bake for 25 to 30 minutes, or until filling is hot and pastry is golden brown. Brush several times during baking. Serve immediately on warm plates.

Yield: 4 to 6 servings.

Oven-Barbecued Chicken Wings

These are great finger foods for a party and are simple to prepare. Allow two wings a person if serving with other dishes.

3 to 4 pounds chicken wings
1 cup soy sauce
1 cup orange, apricot, or peach preserves
3 cloves garlic, finely chopped
1 tablespoon freshly grated ginger
¼ cup dry sherry, gin, or vodka

Place the chicken wings in a heavy plastic bag or nonaluminum bowl. Mix the remaining ingredients and pour over the wings. Seal or cover tightly and refrigerate overnight.

Preheat the oven to 350 degrees.

Remove the chicken from the marinade and place on a wire rack in one layer. Set the rack in a shallow pan and add water to pan to a depth of ½ inch. (This allows the fat to drip into the pan without smoking.)

Bake for 1 hour, or until tender, basting often with the marinade. Arrange on a platter and serve hot.

Yield: 2 to 4 servings.

Chicken Fricassee in Onion-Dill Sauce

This is a delicate chicken dish bathed in a creamy white sauce flecked with green. To bring out its full flavor, prepare it in advance and slowly reheat it at serving time.

2 2½- to 3-pound chickens, cut
    into quarters
3 tablespoons butter
4 large onions, thinly sliced
2 cloves garlic, finely chopped
Salt and freshly ground pepper
3 tablespoons flour
⅓ cup dry white wine
⅓ cup snipped fresh dill

Trim the chicken quarters of all fat and loose skin and set aside.

Melt the butter in a heavy pan. Add the onions and cook over medium heat until limp and transparent, stirring often. Do not let the onions brown. Add the garlic, salt, and pepper. Mix well and cook for another minute or two.

Layer the chicken sections over the bed of onions, cover the pot tightly, and cook over low heat until the chicken is cooked through, 45 to 50 minutes.

Remove the chicken pieces and purée the onions in a blender. Return the purée to the pot and sprinkle with the flour. Cook over medium heat, stirring constantly, until the sauce comes to the boil and is thick and smooth. Reduce the heat, add the wine and snipped dill and mix well. Taste for seasoning and correct. Return the chicken to the pot and cover completely with the sauce. At this point, the chicken may be cooled and covered.

At serving time, heat slowly until warmed through. Serve with rice, noodles, or small new potatoes, steamed in their skins.

Yield: 4 to 6 servings.

Garlic Chicken

Despite the large amount of garlic, you will be surprised at how mild the flavor is. In fact, you might wish to increase the amount you use the next time around.

1 or 2 whole heads of garlic,
    carefully separated into cloves
2 cups water
2 cups chicken broth
3 tablespoons butter
1 3½- to 4-pound chicken, cut into
    quarters
Salt and freshly ground pepper
3 tablespoons flour
½ cup dry white wine

Put the garlic cloves in a small saucepan, cover with the water, and bring to a boil. Lower the heat and simmer for 10 minutes. Drain and rinse under cold water. Carefully slip the skins off the garlic. Do not crush the cloves.

In the same saucepan, bring broth to a boil, add the garlic, and simmer for 30 to 40 minutes. Remove the garlic from the broth and reserve both separately.

Melt the butter in a large skillet or shallow casserole. Add the chicken pieces, skin side down, and brown well on all sides (12

1 whole lemon, peeled of all white membrane and thinly sliced

to 15 minutes total time). Season with salt and pepper. Remove the chicken with tongs or a slotted spoon and reserve.

Preheat the oven to 325 degrees.

Discard all but a thin film of fat from the skillet. Add the flour and stir and cook until golden. Add the wine and stir, scraping the pan to dissolve any browned bits. Add the broth and stir with a whisk or spoon until thickened.

Return the chicken to the skillet or casserole. Scatter garlic cloves and lemon slices over all. Bring to a boil, transfer to the oven, and bake for 45 minutes to 1 hour, or until the chicken is tender.

Arrange the chicken on a warm platter. Skim the fat from the sauce and pour the sauce over the chicken. Serve with noodles or rice.

Yield: 4 servings.

Chicken Livers with Wine

1 pound chicken livers
2 to 3 tablespoons butter
2 to 3 tablespoons vegetable oil
1 pound fresh mushrooms, thinly sliced
¼ cup finely chopped shallots or onion
1½ tablespoons flour
¼ cup Madeira or Marsala
1 cup chicken broth
2 tablespoons lemon juice
Freshly chopped parsley

Trim the livers of fat and bile sac. Separate the halves and dry thoroughly.

Heat 2 tablespoons each butter and oil in a large, heavy skillet. Add the mushrooms and cook, stirring constantly, until liquid evaporates and they begin to brown. With a slotted spoon, remove to a plate and keep warm.

In the same skillet (add additional fat if necessary), cook half the chicken livers, stirring, until they are brown and crusty, about 1½ to 2 minutes. They should remain pink inside. Remove and set aside with the mushrooms. Continue until all the livers are browned.

Add the shallots or onion to the skillet and cook, stirring, until softened. Sprinkle with flour and stir until lightly colored. Add the Madeira and broth and bring to a boil, stirring constantly until smooth and thickened, 5 to 6 minutes. Skim the fat that will collect at the surface.

Return the mushrooms, livers, and any accumulated juices to the sauce. Heat briefly until warmed through. Add lemon juice, sprinkle with parsley, and serve immediately.

Yield: 3 to 4 servings.

Chicken Liver-Mushroom Pâté

With its rich, creamy texture and fine flavor, this pâté makes a delicious appetizer.

1 pound chicken livers
½ pound mushrooms
4 tablespoons butter
1 small onion, coarsely chopped
1 teaspoon paprika
1 clove garlic, crushed
1 tablespoon snipped fresh dill, *or*
  1 teaspoon dried
Few dashes of Tabasco sauce
½ cup (1 stick) cold butter
Salt and freshly ground pepper
½ cup finely minced parsley
6 pitted black olives, cut into
  crescents

Trim livers of fat and bile sack. Dry well on paper towels. Wipe mushrooms with a damp paper towel; trim a thin slice from the stems and discard. Chop the mushrooms coarsely.

In a large skillet, melt the butter and sauté the onion over medium heat until golden. Add the livers, mushrooms, paprika, and garlic and cook for 10 minutes, stirring. Add the dill and cook for 5 to 10 minutes longer, or until the livers are browned and the mushrooms tender. Add the Tabasco.

Drain the chicken liver mixture through a fine strainer. Save the liquid and use it for a sauce or soup; it is delicious, but unless it is completely drained off, it will make the pâté too soft. Place the drained liver and mushroom mixture in a blender or food processor with ½ cup butter cut into chunks. Process until smooth. If you are doing this in a blender, you will have to do it in batches. Remove from the container and add salt and pepper to taste, and perhaps another drop of Tabasco, if you think it needs it. Pack in a lightly oiled 3-cup mold (a small loaf pan will do). It will be quite runny, but it will firm up in the refrigerator. Cover mold with plastic wrap and refrigerate overnight. Unmold to serve. Frost the sides with chopped parsley and decorate the top with crescents of black olives. Serve with melba toast or thin slices of black bread. The pâté will stay fresh in the refrigerator for 3 or 4 days.

Yield: 10 to 12 servings.

Roast Rock Cornish Hens

4 to 6 Rock Cornish hens, fresh or defrosted (1¼ to 1½ pounds each)
½ cup olive or vegetable oil
1 cup dry white wine
⅓ cup lemon juice
1 medium onion, thinly sliced
2 tablespoons finely chopped shallots or scallions (white part only)
2 tablespoons dried tarragon
3 tablespoons flour
2 cups chicken broth

Put the Cornish hens in a large heavy plastic bag or non-aluminum bowl. Combine the remaining ingredients except the flour and broth and pour over the hens. Cover tightly and refrigerate for 24 hours.

Preheat the oven to 425 degrees.

Remove the hens from the marinade, truss, and arrange on a rack in a large roasting pan. Roast for 35 to 45 minutes, basting every 10 minutes with the marinade. Hens are done when the juices run clear and the internal temperature is 170 to 175 degrees.

Transfer to a warm platter. Remove the trussing string and cover lightly while preparing the sauce. Strain the pan juices into a cup or bowl. Skim off all but 3 tablespoons fat. Put the 3 tablespoons of fat in a small saucepan, add the flour, and cook, stirring, until golden. Rinse out the roasting pan with the pan juices and the chicken broth, scraping loose the brown particles, and add to the saucepan. Whisk constantly until thickened and smooth. Serve immediately with the hens.

Yield: 4 to 6 servings.

Cornish Hens with Vinegar Sauce

6 tablespoons butter
4 1-pound Cornish hens, split, or 1 3½- to 4-pound chicken, cut into 8 pieces
Salt and freshly ground pepper
¼ cup finely chopped shallots
½ cup wine vinegar
1 tablespoon dried tarragon
1 cup chicken broth

Preheat the oven to 425 degrees.

Melt 4 tablespoons of butter in a large, flameproof casserole. Brown the hens, lightly, two at a time, on both sides. Do not crowd the pan. Season with salt and pepper. Arrange hens in the pan, cover, and transfer to the oven. Bake for 20 to 30 minutes, or until tender.

Transfer the hens to a serving platter and keep warm while preparing the sauce.

Add the shallots to the casserole and cook on top of the stove until golden. Add the vinegar and tarragon and cook over high heat, stirring constantly, until vinegar is reduced by half. Add the chicken broth and bring to a boil. Add the remaining butter. Remove from the heat and pour over the hens.

Yield: 4 servings.

Roast Turkey

1 12- to 15-pound turkey (reserve neck, giblets, and liver)
1 small onion, peeled and sliced
1 carrot, trimmed and sliced
1 celery stalk, sliced
2 sprigs parsley
1 small bay leaf
Salt and freshly ground pepper
Chicken broth or water

Stuffing:
6 cups cubed bread (use a combination of breads—corn, rye, white—if desired)
3 sticks butter
2 large onions, coarsely chopped
4 to 6 celery stalks, with leaves, peeled and coarsely chopped
1 pound mixed dried fruit, snipped into small pieces with scissors
½ teaspoon dried thyme
½ tablespoon dried basil
¼ teaspoon (scant) dried leaf sage, crumbled
½ cup fresh chopped parsley
2 to 4 tablespoons vegetable oil
Giblet gravy (recipe follows)

Put turkey neck and giblets into a medium-size saucepan along with the onion, carrot, celery, parsley, bay leaf, salt, pepper, and chicken broth or water to cover. Bring to a boil. Partly cover, lower the heat to a simmer, and cook for 1 to 1½ hours. Add the liver during the last 10 minutes. Remove the giblets and neck meat and chop coarsely. Skim fat from broth. Reserve chopped giblets and broth for gravy. Discard the liver and bay leaf.

Scatter the bread cubes on a cookie sheet and dry in a 170- to 180-degree oven until crisp but not brown, 1 to 1½ hours.

Melt 2 sticks of butter in a skillet, add the onion and celery, and cook until softened. Scrape into a large bowl. Add the bread cubes, dried fruit, thyme, basil, sage, parsley, salt, and pepper. Mix well.

Preheat the oven to 325 degrees.

Just before cooking the turkey, lightly stuff the neck and breast cavities. Do not overpack because the stuffing will swell. Leftover stuffing may be dotted with butter and cooked in a baking dish along with the turkey.

Sew or skewer the neck and breast cavities closed, truss well, and rub all over with oil. Arrange a heavily buttered strip of foil on a rack to prevent the breast from sticking.

Arrange the bird breast side down on the rack and set in a shallow pan. Add any remaining butter to the pan. Transfer to the oven.

Cook for 15 to 18 minutes a pound, or until internal temperature is 185 degrees in the thigh and 170 degrees in the breast. Baste the turkey every 15 to 20 minutes with a bulb baster. For the last 30 minutes, carefully turn the bird breast side up. (Use cotton work gloves or pot holders.) Carefully remove the foil and allow the breast to brown. Baste the breast every 10 minutes. Remove from pan, cover loosely with foil, and allow to rest for 20 to 30 minutes before carving.

Yield: 8 to 10 servings.

Giblet Gravy

4 tablespoons fat
4 tablespoons flour
3 cups reserved turkey broth
¼ cup light cream or half-and-half
Reserved turkey giblets

Remove all but 4 tablespoons fat from the roasting pan. Place the pan on top of the stove and add the flour. Stir until golden. Add the turkey broth and whisk until well blended, scraping loose any brown bits that cling to the pan. Simmer 10 minutes, stirring constantly. Add the cream and giblets and heat through but do not boil. Taste and correct seasoning. Serve hot with turkey and stuffing.

Turkey Cannelloni

Turkey breast is a solid, economical piece of meat that can be used in dishes calling for veal scallops or chicken breasts.

2 pounds boneless, skinless turkey breast, cut into 12 slices and pounded thin
Salt and freshly ground pepper
2 tablespoons Dijon or Düsseldorf mustard
¼ teaspoon dried thyme, crumbled
¼ teaspoon dried basil, crumbled
¼ pound Swiss or Fontina cheese, thinly sliced
¼ pound ham, thinly sliced
3 tablespoons olive or vegetable oil
Flour for dredging
1 clove garlic, finely chopped
½ pound fresh mushrooms, thinly sliced
1 1-pound, 12-ounce can Italian plum tomatoes, well drained and chopped (about 1 cup)
2 tablespoons finely chopped parsley

Arrange the turkey slices on a flat surface. Season with salt and pepper. Spread each slice with a dab of mustard. Sprinkle with the thyme and basil. Arrange a slice of cheese and ham on each breast. Roll up jelly-roll fashion. Press closed with your fingers and skewer with a toothpick. Chill until ready to cook.

Heat the oil in a large heavy skillet. Dredge the turkey in flour, shaking off any excess. When the oil is hot, sauté the turkey, turning several times, until well browned on all sides, 6 to 8 minutes. Remove to a warm platter.

Add the garlic and mushrooms to the fat remaining in the pan. Cook, stirring, until the excess moisture evaporates and mushrooms are golden. Add the chopped tomatoes. Bring to a boil and lower the heat. Return the rolls to the pan and cover. Simmer gently until tender, 10 to 15 minutes. Remove toothpicks, arrange rolls on a platter, pour sauce over, and sprinkle with parsley.

Yield: 4 to 6 servings.

Turkey Piccata

1 pound boneless skinless turkey breast, cut into ½-inch slices
Flour for dredging
Salt and freshly ground pepper
2 tablespoons butter
2 tablespoons vegetable oil
2 to 4 tablespoons lemon juice
¼ cup chicken broth
1 lemon, thinly sliced, seeds removed
Fresh parsley sprigs

Place the turkey slices between sheets of wax paper or plastic wrap and pound with a mallet or the bottom of a small cast iron skillet until thin.

Dredge the slices in flour mixed with salt and pepper, shaking off any excess. Heat half the butter and oil in a large nonaluminum skillet. When hot, brown the slices, a few at a time, on both sides. Add more butter and oil as needed. Remove to a platter and keep warm.

Add the lemon juice and broth to the skillet and stir to dissolve any brown bits adhering to the pan. Bring to a boil and pour over the turkey slices. Garnish with lemon and parsley.

Yield: 2 to 4 servings.

Note: Do not flour the turkey slices until just before cooking; otherwise they will become sticky and not brown well. If you can, buy a breast that is skinless and boneless. A 1½-pound skinless, boneless turkey breast will give you 10 to 12 slices. When cutting the breast, slice on the bias and try to cut pieces of about the same size. Chicken breasts, of course, can be used in place of the turkey slices.

Broiled Duck

Broiling produces crisply browned duck that can be cooked rare or well-done.

1 4- to 5-pound duck
½ lemon
Salt and freshly ground pepper

Place the duck in a large kettle, cover with boiling water, and simmer for 20 minutes. Remove from the water, drain thoroughly, and place on a rack. This can be done well in advance of dinner; the final cooking takes less than an hour.

When ready to cook, preheat the broiler for 15 minutes. Split the duck in half, lengthwise, and cut each half in two. Trim away any loose skin and remove as much fat as you can. Pat the duck quarters dry. Rub the bone sides with the cut lemon and rub both skin and bone sides with salt and pepper.

Arrange the duck pieces skin side down on the broiler rack and place the pan 4 inches below the heat. Broil slowly at first and increase the heat as you go along to avoid the danger of burning before the duck is cooked through. Broil on the bone side for 20 minutes. Remove the broiler pan from the oven and pour off the fat. Turn the duck pieces with tongs and prick the skin to release the fat. Return the duck to the oven skin side up, and broil for 20 to 25 minutes longer. If at any time you think that the duck is browning too fast or that the skin is in danger of burning, lower the heat or move the pan farther away, if possible. At this point, the skin should be crisply brown and the duck slightly under-done. Test for doneness by making a cut between the thigh and the body. If the juices are red, cook it a little longer, but if they are slightly tinged with pink, it is done to the rare stage. For well-done, broil 5 minutes longer.

Remove to a heated platter and serve with Orange Sauce or Cherry Sauce (see page 177).

Yield: 2 to 4 servings.

Crisp Roast Duck

This method of roasting duck produces a very crisp skin and juicy meat. If you remove the fat from the pan frequently, you'll have a less smoky kitchen.

1 4½- to 5-pound fresh or
   defrosted duckling
1 carrot
1 celery stalk
1 small onion
2 to 4 sprigs parsley
Water to cover
Salt and freshly ground pepper
1 tablespoon caraway seeds
   (optional)

Reserve the liver and put the duck giblets and wing tips in a saucepan with the carrot, celery, onion, and parsley. Cover with water and bring to a boil, then simmer for 1 to 1½ hours. Strain the broth, skim the fat, and reserve if you are making a sauce.

Remove excess fat from duck. It is not necessary to truss it. Bring a large kettle of water to a boil, add the duck and simmer for 30 minutes. Carefully remove from the water, drain well, and place breast down on a rack or in a shallow roasting pan.

Preheat the oven to 450 degrees.

Sprinkle the duck inside and out with salt, pepper, and caraway seeds. (If preparing a sweet sauce, omit the caraway.) Prick the skin of the duck well, particularly around the legs. Roast for 1 hour. Remove the fat with a bulb baster as it accumulates and discard.

After 1 hour, turn the duck breast side up and continue to cook for 30 to 45 minutes longer, or until the skin is crisp and brown. Transfer to a serving platter and cut with shears or a cleaver into two or four pieces. Serve with sautéed potatoes, red cabbage, and applesauce, if desired. Sauté the reserved duck liver in 1 to 2 tablespoons of butter with 1 small chopped onion, and serve with the duck.

Yield: 2 to 4 servings.

Roast Duck with Cherry Sauce

1 roast duck (see recipe for Crisp Roast Duck, but omit caraway)
1 1-pound can dark pitted cherries
2 tablespoons sugar
½ cup Madeira
1 tablespoon cornstarch

Drain the cherries and reserve the juice.

Remove the duck from the roasting pan and keep warm. Discard all the fat from the pan and place the roaster on top of the stove. Add the sugar and Madeira and scrape with a wooden spoon to dissolve any bits that adhere to the pan. Cook over high heat until the wine almost evaporates. Add the cherry juice, less 2 tablespoons, and bring to a boil. Add cherries and heat through. Add the cornstarch mixed with the 2 tablespoons of cherry juice and stir until thickened. Serve in a gravy boat, with the duck.

Roast Duck with Orange Sauce

1 roast duck (see recipe for Crisp Roast Duck, but omit caraway)
1 tablespoon sugar
1 tablespoon wine vinegar
1 cup reserved duck broth
1 cup freshly squeezed orange juice
2 tablespoons lemon juice
2 tablespoons cornstarch
2 tablespoons cold water
2 tablespoons Grand Marnier (optional)
Orange wedges for garnish
Watercress for garnish

Remove the duck from the roasting pan and keep warm. Discard all the fat from the roaster. Place pan on top the stove and add the sugar and vinegar. Heat slowly until the sugar melts and darkens in color.

Add the duck broth and orange and lemon juices. Stir, scraping loose any brown bits from the bottom of the pan. Simmer for 10 minutes. Add cornstarch mixed with water and stir to mix well. Cook until smooth and thickened, 3 to 4 minutes. Add the Grand Marnier and stir to blend. Remove from heat. Carve the duck into quarters or halves and cover with sauce. Garnish platter with orange slices and watercress, if desired. Pass extra sauce in a gravy boat.

Roast Goose

Goose fat is one of the bonuses of roasting a goose. It is wonderful for cooking chicken livers, browning onions and potatoes, and flavoring sauerkraut and red cabbage.

1 12-pound goose, fresh or
   defrosted, with giblets
2 tablespoons caraway seeds
Salt and freshly ground pepper
1 onion, sliced
1 celery stalk, trimmed and sliced
1 carrot, peeled, trimmed, and
   sliced
3 cups water
4 tablespoons reserved goose fat
2 tablespoons flour
1 small onion, coarsely chopped

Remove excess fat from the goose, render (see page 150), and reserve for cooking. Cut off wings and put in a medium-size saucepan with the giblets (reserve the liver).

Bring a large pot of water to a boil. Carefully plunge the goose into the water and simmer for 25 to 30 minutes.

Preheat the oven to 325 degrees. Season the cavity of the goose with the caraway seeds, salt, and pepper. Arrange on a rack in a shallow roasting pan and roast for 3 to 3½ hours. Remove the fat with a bulb baster as it accumulates and place it in a heatproof jar. (Treat it like liquid gold!)

Meanwhile, add the onion, celery, and carrot to the saucepan with the wings and giblets. Add 3 cups of water and bring to a boil. Lower the heat, partly cover, and simmer for 1 to 1½ hours or until tender. Remove giblets and chop coarsely. Reserve.

Heat 2 tablespoons of reserved goose fat in a small saucepan and add the flour. Cook, stirring, until golden. Whisk in some of the giblet stock and then blend the two. Return giblets to stock. Stir or whisk to mix well. Cook an additional 10 minutes and reserve.

Heat 2 tablespoons goose fat in a small skillet. When hot, cook the goose liver and onion until the onion is golden and the liver still pink inside. Reserve.

When the goose is cooked (the drumstick meat should feel soft to the touch and the joint will move easily), arrange on a warm platter. Lightly cover and let stand for 15 to 20 minutes. Carve into sections and serve with bread dumplings, red cabbage, apple sauce, and cucumber salad. Serve the giblet soup as a first course or reserve for another meal. Serve the goose liver with black bread to two favorite people.

Yield: 6 to 8 servings.

Game Birds

Guinea hen, quail, and pheasant are wild birds that are raised commercially. Their taste is similar to that of other domestic birds, but they are a little gamier and need careful basting or barding to compensate for their dryness. They are in limited supply and expensive, but they bring a festive touch to a special occasion.

The guinea hen, with its bulbous, big-breasted body, is considered the sweater girl of the fowl world. It weighs about 2 pounds or a bit more and will serve two people. Any method of cooking chickens can be adapted to guinea hen. It can be split and grilled, roasted or braised. Roasting takes from 30 to 45 minutes in a 350 degree oven. Cumberland sauce, a sweet-spicy sauce, is a popular accompaniment.

Pheasant weigh 2 to 3 pounds. The hen is recommended over the male because it is larger and a bit fatter, and its meat is smoother, more tender, and less dry. The male must be braised to give it additional juiciness. Allow one bird for two servings.

Quail has a less gamy taste than other game birds and is considered a great delicacy among its admirers. It weighs approximately 3 to 5 ounces and requires two birds per serving. It is almost totally lacking in fat and must be well barded if it is to be roasted.

All game birds, except quail and similar small creatures, should be hung before plucking and eviscerating to tenderize and improve flavor. If a hunter friend happens to give you a freshly killed game bird, the easiest way to handle it is to ask your butcher to hang, dress, and eviscerate it. Game birds are hung, unplucked and undrawn, by their beaks or by their feet in a cool spot. The period of hanging varies, depending on the age of the bird, the weather, and individual taste for degree of gaminess. For really good eating, a game bird should be young. Young birds can be roasted; older ones must be braised. Wild birds that have dined off plants and berries instead of the artificially processed grains on which domesticated stock is nourished are, naturally, leaner than the domestic variety and generally need additional fat. Wrap the breast with a piece of salt pork or bacon, which you will discard after cooking.

Wild Game Birds

Wild game birds—pheasant, quail, partridge, duck, and goose—can be hunted only during special seasons in the United States and Canada, which vary from state to state and province to province. Wild game should not be confused with its commercially raised and domesticated relatives, which can be purchased at any time of the year, often frozen.

Braised Quail

4 tablespoons (½ stick) clarified butter (see page 260)
8 3- to 3½-ounce quail, split down the back and opened flat
½ cup Madeira or Marsala
1 cup chicken broth
Salt and freshly ground pepper

Heat the butter in a large skillet and brown the birds, a few at a time, on both sides. Turn with tongs so you do not pierce the skin. Transfer to a dish as they brown.

Preheat the oven to 325 degrees.

Pour off the fat from the skillet. Add the wine to the remaining juices, stirring to dissolve any brown bits adhering to the pan. Add the broth and bring to a boil. Return the birds to the skillet (or to a heatproof casserole or roaster if the skillet is too small), overlapping if necessary. Season with salt and pepper, cover, and transfer to the oven. Bake for 15 to 20 minutes. Remove cover and continue cooking for 10 to 15 minutes longer, or until quail are brown and tender. Transfer the birds to a warm platter. Skim and discard the fat from pan juices and pour juices over the birds.

Yield: 4 servings.

Braised Pheasant

3 pheasant (2 to 2½ pounds each)
1 large bunch scallions, coarsely chopped
2 large greening or Granny Smith apples, peeled, cored, and thinly sliced
4 tablespoons butter
1 cup dry white or red wine
½ cup chicken broth
½ cup heavy cream or sour cream
Salt and freshly ground pepper
Watercress for garnish (optional)

Remove the livers and chop. Combine with the scallions and apples. Divide evenly and stuff and truss each bird.

Melt the butter in a heavy skillet. Brown the birds well on all sides. Use spoons to turn them so as not to break the skin. Transfer the birds to an ovenproof casserole. (They can fit tightly.)

Preheat the oven to 400 degrees.

Discard the fat in the skillet and add wine and broth. Bring to a boil. Lower the heat and simmer gently for 2 to 3 minutes. Pour over the birds, cover tightly, and transfer to the oven. Cook for 35 to 45 minutes, or until tender. The age of the birds will determine the cooking time. Check often to make sure they don't overcook.

Remove the pheasant to a platter, discard trussing strings, and keep warm while preparing the sauce. Skim any fat from the pan juices. Bring to a boil on top the stove and whisk in the cream. Heat but do not boil the sauce or it will curdle. Taste and adjust the seasonings. Split each pheasant in half with poultry shears and garnish with watercress, if desired. Pour the sauce over the birds or serve separately in a gravy boat.

Yield: 4 to 6 servings.

5
Fish and Shellfish

With its enormous expanse of coastal waters and inland lakes and rivers, the United States possesses one of the world's greatest natural fishery resources. Indeed, the early colonists would have been badly off without the things that swam and crawled in the waters and they learned early to take full advantage of them. Scrod, a young filleted cod, was one of the first distinctively New England dishes and many American fortunes were based on the production and shipping of New England codfish, an industry that has survived to this day.

But as the nation expanded westward in the middle and late nineteenth century and prairie lands replaced seacoast villages and towns, fish lost its dominance in the American diet. Buffalo, elk, caribou, and then the steer became the mainstay of everyday eating. As a result, interest in fish and the quality of fish cookery declined, except in a few areas. Today, however, fish are transported all over the country and frozen fish are available nearly everywhere.

There are few foods that can be more taste-pleasing than a fine fish dish, and there is nothing simpler to prepare. Fish needs only the briefest of cooking and the most delicate of seasonings. If you happen to live near the banks of a well-stocked lake or river, you don't even need a cookbook—just a frying pan, some cooking oil, and salt and pepper.

Types of Fish

There are something like 19,000 species of fish, but only about 200 of them have any commercial importance, which still gives us a huge selection.

Fish are classified as fin fish, those with vertebrae and fins; and as shellfish, those with a hard shell on the outside and no inner skeleton. In the fin fish family are lean fish,

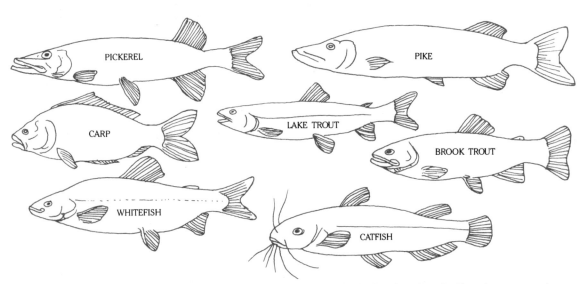

Fresh-water fish are found in our lakes, rivers, and streams. Pike is the brochet *that the French use to make* quenelles de brochet, *or fish dumplings. Some trout migrate like their relative, the salmon, while others remain inland. Brook trout is considered among the best, but even hatchery rainbow trout has delicate flesh. Catfish, so named for its whiskers, is common in the Mississippi Valley and central states.*

Salt-water fish include both lean and fat fish. Not drawn to scale here, some, such as sardine, pompano, or porgy can weigh 8 ounces or less, while the swordfish can weigh 400 pounds. Flat fish such as sole, flounder, fluke, and halibut have both eyes on their upper, dark-skinned side. Most fish sold in America as sole is actually flounder, but the Dover sole, the finest, is sometimes imported.

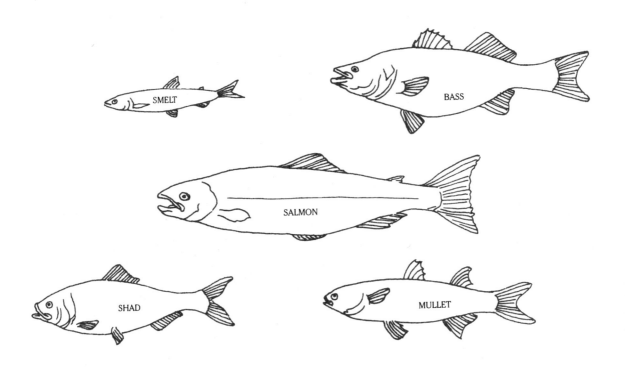

Certain fish have habits that make them seasonal. Many spend most of their lives at sea but return inland to spawn. The most majestic of these is the pink-fleshed salmon. The smelt, its tiny cousin, has similar habits. Certain bass, including striped bass, migrate in similar fashion, as does the shad, a relative of the herring. The gray mullet frequents shallow coastal waters and tastes better caught at sea than in estuaries.

those with a fat content of less than 5 percent, and fat fish, those with a fat content of 5 to 20 percent. Light-fleshed fish, such as bass, carp, cod, flounder, haddock, halibut, perch, sole, swordfish, and red snapper, are among the lean fish. Fat fish usually have darker flesh and include mackerel, salmon, pompano, shad, tuna, and herring. Fin fish are further classified as either fresh-water or salt-water fish, according to the waters in which they spend their adult lives. In the fresh-water category are carp,

catfish, mullet, pickerel, brook trout, lake trout, and whitefish, among others; the salt-water fish include bass, bluefish, cod, lingcod, mackerel, pompano, red snapper, and swordfish. There is still another classification that describes the shape of the body. Fish that have an unusual flattened body and swim on their sides are known as flat fish. In this group are flounder, halibut, plaice, sole, and turbot. The more conventionally shaped fish are known as round fish.

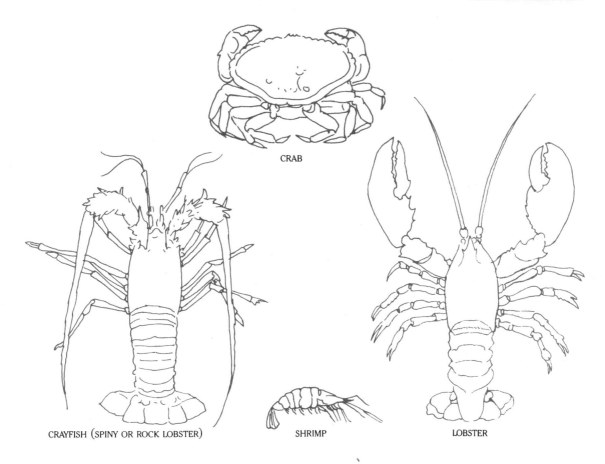

CRAB

CRAYFISH (SPINY OR ROCK LOBSTER)   SHRIMP   LOBSTER

Unlike fish, crustaceans carry their skeletal structures on the outside, and once one gets past the forbidding exterior, there are no bones to worry about, only the tender flesh. Whole crab demands the most work to prepare, while shrimp requires the least: its shell comes off easily. Rock lobster, or spiny lobster, frequently listed as lobster on menus, is really a crayfish. The true lobster is the most desirable of all crustaceans.

The shellfish family consists of crustaceans and mollusks. The difference between them is that the shell of the crustacean is segmented and flexible and the creatures move about in their watery habitat with claws and a tail, while most mollusks have calcified shells with no claws or tails. Crabs, crayfish, lobster, and shrimp are crustaceans; clams, mussels, oysters, and scallops are mollusks. Most mollusks are bivalves, that is, two-shelled, the exceptions being snails and abalone. Also in the mollusk

family is the squid, an active and many-armed swimmer that lives in coastal and oceanic waters.

Nutritive Values

Aside from the pleasure they offer in taste, fish are an excellent source of protein. They offer significant amounts of essential B-complex vitamins, and many valuable minerals. The fattest

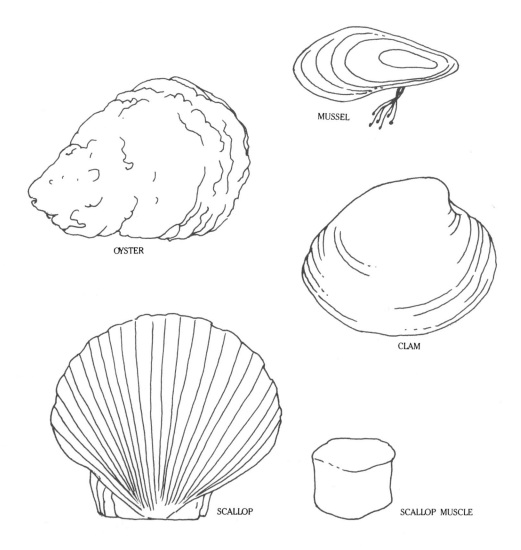

OYSTER

MUSSEL

CLAM

SCALLOP

SCALLOP MUSCLE

Most of the mollusks we eat are bivalves, and their preparation involves cleaning and separating the two shells to remove the meat within. Oysters and clams may be eaten raw, right out of the shell, while mussels require cooking just long enough for the shells to open. Scallops are seldom sold here in their fan-shaped shells. What we buy is the tender muscle the scallop uses to open and close its shell.

fish, for the most part, contain less fat than the leanest meat, and fish fats are a relatively high source of polyunsaturated fatty acids, which makes them of special interest to cholesterol-watchers. Lean fish contains about half the calories found in an equal amount of beef, pork, or lamb. As the fat content of the fish goes up, calories and protein increase. Shellfish are low in fat and calories, but they contain more cholesterol than fin fish. Like meat, fish are low in calcium, except for canned salmon, in which the processing has made the bones virtually soluble. Fish are an excellent source of phosphorus but they have less iron than meat. Carbohydrates are totally absent from fish and occur in low concentrations in shellfish. Salt-water fish contain iodine. Sodium (salt) content is quite low in both salt-water and fresh-water fish, but it is relatively high in most shellfish, except for oysters. Oysters are the only shellfish allowed on a low-sodium diet.

Why Does Fish Cook So Quickly?

Unlike meat, fish does not have to be cooked to become tender. It has only a small amount of connective tissue and its muscle fibers are not tough. Fish flesh is actually edible in its raw state, as evidenced by the growing popularity of the Japanese sashimi, strips of raw fish served with spicy sauces. The only reason we expose fish to heat is to coagulate the muscle fiber proteins so that the flesh will separate into flakes. The flavor of good fish and shellfish is completely lost when too much heat causes the tissues to break down, allowing both juices and flavor to escape. Fish does not have the flavor-producing fat content or muscle tissue of meat and once the natural juices have escaped, the fish becomes dry, tasteless, and even tough.

The basis of good fish cookery is, "How quickly do I cook this fish?" rather than, "How long do I cook it?"

Buying Fish

With today's fast transportation and modern refrigeration, distance is no great deterrent to a fresh fish supply. The average retail fish store will offer the finest quality fish available, generally superior to the selection in supermarkets.

Fresh fish can be bought in the round (whole fish as caught); drawn (eviscerated: entrails removed); dressed (without entrails, fins, and scales and with or without head and tail); steaks (cross sections cut into slices); and as fillets (slices cut parallel to the backbone).

Three-quarters to one pound of fish with bone and from one-third to one-half pound of fillets or boneless steaks will serve one.

Is It Fresh?

Both appearance and odor are clues to a fish's freshness. It is easy to recognize a fresh fish if the head is on. The eyes should be bulging and clear. If they are sunken, dull, or glazed, the fish is not for you. The passage of time and the evaporation of moisture have caused that once golden cornea to become grayish white, which indicates that the fish has had its day. Other indications of freshness are a moist, shiny appearance; firm, resilient flesh that does not remain dented when you touch it but springs back like a well-baked cake; tight shiny scales; and red or clear pink gills under the gill flaps. A brownish coloring in the gills is the result of stale blood. And, finally, your nose will know, for fresh fish do not smell. The slightest sour smell is an instant warning of the onset of

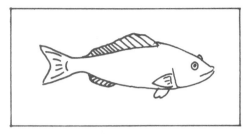 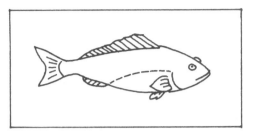

Fish may be sold–or presented to the cook–in the round, just as it comes from the water. It will then be up to the cook to gut it, scale it, remove the fins, and otherwise prepare it for cooking.

When fish is sold drawn, its entrails have been removed, as indicated by the dotted line. The scaling and further preparation are still the cook's responsibility. The head need not be removed.

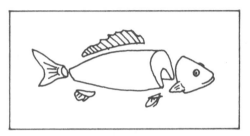

Dressed fish is already gutted, but in addition, it has been scaled, and its head, tail, and fins have been removed. The cook may then cut the fish into steaks or fillets, or cook it just as it is.

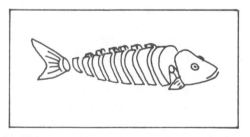 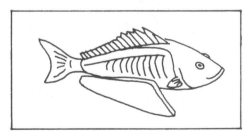

Fish steaks, or slices, need no further preparation before cooking. When cutting steaks yourself, make sure they are uniform in size so that they will cook equally quickly.

Fillets, the sides of the fish cut away from the bony structure, are all ready to cook.

staleness. Salt-water fish should have the "smell of the sea." Undressed fish has the best chance of being fresh because, being most perishable in this form, it has to be sold quickly. Fresh fish fillets should be almost odorless and free of slime.

Frozen Fish

No fish fancier would ever argue the merits of frozen fish over fresh, but there are times when the food shopper has no choice. If the fish has been properly frozen, stored, and thawed, there is no reason why you shouldn't produce a fine cooked result. Flash-freezing at a very low temperature does the least damage to the texture of fish. The faster the freezing, the smaller the ice crystals that form between the fibers, and the less distortion of flavor and texture. However, frozen fish may lose some of its delicate quality and will usually benefit from a well-flavored sauce or a generous amount of moisture and fat in its preparation.

If you are buying frozen fish in a package, select only solidly frozen packages that look sleek and trim. Avoid any that are misshapen, which suggests that they were thawed and refrozen. Store the package immediately in your freezer. When you are planning to use it, remove it from the freezer well in advance and transfer it to the refrigerator in its original package. It may take as long as 24 hours to defrost. Never defrost at room temperature or under running water. Trying to speed up the defrosting process results in loss of natural juices, while slow defrosting at a low temperature allows the ice crystals that have formed within the fibers of the fish to dissolve very slowly. The moisture is retained instead of spilling out and leaving you with dry and tasteless fish.

If you find yourself with more fresh fish than you can use, don't hesitate to freeze it. If it is whole, gut and clean it (see page 190). Wrap it tightly in freezer wrap, slip it into a plastic bag and place it in the freezing compartment of your refrigerator. Don't try to hold it for more than a couple of weeks because the average refrigerator freezer does not reach a sufficiently low temperature for long storage. It has been found that unless fish is held at -10 degrees, enzymatic changes take place that reduce flavor and change fish texture. Fish with a high fat content, such as mackerel, salmon, and shad, do not hold as well as leaner fish in freezer storage.

Storing

Fish is a highly perishable food. You can store it for a day or two, but it is always best to use it as soon as possible after purchase. Rinse it quickly in cold water as soon as you get it home and dry it with a paper towel. Repackage it in an airtight plastic bag and place it in the coldest part of the refrigerator. The purpose of the tight packaging is to prevent moisture loss. Fish may also be kept directly on ice if drainage is provided to keep the fish from soaking up water as the ice melts.

Freshly caught fish should always be eviscerated promptly because of the powerful digestive enzymes present in the intestines that attack the walls of the body cavity and cause spoilage.

Cleaning and Preparing a Fish

Generally the fish dealer cleans and fillets fish, but there may be times when you come face-to-face with a whole fish, perhaps a gift from an angler friend, and you must deal with it yourself. Preparation includes scaling, cleaning, skinning, and filleting.

Start by covering your work table or counter with several thicknesses of newspaper, which will provide automatic wrappings for the discarded parts and make cleaning up easier.

Save fish bones, heads, and trimmings for fish stock. If the fish was dressed and filleted at the market, ask for the head and bones. Fish markets discard pounds of the stuff every day and will probably be cooperative about giving you some. Be sure to specify white-fleshed fish bones and heads only. Oily or strong-flavored fish do not make good-tasting stock.

Removing Fins and Scaling

The fins should be removed before you start scaling; they can be sharp and can nick you. Snipping off the fins with scissors will not remove the little bones at their base. To remove completely, cut around both sides of the fin for its full length, making the cuts meet. Grasp the fin and give a quick pull forward toward the head. The fin and its root bones will lift out.

Wash the fish quickly with cold water; it is easier to remove scales when the fish is wet. Grasp the fish tail firmly with a cloth or paper towel to give you a better hold on it. With a fish scaler or the back of a short-bladed, rigid kitchen knife, use short pushing strokes and gently work against the nap from tail to head. Don't overlook the scales around the base of the head and the fins. Turn fish over and repeat on the other side. Rinse under running water. Wrap the scales in the top layer of newspaper and discard.

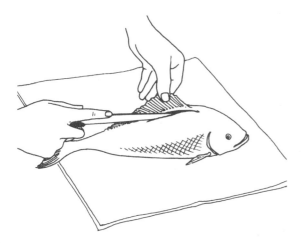

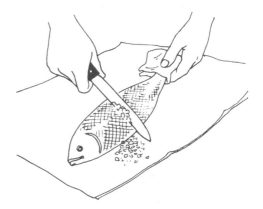

1 *Use a sharp knife to cut along the back of the fish, all around the dorsal fin. Cut deeply enough to free its root bones from the flesh.*

To scale a fish, hold it firmly by the tail while using a fish scaler or the back of a knife to scrape away the scales, working from the tail toward the head. Cleaning up is easier if you work on newspaper.

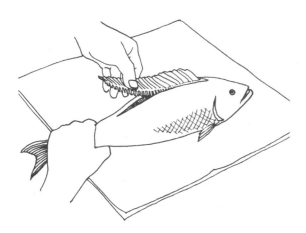

2 *Hold the fin by the end nearer the tail and give it a sharp pull toward the head. The root bones should come away with the fin.*

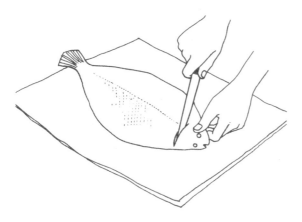

1 *To gut a flat fish, place it on the newspaper with its dark-skinned side toward you. Cut a slit in the form of a semicircle, just behind the head.*

Gutting

The method of gutting depends on the shape of the fish. In round fish, such as mackerel, cod, bluefish, and the like, the entrails lie in the body cavity, but in flat fish such as sole and flounder they are in a cavity behind the head.

Round Fish. Slit the belly from the anal vent to the head and remove everything inside the stomach cavity. Beneath the exposed backbone under a thin membrane lies the blood pocket. Scrape this out with the tip of the knife and rinse under running water to get rid of any clotted blood or bits of viscera or membrane remaining. Dry well inside and out with paper towels. The head and tail may be left on if you are planning to bake or broil the fish whole. Wrap and discard the entrails.

Flat Fish. Make a semicircular cut just behind the head on the dark-skinned side. This opens the cavity containing the entrails. Scrape them out and wash the fish well.

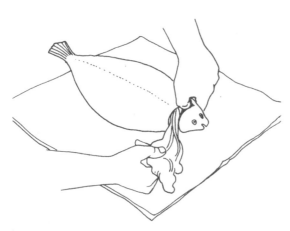

2 *To remove the entrails, put a knife or your finger through the cut you have made and scoop or scrape them out. Rinse well.*

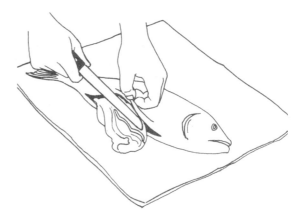

To gut a round fish, make a cut along the underside of the fish, from the anal vent to the head. Remove the entrails and locate the blood pocket beneath the backbone. Remove this and rinse the cavity clean.

Fish Steaks

Begin below the head and slice crosswise into steaks of desired thickness, generally about an inch thick. Make the slices uniform so that all steaks will be done at the same time. Do not remove skin or central bone before cooking.

Filleting a Round Fish

Cut off the head with a diagonal slash. Include the gills and the pectoral fins, the two slender fins on the belly side just behind the gills. If the knife doesn't go through the backbone easily, place the fish on the edge of the table so that the head hangs over and snap the backbone by bending the head down. Cut the full length of the fish along the back. Insert the knife at a slight angle at the head end until you feel the backbone against the knife. Turn the knife flat with the cutting edge toward the tail and gently ease the flesh from the bones with a sliding motion of the knife all the way to the tail. The fillet should be freed and come off in one piece. Turn the fish and repeat on the other side. If the fish is large, the fillets can be cut into serving portions.

1 *To remove the head, make a diagonal cut behind the head, right through the body. Cut at an angle so that the pectoral fins and the gills are cut off with the head.*

2 *Steadying the fish with one hand, cut straight along the backbone from one end to the other, just deeply enough to expose the bone.*

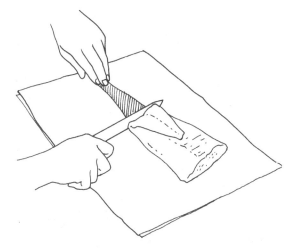

3 *Beginning at the head end again, insert the knife until it touches the backbone. Then, with the knife flat, parallel to the body, ease the flesh away from the bone, gently cutting toward the tail.*

5 *Holding the fillet by the tail, keep the knife flat against the skin and work it toward the head end, between the skin and the flesh.*

To skin, place the fillet skin side down. Hold the tail firmly and cut through the flesh of the fillet about ½ inch above the tail. Flatten the knife against the skin with the blade pointing toward the top of the fillet. Gently push the knife forward as close against the skin as possible while you hold the tail tautly with the other hand.

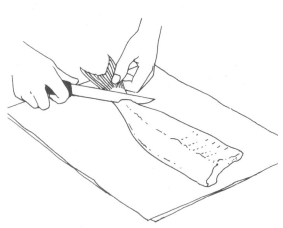

4 *To skin the fillet, start by placing it on the newspaper with the flesh side toward you. Make a cut through the flesh just above the tail, but do not cut through the skin.*

Filleting a Flat Fish

Flat varieties of fish yield four fillets, two on the dark side and two on the light side. Cut off the fins. Start by skinning the fish. Cut a gash through the skin above the tail and peel back the skin for about an inch. Grasp the released skin firmly with one hand and hold the tail with the other. Pull the skin steadily toward the head. It should peel off neatly. With the skin removed, you will see an indentation down the center that separates the double set of fillets. Cut through the flesh on either side of the spine. Slip the knife close to the bone under the fillet and, working toward the outside edge of the fish with short, sharp strokes, cut the fillet loose from the backbone. Make a cut behind the head to release the fillet. Turn the fish around and remove the other fillet the same way. Turn the fish over and remove the fillets on the other side.

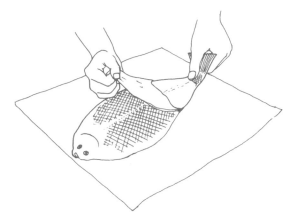

1 *Make a cut through the skin just above the tail. Peel the skin back far enough to get a grip on it, then hold it tightly with one hand and pull it away, holding the tail down firmly with the other hand.*

2 *Flat fish have two fillets on each side. To free them, start by cutting along both sides of the backbone.*

3 *With the knife nearly flat, cut the flesh away from the bones, working the knife from the backbone toward the outside.*

4 *Make a cut behind the head to release the fillet entirely.*

Cooking Methods for Fish

As with meat, fish is cooked either by moist or dry heat. But unlike meat, fish does not have to be tenderized and you, not the cut, determine how it shall be prepared. You can bake it or broil it or poach it or braise it, whether the fish is whole, filleted, or cut into steaks. The essential consideration is that it not be overcooked.

Fish is done when the meat loses its translucency and becomes opaque or solid in appearance. The most accurate way to assess this is to make a cut in the fish about a minute before you think it will be done. If you see a thin line of raw flesh you can remove the fish from the heat. The heat in the fish will continue its cooking job even while the fish rests on a platter on its way to the dining table. With experience, you will develop a feel for fish

cookery and know by just looking at the thickness of a piece of fish how long it will need to cook. The often heard rule about 10 minutes of cooking time per inch of thickness is not completely reliable. It works in some situations and results in grievously overdone fish in others. The directions for "when the fish flakes readily" can also lead to overcooking.

A whole fish will cook more quickly and retain more of its flavorful juices if the head is left on. If you are bothered by the reproachful stare of that lifeless eye gazing out at you, avoid eye contact. You can remove the head before serving if you wish, although many people consider it decorative.

Fish does not take kindly to a wait between preparation and serving. If you think your dinner might have to be delayed, time your preparations accordingly. Sautéeing or poaching takes very little time and your family or guests will hold up better after a 10- or 15-minute delay than the fish will. One of the secrets of successful seafood restaurants is their practice of cooking to order and serving promptly.

Seasonings. A fine fresh fish or fish steak may need only a squirt of lemon juice, a sauce of melted butter, and a sprinkling of salt and pepper to make it outstanding, while a less well-endowed frozen cod or perch fillet might need the help of a sprightly herb-enriched sauce. Herbs and seasonings complementary to fish are basil, bay leaf, capers, caraway, chives, dill, fennel, marjoram, and parsley. Fish responds particularly well to flavorings added during the cooking; poaching in a well-seasoned liquid adds flavor. Butter, olive oil, sweet cream, and wine are among the flavor enhancers useful in preparing fish.

Poaching

Poaching fish means cooking in a liquid that simmers gently; it should not boil or bubble. Cook just until done. If the cooking is prolonged, the fibers start to shrink and the collagen escapes from between the fibers into the water, leaving the fibers dried out.

Small pieces of fish may be poached in a small amount of liquid and a whole fish may be completely submerged in a large amount of liquid. When poaching in a small amount of liquid in the oven, cover the surface of the fish with a piece of buttered wax paper (buttered side resting on the fish) to prevent the surface from drying out. Poaching can be done in a large covered pan on top of the stove or in a shallow baking pan in a 350-degree oven.

Small fish and fillets should be started in boiling liquid, which is then reduced to a simmer. Large whole fish should be started in cold seasoned liquid (previously boiled and allowed to cool), which gives the fish time to take on flavor. Also, if a large fish were plunged into a boiling liquid, the skin could shrink and break. As soon as the liquid reaches the boil, reduce heat to a simmer and cook for 5 to 8

minutes per pound. Figure the time from the point at which the boiling starts. To make removal of a large fish easier, before cooking wrap the fish in cheesecloth with the ends tied together to serve as handles.

The traditional poaching liquid for fish is a court bouillon, which is a mixture of fish stock and wine, punctuated with herbs and seasonings (see page 200).

Braising

Braising is similar to poaching except that the fish is placed on a bed of sautéed chopped vegetables. It is suitable for large pieces of fish such as salmon or halibut or smaller whole fish such as trout or small bass. Butter or oil a baking dish. Layer a bed of two or more of the following vegetables that have been chopped and sautéed in a little butter: onions, carrots, mushrooms, leeks, parsnips, shallots, scallions, and herbs of your choice. Place the fish on the vegetables and cover halfway up with boiling fish stock, or a combination of clam juice and water or clam juice and wine with a bay leaf. Cover the fish with buttered wax paper and bake in the center of a preheated 350-degree oven for about 20 minutes, or until the fish loses its translucency. Lift out the fish, strain the cooking liquid, and cook rapidly, uncovered, to reduce it. It may be thickened with egg yolk, cream, or butter. Cover the fish with the sauce.

Steaming

Steaming highlights every bit of natural fish flavor and is a lovely way to treat a delicate lean fish. Fish must be absolutely fresh for steaming. Fine-textured fish such as porgy, sea bass, red snapper, whiting, yellow pike, or butterfish are first-rate candidates for this cooking method.

In steaming, the fish is cooked over liquid, not in it. The standard steamer has a perforated tray support designed to hold the fish above the water level, but a workable substitute can be improvised if you don't have one. You will need a fairly deep kettle with a tight cover. Place a couple of custard cups on the bottom to support the rack or plate on which you will place the fish. The plate or rack must be well above the level of the liquid you put into the kettle. Add the water, bring it to the boil and place the fish on the rack. Cover the pot and steam the fish over high heat until it loses its translucency. Remove fish from steamer and serve.

Baking

Baking is suitable for whole fish, fish fillets, and steaks. It is important to baste the fish during cooking with the juices from the fish and the fat that you add.

Fillets and Steaks. Brush the fish pieces with melted butter, clarified butter, or oil, and season with lemon juice, salt, and freshly ground pepper. Sprinkle with fresh bread crumbs if you like. Place fish in an oiled or buttered shallow baking dish and bake in a preheated oven at 400 to 425 degrees. Thicker fish should bake at the lower temperature. Fish steaks will need between 12 and 20 minutes, depending on the type of fish and the thickness of the cut. Fillets will be done in 8 to 10 minutes. Baste once or twice during cooking.

Whole Fish. Fish should be cleaned and scaled, and fins removed. Rub inside and out with lemon juice and sprinkle lightly with salt and freshly ground pepper. Leave the head on; the fish will be juicier. Make three slashes on each side of the fish. This will help the heat to penetrate and also prevent the skin from drawing up or splitting. A whole fish may be stuffed with fine fresh bread crumbs seasoned with salt, pepper, herbs, or parsley and moistened with melted butter, or with slices of onion and tomato. If you are using a bread stuffing, spoon it lightly into the fish cavity because it will swell during cooking. Sew the fish closed or secure with small skewers or toothpicks. Place the fish in an oiled or buttered baking pan and brush it with melted butter or butter and oil. Add a splash of dry white wine to use in basting. Bake in a preheated 400-degree oven, basting a few times. Figure 8 to 10 minutes per pound of dressed weight, but much depends on how thick the fish is and its texture. As you approach the end of the cooking time, make a small cut in the fish to see how nearly done it is. Use a baking dish that can be brought to the table; it saves the trauma of transferring to the serving platter, which can be a tricky business.

Broiling

A hot oven is a must for broiling fish. Preheat the broiler to top heat for 10 minutes before cooking the fish. Put the fish on a well-oiled rack, or cover the broiler rack with a sheet of oiled aluminum foil. If you are broiling a fillet, which does not have to be turned, preheat the broiler pan, which will help to cook the underside of the fish.

Fillets and Steaks. Lightly flour the fillets or steaks and brush them with melted butter or oil. Baste them once or twice while they are cooking with butter, oil, wine, or a mixture of melted butter and wine. Place the fish 3 or 4 inches below the heat unit the thinner pieces closer and the thicker pieces farther away. Fillets do not need to be turned; steaks an inch or more thick should be turned once. Save the longer cooking period for the second or turned side so it will be nicely browned when it is served. Allow 6 to 10 minutes total cooking time, depending on the thickness and variety of the fish. Frozen fish needs about double the time. Sprinkle with salt and pepper before serving and pour any of the basting mixture left in the pan over the fish.

Split Fish. To broil a split fish, with or without bone, place it on the broiling rack, skin side down. It does not need to be turned. Broil it 2 or 3 inches from the heat unit and baste it during cooking. It will probably take from 6 to 10 minutes. Sprinkle it with salt and pepper before serving.

Whole Fish. To broil a whole fish, dust it with flour and brush it with melted butter or oil on one side. Flour and oil the second side after you have turned it. Large unboned fish should be scored with three or four diagonal cuts on each side of the body to allow the heat to penetrate evenly and to prevent the skin from splitting while cooking. Place larger fish 5 or 6 inches below the heat unit; smaller fish about 3 inches. Broil the first side 4 or 5 minutes; the second side 5 to 8, depending on the thickness of the fish. Flat fish such as flounder, sole, and fluke are not generally turned. Baste often and sprinkle with salt and pepper before serving.

Pan-Frying and Sautéeing

This is one of the simplest and most popular methods for cooking small whole fish such as trout, smelt, catfish, and sardines, and for fillets and steaks such as haddock, cod, and flounder. The fish may be breaded by dipping it first in flour, then in lightly beaten egg, then in fine bread crumbs, or it may be lightly coated with flour. A sauce is not necessary for sautéed fish, but melted butter and a sprinkling of fresh parsley are especially good with it. It may be accompanied by a wedge of lemon and some tartar sauce.

To sauté fish, heat an equal amount of oil

and butter, or clarified butter (see page 260), in a skillet over moderate heat. Place the floured or breaded fish in the hot fat and sauté until brown on one side; turn and brown the other. Use sufficient fat so that the fish will not stick to the bottom of the pan and will slide easily. Figure approximately 5 to 10 minutes total cooking time, depending on the thickness of the fish. Remove the fish from the pan and drain on absorbent paper.

Deep-Frying

Fish needs a protective coating of egg and bread crumbs or batter when it is deep-fried. Use a deep pan, preferably one equipped with a wire basket. Use a vegetable oil or a melted vegetable fat. You will also need a slotted spoon. Do not fill the pan more than half full. Heat the oil over moderate heat to 375 degrees. If you do not have a thermometer, test the temperature of the fat by dropping a 1-inch cube of day-old bread into the oil. If the bread browns in 60 seconds, the oil is at the correct temperature.

Roll the fish in flour seasoned with a bit of salt and pepper, then in beaten egg, then in fine fresh bread crumbs, or in a batter (see page 208). Fry the fish for 3 to 5 minutes, or until the coating is golden and crisp. Remove cooked pieces with a slotted spoon and drain on absorbent paper. Keep them warm while you cook the next batch. Fry only a few pieces at a time; if you overcrowd the pan, you will lower the temperature of the oil and end up with grease-soaked, soggy fish. Always wait until the oil returns to the proper temperature before adding another batch of fish. If the oil is not hot enough, the fish will absorb the oil instead of being quickly sealed.

Court Bouillon

Bones, heads, and trimmings of
any white-fleshed fish (flounder,
snapper, cod, etc.)
½ cup chopped onion
1 clove garlic, crushed
¾ cup dry white wine, *or* ¼ cup
lemon juice
8 cups water
1 teaspoon salt
10 peppercorns, crushed
1 celery stalk with leaves
½ bay leaf
5 or 6 sprigs parsley
Pinch of dried thyme

Rinse the fish bones and heads in cold water until the water is
clear.

Combine with the remaining ingredients in a stainless steel or
enamel-lined pan (not aluminum) and bring to a boil. Reduce
the heat and simmer for 30 minutes. Strain through a fine sieve
or a double layer of cheesecloth and allow to cool to room
temperature. Refrigerate until ready to use.

The court bouillon should not be discarded. It can be reduced
and used for a sauce or in any way you would use fish stock.

Whole Poached Fish

A whole poached fish makes a stunning presentation.

1 4½- to 5-pound striped bass, sea
bass, or red snapper, cleaned,
with head and tail left on
8 to 10 cups court bouillon
Lemon and parsley for garnish

Rinse the fish well. Wrap it in cheesecloth, leaving a length of the
material on either end to use as handles when you remove the
fish from the poaching liquid.

Place the cold court bouillon in a fish poacher or long oval
roasting pan with a cover. Lower the fish into the liquid, which
should just cover it. Cover and very slowly bring to a boil.
Immediately lower the heat and poach the fish for 5 to 8 minutes
a pound, or until the flesh is opaque. Use a flame-taming device,
if necessary, to keep the liquid at a simmer, not a boil.

Carefully lift the fish out of the liquid and drain on paper towels.
Remove the cheesecloth and pull off or scrape the skin from one
side of the fish. Arrange the fish on a platter skinned side down.
Remove the skin from second side. Garnish with lemon and
parsley.

Serve warm with hollandaise or cold with a mayonnaise-based
sauce (see pages 459 to 462).

Yield: 4 servings.

Baked Stuffed Fish

1 4-pound fish with head and tail
  left on (striped bass, red
  snapper, bluefish, or mackerel)
¼ pound (8 tablespoons) butter
4 to 5 celery stalks, scraped and
  finely chopped
1 small onion, finely chopped
¼ teaspoon dried thyme
Salt and freshly ground pepper
1 egg, lightly beaten
¼ cup dry bread crumbs
Juice of ½ lemon
1 cup dry white wine or vermouth
Lemon wedges
Parsley sprigs

Rinse the fish in cold water and pat dry with paper towels. Make four slashes on each side of the fish. Place in a well-buttered, nonaluminum shallow baking pan large enough to hold the fish.

Melt 4 tablespoons butter in a medium-size skillet. Add the celery and onion and cook until tender, but not too soft or browned. Sprinkle with thyme and add salt and pepper to taste. Set aside to cool for 10 to 15 minutes. Preheat the oven to 400 degrees.

Add the egg, bread crumbs, and lemon juice to the celery and mix well. Lightly stuff the fish cavity, including the head, with the mixture. Skewer the fish closed. Add the wine or vermouth to the pan and dot the fish with the remaining butter. Place the fish in the oven and bake for 25 to 35 minutes, or until the fish loses its translucency. Baste frequently with the pan juices. To serve, remove the skewers and garnish with lemon wedges and parsley sprigs.

Yield: 4 servings.

Baked Striped Bass or Red Snapper

1 3 to 3½-pound striped bass or
  red snapper, boned, with head
  and tail left on
4 tablespoons oil
2 medium onions, thinly sliced
2 medium tomatoes, thinly sliced
Salt and freshly ground pepper
½ teaspoon dried basil
½ cup dry white wine
2 tablespoons chopped parsley

Have the fish boned but left in one piece, which is called butterflying. Wash the fish carefully and pat it dry. Make three slashes on the skin side of the fish. Oil an oval baking pan large enough to hold the fish flat. Preheat the oven to 400 degrees.

Place a layer of thinly sliced onion and tomatoes over the bottom of the pan and sprinkle lightly with salt and pepper. Place the fish over the onion and tomato slices and open it. Salt and pepper the inside of the fish and sprinkle with the basil. Arrange a layer of onion and tomato slices over the bottom half of the fish and cover with the upper half. Skewer the fish closed. Dribble the remainder of the oil over the fish and vegetables and pour the wine over the fish. Bake for 30 minutes, basting from time to time.

Make a small incision in the top of the fish to check its doneness. It is done when the flesh loses its translucency. Sprinkle with parsley and serve with the vegetables and the liquid from the pan.

Yield: 4 servings.

Baked Stuffed Shad

Shad is a great gastronomic delight that, unfortunately, has a very short season. You are best advised to let a professional bone the fish. Otherwise, the distraction of picking out the myriad tiny bones will spoil your enjoyment of the rich, succulent meat.

2 large shad fillets
Salt and freshly ground pepper
1 large onion, chopped
¼ pound mushrooms, chopped
7 tablespoons butter
1 cup fresh bread crumbs
¼ cup finely chopped parsley
½ teaspoon dried thyme
1 hard-boiled egg, coarsely
  chopped
½ cup dry white wine
Lemon slices
Chopped fresh parsley

Grease a shallow baking dish large enough to hold the fish flat. Sprinkle the flesh side of the fillets with salt and pepper and set aside.

In a medium-size skillet, sauté the onion and mushrooms in 4 tablespoons butter until the onion is soft. Add the bread crumbs, parsley, thyme, and egg and mix well. Season to taste with salt and pepper. Preheat the oven to 400 degrees.

Spread the filling over one of the fillets, tucking some underneath the flaps. Smooth it evenly and cover with the other fillet. Tie the fish neatly with string in four or five places to hold it in shape and keep the filling intact. Sprinkle with salt and pepper and rub the skin with 2 tablespoons butter. Transfer the fish to the baking dish and bake for 15 minutes. Spoon 2 tablespoons white wine over the fish and continue baking for 15 minutes longer, basting often with the pan juices. Pour the remaining wine over the fish and bake for 10 minutes more, continuing to baste often.

Remove the fish to a serving platter and add the remaining tablespoon of butter to the juices in the pan. Cut off the strings from the fish and pull off the skin from the top. Pour the pan juices over the fish. Garnish with lemon slices and sprinkle with chopped parsley. Cut in crosswise slices to serve.

Yield: 6 servings.

Shad Roe

Roe are usually sold by the pair and are a great delicacy. They can be sautéed, steamed, or broiled, but poaching them in butter keeps them moist and delicious.

2 pairs shad roe
Milk
Flour
10 tablespoons butter
Salt and freshly ground pepper
3 tablespoons chopped fresh
    parsley
Lemon wedges

Dip shad roe in milk and sprinkle lightly with flour. Melt the butter in a large, heavy skillet with a cover. When the butter is just melted, but not hot or bubbly, dip both sides of the roe in it. Partly cover the pan and simmer over very low heat for 12 to 15 minutes. Use a flame-control device, if necessary, to keep the heat low. Turn once, after 5 or 6 minutes. Shad roe is firm when done, but, to be sure, make a little cut in the side with a sharp knife. If there is no sign of redness, it is done. Sprinkle with salt, pepper, and chopped parsley. Pour the butter from the pan over the roe and garnish with lemon wedges.

Yield: 2 to 4 servings.

Chinese-Style Steamed Sea Bass

Almost any fish can be steamed, as long as it is very fresh.

1 3½-pound sea bass or snapper,
    cleaned, with head and tail left
    on
¼ cup soy sauce (Japanese
    preferred)
¼ cup sherry, gin, or vodka
1 tablespoon finely grated ginger
1 clove garlic, finely chopped
4 thin slices fresh ginger, cut into
    matchlike pieces
2 whole scallions, trimmed and
    cut into matchlike pieces

Make three diagonal slashes on both sides of the fish. Mix the soy sauce, sherry, ginger, and garlic and pour it over the fish. Rub some of the mixture in the fish cavity. Marinate for 1 hour at room temperature, turning the fish several times.

If you don't have a fish steamer, you can improvise one (see page 198). Add about 1 inch of boiling water to the steamer.

Arrange the fish with the marinade on a plate suitable for serving on the steamer rack and sprinkle with the ginger and scallions. Cover tightly and steam for 10 to 12 minutes.

Yield: 2 to 4 servings.

Sautéed Sea Squab

Skinless and with only a single center bone, sea squab is distinguished by its delicate flavor and texture. Sea squab is the edible portion of the rather unattractive puffer, also known as blowfish and globefish. Sea squabs are not uniform in size; they run about eight to the pound, and three to four are an adequate serving for one.

12 to 16 sea squabs
Lemon juice
Salt and freshly ground pepper
½ cup flour
2 tablespoons butter
2 tablespoons oil
Lemon wedges
Tartar sauce

Rinse and dry the fish thoroughly. Sprinkle with lemon juice, salt, and pepper. Place the flour on a square of wax paper and roll the fish in it, shaking off any excess.

Heat the butter and oil in a large, heavy skillet until foamy. Add the fish and cook for 5 minutes on one side, turn carefully with two spoons or tongs, and cook for 3 minutes on the other side. Don't try to crowd too many into the pan at one time. They break easily and you need room to turn them. As they are done, keep them warm in a 200-degree oven and continue cooking the remainder. Add more oil and butter if needed. Serve with lemon wedges and tartar sauce.

Yield: 4 servings.

Trout Amandine

If fresh brook trout are not available, frozen rainbow trout can be used.

4 trout, 10 to 12 ounces each,
    cleaned
Salt and freshly ground pepper
Flour for dredging
12 tablespoons butter
1 cup slivered blanched almonds
2 tablespoons lemon juice
2 tablespoons dry white wine
Fresh chopped parsley

Wash the trout and pat dry with paper towels. Sprinkle with salt and pepper. Place a mound of flour on a square of wax paper and dredge the fish in the flour, shaking off any excess.

Melt 6 tablespoons butter in a large skillet and, when the butter is bubbly, place the trout in the pan. Shake the skillet to make sure that the fish do not stick. Sauté for 5 minutes and turn carefully with two spatulas. Cook for 5 minutes longer. Remove the trout to a hot platter and keep warm in a 200-degree oven. Wipe out the pan with paper towels and add the remaining butter. When hot and bubbly, add the almonds and stir until lightly browned. Add the lemon juice and white wine to the pan and heat through. Spoon the mixture over the trout and sprinkle with chopped parsley.

Yield: 4 servings.

Monkfish Stew

Monkfish, also known as bellyfish, anglerfish, and lotte, has a firm texture that makes it ideal for stew.

2½ pounds monkfish, halibut, or tuna steaks
2 tablespoons olive oil
1 large onion, coarsely chopped
2 tablespoons finely chopped shallots
2 cloves garlic, finely chopped
1 celery stalk, coarsely chopped
1 carrot, coarsely chopped
1 1-pound, 12-ounce can whole tomatoes, drained
½ cup dry white or red wine
3 tablespoons tomato paste
1 teaspoon dried tarragon
¼ teaspoon dried thyme
1 small bay leaf
1 small pinch hot pepper flakes (optional)
2 tablespoons fresh chopped parsley

Remove all the skin and bones from the fish, and cut the fish into large chunks. The monkfish is difficult to skin, but be persistent.

Heat the oil in a large skillet and cook the fish cubes, stirring, until whitened and firm, about 2 minutes. Remove with a slotted spoon and reserve.

To the fat remaining in the skillet, add the onion, shallots, garlic, celery, and carrot. Cook, stirring, until softened and lightly colored. Add the tomatoes, wine, tomato paste, tarragon, thyme, bay leaf, and hot pepper flakes. Bring to a boil, lower heat slightly, and cook briskly until sauce is thickened and reduced. Stir often.

Add the reserved fish cubes, cover, and simmer 7 or 8 minutes. (Halibut and tuna will take less time than monkfish.)

Remove from heat, sprinkle with parsley, and serve immediately with rice.

Yield: 4 servings.

Fish Steaks in Foil

4 salmon, swordfish, halibut, or tuna steaks (about ½ pound each)
¼ cup fresh lemon juice
2 teaspoons dried tarragon, crumbled
Salt and freshly ground pepper
4 slices Spanish onion
4 tablespoons sweet butter

Preheat the oven to 400 degrees.

Sprinkle each steak with lemon juice, tarragon, salt, and pepper. Arrange on a large square of heavy buttered foil. Top each steak with a slice of onion and 1 tablespoon butter. Seal the foil packages well.

Place on a baking sheet in one layer and bake for 7 to 8 minutes. Lower the oven temperature to 375 degrees and continue to cook for 7 minutes.

Remove from the oven and serve the foil packages on individual plates. Each person unwraps his/her own. Serve with creamed mushrooms, grilled tomatoes, and new potatoes. Hollandaise or dill sauce can be served with the fish, if desired.

Yield: 4 servings.

Broiled Swordfish Steak

Swordfish has a hearty, almost meaty quality that makes it popular even among people who are not fish enthusiasts. The herbed sauce in this preparation adds piquancy.

2 pounds swordfish steaks
¼ cup vegetable oil
3 tablespoons chopped scallions
1 whole garlic clove, peeled (optional)
3 tablespoons chopped parsley
¼ teaspoon sweet paprika
1 tablespoon soy sauce (Japanese preferred)
Pinch of dried tarragon
¼ teaspoon dried basil
Salt and freshly ground pepper
Juice and grated rind of 1 lemon

Rinse and dry the swordfish steaks and place them on a foil-lined baking sheet. Heat the oil in a small skillet and cook the scallions and garlic clove until golden. Add the remaining ingredients and cook over very low heat for 2 or 3 minutes longer. Strain the oil and brush it over both sides of the fish. Let stand at room temperature for 1 hour.

Preheat the broiler to very hot and place the fish steaks about 4 inches below the heat. Broil for 5 to 8 minutes on each side, depending on the thickness of the steaks. Brush with oil a few times during the cooking. Test for doneness by making a tiny slit on the top to check. When the fish loses its translucency, remove from the oven. Serve with lemon wedges.

Yield: 4 servings.

Poached Fillets of Sole

The word sole *has become a generic term for any white fish that comes in fillets. The only genuine member of the sole family found in North American waters is the gray sole; the true Channel or Dover sole must be imported and its texture is quite different. Most of the sole we buy comes from one of the numerous members of the flounder family, which in no way diminishes its good eating qualities. But for this fine preparation, we prefer to use gray sole.*

4 large fillets of gray sole
3 tablespoons butter
½ cup carrot, finely diced
1 small onion, finely diced
2 shallots, finely diced
1 tablespoon celery, finely diced
6 large mushroom caps
Salt and freshly ground pepper
⅓ cup dry sherry
1 tablespoon lemon juice
2 teaspoons flour
1 tablespoon water
⅔ cup heavy cream
Parsley sprigs for garnish

Arrange the fillets in a well-buttered baking dish large enough to accommodate them in a single layer. Melt the butter in a small saucepan and add the diced carrot, onion, shallots, celery, and two of the mushrooms, finely diced. Sauté for a few minutes, until the onion becomes limp but not browned. Add salt and pepper and cook, covered, over very low heat for 7 or 8 minutes, or until the vegetables are tender. Add the sherry and heat through. Pour the vegetable mixture over the fish. Poach gently until the fish loses its translucency. Remove the fillets to a platter and keep warm in a 200-degree oven. Cook the remaining mushroom caps for a few minutes in a small amount of water combined with the tablespoon of lemon juice to keep them white. Set aside.

Return the vegetables and liquid to the saucepan and place over low heat. Stir in the flour mixed with water. Bring to a boil and stir until the mixture thickens and reduces. Lower the heat and slowly add the cream, stirring until the sauce coats the spoon. Taste and adjust the seasonings. Serve the fillets covered with a few tablespoons of sauce and topped with a mushroom cap. Garnish the plates with parsley sprigs.

Yield: 4 servings.

Spinach-Stuffed Flounder Rolls

6 tablespoons butter
1 small onion, finely chopped
1 10-ounce package frozen spinach, defrosted, squeezed dry, and finely chopped
½ cup sour cream
¼ cup dry bread crumbs
1 egg, beaten
Salt and freshly ground pepper
Several gratings of nutmeg
1½ to 2 pounds flounder or sole fillets, cut in half lengthwise (about 4 fillets)
White sauce (recipe follows)

Melt the butter in a small skillet and cook the onion until softened. Add the spinach and stir until coated with butter. Remove from the heat and cool for 10 to 15 minutes.

Add the sour cream, bread crumbs, egg, salt, pepper, and nutmeg to the spinach and mix well.

Arrange the cut fillets skinned side up. Spoon some of the mixture evenly along the length of each fillet. Roll each like a jelly roll. Arrange in a buttered shallow casserole, seam side down. Cover with buttered wax paper.

Preheat the oven to 425 degrees.

Bake for 10 to 12 minutes. Serve immediately with white sauce.

Yield: 4 servings.

White Sauce

3 tablespoons butter
3 tablespoons flour
2 cups fish broth, *or* 1 cup clam juice and 1 cup water
Salt and freshly ground pepper
Grating of nutmeg
Lemon juice to taste

Melt the butter in a small saucepan. Add the flour and whisk until bubbly. Add the fish broth and whisk constantly until thickened and smooth. Lower the heat and simmer for 5 to 7 minutes, stirring occasionally. Add salt, pepper, nutmeg, and lemon juice to taste. Serve immediately over fish rolls.

Fish Meunière (Sautéed Fish)

Any boneless fish fillet such as flounder, sole, cod, ocean perch, or any small whole fish such as trout, butterfish, porgies, fresh sardines, smelt, and the like can be cooked by this method.

2 pounds fish fillets or small fish, cleaned
Salt and freshly ground pepper
4 tablespoons milk
½ cup flour
4 tablespoons vegetable oil
4 tablespoons butter
3 tablespoons lemon juice
2 tablespoons finely chopped parsley
Lemon wedges

Rinse the fish. Cut fillets into portion-sized pieces. Add the salt and pepper to the milk in a shallow bowl. Dip the fish into the milk and then into the flour, shaking off any excess. Heat the oil in a pan large enough to hold the fish in a single layer without crowding, or cook them in batches. Add the fish and cook for 2 minutes or longer over moderately high heat until delicately brown on one side. Turn the fish and cook until nicely browned on the other side. If you are cooking the fish in batches, keep the cooked pieces warm in a 200-degree oven. Add more oil if necessary. When all are done, transfer the fish to a warm serving platter, pour off the fat in the skillet, and wipe it out with paper towels. Add the butter and cook over moderately high heat until it foams and starts to darken. Sprinkle the fish with lemon juice and pour the butter over them. Sprinkle each piece with chopped parsley and garnish with a lemon wedge.

Yield: 4 servings.

Deep-Fried Fish

1 cup flour
Salt
1 egg, separated
1 tablespoon salad oil
3 to 4 tablespoons milk
2 pounds white-fleshed fish fillets (flounder, cod, ocean perch)
Vegetable oil for frying

Sift flour and a pinch of salt together in a mixing bowl. Separate the egg and set the white aside. Make a well in the center of the flour and beat in the egg yolk and oil. Add 3 to 4 tablespoons of milk and beat with a wooden spoon until the batter is thick and smooth. This may be done in advance. Just before using, beat the egg white until stiff and fold into the batter.

Sprinkle the fish pieces with salt; dip them lightly in flour and then into the batter. Fry a few pieces of fish at a time in vegetable oil heated to 375 degrees. Fry until golden, 3 to 4 minutes. Remove with a slotted spoon and drain on paper towels. Keep warm in a 200-degree oven until all the pieces are fried. Serve with lemon wedges and tartar sauce.

Yield: 4 servings.

Oven-Fried Fish Fillets

This method of cooking gives the fish a fine crust on the outside and tender, moist texture inside.

2 pounds fish fillets (haddock, flounder, sole, carp) cut into portion-sized pieces
Milk to cover
Salt and freshly ground pepper
1 cup fine dry bread crumbs
6 tablespoons butter, melted
Lemon wedges
Tartar sauce

Place the fish in a shallow pan and cover with the milk seasoned with salt and pepper. Let stand for 15 to 20 minutes. Place the bread crumbs on a large square of wax paper.

Preheat the oven to 500 degrees and place the rack in the upper third of the oven. Remove the fish from the milk and dip into the bread crumbs, making sure that both sides are well covered. Arrange the fillets on a well-buttered baking sheet and dribble the melted butter evenly over each piece.

Bake for 8 to 12 minutes, depending on the thickness of the fish. Transfer to a warmed serving platter and serve with lemon wedges and tartar sauce.

Yield: 4 servings.

Broiled Fish Fillets

Any boneless fish fillet under an inch in thickness—flounder, sole, cod, red snapper, bluefish, haddock, shad—may be broiled by this method. No turning is required.

2 pounds boneless fish fillets
2 to 3 tablespoons butter
Salt and freshly ground pepper
Sprinkling of paprika

Preheat the broiler to high. Rinse the fish fillets and pat dry with paper towels. Use a heatproof shallow baking dish large enough to hold the fish in a single layer, or line a baking sheet with buttered foil. Add the butter to the baking dish and heat under the broiler until the butter melts.

Add the fish fillets flesh side down to coat them with the butter. Then turn them flesh side up. Sprinkle lightly with salt and pepper and gently dust with paprika and place under the broiler 3 or 4 inches from the heat unit, the thinner pieces closer and the thicker pieces farther away. The cooking time will depend on the type and thickness of the fish. A thin fillet such as flounder will need only 3 or 4 minutes; a thicker fillet such as haddock may need 8 to 10. Do not overcook.

Yield: 4 servings.

Escabèche

In this dish of Spanish and Provençal origin, the fish is first sautéed, then marinated in a tangy dressing and served cold as an appetizer course.

A variety of fish may be used. Portion-sized fillets of sole, bluefish, or mackerel, pieces of salmon or fresh tuna, or small fish, such as smelts, mackerel, and fresh sardines, are suitable.

2 pounds fish
⅓ cup lime or lemon juice
½ cup flour
Salt and freshly ground pepper
1 teaspoon sweet paprika
2 tablespoons butter
2 tablespoons oil

Marinade:
2 tablespoons olive oil
½ cup dry vermouth
¼ cup lemon juice
¼ cup pine nuts, lightly toasted in butter
1 large Bermuda onion, thinly sliced

Rinse the fish and dry well. Place the fish in a shallow, non-aluminum bowl and marinate in the lime or lemon juice for 15 minutes. Remove and pat dry with paper towels. Combine the flour, salt, pepper, and paprika on a square of wax paper and blend well. In a heavy skillet, heat the butter and oil until bubbly. Dredge the fish in the seasoned flour, shaking off any excess, and sauté quickly, turning to brown both sides. Cook only as much fish at a time as will fit comfortably in a single layer. Place the cooked pieces as they are done in a large shallow glass or enamel dish.

Wipe out the skillet and heat the oil, vermouth, and lemon juice until warm. Pour the sauce over the fish. Sprinkle with the pine nuts and scatter the onion slices over all. When cool, cover and refrigerate overnight.

Yield: 6 to 8 appetizer servings.

Salt Cod with Potatoes

This is a classic Portuguese dish and a most interesting preparation for dried codfish.

1 pound salt cod
3 large potatoes
½ cup olive oil
2 large onions, sliced
1 clove garlic, finely minced
¼ cup black olives, finely
    chopped
½ teaspoon dillseed
⅓ cup dry white wine
Freshly ground pepper
Chopped parsley

Soak the codfish in cold water overnight, changing the water a few times to remove the salt. Rinse and drain thoroughly. Place it in a skillet or shallow saucepan and cover it with cold water. Bring slowly to a boil and let boil feebly for about 20 minutes, or until the fish flakes easily. Remove the fish and set aside to cool. Reserve the liquid and boil the potatoes in it until tender. Flake the fish when it is cool enough to handle and remove the skin and bones, if there are any. When the potatoes are done, peel and slice them.

Heat the oil in a large skillet and cook the onions until they are golden but not brown, about 10 minutes. Add the flaked codfish, potatoes, garlic, olives, dillseed, wine, and a few grinds of pepper. Cook for about 5 minutes, tossing lightly the whole time. Transfer the mixture to a well-greased 1½-quart casserole and bake in a preheated 400-degree oven for 15 minutes, or until heated through. Garnish with chopped parsley.

Yield: 4 servings.

Gravlax

This special party dish is not cooked. It is cured with salt and seasonings that give it a wonderful texture and flavor.

1 2-pound piece of salmon fillet,
    cut from the tail
3 tablespoons sugar
3 tablespoons coarse salt
1½ tablespoons white or black
    peppercorns, crushed
1 large bunch fresh dill, trimmed
¼ cup Cognac or brandy (use a
    good quality)
¼ cup dry white wine

With the skin side down, sprinkle the salmon with the sugar, salt, and pepper. Scatter the dill on top. Select a shallow, non-aluminum dish in which the fish will fit snugly. Add Cognac or brandy and wine and arrange the fish skin side up in the dish. Cover with plastic wrap, weight with cans (2 to 3 pounds) and refrigerate for 3 days.

Remove from the refrigerator, scrape off the dill, and dry well with paper towels.

Arrange on a carving board and thinly slice on the bias.

Serve as an appetizer with a vinaigrette sauce or as part of a buffet. Serve with black bread spread with sweet butter.

Yield: 8 to 10 appetizer servings.

Codfish Cakes

1 pound salt cod
5 or 6 medium potatoes
6 tablespoons sweet butter
1 large egg
1 teaspoon Worcestershire sauce
Dash of Tabasco sauce
Freshly ground pepper
Oil or butter for frying

Soak the codfish in cold water overnight, changing the water several times to remove the salt. Drain and place in a saucepan. Cover with cold water, bring to a boil, and reduce the heat. Simmer for 20 to 25 minutes, or until the fish flakes easily.

While the codfish is cooking, peel and boil the potatoes until they are tender. The traditional codfish cake has an equal quantity of mashed potatoes and codfish, but you may use more or less potato, according to your taste. When the potatoes are done, drain them well and shake them over the heat in a dry pan until all the moisture is evaporated. While the potatoes are still warm, force them through a food mill or a ricer. Shred the cod with your fingers, removing any skin or bone. Beat together the cod flakes, potatoes, butter, egg, Worcestershire sauce, Tabasco, and a few grinds of black pepper. Taste and correct the seasonings. Form into cakes.

These may be fried in plenty of butter, or rolled in flour or fine bread crumbs and deep-fried.

Yield: 4 servings.

Broiled Finnan Haddie

Finnan haddie, or smoked haddock, comes in fillets and whole fish. (Its name comes from a Scottish fishing port, Findon.) It can be prepared in a variety of ways and this is one of the quickest, simplest, and, we think, nicest.

1½ to 2 pounds finnan haddie
    fillet
4 to 5 tablespoons butter
Freshly ground pepper
2 tablespoons minced chives

Soak the fillet in warm water to cover for 1 hour to reduce saltiness. Drain and dry well. Cut the fillet on the bias into ⅜-inch-thick slices.

Preheat the broiler. Place the slices on the broiler rack and dot each slice generously with butter and a few grinds of pepper. Broil 4 inches from the heat until the finnan haddie is well heated through and the butter bubbly, 3 or 4 minutes. It is not necessary to turn the slices. Remove from the broiler and sprinkle with minced chives. Serve with boiled, parsleyed potatoes.

Yield: 4 servings.

Shellfish

Shellfish are among the great table delicacies of the world. The merest mention of the tasty morsels contained within the shells of clams, crabs, lobster, scallops, and oysters can bring a sparkle to the eyes of even those people for whom fish holds no appeal.

As with all fish, shellfish should not be overcooked. They will respond to this kind of mistreatment even more violently than fin fish. Fin fish reacts to overcooking by becoming dry and tasteless; shellfish becomes tough and rubbery.

Shellfish have a great affinity for one another; they go well together and can often serve as stand-ins for each other in soups, stews, and casserole dishes. You will find that recipes for mussels, oysters, and clams are fairly interchangeable, and you can come up with some interesting and delicious dishes by combining mollusks and crustaceans.

Seafood Stew

¼ cup olive oil

1 large onion, coarsely chopped

2 cloves garlic, finely chopped

1 large bell pepper, coarsely chopped

1 2-pound, 3-ounce can whole tomatoes, drained and crushed

¼ cup tomato paste

2 cups dry white wine

1 small bay leaf

1 teaspoon dried basil, crumbled

½ teaspoon dried oregano, crumbled

½ teaspoon powdered saffron (optional)

1 dozen littleneck clams, cleaned

1½ pounds mussels, scrubbed and cleaned

1 1½-pound lobster (*or* 2 7- to 8-ounce lobster tails), cut into pieces

1 pound firm white-fleshed fish (bass, cod, halibut), cut into large cubes

1 pound large shrimp, shelled and deveined

Salt and freshly ground pepper

Fresh chopped parsley

Heat the oil in a large nonaluminum skillet and cook the onion, garlic, and green pepper, stirring, until soft and lightly colored. Add the tomatoes, tomato paste, wine, bay leaf, basil, oregano, and saffron. Bring to a boil, lower the heat, and simmer for 25 to 35 minutes. Stir frequently to prevent sticking.

Add clams, mussels, and lobster. Cover and simmer until the clams and mussels open, 10 to 12 minutes. Add fish cubes and shrimp and cook for 2 to 5 minutes longer, or until the fish is opaque and the shrimp turn pink. Turn off the heat and let stand, covered, for 5 to 7 minutes. Season to taste and sprinkle with parsley. Serve in soup bowls with warm garlic bread.

Yield: 4 to 6 servings.

Abalone

Abalone is a large sea snail found only in the Pacific Ocean. It has become extremely scarce and no fresh or frozen abalone is allowed to be shipped out of California. However, we do get small amounts of canned or frozen abalone from Mexico and Japan.

Fresh abalone meat needs prodigious tenderizing to soften it before cooking. To remove the edible portion from the shell, run a knife between the shell and the meat. Trim away the dark portion. The meat can be left whole or cut into strips. It must be pounded and pounded with even, firm strokes to ¼-inch thickness. It is ready to cook when it becomes about as limp as overcooked spaghetti. It must be cooked quickly or it will toughen—total cooking time of about a minute for both sides will do it.

Sautéed Abalone

1 pound abalone steaks, cut thin and pounded to ¼-inch thickness
Flour for dredging, seasoned with salt and pepper
1 egg, lightly beaten with 2 teaspoons milk
¾ cup dry bread crumbs
3 tablespoons vegetable oil
1 tablespoon lemon juice

Dip the abalone steaks into the seasoned flour, shaking off any excess, then into egg mixture, then into bread crumbs, patting them to make the crumbs adhere. Heat the oil in a large, heavy skillet and add the abalone slices. Cook them quickly, turning them once, about ½ minute on each side. Sprinkle with lemon juice.

Yield: 2 to 3 servings.

Clams

The American Indians were eating clams on these shores long before the white settlers arrived, and the traditional New England clambake goes back to Indian times.

Many species of clams are found in the tidal flats of America's coastline, with every region having its own particular variety. The two principal East Coast types are the soft-shell or long-neck clam, which is usually steamed, and the roundish hard-shell clam that comes in different sizes.

The largest hard-shell clams are sometimes called quahogs (the white man's somewhat garbled version of an Indian name) and are used for chowders. Very young clams are called littlenecks; the medium size are cherrystones; and a new classification called topnecks has been sandwiched between the two. The smaller hard-shell clams are served raw on the half shell, or they are broiled, baked, and used as an ingredient in seafood dishes.

The most popular of the West Coast varieties is the soft-shell razor clam, which is scalloped, sautéed, deep-fried, or made into fritters and chowders.

Clams are available all year, and are also frozen and canned. The canned minced and chopped clams are flavorful and do nicely in sauces, chowders, and casseroles.

Clams are sold by the pound and shucked

clams by the quart. For steamer clams, figure on about 20 per main-course serving. Four or six small clams on the half shell make an adequate appetizer course for one serving. You will need about one quart of shucked clams for six main-course portions. Eight quarts of un-shucked clams yield about one quart of shucked clams.

If you are buying freshly shucked clams, there should be little or no liquid in the container. The clam meats should be plump, moist, and glistening. The color varies according to locality. If clams are purchased in the shell, the shells should be tightly closed or tighten immediately when tapped. A gaping shell that does not close indicates that the creature is dead and must not be eaten. Good quality clams will keep in the shell in the refrigerator for a week if necessary, but they will gradually lose flavor. It is better to use them within a day or two.

Preparation. Clams can be sandy so you will have to scrub them well with a stiff brush under running water and soak them for 30 minutes in a brine solution, using ⅓ cup salt to every gallon of water to draw out the sand. If you have time, add ¼ cup cornmeal or cornstarch to the water for each quart of clams and leave them in this bath for three hours or so. The clams will feed on the cornmeal and excrete their dirt and grit. Scrub them well to remove all grit and proceed with the preparation. Discard any clams that float to the top or have broken shells.

To Open Clams. Very cold clams will open more quickly because the cold relaxes the muscle that holds the shells together. Press the blade of a clam or oyster knife between the shells and twist it to force the shells apart. Discard the top shell. To free the clams, cut both muscles from the bottom halves of the shells. Open the clams over a pot to save the delicious juice. You may serve the clams raw on the half shell with lemon juice.

1 *Nestle the clam in the palm of the hand, with the hinge resting against the base of the thumb. Slip the knife blade deeply into the seam sideways, then twist the knife to force the shells apart.*

2 *Cut through the muscles to free the clam from its shell.*

Baked Clams

2 dozen cherrystone clams on the half shell
¼ cup freshly grated Parmesan cheese
½ cup dry bread crumbs
½ cup finely chopped fresh parsley
¼ cup olive oil (or more)
2 to 3 cloves garlic, finely chopped
Lemon wedges

Arrange the clams in one layer in a shallow baking pan.

Combine the cheese, crumbs, parsley, oil, and garlic. (The mixture should be pastelike; add more oil if necessary.) Spread the mixture on each clam so that it is completely covered.

Preheat the oven to 425 degrees.

Bake the clams for 15 to 20 minutes, or until golden. Serve immediately with lemon wedges.

Yield: 4 servings.

Broiled Deviled Clams

2 dozen cherrystone clams on the half shell
¼ pound sweet butter at room temperature
¼ cup finely chopped shallots
3 tablespoons Dijon or Düsseldorf mustard
3 tablespoons lemon juice
Salt and freshly ground pepper
¾ cup dry bread crumbs

Arrange the clams in a shallow baking pan. A disposable foil pan with a ridged bottom is good for this because the clams will not tip.

Whisk together the softened butter, shallots, mustard, lemon juice, and salt and pepper until fluffy and light. Spread the mixture evenly over each clam to cover it completely. Cover and chill for 20 to 30 minutes, or until butter is firm. Sprinkle bread crumbs evenly over the clams.

Place the broiler rack so that clams will be 2 inches from the heat source. Broil for 3 to 4 minutes, or until crumbs are golden. Serve immediately.

Yield: 4 servings.

Steamed Clams

1 quart (about 20 clams) per person, thoroughly scrubbed

Place the clams in a deep kettle with ½ inch of water on the bottom. Cover the kettle tightly and steam the clams over moderate heat just until the clams open. This may take from 6 to 10 minutes. Don't overcook or the clams will be tough. With a slotted spoon, remove the clams to large soup bowls. Discard any that do not open. Strain the broth into cups; taste and correct seasoning. Serve the broth and small individual bowls of melted butter along with the clams. To eat the clams, remove from the shell by the neck and dip into broth and then butter. All of the clam is edible except the neck sheath.

Crab

There are three main types of crab on the market: the blue, or common, hard-shell crab found in the North and South Atlantic and the Gulf of Mexico that weighs 5 ounces; the wonderfully flavored Dungeness crab from the Pacific that weighs 2 to 3½ pounds; and the giant Alaskan king crab, the largest edible variety, which weighs from 6 to 20 pounds. Soft-shell crabs are not a separate species; they are the blue crabs found all along the Atlantic coast that have just molted their hard shells in the course of their annual growth process and have been plucked from the waters before the new shell has had time to harden. Normally, crabs have a short shelf life, but soft-shell crabs can be shipped satisfactorily, which is why we see them in the markets.

On the Pacific coast and in a very few places in the East, crab is sold whole and freshly cooked, but in the East—except when soft-shell crabs are available—most crab is in the form of fresh, frozen, or canned crabmeat. Different grades of fresh crabmeat are packaged in ½ - and 1-pound containers: lump meat, lovely, compact snowy white lumps from the large body muscles; flake meat, small pieces of white meat; combinations of lump and flake meat; and claw meat, which has a brownish color. Except for the lump meat, it is necessary to pick over the crab most carefully for small bits of shell and stiff tendons. The lump meat is free of shells and quite wonderful and, as you might expect, the most expensive, but there is no waste and one pound will serve four handsomely. Canned crabmeat does not begin to suggest what good crab really tastes like, but the frozen Alaskan crab can be satisfactory.

Preparation. If you are cooking live crabs, plunge them into boiling salted water to which you have added the juice of half a lemon, a bay leaf, a few sprigs of parsley, and 5 or 6 crushed peppercorns. Allow 8 minutes for each pound of crab. Cook quickly; as soon as the crabs turn bright pink they are done. When the crab is cool enough to handle, snap off the claws and crack them open, reserving them for later eating. Unless the crab is good size, break off and discard the legs. With a sturdy thumbnail

1 *Break off the two large claws. A hammer or nutcracker is useful in cracking them open.*

2 *With the crab on its back, remove the legs by twisting them inwards and pulling them. If the crab is small, discard the legs, which will have very little meat.*

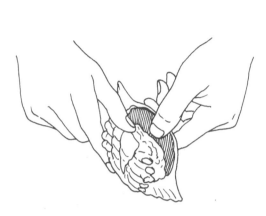

3 *To separate the top shell from the body, pry them apart with your thumb, a knife, or a spoon. The apron will come away.*

5 *It is important to remove the entrails. They may be found either clinging to the body or inside the shell. They should come away in one piece, which must be discarded.*

4 *Pull off the spongy gills, called* dead men's fingers, *and discard them.*

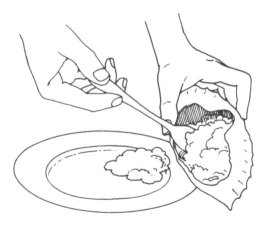

6 *Scoop all the crabmeat out of the shell. The creamy greenish brown substance is the tomalley, which is just as tasty as the more familiar white crabmeat.*

or the tip of a knife, dig under the edge of the back shell and lift it off. Scrape away the spongy gill tissue at the sides and remove the soft entrails. Remove all visible crabmeat, scraping it away from the shell with a spoon. The backfin lumps are the choicest.

Sautéed Soft-Shell Crabs

Spring means soft-shell crabs and fresh asparagus to many food lovers.

8 fresh soft-shell crabs, cleaned
1 cup milk
Salt and freshly ground pepper
Flour for dredging
6 tablespoons clarified butter (see page 260)
¼ cup fresh lemon juice
Lemon wedges
Parsley sprigs

Soak the crabs in milk for 30 minutes. Drain well on paper towels. Season with salt and pepper and dredge in flour, shaking off any excess.

Heat the butter in a large heavy skillet and, when hot, add the crabs, a few at a time. Cook over moderate heat for 3 minutes, turn, and cook for 3 more minutes. Keep warm until all the crabs are cooked.

Arrange on a warm platter and sprinkle with lemon juice. Garnish with lemon wedges and parsley. Serve immediately.

Yield: 2 to 4 servings.

Crab Louis

All recipes for Crab Louis are based on a mound of snowy crabmeat topped with a creamy dressing—a spectacular beginning for a dinner party.

⅔ cup mayonnaise
⅓ cup heavy cream, whipped
3 tablespoons chili sauce
2 teaspoons prepared horseradish
1 tablespoon fresh lemon juice
2 tablespoons chopped fresh parsley
1 tablespoon grated onion
Dash of Tabasco sauce
Salt
2 tablespoons brandy (optional)
1 pound crabmeat, preferably lump or backfin
1 medium head iceberg lettuce
3 hard-boiled eggs, quartered
2 tomatoes, cut into wedges
Watercress sprigs
Lemon wedges

In a small bowl combine the mayonnaise, cream, chili sauce, horseradish, lemon juice, parsley, onion, Tabasco, salt, and the brandy, if using. Cover and refrigerate.

Pick through the crabmeat for any pieces of shell or cartilage, but handle it as little as possible to avoid breaking up the large, firm lumps. Shred the lettuce by cutting the head in half and slicing it thin. Arrange the shredded lettuce on six salad plates. Mound the crabmeat over it, and top with sauce. Garnish each portion with egg, tomato, watercress, and lemon wedges.

Yield: 6 servings.

Crab Cakes with Mustard Sauce

1 pound crabmeat, preferably lump or backfin

½ cup mayonnaise

1 egg white

¼ cup finely minced scallions

2 tablespoons finely minced celery

1 teaspoon Worcestershire sauce

1 tablespoon lemon juice

2 slices white bread, crusts removed, finely shredded

Salt (optional)

½ cup fine dry bread crumbs (or more)

4 tablespoons butter

Mustard sauce (see following recipe)

Pick over the crabmeat to remove any pieces of shell or cartilage, but avoid breaking up the large, firm lumps. In a medium-size bowl, combine the mayonnaise, egg white, scallions, celery, Worcestershire sauce, lemon juice, and shredded bread. Add the crab and fold gently to blend. Taste to see if you want any salt. Chances are it won't be needed.

Preheat the broiler to moderate. Moisten your fingers and divide the mixture into eight portions. Shape into patties. Coat the patties on all sides with the bread crumbs, pressing them in to make them adhere. The crab cakes may be refrigerated and cooked later, if you wish. Heat the butter in a skillet large enough to hold all the patties. Turn them in the butter to coat top and bottom. Transfer them to an oiled baking sheet and place them under the broiler about four inches below the heat. Broil until nicely browned, turn, and brown the other side, about 5 minutes in all. They should be completely cooked through in this time. Cover with mustard sauce. Serve 2 crab cakes per person.

Yield: 4 servings.

Mustard Sauce

2 tablespoons butter

2 tablespoons flour

1 cup milk

½ cup chicken broth

2 tablespoons Dijon mustard

1½ tablespoons Worcestershire sauce

1 teaspoon grated onion

Freshly ground pepper

In a small saucepan, heat the butter. Blend in the flour and stir until it becomes bubbly, about 2 minutes. Remove from the heat, whisk in the milk and chicken broth, return to the heat and whisk vigorously over moderate heat until the sauce becomes thickened and smooth. Add the mustard, Worcestershire sauce, grated onion, and pepper. Taste and correct seasoning. Keep the sauce warm until ready to serve. If it gets too thick (it should be the consistency of heavy cream), thin it out with a bit of broth or milk.

Frogs' Legs

Frogs are not actually fish, but their amphibian family connections give them the right to inclusion in the seafood department.

Frogs' legs are in short supply commercially, but they are available if you happen to live near a frog farm or catch your own. Fish markets have them sporadically, almost always frozen. They are a delicious bit of eating, resembling tender chicken in texture and flavor. The smaller legs are the most tender and the most desirable. You will need from three to six per serving, depending on size. Frogs' legs are usu-ally bought skinned and ready to use. If the frogs are not prepared, cut off the hind legs close to the body. These are the only parts of the frog that are used. Wash them in very cold water and chill, then strip off the skin, begin-ning at the top of the leg. Dry them thoroughly, dust lightly with flour and sauté them in hot fat. They cook quickly, in 6 to 8 minutes. Frogs' legs are bland and are often served with a sauce or seasoned with lemon juice, salt, pep-per, chopped parsley, and a generous amount of garlic to zip up the flavor.

Herbed Frogs' Legs Sauté

8 large frogs' legs
Milk
Flour for dredging
2 tablespoons chopped fresh parsley
2 tablespoons chopped fresh chives
2 tablespoons chopped fresh tarragon, or 2 teaspoons dried
1 cup dry bread crumbs browned in 3 tablespoons butter
3 tablespoons olive oil
3 tablespoons butter
2 cloves garlic, peeled
Salt and freshly ground pepper
Lemon wedges

Soak the frogs' legs in milk for an hour or longer. Dry them well with paper towels and roll them in flour.

Combine the parsley, chives, tarragon, and browned bread crumbs and set aside.

In a skillet large enough to hold all the frogs' legs in a single layer and allow room for turning, heat the oil and butter with the garlic. Add the frogs' legs and sauté them quickly, turning them carefully with two spatulas. They are tender and will stick to the pan if they are not turned often. Remove and discard the garlic cloves when they begin to darken. When the legs are nicely browned, which will take 7 or 8 minutes, add the crumb and herb mixture and mix well with the frogs' legs. Salt and pepper the legs and serve with lemon wedges.

Yield: 4 servings.

Lobster

Lobster is one of the most popular of all shell-fish with a worldwide demand that exceeds supply. They are available all year and are sold live, cooked, or as fresh, frozen, or canned meat, but top honors must go to the lobster you buy live and cook in your own kitchen. Lobsters range from the 1-pound size, commercially graded as chicken lobster, through medium and large to the 4-pound jumbos. Small lobster, up to 3 pounds, are generally better eating. The 1- to 2-pounder is usually adequate for one serving, although a serious trencherman would have no difficulty with a 3- or 4-pounder. In most cases, the weight and number of lobster needed are dictated by purse and appetite.

There is no problem with identifying a live lobster, which is the only kind to buy. It will move its legs and its tail will curl under its body when it is picked up. If the tail hangs flaccid and loose, the lobster is undoubtedly dead and should be passed over. Lobster should be cooked soon after it is bought. Store it only briefly in the refrigerator.

The female is considered superior to the male in tenderness. You can identify the female by the soft, finlike appendages on the under-side, where the body and the tail meet. These appendages are bony in the male. The greenish substance you find in the cavity of lobster is the liver, or tomalley. The female has a roe or coral that reddens in the cooking. Both these sub-stances are delicious and should not be removed unless you wish to put them aside to be used in a sauce or mixed with bread crumbs as a stuffing for a baked or broiled lobster.

Rock, or spiny, lobsters, are shipped from California, Florida, Australia, South Africa, and the Mediterranean. Members of the crayfish family, they are generally frozen or canned and cannot compare in texture and flavor to freshly caught lobster. They have small claws and most of the meat is in the heavy tail. The frozen rock lobster tails range from ¼ to 4 pounds. They may be quickly boiled or broiled and served with melted butter.

To Boil a Live Lobster

Many lobster enthusiasts prefer boiling or steaming over any other cooking method, be-cause the delicate meat is less likely to become dry and tough.

The lobster should be alive when plunged into the water. Should this bother you, perhaps you can find comfort in the opinion of some biologists who maintain that lobster feel no pain because they lack the necessary nervous equipment. If this is not conclusive enough, use a sharp knife to cut between the head and tail shells, which will sever the equivalent of a spinal cord and make the lobster insensitive to the proceedings.

Rinse the lobster in cold, running water. Grasp it firmly by the body and plunge it head first into a large kettle of boiling, salted water— ¼ cup salt to 1 gallon of water. The lobster should be well covered with water; don't put more in than will comfortably fit. Cover the pot and, as soon as the water has returned to a boil, reduce the heat and simmer 5 minutes for the first pound, 3 minutes more for each addi-tional pound. The lobster is done when it turns red.

Remove the lobster from the pot with tongs and place it on its back. As soon as it is cool enough to handle, split the lobster from head to tail with a heavy chef's knife. Crack the large claws and open out the tail so that the meat can be removed easily when served.

The only inedible parts of the lobster are the stomach sac, located about two inches below the head, and the dark intestinal vein that runs down the center and ends at the opening of the tail. Remove them both.

To steam a lobster, follow the directions for steaming fish. Allow 18 to 20 minutes for a 1-pound lobster, and 5 minutes more for each additional pound.

Serve the lobster hot with melted butter and lemon wedges, or cold with mayonnaise.

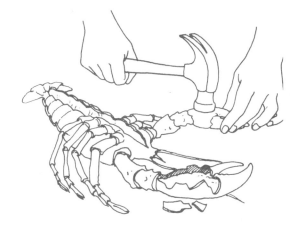

2 *Use a pounder, a hammer, or a nutcracker to break the shells on the large claws. Open out the tail.*

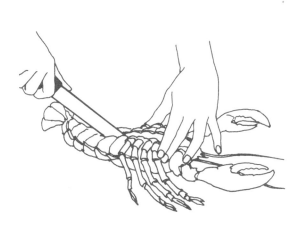

1 *With the lobster on its back, use a sharp, heavy knife to split it open from one end to the other, starting at the head end.*

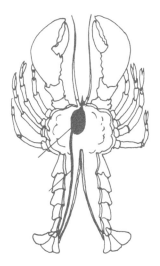

3 *At the head end, you will find the stomach sac. Twist it out and discard it. Locate the intestinal vein, a tube that runs down the middle of the lobster. This must also be discarded.*

Broiled Lobster

Preheat the broiler for 10 minutes. Allow a 1½- to 2-pound lobster per serving. Kill the lobster by inserting a sharp knife where the head meets the shell; this severs the spinal cord. Turn the lobster over on its back and, with a heavy, sharp-pointed knife, split it through the length of the body, cutting right through the back shell. Separate the halves and remove the stomach and the intestinal vein that runs down the tail section close to the back. Leave the orange roe, if present, and the tomalley, which is gray and turns green after cooking. Crack the claws with a mallet. Brush melted butter generously over the flesh side and place the lobster halves on the broiler rack, flesh side up. Broil for 12 to 15 minutes, until they are cooked through, brushing from time to time with the melted butter. Do not turn. Sprinkle with salt and pepper to taste and serve with more melted butter.

Lobster à l'Américaine

2 lobster, about 1½ pounds each
½ cup olive oil
3 tablespoons butter
1 small onion, finely chopped
4 shallots, finely chopped
1 clove garlic, finely minced
3 ripe tomatoes, peeled, seeded, and chopped
2 tablespoons chopped fresh parsley
Pinch of tarragon
1 teaspoon dried thyme
1 small bay leaf
1 cup dry white wine
¼ cup tomato purée
Tabasco sauce
Salt and freshly ground pepper

Kill the lobster by severing the vein at the base of the neck. Cut the tail crosswise into 3 or 4 neat slices following the marks of the joints. Cut off the claws and crack them. Divide the body in half, lengthwise. Remove and discard the stomach and intestinal vein. Reserve the tomalley and the coral, if present, for the sauce.

In a large, heavy skillet, heat the oil and add the pieces of lobster. Toss them around in the hot oil until the shells turn red and the lobster meat is browned. Remove the meat in the shells from the pan and reserve. Add the butter to the oil in the pan and sauté the onion and shallots until golden. Add the garlic, tomatoes, parsley, tarragon, thyme, bay leaf, and wine and simmer slowly, uncovered, for 20 minutes. Add the tomato purée, Tabasco, and salt and pepper to taste. Return the lobster to the sauce, cover the pan, and simmer for 10 to 15 minutes longer. At this point, you can pick out the meat from the claws and tail of the lobster and serve it in the halves of the shells with the sauce (the classic method), or you can serve it as is, in the shells. Whichever way you decide. strain the liquid and return it to the pan with the tomalley and roe and heat through. Pour the sauce over the lobster.

Yield: 4 servings.

Mussels

Mussels are one of our most abundant and unappreciated seafoods. These delicious little blue-black mollusks with their orange-pink flesh are sold alive in the shell and are also canned. Although mussels are available all year, they are not at peak quality during the summer months, from May until the end of August.

Allow about one quart of undrained shucked mussels, or about three quarts of unshucked, for four servings. Mussels are extremely perishable. Store them in the coldest part of the refrigerator and use them within a day of purchase. To test for freshness, try to slide the two halves of the shell across each other. If they slide, they may be filled with mud instead of mussel and must be discarded. Also discard any with open or broken shells.

Cleaning and Preparation. Wash mussels well and scrub them with a stiff brush. Mussels have beards, which should be removed for esthetic reasons. Clip them off with scissors. A splendid procedure for cleaning mussels comes from Virginia Lee, the widely known cooking expert. Place the mussels in a bucket of cold, salted water. Throw in ½ cup or so of cornstarch, corn meal, or flour and a filming of vegetable oil. Soak for an hour or longer. The mussels will feed on the starch and oil and excrete their dirt and grit. Rinse the mussels well and proceed with the preparation.

Unlike clams and oysters, mussels are never eaten raw. They are steamed until their shells open in water or dry white wine (wine is better) and served with their flavorful broth. Discard any mussel whose shell does not open wide during steaming. They are also spendid in seafood stews, soup, cold salad, and on the half shell with a tangy sauce.

Mussels Marinière

1 cup dry white wine
8 tablespoons butter
1 large onion, chopped
1 large garlic clove, crushed
4 parsley sprigs
¼ teaspoon dried thyme
Freshly ground black pepper
3 quarts mussels, cleaned
Salt (if needed)
½ cup chopped parsley

Place the white wine, half the butter, the onion, garlic, parsley, thyme, and a few grinds of pepper in a large kettle and bring to a boil. Add the mussels, cover tightly, and steam over medium heat. Shake the kettle a few times, holding the cover tightly in place (with your hands properly protected with heavy pot holders) so that the mussels change their levels and cook evenly. Cook until the shells open, 5 minutes or so. (If any do not open even after you give them a little extra time, discard them.) Add the remaining butter and chopped parsley. Taste for seasoning and correct; mussels, like clams, often need no additional salt. Serve the mussels in large bowls with some of the broth. You may remove the empty half of the shell, or let your guests take care of that operation themselves. You *must* use your fingers when you separate the shells in eating mussels—there's no other way. Serve plenty of warm, crisp French bread or rolls to sop up the broth.

Yield: 4 servings.

Steamed Mussels in Cream

8 tablespoons butter

3 tablespoons finely minced shallots

3 quarts mussels, cleaned

1 tablespoon celery leaves

1 cup dry white wine

Freshly ground pepper

½ cup cream

1 tablespoon chopped fresh parsley

Melt 3 tablespoons of the butter in a deep kettle. Add the shallots and cook, stirring, until softened. Add the mussels, celery leaves, wine, and a few grinds of pepper. Cover, bring to a boil, and steam over medium heat until the shells open, about 5 minutes. Shake the kettle several times so that the mussels cook evenly. Remove the mussels to a separate pot and keep warm. Boil the stock about 5 minutes, until it reduces a little. Remove and discard the celery leaves. Place the cream in a small, heavy-bottomed saucepan and cook slowly until it thickens. Add cream to stock and swirl in the remaining 5 tablespoons butter, stirring well. Add the parsley and return the mussels to the sauce. Heat through but do not boil. Serve the mussels and sauce in large bowls and pass a basket of warm, crusty French bread.

Yield: 4 servings.

Cold Mussels with Caper Sauce

3 quarts mussels, cleaned

½ cup dry white wine

1 small bay leaf

3 to 4 sprigs fresh parsley

Freshly ground pepper

½ cup mayonnaise, preferably homemade

1 tablespoon Dijon or Düsseldorf mustard

3 tablespoons drained capers

1 clove garlic, finely chopped

2 to 3 tablespoons fresh chopped parsley

Shredded lettuce

Put the mussels in a large deep kettle and add the wine, bay leaf, parsley, and pepper. Cover and steam for 5 minutes, or until mussels are opened. Shake the pot gently several times.

Remove from the heat. Drain and cool, reserving the broth for soup. Remove the mussels from their shells and remove the rubbery band that surrounds each mussel.

Combine the mayonnaise, mustard, capers, garlic, and parsley. Fold in the mussels. Serve at room temperature on a bed of shredded lettuce.

Yield: 4 appetizer servings.

Oysters

Contrary to the folklore that deals with oysters and the advisability of avoiding them in *r*-less months, oysters are safe to eat and available all year. However, they are at their best from September through April. The three species of American oysters are the tiny Olympia oyster, the size of a thumbnail, from the Pacific; the large Japanese or Pacific oyster; and the Eastern oysters from the Atlantic. Among the best known of the Eastern oysters are the Blue Points of Long Island and the Chincoteagues of Chesapeake Bay. Oysters differ in flavor, size, texture, and degree of saltiness according to their point of origin. They can be served raw on the half shell, which many people consider the appetizer course without peer, or they can be broiled, baked, scalloped, fried, and simmered in mouth-watering soups and stews.

Oysters are sold in the shell or on the half shell by the dozen; freshly shucked by the pint or quart. Shucked oysters should be shiny, plump, and sweet-smelling. If you buy them in the shell, they should be alive with the shell tightly closed. If the shells gape and do not close quickly in handling, the oysters are dead and must be discarded. Also discard any with broken shells. For four main-course portions, you will need 24 to 32 oysters in the shell, or about 1 quart of shucked oysters. If you are planning to cook them, it is more convenient to buy them already shucked.

Good quality oysters may be stored safely in the refrigerator for up to five days, but for top flavor they should be eaten immediately. Shucked oysters packed in their natural juices in a tightly closed container that is surrounded by crushed ice can also be refrigerated for the same length of time.

To Shuck an Oyster. Scrub the shells well. Hold the oyster with the flat side up and insert

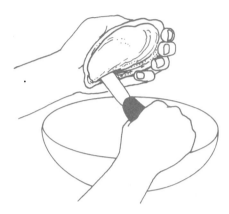

1 *Holding the oyster flat side up in the palm of your hand, insert the tip of the knife near the hinge. Run the knife between the shells, cutting through the muscle at the top as you do so.*

2 *When you have removed the flat upper shell, cut through the muscle where it is attached to the deeper shell. The oyster may be served resting in the shell.*

227

the point of the oyster knife between the shells near the narrow end where the shells are joined. Cut the muscle attached to the flat upper shell and run the knife around the rim. Work over a bowl to catch the juice. Remove the top shell and separate the oyster from the shell by cutting through the bottom portion of the muscle attached to the deep half of the shell. Strain the oyster juice through a linen towel to free it of grit. Serve the oyster resting on the deeper half shell, which will hold the liquor more efficiently than the shallower half.

Before using oysters in any fried or creamed preparation, dry them thoroughly. Bear in mind that oysters, like clams, need only to be warmed and not cooked. They should be added as a last ingredient in a soup or a stew, with the heat turned off when they are added. Oysters will not toughen as much as clams if they're overcooked, but you may not be able to recognize what you are eating.

Fried Oysters

3 eggs
Salt and freshly ground pepper
2 pints shucked oysters, drained and dried
2 cups fine dry bread or cracker crumbs
1½ to 2 cups peanut or corn oil
Tartar sauce and lemon wedges

Beat the eggs well and season lightly with salt and pepper. Dip the oysters in the egg, letting the excess drain back into the bowl, and dredge in crumbs. Shake to get rid of the excess crumbs. For a heavier coating, repeat the process, dipping each oyster in a second coating of egg and crumbs. If you have time, arrange the breaded oysters in a single layer on a rack and let dry for 20 minutes.

Heat the oil in a deep skillet or fryer to 370 degrees, or hot enough to brown a cube of bread in 30 seconds. Slide the oysters into the hot fat, a few at a time. Do not crowd the pan. Cook until golden, about 3 minutes. Remove with a slotted spoon and drain on paper towels. Keep warm in a 200-degree oven while preparing the remaining oysters.

Serve with lemon wedges and tartar sauce.

Yield: 4 servings.

Note: The breaded oysters may also be pan-fried in about ½ inch of a combination of butter and oil. Cook them long enough to brown lightly and get crisp.

Scalloped Oysters

8 tablespoons butter
1 cup crushed cracker crumbs
1 pint oysters
Salt and freshly ground pepper
¼ cup liquid from oysters
¼ cup cream
Tabasco sauce
½ cup fine bread crumbs

Preheat the oven to 400 degrees. Melt the butter in a small skillet and brush a little on the bottom and sides of a shallow baking dish. Reserve a few tablespoons for browning the bread crumbs and toss the rest with the cracker crumbs. (To make the cracker crumbs, put the crackers in a plastic bag and roll them with a rolling pin. They don't have to be finely or uniformly pulverized.) Spread the cracker crumbs over the bottom of the baking dish and arrange the drained oysters over the crumbs. Sprinkle lightly with salt and pepper. Combine the oyster liquid, cream, and a couple of dashes of Tabasco and pour over the oysters. Brown the bread crumbs in the remaining butter and sprinkle over the top. Bake for 25 minutes.

Yield: 6 servings.

Scallops

There are two types of scallops: small bay scallops and larger sea scallops with the contour of a lopsided marshmallow. The scallop morsel that we eat is actually the muscle that the scallop uses to open and close its shell. In the process of closing its shell, the scallop ejects water that propels the bivalve mollusk around the bay or sea bottom. The little creamy pink or amber-colored bay scallop may be ½ inch or less in diameter. It is sweeter and more tender (and more expensive, naturally) than the coarser-flavored sea scallop, which may be as big as 2 inches in diameter, but both are delicious.

The cooking term *scalloped* originally referred to any food that was covered with a cream sauce and bread crumbs and baked in a scalloped mollusk shell. Gradually the term was extended to foods prepared in this manner, regardless of whether they were baked in a scallop shell or a dish with the traditional scallop shape.

Scallops may be sautéed, broiled, deep-fried, poached, or skewered and grilled. Whatever the cooking method, it must be brief or the scallops will become tough and tasteless. Cook them only until they lose their translucency and turn creamy white. Bay scallops are delicious marinated in lime juice and not cooked over heat at all. The acid in the citrus juice accomplishes the cooking. Scallops can be used in any recipe for fish salad or creamed fish. One pound will serve two or three generously. Scallops are available all year, fresh or frozen.

When buying scallops, make sure they have a translucent and glistening appearance and a sweetish odor. Stay away from the dead-white scallop; it may have been frozen and thawed and its flavor will bear no resemblance to that of a fresh scallop, which is never opaque.

Scallops are ready for use just as you buy them. Rinse them quickly in cold water and dry them thoroughly. Sea scallops are not uniform in size and it is a good idea to cut the big ones to match the small ones so that they will all cook in the same length of time.

Seviche of Scallops

This uncooked preparation of Latin American origin, in which the scallops are "cooked" by the action of the acid in citrus juice, makes a lively first course or warm weather luncheon dish.

2 pounds fresh scallops, preferably bay scallops
1 cup lime juice (6 to 8 limes)
1 small red onion, finely chopped
¼ cup finely chopped parsley
⅓ cup olive oil
Dash or two of Tabasco sauce
Salt and freshly ground pepper
2 to 3 ripe avocados, peeled and cut into cubes
Chopped chives or chopped parsley

If you are using the larger sea scallops, slice them thin. Rinse and dry the scallops. Place them in a nonaluminum bowl and pour the lime juice over them. They should be completely covered. Cover the bowl and refrigerate for 3 hours. You will notice that the scallops lose their translucent quality and become opaque, just as when they are exposed to heat. Remove from the refrigerator and allow to stand at room temperature for 1 hour. Stir several times.

Drain well and discard the juice. Toss the scallops with the onion, parsley, oil, Tabasco, salt, pepper, and avocado. Taste and correct the seasonings. Arrange on a lettuce-lined platter or individual dishes. Sprinkle with chopped chives or chopped parsley.

Yield: 6 servings.

Note: You may use slices of fresh flounder or fresh sole fillets in place of the scallops. Cut the fish into ½-inch-thick strips and proceed as above.

Scallops au Gratin (Coquilles Saint-Jacques)

1½ pounds bay or sea scallops
1½ cups dry white wine
6 shallots, finely chopped
1 small bay leaf
4 parsley sprigs
1 tablespoon celery leaves
¼ teaspoon dried thyme
3 tablespoons butter
½ pound mushrooms, thinly sliced
2 tablespoons lemon juice
3 tablespoons flour

If you are using the large sea scallops, cut them into small pieces, about the size of small bay scallops. Rinse the scallops and place them with wine, shallots, bay leaf, parsley sprigs, celery leaves, and thyme in a nonaluminum saucepan and bring very slowly to a boil. Lower the heat and simmer for 4 or 5 minutes, just until the scallops become opaque. Strain the liquid through a fine wire strainer and reserve. Set the scallops aside.

In a good-sized skillet, melt the butter and add the sliced mushrooms and lemon juice. Cook for 5 or 6 minutes over a low flame. Sprinkle with flour and stir until the sauce becomes bubbly. Add 1½ cups of the reserved cooking liquid and stir over

1 cup heavy cream
Salt and freshly ground pepper
Freshly grated Parmesan cheese
½ cup fresh bread crumbs
Melted butter

moderate heat until the sauce thickens and becomes smooth. Strain the sauce, reserving the mushrooms, and return the sauce to the skillet. Add the cream and stir the sauce over low heat until it becomes thick and coats the spoon. Add salt and pepper to taste.

Preheat the oven to 425 degrees. Mix the scallops and mushrooms. Grease 6 baking shells or ramekins. Spoon about 1½ tablespoons sauce into each; add the scallops and mushrooms. Cover with more of the sauce. Sprinkle with Parmesan cheese and bread crumbs and drizzle a little melted butter over each. Bake for 12 to 15 minutes, or until golden brown. These may be made in advance and heated at serving time. If they have been refrigerated, bake for 25 minutes at 350 degrees, or until heated through.

Yield: 6 appetizer servings.

Sautéed Scallops

1½ pounds bay or sea scallops
6 to 8 tablespoons butter
Flour for dredging
½ cup dry vermouth
½ cup heavy cream
Salt and freshly ground pepper
1 tablespoon finely chopped chives
1 tablespoon finely chopped fresh parsley

Rinse the scallops and dry well with paper towels. If using sea scallops, cut the large ones into pieces of equal size so that all will cook evenly.

Melt 6 tablespoons of butter in a large, heavy skillet. Dredge half the scallops in flour, shaking off any excess. (Put the floured scallops in a colander and shake it over the sink to facilitate this; too much flour will make the scallops gummy instead of crisp.) Add the scallops to the hot butter and shake the pan constantly so that the scallops roll about and cook on all sides. Cook them only until they become opaque, 2 or 3 minutes. Remove with a slotted spoon and keep warm while you flour and cook the remaining scallops. Add more butter if necessary.

Add the vermouth to the pan over moderately high heat and scrape up all the browned bits on the bottom of the pan with a wooden spoon. Reduce the heat and add the cream, stirring constantly until thickened, 2 to 3 minutes. Do not let the sauce boil. Season to taste with salt and pepper and pour the sauce over the scallops. Sprinkle with chopped chives and parsley. Serve hot.

Yield: 4 servings.

Broiled Herbed Scallops

2 pounds bay or sea scallops
7 tablespoons butter
2 tablespoons finely chopped
  scallions
½ teaspoon dried basil
½ teaspoon dried tarragon,
  crumbled
2 whole cloves garlic, peeled
2 tablespoons finely chopped
  parsley
Salt and freshly ground pepper
2 tablespoons fine dry bread
  crumbs
Lemon wedges

Preheat the broiler.

Rinse the scallops and pat them dry with paper towels. If you are using sea scallops, cut them so they are uniform in size. Heat the butter in a small skillet and add all the remaining ingredients except the bread crumbs and lemon wedges and cook over low heat for 2 or 3 minutes, stirring. Don't let the butter brown. Discard the garlic, add the bread crumbs, and mix well. Arrange the scallops in a shallow, heatproof baking dish large enough to hold them in a single layer. Pour the bread crumb mixture over them, tossing so that the scallops are well covered.

Place the baking dish on the broiling rack 4 inches from the heat and broil for 6 to 8 minutes, depending on their size. Turn the scallops during cooking to brown on all sides. As soon as they become opaque, they are done. Serve at once with lemon wedges.

Yield: 4 to 6 servings.

Shrimp

The possibilities for the preparation and serving of shrimp are boundless. They can be served hot or cold, in soups or bisques, as an hors d'oeuvre or a salad. They can be broiled, sautéed, curried, creamed, pickled—the list could go on and on. And as varied as they are versatile, shrimp come in all sizes from the tiny ones that need hundreds to make a pound to the giant size with ten or less to the pound. The latter can be woody and tough; you will have more enjoyable eating with the medium or large shrimp. The color of shrimp varies, ranging from a light grayish green to a light tan or pink, depending on the point of origin, and bears no relation to quality.

 You can buy "green shrimp" in the shell (*green* is the industry's term for fresh raw shrimp); or cooked shrimp in the shell; or

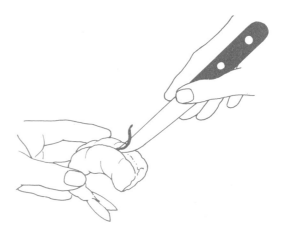

To devein a shrimp, use a knife tip, a toothpick, or your fingertips to tease away the dark vein down the middle of the back. It may not come out in one piece.

cleaned and shelled, cooked or uncooked or flash-frozen shrimp. And then there are canned shrimp. There is a rumor that they were invented by someone who hated shrimp and it may very well be true. This does not apply to the tiny little shrimp that come from the West Coast and the Scandinavian countries and are sold in glass jars. At least they have the virtue of being decorative.

One pound of shrimp in their shells will serve two or three. It takes about 1½ pounds of shell-on shrimp to yield roughly 1 pound of shelled shrimp. Shrimp should be dry and firm when you buy them. If they are limp and appear moist from leaking juices, they may have been frozen and defrosted.

It doesn't matter whether you shell shrimp before or after cooking; do whichever is more comfortable for you. If you shell them before

cooking, include the shells in the cooking liquid for added flavor. The shells are easily removed with your fingers or the tip of a knife. Use the knife tip to remove the black vein that runs down the center of the back. Like the beard on the mussel, it is quite harmless, but it looks unattractive. Leave the shrimp tails for a handle if you are preparing barbecued or grilled shrimp or scampi.

Shrimp must never be overcooked. Unless you know from experience that your fish dealer cooks them properly, you are better advised to buy shrimp raw and cook them yourself. Three to five minutes in boiling water, no longer, will give them color and firmness. After that they become tough and rubbery. Don't cook shrimp before adding them to a sauce or they will be overcooked.

Boiled Shrimp

2 quarts water
1 teaspoon salt
½ bay leaf
2 celery stalks with leaves, cut into 3-inch pieces
4 peppercorns, crushed
1 to 2 pounds raw shrimp, peeled or unpeeled

In a large saucepan, combine the water, salt, bay leaf, celery, and peppercorns. Bring to a boil and boil for 5 minutes.

Add the shrimp and return to the boil. Reduce the heat, cover, and simmer for about 3 minutes. If you are using frozen shrimp, they will need a little more time. As soon as the shrimp turn pink, they are done. Drain at once. When cool enough to handle, remove the shells and devein, if this has not yet been done.

As an appetizer course, four or five shrimp may be served on a bed of greens and topped with a rémoulade sauce or Russian dressing (see page 459).

Shrimp with Feta Cheese

6 to 8 medium tomatoes, *or* a 1-pound, 12-ounce can peeled plum tomatoes

4 tablespoons olive or vegetable oil

2 cloves garlic, finely minced

½ cup dry white wine

2 tablespoons minced fresh parsley

½ teaspoon dried oregano

Salt and freshly ground pepper

2 pounds uncooked shrimp

½ pound feta cheese, crumbled

If you are using fresh tomatoes, peel and seed them. If using canned tomatoes, drain them and reserve the liquid for another use. Chop the tomatoes into small chunks and place them in a large, nonaluminum saucepan with 2 tablespoons oil, the garlic, wine, 1 tablespoon parsley, oregano, salt, and a few grinds of pepper. (Feta cheese may be salty; taste it to judge the amount of salt you need in the sauce.) Simmer, uncovered, over low heat for 25 to 30 minutes, or until the sauce is thickened but not reduced to a purée. The small chunks of tomato lend interest to the finished dish. Stir the sauce from time to time with a wooden spoon to make sure it doesn't scorch.

While the sauce is cooking, prepare the shrimp. Remove the shells and the dark vein. Rinse and dry well with paper towels. Heat the remaining 2 tablespoons oil in a large skillet and sauté the shrimp until they turn pink, 5 minutes or so, tossing them as they cook. Remove with a slotted spoon.

Preheat the oven to 400 degrees. Place the cooked shrimp in a shallow, lightly oiled baking dish large enough to hold them in a single layer. A 9 by 13-inch dish will do nicely. Cover with the tomato sauce and sprinkle with the crumbled feta cheese. Bake for 10 to 15 minutes, until hot and the cheese is very soft. Sprinkle with remaining tablespoon of parsley and serve with hot boiled rice or pasta.

Yield: 6 to 8 appetizer servings, 3 to 4 as a main course.

Scampi

Scampi are the Italian variety of the crustacean that we know as shrimp, generally sautéed in a highly seasoned sauce. They make an excellent hot hors d'oeuvre for parties, or they can serve as a main course.

24 to 30 large shrimp, about 15 to the pound

½ teaspoon salt

5 tablespoons butter

Shell and devein the shrimp, leaving the tail shell on. Sprinkle the shrimp lightly with salt.

3 tablespoons olive oil

3 or 4 large garlic cloves, finely minced

1 teaspoon dried oregano

1 teaspoon dried basil

1 tablespoon finely minced fresh parsley

Lemon wedges

Heat the butter and oil in a large, heavy skillet. Add the garlic, oregano, basil, and parsley. When the oil is hot, add the shrimp, as many as will fit in a single layer in the skillet. If you crowd them, they won't cook properly. Cook them only until they turn pink, 2 or 3 minutes to a side. Stir them with a spoon and shake the pan while they are cooking. When done, remove them with a slotted spoon and continue until all are cooked. Place them in a chafing dish or on a warm platter and pour a little of the seasoned oil in which they were cooked over them. Serve with lemon wedges.

Yield: 8 appetizer servings, 4 to 5 as a main course.

Shrimp Casserole

2 pounds shrimp

1 pound mushrooms, sliced

6 tablespoons butter

1 large clove garlic, peeled and quartered

2 tablespoons chopped fresh parsley

1 28-ounce can Italian plum tomatoes

5 tablespoons flour

½ cup cream

2 tablespoons Worcestershire sauce

¼ cup dry sherry

Dash of Tabasco sauce

Salt and freshly ground pepper

½ cup bread crumbs

Boil the shrimp according to directions on page 233. Drain and set aside.

In a medium-size skillet, sauté the mushrooms in 2 tablespoons of the butter until the liquid evaporates. The mushrooms can cook while you prepare the sauce.

Preheat the oven to 375 degrees.

In a 4-quart saucepan, melt 2 tablespoons butter, add the garlic, and cook slowly until the garlic is golden brown. Remove the garlic with a slotted spoon and discard. Add the parsley and tomatoes, reserving ½ cup of the juice, and cook for 5 minutes, breaking up the tomatoes with a wooden spoon. Make a paste of the flour and the reserved tomato juice and add to the tomatoes. Cook and stir until the sauce comes to a boil and becomes smooth and thickened. Lower the heat and add the cream, mixing well. Stir in the Worcestershire sauce, sherry, and Tabasco. Cook for 5 minutes and remove from the heat. Add the shrimp, mushrooms, salt, and pepper. Taste and correct the seasonings. Pour the mixture into a well-greased 2-quart casserole and sprinkle the top with bread crumbs. Dot with the remaining 2 tablespoons butter. Bake for 20 to 25 minutes, or until hot and bubbly. Serve with boiled rice.

Yield: 6 servings.

Shrimp and Cucumbers

This makes a nice change from the usual cocktail sauce.

1 pound cucumbers, peeled, seeded, and coarsely chopped
2 teaspoons coarse salt
1 large Spanish onion, thinly sliced
1 pound peeled and deveined cooked shrimp
2 tablespoons lemon juice
¼ cup olive oil

Sprinkle cucumbers with 1 teaspoon coarse salt. Allow to stand for 30 to 45 minutes to remove the liquid. Rinse well under cold water and squeeze to remove all water. Set aside.

Add the remaining salt to the sliced onion and allow to stand until soft, 10 to 15 minutes. Rinse in cold water and squeeze dry.

Combine cucumbers, onions, cooked shrimp, lemon juice, and olive oil. Mix well and arrange in a lettuce-lined bowl. Serve as an appetizer or light luncheon dish.

Yield: 4 servings.

Squid

Squid is a small member of the octopus family. For centuries it has been highly regarded among people in the Orient and in the countries bordering the Mediterranean, but it has never been very popular among Americans. However, as other seafoods become scarcer and costlier, more squid is being sold. It has a tougher texture than chicken or beef because it has few connective tissues to break down during cooking, but it has good flavor that is often compared with that of oysters, clams, scallops, mussels, and abalone. The problem of toughness can be overcome by proper cooking.

The smaller squid, 5 to 6 inches long, are preferable to the larger because they are generally more tender. Figure ½ pound per serving. They are available all year, fresh or frozen. Squid can be sautéed, stewed, deep-fried, braised, served cold in a salad, or cooked in a chowder.

To Clean Squid. Fish markets sell cleaned, dressed squid but it is not difficult to do yourself. Hold the tubelike sac or body (also known as the mantle) with one hand and, with the other, gently but firmly pull off the tentacles. All the contents of the sac should come away with the tentacles. Cut the tentacles below the eyes, reserve the tentacles, and discard everything else from the eyes down.

1 *With a pulling and twisting motion, separate the body, or mantle, from the head end, which includes the tentacles. The intestines will remain attached to the head and come out with it.*

Inside the sac is a quill-like bone. Remove it and thoroughly wash out the inside of the sac, rinsing in water several times until the water runs clear. Peel off the sac's outer skin under cold running water and peel off as much of the skin on the tentacles as you can. Dry thoroughly. The squid is now ready to be cooked.

To cut strips or pieces, cut the body lengthwise down the center. Spread the body open and cut into strips. To make rings, cut across instead of lengthwise. The tentacles can be chopped or left whole.

Cooking time varies according to the size and thickness of the squid. When you can pierce the squid easily with a fork, it is done.

2 *Make a cut between the eyes and the tentacles. Discard the head and keep the tentacles.*

4 *After washing the inside of the body thoroughly, pull off the skin on the outside. Sometimes pulling downward on the fin will help the skin to come away. Peel the tentacles as much as possible.*

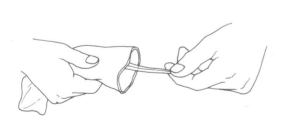

3 *Locate the quill, or pen, inside the body and pull it out. This is the squid's vestigial shell.*

5 *Make a cut down the middle of the body so that it may be opened flat. Cut into strips. Or, if you prefer, do not cut lengthwise, but crosswise, to make rings.*

Braised Squid with Mediterranean Sauce

⅓ cup olive oil

4 cloves garlic, crushed

4 pounds squid, cleaned and sliced into rings

2 sprigs parsley

Salt and freshly ground pepper

2 medium bell peppers (red and/ or green), cut into large dice

1 medium onion, coarsely chopped

3 tablespoons tomato paste

1 tablespoon finely chopped parsley

Heat 2 tablespoons oil in a large, nonaluminum skillet and cook 1 whole clove garlic until golden. Add the squid and stir over medium heat until the squid whitens and just starts to boil. The squid will exude a great deal of liquid. Add the parsley, salt, and pepper. Cover, lower the heat to a simmer, and cook for 45 to 60 minutes, or until the squid is very tender. Do not let it boil because the squid will be tough and rubbery.

About 15 minutes before the squid is done, prepare the sauce. Heat the remaining oil in a medium skillet and add the peppers and onion. Cook briskly, stirring, until the peppers and onion are soft and lightly colored. Add the remaining garlic and stir. Stir in the tomato paste and heat through. (If you cook it too long it will lose its texture. You want the tomato paste to remain separate from the peppers and oil.)

Drain and discard all but 1 or 2 cups of liquid from the squid, depending on taste. Transfer the squid to a warm platter and spoon the sauce on top. Sprinkle with parsley and serve immediately with rice or pasta.

Yield: 4 to 6 servings.

6

Eggs, Dairy Products, and Cooking Oils

Eggs

The egg represents a truly stunning example of natural packaging. It comes with a rich assortment of nutrients all done up in a tidy little container that can double as a cooking pot. It has a broad range of uses, besides serving as a main course for breakfast, lunch, or dinner. Eggs were making cakes rise long before baking powder was ever thought of. They can act as an emulsifier in mayonnaise and salad dressings and as a thickener in soups, sauces, and custards, or they can puff up to gossamer lightness in a soufflé. They will do all this when treated properly. But eggs can really get tough if they're not handled with care.

Composition

A large egg contains about 76 calories, of which the yolk has 59 and the white 17. The yolk contains all the vitamins except C, plus significant amounts of iron, phosphorus, protein, and fat. The fat is saturated and the yolk is high in cholesterol, which may place the egg yolk off-limits for people concerned with a diet low in cholesterol and saturated fat. The white, known as albumen, is pure protein and is acceptable in almost any kind of diet. Both the yolk and the white contain large amounts of water, which adds to their general usefulness, since liquid is essential in baking and cooking. All of the calcium in eggs is in the shell, not in the edible part.

Buying Eggs

Few of us these days live near chicken farms where day-old eggs are available, but most supermarkets do a brisk business with eggs and we can be reasonably sure of their stocks being fresh. A voluntary government inspection program grades the finest eggs as Grade AA Fancy Fresh Quality, followed by Grades A, B, and C. Grades AA and A are recommended for frying, boiling, and poaching, with Grade AA first choice. It has a higher proportion of thick white and a firm, well-centered yolk. As an egg ages, the white becomes thinner and less able to keep the yolk centered in the egg. The yolk itself doesn't do much better. The membrane that confines it begins to stretch and the yolk flattens, making it a poor candidate for a poached or fried egg.

Lower grade eggs, which are naturally less expensive, may be used in muffins, shortened cakes, or in other cooked preparations where the quality of the egg is masked by other ingredients.

There is no difference in flavor or nutritive values between white and brown eggs. The color of the shell is due to the pigment produced by the hen. The color of the egg yolk doesn't mean much, either, and highly colored egg yolks are not necessarily richer in vitamin A. A speck of blood in the yolk is harmless and can be ignored. Lift it out if it bothers you.

When you buy eggs, take an extra minute to open the carton to make sure there are no cracked eggs, because bacteria can seep through the cracks and set up housekeeping inside the egg. This can be dangerous unless the egg is very well cooked. Ten minutes of boiling or an hour of baking in a cake will destroy the bacteria. But to be perfectly safe, stay away from cracked eggs even if they are offered at bargain prices. Do not buy eggs from unrefrigerated counters, because any time out of the cold diminishes the life of an egg.

To Test for Freshness

No one will ever have to tell you when an egg has gone bad. You couldn't possibly miss the odor that seeps out through its porous shell. And it is unlikely that a busy market would offer really stale eggs for sale. But what about the eggs that have been in your refrigerator for a while? How can you know if they are suitable for serving or whether they can be used only in cooking? Place the egg in a bowl of cold water. If it bobs to the surface or floats, it is stale or bad. If it is fresh, it will fall to the bottom of the bowl. The reason is simple. The shell of an egg is porous, and it is lined with a delicate membrane that separates from the large end of the shell to form an air chamber. The size of the air chamber increases as the egg ages. Consequently, a fresh egg is heavier than an old egg and will sink.

Storing

Eggs have one outstanding quality that sets them apart from other foods of animal origin in that, aside from deterioration in quality, they will keep for a considerable length of time. Many factors contribute to their superior keeping qualities. Even though the shell of the egg is porous, the pores are normally filled with organic material that impedes the entrance of microorganisms into the egg, unless the surface is damp. Which is why you *never* wash eggs before you store them. Secondly, the egg comes equipped with two membranes inside the shell that act as further lines of defense against bacterial invasion. And finally, the white itself contains a number of substances with antibacterial action that enable it to resist microorganisms that might invade it. However, once an eggshell is broken, its defenses are down and it is susceptible to bacteria.

Store eggs in the refrigerator, preferably in the carton in which you bought them rather than on the open shelves provided by well-meaning refrigerator designers. The closed container protects the eggs from air penetration, which slows the loss of moisture and carbon dioxide, preserving freshness. The United States Department of Agriculture recommends that eggs be stored with the blunt end up, which keeps the yolks centered.

If you have some leftover egg yolks or whites, you can store them in the refrigerator for three or four days. Egg yolks can be used for emulsified sauces, such as mayonnaise, hollandaise, and béarnaise, to enrich sauces, and in rich custards. Egg whites can be used for meringues, angel food cake, or for clarifying stock. Store the unbroken yolk in a covered container with enough cold water to cover the entire yolk, which will keep it from hardening. Store the whites in a covered container.

Yolks and whites can also be frozen. To keep the yolks from coagulating, gently stir in 1 teaspoon sugar or ½ teaspoon salt for every 6 egg yolks. Use the sweetened egg yolks for dessert and the salted ones for sauces or to add to egg dishes. Frozen egg whites can be thawed and used exactly like fresh ones. Place the egg whites in a glass or plastic container, cover tightly, and label the container with the number of egg whites it holds. Allow a little room in the container for expansion. Defrost at room temperature. They will take about an hour to thaw. Whites may also be frozen in ice cube trays. Each cube is roughly the equivalent of one egg white. After the egg white cubes are frozen, remove them from the trays and store in a plastic bag in the freezer. Use as needed.

Measuring Eggs

The size of an egg is no reflection of quality or nutritive value. Egg sizes are standardized by the government, which classifies them according to the minimum weight of a dozen eggs. There are six classes: jumbo, weighing 30 ounces; extra large, 27 ounces; large, 24 ounces; medium, 21 ounces; small, 18 ounces; and peewee, or pullet, 15 ounces. Most recipes, including those in this book, are based on large eggs, 24 ounces per dozen. If you are using a different size, the following measurements by volume may help you to figure the substitutions. For an 8-ounce cup you will use about:

	Whole eggs	Egg whites	Egg yolks
Extra large	4	6	10-11
Large	5	8	12
Medium	6	9-11	13-14
Small	7	11-12	15-16

The yolk of an egg is about 1⅓ tablespoons and the white about 2 tablespoons. If you need only a portion of an egg when increasing or decreasing a recipe, beat it slightly and measure about 1½ tablespoons for half an egg and about 1 tablespoon for a third.

Separating Eggs

It is easier to separate the yolk from the white when the egg is cold, but this observation may be academic if you plan to beat the whites or

As the yolk is passed from one half of the shell to the other, the white drips down into the bowl or cup. Because it is important not to let a single speck of yolk get mixed with the whites, it is safer to break one egg at a time over a small bowl and then transfer each egg white to another, larger bowl before breaking the next egg. That way, if you make a mistake, you only lose one egg white.

A different way to separate an egg is to break it into your hand. Let the white drip through your separated fingers; the yolk will remain in your hand. Put the yolk in another bowl and transfer the white to a third, larger bowl.

yolks immediately, since they should always be at room temperature if you hope to achieve maximum volume.

If you are going to beat the whites, you will need two small bowls and one large one. Crack the center of the egg on the rim of the bowl or use the blunt side of a knife (the sharp side could break the yolk) and divide the shell in two. Hold the egg over one of the small bowls and pass the yolk from one half-shell to the other, letting the white drip into the bowl. When all the white has dripped out, slip the egg yolk into the second small bowl and transfer the white to the large bowl to be used for beating. This extra small bowl maneuver is a safety measure in case some egg yolk gets mixed with the white, which could ruin your whole bowl of egg whites. This way, you stand to lose only one egg white.

There is another method of separating eggs

that you might like better once you get used to it. Crack the egg and drop the whole egg into the palm of your hand. Separate your fingers slightly and let the white dribble between them into a bowl. Your hand is softer than the egg-shell and less likely to pierce the yolk.

When you separate the yolk from the white, you will see two twisted mucilaginous projections that anchor the yolk in the thick white and keep it centered in the egg. These are known as *chalazas* and are whipped along with the rest of the white in the beating process.

Beating Egg Whites

The success of a spectacular soufflé is dependent on a number of things, chief among them the amount of air bubbles that are beaten into the egg white. The air bubbles become trapped within the walls of protein, where they keep expanding. The longer the whipping, the more the bubbling and the firmer the foam. Too few air bubbles and the soufflé is a flop. However, too many will make the egg white incapable of further expansion during baking, producing another kind of disaster. The object is to beat the egg whites to just the proper degree of stiffness—a not impossible task.

Start with the right utensils. Use a stainless steel, unlined copper, glass, or china bowl—not aluminum or plastic. Aluminum will tinge the egg white gray, and plastic is unsatisfactory because traces of fat from other uses have a way of clinging to a plastic surface and are difficult to remove. A deep, round-bottomed bowl that is narrower at the base is the best shape so that the whole mass of egg whites stays in motion. The bowl should be large enough to allow for expansion—it is possible for egg whites to increase to six or seven times their original volume. The bowl and beaters must be absolutely clean and free of fat and moisture and without the tiniest trace of egg yolk. With egg yolk present, the water in the egg white will emulsify the fat in the egg yolk, hindering the formation of air cells.

There has been continuing controversy over the relative merits of beating egg whites with a balloon whisk in an unlined copper bowl, where the acidity of the metal helps the whites to rise and keep their stability after they have risen, versus beating them in a stainless steel or glass bowl, where you need to add a pinch of cream of tartar to supply the acidity. Let's lay the controversy to rest. We have yet to meet anybody (ourselves included) who could spot the difference in a properly made soufflé regardless of how the egg whites were beaten. A hand beater or an electric one works just as well as a whisk, and certainly an electric appliance produces less wear and tear on the cook.

Be sure to have your egg whites at room temperature—about 70 degrees. The proteins will expand more rapidly when the egg whites are not chilled. If you haven't had time to bring them to room temperature, set the bowl of egg whites in a basin of warm water and stir them about gently to unchill them.

When using an electric mixer, start on low speed until the whites are foamy. When this point is reached, add $\frac{1}{4}$ teaspoon cream of tartar for each 4 egg whites to supply the acid, and a pinch of salt. Both salt and cream of tartar will delay the foaming action, which is why you wait until the foam has started to form before adding them. Do not attempt to beat egg whites stiff in a blender or a food processor. It won't work because the blades can't pull in enough air to lighten them. If you are using a hand-held electric mixer, keep turning the bowl from left to right and move the beaters up and down the sides of the bowl to make sure that the whole bulk of whites is kept in motion.

When making a meringue, never add sugar to whites until the whites have reached the point where they stand up in peaks. Then add the sugar slowly, a little at a time, whipping as you go. If you add the sugar too early or too rapidly, you will end up with a marshmallow sauce that will never firm up.

After a minute or two of beating the egg whites you can increase the speed to fast and beat until the whisk or beater, when removed from the mixture, pulls with it stiff peaks that have a shiny, glossy surface. This is what is meant by "stiff but not dry." Your clues are the gloss and the shine. Overbeaten egg whites become dry and opaque. They may have greater volume but their cells will not stretch to capacity when heated. If you have overbeaten, add another egg white and beat again; the shiny, satiny peaks will return. Once egg whites are beaten, they should be combined with other ingredients at once, before the air you have just pumped into them starts to diminish.

Folding Egg Whites with a Spatula

Folding Egg Whites by Hand

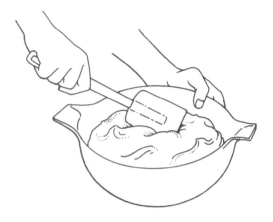

1 *Once you have gently stirred a quarter of the beaten egg white into the base, put the rest of the whites on top and cut down through the middle of the mixture with the spatula.*

1 *Having mixed a quarter of the beaten whites into the base and added the remaining whites to the bowl, plunge your hand to the bottom and lift the heavier mixture up toward the top.*

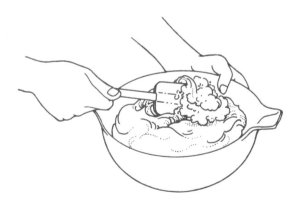

2 *Scoop the base from the bottom, drawing it upward and toward the side of the bowl with the spatula. Repeat both steps, turning the bowl as you do so, until the two preparations are combined.*

2 *With your hand straight and stiff, use a slicing motion to cut down through the contents of the bowl. Continue scooping and slicing motions, turning the bowl with each stroke.*

Folding Egg Whites

Adding beaten egg whites to a batter or a sauce base must be done quickly and gently in order to retain as much air in the whites as possible. Rough handling will lose you some of the air bubbles you just pumped into them. Always fold the light whites into the heavier mixture. Begin by stirring one-quarter of the egg whites into the heavier mixture to lighten it. Then scoop the remaining egg whites on the top. Combine them by plunging a wide rubber spatula down through the center of the mixture to the bottom of the pan. Lift up the batter and deposit it on top of the foam. Move the bowl a quarter of a turn with each stroke and continue rapidly, bringing up the sauce base and folding. Do not overfold or the egg whites will deflate. It should not take more than a minute to complete the folding process.

The folding can also be done with your hands. After you have lightened the mixture and added the remainder of the beaten egg white, use your hand to scoop up the heavy material on the bottom and cover the whites. Then cut it in with a sharp, clean motion of your hand to the base of the mixing bowl, as though cutting a cake. With your other hand, turn the bowl slightly each time you repeat these slicing and lifting motions. You will find the blending is quickly and easily accomplished.

Beating Egg Yolks

Egg yolks may be beaten with a wire whisk or with an electric beater. As they are beaten, they thicken and become lighter in color. The recipe that directs you to beat egg yolks and sugar until "thick and lemon-colored" is not precise enough in describing when that point is reached. What is not always stated in recipes is that the egg yolk and sugar should be beaten

Ribboning *is what the batter does when it has been sufficiently beaten. It will run from the whisk or spoon in a thick ribbon that folds back on itself and remains on the surface for a few seconds.*

until the mixture runs in a broad ribbon (hence the term *ribboning*) from the side of the spoon or beater and folds on itself as a ribbon would. When that point is reached, you can be sure that the mixture will heat with no danger of being grainy. The beater has forced air into the protein of the yolk and, at the same time, the sugar is absorbing the moisture contained in the yolk, forming a syrup.

The beating process will take from 5 to 8 minutes. Beat the egg yolks in the small bowl of an electric mixer for 3 minutes, until they are pale lemon-colored. Reduce speed and add sugar. Then increase speed and beat for 5 minutes longer. Test for ribboning.

Egg Yolks as Thickeners. Egg yolks are splendid as thickeners or enrichment for hot mixtures such as soups and sauces, but they must be added carefully, just before serving. The yolks must be heated slowly before being added or you run the risk of a frosting of scrambled eggs on whatever it is you are preparing.

Beat the eggs lightly in a bowl or large cup and add half of the hot sauce or soup slowly, bit by bit, to heat the yolks. When this mixture is smooth and thick, return it to the original pot of simmering liquid, whisking it in gradually. Don't let the mixture boil or it will curdle. There is an exception to this, however. If the mixture contains a starch, such as flour or cornstarch, let it come to a boil until just one or two bubbles appear—no more than that— and reduce the heat so that the liquid remains at a simmer.

Egg Cookery

Eggs are not capricious; you can depend on them to proceed along predictable lines. For one thing, fresh eggs will always be superior to old eggs in taste and texture (except for hard-boiled eggs, which we will get to later.) And for another, eggs will get tough if they are cooked too long or over too intense a heat. Egg proteins respond quickly to heat. The whites begin to become jellylike when heated to about 140 degrees, the yolks begin to coagulate at about 149 degrees, and the whole egg begins to coagulate at about 156 degrees. As you can see, this is well below the boiling point of 212 degrees. At very high temperatures, the rate of coagulation is so rapid as to be almost instantaneous. Except for omelets, eggs must always be cooked over low, gentle heat.

You will have better texture and volume in eggs, whether you cook them or beat them, if the eggs are at room temperature, about 70 degrees. You can warm cold eggs by placing them in a bowl of lukewarm water for 30 minutes or so. Always let the eggs reach room temperature in their shells. If exposed to air, the yolks become dry and harden.

When cooking an egg in its shell, you can

lessen the danger of having its innards leak out through a crack if you pierce it first. Make a pinhole in the large end, penetrating about ¼ inch so that the pin goes through the membrane surrounding the air pocket. As the air from the pocket expands in the hot water, it will use the pinhole as an escape hatch, thereby releasing the pressure that might otherwise crack the shell. You can buy an egg piercer, but this represents the epitome of specialized gadgetry when a common pin or needle will do as well.

Eggs can be cooked soft, medium hard, hard, coddled, poached, scrambled, or fried, with a variety of modifications of each process. The difference between hard-boiled, soft-boiled, medium-boiled, and coddled is a matter of timing rather than of method. There are any number of ways of boiling eggs. They can be started in cold water or boiling water, or brought to a boil and allowed to rest in the water for a certain length of time. The method described here is simple and satisfactory. Just watch the clock.

Soft-Boiled, Medium-Boiled, and Coddled Eggs

Soft-boiled eggs have runny yolks and soft whites. Have enough boiling water in a saucepan, preferably enamel or glass, which won't discolor, to cover the eggs by at least an inch. Pierce the blunt end of the egg and lower it carefully into the boiling water with a spoon. When the water returns to the boil, reduce the heat so that the water just simmers and start timing. Simmer for 3 minutes and remove from the water. A jumbo-size egg will need 30 seconds more; if the egg came directly from the refrigerator, it will need about 1 minute longer.

A medium-cooked egg has a firm opaque

white and soft yolk. It will need about 4 minutes of simmering.

The French *oeufs mollets* translates into a medium-boiled egg with the white firm enough for handling and the yolk runny—rather like an egg poached in its shell. They are used for eggs in aspic and similar dishes and can be served hot or cold. They are cooked as in the preceding directions, but for 6 minutes. Plunge them immediately into cold water to stop the cooking. Peel as soon as the shell is cool.

Coddling produces eggs with wonderfully tender whites and no yolk discoloration. With a spoon, lower the egg into a pan of boiling water that covers it by at least an inch. Cover the pan and turn off the heat. The length of time the egg remains in the water determines how well-done it is. For soft, lightly coddled eggs, allow 6 minutes; for firmly coddled eggs, 8 minutes.

Hard-Boiled Eggs

Hard-boiled eggs present an exception to the rule that an egg can never be too fresh, for a very fresh boiled egg will not peel smoothly. The next time you have to deal with a hard-boiled egg that refuses to give up its shell neatly, don't blame yourself. Not enough time elapsed in the journey from the chicken coop to your kitchen. The reason lies in the acidity of a newly laid egg. After a few days a normal chemical change takes place in which the acidity of the egg changes to alkalinity. When the egg becomes alkaline, it will part with its shell nicely. Sometimes eggs are sprayed with a fine mist of tasteless mineral oil to retard air penetration and preserve their freshness. Here again, we'll have a too-fresh egg and an egg-peeling problem. In an interesting experiment, an egg less than 2 hours old was made alkaline by exposure to ammonia vapor for 10 minutes, and the shell was peeled off cleanly.

Another egg idiosyncrasy that distresses some cooks is the grayish green discoloration that can appear around the yolk of a hard-boiled egg. The cooks may not have to take the onus for eggs that won't peel smoothly, but this one can be laid directly at their door. It is caused by cooking the eggs at too high a temperature and for too long a time. The discoloration is not harmful, but it isn't attractive, either. It is due to the iron sulfide that forms as a chemical reaction between the iron in the yolk and the hydrogen sulfide liberated from the sulfur-containing proteins in the white. It is similar to the discoloration on the tines of the silver fork with which you ate the eggs, except that the deposit on the fork is silver sulfide.

To hard-boil an egg, pierce the blunt end of the egg with a pin and lower the egg carefully into a pan of boiling water that covers the egg by an inch. As soon as the water returns to the boil, reduce the heat so that the water simmers gently. Simmer for about 10 minutes, depending on the size of the egg (see chart below). When the time is up, drain the eggs, crack the shells lightly with the back of a spoon, plunge the eggs into cold water, and peel them.

These are the cooking times for hard-boiling eggs. If they are taken directly from the refrigerator, add 1 minute.

U.S. Graded Eggs	Time
Small and Medium	10 minutes
Large	11 minutes
Extra large	12 minutes
Jumbo	13 minutes

Shirred Eggs

Shirred eggs are baked in small, shallow dishes just large enough to hold one or two eggs (you can use glass custard cups). They are cooked quickly in a hot oven until barely set—the white coagulated but not hardened and the yolk runny. The egg will continue to cook in the hot dish even after it is removed from the oven.

Preheat the oven to 425 degrees. Place the oven rack in the upper third of the oven, the hottest part. Melt 1 teaspoon butter in each baking dish and swirl it around to coat the bottom and the sides. Place the dishes on a cookie sheet. Break one or two eggs into each dish and sprinkle the tops with 1 teaspoon cream or butter. Cover with aluminum foil, which will hold the steam as it condenses and helps to cook the yolk. Bake for 5 minutes. Remove from the oven, uncover, and sprinkle lightly with salt and freshly ground pepper.

If you wish, you can garnish the shirred eggs with pieces of sautéed chicken livers, grated Parmesan cheese, small pieces of cooked pork sausage, or a light dusting of fine bread crumbs.

Poached Eggs

A poached egg is cooked in simmering water until the white is coagulated and the yolk still runny. Eggs for poaching should be very fresh with firm whites and plump yolks. Use a nonstick or a buttered fry pan. Add water to a depth of 2 or 3 inches. Bring the water to a boil and add 1 tablespoon of plain white vinegar to help the egg coagulate faster. Reduce the heat so that the water barely simmers.

To keep the egg from spreading, break each egg individually into a small cup (a ½-cup measuring cup works well), lower the cup into the water and gently tilt out the egg. Don't try to cook too many at a time—perhaps just two or three—and distribute them in the water so they don't impinge on each other. Spoon the simmering liquid over the egg for 3 or 4 minutes, until the white becomes opaque and the yolk feels just resistant to the touch. Or you may

cover the pan and let it stand off the heat for about 8 minutes. By that time, the whites and the yolks should be sufficiently firm. Remove with a slotted spoon or a skimmer and drain thoroughly. If you are not using the eggs at once, plunge them into cold water to stop the cooking. If you wish to keep the eggs for use on the following day, store them in the refrigerator in a bowl of cold water. In either case, reheat the eggs by placing them in a bowl of lightly salted hot, not boiling, water for a few minutes.

If the eggs look a bit ragged, trim them with scissors.

Fried Eggs

Eggs must be fried over very low heat. If the pan is too hot, the under surface of the egg will be overcoagulated and toughened before the heat reaches the upper surface. A tough brown edge on a fried egg is coagulated, dehydrated, and partly scorched protein. It is called cracked protein and it has its own distinctive flavor, which some people like. If you happen to be one of them, you will know what to do. For most people, a perfect fried egg has a thick compact white, uniformly coagulated and tender, and an unbroken yolk covered with a layer of coagulated white.

You can fry eggs in any fat of your choice—butter, margarine, oil, or bacon fat. The more fat you use, the faster the heat penetration will be. Heat the fat in a skillet before adding the egg. The hot fat will coagulate the egg quickly and prevent it from spreading. Crack the egg into a shallow bowl and slide it into the heated, greased pan. Cook until the eggs are firm. You can speed up the cooking by basting the top of the egg with hot fat or you can cover the skillet during the last 2 minutes of cooking time to finish cooking the top. Sprinkle lightly with salt and freshly ground pepper. Salt hardens egg proteins, so use very little.

Scrambled Eggs

Some people like scrambled eggs dry; others prefer them moist and creamy. The same process will produce either result, depending on when you remove the pan from the heat. Longer cooking will produce drier eggs.

Use a heavy cast aluminum, enameled cast-iron, or nonstick pan. Beat the eggs well in a bowl with salt and freshly ground pepper. Use very little salt because salt hardens egg proteins. For lighter eggs, add 1 teaspoon water or cream, but if you like them thick and eggier, omit the additional liquid. Heat 1 tablespoon butter per egg, add the beaten egg, and turn the heat very low. The secret of making good scrambled eggs is to heat the mixture slowly and scrape the egg from the bottom and sides of the pan as it coagulates. Stir the mixture gently with a whisk (a rubber spatula if you are using a nonstick pan), lifting the egg mixture up and over from the bottom as it thickens and curds form. Keep breaking up the curds; the eggs will be softer and creamier if the curds are small. Eggs dry out very quickly toward the end of the cooking, so remove the pan from the heat when the eggs are about three-quarters done if you want them moist. The heat in the eggs will continue to cook them and they will be just right by the time they are transferred to the plate.

You can add small amounts of any of the following, stirring them into the egg mixture before scrambling: crisp bacon bits, pieces of cooked sausage, finely chopped ham, or chopped herbs, such as parsley and chives.

Any water-producing vegetables such as scallions, onions, tomatoes, and mushrooms should be lightly sautéed before being added, or they will interfere with the creaminess of the

eggs. Finely cut smoked salmon should be heated in the butter before the eggs are added and scrambled.

Omelets

Although there are many cooks who have achieved a degree of popular acclaim because of their way with a fry pan and a couple of lightly beaten eggs, omelet making is not beyond the scope of anyone who appreciates eating one. It requires some dexterity and speed, but chiefly practice.

It is generally more satisfactory to make a 2- or 3-egg omelet for individual servings than a huge one to serve two, three, or more. The size and shape of the pan are important; a 7- or 8-inch skillet with a rim that flares is a good one for individual omelets, and if it has a nonstick surface, so much the better. The non-stick pans make special omelet pans unnecessary.

Have the eggs at room temperature. Break 2 large or 3 small eggs into a mixing bowl with a pinch of salt and a few grinds of pepper and beat or whisk them lightly with a fork or small whisk. Mix them just enough to blend the yolks and whites. You can ruin an omelet before it is even started by vigorous beating. If the egg protein is overbeaten, it liquefies and loses its ability to develop volume, resulting in a hard, flat pancake instead of a light fluffy omelet.

Heat the empty omelet pan over high heat. It will be at the right temperature when a single drop of water dribbled on the surface bounces off. Add 1 tablespoon of butter and swirl it around to grease the sides and bottom. If the pan is at the proper heat, the butter should melt and foam almost at once. When the foam diminishes, the butter will be at the right temperature. The hot fat is essential because it insulates the egg mixture from the bottom of the pan. If it were only warm, the butter would mix with the eggs, the omelet would stick, and you would end up with something more like scrambled eggs than an omelet.

When the butter stops foaming, quickly pour in the eggs. From this point on, speed is the keynote. The eggs will frill around the edges almost at once. With a spatula, lift an edge of the omelet and tilt the pan to run the liquid egg underneath. Continue to do this until there is no more liquid egg to run underneath. Even if there are some shiny little pools of egg, they will continue to cook on their way to the table. Turn off the heat. A perfect omelet is soft inside with the eggs barely set. With the spatula, start rolling the omelet, beginning at the end of the pan near the handle, and tilt the pan forward so that the omelet rolls itself. Grasp the handle of the pan, palm underneath with the fingers on top, and hold a warm plate in the other hand. Quickly invert the pan and tilt the omelet onto the plate in a nice, neat roll. From the moment the eggs go into the pan until the omelet is turned into the serving dish will be under a minute. Serve at once. If you are making a succession of omelets, wipe the pan with a paper towel after each, reheat the pan, add butter, and continue.

Filled Omelets. Set the filling at the very center of the omelet before folding. Use about 3

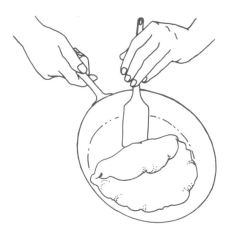

2 *To roll the omelet, tilt the skillet away from the handle. Use the spatula to give the omelet a nudge. It should roll itself.*

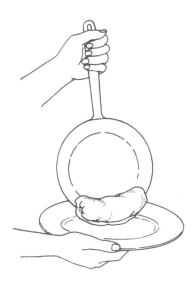

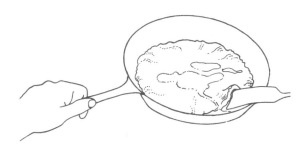

1 *As soon as the egg is poured in, it begins to set. Lift a corner of the omelet and tilt the skillet toward that corner so that the uncooked egg runs under it. Continue until there is no more runny egg.*

3 *Supporting the handle with the palm of your hand, tip the skillet so that the omelet rolls out onto the plate, seam side down.*

tablespoons of filling—creamed fish or chicken; dried beef; sautéed chicken livers; sliced mushrooms, sautéed or creamed; ripe tomatoes that have been peeled, seeded, chopped, and sautéed; sautéed potatoes and onions; or any other mixture that appeals to you.

Grated cheese should never be added to the omelet mixture before cooking as it will make the omelet stick to the pan. Instead, sprinkle 2 or 3 tablespoons of coarsely grated Swiss or Cheddar cheese over the omelet just before folding. The heat of the omelet will melt the cheese.

One tablespoon of fresh minced herbs, such as parsley, chives, chervil, or tarragon, may be mixed into the eggs before making the omelet. Finely chopped watercress leaves and stems also make an interesting addition, and ¼ teaspoon each of dried rosemary, thyme, savory, and marjoram are a pleasant combination.

Soufflés

In spite of the aura of mystery that surrounds a soufflé, nothing is simpler to prepare. A soufflé is made up of two parts—the base, which can be a heavy cream sauce, or beaten egg yolk mixed with the flavoring ingredients; and stiffly beaten egg white, which is the essential ingredient. The air bubbles beaten into the egg whites expand in the oven heat, making the soufflé light and puffy. (A cold soufflé is a kind of mousse and is not to be confused with a true soufflé, which is always baked. Recipes for cold soufflés will be found on page 562.) The egg white is beaten until stiff but not dry, and then folded into the soufflé base gently so as to disturb the air bubbles as little as possible. To insure a light soufflé, add one more egg white than yolk. Beaten egg white deflates rapidly and should be combined with the other ingredients at once.

The classic soufflé dish is a round, porcelain dish with striated sides, but it is not necessary to confine yourself to this type. You can use a metal charlotte mold or heatproof glass casserole.

Always bake the soufflé on a rack placed in the lowest third of the oven. The bottom of the dish will get a concentrated blast of heat that gives the soufflé the upward push it needs to help it rise nicely. For a soufflé with a crisp outside, bake directly on the rack. If you don't want a crust on the bottom and sides, bake the soufflé in a pan of hot (but not boiling) water. Serve soufflés at once; they do not take kindly to waiting.

Basic Soufflé

Heat 4 tablespoons of butter and stir in 4 tablespoons of flour. Cook and stir until bubbly, about 2 minutes. Remove from the heat and add 1½ cups of milk all at once, stirring vigorously with a wire whisk. Return to the heat and cook and stir until the sauce is smooth and thickened. This is the soufflé base. To it, you may add 1 cup puréed or finely chopped vegetables, grated cheese, or finely chopped poultry, meat, or fish. Add seasonings to taste– salt, freshly ground pepper, Tabasco, Worcestershire sauce, dry mustard, or whatever you think will enhance the flavor. Beat 5 egg yolks until thick and add slowly to the cooled mixture. Fold in 6 stiffly beaten egg whites and spoon into a well-buttered 2-quart baking dish. Bake in a preheated 350-degree oven for 35 to 45 minutes, or until the soufflé is well-puffed and brown. The shorter baking time will give you a soufflé that is moist and even slightly runny in the center; the longer time will give you a soufflé that is firm all the way through.

Milk

Milk and milk products occupy an important place in American eating and cooking habits. Milk provides proteins and fats, and is rich in calcium, a bone-building material not present in large quantities in most other foods. Cow's milk is also a source of vitamins A, D, E, and B, and it contains traces of many minerals, but it is a poor source of iron. Any adult who depended solely on milk products would be likely to develop iron-deficiency anemia. Milk does not taste as sweet as its 5 percent sugar content might lead you to expect, because milk sugar, lactose, is less sweet-tasting than cane sugar.

Not all physicians and nutritionists agree about the value of milk in the adult diet. Some contend that adults do not need large amounts of calcium and that the fat and cholesterol in milk products are in fact bad for us. Despite the controversy, most of us would be at a disadvantage if we were obliged to cook or bake without dairy products.

Whole milk is fresh, fluid milk that contains between 3.25 and 4 percent milk fat and at least 8.25 percent nonfat solids, which are the source of the proteins, minerals, and vitamins. Most milk is fortified with vitamin D, and some with vitamin A.

Homogenized milk is whole milk that is mechanically blended to distribute the fat particles evenly throughout the milk. Consequently, the cream does not rise to the top. The disadvantages in cooking with homogenized milk are that it curdles easily when heated; custards made with it take longer to cook; it produces a slightly different texture in cooking from that of whole milk; sauces are stiffer; and fat separation is greater. However, since virtually all whole milk and cream are homogenized today, there is often no choice.

Skim milk is whole milk from which some of the fat has been removed. It contains all the protein, calcium, and B vitamins of whole milk, but it has lost some of the fat-soluble vitamins. There are two types of skim milk—*low-fat milk,* also called *partly skim milk,* and *skim milk,* also called *nonfat milk.* Both types are usually labeled "fortified," which means that some of the vitamins that were lost with the fat have been replaced. Low-fat milk contains between .5 and 2 percent milk fat and it looks and tastes more like whole milk than does skim milk. Skim milk contains less than .5 percent milk fat.

Skim milk is the milk of choice for people who must restrict fats and cholesterol in their diets, or for those concerned with calories. Either type can be used in place of whole milk in cooking or baking. Sauces and cream soups may not have as rich a taste as those made with whole milk or cream, but they should have a smooth, velvety texture and be most palatable.

Raw milk is whole milk that has not been pasteurized or homogenized. There are people who feel that pasteurization destroys not only the natural taste of milk, but also some of the vitamins and the useful bacteria along with the bad. Raw milk is sold in health food and specialty shops. Because of the small amount produced and the special care that must be taken to produce it, the cost is about twice that of pasteurized milk.

Buttermilk was traditionally the liquid that remained in the churn after the butter was made, but these days this lovely natural stuff is available only to those who live on or near a dairy farm. Buttermilk is now a cultured product, made by artificially fermenting whole milk or skim milk with a bacterial culture. Buttermilk may be substituted for sour milk in any recipe.

Dry whole milk solids are pasteurized milk particles made by air drying the milk and removing the water. There are also dry milk solids from which the fat has been removed. Both can be reconstituted with water or added directly to food for additional enrichment. The usual proportion is 2 to 4 ounces of dry milk to an 8-ounce cup of water. Reconstituted dry milk improves in flavor if you allow it to stand for several hours in the refrigerator before using. This is because the milk sugar, or lactose, is less soluble than the table sugar we ordinarily use and it takes a while before it fully dissolves.

Evaporated milk is a canned milk concentrate prepared by evaporating half the moisture from fresh whole milk. It can be used in its concentrated form in cooking or returned to its original volume by adding an equal amount of water. It has a slight caramelized taste and color caused by the heat used in processing. It is a convenient product to have on hand as a substitute for cream in sauces and soup, but once opened, it must be refrigerated and treated like regular milk. Unopened cans should not be held longer than six months. Evaporated milk, either whole or skim, which is also available, can be whipped. Chill the milk in an ice cube tray in the freezer until ice crystals form around the edges. It will beat up in glossy peaks. Use it promptly.

Sweetened condensed milk is whole milk in which the water content is reduced about 60 percent and the sugar content is raised to 40 to 44 percent. It is not sterilized because of its high concentration of sugar. Unopened cans should not be held longer than six months. Once opened, it should be refrigerated in its original container. The sugar acts as a preservative and it will remain in good condition for at least ten days. Because of its high sugar content, it cannot be used interchangeably with evaporated milk in recipes. It is used principally for candies and desserts.

Yogurt is a thick, custardlike product with an acid, tangy flavor that results from milk being fermented with special bacterial cultures. It is made from either whole milk or skim milk, and it comes unflavored and in a wide variety of flavors and fruit combinations. Unflavored yogurt is used in dips, salad dressings, and as a substitute for sour cream.

Cream

There are several kinds of cream on the market, each designed for a different use. They are pasteurized or ultrapasteurized, the latter to increase their shelf life.

Half-and-half is a mixture of milk and cream that more nearly resembles milk. It contains a little more milk fat (10.5 percent) than whole milk and may be used in place of light cream. Its purpose is to impart the taste of cream with fewer calories. It will not whip.

Light cream, also called coffee cream or table cream, is cream that contains at least 18 percent milk fat. It will not whip.

Whipping cream, or heavy cream, is the richest cream available, containing at least 36 percent milk fat. Most of the heavy cream today is ultrapasteurized, a process that exposes cream to very high heat. This extends its shelf life and keeps it fresh for 60 to 90 days. Unfortunately, ultrapasteurized cream does not have as pure a taste as heavy cream not so treated, but the subtle difference in flavor can be masked if the whipped product is flavored and sweetened.

To Whip Cream. Chill the bowl and beaters and have the cream very cold before whipping so that the butterfat remains firm. The colder the utensils and cream, the lighter the whipped cream. If the butterfat gets warm, it will be unable to support the bubbles of air that you are pumping in, and the cream will not foam or thicken. To avoid spattering, whip the cream in a high narrow bowl rather than a low wide one. Cream will double in volume when whipped. Use a whisk, a rotary beater, or an electric beater. Beat slowly in the beginning, then gradually increase speed, but slow down when soft peaks begin to form. It is important to recognize when to stop, because only a few extra turns of the beater can change your snowy white froth into a lump of butter. If the cream threatens to turn into butter, carefully whip in 2 tablespoons cold milk.

You can add sweetening at any time during the whipping. Sugar delays the clumping of the fat and there is less danger of overbeating once it is added. If you are using a flavoring extract or a liqueur, add it when the cream starts to thicken. Use 1 to 1½ tablespoons liqueur for each cup of cream. For mousses, Bavarian creams and frozen soufflés, whip the cream only until it barely mounds, halfway between the pouring and spooning stages. If the cream is whipped too stiffly, it will cause a buttery taste.

Stabilizing Whipped Cream. If a cake is to be filled or decorated with whipped cream in advance, the cream will need to be stabilized so that it will stay firm. For each cup of cream to be whipped, dissolve 1 teaspoon unflavored gelatin in 2 tablespoons cold water and heat until it is thoroughly melted. Let it cool. Whip the cream until it barely mounds. Pour the gelatin slowly into the cream as you continue to beat until it is stiff. This changes the texture slightly, but it gives the cream stability. A little confectioners' sugar also acts as a stabilizer because of the cornstarch in it.

Crème fraîche, which has recently become popular in American kitchens, is a matured, thickened heavy cream with a slightly sour flavor tinged with the taste of crushed almonds. Cream in France is not pasteurized and contains the lactic acid bacteria that allow it to thicken and sour naturally. However, by adding sour cream, yogurt, or buttermilk to our pasteurized heavy cream, you restore the necessary ferments and can make a reasonable facsimile of *crème fraîche* in your own kitchen. It is lovely over fresh fruit and, unlike sour cream, it can be boiled without curdling. It will keep for two weeks or longer in the refrigerator, so that you can always have some thick cream on hand.

Blend together in a saucepan 1 pint heavy cream with ½ pint sour cream or yogurt. If you are using buttermilk, 2 teaspoons will do for 1 pint of cream. Heat very gently just to remove the chill and get the action started, to no higher than 90 degrees. Remember that your index finger normally registers about 98 degrees, so that when you touch the cream, it should feel just slightly cool. If it is too hot, you

will kill the bacilli and nothing will happen. Transfer the mixture to a container, partly cover, and let stand at room temperature, on the pilot light of a stove, or in an oven kept warm by its pilot light. Depending on the temperature, it will thicken in 8 to 24 hours. Every 8 hours or so, take a peek and stir it. This procedure will work with ultrapasteurized cream as well as with regular cream, but the ultrapasteurized may take a little longer to thicken. As soon as it has thickened sufficiently, cover the container and refrigerate.

Nondairy coffee cream is frequently bought by people who are under the impression that it is unsaturated and low in calories because it contains no dairy products. Actually, most nondairy creams are made with chemicals, artificial flavorings, and coconut oil, which is highly saturated. Buyers would be better off with the calories and fat content of light cream. If you are in doubt about a product, write the manufacturer for information about the kind of oil that is used.

Sour cream is sweet cream that has been inoculated with a lactic acid culture, in contrast to the natural product of a bygone era that was made by allowing unpasteurized heavy cream to sour naturally in a warm spot behind the stove. Sour cream has a slightly acid taste and is used for dips, in sauces, and in baking.

Sour half-and-half has fewer calories than the regular sour cream. Do not substitute it for sour cream in baking, but it can be used in dressings, as a topping for fruits and baked potatoes, and for any noncooking purpose for which you might choose regular sour cream.

Storing

All milk products should be kept cold and covered. Fluid milk can be frozen in its container. It takes about 2 days in the refrigerator or about 6 hours at room temperature to defrost completely. Sometimes small flecks of solids form.

Not all heavy cream will whip successfully after being frozen. It is safer not to attempt to freeze it, but whipped cream freezes very well. Whip it, sweeten and flavor it, and freeze it in individual servings for future uses.

Dairy sour cream and yogurt should not be frozen, although there are some dishes prepared with them that freeze very well.

Cooking with Milk and Cream

Anyone who has ever heated milk knows how quickly it can scorch and how little time it needs to boil over. The skin that forms on the surface of the milk as it is heating in an uncovered pot acts as a lid, holding in the steam. The steam is just as determined to escape—and there you are, with a milky mess. The formation of the skin is due to the evaporation of water from the surface and the effect of the heat on the milk fat and calcium salts. The brownish color and objectionable flavor that develop in scorched milk come from the caramelization or burning of lactose, the sugar contained in milk.

To avoid these minor disasters, never boil milk; heat it until bubbles form around the sides of the pan and steam escapes. This is known as *scalding*. Formerly milk was scalded to kill bacteria, but this is no longer necessary. Now we scald milk only to speed up the preparation and cooking time of breads and custards. Scalding hastens the dissolving of sugar and the melting of fat. Heating may be done over direct heat or in the top of a double boiler over hot water. It is helpful to rinse the pan with cold water before heating milk in it. The water reacts with the metal of the saucepan to form a film, making it easier to scald the milk without burning the pan. It is also helpful to stir the milk gently while it is heating to create a froth. The froth will minimize the formation of a skin.

Cream can be reduced for a rich sauce by boiling it until it becomes thickened and takes on a pale golden color. But when adding cream to any dish cooked on top of the stove, do not let it boil because it will curdle. Always heat dishes containing cream over a low heat, stirring often.

Never allow a mixture that contains sour cream to boil, either, or it will curdle. If you are preparing a sour cream sauce, add the sour cream at the end, after the sauce is cooked. Use salt sparingly in sour cream recipes, as salt also tends to cause curdling.

About Curdling. A velvety cream sauce or soup that suddenly separates, or curdles, is an unwelcome sight for any cook. Curdling does not affect the flavor of a preparation, but it looks unattractive. Different kinds of milk have different tolerances to heat. Evaporated milk does not curdle easily; next in stability is fresh milk; and the least stable is dry milk. A major cause of curdling in cooking milk products is cooking over too high a heat and for too long a time. The addition of a small amount of flour or cornstarch to the cold milk will discourage curdling. An egg yolk custard will be less likely to curdle if you beat 1 teaspoon cornstarch or flour into the cold milk for every 4 egg yolks used. You can sometimes rescue a custard that has begun to curdle during boiling by pouring it at once into a cold bowl and beating it vigorously with a whisk.

There is also a danger of curdling if you add a milk product to an acid food. But if you reverse the process and add the acid food slowly to the milk, you prevent curdling. In making cream of tomato soup, for instance, add the hot tomatoes to the hot milk and you can be sure of a creamy, smooth result. Again, a thickening such as flour added either to the tomatoes or to the milk before they are combined will also help to stabilize the fat molecules and prevent curdling.

Butter, Cooking Fats, and Oils

Cooking fats are the culinary maids-of-all-work. Used properly, they heighten food flavors; they provide the medium that browns and cooks; they bring lightness and moisture to baked products; and they form the emulsifying agents in gravies and mayonnaise. We would have a hard time cooking without them.

Fats for cooking include both solid fats and cooking oils. Among the solid fats are butter, margarine, vegetable shortenings, and lard. Many of these are interchangeable in terms of bringing a dish to completion, but different fats will result in differences in flavors and textures. Liquid oils can be substituted for melted butter in most baking and cooking recipes, but the butter flavor will be missing. The one thing that won't be affected is the calorie count, for fat is fat, whether it comes from a cow or from corn. One tablespoon of butter or margarine is 102 calories; one tablespoon of corn, cottonseed, sesame, soybean, or safflower oil is 120 calories; one tablespoon of peanut or olive oil is 119 calories; one tablespoon of lard is 117 calories; and a tablespoon of vegetable shortening is 111. Butter and margarine are the lowest because they are only 80 percent fat; the others are 100 percent fat.

About Saturated and Polyunsaturated Fats. In today's cholesterol-conscious society, we hear a great deal about polyunsaturated and saturated fats. These terms apply only to the chemical properties of the fats and have nothing to do with their taste, consistency, or cooking qualities. Fats are composed of three types of fatty acids, depending on their chemical composition. Saturated fatty acids have the effect of raising the cholesterol level in the blood, poly-unsaturated fatty acids tend to lower it, and monounsaturated fatty acids are neutral in their effect, neither raising it nor lowering it to any extent. Olive oil is the prime example of a monounsaturated fat.

Polyunsaturated fats are usually liquid oils of vegetable origin, such as corn, cottonseed, soybean, safflower, and sunflower. Although coconut oil is a liquid vegetable oil, it is highly saturated. Peanut oil is lower in polyunsaturates than the other vegetable oils and therefore less desirable. Saturated fats are usually of animal origin and are solid at room temperature—butter, lard, meat fats, and products made from whole milk, such as sweet and sour cream, cheeses, and the like. Although solid shortenings such as Crisco and Spry are made from liquid oils, the process of hydrogenation that changed them into a creamy solid with a long shelf life also alters their chemical composition and turns them into saturated fat.

Butter

All butter is made from fresh sweet or soured cream and by law it must contain at least 80 percent fat. The remaining 20 percent consists of water with some milk solids. Small amounts of salt for flavor and preservation are sometimes added. Butter is the least nutritious of all the dairy products, supplying vitamin A and fat and little else. However, its taste and the delicate, distinctive flavor it brings to baked and cooked foods have made it an essential kitchen ingredient for cooks all over the world.

Butter comes in several types and grades. It

is graded by United States government inspectors on the basis of taste, aroma, body, and texture. The top quality is Grade AA, or U.S. 93 Score. Grade A is close to Grade AA. The lower grades are made from soured cream and may have an acid or even musty taste and poor texture.

Salted butter contains about 2 percent salt. Unsalted or sweet butter—the terms are synonymous—is more delicate in flavor and is preferred by many discriminating cooks. Since salt can mask an off-flavor, some cooks feel that they are more assured of freshness when they buy unsalted butter. Sweet butter and salted butter are interchangeable in recipes, unless one or the other is specifically called for.

Whipped butter is butter with air or inert gas incorporated to make it soft and easy to spread. Whipping increases not only the volume but also the price. You can make your own by whipping regular bar butter. Allow it to soften at room temperature, then beat very well with an

To measure bulk butter, fill a measuring cup with water in an amount equal to the difference between 1 full cup and the required amount of butter. Add butter until the water level reaches 1 cup.

electric beater until it becomes light and fluffy. Do not substitute whipped butter for butter in recipes because the additional air makes it difficult to gauge the actual amount of butter you are adding.

Buying and Storing
To be sure of quality, buy Grade AA. Sniff the package—a rancid odor will seep through packaging. Butter is sold in 1-pound and ½-pound packages, and in individually wrapped sticks of 4 ounces (¼ pound) each. The undivided 1-pound blocks are often cheaper than cut butter because they are less expensive to package.

Store butter in the coldest part of your refrigerator in a tightly covered container or in its original package. If uncovered, it will absorb flavors of other foods. Butter for immediate use should be kept in the butter compartment, if your refrigerator has one. Well-wrapped sweet butter will keep in the refrigerator for about a week; salted butter for 10 days to 2 weeks. Butter freezes very well and can be kept frozen for months. Wrap the package in moisture-proof freezer wrappings and seal it tightly to prevent moisture loss. It should be thawed slowly in the refrigerator.

Measuring Butter. Butter that comes in quarter-pound sticks practically measures itself. Each quarter-pound stick consists of 8 tablespoons, or ½ cup. There are 2 cups to the pound.

To measure bulk butter, use the simple water displacement method. A solid will displace its own weight in liquid. If you want ½ cup butter, fill a measuring cup with ½ cup cold water and add butter until the water reaches the 1-cup mark. Drain off the water.

Cooking with Butter
Butter has a low smoking point and must be heated over moderate heat or it will brown and burn. As butter begins to get hot, it foams up,

and then the foam begins to subside. This is the point when the butter is at the proper temperature for sautéeing.

Because of its low smoking point, butter is often combined with cooking oil for sautéeing. Oil has a higher smoking point and this enables the fat to reach a higher temperature without burning. But it is still possible to brown butter for a sauce by allowing the butter to heat very slowly so that it will brown evenly without burning. Don't try to hurry it and don't let it get too dark; butter that is burned has a bitter taste.

Clarifying butter is still another way to prevent it from becoming overheated and burning. Drawn or clarified butter is merely melted butter with the milk solids—the whey and the casein—removed. These milk solids separate from the liquid when butter is heated to a high temperature. They settle to the bottom of the pan, discolor, and become bitter. Using clarified butter allows you to do the most delicate sautés without burning or discoloration. Adding oil to unmelted butter will serve as a substitute for clarified butter in most sautéeing or frying, but it will not be quite as elegant as a sauté prepared with the clarified butter alone.

Clarifying Butter. Cut the butter into small pieces and melt it over moderate heat. With a spoon, skim off the foam, remove the pan from the heat and let it stand for a few minutes to allow the milk solids to settle. Skim the clear yellow liquid off the milky residue left on the bottom of the pan and store it in a covered jar in the refrigerator. This clear liquid is the clarified butter. Discard the residue; it is the whey and it is unusable. The foam is the casein and may be used to season vegetables. Clarified butter will last for weeks because the whey and casein, which are subject to bacterial change, have been removed. Clarified butter is the *ghee* used in the cooking of India, and for centuries it has provided the answer to preserving butter in a country with a hot climate and limited refrigeration.

Creaming Butter. Creaming butter introduces air into the butter, which acts as an important leavening in cake making. The butter should be at room temperature. If it is very firm, squeeze it with your fingers to soften it. To cream, use a wooden spoon, a hand whisk, an electric mixer, or your fingers. Beat it until it becomes fluffy, light, and creamy. As the butter becomes aerated, you will see it turning whiter and lighter.

Margarine

Like butter, margarine must contain 80 percent fat by law. The remaining 20 percent consists of water, milk solids, and salt, unless the margarine is unsalted. Almost all margarines are enriched with added vitamins and are tinted to give them a butter color. Margarines are usually emulsions of milk and refined vegetable oils, although some have added animal or dairy fats. If you are using margarine because you are concerned with cholesterol, read the label carefully and choose a margarine that lists *liquid* corn, safflower, sunflower, or soybean oil as its first ingredient.

Margarines are perishable and must be kept covered and refrigerated. Salt-free margarine should be stored in the freezer. Margarine may be substituted for butter in the same quantities in any recipe. In some instances, the texture it produces in baking and cooking may be somewhat different from that provided by butter, and the butter flavor will be missing. Use the stick margarine for baking. The soft tub margarine is suitable as a table spread and for dressing cooked vegetables, but it burns too quickly to be used for pan-frying. Diet margarine cannot be used for any kind of cooking because it is largely water.

Vegetable Shortenings

Vegetable shortenings are bland, solid shortenings based on oils like corn, cottonseed, peanut, and the like, that have been hydrogenated (treated with hydrogen). The process of hydrogenation converts them into a solid state and they can be stored in a covered tin at room temperature, which is probably their chief virtue. Solidifying the oil changes its essential fatty acids from polyunsaturated to saturated. Vegetable shortenings are acceptable for baking and may be substituted for butter in the same quantities.

Lard

Lard is fat rendered from pork. Leaf lard, which comes from the layered fat around the kidneys rather than from trimmings and incidental fatty areas, is considered the best. Good lard, particularly leaf lard, creates a very short, flaky texture in pastry and biscuits because of its chemical structure, but it is used less successfully in cake baking. Lard is also used in frying and sautéeing, although it is not as popular as it once was, since we have become accustomed to vegetable shortenings. Lard should be refrigerated in covered containers.

Cooking Oils

Cooks and nutritionists value liquid vegetable oils for their cooking properties, for their flavors, or, in some cases, their neutral taste, as well as for the polyunsaturated fatty acids contained in oils such as safflower, soybean, corn, cottonseed, and sunflower.

Serious cooks may wish to keep more than one kind of oil on hand for different purposes—a delicate olive oil and perhaps a walnut or hazelnut oil to blend together for salad dressings, and one of the standard vegetable oils such as corn, safflower, or peanut oil for general use. Most oils are similar to each other in blandness, but olive oil is an exception. Olive oils vary greatly in quality, taste, and cost. The French, Greek, Italian, and Spanish all have differences in flavor, influenced by the soils in which they were grown. Virgin oil from the first pressing is the best quality, and cold-pressed oil is preferable. Experiment with a few until you find one to your liking. The strong, fruity-flavored olive oils should not be used in baking, or in any cooking where their distinctive taste might overpower the other flavors. The milder vegetable oils are recommended for general cooking and baking, and, alone or in combination with olive oil, for mayonnaise. Their high smoking point adds to their usefulness and they are often combined with butter in the sauté pan, so that food can be cooked at a higher temperature without danger of burning. Do not attempt to use liquid oil in place of solid fats in baking without the adjustment of other ingredients.

Store oils away from strong light and preferably in a cool place. Good quality oils are stable and do not require refrigeration. You will find that some oils become cloudy when refrigerated, but they will clear when brought to room temperature.

Fats for Deep-Frying

Butter and margarine are unsuitable for deep-frying because of their low smoking point, but any of the vegetable oils may be used. In spite of airy reassurances from some quarters that oils may be reused again and again, it is generally safest not to use the same oil more than twice. However, if the oil hasn't darkened the tiniest bit, you might consider a third use, although discarding it could be a justifiable extravagance. Each time an oil is heated, the smoking temperature is lowered because of chemical changes in the fat molecules, and overuse will make the oil smelly and produce an off-taste. Successive heatings also diminish the polyunsaturated quality of the oil and make it more saturated. If you must reuse oil, strain it through a fine strainer lined with cheesecloth while it is still warm to strain out all the little burned bits, and refrigerate it in a closed bottle.

Be careful when deep-frying to keep the oil at the proper temperature. It must never be hot enough to smoke, which will overbrown the food and fill the air in your house with an unpleasant, greasy odor. Underheated oil, on the other hand, will soak into the food and, instead of searing it quickly and making it brown and crisp, will give you a soggy, grease-soaked product.

Cheese

Cheese is made nearly everywhere in the world where animals are milked and where there is a surplus of milk over what the people need to drink. Cheesemaking represents the ultimate in variations on a theme, with more than 800 kinds of natural cheese. Most cheese is made from cow's milk, simply because more cows are milked throughout the world than any other animal. Smaller quantities are made from the milk of goats and ewes, and in some countries the milk of other animals such as camels, mares, reindeer, and water buffalo is used. Milk from any mammal can be made into cheese.

Ancient records indicate that the art of cheesemaking was known over 4,000 years ago, and, judging from the ever-growing assortment of cheeses on the market, it is still a popular one. And with good reason, for cheese is a most versatile food. It can serve as an appetizer, a main course or salad ingredient, a snack or sandwich, and it lends a distinctive flavor to soups, sauces, and other foods. A wedge of cheese accompanied by a crisp apple or a succulent pear makes a first-rate dessert and a platter of assorted cheeses with a variety of breads and crackers can provide satisfactory nibbles for a room full of guests. It is highly nutritious, containing in a concentrated form almost all the protein and usually most of the fat (cottage cheese excepted) as well as essential minerals, vitamins, and other nutrients of milk. Most cheeses are also high in calories and sodium, although there are a few low-fat and low-sodium cheeses available. Among the low-sodium cheeses are a Dutch Gouda and a domestic Cheddar.

Kinds of Cheese

It is difficult to classify cheese, but we can differentiate natural cheese, process and blended cheese, and fresh or uncured cheese.

Natural Cheese
Natural cheese is made by heating milk with rennet (a substance obtained from the stomach linings of young calves), or a bacterial culture, or both, which causes the milk to coagulate or curdle. Once the milk has separated into curds (soft white lumps) and whey (the watery liquid remaining after the curds have been removed), the curds are drained, pressed into molds, and allowed to ripen through the action of harmless bacteria that are added. Both milk and cream are used for certain types of cheeses; for other

types, skim milk, whey, and mixtures of all of these are used. Flavor and texture are achieved by curing, a process of holding the cheese for a certain length of time at a controlled temperature and humidity while it ripens and blossoms in taste.

Process Cheese

Process cheese is made from one or more natural cheeses that are ground, pasteurized, and stirred with an emulsifier, stabilizer, and water into a smooth, homogeneous mass that can be rolled flat or packed into blocks. Sometimes flavorings and colorings are added. The pasteurization prevents further ripening so that the development of flavor in process cheese comes to a halt during its preparation. In natural cheese, the flavor improves as it ages. Process cheeses have no rind. They spread and melt easily, are conveniently packaged in neat little blocks or slices, and they store well. Their major drawbacks are their bland taste and gummy texture.

The package information will indicate the type of cheese used, such as American, Swiss, Limburger, or any combination of them, as well as other ingredients. Some process cheeses have a smoked flavor added. Much of the process cheese goes into cheeseburgers, grilled cheese sandwiches, gratin dishes, and the like.

Processed cheese food is made the same way as process cheese, except that it needs to contain only 51 percent cheese, with the balance made up of milk, nonfat dry milk, cream, or whey solids. Fruit, vegetables, meat, spices, and flavorings may be added. Process cheese spread is process cheese with higher moisture and lower milk fat content.

Cold pack cheese, or club cheese, is made by grinding one or more cheeses and combining without heating into a smooth, spreadable mixture. It is packed in jars, rolls, or links. Cold pack cheese food is similar, but it includes

other dairy ingredients such as concentrated whey or skim milk.

"Filled" or imitation cheese is cheese in which part of the natural milk fat has been replaced by vegetable oil.

Fresh Cheese

Fresh cheese is not allowed to ripen and it must be used soon after it is made. Heading the popularity list among fresh cheeses is cottage cheese, which is a soft, white, acid-tasting cheese made from skim milk that has been curdled by the action of lactic bacteria. It is available in special diet brands (uncreamed, no salt added) and creamed, in which milk or cream is added for a richer taste.

Pot cheese differs from cottage cheese in that it contains less moisture and is never creamed. Farmer cheese is a firm pressed white cheese usually made from whole milk, sometimes from partly skimmed milk. It is sometimes used as a substitute for cream cheese. Cream cheese is made from cream, or a mixture of cream and milk. Neufchâtel is a type of cream cheese that originated in France. It is made with more milk and less cream than cream cheese and consequently contains less fat and fewer calories. Gournay is a soft French cheese that is flavored with either pepper or garlic and herbs. It is packaged in 5-ounce foil containers and is marketed under such trade names as Boursin, La Bourse, and Tartare Provençal. Other un-cured cheeses are the bland, mild-tasting mozzarella that originated in Italy, and feta, of Greek origin, a soft white cheese pickled in salt, both of which are also made in this country.

Fresh cheeses are also made from whey, the part of the milk that is usually drained off in other cheese-making processes. Among them are the Italian-inspired ricotta, which resembles cottage cheese in color and texture but has a slightly richer and sweeter taste, and Mysost, of

Norwegian origin, which is light brown in color and has a buttery consistency.

What Makes Cheeses Differ?

Although all cheeses come from a common source, they differ widely in taste and texture. The differences are related to a number of factors—the kind of milk used; the method employed for coagulating the milk and for cutting, curing, and forming the curd; the types of bacteria or mold culture used in ripening the cheese; the degree of salting; and the conditions under which the cheese was ripened, such as the temperature, humidity, and length of time. A minor change in any of these can create a totally different product.

Cheeses, like people, tend to migrate, and we find versions of the same cheeses being made in many countries, far removed from their places of origin. The Italian-born Parmesan, Romano, and Provolone, for example, are made in considerable quantities in the United States. English Cheddar is much the same as the Cheddar made in the United States and Canada. Among other North American versions of European cheeses are mozzarella, Limburger, and Port Salut.

Cheese experts are frequently given to passionate discussions over the relative merits of American-made cheeses versus European cheeses. It is generally agreed that American-made cheeses are more uniform in quality, because they are always made from pasteurized milk, but they lack the full character and distinctiveness of European cheeses. Some of the benign bacteria in unpasteurized milk that add to the cheese's personality have been destroyed. Nor can we duplicate some of the natural conditions that play an essential role in the taste and texture of some of the great European cheeses—the sweet grass of the high Alps that nourishes the cows whose milk makes Swiss cheese, or the caves of Roquefort, where the cheese of the same name is ripened. But certain European cheeses made in America are better than others and, when well aged, are every bit as good as their Old World counterparts. Cheddar is an outstanding example.

Do not confuse the Gruyère cheese that comes in foil-wrapped triangular wedges packed in round boxes that we find in our supermarkets with genuine Gruyère cheese. Eat it if you like but do not substitute it for Swiss cheese in cooking. It will add little in flavor. True Swiss cheese is the world-famous Emmentaler from Switzerland, or the French or Swiss Gruyère, and they are well worth shopping for.

Buying Cheese

The quality of natural cheeses can vary with the season. Sometimes the best milk is available in the early spring, sometimes in the late summer, and this will affect the cheese. The best advice is to find a reliable cheese store with a knowledgeable staff. Try to buy cheese the way you buy grapes or cherries—taste first. Generally cheese merchants are a friendly lot and will give you taste samples of various cheeses, which can turn a cheese shopping expedition into a pleasant eating spree.

Storing

Store cheese, tightly wrapped, in the warmest, not the coldest, part of the refrigerator. Cheeses that have a strong odor, such as Limburger and Liederkranz, should be stored wrapped in a tightly covered container. If you are storing a large piece of hard cheese after cutting, butter the cut edges before wrapping in foil and refrigerating. The butter will act as a seal and help to prevent the cheese from drying out.

If any surface mold develops on hard cheese, trim it off before serving. Of course, this does not apply to the mold-ripened cheeses such as Roquefort and Stilton, where the mold is an important part of the cheese and meant to be eaten. If mold penetrates the interior of cheeses, such as Swiss or Cheddar, you have the choice of cutting away the moldy parts if they are not too extensive or discarding the cheese.

Freezing is not recommended for most cheeses because their texture changes and they become crumbly when thawed. But you can freeze Roquefort, Gorgonzola, or other blue cheeses for use in salads when a crumbly texture is desirable.

Cooking with Cheese

High heat and long cooking make cheese tough and stringy. This is because the protein in cheese coagulates and shrinks when it is heated above a certain temperature, overbalancing the tendency of the cheese to soften as the fat melts. Cheese needs just enough heat to melt the fat so that it can blend with the other ingredients.

When making a cheese sauce, add the cheese at the last minute and cook only until it melts. If the cheese is grated or shredded, it will melt more quickly. Just keep your cooking time as brief as possible, even when you are browning a cheese sauce under the broiler.

The hard natural cheeses such as Swiss, Cheddar, Provolone, and the like are excellent for cooking. Preferred are the "aged" or "sharp" cheeses, which are cheeses aged over six months. They melt more easily, blend well with other ingredients, and add richer flavor than younger cheeses. (Aged cheeses cost a little more because of added costs of curing.) Pro-

cess cheeses make a smooth sauce because of the emulsifiers in them, but the sauce will have a tacky, rubbery consistency. Cheese sauces made with natural cheese might seem grainy by comparison, but the cheese flavor is vastly superior.

Grating Cheese. Parmesan, Romano, and Cheddar are the cheeses used most often for grating, but any cheese that has become hardened in your refrigerator can be grated and used as a topping or flavoring. Four ounces of cheese will yield one cup of grated cheese.

It is always better to grate your own. The flavor is much stronger and fresher than that in the prepacked products. Cold cheese taken directly from the refrigerator can be grated more easily than a cheese at room temperature. It can be cut into small pieces and grated in the food processor or blender if it is not too hard. Otherwise, the standard four-sided kitchen grater is effective.

Serving Cheese. Except for soft, unripened cheeses such as cottage cheese, cream cheese, farmer cheese, Boursin, and the like, which must be kept refrigerated until served, all cheese tastes better unchilled. Remove them from the refrigerator so they can have an hour or longer at room temperature before serving. A soft, runny cheese like Brie may need longer, depending on how ripe it is.

Eggs

Soft-Boiled, Medium-Boiled, Coddled, Hard-Boiled Eggs, see page 247
Poached, Fried, Scrambled Eggs, see page 249
Omelets, see page 250
Soufflés, see page 252

Eggs Benedict

A perennial favorite for brunch.

6 halves English muffins, toasted
6 thin slices ham, hot or cold
6 hot poached eggs (see page 249)
Hollandaise sauce (see page 461)

Arrange the ham and poached eggs on the toasted muffin rounds. Cover with hollandaise. Serve at once.

Yield: 6 servings.

Baked Cheese Omelet

12 eggs at room temperature
2 cups grated sharp Cheddar cheese, about ½ pound
4 tablespoons melted butter
Salt and freshly ground pepper
2 tablespoons dry mustard
1 cup milk

Butter a 2-quart baking dish. Preheat the oven to 325 degrees.

Break the eggs into a large bowl and beat until frothy and light. Add the remaining ingredients and blend well. Pour into the prepared baking dish, cover tightly, and bake for 40 minutes, or until set. Serve hot.

Yield: 6 to 8 servings.

Eggs with Peppers and Onions

5 large bell peppers, or 8 to 10
   Italian frying peppers
4 tablespoons olive oil
1 large onion, thinly sliced
1 clove garlic, crushed
4 to 6 eggs, well beaten
Salt and freshly ground pepper
Freshly grated Parmesan cheese
   (optional)

Remove the seeds and membranes from the peppers. Slice lengthwise into 1- to 1½-inch strips. Heat the oil in a large skillet. Add the onion, garlic, and peppers and sauté until lightly colored, 5 to 7 minutes. Cover the pan, lower the heat, and cook until peppers are soft, 10 to 15 minutes. Shake the pan occasionally.

Remove the cover and cook over high heat, shaking the pan constantly, until moisture has evaporated. Lower the heat and add the beaten eggs. Season with salt and pepper. Stir until cooked to your preference.

Remove from the heat and serve on hero rolls or with a good Italian or French bread. Sprinkle with cheese if desired.

Yield: 2 to 3 servings.

Eggs Florentine

5 tablespoons butter
3 tablespoons flour
1½ cups milk
½ cup light cream
Salt and freshly ground pepper
1 pound fresh spinach, or 1 10-
   ounce package frozen spinach,
   cooked, well-drained, and finely
   chopped
Freshly grated nutmeg
6 poached eggs (see page 249)
3 tablespoons freshly grated
   Parmesan cheese

Melt 3 tablespoons of the butter in a heavy-bottomed saucepan and stir in the flour. Cook until the mixture is bubbly, about 2 minutes. Remove from the heat, stir in the milk and cream all at once, whisk vigorously, and return to the heat. Cook and stir until the sauce is thickened and smooth. Season with salt and pepper to taste.

Heat the chopped spinach, some grated nutmeg, and ½ cup cream sauce in a saucepan, but do not boil. Butter a shallow, heatproof baking dish, about 9 by 13 inches, and arrange the spinach in the bottom. Place the poached eggs over the spinach.

Stir 1 tablespoon Parmesan cheese into the remaining cream sauce and spoon the sauce over the eggs. Sprinkle with the rest of the Parmesan cheese, dot with butter, and brown lightly under the broiler. Serve hot.

Yield: 3 to 6 servings.

Spinach Omelet

A crustless quiche that makes fine picnic fare.

1 pound spinach, washed and stems removed, *or* 1 10-ounce package frozen spinach
4 tablespoons butter
1 clove garlic, crushed
Salt and freshly ground pepper
6 eggs, lightly beaten
½ pound feta cheese, crumbled
Freshly grated nutmeg
1 tablespoon olive oil

Cook the spinach in a covered pot in the water clinging to the leaves until wilted. Drain and squeeze dry in a towel. Chop fine.

Melt 2 tablespoons of butter in a 10-inch cast-iron skillet. Add the spinach, garlic, salt, and pepper. Cook until the spinach is soft, about 5 minutes. Transfer to a large bowl and add the eggs, feta, and nutmeg. Mix well.

In the same skillet, heat the remaining butter and the olive oil. When hot, add the egg mixture. Cover and cook over very low heat until the bottom is set, 8 to 10 minutes. Run the pan under the broiler briefly if the top is still uncooked. You may also bake the omelet in a 350-degree oven for 12 to 15 minutes, so that the center will still be soft.

Invert the omelet onto a serving platter and cut into wedges. Serve hot or at room temperature.

Yield: 4 servings.

Country Omelet

½ pound bacon or cooked ham, diced
3 tablespoons butter or oil
2 to 3 baking potatoes, peeled and cut into small dice
1 large onion, coarsely chopped
1 to 2 large bell peppers, seeded and coarsely chopped
1 clove garlic, finely chopped
8 eggs, lightly beaten
2 ripe tomatoes, peeled and thinly sliced (optional)
Salt and freshly ground pepper
1 to 2 tablespoons fresh parsley, finely chopped

In a 10-inch cast-iron skillet, cook the diced bacon until crisp. Remove with a slotted spoon and reserve. Discard all but 1 tablespoon fat. Add the butter and potatoes and cook over medium heat until golden. Add the onion and peppers and cook, stirring, until softened and lightly colored and the potatoes are tender. Add the garlic and cook, stirring, until golden.

Pour in the eggs and add the sliced tomatoes. Season with salt and pepper. Cover and cook over low heat until set, 6 to 7 minutes. If top is still too soft, run the pan under the broiler briefly. Sprinkle with parsley.

Serve hot or cool, cut into wedges.

Yield: 4 to 6 servings.

Zucchini Frittata

A frittata is an Italian omelet that is flat, not folded. It makes a nice appetizer course, or a luncheon or supper dish.

8 zucchini, about 2 pounds
2 tablespoons salt
3 tablespoons olive oil
3 tablespoons butter
8 eggs, beaten
Salt and freshly ground pepper
½ cup freshly grated Parmesan, Romano, Swiss, or any combination of cheeses

Wash and shred the unpeeled zucchini. Place it in a colander set over a bowl or dish. Sprinkle with the salt and toss to blend. Let stand for 1 hour. Rinse the zucchini in cold water and squeeze dry in a towel.

Heat the oil and butter in a 10-inch cast-iron skillet. Add the zucchini and stir just to coat with fat. Add the eggs seasoned with salt and pepper. Stir to mix well. Cover and lower the heat. Cook just until set, about 15 minutes. The top will still be soft. You may also bake the frittata in a preheated 350-degree oven for 20 to 25 minutes, or until almost firm in the center.

Sprinkle with the cheese and run under the broiler to brown lightly and to complete the cooking.

Remove and serve warm or cool, cut into wedges.

Yield: 4 to 6 servings.

Quiche Lorraine

1 10-inch tart crust (see page 501)
½ pound bacon, cut into small pieces
2 medium onions, coarsely chopped
½ pound Gruyère or Swiss cheese (or a combination), shredded
3 eggs, lightly beaten
1½ cups half-and-half
Salt and freshly ground pepper
Freshly grated nutmeg

Prepare the tart crust. Prick the crust and bake at 400 degrees for 10 to 12 minutes. Brush the bottom with lightly beaten egg and bake for 2 minutes longer. Let cool. (This may be done in advance.)

Preheat the oven to 350 degrees.

Cook the bacon until crisp. Remove with a slotted spoon and drain. Discard all but three tablespoons fat. Add the onion and cook until softened, 3 to 5 minutes.

Spread the cheese in the quiche shell and sprinkle the bacon evenly over the cheese. Blend the 3 eggs with the half-and-half, salt, pepper, and nutmeg and pour into the quiche shell. Bake for 35 to 40 minutes, or until the center is almost firm and the top puffed and lightly brown.

Yield: 6 to 8 servings.

Broccoli Quiche

1 9-inch tart crust (see page 501)
Dijon mustard
1 10-ounce package frozen
  chopped broccoli
3 eggs
⅔ cup grated Swiss cheese
¾ cup milk
½ cup cream
Salt and freshly ground pepper
Freshly grated nutmeg
2 teaspoons Worcestershire sauce
2 tablespoons freshly grated
  Parmesan cheese

Prick the crust well and bake it in a 400-degree oven for 10 to 12 minutes, just until the bottom is set and the edges lightly golden. Remove from the oven and brush the bottom lightly with Dijon mustard. This acts as a seal and helps to prevent the crust from becoming soggy. Return to the oven for 2 minutes.

Cook the broccoli according to package directions and drain well. Spread over the pastry shell. Beat the eggs lightly and add the grated cheese, milk, cream, salt, pepper, nutmeg, and Worcestershire. Blend well and pour over the broccoli. Sprinkle Parmesan cheese over the top.

Bake in a 375-degree oven for 30 minutes, or until the custard is just set. Allow the quiche to cool and settle for a few minutes before serving.

Yield: 6 servings.

Grand Marnier Soufflé

¾ cup sugar
2 cups milk
5 tablespoons sweet butter
¼ cup flour
2 teaspoons cornstarch mixed
  with 1 tablespoon cold water
4 tablespoons Grand Marnier
5 egg yolks
7 egg whites
Pinch of salt

Place oven rack in lowest third of the oven and preheat the oven to 400 degrees. Butter a 2-quart soufflé dish and place a couple of tablespoons of sugar in the dish. Tilt and tap it to coat the sides and bottom. Shake out any excess.

Reserve 2 tablespoons of the ¾ cup sugar and combine the remaining sugar and milk in a small saucepan. Heat until small bubbles appear around the outside edges and the mixture begins to boil. Remove from the heat. In a small, heavy-bottomed saucepan, melt the butter and add the flour. Cook and stir until it bubbles, about 2 minutes. Whisk in the hot milk and cook and stir gently until smooth. Add the dissolved cornstarch and continue to cook over moderate heat until the sauce is thickened. Remove from the heat and stir in the Grand Marnier.

Beat the egg yolks at high speed in the small bowl of an electric mixer for 4 or 5 minutes, or until pale lemon-colored. Add half a cup or so of the sauce to the egg yolks to warm them and slowly stir the warmed yolks into the sauce. Beat only until well blended.

You can complete the soufflé now or cover the sauce mixture and set it aside at room temperature to be completed later. The egg whites must be beaten and folded into the sauce at the last minute. In a large bowl, beat the egg whites until foamy. Add a pinch of salt and continue to beat, gradually adding the remaining 2 tablespoons of sugar. Beat until stiff, but not dry. Gently fold in about one-quarter of the beaten whites to the sauce mixture to lighten it and then fold in the remaining whites as rapidly and lightly as you can and only until both mixtures are blended. Spoon the mixture into the soufflé dish and smooth the top with a rubber spatula.

Place in the oven and turn down the heat to 375 degrees. Bake for 25 to 30 minutes. It should be firm on the sides and creamy in the center. Serve the soufflé the moment you take it from the oven—it won't wait.

Yield: 6 to 8 servings.

Cheese Soufflé

6 ounces sharp Cheddar cheese
6 large eggs, at room temperature
1 extra egg white
6 tablespoons butter
6 tablespoons flour
½ teaspoon paprika
Pinch of ground red pepper
1½ cups milk

Butter a 2-quart soufflé dish. Preheat the oven to 350 degrees and place rack in the lowest third of the oven.

Grate the cheese and set aside. Separate the yolks and whites of the eggs.

In a large, heavy-bottomed saucepan, melt the butter over low heat and blend in the flour, paprika, and red pepper. Stir and cook until the mixture is bubbly, about 2 minutes. Remove from the heat and add the milk, whisking vigorously. Return to moderate heat and cook and stir until the sauce is smooth and thickened. Reduce the heat to very low, add the cheese, and stir until it is melted. Remove from the heat. While the sauce is cooling, beat the egg yolks until thick and lemon-colored. Pour a half cup or so of sauce into the beaten egg yolks to warm them, and slowly stir the yolks into the cheese mixture, blending thoroughly.

In a large bowl, beat the egg whites until stiff but not dry. Whisk about one-quarter of the whites into the cooled sauce to lighten it and then add the remainder of the whites. Fold gently until well blended and no large clumps of whites are evident. Don't overfold or you will deflate the whites. Spoon carefully into the soufflé dish. Bake uncovered for 35 to 45 minutes, or until puffed and golden brown. Serve at once.

Yield: 6 servings.

Chocolate Soufflé

6 ounces dark sweet chocolate
1 cup milk
10 egg whites
Pinch of salt
¼ teaspoon cream of tartar
4 tablespoons confectioners' sugar
Lightly beaten and sweetened
  whipped cream (optional)

Preheat the oven to 350 degrees. Butter a 2-quart soufflé dish. Place a couple of tablespoons of granulated sugar in the dish and tilt it to cover the sides and bottom. Shake out any excess.

Melt the chocolate in a heavy-bottomed saucepan over very low heat with the cup of milk. Watch it carefully and stir until dissolved. Set aside and let cool.

In a large bowl, beat the egg whites until foamy. Add a dash of salt and the cream of tartar. As the whites begin to stiffen, add the confectioners' sugar gradually and continue to beat until soft peaks form and it becomes stiff but not dry. Fold the melted chocolate gently into the egg whites, cutting it in with a rubber spatula until blended. Spoon the mixture into the soufflé dish, piling it so that the center is higher than the sides. Place the dish on the rack in the lowest third of the oven and bake for 30 minutes. The top will be firm and puffy and the inside soft and runny. If you want a less moist soufflé, bake it for 5 to 10 minutes longer. Serve at once with softly whipped cream, if desired.

Yield: 6 servings.

Creamy Rice Pudding

Rich and creamy—the stuff of which dreams of rice pudding are made.

3 cups milk
2 cups half-and-half
½ cup long-grain rice
3 eggs, separated
½ cup sugar
¼ teaspoon salt
2 tablespoons Grand Marnier or
  Cointreau
Grated peel of 1 orange (optional)
1 teaspoon vanilla extract
Freshly grated nutmeg

Rinse a large, heavy saucepan with cold water and drain, but do not dry.

Combine the milk and half-and-half in the saucepan and bring slowly to the boiling point. Add the rice and return to the boil. Lower the heat, cover, and simmer very gently for 1 to 1¼ hours, or until the rice is tender and most of the milk has been absorbed, although it will still be somewhat soupy. Use a flame control device over the heat unit if necessary to minimize the danger of scorching. Stir frequently. Remove from the stove and let cool to lukewarm.

In a small bowl, beat the egg yolks until frothy. Add ¼ cup of sugar and the salt and continue to beat until thick and lemon-colored (see page 246). Blend into the cooled rice and stir in the Grand Marnier, grated peel, and vanilla extract.

Preheat the oven to 350 degrees. Butter a 2-quart casserole or soufflé dish.

In a medium-size bowl, beat the egg whites until soft peaks form. Slowly add the remaining ¼ cup of sugar and continue beating until glossy and stiff. Stir one-quarter of the whites into the rice mixture. Carefully fold in the remaining whites.

Spoon the pudding mixture into the baking dish. Sprinkle the top lightly with some grated fresh nutmeg. Set the dish into a larger pan. Place on the oven rack and fill the larger pan with hot water to a depth of 2 or 3 inches. Bake for 30 minutes, or until lightly browned and puffed. Don't overcook.

Remove from the water bath and cool on a wire rack. Serve warm or at room temperature.

Yield: 6 servings.

Boiled Custard

This is also known as soft custard, stirred custard, or crème Anglaise. *It can be served by itself, or poured over fruits, cakes, or puddings.*

6 egg yolks
½ cup sugar
¼ teaspoon salt
2 cups milk or light cream, *or* 1 cup of each, scalded
1½ teaspoons vanilla extract
2 tablespoons Grand Marnier, Cointreau, or kirsch

In a heavy-bottomed saucepan, mix the egg yolks, sugar, and salt and whisk only until well blended. Add the hot milk very slowly, stirring well. Cook over medium heat, stirring constantly with a wooden spoon, until the mixture coats the spoon, 6 to 8 minutes. Do not let it boil or the eggs will curdle. If you see small bubbles beginning to form around the edge of the pan, remove it quickly from the heat.

Strain the sauce into a bowl and add the vanilla extract and the liqueur and mix. Let cool to room temperature and stir from time to time to prevent a film from forming on the custard's surface. Cover and chill when cooled.

Yield: 2½ cups.

Variation: Add 1½ teaspoons ground cardamom to the ingredients after the hot milk is added. Pour the cooked custard after it has cooled into four individual serving dishes. Sprinkle with toasted pistachio nuts that have been tossed in about a tablespoon of sugar. Refrigerate until ready to serve.

Baked Caramel Custard

A silky, smooth custard that never goes out of style. It may be baked in six individual custard cups, but it looks more elegant when prepared in one large baking dish and served at the table with its crown of caramel.

1½ cups sugar

1 tablespoon water

3 whole eggs

2 egg yolks

Pinch of salt

2 cups milk, *or* 1 cup milk and 1 cup light cream

Half a vanilla bean, split, *or* 1½ teaspoons vanilla extract

Preheat the oven to 325 degrees.

Have ready a 1½-quart baking dish, ovenproof glass, metal, or porcelain. Heat 1 cup of sugar and 1 tablespoon of water in a heavy-bottomed saucepan over low heat. Stir with a long-handled spoon until the sugar melts, about 10 minutes. Continue to cook until it turns deep amber-colored. Watch it carefully and as soon as the proper color is reached, turn off the heat. Pour the syrup into the ungreased custard mold and tilt the mold back and forth so that the syrup coats the bottom and sides evenly. When the caramel starts to set, invert the mold over a plate so that the syrup can trickle down the sides. For easy removal of the custard, lightly butter whatever parts of the mold are not covered with caramel.

In a mixing bowl, combine the whole eggs and egg yolks and beat just enough to blend well. Overbeating the eggs will create air pockets and result in a custard with little holes. Stir in the remaining ½ cup of sugar and the salt.

Heat the milk with the vanilla bean in a heavy saucepan over medium heat, stirring occasionally to prevent scorching, until tiny bubbles appear around the edges and the surface begins to move. Remove from the heat and pour slowly into the egg mixture, stirring constantly. Do not whip. If you overbeat the egg and milk mixture you will create a foam, which will prevent the custard from having a smooth top surface. Remove and discard the vanilla bean. If you are using vanilla extract, add it.

Strain the mixture into the prepared mold. Place the mold in a roasting pan in the center of the middle rack of the oven. Pour hot water into the roasting pan to reach two-thirds the depth of the baking dish. The hot water bath will prevent the custard from overcooking or curdling.

Bake for 45 to 50 minutes, or until a skewer or thin-bladed knife inserted into it comes out clean. When baked, remove the mold from the water bath and allow to cool completely. When cool, cover with plastic wrap and refrigerate until serving time. It should be unmolded only after chilling for several hours.

To serve, run a knife around the edges, place a round serving dish over the mold and invert. The custard should slide out of the mold easily.

Yield: 6 to 8 servings.

Baked French Toast

4 eggs
½ cup milk
6 slices firm white bread, challah,
  or brioche

Combine the eggs and the milk in a blender and process until smooth. Place the bread in a 9 by 13-inch baking dish and pour the egg over it. You may need more egg and milk if the slices are very thick. The bread should be well coated. Cover and refrigerate for several hours or overnight.

Preheat the oven to 500 degrees.

Arrange the bread slices on a well-greased baking sheet and bake for 2 to 3 minutes. Turn and continue to bake until golden, 1 to 2 minutes more.

Serve hot with butter, syrup, cinnamon sugar, or fruit preserves.

Yield: 3 to 6 servings.

Pancakes

2 cups all-purpose flour
2 teaspoons baking powder
4 tablespoons sugar
Salt
2 eggs
3 tablespoons melted butter
2 cups milk

Combine the flour, baking powder, sugar, and salt in a large bowl and blend well. In a separate bowl, beat the eggs lightly and mix well with the melted butter and milk. Add the milk mixture to the flour and stir just enough to make a somewhat creamy batter with some lumps. Do not overbeat.

Heat a griddle or a 10-inch cast-iron skillet. Grease it lightly with a paper towel dipped in oil. Test the heat of the griddle by sprinkling a few drops of cold water over it. If the drops sputter and bounce, the griddle is just right. If the water just sits there and boils, it is not hot enough; if the water vanishes, the griddle is too hot. Cool the pan by removing it from the heat for a minute or two. Spoon or ladle the batter onto the hot griddle. When bubbles appear on the top and the edges look dry, lift the pancake with a spatula to see how well it has browned. Two or three minutes on the first side should do it. Turn the pancakes only once and continue cooking until the second side is done. The second side will take only about half as long as the first.

Serve with butter and maple syrup.

Yield: 18 4-inch pancakes.

Whole Wheat Pancakes. Substitute 1 cup whole wheat flour for 1 cup of the white flour.

Blueberry Pancakes. Lightly fold 1 cup well-drained blueberries into the batter after it is mixed.

Buttermilk Pancakes. Substitute the same quantity of buttermilk for the milk, and use ½ teaspoon of baking soda and 1 teaspoon of baking powder in place of the 2 teaspoons baking powder.

Fruit Pancakes. Add 1 cup finely chopped apples or ½ cup finely chopped dates and raisins to batter after it is mixed.

Apple Pancake

This gives a good account of itself for breakfast, brunch, supper, or as a dessert.

3 large tart apples (about 1½ pounds)
3 tablespoons butter
¼ cup sugar
¼ teaspoon ground cinnamon
¼ teaspoon freshly grated nutmeg
Grated rind of 1 lemon

Pancake:
2 eggs
½ cup milk
½ cup flour
Salt
2 tablespoons butter

Topping:
4 tablespoons sugar
1 tablespoon lemon juice

Preheat the oven to 450 degrees.

Pare, core, and thinly slice the apples. Melt the butter in a large skillet and cook the apple slices over low heat for 5 minutes. Mix together the sugar, cinnamon, nutmeg, and lemon rind. Add to the apples and cook, covered, for 5 to 7 minutes longer, or until the apples are crisp-tender. Don't overcook. Remove from the heat and keep warm.

To make the pancake, beat the eggs with a wire whisk or an electric beater until they are thick and lemon-colored. Add the milk, flour, and salt and beat until smooth. Melt the butter in a 9-inch ovenproof round shallow baking dish or a glass pie plate. Pour the batter into it and place in the oven for 15 minutes. After the first few minutes, the pancake will begin to puff up. Prick the batter and continue to prick it each time it puffs. After the first 15 minutes, reduce the heat to 350 degrees and cook for 10 minutes longer, or until the pancake becomes golden and crisp and looks done.

Remove from the oven and loosen the bottom of the pancake with a spatula. Sprinkle 2 tablespoons of the topping sugar over the pancake. Place the apple mixture over half the pancake, sprinkle the apples with 1 tablespoon of lemon juice, and fold over the other half of the pancake. With a broad spatula, transfer the pancake to a warmed platter. Sprinkle the top with the remaining 2 tablespoons of sugar and serve at once.

Yield: 2 or 3 servings.

Crêpes

A well-known chef and restaurant owner observed that he could sell almost any food that was wrapped in a crêpe. This is also true in homes because crêpes are perfect vehicles for poultry, seafood, mushrooms, and meat and vegetable combinations, turning small amounts of leftovers into party fare. Or the same crêpes with a bit of sugar added to the batter make wonderful desserts, sauced and flamed, or bulging with ice cream and topped with a sauce.

These small, delicate pancakes are simple to make and should not intimidate even the most inexperienced cook. You can use an iron crêpe pan or a small, nonstick skillet, which is our choice. A pan with a 6-inch bottom and sides that slope out to an 8- or 9-inch diameter is an excellent size.

Make the batter an hour or two ahead of time, cover it with plastic wrap, and let it stand at room temperature. This gives the flour time to absorb some of the liquid and expand. Without this resting period, the crêpes will not cook as well. You may also refrigerate the batter overnight.

Entrée Crêpes

3 large eggs
Pinch of salt
1½ cups milk
1 cup all-purpose flour
4 tablespoons melted butter
2 to 3 tablespoons melted butter
  for greasing pan

Break the eggs into a mixing bowl and whisk until well blended. Add the salt and milk and mix well. Stir in the flour and 4 tablespoons melted butter and beat until smooth and free of lumps. You can use a whisk or electric beater, or put all the ingredients in a food processor or blender and process until smooth. The batter should have the consistency of heavy cream. It will thicken a bit as it stands, but if it becomes too thick, you can thin it with a teaspoon or two of water or milk.

When you are ready to cook, heat the skillet over moderate heat and test with a drop of water. It is at the right temperature if the water sizzles and bounces off. Brush the bottom of the pan lightly with melted butter. Dip a ladle or measuring cup into the batter and pour just enough batter into the pan to cover the bottom in a thin layer. Raise the pan and tilt it quickly so that the entire bottom is covered. If there is too much batter, pour the excess back into the bowl. If not quite enough batter to cover, add more. You will probably need about 3 tablespoons of batter per crêpe.

Cook over medium heat until the underside is delicately brown. It should be done in 1 or 1½ minutes. Slide the spatula between the crêpe and the pan to loosen the edge, and flip it over, either with your fingers or the spatula. There is less chance of cutting the crêpe if you use your fingers. Brown the second side, about 30 seconds. It will not brown as evenly as the first side, but put the filling on this side. Transfer the finished crêpe to a towel and continue to cook until all the batter is used. Brush the pan with butter as needed; it will not be necessary to grease the pan for each crêpe. You can stack the crêpes as they are cooled.

To freeze or refrigerate, wrap the stacked crêpes in aluminum foil. The individual crêpes do not need to be separated with wax paper. If the outside edges of the crêpes look crusty or ragged, trim them with a sharp knife or scissors.

Yield: 18 to 20 6-inch crêpes.

Variations: Crêpes can be flavored with a variety of herbs or with spinach. For herb-flavored crêpes, add 2 tablespoons minced chives and parsley, or 2 tablespoons minced fresh dill, to the batter and blend for 30 seconds. For spinach-flavored crêpes, add ½ cup cooked, well-drained and chopped spinach to the batter and blend for 30 seconds.

Dessert Crêpes. Add 2 tablespoons sugar and 2 tablespoons brandy to the entrée crêpe batter and proceed as for entrée crêpes.

Crêpes with Curried Crabmeat

A delicious appetizer or a luncheon or supper dish that can be prepared well in advance and baked just before serving.

12 entrée crêpes
½ pound crabmeat, preferably lump
1 tablespoon butter
1 tablespoon chopped shallots
½ cup dry white wine
1 teaspoon curry powder
Dash of Worcestershire sauce
Salt and freshly ground pepper
2½ cups medium white sauce (see page 451)
4 tablespoons butter, melted
¼ cup cream
2 tablespoons lemon juice
Freshly grated Parmesan cheese

Pick over crabmeat and remove bits of shell and tendon. Set aside. In a medium-size skillet, heat the butter and add the shallots. Cook, stirring, until softened. Add the wine, curry powder, Worcestershire, salt, and pepper, and 1 cup white sauce. Cook for 2 minutes, stirring. Stir in the crabmeat and mix well.

Preheat the oven to 350 degrees.

Spoon 1½ to 2 tablespoons of filling into the center of each crêpe and roll the crêpe around the filling. Arrange seam side down in a greased, shallow baking dish. Bake for 15 to 20 minutes, or until hot.

In a small saucepan, combine the remaining white sauce with the melted butter, cream, and lemon juice. Heat gently and pour over the crêpes. Sprinkle with Parmesan cheese and broil 4 to 6 inches from the heat until lightly browned and bubbling.

Yield: 4 to 6 servings.

Orange Dessert Crêpes

In addition to its good taste and party airs, the virtue of this preparation is that it can be completed well in advance and popped into the oven 10 minutes before it is to be served.

18 to 20 dessert crêpes (see page 279)

¾ cup sugar

8 tablespoons butter

Grated rind of 1 orange

Juice of 2 oranges

2 tablespoons lemon juice

⅓ cup orange liqueur (Grand Marnier, Curaçao, etc.)

2 tablespoons brandy

⅓ cup slivered almonds

1 teaspoon butter

3 tablespoons brandy for flaming (optional)

Heat the sugar and butter in a heavy-bottomed pan over a low flame, stirring constantly, for 10 to 12 minutes, until it becomes spongy and darkens a bit. Remove from the heat and stir in the grated rind, orange and lemon juice. Return to the heat and cook and stir for 2 minutes longer to make a smooth sauce. Mix in the orange liqueur and brandy and remove from the heat.

Spoon about 1 tablespoon of sauce over each crêpe and fold in quarters, like a handkerchief. Pour a thin film of sauce over the bottom of a shallow, ovenproof baking dish—a 12-inch-long oval dish is a good size. Arrange the folded crêpes with the point up and slightly overlapping in the dish. Cover the crêpes with the remaining sauce. Brown the slivered almonds in a small skillet with 1 teaspoon of butter. They burn easily, so shake the pan as they cook and watch them closely. Sprinkle the toasted almonds over the crêpes. Cover the baking dish with plastic wrap until ready to serve.

At serving time, warm the crêpes, uncovered, in a 350-degree oven for 10 minutes. The crêpes may be flamed at the table in the baking dish, if desired. Heat the brandy, ignite it with a match, and pour it, flaming, over the crêpes. Protect your fingers and shake the dish until the flame dies. Serve immediately.

Yield: 6 to 7 servings.

Crêpes with Jam. Crêpes may be filled with any kind of fruit preserves. If you are making them at the last minute, spread them with the preserves, roll them, sprinkle with confectioners' sugar, and serve at once. If done in advance, place the rolled crêpes in a buttered baking dish, sprinkle them lightly with sugar, and flame them with ⅓ cup warmed brandy.

Apricot Crêpes. Spread crêpes with apricot preserves, roll, and place in a buttered baking dish. Cover with Apricot Sauce (see page 465) and heat in a 350-degree oven for 10 minutes. Serve with additional warmed sauce and canned apricot halves.

Crêpes with Ice Cream. Roll the crêpes around finger-shaped wedges of ice cream and serve topped with hot Chocolate Sauce (see page 468) or hot Blueberry Sauce (see page 466).

Cheese Blintzes

A cheese blintz is a sturdy crêpe filled with a rich cheese mixture. It is a good lunch dish, or it can be used as a substantial dessert for a light meal.

Batter:
2 eggs
1 cup all-purpose flour
1 teaspoon salt
1 cup milk
⅓ cup water

Filling:
1 pound farmer cheese
2 eggs
Salt
2 tablespoons sugar
1 teaspoon vanilla
½ teaspoon grated lemon rind

½ cup clarified butter for frying
  (see page 260)
Sour cream

In a large bowl, beat the eggs well. Mix together the flour and salt. Add the flour alternately with the milk and water to the beaten eggs to make a smooth batter. Or you may place all the ingredients in a blender or food processor and process until smooth. Let the batter stand at room temperature, covered, for at least 1 hour.

When ready to cook, heat an 8-inch crêpe pan or iron skillet. When hot enough for a drop of water to sputter and bounce off, brush the bottom of the pan lightly with melted butter. Pour in enough batter to cover the bottom of the pan in a thin layer, tilting and rotating the pan so that the batter covers the bottom. Cook on one side only until lightly browned. Slide out onto a clean kitchen towel, cooked side up. Continue until all are cooked, greasing the pan lightly between each pancake.

Combine the farmer cheese, eggs, salt, sugar, vanilla, and lemon rind and beat with a wooden spoon until well blended.

Place 2 tablespoons of the cheese mixture on the cooked side of each pancake. Fold in three sides, press lightly to flatten and spread the filling, and roll. Place seam side down on a baking sheet. Continue until all are done. The blintzes may be covered and refrigerated at this point, or securely wrapped and frozen.

When ready to cook, heat 3 or 4 tablespoons of clarified butter in a large skillet. When hot, add the blintzes, seam side down. Cook for 3 to 5 minutes, or until golden brown. Turn carefully and cook the other side. Continue until all are done, adding butter as needed. Transfer to a warm platter as they are completed.

Serve topped with sour cream. Sweetened blueberries or strawberries are delicious served along with the sour cream.

Yield: About 6 servings.

Yogurt

1 quart milk, regular, low-fat, or skim

1 tablespoon commercial plain yogurt

Heat the milk slowly and bring it to the boil for a minute. Remove from the heat and allow it to cool, stirring frequently, until lukewarm, about 110 degrees. (It will feel warm to the touch, but not hot.) This may take an hour. Mix in the tablespoon of yogurt and stir well. In case you are tempted to use more yogurt as a starter in the hope of getting a better result, don't. If the bacillus is overcrowded, it gives a sour, watery product. The culture needs room to grow if the yogurt is to be mild and creamy.

Pour the mixture into clean glass jars or a glass or crockery bowl. Cover with plastic wrap and a heavy towel and place in a warm, draft-free spot, such as an oven with a pilot light, a Styrofoam cooler, or a cupboard warmed by counter lights. The activator in yogurt is a living organism that needs warmth and undisturbed rest until it is set. Handle it as little as possible until then. Check the yogurt in 7 or 8 hours to see if it has reached a thick, custardy consistency. To determine the thickness of the yogurt, tilt the bowl or jars to see if it holds together. As soon as it has reached the proper consistency, cover and refrigerate. It will firm up a bit more when chilled. If it is allowed to incubate too long, it can become very sour. The yogurt will stay fresh for 6 or 7 days. Save a tablespoon to serve as a starter for the next batch.

This yogurt is generally less firm than the commercially prepared one and will be bland. For flavor and variety, add sugar, vanilla, cinnamon, or any flavor of jam or fruit purée, such as mashed bananas, prunes, apricots, or berries.

Labneh (Arabic Cream Cheese)

Long a dairy staple in the Middle East, labneh, *a thickened yogurt, is gaining increasing popularity in this country. It is used as a dip, as a substitute for sour cream, as a side dish with lamb, and as a cheese spread. It has a tangy, slightly sour and refreshing taste.*

To prepare, line a colander or a strainer with a few thicknesses of cheesecloth or a large square of discarded sheet and set it over a bowl. A jelly bag suspended over the kitchen sink will also do nicely. Spoon in a quart or more of homemade or commercial yogurt and allow it to drain for 2 or 3 hours, or overnight. The longer the yogurt drains, the firmer the end product will be. It will reach the consistency of sour cream in 2 or 3 hours; an overnight period will give it the consistency of soft cream cheese. The draining can be done in the refrigerator or at room temperature if the kitchen is not overly hot. When done, transfer to a covered container and refrigerate.

To serve as a dip, mound the labneh in a bowl and accompany with crackers, breads, or assorted raw vegetables.

Liptauer Cheese

½ pound cream cheese, softened

4 tablespoons sweet butter

¼ cup sour cream

4 anchovy fillets, *or* 2 teaspoons anchovy paste

1 teaspoon drained capers, chopped

2 teaspoons Dijon mustard

1 teaspoon caraway seeds, bruised

2 tablespoons Hungarian paprika

2 tablespoons finely chopped chives or scallions

Blend all the ingredients in a food processor, or mix with an electric mixer. Pack into a small plastic-lined bowl. Chill until firm. Unmold and serve with thinly sliced pumpernickel or rye bread.

Yield: About 1½ cups.

Berry Cheese Spread

Serve this as part of a cheese tray assortment for dessert.

1 8-ounce container whipped cream cheese, softened slightly

1 pint fresh strawberries or raspberries, hulled, sliced, and sugared to taste

Combine the ingredients in a bowl and mix well with a fork. Pack into a small bowl lined with plastic wrap. Chill until firm. Unmold and serve with dark bread or crackers.

Yield: About 1¼ cups.

Note: If fresh berries are not available, drain a 1-pound container of frozen berries and purée or chop them coarsely.

Mock Boursin

1 8-ounce package cream cheese, softened
2 tablespoons heavy cream
1 clove garlic, finely chopped
½ teaspoon dried basil
½ teaspoon dried dill
½ teaspoon dried thyme
Lemon pepper

Combine all the ingredients except the lemon pepper in a food processor or mixing bowl. Process or beat until well blended. Pack into a small, plastic-lined bowl and refrigerate.

When ready to serve, remove plastic, arrange on a serving dish and sprinkle with lemon pepper. Serve with crackers, bread, or fresh vegetables.

Yield: 1 cup.

Note: Lemon pepper is an interesting addition to the spice shelf. It is good on broiled chicken, steak, or fish.

Cheese Spread

2 8-ounce packages cream cheese, softened
¼ pound blue or Roquefort cheese, crumbled
1 tablespoon drained, prepared horseradish
Parsley sprigs

Combine the cheeses and horseradish and blend well. Pack into a plastic-lined bowl and refrigerate for at least 2 hours. Remove from the bowl and garnish with parsley. Serve at room temperature with fruit and crackers.

Yield: 2¼ cups.

Cheese Puffs

A tangy, melt-in-the-mouth hors d'oeuvre.

4 tablespoons butter

8 ounces sharp Cheddar cheese, shredded, about 2 cups

1 teaspoon Worcestershire sauce

½ teaspoon dry mustard

Dash of ground red pepper

1 tablespoon chili sauce

1 cup all-purpose flour

For easy blending, have the butter and cheese at room temperature. Combine the butter, cheese, Worcestershire sauce, dry mustard, pepper, and chili sauce in a bowl and beat until well mixed. Slowly add the flour and mix well with your fingers. Shape the dough into ¾-inch balls and arrange on baking sheets. Leave a little space between the balls as they will spread a bit. Cover with plastic wrap and refrigerate until ready to bake. Bake in a preheated 350-degree oven for 16 to 18 minutes, or until they are set. They will have a flattened base and a domed top.

Yield: 60 to 70 puffs.

Feta Cheese Spread

4 ounces feta cheese, softened

1 8-ounce package cream cheese, softened

1 clove garlic, finely chopped

3 whole scallions, trimmed and finely chopped

1 tablespoon sour cream

2 to 3 sprigs fresh dill, snipped

Freshly ground pepper

Fresh chopped parsley

Combine all the ingredients except parsley in a bowl and blend well with a fork or wooden spoon. Pack into a small, plastic-lined bowl and chill until firm.

Roll the cheese ball in parsley and arrange on a platter with vegetable crudités, crackers, or bread.

Yield: 1½ cups.

Baked Brie

This gives a piece of leftover or over-aged Brie a new lease on life and provides the makings of an excellent dessert.

Remove and discard the crust from the top and sides of the cheese and cover the surfaces with lightly crushed cornflakes, pressing them in to make them adhere. Drizzle with melted butter and, just before serving, place in a preheated 450-degree oven for 4 or 5 minutes, or until runny and heated through. Serve with crackers or slices of crusty French bread.

Fried Mozzarella

For a vegetarian meal, serve with rice or pasta and a vegetable casserole, such as zucchini, eggplant, and tomatoes.

1 pound whole- or skim-milk
   mozzarella, cut into ½-inch-thick
   slices
1 cup flour
2 eggs, beaten
1 cup dry bread crumbs
Corn oil
Fresh chopped parsley
Tomato sauce (optional)

Dredge each slice of mozzarella in flour and shake to remove excess. Dip in egg and then in bread crumbs. Pat with the fingers so that the crumbs adhere.

Arrange in one layer on a baking sheet. When ready to serve, add corn oil to a depth of ½ inch in a large skillet. When hot, add the mozzarella in one layer and fry until golden on both sides, about 5 minutes. Drain on paper towels or a wire rack. Sprinkle with parsley and serve immediately.

Yield: 3 to 4 servings.

7
Cereals, Legumes, and Pastas

Cereals, legumes, and pastas are the mainstay of food and nourishment for more than half the peoples of the world. They are an extraordinarily versatile food group, stretching a meager food supply when meat, fish, and fresh vegetables and fruits are limited (or expensive) and adding substance and glamour to even well-stocked tables. They lend themselves to happy combinations with other foods to produce lusty, appetite-provoking dishes.

Cereals

Our word *cereal* is derived from the name of the Roman goddess of grain, Ceres, and, judging by the stacks of seductively packaged cereals that line supermarket shelves, her immortality is assured. The vast array of grains that provide us with cereal products includes wheat, rice, corn, rye, barley, millet, and oats. From them we get our breakfast foods, the starch products that provide side dishes, and flours. (For more about flours, see page 470.)

The importance of cereals in the national diet and the kind of cereal consumed vary from country to country. In rich countries like the United States and Canada, which enjoy a high standard of living, the percentage of calories in the national diet from cereals is comparatively low, somewhere from one-fifth to one-quarter of total calories. In poorer countries where there is a shortage of other agricultural products, cereals may represent three-fifths or more of the total calories. Wheat is the main cereal in the United States and Canada; rice is the main cereal in China, Japan, and India; rye is the main cereal in Russia and Central Europe. Corn is popular in Mexico and South America as well as in the United States. Oats are used to a more limited extent for human food.

Nutritive Values

Cereals are uniquely inexpensive sources of energy. They contain 75 percent carbohydrate and from 7 to 14 percent protein. Although the protein is not as high in quality as that found in meat, milk, and eggs, it can be fortified when the cereals are combined with other proteins such as milk, cheese, eggs, legumes, or small quantities of meat or fish. Indeed, a combination of rice and beans is a food staple in many cultures.

The vitamins and minerals of grains are contained mostly in the outer layers. Cereal grains are composed of three different parts—the outside layer, or the *bran*; the embryo, or the *germ*; and the *endosperm*, which is the major portion and the part that contains the starch cells. The bran in the outside layer contains cellulose, an indigestible material that provides important bulk to the gastrointestinal tract. It also contains minerals, mostly iron, and important B vitamins—niacin and thiamine—and is a fair source of riboflavin and protein. The germ is rich in unsaturated fat, but these cells are not too stable and the germ is removed from most cereal products to prevent them from becoming rancid.

Despite the nutritive values in whole grain cereals, most cereals are milled or refined before they are put on the market. There are a number of reasons, most of them having to do with popular preferences. Many people find cereals without the outer bran layer more palatable. Also, the refined cereals take much less time to cook than do the whole grain cereals.

Various methods of refining are used, depending on the type of grain. The bran on rice and barley may be removed by abrasion. Wheat kernels are passed between rollers operating at high speed. Heat from the rollers causes the fat in the germ to melt, and the germ and the bran come off in flakes. The endosperm is extracted and passes through rollers that subdivide it into smaller and smaller particles. However, with the bran and germ go a high proportion of the nutrients, except for the starch and protein. This should make it obvious that whole grain cereals are more nutritious than refined cereals, even though the enrichment of many breakfast cereals has become a standard procedure in the food industry.

Types of Cereal

Barley

Barley may have been one of the very first cereals that was cultivated. It was known to the ancient Greeks, Romans, Chinese, and Egyptians and it was the chief bread material in Europe as late as the sixteenth century. It is a hardy plant that can grow in poor soil with little water. The Plymouth colonists valued it highly and used it in soups, cereals, bread, and beer.

In cookery, barley is used in the form of hulled barley and pearl barley. Hulled barley has had the outer hull removed and pearl barley has been processed to remove both hull and germ, leaving a small cream-colored ball that looks like a tiny, irregularly shaped freshwater pearl. A classic use of barley is as an accompaniment for braised lamb, but it goes equally well with all meats. Too often barley is thought of only as a soup ingredient, but it gives a lovely account of itself in a baked casserole preparation.

Bulgur

Bulgur, parched cracked wheat, is light golden brown in color with a nutty taste and texture. While not widely used in this country, it has a long gastronomical history. The ancient Persians mixed it with raisins, peas, or pine nuts as a stuffing for whole baby lambs and chickens, or they cooked it with nuts in olive oil and used the mixture as a stuffing for eggplant.

Bulgur is made of whole wheat grains that have been boiled and dried. It can be used raw in a salad after being reconstituted by soaking in water for an hour. It is cooked in liquid in the proportion of one cup of bulgur to two cups of liquid and it will increase when cooked to nearly four times its original volume. It is used in soups, in stuffings, or as a starch with a meat or poultry main course.

Cornmeal

No product that we use in our kitchens is more truly American than corn. Until Columbus returned to Spain with the first kernels of maize from the New World, no European had ever seen corn. In England, "corn" was the seed of any grain, from wheat to barley. The starchy part of the corn kernel is marketed whole as hominy, cracked as groats, and ground as cornmeal. Cornmeal comes from either white or yellow corn. White and yellow cornmeal taste much the same and can be used interchangeably, although regional preferences may favor one over the other. Commercially ground cornmeal is made from grains with the germ removed, and water-ground meal retains the vitamin-rich germ. The texture of cornmeal ranges from fine to coarse. The coarse water-ground is recommended for cornmeal mush or Italian polenta, and the finer grinds for muffins and bread, although it is a matter of choice. Cornmeal mush may be served as a starch vegetable or a breakfast dish.

Groats

See Kasha.

Hominy

Hominy is dried corn with the hull and germ removed, often by being soaked in a weak solution of lye or soda. Hominy grits are ground hominy grains, slightly coarser than cornmeal. They are popular in southern United States. They are boiled and served as a breakfast cereal or as an accompaniment for fish or ham, or shaped into patties and fried.

Kasha

Kasha is buckwheat seed that has been parboiled, dried, and coarsely ground. In spite of its name, buckwheat is not even a distant relative of wheat and is neither a grain nor a cereal. It is the common name for a family of herbs and shrubs that produces a seed used primarily as flour. Buckwheat has been cultivated in Europe since the Middle Ages and the flour is used in the United States, Japan, and eastern Europe. *Groats* is a generic term that may stand for cracked wheat, buckwheat, or oats, but the groats that come from buckwheat are called *kasha*. Kasha has a nutty, distinctive flavor and makes a hearty, delicious side dish with poultry, pot roast, and game.

Rice

Rice is a universal food staple; more than half the world's population eats it three times a day. It has been cultivated in China for over 4,000 years. It was introduced to the American colonies in the mid-seventeenth century and it became an important crop.

A good deal of the rice we eat has had the bran removed to yield white, or polished, rice. The practice of polishing natural brown rice to a creamy whiteness is standard in the West but less common in the Orient. Unfortunately, a high proportion of the nutrients, except the starch and protein, go along with the bran and germ when they are removed, which encour-

ages the use of natural brown rice over the white.

Rice is an excellent ingredient for stuffings, salads, and desserts, besides its common use as a starch side dish. A bland food, it lends itself admirably to all manner of flavorings and seasonings. It may be boiled, steamed, or baked.

White Rice. Regular milled white rice has had the inedible outer hull and the inner coating of bran removed. It is available in long-, short-, and medium-grain varieties. The long grain tends to separate into light fluffy grains when cooked. The short and medium grains have a tendency to cling together and are useful for puddings, croquettes, rice rings, the creamy Italian risotto, or any dish that requires tender, easily molded rice. However, long-grain rice also works well for these purposes.

Converted Rice. Converted rice is long-grain rice that has been steamed under pressure before milling so that many of the vitamins and minerals of the whole grain are retained. After steaming, the rice is dried and then polished as white rice is. It requires a little more liquid to cook than regular milled rice. When cooked, the grains are fluffy, plump, and separate.

Precooked Rice. Known commercially as Minute or Instant Rice, this is a form of long-grain rice that has been cooked before being packaged. It requires only a few minutes in boiling water to be ready to serve. This is its chief and, in the opinion of some cooks, its only virtue.

Brown Rice. Brown rice is rice closest to its natural state. Only the hull and some of the bran have been removed and it is rich in vitamins and minerals, nutritionally superior to white rice. It has a subtle, nutlike flavor and, when cooked, does not look much browner than white rice. As with any whole grain cereal, it requires a slightly longer cooking time and a little more liquid than the same cereal after it has been milled.

Wild Rice. Wild rice is not really rice, but the seed of a grass that grows wild in the Great Lakes region. It is dark brown and rich in flavor, with an interesting texture. The wild rice crop must be gathered by hand and it is so limited that the price is deplorably high. Which is too bad, because it is a lovely, festive product, excellent as a stuffing for game birds and as a side dish with poultry.

Barley Casserole

Barley is an interesting grain that is not used often enough as a starch course. This is a hearty casserole that goes well with lamb, beef, or veal roasts.

6 tablespoons butter

⅓ cup pine nuts or slivered almonds

1 onion, finely chopped

1 cup pearl barley

¼ pound mushrooms, sliced

½ cup minced fresh parsley

¼ cup minced chives, or sliced scallions

3½ cups beef or chicken stock

Salt and freshly ground pepper

Grease a 1½-quart casserole.

In a large skillet, melt 2 tablespoons of butter. Add the pine nuts and brown them lightly, stirring often. They burn quickly, so keep an eye on them. Remove the nuts from the skillet and set aside.

Melt the remaining 4 tablespoons butter in the same skillet. Sauté the onion until slightly wilted. Add the barley and mushrooms and stir constantly until the barley is slightly toasted.

Remove the pan from the heat.

Stir in the nuts, parsley, and chives and transfer to the buttered casserole. Heat the broth to the boiling point, pour over the barley, and stir. Add salt and pepper to taste. The amount of salt depends on the saltiness of the stock, so taste as you go. Bake for 1 hour in a 375-degree oven, or until the barley is tender and the liquid absorbed.

Yield: 5 to 6 servings.

Bulgur

Bulgur, or cracked wheat, can add interesting variety to your starch repertoire.

2 tablespoons butter
1 onion, finely chopped
1 cup bulgur
2 cups hot chicken or beef broth
Salt and freshly ground pepper

Melt the butter in a heavy saucepan. Add the onion and cook over low heat until lightly browned. Stir in the bulgur and mix until the grains are coated with the fat and lightly toasted. Stir in the hot broth and taste to see if more seasoning is needed. You may want only a few grinds of pepper. Cover the pot and simmer over low heat for 15 minutes, or until all the liquid is absorbed. Remove from the heat and leave covered in a warm place until ready to serve.

Yield: 4 servings.

Variations: Prepare the above recipe and keep warm. Melt 1 tablespoon of butter in a skillet and add 1 small onion, chopped, ½ green pepper, chopped, and 1 clove of garlic, finely minced. Cook until the onion is limp and add 1 medium tomato, chopped, ½ teaspoon dried oregano, 1 teaspoon dried mint, and a few grinds of pepper. Toss the mixture with the cooked bulgur.

Add to the cooked bulgur ½ cup cooked baby lima beans and toss.

Polenta

6 cups water
1 tablespoon salt
2 cups stone-ground cornmeal
2 tablespoons butter
½ cup grated Parmesan or
    Romano cheese

Bring the water and salt to a boil. Trickle the cornmeal very slowly into the water, stirring constantly. You can use a whisk at first but as it begins to thicken, use a long-handled wooden spoon or spatula to stir the bottom and sides of the mixture.

When all the cornmeal has been added, lower the heat to a quiet, steady simmer and cook for about 40 minutes, stirring frequently, until the polenta is stiff and leaves the sides of the pan as you stir.

Spoon into a serving dish and mix with the butter and cheese. Serve immediately as an appetizer course, a main course, or a starch vegetable with poultry, pork, lamb, or chili.

Yield: 4 to 6 servings.

Southern Spoon Bread

2 cups milk
Salt
¾ cup cornmeal
4 tablespoons butter
4 eggs

Heat the oven to 375 degrees. Heat the milk and salt to the boiling point and lower the heat to a simmer. Add the cornmeal and stir and cook until it becomes thick. Add the butter and remove from the heat. In a small bowl, beat the eggs until thick and lemon-colored. Add them to the cooled cornmeal mixture and blend well. Pour into a buttered 9-inch-square baking dish and bake for 1 hour, or until a cake tester comes out dry.

Yield: 6 servings.

Hominy Grits

To prepare 1 cup grits, bring 4 cups water and 1 teaspoon salt to a boil. Slowly stir in the grits over moderate heat and cook, stirring from time to time, until thick, about 20 minutes. If you are using quick-cooking grits, follow the directions on the package.

Yield: 4 servings.

Kasha (Buckwheat Groats)

Try this for a change from other grains or cereals as an accompaniment for meat or poultry.

1 cup kasha
1 egg, lightly beaten
2 cups chicken or beef broth
3 tablespoons butter
Salt

In a heated skillet, combine the kasha and egg. Cook and stir vigorously over high heat until each grain is separate and dry. Bring the broth to a boil and add to the kasha. Cover and reduce heat to a simmer. Cook for 20 minutes, or until all the liquid is absorbed. Stir in the butter and add salt to taste.

Fluff with a fork before serving.

Yield: 4 servings.

Variations: At the time you add the boiling broth, add to the kasha 1 chopped onion or green pepper, or 1 cup sliced mushrooms that have been sautéed in oil or butter.

Steamed Rice

There are many schools of thought about rice cookery and countless theories on the best technique for producing perfect rice. First-rate cooks differ widely in their views about cold water versus boiling water, a lot of water versus carefully measured water, a covered pot versus an uncovered pot, and so on. Perfect rice and equally perfect disasters have been produced with virtually every method. It is of interest that a group of food scientists using seven different cooking methods compared the results and came to the conclusion that the quality of the cooked rice appeared to stem more from the characteristics inherent in the rice than from the cooking method used. On that inconclusive note we give you our steamed rice, which has always turned out fluffy and fine, with well-separated grains.

1 cup long-grain rice (see note)
1¾ cups water or broth
1 tablespoon butter (optional)
¾ teaspoon salt

Combine the rice, water, butter, and salt in a heavy-bottomed 2-quart saucepan. Bring to a boil over moderately high heat, reduce the heat to a low simmer, and cover the saucepan with a tight lid. Simmer without lifting the lid for 15 minutes, or until most of the water is absorbed and the rice is tender. Don't stir rice once it has come to a boil because stirring mashes the grains and makes them gummy. Lifting the lid will allow steam to escape, thereby lowering the temperature, which can result in the rice's sticking to the pot. When the rice is done, remove the pot from the heat and allow it to stand, covered, for 15 to 20 minutes. Remove the cover and fluff with a fork. If you wish, add a tablespoon or two of soft butter to the cooked rice and toss it with a fork until the grains are coated. Always stir cooked rice with a fork. A spoon will bruise the grains and make them gummy.

Yield: 3 cups, or 4 servings.

Note: Brown rice may be substituted for white rice, but increase the liquid to 2½ cups and double the cooking time. If you use converted rice, allow ¼ cup more liquid for each cup of rice. One cup of raw converted rice yields about 4 cups cooked rice.

To increase quantity: For 2 cups of long-grain rice, use 3¼ cups of water. If you plan to prepare more than 2 cups of rice, use a large shallow heavy skillet in preference to a deep casserole and the rice will be fluffy. In a deep pot it becomes compacted because of the weight and volume, thus increasing the chances of its being sticky.

Rice with Peas. Lightly cook half of a 10-ounce package of frozen green peas. Stir into the cooked rice and sprinkle with grated Parmesan cheese.

Saffron Rice. Crumble ½ teaspoon loosely packed saffron threads. Add it to the liquid in the saucepan and stir before adding the uncooked rice.

Green Rice. Toss 4 cups cooked rice with 4 tablespoons melted butter and ½ cup each minced parsley and chopped chives or scallions, both the green and white parts. Finely chopped fresh basil may also be used.

Rice with Nuts. To 4 cups cooked rice, add about 1 cup crisply toasted almonds, walnuts, or pecans, coarsely chopped. You may also use whole pine nuts or thinly sliced water chestnuts. Toss with 4 or 5 tablespoons melted butter.

Baked Rice

An effortless way to produce a perfect rice dish.

2 tablespoons butter
1 small onion, finely chopped
½ cup chopped mushrooms
1 cup long-grain rice
2 cups chicken or beef broth
Salt and freshly ground pepper

Preheat the oven to 350 degrees.

Melt the butter in a 1½-quart flameproof casserole and cook the onion until it is limp and transparent. Add the mushrooms and cook for 2 minutes longer. Add the rice and stir with a wooden spoon until the grains are well coated. Add the broth and bring to a boil. Taste to see if salt and pepper are needed. Cover the casserole tightly and bake for 30 minutes. The liquid should be absorbed and the rice tender.

Yield: 4 to 5 servings.

Baked Brown Rice

4 tablespoons butter
1 medium onion, finely chopped
½ cup raisins
½ teaspoon cinnamon
Pinch of ground cloves
¼ teaspoon curry powder
1 cup short-grain brown rice
2 cups chicken broth
¼ cup slivered almonds or whole pine nuts, sautéed in 1 tablespoon butter until golden

Preheat the oven to 350 degrees.

Melt the butter in a 1½-quart flameproof casserole and add the onion and raisins. Cook, stirring, until the onion is softened and lightly colored. Add the cinnamon, cloves, curry powder, and rice and stir until the rice grains are coated.

Add the broth and bring to a boil. Cover and transfer to the oven. Bake for 50 to 60 minutes, or until the liquid is absorbed and the rice tender. Remove from the oven and stir in the nuts.

Yield: 4 servings.

Note: This may also be cooked on top of the stove over low heat, tightly covered.

Risotto Milanese

Italian risotto is a frequently misunderstood preparation. It is not boiled rice, but rice that has been cooked to creamy tenderness by the gradual addition of hot broth, which causes the rice grains to swell but still retain their firm-to-the-bite quality. Risotto is generally served as a first course, although it may be served as a starch, albeit a rich one, with any dish.

4 tablespoons clarified butter (see page 260), or half butter and half vegetable oil

Marrow scraped from 2 or 3 beef bones (optional)

1 small onion, finely chopped

2 cups Italian short-grain rice, or long-grain converted rice

4 cups hot beef broth

1 teaspoon loosely packed saffron threads

½ cup freshly grated Parmesan cheese

Heat the butter and beef marrow (if using) in a heavy-bottomed 2-quart skillet. Add the onion and cook, stirring, until it becomes limp and transparent. Add the rice and stir for 1 or 2 minutes until the grains are well coated with fat and become translucent.

Keep the broth at a low simmer on another burner. Add a cup of the simmering broth to the rice and stir while cooking, always loosening the rice from the bottom of the pan to prevent its sticking. When the liquid is almost absorbed, add an additional cup of broth and continue to stir. The rice will gradually soften and become creamy. When this happens, add the stock more slowly, always waiting until it is absorbed before adding more. You don't want to drown the rice, only to give it as much liquid as it can absorb. Add the saffron dissolved in some of the hot broth after 10 or 15 minutes. The Italian rice should be cooked in about 30 minutes; the long-grain in 20 to 25. The quantity of liquid called for in this recipe is approximate; you may end up using less or slightly more. When done, the risotto should be creamy but *al dente*, firm to the bite in the center, and all the liquid absorbed. Continue to stir even in the final cooking to prevent the rice from sticking to the pan. When done, stir in the cheese with a fork and serve hot.

Yield: 4 to 6 servings.

Note: The beef marrow is not a necessity, but it gives a special flavor. The rice of choice for this dish is the Italian Arborio rice, but, if properly made, you can have a splendid risotto with a good long-grain rice.

Mushroom-Rice Ring with Almonds

Fill the center of the ring with cooked green peas for an attractive party dish.

4 tablespoons butter

½ pound mushrooms, sliced (about 2½ cups)

2 medium onions, finely chopped

1¾ cups converted rice

3½ cups chicken broth

1 tablespoon Worcestershire sauce

Salt

½ cup sliced almonds browned in 2 teaspoons butter

½ cup finely minced parsley

2 10-ounce packages frozen peas (optional)

Melt the butter in a large skillet. Add the mushrooms and onions and sauté until the onions are limp and transparent, about 5 minutes. Stir in the rice and coat with fat. Add the broth and Worcestershire sauce and taste to see if salt is needed. Bring to the boil, reduce the heat, cover, and simmer until the rice is tender and the liquid is absorbed, about 15 minutes. Remove from the heat and let stand, covered, for 15 to 20 minutes. Stir in the toasted almonds and parsley and toss well with a fork to distribute. Butter a 6-cup ring mold generously and pack the hot rice into the mold, pressing it in firmly. Cover the mold with a hot serving dish and invert. Remove the mold carefully.

Fill the center with hot cooked green peas if desired.

Yield: 6 servings.

Baked Rice and Chick-peas

½ cup olive oil

2 cloves garlic, finely chopped

2 cups long-grain white rice, *or* 1 cup short-grain brown rice

¼ cup chopped tomatoes

2 cups cooked chick-peas, *or* 1 1-pound, 4-ounce can, drained

3 cups chicken broth

Pinch of cinnamon

Salt and freshly ground pepper

Preheat the oven to 350 degrees.

Heat the oil in a casserole and cook the garlic until golden. Add the rice and cook, stirring, until translucent and coated with fat. Add the tomatoes, chick-peas, chicken broth, cinnamon, salt, and pepper.

Bring to the boil, cover, and transfer to the oven. Bake the white rice for 25 to 30 minutes, or until tender. Brown rice will take 50 to 60 minutes.

Yield: 4 to 6 servings.

Eastern Rice Pilaf

Aromatic and textured with fruits and nuts, this can be a side dish or, flecked with cooked meat, poultry, or fish, a supper dish.

4 tablespoons butter
2 cups long-grain rice
¼ cup pine nuts
3½ cups beef broth (or a mixture of broth and water)
⅓ cup seedless white raisins
½ teaspoon ground allspice
½ teaspoon freshly grated nutmeg
½ teaspoon ground cinnamon
2 teaspoons Worcestershire sauce

Melt the butter in a large skillet. Add the rice and pine nuts and stir over moderate heat until the rice and nuts take on color, about 5 minutes. Stir in the remaining ingredients and bring to a boil. Reduce the heat and simmer, covered, until the rice is tender and the liquid absorbed, for 20 to 25 minutes. Let stand, covered, for 10 minutes removed from the heat. Fluff with a fork and transfer to a heated bowl.

Yield: 8 servings.

Tomato Pilaf

2 medium-size ripe tomatoes, coarsely chopped
4 tablespoons butter
Salt and freshly ground pepper
2 cups beef stock
1 teaspoon tomato paste
1 cup long-grain rice
1 teaspoon dried basil
2 tablespoons melted butter

In a large heavy-bottomed nonaluminum saucepan, combine the tomatoes, butter, salt, and pepper. Cook over moderate heat for 5 minutes, or until the mixture is thick and fairly smooth. Stir and mash the tomatoes with a wooden spoon while cooking. Add the stock and tomato paste and bring to a boil. Cook briskly for 5 minutes. Purée the mixture through a food mill, or force it through a strainer. Discard the seeds and coarse pulp. There should be 2 cups of the purée. Boil it briskly until it is reduced to 1¾ cups. If there is less than this amount, add stock. Add the rice and basil to the tomato purée and bring to a boil. Reduce the heat, cover, and simmer for 15 minutes, or until the rice is tender and the liquid absorbed. Remove from the heat, add the 2 tablespoons of melted butter, and toss with a fork. Cover and let stand for 10 minutes before serving. Fluff with a fork and transfer to a heated serving bowl.

Yield: 4 servings.

Rice and Cheese Pudding

2 tablespoons butter
1 large clove garlic, finely minced
1 small onion, finely chopped
1½ cups cooked rice
2 eggs, lightly beaten
1 cup milk
2 teaspoons Worcestershire sauce
1 cup grated Cheddar cheese or
　any other sharp cheese, about 4
　ounces
Salt and freshly ground pepper
½ cup minced fresh parsley
1 tablespoon minced chives, green
　and white parts

Preheat the oven to 350 degrees. Grease a 1-quart baking dish.

In a small skillet, melt the butter and sauté the garlic and onion until softened. In a medium-size bowl, combine the rice with the remaining ingredients and blend well. Stir in the garlic-onion mixture. Pour into the baking dish, cover tightly, and bake for 40 to 45 minutes, or until set. Uncover for the last 10 minutes of cooking so that the top will brown a bit.

Yield: 6 servings.

Wild Rice Casserole

This makes a lot out of a little wild rice and offers an interesting variety of textures.

½ cup wild rice
7 cups lightly salted water or stock
½ cup long-grain rice
4 tablespoons butter
1 medium onion, finely chopped
2 celery stalks, finely chopped
½ pound mushrooms, sliced
1 8-ounce can water chestnuts,
　drained and sliced
1 tablespoon soy sauce (Japanese
　preferred)
½ cup slivered almonds, browned
　in 1 tablespoon oil

Preheat the oven to 350 degrees.

Wash the wild rice in cold water, changing the water several times until it is completely clear. Soak it in cold water to cover for a few hours. Drain. In a large pot, bring the water or stock to a boil and cook the wild rice for 20 minutes, covered. Add the white rice, and continue to cook for another 15 or 20 minutes, or until tender. Drain.

In a medium-size skillet, melt the butter, and cook the onion until limp and transparent but not browned. Add the celery and mushrooms and cook for an additional 5 minutes. Don't overcook the celery; it should be crisp-tender. To the drained rice add the onion, celery, mushrooms, water chestnuts, and soy sauce and mix well. Taste for seasoning and correct. You may want to add a bit of salt or a bit more soy sauce. Transfer to a greased 6-cup casserole. Bake uncovered until heated through, about 30 minutes.

While the rice is in the oven, brown the almonds in a small skillet, shaking the skillet from time to time so that they will brown evenly. Before serving, sprinkle the browned almonds over the rice.

Yield: 6 servings.

Legumes

A combination of increased public awareness of nutrition and ever-spiraling food costs have brought new glamour and interest to legumes. Legumes—beans, peas, and lentils—are the dried seeds from plants that belong to the *Leguminosae* family, hence the name. They are inexpensive, hearty, chockablock with nutrients, and can be prepared in all sorts of delicious ways.

As a group, legumes contain approximately twice as much protein as cereals, and on a per-serving basis, about half as much protein as lean meat.They are richer than cereals as a source of some of the essential amino acids. Beans and peas are low in fat and high in carbohydrates. A cup of cooked beans, depending on the variety, contains between 210 and 224 calories. Peanuts and soybeans are exceptions. Peanuts, which are actually a legume although they are classed with nuts, are high in fat; soybeans are high in protein as well as fat. Legumes compare favorably with lean meat as a source of iron and some of the B vitamins.

There are more than two dozen different varieties of packaged legumes in our markets. The following are among the most commonly known:

Black Beans. These are a food staple in their native South America and are popular in the Caribbean and in the Southwest. Oval-shaped and black-skinned, they are sometimes called turtle beans. They have achieved everlasting distinction in black bean soup, and they can also be boiled and mashed.

Blackeye or Yelloweye Beans, or Cowpeas. These are kidney-shaped peas with either a black or a yellow spot on a white seed. When Southerners speak of peas, they are generally referring to cowpeas. Serve them in a soup or cooked with a hambone and seasonings as a side dish.

Chick-peas. Also called garbanzos, ceci, or gram, depending on the language. They are small, round, beige-yellow beans, popular in Mediterranean countries. They are used in stews, salads, and purées and are the essential ingredient in the Middle Eastern dish called hummus. They are hard and take a long time to cook.

Flageolets. Pale green and kidney-shaped, similar to baby limas, flageolets are the French beans used as a classic accompaniment for lamb. They make a delicious purée.

Lima Beans. Dried lima beans are a popular ingredient in soups, salads, and casseroles, and can be simply laced with butter as a side dish with meats.

Lentils. About the size of split peas, lentils are small flat seeds that come in a variety of colors, most generally brown or greenish. They make lovely soups or purées, or they can be used in vegetable stews or curried with rice.

Pinto and Pink Beans. These are similar in flavor to red kidney beans and can be used interchangeably with them. They are often used in Mexican dishes.

Red Beans and Red Kidney Beans. Red beans are dark and oval-shaped; red kidney beans are large and bright red. They are often served in chili con carne as well as in soups, salads, and casseroles.

Split Peas, Green and Yellow. Split peas are, as the name suggests, peas that have been dried and split. Split peas of either color are used in hearty soups or as a thick purée with pork or ham, a classic combination.

Soybeans. These small hard legumes are the highest in protein and amino acids of all legumes. They are a most important crop because of their nutritional value. Soybeans are used for flour, soy sauce, bean curd, oil, and in soups and salads.

White Beans. The white bean group includes pea beans, Great Northern beans, navy beans, and marrow beans. Pea beans and navy beans are used for Boston baked beans.

Cooking Legumes

Preparation. Beans must be picked over carefully before using because pebbles and other little expendables can get mixed up with them. Place the beans in a good-size bowl and cover them with cold water. Foreign particles will rise to the surface for easy removal. Also sift through the beans with your fingers and remove anything that doesn't look like a bean.

Because of their low moisture content, dried beans cook faster if they are first soaked overnight. This need not be done to beans whose packages direct that no soaking is necessary, or to lentils or split peas, which cook satisfactorily without prior soaking. As an alternative to overnight soaking, boil the beans for 2 minutes, remove the pot from the heat, cover the pot, and let it stand for 1 hour. This gives as good a result as the overnight soak. The usual proportion for soaking and cooking dried legumes is 2½ to 3 cups of water for every cup of beans.

Cooking. Legumes contain natural plant toxins that can be harmful. However, the heat used in cooking effectively neutralizes these toxins, which is why it is important to cook legumes. *Never* eat them raw. Discard the soaking water, rinse the beans, and cook in fresh water.

Add 1 teaspoon of salt for each cup of beans and water to cover. Cover the pot and simmer gently until the beans become tender. Be sure that the beans remain covered with water during the whole cooking period. To test for doneness, you cannot improve on the old-fashioned method of removing two or three beans on a spoon and blowing on them. If the skin breaks and peels away, the beans have reached the right stage of tenderness. You can also taste for tenderness.

The amount of time needed to cook beans can vary according to the moisture content and the conditions under which the beans were stored. Since you have no way of knowing this in advance, you will have to test and taste.

The addition of baking soda reduces the cooking time by about one-fourth, but the amount must not exceed ⅛ teaspoon of soda for each cup of beans, and the soda must be measured exactly. Too much soda will affect the flavor and nutritive value of beans, and also make them dark and mushy. Laboratory tests have shown that this small amount of soda does not diminish the vitamin content nor does it appreciably alter the quality of the cooked bean. Baking soda is worth using when cooking chick-peas, which can take many, many hours to soften.

If acid ingredients such as tomatoes, ketchup, or vinegar are included in a recipe, add them after the beans are partly cooked, because acid prevents softening of the beans and the cooking time will be prolonged. Molasses, too, should be added after the beans become tender, because the calcium in the molasses has the same hardening effect on the beans. Some experts recommend adding the salt after the beans are soft.

Boston Baked Beans

1 pound navy or pea beans
6 cups water
Salt
3 medium onions, sliced thin
⅓ cup unsulfured molasses
¼ cup sugar
2 teaspoons dry mustard
½ teaspoon ground ginger
Freshly ground pepper
¼ pound salt pork, cut into ¼-inch-thick slices

Soak the beans overnight in 6 cups of water, or use the quick-soak method (page 301). Drain and add salt and fresh water to cover. Add half the onions and bring to a boil. Cover the pot, lower the heat, and simmer for 45 minutes, or until just tender.

Preheat the oven to 300 degrees. Drain the beans when tender, reserving the liquid. Place the beans and remaining onions in a 2-quart casserole or bean pot. Combine the remaining ingredients, except the salt pork, with 1 cup of the reserved bean liquid. Pour over the beans and stir thoroughly but gently. Push in the slices of salt pork, distributing them evenly. Add additional bean liquid to cover the beans by ½ inch.

Cover the pot tightly with foil and the pot lid, and transfer to the oven. Bake for 5 to 6 hours, or until tender. Add additional bean liquid as needed.

An hour before the beans are done, remove the foil and lid so that the top can be brown and crusty.

Yield: 6 to 8 servings.

Note: Beans can be cooked in a slow cooker overnight. You probably will not have to add as much liquid as when oven-baked. The flavor is somewhat different, but good.

Bean Purée

A pleasant side dish, compatible with almost any meat.

2 cups dried white beans
1 small onion, coarsely chopped
4 tablespoons butter
½ to ¾ cup heavy cream
Salt and freshly ground pepper

Soak the beans overnight or use the quick-soak method (page 301). Cook with the onion as in preceding recipe until soft. Drain well and purée in a food mill to remove the skins. Blend in the butter and enough cream to make a creamy mixture. Season with salt and pepper and serve hot.

Yield: 6 servings.

Mediterranean Beans

1 pound navy or pea beans
2 tablespoons olive oil
1 small onion, finely chopped
1 clove garlic, finely chopped
¼ cup tomato sauce
2 tablespoons tomato paste
1 teaspoon ground cumin
2 tablespoons finely chopped
  fresh parsley

Soak the beans overnight, or use the quick-soak method (page 301).

Drain and place in a kettle. Add the remaining ingredients, except the parsley. Cover with water and bring to a boil. Lower the heat and simmer until tender, 1 to 1½ hours. Transfer to a warm serving bowl and sprinkle with parsley.

Serve hot with any pork or lamb dish.

Yield: 4 to 6 servings.

Breton-Style Beans

For a special treat, particularly with a lamb dish, use flageolets, the delicate green French dried bean.

2 cups dried white beans or
  flageolets
Water
1 onion stuck with 2 cloves
¼ pound salt pork
1 large carrot, scraped and cut in
  half
1 bay leaf
Salt
2 tablespoons butter
2 medium onions, finely chopped
2 shallots, finely chopped
1 large garlic clove, finely
  chopped
½ teaspoon dried thyme
3 cups peeled and chopped
  tomatoes, fresh or canned
2 tablespoons chopped fresh
  parsley

Soak the beans in water overnight or use the quick-soak method (page 301). Drain the beans and return to the kettle with water to cover. Add the whole onion, salt pork, carrot, bay leaf, and salt and bring to a boil. Cover, reduce the heat, and simmer for 45 minutes.

Remove the salt pork and cut into small cubes. Reserve. Cook the beans for 15 to 30 minutes longer, or until tender.

Melt the butter in a skillet and cook the salt pork cubes until nicely browned. Add the chopped onion, shallots, garlic, and thyme and cook until the onions are limp. Add the tomatoes and cook, stirring, until the sauce is thickened.

Drain the beans but reserve the liquid. Discard the onion, carrot, and bay leaf. Combine the beans with the tomato sauce and mix gently. Simmer for 10 minutes. If the beans seem dry, add a bit of the reserved bean liquid. Serve sprinkled with chopped parsley.

Yield: 6 to 8 servings.

Red Beans and Rice

A complete meal, hearty and satisfying.

2 cups dried red beans or kidney beans

¼ pound cooked ham, cubed

¼ pound salt pork, cut into ¼-inch-thick slices

1 ham hock

1 medium onion, coarsely chopped

4 whole scallions, trimmed and chopped

1 medium bell pepper, seeded and coarsely chopped

2 tablespoons chopped fresh parsley

2 cloves garlic, finely chopped

½ teaspoon dried thyme

2 small bay leaves

¼ teaspoon dried hot red pepper flakes

Salt and freshly ground pepper

4 cups hot cooked rice

Sliced oranges (optional)

Soak the beans in water overnight or use the quick-soak method (page 301). Drain the beans and put in a large kettle with the remaining ingredients, except the rice and oranges. Add cold water to cover.

Cover and bring to a boil. Lower the heat and simmer gently for 2½ to 3 hours. Remove meat from ham hock and discard the bones. Remove the bay leaves. Return the meat to the beans. Add salt and pepper to taste.

Serve with hot rice and garnish with orange slices, if desired.

Yield: 6 servings.

Purée of Green Split Peas

Purée of split peas makes a fine vegetable.

1 pound green split peas

Chicken broth to cover

1 onion, chopped

1 bay leaf

½ teaspoon dried mint

Salt and freshly ground pepper

4 tablespoons butter

Wash the peas in several changes of water and pick them over. Drain. Place in a heavy pot and cover with broth. Add the onion, bay leaf, mint, salt, and pepper. Cover and bring to a boil. Reduce the heat and simmer slowly until the peas are tender, about 45 minutes. Drain, discard the bay leaf, and reserve the broth. Purée the peas in a blender or food processor, adding a bit of the broth if too thick. Scrape into a warm serving bowl and fluff in the butter. Taste and correct seasoning.

Yield: 4 servings.

Glazed Chick-peas

Shiny and golden with glaze, these chick-peas are an unusual side dish that goes well with a simple roasted meat or chicken.

3 cups cooked chick-peas
¼ cup brown sugar
⅓ cup white corn syrup
2 tablespoons butter

Preheat the oven to 350 degrees. Lightly oil a large flat pan, such as a jelly roll pan. Spread the chick-peas over it and sprinkle with the brown sugar and the corn syrup. Mix well. Dot with butter and bake for 20 to 35 minutes, stirring the chick-peas from time to time so that they are well coated with the syrup. They are done when they are shiny and burnished and the syrup is mostly absorbed. Transfer to a warm serving bowl and serve hot.

Yield: 5 or 6 servings.

Hummus (Purée of Chick-peas)

A Middle Eastern specialty that makes a lovely hors d'oeuvre served with pita bread or melba toast, or as a dip with raw fresh vegetables. Tahini (sesame seed paste) is available in health and specialty food stores.

⅔ cup sesame seed paste (tahini)
3 tablespoons water (or more)
⅓ cup fresh lemon juice
2 cloves garlic, crushed
2 cups cooked chick-peas
Salt and freshly ground pepper
3 scallions, finely chopped (green and white parts)

Combine the sesame seed paste, water, lemon juice, and garlic in a blender or food processor. Blend until smooth and creamy. Add the chick-peas and blend until smooth. Push down with a spatula as needed. You may wish to add an additional 1 to 2 tablespoons of water if the mixture is too thick.

Scrape out into a serving bowl and season to taste. Sprinkle with scallions.

Yield: 4 to 8 servings.

Variation: If you are not able to get sesame paste, the following makes an excellent purée: 2 cups cooked chick-peas (or a 1-pound, 4-ounce can), 3 tablespoons oil, ½ teaspoon sesame seeds, salt and freshly ground pepper, 1 or 2 cloves garlic, crushed, 2 tablespoons chopped parsley, 4 tablespoons lemon juice, and a few dashes of paprika. Whir in a blender or processor until smooth and creamy.

Monastery-Style Lentils

1 cup dried lentils
3 cups (or more) water
Salt
⅛ teaspoon dried thyme
⅛ teaspoon dried marjoram
3 onions, chopped
1 carrot, finely chopped
¼ cup olive oil
¼ cup finely minced fresh parsley
2 tomatoes, peeled and chopped
4 tablespoons dry sherry
4 tablespoons grated Swiss cheese

Wash the lentils in several changes of cold water, picking them over carefully. Drain and place in a heavy saucepan with 3 cups of water, salt, thyme, and marjoram. Cover, bring to a boil, reduce the heat, and simmer for 15 minutes.

In a small skillet, cook the onion and carrot in the olive oil until soft, about 5 minutes. Add to the lentils with the parsley, tomatoes, and sherry. Cover and simmer until the lentils are tender, 30 to 40 minutes longer. Add a bit more water, if necessary. Taste and correct seasoning. Transfer to a warmed bowl and sprinkle with grated cheese.

Yield: 3 or 4 servings.

Curried Lentils and Brown Rice

2 tablespoons butter
2 tablespoons vegetable oil
1 teaspoon curry powder
1 teaspoon salt
Freshly ground pepper
Pinch of ground cloves
Few dashes of Tabasco sauce
1 medium onion, finely chopped
1 clove garlic, finely minced
½ cup lentils, washed, picked over, and drained
2 cups water
½ cup brown rice
1½ cups water
Minced fresh parsley

In a medium-size saucepan, melt the butter and oil and add the curry powder, salt, pepper, cloves, and Tabasco sauce. Heat and stir for a minute. Add the onion and garlic and cook, stirring, until the onion becomes limp. Add the lentils with 2 cups of water. Bring to a boil, cover the pot, lower the heat, and simmer for 45 minutes, or until the lentils are tender but still firm. Check the pot from time to time to see that there is enough liquid and add in small amounts as needed. The liquid should all be absorbed at the end of the cooking time. While the lentils are cooking, cook the brown rice in 1½ cups of water in a covered pot until tender, about 40 minutes. Blend together the rice and lentils in a warm serving bowl, sprinkle with minced parsley, and serve at once.

Yield: 4 servings.

Lima Beans in Sour Cream

1 pound dried lima beans
4 tablespoons butter
2 large onions, finely chopped
½ pound mushrooms, sliced
2 tablespoons sweet paprika
Salt
1 tablespoon flour
1½ cups (or more) sour cream or
  crème fraîche
1 cup finely minced fresh parsley

Soak the beans in water overnight, or use the quick-soak method (page 301). Drain, cover with water, add salt, and bring to a boil. Reduce the heat, cover, and simmer until the beans are tender, hour or a little more. While the beans are cooking, melt the butter in a large, heavy skillet and sauté the onions until limp and transparent. Add the mushrooms and cook for 3 or 4 minutes. Sprinkle with paprika, salt, and flour and cook for 3 or 4 minutes longer, stirring constantly. Add the drained beans, sour cream, and parsley, mix gently, and heat through. Taste and correct the seasonings. Transfer to a heated bowl to serve.

Yield: 8 servings.

Baked Lima Beans

1 pound dried lima beans
3 cups water
Salt and freshly ground pepper
½ teaspoon dried thyme
¼ teaspoon freshly grated nutmeg
⅓ pound salt pork, cut into ¼-
  inch cubes
2 onions, sliced
4 carrots, thinly sliced
¼ cup minced fresh parsley

Soak the beans overnight and drain, or use the quick-soak method (page 301). Place the beans in a large kettle with 3 cups water, salt, pepper, thyme, and nutmeg. Simmer, covered, until almost soft, 20 to 30 minutes. While the beans are cooking, brown the salt pork in a skillet and drain on paper towels. Pour off all but 3 tablespoons fat from the skillet. Brown the onions and carrots in the pork fat. Combine with the salt pork and beans and transfer to a 3-quart casserole.

Bake, uncovered, in a 350-degree oven for about 1 hour, or until beans and carrots are tender. Add water if the mixture seems dry. Before serving, stir in the minced parsley.

Yield: 8 servings.

Pasta

Pasta is the generic name in Italian for all the dried starch products, such as spaghetti, macaroni, and noodles, that come in shapes and sizes as varied as nature's own forms. They are all made from a basic flour and water dough, either with or without egg, and they owe their names and their personalities to the shapes in which they are fashioned—strands, shells, bows, twists, spirals, and the like. Green pasta is simply pasta to which spinach has been added. It makes it a bit softer and creamier but has no significant effect on the flavor. The difference is mainly visual—green noodles look most attractive when served with a white or red sauce.

Whether viewed from a gastronomic, nutritional, or budgetary viewpoint, pasta is a splendid foodstuff. It is high in energy-producing carbohydrate and, when complemented with sauces of fresh vegetables, cheeses, meats, seafood, or tomatoes, provides a well-balanced meal. Its uses are legion: as an appetizer, a main course, a side dish, a family dinner, or an informal company buffet.

Imported Italian pasta is generally superior to the American factory-made variety. It is made of the heart of hard durum wheat and will cook up both tender and firm at the same time. The American-made pastas use a different flour and can become gummy unless carefully cooked. The Italian level of excellence for cooked pasta is *al dente*, firm to the bite, with a texture and consistency that let you know what you are eating. It is a good idea to try different imported and domestic products until you find one that pleases you.

We are finding an increasing number of shops in more and more cities that sell excellent freshly made pasta. It is not dried until hard like the commercial packaged products, and it cooks in very little time, often just a couple of minutes. It should be used at once, or it can be frozen. Only the ribbony kinds of pasta such as fettucine, tagliatelle, and broad lasagna noodles can be bought fresh. The tubular pastas such as ziti and cannelloni are shaped into cylinders through a machine and must almost always be bought dry. There are many electric or hand-operated pasta machines on the market, and many people have begun to make their own pasta with great success.

Cooking Pasta

For 1 pound of pasta, bring 4 quarts of water seasoned with 1½ heaping tablespoons of salt to a boil in an 8-quart covered pot. There are valid reasons for using a large quantity of water. First, there has to be room for the pasta to expand and move around. Even more important for perfect pasta, the fast boil must be continued throughout the cooking. Introducing foods into the pot can interrupt the boiling, but if the quantity of water is at least three times as much as will cover the food, the boiling process will not be halted.

When the fast rolling boil is reached, remove the cover, add 1 or 2 teaspoons of oil, and drop in the pasta. (If the boil slows down, cover the pot briefly until it returns to a lively boil.) Make sure all the pasta is covered by the water. Long, thin strands of spaghetti or linguine may need a push with a long-handled wooden spoon to submerge all the strands below the surface of the water once they begin to soften. Let it be a gentle push, just enough to bend them and not break them. You want all the strands uniform in length. Stir the pasta from time to time.

If you are cooking commercial pasta, start

testing after 5 minutes. Freshly made pasta will cook more quickly, in a matter of 2 or 3 minutes. You can test only by tasting. Fish out a strand with kitchen tongs and bite into it. Cooking times will vary with different pasta. Don't pay attention to package directions; the cooking time is invariably too long and you must be the judge of when the pasta has reached the done stage. It should be tender with no suggestion of a raw center, but *al dente*, firm to the bite. Don't overcook it.

The moment it is done, drain it in a colander. Some cooks recommend rinsing it in cold water to stop the cooking, but this will not be necessary if you quickly empty the pot into the colander and let the hot water drain off. Immediately after draining it, transfer it to the pot or a warmed serving bowl and, using two forks, toss it with the sauce. You may add the sauce at once, which will prevent the pasta from sticking together. In addition to the sauces in this chapter, see page 456 for basic tomato sauces.

Unsauced cooked pasta will store very well, in the event that you have cooked more than you need. Toss it in oil and refrigerate it in a covered container. When you are ready to use it, place it in a pot of boiling water for no longer than it takes to heat through, 1 to 2 minutes. Drain and serve at once. Cooked pasta will not store as successfully if it is in a sauce; the sauce softens the pasta and affects the texture.

Pasta can be dressed simply with cheese and butter or oil and garlic, or with fresh vegetables cooked in butter and oil. The combinations are endless.

Cold Pasta

Cold pasta is a delicious budget-stretcher that is gaining in popularity. Tortellini, bows (butterflies), or shell-shaped pasta are good choices for this preparation. Cook the pasta in chicken broth only until *al dente*. Don't overcook. Rinse in cold water and drain thoroughly. Toss with a good quality olive oil. Blend in some mayonnaise flavored with Dijon mustard, a splash of tarragon vinegar, and a generous amount of chopped fresh basil. If you wish, you can add some fresh chopped, seeded, and peeled tomatoes. Add salt and pepper to taste. Or mix the cooked pasta with some diced leftover chicken or meat or a small quantity of cooked shrimp, lobster, or crabmeat and toss with a sprightly vinaigrette seasoned with Dijon mustard.

Bolognese Sauce

Bolognese sauce is one of the most famous of pasta sauces and has many variations. This is a classic and delicious version. It is sufficient for 1 pound of pasta.

¼ pound chopped bacon

1 medium onion, finely chopped

1 celery stalk, finely chopped

1 medium carrot, scraped and finely chopped

3 tablespoons olive oil

1 pound lean ground beef (or a combination of beef, veal, and pork)

1 cup chicken or beef broth

1 cup dry white wine

2 cups canned peeled Italian tomatoes, roughly cut, with juice

1 teaspoon salt

Freshly ground pepper

⅛ teaspoon freshly grated nutmeg

½ cup light or heavy cream

In a deep, heavy nonaluminum kettle—an enameled cast iron casserole will do—combine the bacon and vegetables with the oil. Cook, stirring, over low heat until the onions are translucent and the vegetables softened. Add the meat, using a wooden spoon to break up any lumps. Cook only until the meat loses its raw red color. Do not let it brown. Add the broth and wine, raise the heat and cook until the sauce thickens a little. Add the tomatoes, salt, pepper, and nutmeg and stir well. Taste and adjust the seasonings. When the sauce begins to bubble, lower the heat and simmer very slowly, partly covered, for about 4 hours. You might want to use a flame control device to keep the simmer very low with no more than an occasional lazy bubble. Stir occasionally to prevent sticking. Just before serving, mix in the cream. Taste again for seasoning and adjust.

Yield: About 3 cups, or enough for 4 to 6 servings.

Note: This recipe can easily be doubled and freezes well. It can be kept in the refrigerator for 5 or 6 days. If using after refrigerating or freezing, bring to a boil and simmer slowly for 15 minutes before adding to the pasta.

Fresh Tomato Sauce

Save this for the time of year when vine-ripened, juicy tomatoes are in season. It is basically an uncooked sauce with the tomatoes briefly warmed and tossed with 1 pound of hot, cooked pasta.

½ cup olive oil

1 to 2 cloves garlic

2 to 3 pounds red, ripe tomatoes, peeled, seeded, and coarsely chopped

¼ cup finely chopped fresh parsley

3 tablespoons finely chopped fresh basil, *or* 2 teaspoons dried

Heat the oil and garlic in a large skillet. When the garlic turns golden, remove and discard. Add the tomatoes, parsley, and hot pasta and toss until well blended. Serve hot.

Yield: 4 to 5 cups, or enough for 4 to 6 servings.

Chicken Liver Sauce

Serve over egg noodles or fettucine. This is sufficient sauce for 1 pound of pasta.

2 ounces salt pork, cut into small cubes

2 to 4 tablespoons butter

½ pound chicken livers, trimmed and cut into quarters

1 cup light cream

Salt and freshly ground pepper

Blanch the pork in boiling water for 3 minutes and drain well. Melt the butter in a medium-size skillet and add the pork and chicken livers, well dried. Sauté until lightly browned, shaking the skillet and tossing. The livers should be slightly pink inside. Add the cream, salt, and pepper and heat through, but do not boil. Serve hot over freshly cooked hot pasta.

Yield: 4 servings.

Pesto

Pesto, an uncooked sauce made of fresh basil leaves, garlic, oil, cheese, and pine nuts, is loaded with wonderful tastes. Make it in quantity when fresh basil is in season and freeze it. It will liven up your winter menus. (See note for freezing instructions.)

2 cups basil leaves, rinsed and patted dry (discard the stems)

1 to 2 garlic cloves, peeled and lightly crushed

¼ cup chopped fresh parsley

8 to 10 grinds of black pepper

Pinch of salt

3 tablespoons pine nuts

½ cup olive oil

2 tablespoons butter

½ cup freshly grated Parmesan cheese

2 tablespoons grated Romano cheese

Place the basil leaves, garlic, parsley, pepper, salt, pine nuts, and olive oil in the container of a blender or food processor. Blend at high speed, scraping down with a rubber spatula from time to time. The mixture does not need to be completely liquefied; bits of basil may remain.

Scrape into a bowl and beat in the butter and cheeses. Before spooning the pesto over the pasta, thin it with a tablespoon or two of the hot water in which the pasta has been cooked.

Yield: 2 to 2½ cups, or enough for 5 to 6 servings.

Note: To freeze pesto, make the pesto as above, eliminating both the cheese and the butter. Store in tightly sealed containers in the freezer compartment. Thaw in the refrigerator overnight before using. After thawing, stir in the butter and cheese. Adding the butter and cheese just before using gives the sauce a much fresher taste.

Walnut Sauce

An unusual walnut-flavored sauce, to be used with any short, tubular pasta such as penne, ziti, or ditali. This is enough sauce for 1 pound of pasta.

½ cup olive oil

2 cloves garlic, finely chopped

½ cup finely chopped walnuts

½ cup ricotta cheese

Salt and freshly ground pepper

½ cup dry white wine

¼ cup finely chopped fresh parsley

Grated Parmesan or Romano cheese (optional)

Heat the olive oil in a large skillet. Cook the garlic until it is lightly colored. Add the walnuts, ricotta cheese, salt, pepper, and wine. Stir over low heat until blended and hot. Stir in the parsley. Add drained, freshly cooked pasta and stir until well coated. Serve hot with grated cheese, if desired.

Yield: 4 to 6 servings.

Fettucine in Cream and Butter

This simple preparation, widely known as Fettuccine Alfredo *(named for the Roman restaurateur who originated it) is a lovely first course.*

1 cup heavy cream
8 tablespoons butter
1 pound fettucine
¾ cup freshly grated Parmesan cheese
Salt and freshly ground pepper

In a flameproof bowl or casserole that can be brought to the table, warm the cream and butter over low heat until the butter is melted, about 1 minute. Turn off the heat. Cook the fettucine in 4 quarts of boiling salted water until just done. The noodles should be firm because they will cook a bit more. Drain well and add to the bowl with the butter and cream. Over very low heat, toss the fettucine until well coated. Add the Parmesan, salt, and pepper and toss again briefly, until all the noodles are well coated. Serve at once with additional grated cheese, if desired.

Yield: 6 to 8 servings.

Pasta Primavera

¼ cup sweet butter
1 medium onion, finely chopped
1 pound asparagus, trimmed, peeled, and cut diagonally into 1- to 2-inch slices.
1 cup cauliflower, broken into small flowerets
2 to 3 medium zucchini, thinly sliced
1½ cups broccoli, separated into small flowerets, stems peeled and thinly sliced
½ pound mushrooms, thinly sliced
1 clove garlic, finely minced
1 pound spaghetti or linguine
1 cup cream (light or heavy)
½ cup (or more) pesto (see page 312)
Salt and freshly ground pepper
1 cup freshly grated Parmesan or Romano cheese
3 tablespoons finely chopped fresh parsley

Fill a large pot with water, cover, and start heating it for the pasta. Wash, trim, and prepare the vegetables.

Heat the butter in a large skillet. Add the onion and cook until limp and transparent. Add the asparagus, cauliflower, zucchini, broccoli, mushrooms, and garlic. Cook, stirring with a wooden spoon, until the asparagus turns bright green, 3 or 4 minutes.

Add the pasta and 1 tablespoon of salt to the rapidly boiling water and stir.

Add the cream and pesto to the vegetables and mix through. Cover the pot and simmer gently for 2 to 3 minutes. The vegetables should be just crisp-tender. Taste to see if salt and pepper are needed, bearing in mind that the cheese is salty.

Check the pasta by fishing a strand out of the water and biting it to see if it is *al dente*. Drain the pasta in a colander and return to the pot while it is still hot. Add the vegetables and cheese and toss with forks until well combined. Transfer to a large bowl and sprinkle with parsley.

Yield: 4 to 6 servings.

Spaghetti Carbonara

Literally "burned" spaghetti. A delicious dish, quickly prepared.

½ pound bacon, cut into pieces
6 tablespoons butter
½ cup white wine
2 eggs
½ cup cream, heavy or light
1 pound spaghetti
¾ to 1 cup freshly grated
    Parmesan cheese
Salt and freshly ground pepper

Cook the bacon in a large skillet until crisp. Remove with a slotted spoon and keep warm. Discard all but 2 tablespoons of the bacon fat. Add the butter and wine to the skillet. Cook until the wine is reduced, about 1 to 2 minutes, and set aside. Beat the eggs with the cream and set aside.

Cook the pasta in 4 quarts of boiling salted water until *al dente*. Drain and add to the skillet.

Over medium heat, stir and toss the pasta in the butter mixture until very hot, 1 to 2 minutes. Remove from the heat and stir in the eggs beaten with the cream, half the cheese, and the reserved bacon. Stir and toss quickly so that all is coated with the egg mixture. The heat of the pasta will cook the eggs.

Spoon into a serving platter, sprinkle with the remaining cheese, and serve hot.

Yield: 4 servings.

Pasta with Ricotta and Spinach

1 pound fresh spinach, *or* 1 10-
    ounce package frozen
8 tablespoons butter
2 tablespoons finely chopped
    shallots
Salt and freshly ground pepper
Several gratings of nutmeg
½ cup cream or half-and-half
1 pound ricotta cheese
1 pound fusilli, penne, ziti, or egg
    noodles
½ cup freshly grated Parmesan
    cheese

Cook the spinach in the water clinging to the leaves after it is washed. Or cook frozen spinach until thawed. Place in a sieve and press out all the water. Chop fine and set aside.

Melt the butter in a small skillet and add the shallots. Cook until softened. Add the spinach, salt, pepper, nutmeg, and cream and stir to mix well. Add the ricotta and heat through. Taste and adjust seasoning.

Meanwhile, bring 4 quarts of salted water to a boil. Cook the pasta until *al dente*, drain well, and return to the pot.

Pour the hot spinach-ricotta mixture over the pasta and mix well. Transfer to a warm serving platter, sprinkle with cheese, and serve hot.

Yield: 6 to 8 servings.

Linguine and Clam Sauce

24 to 36 littleneck or cherrystone clams (enough for 1 cup chopped clams and 2 cups clam liquid)
1 pound linguine
2 8-ounce bottles clam juice
½ cup olive oil
3 to 4 cloves garlic, finely minced
⅓ cup chopped fresh parsley

Whether you or your fish man opens the clams, be sure to save all the juice. You should have about 2 cups. Filter the juice through a strainer lined with paper towels to strain out all the sand and set aside. Chop the clams (do not use a blender or food processor) and set aside.

Bring 3 quarts of water and the 2 bottles of clam juice to a brisk boil. Add the linguine and boil for 5 minutes only. It will have additional cooking later. Drain at once, discarding the liquid, and toss with 2 tablespoons of the olive oil.

In a small saucepan, heat the remaining oil and garlic. When the garlic turns lightly golden, add the clams and turn them quickly in the hot oil for a minute or two. Remove the pan from the heat and stir in the parsley.

Place the 2 cups of reserved clam liquid in the kettle in which the pasta was cooked. Bring to a boil and add the drained pasta. Cook, stirring, until the clam juice is mostly absorbed and the linguine is tender. Arrange the linguine on a warm platter, spoon the clam mixture over, and serve immediately in warmed large shallow bowls.

Yield: 4 to 6 servings.

Note: Cheese is not generally served with Italian clam sauce, although there are exceptions.

Ravioli Casserole

This features the flavor, but not the form, of meat-and-spinach ravioli.

½ pound bow tie macaroni or ziti, cooked *al dente*, rinsed in cold water and drained well

1 pound lean ground beef

¼ cup olive or vegetable oil

1 small onion, finely chopped

2 cloves garlic, finely chopped

½ pound fresh mushrooms, thinly sliced

2 cups homemade tomato sauce (see page 456)

¾ cup beef broth

½ teaspoon dried basil

½ teaspoon dried oregano

½ teaspoon dried thyme

Salt and freshly ground pepper

2 10-ounce packages frozen spinach, cooked, well drained, and finely chopped

½ cup dry bread crumbs

½ cup finely chopped parsley

½ cup freshly grated Parmesan cheese

Preheat the oven to 350 degrees. Prepare pasta and set aside. Do not overcook because it will be baked later. Butter a 3-quart casserole and set aside.

Brown the meat in a large skillet until it loses its raw color. Remove with a slotted spoon and set aside. Discard any accumulated fat. To the same skillet add 2 tablespoons oil, the onion, garlic, and mushrooms. Cook until the moisture evaporates and the onion is lightly colored.

Return the meat to the skillet and add the tomato sauce, beef broth, basil, oregano, thyme, salt, and pepper. Simmer gently, uncovered, for 10 minutes.

In a bowl, combine the reserved pasta with the spinach, bread crumbs, parsley, and cheese. Add additional salt and pepper, if necessary.

Spoon a layer of meat sauce into the casserole. Evenly spread a layer of macaroni spinach mixture over this, then another layer of meat sauce. Continue alternating layers until the dish is full, ending with a layer of meat sauce.

Bake for 30 to 40 minutes, or until bubbly and hot. Allow to stand for 5 to 7 minutes before serving.

Yield: 4 to 6 servings.

Baked Macaroni and Cheese

This is a standard baked macaroni and cheese dish that has never ceased to delight. Serve with a tossed salad, followed by fresh fruit, and you have a nutritionally adequate and satisfying supper menu. You can use any pasta, but the small shells are particularly successful.

10 ounces small pasta shells

4 tablespoons butter

4 tablespoons flour

2½ cups milk

Cook the pasta according to package directions, being careful not to overcook because it will be further baked in the oven. Drain well and set aside.

10 ounces Cheddar cheese, shredded (about 2½ cups)
¼ teaspoon dry mustard
Dash of Worcestershire sauce

Preheat the oven to 375 degrees. In a medium-size saucepan, melt the butter and add the flour. Whisk until bubbly. Remove from the heat and add the milk all at once, whisking vigorously. Return to moderate heat and cook and stir until thickened and smooth. Turn heat to very low and add the cheese, reserving ½ cup to use for the topping. Stir until the cheese is melted. Blend in the dry mustard and Worcestershire sauce.

Combine the cheese sauce and pasta, mixing well. Transfer to a greased 2-quart casserole, sprinkle the remaining cheese over the top, and bake for 30 minutes.

Yield: 4 to 6 servings.

Lasagna

A universal favorite that is great party or everyday fare.

½ to ¾ pound lasagna noodles
2 tablespoons olive or vegetable oil
1 pound ricotta cheese
2 eggs
4 cups Bolognese sauce (see page 310)
2 tablespoons finely chopped fresh parsley
½ cup freshly grated Parmesan cheese
½ pound Mozzarella cheese, shredded or cubed

Preheat the oven to 350 degrees. Butter a lasagna pan; an 8 by 14 or 10½ by 12-inch will do, as long as it is 2 inches deep. Set aside.

Cook the noodles in boiling, salted water with 2 tablespoons of oil added, until just firm. Do not overcook. Drain and drop into cold water until ready to use.

Combine the ricotta, eggs, 2 to 3 tablespoons Bolognese sauce, parsley, and 2 tablespoons of Parmesan in a bowl and mix well.

To assemble, drain and dry the pasta well. Spoon a thin layer of meat sauce over the bottom of the pan and arrange a single layer of pasta, overlapping slightly, over the sauce. Spread with a layer of meat sauce, a layer of ricotta, and sprinkle with mozzarella. Repeat with a second layer of pasta, meat sauce, ricotta, and mozzarella. Repeat the layering again, ending with pasta and meat sauce. Sprinkle top with Parmesan. Allow ½ inch between the lasagna and the top of the pan.

Cover tightly with foil and press down lightly to compact. Place on a baking sheet or piece of foil to collect drippings. Bake for 50 minutes to 1 hour, or until bubbly and hot. Remove foil 15 to 20 minutes before it is done to brown the top. Remove from the oven and allow to settle for 15 to 20 minutes before cutting in squares. Serve with garlic bread and a tossed green salad.

Yield: 6 to 8 servings.

Potato Gnocchi

3 large baking potatoes (1½ to 1¾ pounds)
2 cups all-purpose flour
2 eggs, lightly beaten
½ cup butter, melted
½ cup freshly grated Parmesan cheese

Cook the potatoes in boiling water until tender. Peel and rice (or mash) while still hot. Measure the flour into a large bowl. Make a well in the center of the flour and add the eggs and potatoes. Combine with a wooden spoon until well mixed. Turn out on a lightly floured surface and knead, adding more flour if necessary, until the dough is smooth. Shape bits of dough into thin, sausagelike rolls. Cut into pieces ¾ to 1 inch long. Shape each piece into a small crescent by pulling the center of the dough toward you with the index finger. Preheat the oven to 325 degrees.

Bring a large kettle of water to a boil. Add the gnocchi in two or three batches and simmer gently for 8 to 10 minutes, or until they rise to the surface. Remove with a strainer and keep warm. Continue until all gnocchi are done. Place the gnocchi in a buttered baking dish and dribble with the butter. Sprinkle with the cheese and bake for 10 to 12 minutes, or until hot. Or, toss with your choice of sauce.

Yield: 4 to 6 servings.

Gnocchi di Ricotta (Ricotta Dumplings)

1 pound ricotta cheese
Several gratings of nutmeg
Salt to taste
2¼ to 2¾ cups flour
Bolognese sauce or pesto (see pages 310 and 312)
Freshly grated Parmesan cheese

Put the ricotta, nutmeg, and salt in a bowl and slowly stir in the flour until a soft dough is formed. Wrap in plastic and chill thoroughly or overnight.

Lightly flour your hands and pinch off walnut-size pieces of dough. Roll between the palms of your hands until about 1½ inches long and tapered at each end. Arrange on a lightly floured cookie sheet in one layer. Do not allow to touch or they will stick together. Preheat the oven to 325 degrees.

Bring 6 quarts of salted water to a boil. Add a handful of gnocchi to the water and simmer for 10 minutes. Remove with a sieve, drain, and place in a baking dish. Continue to cook gnocchi in batches in the same way.

Spoon 2 to 2½ cups of Bolognese sauce or ¾ cup of pesto sauce over the gnocchi and toss to blend. Sprinkle with cheese and heat in the oven until bubbling and hot. Serve immediately.

Yield: 4 to 6 servings.

8
Vegetables

A benign revolution has been taking place in American eating habits over the last few years, as evidenced by a surge of interest in vegetables that have never been inside a processing plant. Supermarket managers report that sales of fresh produce are up; open-air farmers' markets in urban areas are proliferating, as are small neighborhood greengrocers' shops whose display bins overflow with the brilliant colors and joyous aromas of lovely fresh fruits and vegetables.

Vegetables are finally emerging from the era when they were served and eaten as a penance ("Finish the string beans or no dessert") and the public is coming to appreciate the eating pleasure to be found in fresh, glowing vegetables cooked to crisp-tender perfection. It would be difficult to imagine a meal that was visually pleasing without the variety of color and texture that vegetables offer.

As further proof of progress in the vegetable world, consider some items that have appeared only recently. We have the interesting and unusual spaghetti squash, in which nature has succeeded in duplicating the handiwork of pasta makers, and plump, crunchy sugar peas that combine all the best qualities of green peas and snow peas. And who can predict what surprises lie ahead?

Composition

As a group, vegetables are richer in minerals and vitamins than are fruits. The dark green leafy vegetables are high in iron, some of the B-complex vitamins, vitamin C, and carotene, the substance that the body ultimately changes into vitamin A. Vegetables are uniformly low in fat and have a high moisture content, and, except for peas and beans, are low in protein. Almost all vegetables, with the exception of potatoes, corn, peas, and beans, are low in carbohy-

drates, which gives them added value in these diet-conscious times. They also contain quantities of the cellulose that provides needed bulk in our diets. By mixing a rich palette of colors that ranges from white through shades of green, yellow, and red to deep purple, we can provide visual pleasure at meals and fulfill our varied mineral and vitamin requirements at the same time.

Nutritive Value of Cooked Vegetables

It is inevitable that there will be some nutritive losses during cooking, but this does not mean that we should eat only raw vegetables. In some cases, vegetables have more nutrients available for absorption by the body after they are cooked than when they are raw. Cooking vegetables in as little liquid and for as short a time as possible is the best way to reduce loss of nutrients. Minerals are not affected by cooking, nor are starches or sugars, unless the vegetable is scorched. Vitamin C is the most vulnerable; it not only dissolves in the cooking water, it also diminishes just by exposure to air. The greatest destruction of vitamin C is during the first minute or two of the cooking period, but this can be minimized if the water is boiling vigorously when the vegetable is added to the pot. No one method of cooking vegetables is superior to all others, but those processes that retain the best color and flavor are likely to retain the most nutrients.

Buying

The quality of a cooked vegetable will depend on what it was like in its raw state; a tired, limp thing is not likely to turn into a crisp-tender morsel after a bath in boiling water. Concentrate on what is freshest and best in the market. Don't shop with a firm commitment to a preconceived plan. The fresh asparagus you had in mind could turn out to have skinny, ridged stalks; you'd be better off in that case with crisp, fresh carrots. Not as elegant, perhaps, but they will taste and look better. The younger the vegetable, the more tender it will be and the less time it will need to cook. When vegetables age, they often become woody and tough and, in the vegetable world, bigger is not necessarily better. Small beets and turnips, for example, are often better than big ones. Consider each vegetable in relation to the recommendations for ripeness and freshness described in the recipe section.

Buy vegetables shortly before you plan to use them. Some, such as celery, carrots, winter squash, onions, and potatoes, store well, but most will be better the sooner they are cooked. The sugar content of some vegetables decreases as the vegetables mature and drops strikingly after they are harvested. This is particularly true of starchy vegetables such as peas and corn, which are at their sweetest immediately after being picked.

Storing

Most vegetables should be stored in the refrigerator because the cold slows down enzyme activity and delays spoilage. Place vegetables, unwashed, in the vegetable crisper or in plastic bags to keep them from drying out. It is loss of moisture that causes vegetables to wilt. Always remove the tops from vegetables such as carrots and beets before storing. If left on, the flow of sap continues to the leaves and the vegetable becomes limp and dry. Potatoes do not do well in the refrigerator because the cold causes the starch to change to sugar. Ideally, potatoes, onions, and thick-skinned winter squashes should be stored in a cool, dry place at a temperature between 55 and 65 degrees.

Certain vegetables and fruits make poor roommates and should not be stored together. Onions give off a gas that hastens the spoilage of potatoes, so keep them apart. Apples give off an ethylene gas that gives carrots a bitter taste.

Preparation for Cooking

Since vegetables grow in or near the soil, they need thorough washing to remove particles of soil and any microorganisms that may be in it. Lukewarm water will do a better job of cleansing than cold. Wash the vegetables in several changes of water, lifting them out so that the soil remains in the water. Or hold them under running water.

Many of the vitamins in vegetables lie near the skin, and if you pare the vegetable too deep, you will lose them. The best instrument for paring—far better than a paring knife—is a swivel-bladed vegetable peeler. It is constructed so that it removes the skin with only a minimum amount of edible material that lies underneath it. For best results, use it with a light whittling motion and without pressure.

Prepare your vegetables just before you use them. When they are exposed to air or soaked in water after being cut or pared, their vitamin content is diminished. If you are cutting a number of vegetables that are to be cooked at one time, cut them uniformly so they will all become tender at the same time. Oriental cooks have been observing this practice for centuries and it is an example worth following.

Cooking Methods for Vegetables

The natural glowing color of vegetables adds to the pleasure of eating them, but too often something happens to their brightness in the cooking pot. This is particularly true of green vegetables, which often come to the table a dull olive green. When the green vegetable is cooked in a covered pot, the chlorophyll, which is the pigment that causes the green color, is acted upon by the acid that is also present in the vegetable. The volatile acid is trapped in the cooking pot instead of escaping into the atmosphere. It condenses on the pot lid and falls back into the pot, diminishing the chlorophyll. To avoid this, boil green vegetables uncovered, using a large quantity of water, which will help to dilute some of the acids in the vegetable. Boil them as quickly as possible, until they are tender but still crisp. Although this contradicts the rule about using as little liquid as possible in cooking vegetables, the advantages of retaining color and texture outweigh the disadvantages in this case.

It used to be a popular practice for cooks to add baking soda to green vegetables to make them bright. And bright they were, with an intense, artificial green, as vivid as a make-believe lawn in a stage set. The baking soda neutralized the acid and reacted with the chlorophyll to produce this unnatural hue. It also made the vegetable mushy and destroyed vitamins. We know better now and few people follow this procedure.

Red cabbage presents another kind of problem. Its red pigment, called anthocyanin, leaches out during cooking, causing the cabbage to fade to a dull and unappetizing blue. You can prevent this by adding a sour apple or some vinegar to the red cabbage, which will preserve the bright red color. Certain minerals also react with the pigments in cabbage. Always use stainless steel knives to cut cabbage; carbon steel may leave dark blotches on the leaves. To keep beets from becoming pale and anemic-looking during cooking, cook them with skins, roots, and one or two inches of stem left intact. This will prevent the red pig-

ment from leaching out. To keep white vegetables from yellowing, add a pinch of cream of tartar to the cooking water. The cream of tartar is an acid and has the effect of bleaching the vegetable.

The unpleasant odors associated with cooking cauliflower, turnips, and white cabbage are the result of their being cooked in a covered pan for a long period. The disagreeable odor comes from hydrogen sulfide being liberated from the sulfur-containing compounds in these vegetables. You can avoid it easily by not covering the pan and by cooking only until crisp-tender.

Boiling

Add uncooked vegetables to a pot containing a very small amount of boiling, salted water. Use just enough water to prevent scorching. As soon as the water has returned to a boil, cover the pot and cook until the vegetables are crisp-tender. Taste them frequently to prevent overcooking. Season and serve at once.

A number of vegetables can be cooked in this manner. Exceptions are the cabbage and onion families, turnips, and parsnips, which should be cooked uncovered to prevent unpleasant odors, and green vegetables, where we wish to preserve color.

To keep green vegetables as bright as possible, use a large quantity of water. The more water you use, the faster it will return to a boil after adding the vegetables and the less time the vegetables will need to remain in the hot water bath. Season the water with about 1 teaspoon of salt per quart. Add the vegetable gradually to the boiling water so as to interrupt the boiling process as little as possible. Cook just until the vegetable becomes tender but retains its crispness. Tasting is the only way to tell when this point is reached. With a slotted spoon or tongs, lift out a morsel and taste it.

As soon as the vegetable has reached the

proper state of doneness, drain it through a strainer or colander, return it to the pot or warmed serving bowl, and add butter. Never cover a vegetable completely after it is cooked; allow the steam to escape and it will have better color. If the vegetable is not to be served immediately, or if it is to be served cold, plunge it into a large amount of cold water, which is called *refreshing*. This will arrest the cooking process, set the color, and preserve texture and flavor. The vegetable can then be reheated briefly in a saucepan of hot water or with a little melted butter at serving time. This is how first-rate restaurants manage to serve green vegetables that look as if they were freshly cooked, in contrast to the olive green ones, faded from

Once the water in the pot is boiling rapidly, fit the steamer basket into the pot, making sure that the legs of the steamer keep the vegetables above the water level. Cover tightly.

their interlude on a steam table, that are standard in second-rate restaurants.

Parboiling, or *blanching*, refers to a brief boiling period or immersion in boiling water to set color or soften the food a bit. It is frequently done as a preliminary step to further cooking. Blanching also refers specifically to pouring boiling water over foods such as tomatoes, to make peeling easier.

Steaming

Most vegetables can be steamed, and this is highly satisfactory from a nutritional standpoint because the only water that the vegetable comes in contact with has been converted to steam. Consequently, there is less vitamin loss and the full flavor of the vegetable is realized. In steaming, the vegetable is suspended in a perforated container that is supported above the level of rapidly boiling water. There are specially designed steamer pots or there is an adjustable, collapsible metal basket that fits into almost any pot. The disadvantages of steaming are that it takes longer than boiling and it causes green vegetables to lose color. Small new red potatoes, sliced celery, and various winter squashes are only a few of the many vegetables that are delicious when steamed.

Baking

You can bake any vegetable that is high in moisture and contains enough cellulose to hold its shape. The moisture is necessary to soften the cellulose so that the vegetable will become tender. The prime example of a baked vegetable is, of course, the fine, fluffy Idaho potato that adds substance to so many meals. Vegetables may be baked either in their skins or pared. Winter squash may be baked with the skin on, either cut into portions or left whole. Parsnips bake well in their jackets and are easier to peel after cooking. Corn on the cob can be baked in the husk, or shucked, buttered, seasoned, and wrapped in aluminum foil. Tomatoes are most successful candidates for baking and take very little time. Onions and beets bake well but they take a long time, and it is often a help to parboil for 3 or 4 minutes to speed up the cooking process. Carrots, eggplant, cucumbers, and artichokes also bake well if they are partly cooked first. If you are going to stuff and bake vegetables such as zucchini, green pepper, and eggplant, parboil them first.

Always prick the skins of starchy vegetables before baking to allow room for the steam generated within to escape and to prevent the vegetable from exploding in the oven.

Panning

Panning, or braising, is cooking in a small amount of fat in a covered skillet. It is excellent for tender young vegetables and those that are finely cut and evenly sliced. In panning, the vegetable is cooked to a large extent in steam that seeps out of the cut tissues. It is important for the cooking to start promptly as soon as the vegetable is added so have the fat hot—about 1 tablespoon of oil or butter to each pound of vegetable. Add the vegetable and cover with a tight-fitting lid to retain the steam. If the vegetables are dry, sprinkle them lightly with water before adding them to the hot fat. When the steam comes up briskly, reduce the heat and cook over low heat until the vegetable is just tender. Shake the pan frequently to make sure that the contents are not sticking.

The secret of success in panning is to have the vegetable pieces thinly cut so that the heat penetrates readily. Panning has all the advantages of cooking in a small amount of water plus a shorter cooking time because the vegetable is shredded or cut into thin slices. Five to seven minutes in a covered pan will not affect the green color of vegetables. Among the vegetables that can be panned are kale, cabbage, okra, celery or celery cabbage, spinach or chard, very young tender green beans, or broccoli flowerets, finely cut.

Stir-Frying

Oriental cooking is distinguished for its way with fresh vegetables; they are crisp and crunchy and retain all the vivid coloring that nature provided. The secret lies in the fast cooking that is traditional in Oriental cuisine, giving us a perfect example of a virtue being created out of a necessity. China has always suffered from a shortage of fuel and it was essential that cooking be done using as little as possible. Since small pieces of food cook more quickly than large pieces, the pattern of Oriental cookery evolved, shaped by deft hands and creative imaginations, and it became one of the great cuisines of the world.

But without regard to the relevance of fuel shortages in our present society, stir-frying can stand on its own as an ideal method for cooking an assortment of tender young vegetables. It takes only about 4 or 5 minutes. The time-consuming part is the preparation, for all the vegetables must be uniformly small in size if they are to cook evenly. The vegetables that need longer cooking are put in first, followed by the tenderer ones, so that they are all done at the same time. The traditional Chinese cooking pot, the wok, is designed to distribute the heat over a wide surface. The cooking oil is concentrated in the conical bottom of the pot and you can swish the food in and out of the hot oil easily. The wok is a convenience but not a must; you can use a good heavy skillet for stir-frying.

Heat the pan and add the oil, about 1 tablespoon to 1 pound of vegetables. You might want to heat a clove or two of garlic or a couple of slices of fresh ginger for flavor and remove them before you add the vegetables. When the oil is hot, add the vegetables and stir and toss them until all are well-coated with the oil. Continue to cook, stirring, until the vegetables are crisp-tender.

Deep-Frying

Deep-fried vegetables add crunch and crisp texture to fish, meat, or poultry main courses and a platter of deep-fried vegetables makes a lovely appetizer course. Starchy vegetables such as potatoes can be deep-fried without a coating, but most vegetables need the protection of a batter before being placed in their hot oil bath (see Fritter Batter, page 208). Among the vegetables that can be deep-fried are broccoli, cauliflower, asparagus, whole green beans, eggplant and zucchini slices or cubes, and whole mushroom caps.

Puréed Vegetables

Food processors were made to order for vegetable purées and vegetable purées were made to order for the times when you would like to prepare your vegetable well in advance. Puréed vegetables won't wilt while waiting, which may account for their popularity in restaurants. Puréed carrots, peas, and broccoli are all delicious and look equally inviting. Puréed combinations of potatoes with vegetables such as turnips, parsnips, or celery root also make wonderful vegetable courses.

For a vegetable purée, cook the vegetable until soft. Drain and reserve the cooking liquid. You can mash the vegetable with a potato masher, or strain it through a sieve or a food mill, or purée it in a food processor or blender. You will need a little of the cooking liquid if you use the blender. Return the purée to a saucepan and stir in butter. Season with salt and pepper and perhaps a pinch of freshly grated nutmeg. Cook over medium heat, stirring constantly, until the purée is on the dry side. Purées should be creamy but not soupy. If you wish, you can stir in about 2 tablespoons of cream.

Pressure Cooking

Pressure cooking of vegetables saves nutrients and flavor, as well as time. Pressure cookers are usually operated at 15 pounds of steam pressure and a temperature of 250 degrees, compared with the 212-degree boiling point that is as high a temperature as can be achieved in stovetop cooking. Naturally the higher heat will cook food in a fraction of the time needed for other methods. But this may not be as advantageous as it sounds because a few seconds too long in a pressure cooker can result in a sadly overdone vegetable. Vegetables are not uniform in texture; some may need a little more cooking time and some a little less, which is impossible to gauge in a pressure cooker.

Leftover Vegetables

The least attractive thing you can do with leftover vegetables is to reheat them and present them in the same form in which they previously appeared. It can make indifferent vegetable eaters openly rebellious and it is not even sound nutritionally, because a prolonged second heating further destroys nutrients. Toss them with a tangy vinaigrette sauce and a bit of chopped red onion. Or cut them finely and mix them in a cold rice or bulgur salad. Don't add them to a bowl of mixed greens; they will dilute the crispness of the salad and add nothing in the way of taste or texture. However, they could be used in a frittata or an omelet, where they require very little reheating, or they can be puréed and added to a soup. If the amount is considerable, you can bake them in a cream or cheese sauce, allowing about one-quarter as much sauce as vegetable. This is a very acceptable way to serve previously cooked vegetables.

Frozen and Canned Vegetables

You cannot compare the flavor and texture of most canned and frozen vegetables with the fresh, but there are times when it might be expedient to go with canned or frozen. The recipes will recommend where they may be used. If there is a choice between frozen and canned, choose the frozen. They are generally superior, both nutritionally and in flavor. If you compare the taste of canned peas or canned carrots with the same vegetables frozen, you will have a striking example of the effects of prolonged cooking and high temperatures on the flavors of what were originally flavorful vegetables. These changes are unavoidable because the canning process requires overcooking. Freezing, on the other hand, deals more gently with both texture and taste, preserving each. Frozen green peas are much closer to the fresh than the canned are, and they can be a comfort when fresh peas are out of season or so astronomically priced that buying them would throw the week's food budget out of balance.

Frozen vegetables cook more quickly than fresh because they are blanched before being frozen. To minimize the loss of vitamin C, cook the frozen vegetable while still frozen, before it has had a chance to thaw.

Having made a case for the general superiority of frozen vegetables, let's go on to some of the indispensable canned products. Heading the list are canned tomatoes. The peeled Italian plum tomatoes in tomato purée are ever so much better for sauces and soups than the tasteless, mealy objects that pass for tomatoes in urban markets, particularly during the winter months. There are also baby sliced canned tomatoes, which are a useful product with good flavor and color. They do well in preparations in which you want to suggest the presence of tomato slices. Canned Italian tomato paste, a highly concentrated purée of tomatoes, is valuable in adding body, flavor, and color to sauces and stews. Often a small quantity, a tablespoon or less, is all that is needed. Transfer the leftover tomato paste to a screw-top glass jar. Add a light coating of vegetable oil or a little vinegar to keep it from developing mold and store in the refrigerator. Canned artichoke hearts and canned baby beets are also good products, difficult to duplicate in their fresh state.

Of all methods of commercial processing of vegetables, the one that takes the greatest toll in nutrients is dehydration. Whether frozen of nonfrozen, a dehydrated vegetable is left with only a small part of its original food value.

Artichokes

Selection: Choose heavy, compact artichokes with tightly closed petals and good green color. A few darkish spots have no significance, nor does size affect quality or flavor. Allow one artichoke for each serving.

Peak Season: March through May.

Methods of Preparation: Boiled, stuffed and baked, or braised.

Preparing Artichokes

1 *Cut off the stem and pull off the coarse leaves at the base. Then, with the artichoke on its side, cut across the top of the cone, about ½ inch from the point.*

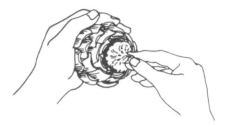

3 *If you wish to remove the choke, or fuzz, before cooking, gently spread the leaves apart and pull out the central core of tender, spiky young leaves. This will expose the choke.*

2 *Cut off the prickly tips of the leaves with a pair of scissors.*

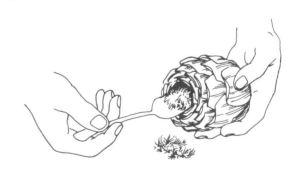

4 *Use the point of a spoon to scrape out the hairy fibers of the choke. Rub the exposed bottom with lemon juice and press the leaves closed again.*

Whole Boiled Artichokes

Whole artichokes with a dressing make a fine appetizer course, a side dish, or a hot weather luncheon entrée. They may be served hot, warm, or well-chilled.

4 artichokes
Boiling water to cover
1 teaspoon salt
¼ cup lemon juice or vinegar
Lemon wedges

Wash the artichokes well. With a sharp knife, trim off the stem end of each artichoke flush with the bottom petal bases so that the artichoke will sit firmly on the plate when served. Pull off any tough petals at the base. Place the artichoke on its side and slice off a good ½ inch or more from the top. Shorten the rest of the leaves neatly and evenly with scissors, cutting them to about two-thirds of their original height to get rid of the prickly tops.

Place the artichokes, bases down, in a deep enamel or stainless steel kettle (aluminum turns artichokes grayish). Cover with boiling water, add the salt and lemon juice or vinegar, and cook, uncovered, for 30 to 45 minutes, depending on the size and age of the artichokes. If the water level gets low during the cooking, add more boiling water to cover. Start testing after 30 minutes by piercing the bottom of the artichoke with a small, sharp-pointed knife. When the knife goes in easily, the artichoke is done.

Remove from the water with kitchen tongs or two long-handled spoons. Place the artichokes upside down on paper towels and let them drain for 10 minutes, by which time they will be cool enough to handle.

To remove the chokes, spread the center leaves so that you can grasp the center core and twist it out. With a pointed teaspoon, scoop out the fuzzy choke and rub the bottom with a lemon wedge to prevent darkening.

Serve warm with hollandaise sauce (page 461) or melted butter, or cold with vinaigrette dressing (page 392) or mustard mayonnaise (page 459).

Yield: 4 servings.

Note: Cooked artichoke leaves make a lovely base for hors d'oeuvre, for which calorie counters will thank you. Detach the leaves after the artichoke is cooked and place a small mound of minced cold fish, chicken, mushroom, crabmeat, or shrimp salad over the edible portion of each leaf.

Stuffed Baked Artichokes

4 cooked artichokes
1 cup bread crumbs
1 large clove garlic, finely minced
2 tablespoons fresh minced parsley
4 shallots, finely chopped
1 tablespoon capers
½ teaspoon dried marjoram
½ teaspoon salt
Freshly ground pepper
6 tablespoons olive oil
2 tablespoons lemon juice

1 cup basic vinaigrette (see page 392)
1 hard-boiled egg
1 tablespoon minced fresh parsley
1 tablespoon minced celery leaves
1 tablespoon snipped chives
½ teaspoon dry mustard
1 teaspoon Worcestershire sauce

Prepare the artichokes as in the preceding recipe, but undercook them a bit—about 25 minutes in boiling water.

In a small bowl, mix together the bread crumbs, garlic, parsley, shallots, capers, marjoram, salt, pepper, and 2 tablespoons of the oil. Pack the mixture into the centers of the artichokes and between the leaves. Arrange the artichokes in a well-oiled shallow baking dish that will hold them snugly upright. Drizzle over them the remaining 4 tablespoons of oil and the lemon juice. Place a scant ½ inch of hot water in the bottom of the baking dish and bake them for 25 to 30 minutes, uncovered, basting them frequently. Serve with hot vinaigrette sauce.

Yield: 4 servings.

Hot Vinaigrette Sauce
In a small saucepan, heat the vinaigrette to the boiling point. Mince the hard-boiled egg or push it through a coarse strainer. Add it and the rest of the ingredients to the vinaigrette and beat until it is well combined. Pour hot over stuffed artichokes.

Yield: About 1⅓ cups.

329

Asparagus

Selection: Choose straight, well-rounded stalks that are bright green, with compact pointed tips. The thicker the spear, the more tender it is likely to be. Allow 4 to 8 stalks per serving, depending on size.

Peak Season: April to June.

Methods of Preparation: Usually boiled, but may also be blanched and deep-fried or stir-fried.

Boiled Asparagus

What better way to announce spring than the first appearance in the markets of fresh green asparagus? Unfortunately, it enjoys a relatively short season and the canned and frozen varieties are poor substitutes (if, indeed, they can be considered substitutes) for the fresh.

24 asparagus stalks
1 teaspoon salt
4 cups water, approximately

Wash the asparagus well in a couple of changes of warm water if it seems at all sandy. Cut or break off the tough white ends. Peel the asparagus stalks carefully, starting about 2 inches below the tips. A swivel-bladed vegetable peeler does a perfect job.

Asparagus can be steamed upright in a tall pot, but once the stems are peeled there is no need for this procedure because they will cook as quickly as the more tender tips. Use a large skillet or casserole in which the asparagus can lie flat. Allow about 2 cups of water per pound of asparagus.

Bring the salted water to a boil, add the peeled asparagus and bring the water to a second boil. Boil uncovered for 8 to 12 minutes, depending on the thickness of the stalks. Test by picking up a stalk with kitchen tongs. If the stalk bends ever so slightly, consider it done. It is a pity to overcook asparagus—a fact known even in ancient times. It is said that the Roman emperor Augustus originated the saying "Quicker than you can cook asparagus," nearly 2,000 years ago.

The moment the asparagus is done, remove it from the water with tongs and drain it on a folded kitchen towel. If it is to be served cold, refrigerate it; if hot, transfer it to a warmed serving platter.

Asparagus makes a splendid first course, served cold on a bed of greens, dressed with a vinaigrette sauce and perhaps a strip of pimiento for color. Hollandaise, melted butter, or a sprinkling of browned bread crumbs are appropriate for hot asparagus.

Yield: 4 servings.

Asparagus Souffle

For leftover cooked asparagus (or broccoli).

1 teaspoon butter
2 tablespoons bread crumbs
4 tablespoons butter
4 tablespoons flour
1⅓ cups milk
Salt and freshly ground pepper
1 teaspoon grated onion
3 tablespoons grated sharp
  Cheddar cheese
4 egg yolks
1¼ cups cooked asparagus (or
  broccoli), finely chopped
Pinch of dried tarragon
5 egg whites at room temperature

Preheat the oven to 400 degrees and place the baking rack in the lowest third of the oven.

Butter a 1½-quart casserole with the teaspoon of butter and sprinkle with crumbs to coat the sides and bottom evenly. Shake out any excess crumbs.

Melt 4 tablespoons butter in a medium-size saucepan. When the foam subsides, add the flour and stir well with a wire whisk. Cook over moderate heat until the mixture bubbles. Pour in the milk all at once, beating vigorously with the wire whisk until the mixture is thickened and smooth. Remove from the heat and stir in the salt, pepper, onion, and cheese; stir until the cheese is melted. Add the egg yolks one at a time, beating well after each addition. Stir in asparagus and tarragon and blend. Transfer the egg yolk mixture to a large bowl.

Beat the egg whites until stiff but not dry. Stir about a quarter of the egg whites into the asparagus mixture to lighten it and then gently fold in the remainder of the egg white. Spoon the mixture into the prepared soufflé dish, piling it so that the center is higher than the sides. Place in the preheated oven and immediately reduce the temperature to 375 degrees. Bake for 35 to 40 minutes, or until the soufflé is puffed and browned on top. Serve at once.

Yield: 4 servings.

Avocados

Like tomatoes, avocados are botanically a fruit but are commonly classified as a vegetable. Avocados are pleasantly bland, with a rich, buttery taste.

Selection: For immediate use, buy fruits that yield to light pressure. Avoid any with dark sunken spots or signs of bruising. They may also be purchased underripe and ripened at room temperature. Store a ripe avocado in the refrigerator and use it before it gets too soft.

Peak Season: December to early spring, but available all year.

Methods of Preparation: An avocado may be peeled and sliced or cut in half lengthwise, with the large center pit removed. Use a stainless steel knife to retard darkening. Avocado flesh discolors rapidly when exposed to the air unless sprinkled with lemon or lime juice. Avocados are used raw in salads, puréed in soups, mashed to make a dip, or eaten right from the shell with a vinaigrette dressing or a dash of lemon juice, salt, and pepper. The cavity in the avocado forms a natural container for a stuffing and half an avocado filled with a poultry or seafood salad makes an elegant appetizer or main luncheon course.

Guacamole

This piquant dip of Mexican inspiration is one of the avocado's chief claims to fame. Serve it with an assortment of crackers, or as a stuffing for hollowed-out cherry tomatoes.

2 large, ripe avocados
2 medium-size tomatoes, peeled, seeded, and chopped
1 bunch scallions, very finely chopped
2 tablespoons lemon juice
½ teaspoon Tabasco sauce
Salt and freshly ground pepper
Pinch of sugar

Peel the avocados and mash with a fork. Add the rest of the ingredients and blend well. Mound into a serving bowl and cover tightly with plastic wrap or aluminum foil and chill in the refrigerator. Make it as close to serving time as you can to keep its fresh green color. There is a rumor that the inclusion of the avocado pit will retard darkening; not so.

Yield: 3 cups.

Green or Yellow (Wax) Beans

Selection: Choose brightly colored beans, green or yellow, with slender pods and without blemishes. The pod should break crisply in your fingers. If the pods look ridged and bulgy, pass them up. Allow 1 pound for 3 or 4 servings.

Peak Season: May to October, but available all year.

Methods of Preparation: Beans may be served hot as a side dish or in soups and stews; cold in a salad; or raw with a dip. They may be boiled, steamed, or stir-fried. If they are young and tender, cook them whole. Otherwise, cut into 1- or 2-inch lengths, in thin slivers, or on the bias.

To Cook: We think that the French way, in which the beans are cooked in a large quantity of boiling water, is the most satisfactory. The greater the quantity of water, the faster the water will return to a boil after the beans are added, and the more quickly the beans will cook.

Wash the beans and snap off the ends. Most beans today are stringless, but occasionally some of the old-fashioned variety show up and you will have to pull off the strings. If the beans are young and tender, leave them whole; they are most flavorful in that form.

Have a large pot of boiling, salted water prepared. Drop the beans in gradually so as to disturb the boiling process as little as possible. Cook them uncovered to retain their color. After all the beans are added and the water has returned to a full boil, reduce the heat. Cooking time depends on the variety, age, and size of the beans. Young cut beans may be done in 5 minutes; larger, more mature ones may take as much as 15. Start testing after 5 minutes. The beans should be crisp-tender and should cook for the shortest time possible. As soon as they are done, drain them well, return to the pot, and season with salt and pepper.

If you are cooking them in advance to serve later, drain them and plunge them into cold water to stop the cooking and set the color. Reheat at serving time with butter, salt, and pepper, or you can give them a quick dunk in boiling water just to heat them through.

Herbed Green Beans. Cook beans as above and toss them with butter to which you have added 1½ teaspoons fresh herbs or ½ teaspoon dried. Use dill, summer savory, thyme, rosemary, or mint.

Garnishes for Beans. Brown slivered almonds, sliced water chestnuts, or thinly sliced mushrooms in a little oil or butter and toss with the beans.

Green Beans Provençale. Heat 2 tablespoons olive oil and 1 tablespoon butter in a large skillet or saucepan. Add 1 medium-size onion, chopped; ½ green pepper, coarsely chopped, 1 clove garlic, finely minced, and cook until tender. Add 2 large tomatoes, peeled, seeded, and chopped, salt, freshly ground pepper, ¼ cup minced fresh basil or 1 tablespoon dried basil, and ¼ cup minced fresh parsley. Cook and stir until tomatoes are softened, about 10 minutes. Add 1½ pounds cooked beans and toss until heated through.

Yield: 5 to 6 servings.

Fava Beans

Fava beans, also known as broad beans, have large, velvety pods and big flat seeds. They resemble lima beans, for which they can be substituted. Young fava beans are tender, but as they mature, the skin covering the bean becomes coarser and tougher and must be removed before they are eaten. Because of this, always try to find the smallest, youngest broad beans. They are generally available in the spring and early summer.

The pods and skins of the fava beans are heavy and you will need from ¾ to 1 pound per serving. When young and tender, or when peeled, fresh fava beans may be cooked like lima beans and served with melted butter, or with oil and garlic and a sprinkling of lemon juice.

Piquant Fava Beans

4 pounds fava beans in the pod
3 slices bacon, chopped
1 onion, finely minced
1 tablespoon olive or vegetable oil
1 teaspoon dried oregano
Beef broth or water
Salt and freshly ground pepper
1 tablespoon butter
1 tablespoon chopped fresh
  parsley

Shell the fava beans. If they are large, remove the tough skin with the tip of a sharp-pointed knife. In a medium-size saucepan, sauté the bacon until crisp. Remove the bacon and reserve. Add the onion to the bacon fat and cook until tender. Add a table-spoon of oil if needed. Add the beans and oregano and enough broth or water to cover. Simmer over low heat until the beans begin to soften. Add salt and pepper to taste. They will need from 15 to 20 minutes or longer, depending on the size and toughness of the beans. Stir them frequently and taste for doneness. When tender, drain the beans and toss with butter, the crisp bacon bits, and parsley.

Yield: 4 servings.

Lima Beans

Most of the lima beans harvested are frozen, canned, or dried, but fresh beans, if you can find them, are especially good, with a deli-cious, delicate taste and slightly mealy texture.

Selection: Look for clean, bright, dark green pods that are properly filled. The shelled bean should be plump with tender skin and a good green or greenish white color. Allow ¾ to 1

pound per serving. Two pounds unshelled gives about 2½ cups shelled.

Peak Season: July until October but available all year.

Method of Preparation: Boiled and served as a main course accompaniment; in soups, stews, puréed, or cold in salads.

Lima Beans in Cream

3 pounds lima beans in the pod
3 tablespoons butter
⅔ cup heavy cream
Salt and freshly ground pepper
Freshly grated nutmeg
2 tablespoons finely chopped
  fresh parsley

Shell beans by snapping the pod open or use a knife or scissors to cut a thin strip lengthwise along the inner edge and remove the beans. Cook the beans in boiling water to cover until tender, from 10 to 20 minutes, according to size. Drain. Stir in the butter and heat for a minute or two, stirring to coat the beans. Add the cream and season to taste with salt, pepper, and nutmeg. Cook over low heat for 3 minutes, until the cream is heated and thickens slightly. Stir the beans gently from time to time so that they don't stick. Transfer to a heated bowl, sprinkle with parsley, and serve hot.

Yield: 4 servings.

Succotash. Lima beans or fava beans may be combined with fresh, frozen, or canned whole kernel corn, butter, cream, salt, and pepper to make succotash, an Indian dish that the Pilgrims adopted almost immediately upon their arrival on these shores. It is chronicled that the Indians made succotash of corn and kidney beans and perhaps dog meat, all cooked in bear grease, but you might be more disposed toward today's version. Use equal quantities of beans and corn. You might like to zip it up a bit with a few shakes of Tabasco or Worcestershire sauce.

Dried Beans. See Legumes (page 300).

Beets

Selection: Look for firm small or medium-size beets; the large ones tend to be tough and tasteless. The beets should have a good round shape, firm flesh, and a deep red color. Tired-looking beet tops are not necessarily a sign of poor quality because beet tops deteriorate rapidly without affecting the quality of the root. Fresh, thin-ribbed, clean beet tops can be used in salad or as cooked greens or potherbs. Allow 1 pound for 3 servings.

Peak Season: June through October, but available all year.

Methods of Preparation: Boiled or baked and served hot with butter or a sauce, cold in salad, or pickled as a relish. In a salad, their sweetness makes a lovely counterpoint to the slightly bitter taste of Belgian endive.

Beets are such a flavorful vegetable that they need little embellishment. After being boiled, they can be sliced and heated in a saucepan with a few tablespoons of butter, a generous splash of lemon juice, and some salt and freshly ground pepper.

To Cook: To preserve the deep red color, cook beets whole with their skins intact, and peel them after cooking. Cut off the stem an inch above the bulb and leave the rootlets on, which will prevent the juice from escaping. Boil the beets in salted water to cover until tender.

Young beets will take from 30 to 45 minutes; older ones an hour or more. Don't test with a fork, which will also give the juice the opportunity to bleed; rather, remove a beet from the pot with a spoon and feel it. If it gives a bit and is tender to the touch, it is done.

Drain the beets, rinse them quickly in cold water for a minute or two to cool them, and peel them by slipping off the skins. Leave them whole if small; otherwise slice, quarter or cut into julienne strips. Toss with butter, salt, and pepper.

Baked Beets. Wash the beets in cold water. Leave an inch of stem and the rootlets. Wrap the beets together in aluminum foil in a snug package. Place on a baking sheet and bake in a 400-degree oven on the middle rack until tender. Small beets will take about 1½ hours; larger ones about 2 hours. When they give a bit and are tender to the touch, they are done. When cool enough to handle, peel off the skins and slice them. You can toss them with a little butter, salt, and pepper to serve as a hot vegetable, or dress them with some olive oil, wine vinegar, salt, and pepper and serve them at room temperature or chilled. Try them cooled and lightly bathed in sour cream or plain yogurt seasoned with salt and pepper.

Pickled Beets. Boil together ½ cup white or cider vinegar, ¼ cup water, ¼ cup sugar, ½ teaspoon salt, and freshly ground pepper for 5 minutes. Add 2 teaspoons caraway seeds and let cool. Put 1 pound of cooked beets, peeled and thinly sliced, into a deep bowl and pour the dressing over them. Let stand for a few hours or refrigerate overnight. Drain before serving. Serve cold or at room temperature.

Belgian Endive

Belgian endive is also called French endive and witloof.

Selection: Look for crisp, firm, tightly closed heads that are fresh looking, without stains or blemishes.

Peak Season: November through April, but available September through May.

Methods of Preparation: Belgian endives are so pampered in their cultivation that they need little washing. Trim off a bit at the root end, remove any wilted or broken outer leaves, and wipe with a damp cloth. For use raw in salads, the leaves can be separated and served whole or cut into strips, or the whole head can be sliced into ½-inch rounds. It makes a notable hot vegetable, braised or sautéed and served with poultry or roasts.

Braised Endive

Endive may be cooked whole or cut lengthwise into halves.

6 heads Belgian endive
4 tablespoons butter
2 tablespoons fresh lemon juice
Salt
½ cup chicken broth
Pinch of sugar

Remove any broken outer leaves from endives and wipe with a damp cloth. In a skillet large enough to hold the endives in a single layer, heat the butter and lemon juice, add the endives, and sauté for 5 minutes, turning them on all sides.

Add salt, broth, and sugar and simmer slowly, covered, until the endives are tender, but firm enough to hold their shape. Remove the endives and keep warm. Increase the heat and boil the pan juices until reduced to 2 or 3 tablespoons. Pour over endives and serve hot.

Yield: 6 servings.

Variations: Add ½ teaspoon dried basil to the pan juices as you reduce them. Or sprinkle the cooked endives with 2 tablespoons coarsely chopped walnuts, lightly browned in a tablespoon or two of butter.

Broccoli

Selection: Look for tightly packed heads with no yellow flowers showing inside the buds. Depending on the variety, the color ranges from dark green to a green with a purplish cast. Stalks and stems should be tender and firm with fresh leaves. Allow ½ pound per serving.

Peak Season: October to May, but available all year.

Methods of Preparation: The buds, or flowerets, may be served raw with a dip or in a tossed salad. Broccoli may be steamed, sautéed, boiled, puréed, or used in soups and vegetable quiches. Broccoli stems, too often discarded or ignored, have a delicious flavor and make a splendid vegetable by themselves.

To Cook: The cardinal rule in preparing broccoli is to undercook it so that it remains bright green and has a bit of crunch. The stems are tougher than the flowerets and need longer cooking. Cut off the flowerets a little below the base where they meet the stalks. Boil the stalks for 4 or 5 minutes, and then add the flowerets for 2 or 3 minutes. Or, you can divide the broccoli into flowerets leaving about 4 inches of stem. Peel the stems, removing the thick outer covering. Boil, covered, in a large quantity of salted water for 5 minutes. This short cooking period will not diminish the green color. Drain carefully so as not to break the flowerets and plunge into cold water to stop the cooking. Drain again. When you are ready to serve, reheat the broccoli for a moment in boiling water or quickly stir-fry in a skillet with hot butter and seasonings.

Serve with a warm dressing such as hollandaise sauce, or melted butter in which you have browned some sesame seeds.

Broccoli Soufflé. See Asparagus Soufflé, (page 331).

Broccoli with Ripe Olive Sauce. Heat 1 clove crushed garlic in 4 tablespoons butter. Discard the garlic when it turns brown and stir in ½ cup chopped ripe olives, 1 teaspoon lemon juice, and salt and pepper to taste. Pour over cooked broccoli.

Broccoli-Potato Purée

1 large bunch broccoli, about 2 pounds
3 or 4 large potatoes
3 tablespoons butter
Salt and freshly ground pepper
2 tablespoons cream
½ cup freshly grated Parmesan cheese
½ cup fine bread crumbs

Cut off and discard the tough stem ends and coarse outer leaves of the broccoli. Cut the broccoli into pieces and cook, uncovered, in a large quantity of boiling salted water until very soft. While it is cooking, boil and mash the potatoes. Drain the broccoli and purée it in a food mill or food processor.

Preheat the oven to 350 degrees.

Combine the potato and broccoli purées, butter, salt, pepper, cream, and Parmesan cheese and blend well. Transfer to a greased 2-quart baking dish and sprinkle with bread crumbs. Bake for 30 minutes, or until heated through.

Yield: 4 to 6 servings.

Broccoli Rabe

Broccoli rabe is a member of the cabbage family with a slightly bitter and assertive flavor. It comes in long clusters of skinny leaves topped with pale yellow buds and is generally available in Italian markets. Allow ½ pound per serving.

Selection: Look for thin, firm stems that look crisp and fresh.

Peak Season: Summer and fall.

Methods of Preparation: Boiled or steamed and then sautéed. It may be combined with cooked spinach or cabbage, which will soften its bitter taste. It goes well as a vegetable accompaniment for pork or sausage dishes, and can be used in soups and stews or cooked and served cold in salads.

Sautéed Broccoli Rabe and Spinach

1 pound broccoli rabe
1 pound fresh spinach
3 tablespoons olive or vegetable oil
2 or 3 large cloves of garlic, minced
Salt and freshly ground pepper
3 tablespoons lemon juice

Discard the tough outer leaves and wash the broccoli rabe in several changes of water to remove all traces of sand. Drain well and cut off any tough stems. Cut the leaves and stems into 2-inch pieces. Drop into a large saucepan filled with rapidly boiling water and cook for a minute or two after the water returns to a boil. Drain and set aside.

Discard the tough stems of the spinach and wash it as you did the broccoli rabe. Cook the spinach in a covered pan with just the water that adheres to the leaves for about 5 minutes, or until not quite tender. Drain and set aside.

Using your hands, squeeze all the moisture you can out of the broccoli rabe and the spinach. Chop them coarsely.

Heat the oil and garlic in a large skillet until the garlic colors slightly. Add the chopped greens, turning them so they are coated with oil. Sauté over medium heat, stirring frequently, until tender, about 10 minutes. Season to taste, sprinkle with lemon juice, and serve hot.

Yield: 4 to 5 servings.

Brussels Sprouts

Selection: Look for sprouts with fresh, bright green color and firm, tight little buds. Smallest are best. Allow 1 pound for 3 or 4 servings.

Peak Season: October through February, but available most of the year.

Methods of Preparation: Generally boiled and

served hot as a vegetable with melted butter or a variety of toppings. Frozen baby Brussels sprouts are a good product; cook them briefly in boiling salted water, covered, for 4 or 5 minutes.

When properly cooked, Brussels sprouts can be crisp, crunchy, and well-flavored, but they become mushy if overcooked, which probably accounts for their tarnished reputation. They are a hearty vegetable and should not accompany foods in subtle wine or herb sauces, which will be overpowered by the assertiveness of the sprouts.

To Cook: Wash thoroughly and trim off stem ends and loose leaves. Cut a cross in the bottom of each so that the sprouts will cook more quickly. Place them in a saucepan with enough boiling water to come halfway up the sprouts. When the water has returned to a boil, cover and simmer for 7 or 8 minutes, until just tender. The time will vary according to the age and size of the sprouts. Taste one for doneness. Drain and return to the pan. Add a few tablespoons of butter and toss until coated. Sprinkle with salt and pepper.

Variations: Cooked Brussels sprouts may be combined with sautéed sliced mushrooms, sesame seeds, or sliced almonds browned in butter.

You can also combine 1 pound of cooked Brussels sprouts with ½ pound cooked and peeled whole chestnuts in a saucepan and toss with butter, salt, pepper, and a few gratings of fresh nutmeg. Add 4 tablespoons heavy cream and cook a minute longer. Transfer to a heated bowl and sprinkle with minced parsley.

Cabbage

Selection: The three most commonly seen cabbages are the familiar green and white cabbage, red cabbage, and the curly-leafed Savoy cabbage. They may be used interchangeably. Look for firm heads that are heavy for their size. Outer leaves should be a good green or red color, not wilted or yellowed. Allow 2 pounds for 4 to 6 servings.

Peak Season: Year round. Savoy cabbage is available September through March.

Methods of Preparation: Shredded raw for salad, pickled, braised, boiled, stuffed, or steamed, and as a soup ingredient.

Cabbage is a splendid vegetable that has withstood centuries of poor preparation. Its undeserved reputation of being mushy and having an offensive cooking odor must be blamed on the cooking method, not the cabbage. Cabbage that is cooked quickly and served crisp-tender is a joy to eat and its aroma does not linger in the air.

To Cook: Wash head and discard any wilted leaves. Cut into wedges or shred coarsely and remove hard white core. Cook, covered, in 2 inches of boiling salted water. Shredded cabbage will need 4 to 5 minutes and wedges 8 to 12 minutes.

To braise cabbage, melt just enough butter or fat to film the bottom of a large saucepan or skillet. Add cabbage wedges or shreds. Cook over medium-low heat for 3 or 4 minutes, stirring with a fork so that all the pieces are coated with the fat. Add a couple of tablespoons of water, cover the pan, and steam for 5 to 10 minutes, depending on the size of the cabbage pieces. Season when cooked.

Red cabbage may be cooked by either of these methods, but add a little lemon juice, vinegar, or pieces of tart apple. The acid is necessary to hold the color. Red cabbage needs longer cooking time than white.

Braised Cabbage with Caraway Seeds

This may change the minds of people who think they don't like cabbage.

2 pounds cabbage
4 tablespoons butter
1 large onion, sliced
Salt and freshly ground pepper
1 tablespoon caraway seeds
1 teaspoon dried basil

Cut the cabbage into quarters, remove the core, and cut into thick slices. Melt the butter in a large skillet, add the onion, and cook until the onion is limp and transparent but not brown. Add the cabbage, turning it with a fork to coat with oil and distribute the onion. Sprinkle lightly with salt and pepper, add the caraway seeds and basil, and mix through. Cover the pan and cook over low heat until crisp-tender, 6 to 8 minutes. Shake the pan from time to time. Serve hot.

Yield: 6 servings.

Hot Sauerkraut

The tart flavor of sauerkraut can add interest to a bland dish like boiled beef, or to pork or game dishes. The sauerkraut packaged in plastic bags or canned sauerkraut may be used.

2 pounds sauerkraut
2 tablespoons butter
½ green pepper, diced
1 large onion, chopped
2 teaspoons flour
1 cup tomato purée
Freshly ground pepper
Pinch of sugar
Salt

Sauerkraut is very salty; rinse it well under cold running water and squeeze out the excess moisture.

Melt the butter in a large skillet and add the green pepper and onion and cook until tender. Add the drained sauerkraut, sprinkle with flour, and mix well. Add the tomato purée, pepper, and a pinch of sugar. Cover the pot and cook over low heat, stirring occasionally to keep it loose. Cook for 40 to 45 minutes or longer—the longer it cooks, the better it tastes. The sauerkraut should be moist but not soupy. If necessary, cook uncovered to thicken. Taste to see if salt is needed and correct the seasoning. Serve hot.

Yield: 4 to 6 servings.

Sweet and Sour Red Cabbage

A classic accompaniment for pot roast.

1 medium-size red cabbage, about
  2 pounds
2 tablespoons butter
1 onion, chopped
2 tablespoons brown sugar
2 tart apples, peeled, cored, and
  thinly sliced
¼ cup cider vinegar
Freshly grated nutmeg
½ cup dry red wine
Salt

Wash the cabbage, cut it into quarters, remove the core, and cut into thin slices.

Melt the butter in a large skillet, add the chopped onion, and cook until golden. Add the brown sugar and mix well. Add the cabbage, apples, vinegar, nutmeg, and red wine. Cook covered for 10 minutes, then partly cover and cook over low heat for 35 to 40 minutes longer, or until the cabbage is tender. Stir from time to time. Taste and correct the seasonings; it may need salt, more sugar, or a squirt of lemon juice.

Yield: 4 to 5 servings.

Oriental Cabbage

Two popular Oriental cabbages that we see with increasing frequency in the markets are Chinese cabbage, known as celery cabbage or pe-tsai; and Chinese chard, called bok choy. To add to the confusion, they are both called Chinese cabbages.

Chinese cabbage looks very much like a pale head of romaine lettuce. It has a long oval head with broad-ribbed pale green leaves that are strong-veined and somewhat crinkled.

Selection: Look for heads with crisp outer leaves. Pass up the very large or very firm heads; they have a strong flavor. Two pounds will serve four to six.

Peak Season: Year round.

Methods of Preparation: Cook as you would any other cabbage—stir-fry, steam, or boil. It has a more delicate flavor than other cabbages and practically no odor while cooking. It is delicious raw in salad—crisp and crunchy.

Bok choy resembles both chard and celery. It has a light, delicate flavor and crisp texture. Long cooking will ruin it. It is a leafy vegetable with white stems and green leaves and is a popular ingredient in many Oriental dishes.

Selection: Look for leaves that are dark green, shiny, and fresh looking. Avoid those that look wilted or limp.

Peak Season: Year round.

Methods of Preparation: Cook like Swiss chard. If mature, cook stalks and leaves separately because the stems will take a longer time. The leaves may be cut in squares and cooked like spinach or cut into bite-size pieces and stir-fried. Use in meat or vegetable combinations where some crisp texture is wanted. The hearts may be used raw in salads or blanched and seasoned with butter, salt, and pepper. If used in soup, add during the last 10 minutes of cooking to retain crispness.

Carrots

Selection: Look for firm, smooth, well-formed, and deeply colored carrots. Carrots with a bright orange color are more nutritious than the paler ones because they are richer in carotene, the substance that the body converts into vitamin A. Carrots are sold topped and prepackaged, and in bunches with their tops on. Allow 1 pound or 1 medium bunch for 3 or 4 servings. One pound of shredded or grated carrots yields about 3 cups.

Peak Season: Year round.

Methods of Preparation: Raw for salads, nibbles, and juice. Boiled, steamed, braised, baked in soups, stews, as a flavoring vegetable with roasts, in cakes, cookies, and breads.

To Cook: Small, young, tender carrots may simply be scrubbed with a firm-bristled vegetable brush; older, larger ones should be scraped with a vegetable peeler. They may be diced, sliced diagonally or in rounds, cut into julienne strips, shredded, grated, or left whole.

Cook carrots in an inch or two of boiling salted water until crisp-tender, or slightly softer if you are going to purée them. Cooking time varies with the age and size of the carrots.

Whole mature carrots take from 15 to 20 minutes; whole baby carrots 8 to 10 minutes; cut, sliced, or shredded carrots 4 to 10 minutes. Carrots bake more successfully if they are parboiled first. Peel and parboil them until half done and then place in the roasting pan with the meat for the last 30 minutes.

Carrot Curls. Peel large carrots. With a swivel-bladed peeler, cut lengthwise paper-thin strips. Roll each strip tightly and fasten with a toothpick. Chill in ice water for 1 hour. Remove toothpick for serving.

Puréed Carrots. Scrape carrots and cut them into chunks. Simmer in boiling salted water until soft. Drain well and purée them through a food mill or in a food processor. Add a good chunk of butter and season with salt, if needed. Serve in a heated bowl and sprinkle with chopped fresh parsley. If you wish, blend in a few tablespoons of heavy cream.

You may also combine the carrot purée with an equal quantity of finely mashed potatoes, 3 tablespoons of heavy cream, and a large chunk of butter. Beat together until smooth and creamy.

Honeyed Carrots

3 tablespoons butter
3 tablespoons orange juice
1 tablespoon lemon juice
¼ teaspoon ground ginger
4 tablespoons honey
½ teaspoon salt
1 pound carrots, scraped and cut in julienne strips

In a large, heavy skillet with a cover, combine the butter, orange and lemon juices, ginger, honey, and salt and heat to the boiling point. Add the carrots and cook, covered, over low heat for 5 to 10 minutes, or until the carrots are crisp-tender. Stir them frequently while they are cooking to prevent scorching and so that they will take on an even glaze. Serve hot.

Yield: 3 to 4 servings.

Savory Carrots

A Middle East preparation with a provocative and different flavor.

1 pound carrots
½ cup olive oil
6 tablespoons red wine vinegar
1 bunch fresh parsley, minced
1 tablespoon ground cumin
1½ tablespoons sweet paprika
3 garlic cloves, finely chopped
Salt and freshly ground pepper

Scrape carrots and cut them diagonally into ½-inch-thick slices. Cook over medium heat in a small amount of boiling salted water, covered, until tender but still firm. The time needed depends on the freshness of the carrots; test for tenderness by piercing them with the tip of a sharp-pointed knife.

While the carrots are cooking, whisk together the oil and vinegar in a small bowl. Add the remaining ingredients and mix well. When the carrots are done, drain them thoroughly and pour the sauce over while they are still warm. Toss well. The carrots may be served hot or at room temperature.

Yield: 4 servings.

Cauliflower

Selection: Look for a crisp, heavy head with clean, firm, creamy white flowerets and fresh green outer leaves. Avoid heads that are spotted, speckled or bruised. Allow 1 medium head, about 1½ pounds, for 4 servings.

Peak Season: September through November, but available all year.

Methods of Preparation: Raw, with a dip; cooked or raw in salads and mixed pickles. Boiled, steamed, deep-fried, in soups, and puréed or sautéed after boiling.

To Cook: The head may be left whole or separated into flowerets. Wash well and drain. Steam in a steamer basket over boiling water or boil in a covered pot in 2 inches of boiling salted water. A tablespoon or two of lemon juice or milk added to the boiling liquid will help to preserve the white color. Flowerets will take 5 to 8 minutes; the whole head (boiled top down) takes 15 to 25 minutes. The age and size of the vegetable will determine the cooking

time. If you are cooking the cauliflower for later use, drain and plunge immediately into cold water to stop the cooking. Drain it again and refrigerate, covered. Overcooking cauliflower makes it mushy and spoils color and flavor.

Serve with melted butter and lemon juice, herb-flavored butter, or a sprinkling of Parmesan cheese and bread crumbs.

Cauliflower au Gratin. Arrange cooked flowerets in a shallow greased baking dish that can be used for serving. Cover flowerets with a medium white sauce (page 451), sprinkle with grated Parmesan or Cheddar cheese, top with browned bread crumbs, and bake in a 375-degree oven until the cheese melts and the top is browned, about 20 minutes.

For extra eye and taste appeal, combine cauliflower flowerets with broccoli flowerets; the white and green provide an interesting contrast.

Celeriac

Celeriac is a round, knobby brownish root with a rough skin, also called celery root and knob celery. It is a variety of celery grown for its enlarged root and not for its stalks and leaves, as is ordinary celery. It has an intense celery flavor with smoky overtones.

Selection: Choose unwilted firm knobs that are small. The larger heads tend to be woody. Allow 1 pound for 3 servings.

Peak Season: September through April.

Methods of Preparation: Raw and cooked in salads; boiled and braised; in combination with other vegetables, particularly potatoes. It is notable when served in a mustard mayonnaise (see Céleri-Rave Rémoulade, page 398). It must always be peeled, either before or after cooking, and discolors rapidly when exposed to air.

To Cook: Celeriac may be cooked whole or sliced. Scrub well and cut off leaves and rootlets. Cook in a covered pot with enough boiling salted water to cover, until tender. Add a little vinegar or lemon juice to the water to keep the celeriac white. Whole knobs may take from 25 to 35 minutes, depending on size; slices or wedges may be tender in anywhere from 6 to 15 minutes. Do not overcook; it tends to get mushy if overdone. Peel when cool enough to handle and cut as desired. Toss in melted butter and sprinkle with chopped chives or parsley.

Purée of Celeriac and Potatoes. Use equal quantities of celeriac and potatoes. Trim and peel celeriac and cut into eighths. Peel potatoes and cut the same size. Cover with boiling salted water and simmer in a covered saucepan until tender. Drain well and purée through a sieve or a food mill—not a blender or a food processor. Beat in 3 or 4 tablespoons of butter and season with salt and pepper. Beat in 1/3 cup or more of heavy cream and beat again over low heat until light and fluffy. If you are not going to serve immediately, keep hot in the top of a double boiler. Serve sprinkled with chopped parsley.

Celery

Selection: Choose celery with fresh leaves and firm, glossy stalks brittle enough to snap easily. Allow 1 medium bunch for 4 to 6 servings, and 1 heart for 2 servings.

Peak Season: All year.

Methods of Preparation: Raw, as a nibble and in salads; cooked in stews and soups as an aromatic vegetable; boiled, braised, creamed, sautéed. Do not discard the leaves; their concentrated flavor enhances stews, salads, roasts, and soups. If celery is stringy, peel lightly to remove the strings.

To make celery hearts, trim off all the outer stalks. Slice the heart lengthwise in two and crisp in ice water.

To Cook: Cut celery ribs crosswise into thick or thin slices, straight or on the diagonal. Or cut into strips or chop, depending on the use. Cook, covered, in an inch of boiling water or in beef or chicken broth for 4 to 8 minutes, until crisp-tender. Cooking time depends on the size of the pieces. Drain and toss with butter, herb butter, or cheese or white sauce.

Celery Parmesan

Celery is too often overlooked as a cooked vegetable. The sliced celery stalks look most attractive—somewhat like arrowheads—and provide a crisp, crunchy vegetable accompaniment to a meat, fish, or poultry main course.

6 large celery stalks
Water, or chicken or beef broth
Salt and freshly ground pepper
1 cup sour cream
⅓ cup freshly grated Parmesan cheese
2 tablespoons chopped fresh parsley

Wash the celery and remove the strings with a vegetable peeler. Cut the stalks crosswise into 1-inch-thick diagonal slices. Cook, covered, in 1 inch of boiling water or broth for 4 to 8 minutes, or until crisp-tender. Drain and transfer to a shallow greased baking dish. Sprinkle lightly with salt and pepper. Spread sour-cream over the top and sprinkle with Parmesan cheese and chopped parsley. Place in a 350-degree oven until warmed through.

Yield: 4 servings.

Braised Celery

The prepackaged trimmed celery containing two bunches per package is recommended for this.

2 bunches celery
3 tablespoons butter
1 large onion, finely chopped
1 carrot, coarsely grated
½ cup chicken or beef broth
1 clove garlic, minced
Salt and freshly ground pepper

Remove the tough outer stalks of celery. Trim the roots, but leave enough to hold the bunch together. Slice off the top and leaves, leaving the celery heart about 6 inches long. Split the hearts in two, lengthwise. Save the celery you cut off for soups, stews, and such.

Wash the celery well, making sure that all traces of sand are removed. Parboil the celery hearts in an inch of boiling salted water, covered, for 5 minutes. Drain.

In a large heavy skillet, melt the butter and cook the onion and carrot until the onion is golden. Push them to one side of the pan (or remove them if the pan is too small), add the celery, and brown on both sides. Spread the chopped vegetables over the celery, add the broth, garlic, salt, and pepper. Cover the pot and cook over low heat until the celery is tender but still crisp, 10 to 15 minutes. To serve, spoon the liquid and vegetables over each portion of celery.

Yield: 4 servings.

Chestnuts

Selection: Choose fresh-looking nuts that are plump and glossy and heavy for their size, without blemishes. One pound of shelled, peeled chestnuts yields approximately 2½ cups.

Peak Season: December and January, but available October through March.

Methods of Preparation: The hard outer shells and the thin brown bitter inner peel must be removed before chestnuts can be used. They're a nuisance to peel, but the unique flavor and texture of chestnuts compensate for the effort and the damaged fingernails. Roasted chestnuts are a beautiful snack; braised, they are delicious in stuffings, as an accompaniment to other vegetables such as Brussels sprouts, or simply on their own. Cream-enriched sweetened chestnut purée makes a sublime dessert. Canned chestnuts are also an excellent product.

Chestnuts can be cooked and mashed like potatoes, pressed through a sieve, or whirled in a blender, with a little of the cooking liquid added.

To Peel: With a sharp knife, slash an X in the flat side of the chestnut. Place the chestnuts in a saucepan with enough cold water to cover. Bring to a boil, and boil for 3 minutes. Remove pot from the heat. Remove the chestnuts from the water, a few at a time. With a sharp-pointed knife, remove the outer shell and the inner skin. Keep the unpeeled chestnuts in the hot water until you get to them or the inner skin won't come off. Reheat the water if it gets cold. Don't expect that all the chestnuts will be intact and in one piece when peeled; some will inevitably be broken.

Braised Chestnuts

1 cup chicken or beef broth
2 tablespoons dry white wine
½ teaspoon salt
Freshly ground pepper
1 pound chestnuts, peeled
3 tablespoons butter

In a medium-size saucepan, combine the broth, wine, salt, and pepper. Bring to a boil, add the chestnuts, reduce the heat, cover, and simmer for 15 to 20 minutes, or until the chestnuts are tender. Drain, return to the heat, and toss with butter. Serve hot.

Yield: 3 to 4 servings.

Creamed Chestnuts. Follow the preceding directions and add ¼ cup heavy cream to the butter before tossing.

Chestnuts and Brussels Sprouts. Combine cooked chestnuts with 1 pound of cooked Brussels sprouts and heat together.

Collards

Selection: Look for crisp, fresh, clean, tender young leaves free from insect injury. Allow 1 pound for 2 servings.

Peak Season: January through April, but a fairly constant supply all year.

Methods of Preparation: Boiled and served as a vegetable.

To Cook: Wash collard greens in several changes of water to remove all traces of earth or sand. Trim off the tough stems and tear or cut the large leaves into pieces or shred like cabbage. In the traditional Southern style, collards are boiled for about 2 hours with one of a variety of pork products, but generally 20 minutes or so in boiling salted water in a covered pot will make them tender enough to eat. The "pot likker" that we find referred to in stories laid in the South is the juice that results from cooking collards with some type of pork. It is a liquid rich in vitamins and minerals, to be sopped up with corn bread.

Southern Style Collard Greens

Kale, chard, and turnip, beet, or mustard greens may be used interchangeably with collard greens in this receipe. Try combining two or more for variety.

4 pounds fresh collards, washed and prepared for cooking

1 meaty ham hock, *or* ½ pound salt pork, cut into small cubes

1½ quarts water, approximately

Salt and freshly ground pepper

Place the prepared collards in a large pot with the ham hock or salt pork and cover with water. Bring slowly to a boil, lower the heat, cover, and simmer for 1½ to 2 hours. Stir from time to time. At the end of this time the water should have evaporated and the salt pork melted. If you have used a ham hock, scrape off the pieces of meat, return them to the pot, and discard the bone. Drain the greens if there is excess liquid. Season with salt and pepper.

Yield: 6 to 8 servings.

Corn

Selection: Look for corn that has fresh green husks and is free from decay where the silk ends. Pull back the husk and puncture a kernel with your fingernail. If fresh, a milky liquid will exude; if unripe, it will be water; and if past its prime, the milk will be doughy. Allow 1 to 2 ears per serving.

Peak Season: Heaviest supply spring and summer, but available fresh all year, depending on locality.

Methods of Preparation: Boiled, roasted, or grilled over an open fire in the husk or husked; cooked and husked in salads, fritters, soufflés, puddings.

To Cook: The perfect way to boil fresh corn is to deal with perfect corn—that is, corn that has just been picked. The sooner it is used after leaving the field, the sweeter and more tender it will be. Shortly after corn is picked, the sugar begins to turn to starch. High temperatures also hasten this process, which is why you must always keep corn in the coldest part of the refrigerator if you have to store it.

Remove the husks and silk; cut off the stems and, if you wish, the tips. Place the shucked corn in a kettle containing enough boiling water to cover it. Do not use salt in the water— it will toughen the corn. Cover the pot and, when the water returns to a lively boil, turn off the heat, keep the pot covered, and let the corn stand in the water 5 minutes. Serve without further cooking. Remove only enough ears for the first serving; the remaining corn may stay in the water for as long as 15 minutes or so

without damage to flavor or quality. Serve with butter and salt.

To roast corn in the oven, preheat the oven to 400 degrees. Remove the husks, spread the ears with butter, sprinkle with salt and pepper, and wrap in a square of aluminum foil. Bake for 15 minutes. Turn the ears over and bake an additional 10 to 15 minutes.

Leftover corn should be cut off the cob and stored, covered, in the refrigerator. Use it for corn pudding or fritters, or combine it with an equal amount of cooked lima beans to make succotash (see page 335).

Corn Pudding

Light and custardy.

3 eggs
2 cups light cream
2 cups corn, cut from the cob (about 4 ears)
1 tablespoon butter, melted
2 teaspoons sugar
Salt and freshly ground pepper
1 teaspoon Worcestershire sauce

Heat the oven to 350 degrees. Butter a 1½-quart casserole.

Beat the eggs and cream together until light, frothy, and well blended. Stir in the corn, butter, sugar, salt, pepper, and Worcestershire sauce. Pour into the prepared casserole and place the casserole in a large baking pan. Add 1 inch of boiling water to the pan. Bake for 1 hour, or until set. Cool for 5 minutes before serving.

Yield: 4 servings.

Corn Fritters

2 egg yolks, slightly beaten
2 cups fresh corn, cut from the cob (about 4 ears)
½ teaspoon salt
Freshly ground pepper
¼ cup all-purpose flour
¼ teaspoon baking powder
2 egg whites
2 tablespoons oil
2 tablespoons butter

Mix together the egg yolks, corn, salt, and pepper. Add the flour and baking powder and stir until smooth. In a separate bowl, beat the egg whites until they stand in peaks and are stiff but not dry. Gently fold the beaten egg whites into the corn mixture.

Over a moderately high flame, heat the oil and butter in a large skillet until foamy. Drop the batter by tablespoons into the hot fat and cook until golden brown. Turn and brown the other side. Keep warm in a 200-degree oven while cooking the rest of the batter. Add more oil if needed.

Yield: 4 to 6 servings.

Cucumbers

Selection: Look for cucumbers that are slender, firm, and of good green color. Avoid fat cucumbers that feel soft inside. If possible, buy the unwaxed cucumbers that don't need to be peeled; a good deal of the flavor lies in the skin. Allow 1 medium cucumber for 2 servings.

Peak Season: Summer months, but available all year.

Methods of Preparation: Raw as a nibble, in salads, sandwiches and sauces; pickled; cooked in soups; sautéed, poached, or stuffed and baked.

To Cook: Peel, if the cucumbers are waxed, and cut into thick rounds or strips. Cook in an inch of boiling water for 3 to 5 minutes. Drain and serve with butter seasoned with tarragon, chervil, or dill and a sprinkle of lemon juice. To sauté, dip slices in flour and sauté in butter.

Cucumber Hors d'Oeuvre. Cucumber baskets make excellent containers for hors d'oeuvre preparations. Cut peeled cucumbers into wedges 2 inches long. Scrape out the insides, leaving a substantial rim and bottom to contain the filling. Fill with a mixture of cottage cheese and chopped scallions; tuna fish mixed with cream cheese and a bit of mayonnaise; cream cheese mixed with chopped smoked salmon and capers; or a filling of your own inspiration.

Sautéed Cucumbers

A good accompaniment for fish dishes.

3 large cucumbers
⅓ cup flour
4 tablespoons butter
1 tablespoon minced onion
Salt and freshly ground pepper
2 tablespoons chopped dill

Wash and peel the cucumbers, if necessary. Cut into diagonal slices, ½ inch thick. Pat dry with paper towels. Put the flour in a paper bag. Add a few cucumber slices at a time and shake the bag to coat the slices. Shake off any excess flour from the slices. Melt the butter in a large skillet, add the onion and cook until golden. Add the floured cucumber slices and cook over moderately high heat, browning on both sides. Drain the slices on paper towels. Salt and pepper lightly and serve sprinkled with dill.

Yield: 4 to 6 servings.

Eggplant

Selection: Look for firm eggplant with clear, dark satiny color, unscarred, with no soft or brown spots. Medium-size ones, weighing about 1½ pounds, are generally the best. A large, heavy eggplant will usually have more seeds than the slimmer, lighter ones. Allow 1 medium eggplant (about 1½ pounds) for 4 servings.

Peak Season: August and September, but available all year.

Methods of Preparation: Eggplant is never eaten raw. It can be baked, steamed, sautéed, deep-fried, or broiled. Eggplant can be halved and stuffed; sliced, cubed, or diced; served alone or in casserole combinations with meat, vegetables, and cheeses; served hot, at room temperature, or chilled as a cold salad. It combines well with tomatoes, garlic, onions, herbs, meats, and cheeses.

Young, tender eggplant need not be peeled, but if the skin is tough, it should be removed. Eggplant contains a good deal of water that can have a slightly bitter taste. There are two schools of thought about whether the eggplant should be salted before cooking in order to draw out the water. People on a low-sodium diet will naturally skip the salting; others can try it both ways and decide for themselves. If you wish to draw out the water, liberally salt the cut and peeled pieces and place them in a colander with a plate under it to catch the drippings. Let stand at least 30 minutes—longer if possible—and blot thoroughly with paper towels before cooking.

Leftover cooked eggplant whirred in a blender into a paste and seasoned with lemon juice, salt, and pepper makes a delicious dip.

Broiled Eggplant

Eggplant absorbs a great deal of fat when sautéed. Broiling the slices does a very good job of cooking them and requires much less fat.

2 medium-size eggplant
3 garlic cloves, finely chopped
½ cup olive oil
Salt and freshly ground pepper
Freshly grated Parmesan cheese

Wash eggplant, trim off stem end and slice off the rounded end. Leave the skin or pare it, depending on how tough or tender it is. Cut into ½-inch-thick slices. Salt the slices if you wish and let stand for 30 minutes to drain. Blot dry with paper towels.

Combine the garlic and olive oil and mix well. Heat the broiler.

Line a baking sheet with aluminum foil and oil it lightly. Place the broiler rack about 5 inches below the heat source. Arrange the eggplant slices in a single layer on the baking sheet; you may have to do this in two batches. Brush the slices generously with the garlic-flavored oil and sprinkle lightly with salt and pepper. Broil for 5 minutes, or until lightly brown. Brush with more oil if they seem to be getting dry. When browned, turn the slices with a broad metal spatula, repeat the application of oil, salt, and pepper, and broil until lightly browned on the other side, about 5 minutes. The slices should be just cooked through, and not too soft or limp. A minute or two before they are finished, sprinkle Parmesan cheese over the slices. Serve hot.

Yield: 6 to 8 servings.

Variation: Undercook the eggplant slices. Transfer them to a shallow greased 9 by 13-inch baking dish. Top each eggplant slice with a thin slice of tomato, some coarsely grated mozzarella cheese, and a sprinkling of freshly grated Parmesan cheese. Reduce oven heat to 350 degrees and bake until the cheese melts, about 7 to 10 minutes.

Sautéed Eggplant

2 medium eggplant
2 garlic cloves, finely minced
½ cup olive oil (approximately)
4 anchovy fillets, finely minced
1 teaspoon dried chervil or thyme
Freshly ground pepper and salt, if
   necessary
2 tablespoons finely chopped
   fresh parsley

Peel eggplant and cut into 1-inch-thick slices. Cut slices into 1-inch cubes. Sprinkle with salt if you wish and let drain for 30 minutes. Blot dry with paper towels.

In a large skillet, heat half the oil and sauté the garlic until golden. Add the eggplant cubes, turning them often, and shake the pan so that the cubes cook evenly. After 10 minutes, add the anchovy fillets and chervil or thyme. Add more oil if needed. Continue to cook, shaking the pan frequently, until the eggplant is tender and cooked through but still firm, 30 to 40 minutes in all. Add pepper and taste to see if you need salt. The anchovies might provide all you need. Serve sprinkled with chopped parsley.

Yield: 6 to 8 servings.

Stuffed Eggplant

This can serve as an appetizer or a luncheon course.

6 small eggplant, *or* 3 1-pound
   size
Salt
½ cup olive oil
1 onion, chopped
4 tomatoes, peeled, seeded, and
   finely chopped
1 cup bread crumbs
1 7-ounce can Italian tuna
5 tablespoons finely chopped
   fresh parsley
2 cloves garlic, finely minced
½ cup green olives, finely
   chopped
1 tablespoon fresh basil, finely
   chopped, *or* 1 teaspoon dried
6 anchovy fillets, mashed
2 tablespoons drained capers,
   chopped
Freshly ground black pepper

Cut the eggplant in half lengthwise and scoop out flesh, leaving a ¼-inch shell. Chop the pulp finely. Sprinkle the inside of the eggplant shells with salt and drain them upside down on paper towels.

Heat 4 tablespoons of the oil in a large skillet. Add the onion and cook until limp. Add the eggplant pulp to the skillet and cook until lightly brown, about 10 minutes. Add the tomatoes and cook over high heat, stirring often, until soft and thickened and the liquid evaporated. Add bread crumbs, tuna, 2 tablespoons parsley, garlic, olives, basil, anchovies, and capers and cook for 2 or 3 minutes, or until heated through. Season with salt and pepper to taste.

Blot eggplant shells with paper towels. Stuff with the mixture and dribble the remaining oil over each half. Place the filled halves in a 9 by 13-inch shallow baking dish and add ½ inch of hot water to the bottom of the dish. Bake in a 375-degree oven for 45 to 50 minutes. Sprinkle with remaining chopped parsley. Serve warm or at room temperature.

If you wish, you may serve this with a fresh tomato sauce.

Yield: 6 servings.

Fennel

Sweet fennel is also known as Florence fennel, finocchio, fenucchi, or anise. It is used as a vegetable and is not to be confused with the common fennel that is grown for use as a seasoning. Florence fennel is a bulbous vegetable made up of broad-leaf stalks that overlap each other at the base of a stem, to form a bulb that is firm, crisp, and 3 to 4 inches across.

Selection: Look for firm, crisp bulbs, pale greenish white in color, with fresh looking green tops. Allow 1 medium bulb for 2 servings.

Peak Season: A winter vegetable, available October through April.

Methods of Preparation: Sliced and used raw, like celery, in salads or as a nibble. Braised as a vegetable or a flavoring vegetable in casserole dishes or vegetable mixtures.

To Cook: To prepare for cooking, trim off the tops of the stalks down to the knobs. The stalks are excellent for soups and stews. Cut off the hard base. If the bulbs are large, cut them into halves or quarters lengthwise. Cover with boiling water or beef stock and cook, covered, for 5 minutes, until tender but still firm. Toss with melted butter, season with salt and pepper, and serve.

Braised Fennel

Fennel is sweeter and has a less pronounced anise taste when cooked. It goes well with roast lamb, chicken, and veal.

3 large heads fennel
1 cup boiling chicken or beef broth
Salt and freshly ground pepper
3 tablespoons freshly grated Parmesan cheese
6 tablespoons butter, melted

Cut off the tops of the fennel at the point where the bulbous part begins. Trim away any tough, wilted, or stringy outer leaves. Cut bulbs lengthwise into halves or quarters.

Put the fennel bulbs in a saucepan and add boiling broth to barely cover. Cook, covered, over low heat for 5 or 6 minutes, or until the fennel has softened just the least bit. Drain well, reserving the broth. Transfer the fennel to a generously buttered shallow baking dish. Add ½ cup of the reserved broth and sprinkle lightly with salt and pepper. Cover the dish tightly with aluminum foil and bake in a 350-degree oven for 30 minutes. Remove the foil; sprinkle with Parmesan cheese and melted butter. Bake for 20 minutes longer, or until the fennel is lightly colored and just tender when pierced with a sharp-pointed knife. The fennel need not be uniformly soft; the firm parts will retain a little crunchiness. Transfer to a heated platter and serve hot.

Yield: 4 to 6 servings.

Jerusalem Artichokes (Sunchokes)

Jerusalem artichokes are the root of a variety of sunflower plant and have nothing whatever to do with either Jerusalem or artichokes. In appearance, they are something between a knobby potato and ginger root. They have a lovely, crisp texture and nutlike flavor.

Selection: Look for firm tubers that are neither soft nor spongy. The flesh under the skin should be creamy white. Allow 1 pound for 3 servings.

Peak Season: October to March.

Methods of Preparation: Raw, as an hors d'oeuvre with a dip or in a salad; boiled, broiled, sautéed, mashed, or baked in their jackets—any cooking method you use for a potato.

The skins of Jerusalem artichokes are tender and don't really need to be peeled, but you can scrape them with a vegetable peeler as you do a potato and plunge them immediately into cold water with salt and lemon juice to keep them from discoloring. Don't worry about bits of skin that remain between the knobs; ignore them as you do the skins of new potatoes.

To Cook: Scrub the artichokes thoroughly under cold running water, using a stiff vegetable brush. Cover with boiling salted water and cook, covered, until tender but firm when tested with a sharp-pointed knife, about 10 to 12 minutes, depending on their size. They can get mushy quickly and they need to be watched. When done, drain well and slice them. Toss with butter, season with salt and pepper, and sprinkle with fresh chopped parsley.

Creamed Jerusalem Artichokes. Cook and slice artichokes as above. Add heated heavy cream, a dash of Tabasco, and, if you like, chopped chives or chopped parsley.

Sautéed Jerusalem Artichokes. Blanch the peeled or scrubbed artichokes in boiling salted water for 2 minutes. Remove from the water and drain. Cut into ¼-inch slices and sauté until tender in oil to which you have added 1 or 2 cloves of garlic, chopped. Season with salt and pepper. Stir the slices during cooking and taste for tenderness. When done, stir in a couple of tablespoons of fresh chopped parsley and serve hot.

Kale

Selection: Look for crisp leaves with a good dark green color.

Peak Season: December through April, but available all year. Allow 1 pound for 2 servings.

Method of Preparation: Boil, as for collards and other greens.

To Cook: Remove and discard tough outer leaves and thick midribs. Cut or break large leaves into pieces. Wash thoroughly and shake leaves to get rid of some of the moisture. Cook, covered, in boiling salted water until tender. Cooking time can vary from 15 to 40 minutes, depending on how young and tender the leaves are. Kale, like other greens, combines well with pork products such as sausage, bacon, salt pork, and ham bones.

Kohlrabi

Kohlrabi is a member of the cabbage family but is different in appearance from any of its relatives. Both its bulb and the stems that shoot from it are good to eat. Young small bulbs have a mild, turniplike flavor and crisp, tender texture.

Selection: Look for small or medium-size kohlrabi bulbs with fresh green leaves and a thin rind that can be pierced with your fingernail. Allow 1 medium or 2 or 3 small kohlrabi per person.

Peak Season: June and July, but available May through November.

Methods of Preparation: Raw in mixed salads or as an hors d'oeuvre served with a dip; boiled or steamed and served as a vegetable.

To Cook: Cut off and discard the leaves. Wash and drain the stems and chop them. They may be cooked with the kohlrabi bulbs in boiling salted water and served together with them, or they can be boiled separately.

Young tender bulbs do not need to be peeled, but it is desirable to remove the tough outer skins of more mature ones. Slice, dice, or cut into julienne strips and boil in salted water, uncovered, until tender, 20 to 30 minutes. Drain. Toss with melted butter and season with salt and freshly ground pepper.

Creamed Kohlrabi. Combine cooked kohlrabi slices with a medium white sauce (page 451). Figure 1 cup of sauce to 2 cups of the cooked vegetable. If you wish, you can purée the cooked stems and add them to the sauce. Mix in a tablespoon or two of grated Parmesan cheese.

Leeks

Leeks are the sweetest and mildest members of the onion family.

Selection: Look for tightly rolled leaves with fresh green tops. Small or medium leeks are more tender. They should "give" a bit to the touch. Allow 1 to 2 medium leeks per serving.

Peak Season: Fall until early spring, but available all year.

Methods of Preparation: Leeks are a deservedly popular aromatic vegetable in soups, stews, and braised dishes. They may be braised, boiled, or puréed as a vegetable accompaniment to roasted meat or fowl.

To Cook: The bottoms of leeks grow underground and dirt may seep in between the layers of the leaves. To remove it, trim the ends of the leeks and split the stems lengthwise down the center almost but not quite to the end. Rinse well between the leaves. Trim off the rootlets.

You may also cut the leeks into 2-inch slices and swish them around in a bowl of water, changing it a few times, until no dirt remains in the bottom of the bowl. Drain well.

Put leeks in a saucepan with boiling water to cover. When water returns to the boil, reduce heat and simmer until tender, 5 to 10 minutes, depending on the quality and freshness of the leeks. Test with a fork or taste to determine doneness. Drain well. Season with salt, freshly ground pepper, and melted butter, or a sprinkling of Parmesan cheese.

Purée of Leeks. Cook leeks as described above. Drain well and purée in food processor. Transfer to a bowl and blend in 2 tablespoons butter and 5 tablespoons heavy cream for each pound of leeks. Season with salt, pepper, and a few gratings of fresh nutmeg. Blend well.

Mushrooms

Once a delicacy for a favored few, mushrooms are now a standard supermarket product.

Selection: Look for plump, unblemished mushrooms with the cap closed tightly around the stems. Avoid those markedly pitted or discolored with wide-open caps and dark gills. The washed mushrooms that come wrapped in plastic have less flavor than the loose ones. Allow 1 pound of mushrooms for 4 servings.

Peak Season: Fall until spring, but available all year. August low point of production.

Methods of Preparation: Raw, pickled; sautéed, baked, broiled, creamed, deep-fried in batter, stuffed; in soups, sauces, stews, casserole dishes, soufflés, and quiches.

Dried mushrooms bring a distinctive taste to soups and stews. They are expensive, but a little goes a long way. To reconstitute, wash them in lukewarm water to remove grit and then soak in warm water to cover for 30 mintues or longer. Use the soaking water as part of the liquid in the dish you are preparing. About 3 ounces of dried mushrooms are the equivalent of 1 pound of fresh.

To Cook: Wipe mushrooms with a damp towel. If they are very dirty, wash them quickly and wipe dry with paper towels. Mushrooms should not be soaked as they quickly become waterlogged. Cut a thin slice from the stem and discard. Do not peel mushrooms; much of the flavor and nutritive value is in the skin.

To sauté sliced or whole mushrooms, cook them quickly in butter or a combination of butter and oil with some chopped garlic added to the fat, if you like. Cook them for 3 to 5 minutes, uncovered, stirring often. Season with salt and pepper and a squirt of lemon juice.

To broil, brush large mushroom caps with melted butter. Sprinkle with salt and pepper. Arrange mushrooms in a baking dish and broil 4 inches below the heat source, 5 minutes on each side. They will be juicier if you broil them hollow side up first, then turn cap side up.

Creamed Mushrooms

1½ pounds mushrooms
4 tablespoons butter
2 tablespoons oil
3 or 4 shallots or scallions, finely minced
1 teaspoon flour
⅔ cup heavy cream, warmed
2 or 3 tablespoons Madeira or dry sherry (optional)
Salt and freshly ground pepper

Clean the mushrooms and cut a thin slice from the stem end and discard. Leave the mushrooms whole if small, or slice or quarter them. Sauté them in the butter and oil for 3 minutes; add the shallots or scallions and stir over moderate heat for 3 minutes longer. Add the flour and cook 3 minutes longer, stirring constantly.

Remove from the heat and add the warmed heavy cream and wine. Return to low heat and cook until the cream has reduced and thickened. Shake the pan back and forth until the cream coats the mushrooms. Add salt and pepper to taste. Do not overcook.

Yield: 4 to 6 servings.

Stuffed Mushrooms

A delicious and edible garnish for a meat or poultry course that can also serve as a second vegetable.

12 large mushrooms
3 tablespoons butter
1 onion, finely chopped
1 clove garlic, minced
4 anchovy fillets, mashed
3 tablespoons chopped fresh
 parsley
½ teaspoon dried thyme
Freshly ground pepper
2 slices bread, crusts trimmed,
 soaked in water and squeezed
 dry
1 teaspoon mayonnaise
2 tablespoons freshly grated
 Parmesan cheese
2 tablespoons fine bread crumbs

Wipe the mushrooms with a damp cloth. Trim off a thin slice from the stem and discard. Remove the stems and chop fine. Reserve the caps.

Melt the butter in a skillet and cook the chopped stems and onion for 5 minutes, stirring a few times. Add the garlic, anchovies, parsley, thyme, and pepper and cook for 5 minutes over medium-high heat. Remove from the heat and mix in the bread, blending well. Add the mayonnaise to moisten and bind the mixture. Taste and correct the seasonings. The anchovies may have added enough salt, but you may want more.

Grease a shallow baking dish and arrange the mushrooms in it, hollow side up. Fill the caps with the stuffing, mounding it nicely with your fingers. Sprinkle with the Parmesan cheese and bread crumbs. Bake for 20 minutes in a preheated 350-degree oven.

Yield: 4 servings.

Pickled Mushrooms

Serve on toothpicks as an hors d'oeuvre, or in a salad. Use only firm, fresh, white, uniformly sized mushrooms.

1 pound mushrooms
1 cup olive or vegetable oil
3 tablespoons wine vinegar
3 tablespoons lemon juice
5 scallions, chopped
Salt and freshly ground pepper
½ teaspoon dried oregano
½ teaspoon dried rosemary leaves,
 crushed
½ teaspoon dry mustard
Pinch of sugar

Separate the stems from the caps and save the stems for another use. Wipe the mushrooms with a damp cloth. Mix together the remaining ingredients in a large glass jar with a cover. Taste the dressing and correct the seasonings. Add the mushrooms to the jar and shake it gently so that they are well bathed in the dressing. Cover the jar and refrigerate for at least 12 hours. Don't worry about there not being enough dressing to cover; the mushrooms reduce in bulk after a while and duck down nicely in the marinade. Drain the mushrooms to serve.

Yield: 6 to 10 appetizer servings.

Duxelles

Duxelles is a rich and flavorful paste made of minced mushrooms used in stuffings and sauces, in soups, added to scrambled eggs or omelets, or as an hors d'oeuvre spread on toast. It's a splendid way to use mushroom stems or mushrooms that have become discolored and lost their chance to appear in your salad. Duxelles keeps well in the refrigerator for a couple of weeks, or it can be frozen in small individual containers to be used as needed.

1 pound mushrooms, very finely chopped
6 tablespoons butter
2 shallots, finely chopped
2 tablespoons onion, finely chopped
Salt and freshly ground pepper
¼ cup Madeira (optional)

Squeeze the finely chopped mushrooms in a towel to extract most of the juice. Save the juice for a soup or sauce.

Melt the butter in a large skillet and add the shallots and onion. Cook for a few minutes, stirring. Add the chopped mushrooms and sauté over low heat, stirring frequently, until dry and dark in color. Add salt and pepper to taste. Add the Madeira, if desired, and boil down rapidly until completely evaporated.

Allow to cool if not to be used immediately and place in a covered jar. Refrigerate or freeze.

Yield: 1½ cups.

Mustard Greens

Mustard greens are a minor leafy vegetable, popular in the South and also used in a number of Italian and Chinese dishes.

Selection: Look for fresh, crisp, clean mustard greens with tender leaves and good green color. Some varieties are lighter green, others have a slight bronze tinge.

Peak Season: December through April, but available all year. Allow 2 pounds for 4 servings.

Methods of Preparation: Tender young leaves can be used raw in salad, either alone or in combination with other greens. Older leaves must be cooked and can be served as a hot vegetable or puréed.

To Cook: Discard browned or faded leaves, roots, and tough stems. Wash thoroughly in a bowl of water, lifting the greens out of the water and changing the water until no traces of sand remain. Cut large leaves into pieces. Cook in a large pot of boiling salted water, covered, for 10 to 15 minutes, or until tender. Drain well, season with salt, pepper, butter, and a few squirts of lemon juice or vinegar, or cook Southern-style with pork (see Collards, page 347).

357

Okra

Okra is a pod vegetable that is distinctive for the thick, gummy sap that oozes out of the sliced pods as they are cooked, thickening soups and stews. Outside of the United States, it is called gumbo, which is also the name for the Louisiana stew made with okra. Allow 1 pound for 3 or 4 servings.

Selection: Look for young, tender, fresh, clean pods 2 to 4 inches long. Avoid flabby, dull, dry, or discolored pods.

Peak Season: July through October, but available all year, especially in the Southern states.

Methods of Preparation: Okra must always be cooked—steamed, sautéed, boiled, deep-fried. Used in salads, as a thickener in gumbos and Creole stews, cooked by itself or in combination with other vegetables, particularly corn and tomatoes.

To Cook: Wash and trim off the stem ends. Leave small pods whole. Cook covered in an inch of boiling salted water until barely tender, 3 to 5 minutes. Drain at once, season and serve with butter and lemon juice, tomato juice, or buttered bread crumbs. Okra must be timed carefully when cooking; overcooking makes it slippery and dulls its color, but when cooked quickly, the juice will not run out and the pods will have a crisp, crunchy texture. However, long cooking is desirable in a stew or gumbo, where the thickening is an integral part of the preparation.

Okra Appetizer

1 pound small, uniformly sized
  okra with stems
½ cup mayonnaise
½ cup plain yogurt
½ teaspoon Dijon mustard
2 teaspoons chopped onion

Wash the okra, leaving the stems, which will be used as handles. Plunge the okra into boiling salted water and boil for exactly 3 minutes. Time from the moment the water returns to the boil. Drain immediately and chill.

Arrange the okra on individual plates, placing them like the spokes of a wheel. Combine the remaining ingredients and spoon into a lettuce cup or a small individual bowl in the center of each plate. The pods are then dipped into the sauce and eaten out of hand.

Yield: 4 servings.

Variation: Serve the okra warm and in the same manner with either hollandaise sauce or melted butter.

Creole Okra

4 tablespoons butter

2 medium onions, sliced

1 small green pepper, cut into strips

1 pound okra, trimmed and cut into ½-inch-thick slices

4 tomatoes, peeled, seeded, and chopped

1 cup corn kernels

2 teaspoons dried basil

Tabasco sauce

Salt and freshly ground pepper

¼ cup minced fresh parsley

Melt butter in a large skillet and add the onions and green pepper. Cook, stirring frequently, until the onions are limp. Add the okra and tomatoes, cover, and simmer until the tomatoes soften and the okra is tender, about 15 minutes. Stir from time to time. Add the corn, basil, 4 or 5 shakes of Tabasco, salt, and pepper and simmer for another 3 or 4 minutes. Taste and correct the seasonings. Serve hot, sprinkled with minced parsley.

Yield: 6 servings.

Onions

A food writer once observed that onions would be prized above truffles and caviar if they were not so abundant. They are surely one of the most indispensable flavoring vegetables and most cooks would find it a hardship to cook without them.

Selection: Look for onions that are firm and well shaped, with dry, paperlike skins. Avoid onions that are sprouting or have wet, soggy necks. The size of an onion does not affect its quality. Allow 1 pound for 4 servings; 4 to 6 small white onions per serving.

Peak Season: All year.

Methods of Preparation: Raw in salads and sandwiches; cooked in soups, stews, casseroles, quiches, sauces, and more. Onions may be sautéed, baked, boiled, braised, roasted, or deep-fried. Cooking brings out their mellow sweetness and flavor.

There are many varieties of onions, some suited to particular uses: the sweet red Italian onion, wonderful raw in sandwiches and salads but too mild for cooking; the sweet Bermuda or Spanish onions, gentle enough to be eaten raw, but with enough character to be cooked; the small white boilers that can be glazed, creamed, or cooked in a stew; the yellow globe onions, the workhorses of the onion family; and, of course, the babies of the onion family, chives, scallions, and shallots, discussed on page 15 .

Braised Onion Slices

Excellent with roasted meats or poultry.

4 large Bermuda onions
2 tablespoons oil
2 tablespoons butter
Salt and freshly ground pepper
⅓ cup chicken broth
1 teaspoon dried thyme
Paprika

Peel the onions and cut them into 1-inch-thick slices. In a large skillet or sauté pan, heat the oil and butter, add the onion slices, and toss them about for a few minutes in the hot fat. Add the salt, pepper, broth, and thyme and mix well. Cover the pan and reduce the heat to low. Simmer for about 15 minutes, or until the onions are just crisp-tender. Stir from time to time. Sprinkle lightly with paprika and serve hot.

Yield: 5 to 6 servings.

Baked Onions

Every bit of the natural sweetness in onions is enhanced by long, slow baking. They take a long time, but they require no attention.

6 very large yellow or, preferably, Bermuda onions
4 tablespoons butter
Salt
Parsley sprigs

Preheat the oven to 350 degrees.

Line a baking pan with aluminum foil to make the cleaning up easier. Onions exude a syrup that will make them stick to the pan. Leave the skins on the onions but trim off the roots. Arrange the onions standing upright and bake in a preheated oven on the center rack for 2 hours, or until tender. When you can pierce them easily with a sharp-pointed knife, they are done.

Remove from the oven and peel off the skins. Transfer to a heated serving platter. Spread the tops open with the point of a knife and insert a lump of butter in each. Sprinkle lightly with salt and top with a sprig or two of fresh parsley.

Yield: 6 servings.

Stuffed Onions

Stuffed onions are an interesting departure from the usual. Allow 1 large onion per serving. Peel them and boil in salted water for 10 minutes. Drain well and let them cool until you can comfortably handle them. Remove the centers, leaving about ½ inch of shell all around. Be careful not to cut through the bottom so you will have a firm base to hold the filling. Season the inside of the shells with salt and pepper. Chop the onion that was removed from the center and mix with leftover meat or poultry, cooked rice, duxelles (page 357), or whatever else appeals to you. Season the mixture with salt and pepper to taste. Fill the onions with the mixture, sprinkle the tops with bread crumbs and a bit of melted butter, and arrange in a heatproof serving dish. Add stock or tomato juice to the dish to come halfway up the onions. Bake in a 400-degree oven until the tops are browned, 20 to 25 minutes.

Creamed Onions

1 pound small white onions
4 tablespoons butter
1 teaspoon sugar
¼ cup water
1 cup heavy cream
Pinch of ground red pepper, or a few drops of Tabasco sauce
½ teaspoon dried thyme
Salt and freshly ground pepper
½ cup bread crumbs

It is always easier to slip the skins off the small white onions if you blanch them for a few minutes and then peel them. Fill a large saucepan with salted water, bring to a boil, and put in the onions. Cook over a low heat for 7 minutes. Drain and refresh under cold water. Peel the onions and cut a cross in the root end. This will prevent the center from popping out during cooking.

Melt the butter in a large skillet and add the onions. Sprinkle them with the sugar and brown them slowly, turning often. They won't brown evenly so don't try. When they are partly browned and a bit tender, transfer them to a greased shallow baking dish. Add the cold water to the butter-sugar mixture in the skillet and cook until the liquid is syrupy and brown. Stir in 1 cup of heavy cream (or 1 cup medium white sauce, see page 451), the ground red pepper, thyme, salt, and pepper. Pour over the onions. Sprinkle fine bread crumbs over all. Bake in a 350-degree oven for 20 to 25 minutes, or until the onions are tender.

Yield: 4 servings.

Honey-Glazed Onions

1 pound small white onions
4 tablespoons butter
4 tablespoons honey
Salt
2 tablespoons chopped fresh parsley

Blanch onions for 5 minutes in rapidly boiling water. Drain and refresh under cold water. Peel. Make a cross gash at the root end. Melt the butter in a large skillet and add the honey. Stir until the mixture is blended. Add the onions and cook slowly, turning them often, until they are tender and glazed, 30 to 40 minutes. Sprinkle lightly with salt and minced parsley.

Yield: 4 servings.

Parsnips

The parsnip looks a bit like a dingy white carrot, but it is a delicious and satisfying vegetable that deserves more usage than it gets. The flavor of parsnips improves after a frost, which changes the starch in the root into sugar, giving it a sweeter taste. Allow 1 pound for 2 or 3 servings; 2 pounds for puréed parsnips to serve three or four.

Selection: Look for small to medium-size parsnips, firm, well shaped, and smooth.

Peak Season: September through May, but available all year.

Methods of Preparation: Raw in salads; used sparingly, in soups and stews; as a vegetable, they can be braised, boiled, steamed, deep-fried in thin slices in batter, creamed, or puréed with potatoes.

To Cook: Parsnips may be skinned either before or after boiling. Peeling them after they are cooked keeps them from discoloring. Slice them lengthwise to remove the woody core. Parsnips may be cooked whole, or in slices, strips, or dice. Cook whole parsnips in boiling salted water for 20 to 40 minutes, depending on the age and quality. Cut-up parsnips will take much less time. They may also be baked, covered, in a 350-degree oven for 20 to 30 minutes, depending on size. They should not be overcooked; when crisp-tender, they have a sweet, nutty flavor.

Puréed Parsnips

This is one of the nicest ways to serve parsnips and it is a delicious accompaniment to poultry, game, or a roast.

3 pounds parsnips
3 tablespoons butter
⅓ cup heavy cream
Salt and freshly ground pepper
Buttered bread crumbs (optional)

Put the parsnips in enough boiling salted water to cover and simmer, covered, for 20 to 40 minutes, or until tender. Do not overcook. Drain the parsnips and plunge them into cold water. Drain and peel. Purée the parsnips in a food mill or food processor. Return to the saucepan and beat in the butter, cream, salt, and pepper. This may be kept hot in the top of a double boiler, or put into a greased 1-quart baking dish, sprinkled with buttered bread crumbs, and baked in a 350-degree oven for 20 to 25 minutes, or until heated through.

Yield: 5 or 6 servings.

Peas

About 95 percent of the national pea crop ends up in cans, boxes, or plastic bags, and one must search diligently for the fresh green pods bulging with their tender sweet pellets.

Selection: Look for fairly large, bright green pods that are well filled. Don't guess at their contents; open a pod and taste the pea. It should be plump, sweet, tender, and a fresh, bright green. Allow ¾ to 1 pound of peas in the shell per serving; 1 pound of peas in the shell yields approximately 1 cup of shelled peas.

Peak Season: March through November, but may be available at other times.

Methods of Preparation: If small and tender, use raw in salads. Boiled or braised, served as a vegetable or in casseroles, stews, soups, and in combination with other vegetables.

To Cook: Shell peas just before using. Cook in a covered pan with as little water as possible and for as short a time as possible, until just tender. Do not salt until *after* they are cooked; salt will toughen them. Young peas may take 5 or 6 minutes; older ones perhaps double that time. Taste one to check for doneness. Dress with melted butter and a light sprinkling of salt and pepper.

The French method of cooking peas is actually a form of braising. Line a heavy skillet with wet lettuce leaves, pour in the shelled peas, and cover with more wet lettuce. Cover the skillet and cook over medium heat 20 to 35 minutes, or until the peas are tender. Serve with or without the lettuce.

For purées and soups, boil peas until very soft. Add some heavy cream and butter to the peas and purée through a food mill or in a food processor.

If you are using frozen peas—the tiny ones are the best—ignore the package directions. Just heat them through with boiling water for a minute or two and drain.

Snow Peas

Time was when these crunchy things were the sole property of first-class Chinese restaurants, but now they are generally available, for which we give thanks. Known also as Chinese peas, *mangetout* (eat all), sugar peas, and Chinese pea pods, these firm, crisp, flattened pods that taper at both ends need only the briefest immersion in boiling water and the simplest dressing of butter, salt, and pepper to provide a delicious taste treat. Allow 1 pound for 4 servings. Snip off the tips before cooking and remove strings if present. They may also be stir-fried for 2 minutes, just until they turn bright green. They are lovely cut into julienne strips and combined with other julienne vegetables or mixed with mushrooms sautéed in butter. This last is a most pleasing combination of contrasting tastes, colors, and textures.

Sugar Snap Peas

A new entry into the vegetable world, this was awarded the All America Gold Medal in 1979, a most unusual honor for a vegetable. This plump little green vegetable represents the best aspects of regular peas and snow peas with its crisp edible pod nestling tender peas. Snip off the tips, remove the strings, and cook the sugar snaps just as you do snow peas—a minute in boiling water. Drain and dress with butter, salt, and pepper. They are also good raw. Allow 1 pound for 4 servings.

Peppers

Peppers, also known as sweet peppers, bell peppers, and globe peppers, are green when mature but they turn red as they continue to ripen. Less commonly seen are the yellow variety.

Selection: Look for firm, well-shaped, thick-fleshed peppers with glossy red or green color, without soft spots or wrinkled skin. Allow 1 per serving.

Peak Season: May through October. Green peppers are available all year, the red ones seasonally.

Methods of Preparation: Raw in salads or cut into strips and served with a dip; pickled; or a flavoring ingredient in casseroles, stews, soups. To cook, sauté, stir-fry, bake, broil, or stuff.

Varieties: Small, thin, light green Italian peppers are mild in flavor, good for flavoring or for sautéeing.

Pimiento is a sweet pepper available skinned and processed and only in jars. Colorful and mild, it is used primarily as a garnish to add color contrast to a dish.

Hot chili peppers vary in strength. Unless you want an incendiary dish, be sure to remove all the tiny seeds, which are the hottest part. The juice from chilies is highly irritating to the skin and eyes. Wear rubber gloves and wash them well before removing them.

Tabasco sauce is made from salted and pickled Tabasco chilies. It may be used in place of ground red pepper (Cayenne).

To Cook: Wash peppers thoroughly and slice off the stem end. Remove the pith, seeds, and membranes, leaving only the shells. Rinse to get rid of any remaining seeds, which can be bitter. Peppers can be used whole, cut into quarters, sliced, chopped, cut into julienne strips, or in rounds. They make natural containers for stuffing.

To sauté, cut green and red peppers into ¼-inch strips. Heat 2 tablespoons of butter and 2 tablespoons of oil and add a crushed clove of garlic and a thinly sliced onion. Cook until limp. Add the julienne strips and toss and cook until they are crisp-tender, 5 or 6 minutes. Serve hot or at room temperature as a vegetable.

Veal-Stuffed Peppers

6 large bell peppers, tops and seeds removed

3 tablespoons olive or vegetable oil

1 large onion, finely chopped

1 clove garlic, finely chopped

3 tablespoons pine nuts

1½ pounds ground veal

2 cups cooked white or brown rice, cooled

Blanch peppers in a large amount of boiling water for 3 minutes. Turn them in the water so they cook evenly. Remove and drain the peppers.

Heat the oil in a large, heavy skillet. Add the onion, garlic, and pine nuts and cook, stirring, until the onion is soft and pine nuts are golden.

Add the veal and break up the lumps with a spoon. Cook until the veal loses its raw color. Scrape the mixture into a large mixing bowl and add the rice, half the cheese, the chopped

¼ pound Monterey Jack or Cheddar cheese, grated

¼ cup finely chopped fresh parsley

1 teaspoon dried oregano or marjoram

2 eggs

Salt and freshly ground pepper

1 cup beef broth

2 cups tomato purée

2 sprigs parsley

1 bay leaf

parsley, oregano, eggs, salt, and pepper. Mix well with your hands or a fork. Taste a bit of the mixture and adjust the seasonings if necessary.

Preheat the oven to 375 degrees.

Select a baking dish just large enough to hold the peppers snugly. Stuff the peppers and place them in the baking dish.

In a saucepan, combine the broth, tomato purée, parsley sprigs, and bay leaf and bring to a boil. Pour the sauce around the peppers. Cover with foil and bake for 30 to 45 minutes. Remove the foil, sprinkle the remaining cheese on top of the peppers, and serve hot or at room temperature.

Yield: 4 to 6 servings.

Variation: For a nonmeat dish, stuff the peppers with a mixture of 3 cups fresh bread crumbs, 8 anchovy fillets, rinsed and chopped, ½ cup chopped black olives, ½ cup chopped water chestnuts, 2 tablespoons drained chopped capers, and 2 tablespoons minced parsley. Top each pepper with a small piece of butter and bake as above.

Stewed Peppers

4 tablespoons olive oil

1 large onion, sliced

4 large peppers, trimmed and cut into 1-inch strips

2 pounds fresh plum tomatoes, peeled and chopped

1 garlic clove, finely minced

½ cup chopped fresh Italian parsley

¼ cup coarsely chopped pitted black olives

½ cup fresh basil leaves, minced, or 1 tablespoon dried

Tabasco sauce

Salt and freshly ground pepper

In a large saucepan, heat the oil and add the onion and peppers. Cook for 3 minutes, stirring constantly. Add the tomatoes, garlic, parsley, olives, basil, and a few shakes of Tabasco. Cover and simmer over low heat until tender, 12 to 15 minutes. Add salt and pepper to taste. Serve warm or at room temperature.

Yield: 6 servings.

Potatoes

Potatoes are the world's most important vegetable, and one of the most maligned by dieters. A medium-size baked potato contains about 90 calories—the same as an apple or an orange—and if you don't heap it with butter or sour cream you will get 90 calories of good nutrition. Try it with a favorite herb, some freshly ground black pepper, or a spot of plain yogurt if you are concerned about your weight.

Selection: Look for firm potatoes that are well shaped, relatively smooth, without bruises, sprouting eyes, or large areas of green-tinged skin. Allow 1 baking potato, or 2 to 4 new potatoes, depending on size, per serving.

Peak Season: Available all year. Peak season for new potatoes is March to August.

Methods of Preparation: Always cooked, potatoes may be baked, boiled, sautéed, roasted, deep-fried, steamed, creamed, used in soups, stews, puddings, and pancakes; cold in salads and soups. If potatoes are not cooked immediately after peeling, keep them in cold water to prevent darkening.

"Greening" on Potatoes: The greening on a potato is caused by exposure to light. The green areas contain solanin, a glycol alkaloid, which, if eaten in very large quantities, can cause illness. However, it does not affect the rest of the potato, and the potato may be eaten with complete safety if the green is cut away. Store potatoes in a cool, dark area, not the refrigerator. Extreme cold converts the potato starch to sugar, which does not improve flavor.

Varieties: Potatoes differ in every region of the country. Get to know those in your area, and which variety is best suited to a particular purpose. It is the starch content that determines the cooking quality of the potato, and this varies. Those highest in starch, such as the russet Burbank, known as the Idaho, are mealy and best for baking, mashing, and for French fries. Red or brown "new" potatoes, so-called because they have not been kept in storage, have a waxy quality; they keep their shape and will not soak up dressing, which makes them ideal for salads and creaming, and for boiling and steaming whole. Mature potatoes of many varieties are the all-purpose potato; they may be boiled, scalloped, mashed, fried and even baked.

Baked Potatoes

The mealy Idaho is the number one choice for baking. Baking the potatoes in a hot oven allows the starch granules to expand, making the inside of the potato fluffy and the skin crisp.

Preheat the oven to 425 degrees.

Scrub the potato with a stiff vegetable brush and prick the potato in a few places with a fork. This provides an escape hatch for the steam that develops and prevents the skin from bursting. If you want the skin soft, rub it with oil or butter. An aluminum or stainless steel baking nail speeds up the baking time a little, acting as a heat conductor, like the bone in a roast.

Place the potatoes on the center rack of the preheated oven and bake for 45 minutes to 1¼ hours, depending on the size of the potatoes. To test, protect your hand with a potholder and gently squeeze the potato. If it gives a little and feels soft, it is done. Remove from the oven and, with a sharp-pointed knife, make a slit across the top. Protecting your hands, squeeze the ends of the potato to release the steam, which will keep the potato mealy. Never bake potatoes wrapped in little foil packages; you will have steamed potatoes lacking in the dry, mealy texture that makes baked potatoes so distinctive. If you wish to bake potatoes in an oven set at 350 degrees, in which other foods are roasting, increase the baking time.

Top the baked potato with salt, pepper, and a lump of butter, or a dollop of sour cream or plain yogurt and some chopped chives.

Stuffed Baked Potatoes. If the potatoes are very large, split them in half lengthwise after they are baked. If the potato is for an individual portion, cut a large oval opening the length of the potato. Scoop out the cooked pulp, leaving the shell intact. Mash with salt, pepper, butter, warmed milk or cream (about 2 teaspoons per potato), and beat until light and fluffy. You can add a little grated Cheddar cheese and some chopped chives, if you like. Refill the shells, sprinkle the top with some grated Parmesan cheese, and dot with butter. These may be done early in the day. Reheat the potatoes at serving time in a 375-degree oven for 15 to 20 minutes, until heated through and the tops nicely browned.

Boiled Potatoes

The loss of Vitamic C is least when the potatoes are boiled in their skins in as little water as possible for as short a time as possible. A good deal of the nutritive value of the potato is found in and under the skin.

Put the potatoes in a pot of boiling, salted water, cover the pot, and cook until the potatoes are tender when pricked with a fork. They will take from 20 to 45 minutes, depending on size. When done, drain. Return to the pot and shake over low heat until dry.

Peel the potatoes while they are still warm; the skin comes off more easily than when cold.

New Potatoes

Small new potatoes, like small children, are at their best when dressed simply.

Scrub the potatoes well, leaving the skins on. Peel a thin strip from around the center to keep them from bursting. Boil, or better still, steam. Depending on their size, they will take from 15 to 20 minutes. Watch them carefully and don't overcook. To test, pierce them with a sharp-pointed knife. They should be a bit underdone. When tender, drain them and return to the pan. Shake the pan over low heat until the potatoes are dry. Add a few tablespoons of butter and chopped parsley and shake the pan to coat the potatoes. Season to taste with salt and pepper. Serve hot.

Mashed Potatoes

Mashed potatoes can be wonderful or undistinguished, depending on the tender loving care they have received. The potatoes must not be overcooked, or they will be watery and not have good flavor.

Peel 1 pound of potatoes and cut into halves or quarters. Half an onion in the cooking water will add a little flavor. Cook in boiling, salted water for 25 to 30 minutes, or until the potatoes are tender. They should just break under the pressure of a fork but not be mushy. Drain, return to the pot, and shake the pan over low heat until the potatoes are dry. Press the potatoes through a sieve or a food mill, return them to the pan, and beat with a wooden spoon or spatula until smooth. Add salt, pepper, and 2 tablespoons of butter, then add from ½ to 1 cup warm milk, little by little. Potatoes vary in consistency and in their ability to absorb fats and liquids. Thus it is impossible to establish a firm rule for how much must be added. Start with smaller quantities and add gradually. It is essential that the liquid be hot if the potatoes are to be fluffy. Mix over low heat, adding the liquid a little at a time, until you reach the desired consistency. It is best if served at once, but if it must be held, transfer to a buttered baking dish, dot with additional butter, and keep warm in a 250-degree oven. Serve as soon as possible.

Yield: 3 to 4 servings.

Pan-Roasted Potatoes

To pan-roast potatoes along with meat, use peeled large potatoes or new potatoes. Parboil them for about 10 minutes, until barely tender, and drain well. About an hour before the roast is done, add the potatoes to the baking pan and turn them in the drippings from the meat. Turn them a few times during cooking so that they will roast evenly. Baste frequently with the pan drippings to keep them moist and juicy.

Pan-Crisped Potatoes

These are crunchy and crusty outside and mealy inside.

Cut 5 or 6 boiled and peeled potatoes lengthwise into eighths. Film the bottom of a large, heavy skillet with ⅛ inch of oil and heat. Add the potato pieces and sprinkle with salt, pepper, and paprika. Cook over medium heat for 15 or 20 minutes, shaking the pan frequently and turning the potatoes with a spatula so that they get brown and crusty all around. Serve hot.

Yield: 4 to 6 servings.

Country-Style Fried Potatoes

Roughly cut 4 or 5 boiled and peeled potatoes into 1-inch cubes. Film a large, heavy skillet with ⅛ inch of vegetable oil and cook 2 large chopped onions until golden. Add the potato cubes, sprinkle with salt, pepper, and paprika, and toss until golden, 10 or 15 minutes. Add more oil if needed. Sprinkle with chopped fresh parsley.

Yield: 3 to 4 servings.

French-Fried Potatoes

Peel the potatoes and cut them into long strips less than ½ inch wide and thick. They are best peeled and cut just before you use them, but if this is not possible, put them in a bowl of cold water and take them out just before frying time. Pat them dry with paper towels and be sure that they are thoroughly dry before going into the hot oil or they will spatter.

Heat the oil in a deep fryer. You need several inches of fat—enough to completely submerge the potatoes. Heat the fat to 325 degrees. Use a frying basket if you have one; otherwise, use a slotted spoon to remove the potatoes. Add a handful of potatoes and cook for about 6 minutes, until soft but not very brown. Move the pieces about as they cook so that they do not stick together. Remove the potatoes from the fat as they are cooked and drain them on paper towels. Continue until all are done.

They may remain at room temperature for an hour or so, until the final frying. When ready to serve, reheat the fat to 375 degrees. Return the fried potatoes in batches and cook 2 to 3 minutes, or until crisp and golden brown. Remove from the fat and drain well on paper towels to remove the excess fat. Season with salt and serve immediately. Do not cover French-fried potatoes after they are cooked or they will get soggy.

Scalloped Potatoes

5 medium potatoes, peeled and
 thinly sliced
Salt and freshly ground pepper
Grating of fresh nutmeg
2 tablespoons flour
1 medium onion, thinly sliced
4 tablespoons butter
1½ cups hot milk (approximately)

Preheat the oven to 350 degrees. Grease a 1½-quart baking dish. Spread a layer of potatoes over the bottom of the dish. In a cup, combine salt, pepper, nutmeg, and flour. Sprinkle the potato layer with the flour mixture, add a few slices of onion and dot with butter. Repeat with layers of potatoes and seasoned flour until all are used. Pour hot milk almost to the top layer. Dot the top with butter. Bake, covered, for 30 minutes. Uncover and bake for 30 minutes longer, or until potatoes are fork-tender.

Yield: 4 servings.

Potatoes O'Brien

6 medium potatoes, cut into ½-
inch cubes
2 tablespoons butter
2 tablespoons oil
1 small onion, chopped
3 tablespoons diced green pepper
3 tablespoons diced pimiento
Salt and freshly ground pepper

Cook the potato cubes, covered, in boiling salted water until barely tender, about 10 minutes. Drain well. Heat the butter and oil in a large skillet and add the onion and green pepper. Sauté until soft but not brown, about 5 minutes.

Add the pimiento and diced potatoes, sprinkle with salt and pepper, and sauté until potatoes are browned, stirring from time to time.

Yield: 4 to 6 servings.

Delmonico Potatoes

Creamed potatoes with a cheese topping.

6 medium potatoes, cut into ½-
inch cubes
2 tablespoons butter
2 tablespoons flour
1½ cups milk
Salt and freshly ground pepper
½ cup grated sharp Cheddar
cheese
1 cup buttered bread crumbs
(see page 27)

Cook the potato cubes, covered, in boiling salted water until barely tender, about 10 minutes. Drain well. Heat the butter in a heavy skillet over low heat. Whisk in the flour and cook, stirring, for 3 minutes. Add the milk and stir vigorously over medium-high heat until the sauce comes to a boil. Season with salt and pepper. Reduce the heat and add the potatoes, tossing them well in the sauce. Transfer the creamed potatoes to a buttered shallow baking dish, 9 by 13 inches. Sprinkle with cheese and buttered bread crumbs. Bake in a 400-degree oven until heated through, 10 to 15 minutes.

Yield: 4 to 6 servings.

Pumpkin

Pumpkin is a member of the large family that includes squashes. Since it has become a symbol of Halloween and Thanksgiving-dinner desserts, the pumpkin is too often overlooked as a fine vegetable.

Selection: Look for bright-colored, firm, unblemished pumpkins. The shape is unimportant unless you are planning to make a jack-o'-lantern. For cooking, the smaller ones have less waste and are usually more tender. Allow 3 pounds of fresh pumpkin, which will yield about 3 cups of cooked and mashed pumpkin, for 3 or 4 servings.

Peak Season: Fall, but available throughout the year in different parts of the country.

Methods of Preparation: May be prepared in any fashion in which you cook winter squash—boiled, baked, steamed—and in breads, pies, and soups. Canned pumpkin may be substituted in any recipe calling for mashed or puréed pumpkin.

To boil, halve or quarter the pumpkin and

remove the seeds and center fibers. Cut into chunks and cook, covered, in a small amount of boiling, salted water for 25 to 40 minutes, or until the pulp is soft. Pumpkin is a watery vegetable and does not require a large amount of water. Drain after cooking and scrape the pulp away from the skin. Mash well, then place in a strainer and allow to drain for 30 minutes to get rid of the excess liquid. Use the purée for soups, breads, or desserts. To serve as a vegetable, add a lump of butter and season with salt, pepper, and a few gratings of fresh nutmeg, or a pinch of powdered ginger.

To bake, cut the pumpkin into portion-size wedges and remove seeds and center fibers. Place cut side down in a baking pan, add an inch of water, and bake in a 350-degree oven for 30 to 45 minutes, or until the pulp is soft. Turn right side up and season the cavity with salt, pepper, and a little scraped onion, if you like, or a sprinkling of sesame seeds, or brown sugar, maple syrup, or molasses and butter. Bake 5 to 10 minutes longer.

Pumpkin in Cream Sauce

1½ pounds pumpkin
2 tablespoons butter
1 onion, finely chopped
2 tablespoons flour
1 cup chicken broth
Salt and freshly ground pepper
1 tablespoon finely chopped fresh dill, *or* 1 teaspoon dried
2 teaspoons lemon juice
½ cup cream

Peel pumpkin and cut into julienne strips 2 to 2½ inches long. You should have about 3 cups.

Melt the butter in a 2-quart saucepan and cook the onion until lightly browned, stirring often. Stir in the flour and cook for 2 minutes, continuing to stir. Whisk in the chicken broth and stir over medium-high heat until the mixture is thickened and smooth. Add the pumpkin, salt, pepper, and dill. Reduce the heat to very low, cover the pan, and simmer slowly for 20 to 30 minutes, or until the pumpkin is tender. Add the lemon juice and cream and heat through, but do not boil.

Yield: 3 to 4 servings.

Variation: Cook julienne pumpkin strips in a tomato sauce flavored with basil.

Rutabagas

The rutabaga is a root vegetable that is often called yellow turnip, although it is believed to be a hybrid of turnip and cabbage. It is also called Swedish turnip or Swede. Rutabagas look like elongated globes, more yellow and firmer fleshed than turnips and with a strong flavor.

Selection: Look for firm, solid rutabagas, smooth-skinned and heavy for their size. Size does not affect quality. Allow ½ pound per serving.

Peak Season: October through February, but available all year.

Methods of Preparation: Rutabagas must be peeled before cooking. Raw, in slices or sticks; creamed, puréed, as fritters or pancakes, in stews and casserole dishes, soup, glazed, or baked.

To Cook: Peel the rutabagas and cut into chunks, dice, julienne strips, or slices. Drop them into a large quantity of boiling salted water until tender, 5 to 15 minutes, depending on size. Do not overcook. Drain, toss with butter, and season with salt and pepper and a dash of lemon juice. You can add ½ teaspoon of sugar to the cooking water if you like, which some people feel improves the flavor.

Purée of Rutabagas. Drain the cooked rutabagas and mash them with a ricer, or purée them in a food processor. Return to the saucepan and stir in a few tablespoons of butter. Season with salt, pepper, and a pinch of mace. Beat vigorously, as you do for mashed potatoes, and beat in a little cream.

Rutabaga and Onion Casserole

2 pounds rutabagas
4 cups thinly sliced onion
Salt and freshly ground pepper
½ cup chicken broth, heated
2 tablespoons butter

Preheat the oven to 350 degrees. Peel the rutabagas, cut them in half lengthwise and then into thin crosswise slices. Grease a 2½-quart casserole. Arrange layers of rutabagas and onions and sprinkle lightly with salt and pepper. Pour hot broth over the vegetables. Dot with butter. Cover the casserole tightly with aluminum foil and bake for 2 hours, or until the rutabagas are tender.

Yield: 4 to 6 servings.

Salsify (Oyster Plant)

A bland, pleasant root vegetable that was given the name of oyster plant because its flavor is reputed to resemble that of an oyster, although the similarity eludes many people, including this writer. Salsify looks somewhat like parsnip and, like parsnip, its flavor improves if harvested after the first heavy frost.

Selection: Look for well-formed, firm clean roots with either black or white skin. Allow 1 pound for 2 or 3 servings.

Peak Season: October and November.

Methods of Preparation: Cooked and sliced, diced, cut into julienne strips and tossed with butter or a delicate cream or hollandaise sauce, or served cold, marinated in a vinaigrette.

To Cook: Like celeriac and artichokes, salsify discolors on exposure to air. Before preparing it, have ready a bowl of water to which lemon juice has been added, in which to keep the

pieces until they are ready to be cooked. Trim and scrape the roots; cut them into julienne strips or ½-inch-thick slices about 2 inches long. Cook in a large pot of boiling salted water to which you have added some lemon juice or vinegar. Cover the pot and simmer for 5 to 10 minutes, or until tender, depending on the size of the pieces. Do not overcook. Drain well, season with salt, pepper, and lemon juice and toss in melted butter. Sprinkle with parsley.

Creamed Salsify. Cook 2 pounds of trimmed and scraped salsify until tender. Cut into thin slices. Prepare 1½ cups medium white sauce (see page 451). Alternate layers of salsify with cream sauce in a 1½-quart greased baking dish until all are used. Top with a layer of buttered bread crumbs. Bake in a 350-degree oven until heated through and bubbling, 20 to 25 minutes. Serves 6.

Sorrel (Sourgrass)

An arrow-shaped green leaf with a sour, pungent, refreshing sharpness. Usually sold in bunches.

Selection: Look for young, fresh-looking, unblemished green leaves. Allow 2 to 3 pounds of sorrel for 4 people.

Peak Season: Spring and summer, but available in limited quantities all year.

Methods of Preparation: Raw, in salads; cooked, in soups or as a vegetable, like any other flavorful green.

To Cook: Trim the sorrel and discard wilted leaves and coarse stems. Wash well in several changes of water. Cook in the moisture that adheres to the leaves after washing. Cook, uncovered, over low heat about 10 minutes, until wilted, stirring a few times. Drain well, chop the leaves, and season with salt, pepper, butter, and a few tablespoons of cream. Heat through but do not allow to boil. Serve hot.

Spinach

It is too bad that the public was ever urged to eat spinach because it was "good" for them. If it had no merits other than its delicious flavor, appetite-provoking color, and versatility, it would still be a wonderful vegetable.

Selection: Look for fresh, crisp, flat or crinkled dark green leaves. Prepackaged spinach in plastic bags varies in quality and must take second place to loose spinach. Frozen spinach works very well in many recipes and is a great convenience for cooks in a hurry (or for lazy cooks). Allow 1 pound fresh spinach for 2 servings.

Peak Season: Early spring but available all year.

Methods of Preparation: Young, tender leaves may be used raw in salads; cooked as a vegetable, it may be sautéed, steamed, chopped, or puréed. Used in soup, quiches, soufflés; often served as a base for eggs, chicken, fish, or meat with a hollandaise, cream, or cheese sauce, browned under the broiler. Foods prepared this way are called *Florentine*.

To Cook: Since spinach grows close to the ground, it must be washed carefully to remove grit and sand. Trim off the roots and heavier stems and swish the leaves around in a sinkful of lukewarm water to which a little salt has been added; this will remove dirt more effectively than cold water. Lift the spinach leaves out of the water and repeat in a cold water bath until no signs of sand remain. Cook spinach, covered, for 3 to 5 minutes in the water that remains on the leaves after washing, until the leaves are wilted. Drain in a strainer, pressing out the moisture with a spoon, or squeeze dry with your hands. Leave whole or chop, season with salt and pepper and a few drops of lemon juice or a few gratings of fresh nutmeg, and butter or oil.

Puréed Spinach. Cook and drain spinach as above. Purée in a blender or processor. Reheat with butter, salt, and pepper.

Creamed Spinach. For 4 people, cook 3 pounds of spinach as above. Drain well and chop fine. In a large saucepan, melt a tablespoon or two of butter. Add 2 teaspoons of flour and cook for 3 minutes, stirring, until it becomes bubbly and golden. Add spinach, mix well, and cook for a minute. Season with salt, a few grinds of pepper, freshly grated nutmeg, and ½ cup hot milk or cream. Mix well, bring to a boil, reduce heat, and cook a minute or two longer.

Stir-Fried Spinach

This is one of the simplest and nicest ways to prepare spinach.

2 pounds fresh, young spinach
3 tablespoons vegetable oil
1 large garlic clove, finely minced
Salt and freshly ground pepper

Remove the coarse stems, leaving the spinach leaves whole, and wash the leaves in several changes of water until all sand is removed. Steam, covered, in a large pot in the water remaining on the leaves, until just wilted. Place in a large colander and let them drain. This can be done in advance of the cooking, which will then take just a few minutes.

When ready to serve, heat the vegetable oil and garlic in a large skillet. Add the drained spinach and stir and cook until heated through and the leaves are glossy with the oil. Season lightly with salt and pepper and serve at once.

Note: Spinach prepared in this manner may be used as a bed for steamed or poached fish.

Yield: 4 servings.

Baked Spinach and Cheese

2 pounds spinach, *or* 2 10-ounce packages frozen, chopped spinach
1 tablespoon butter
1 medium onion, finely chopped
3 eggs, well beaten
¾ cup milk
¾ cup sharp Cheddar cheese, shredded
Salt and freshly ground pepper
2 tablespoons melted butter
¾ cup bread crumbs

Cook the spinach and drain it well, squeezing out every bit of moisture. If using fresh spinach, chop it. Preheat the oven to 350 degrees.

In a small pan, melt the butter and cook the onion until limp and golden, but not brown. Mix together in a bowl the beaten eggs, milk, ½ cup of the shredded cheese, and salt and pepper to taste. Add the onion and drained spinach and mix well. Transfer to a well-greased 8 by 8 by 2-inch baking pan. Place in the oven and bake for 25 minutes. Combine the remaining ¼ cup of cheese, the melted butter, and bread crumbs and sprinkle over the spinach. Continue to bake for 10 or 15 minutes longer, or until a knife inserted near but not in the center comes out clean. Remove from the oven and let stand for 5 minutes before serving. Cut into oblongs to serve.

Yield: 6 servings.

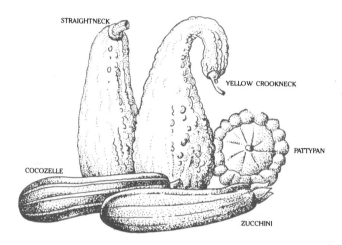

STRAIGHTNECK

YELLOW CROOKNECK

PATTYPAN

COCOZELLE

ZUCCHINI

Harvested before they mature, summer squashes have thin, delicate skins and seeds that are still small and tender. They do not keep well and should be bought, cooked, and eaten soon after they are picked. They need no peeling and may be eaten raw or cooked.

Squash

The squash family is a large one that, for purposes of classification, is divided into summer and winter categories. This is not quite accurate because summer squashes are to be found all winter and winter squashes abound when the weather is balmy. The main difference between the two is that summer squashes have soft skins and tender, edible seeds; they are picked and eaten while still immature, before the seeds and rinds harden. The winter types are all hard-shelled with fully formed seeds and lend themselves to long storage.

Summer Squash

The popular varieties of summer squash are yellow crookneck or yellow straightneck; cocozelle (similar to zucchini) and zucchini; and pattypan, also known as cymling, or scallop.

Selection: Look for firm, young, fresh squashes, fairly heavy for their size and without blemishes. Allow 1 pound for 3 servings.

Peak Season: May to August, but available all year.

Methods of Preparation: Raw as an hors d'oeuvre or in salads; cooked in soups, stews, combined with other vegetables, stuffed.

To Cook: Summer squashes are never peeled but they should be scrubbed well. Cut slices from the stem and blossom ends. Cut into cubes, slices, chunks, or julienne strips, according to recipe directions. To boil, simmer in a covered pan, using a small amount of boiling, salted water, for 4 to 5 minutes, until just tender.

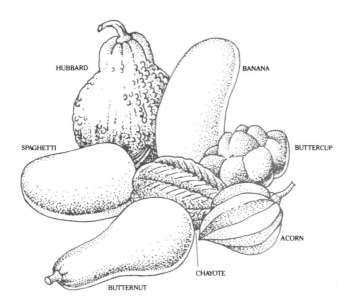

HUBBARD

BANANA

SPAGHETTI

BUTTERCUP

ACORN

CHAYOTE

BUTTERNUT

The winter squashes have tough rinds and seeds, since they have been allowed to mature before they are picked. They can be kept for longer than summer varieties, and many, if kept in a cool, dry place and given sufficient ventilation, may be stored all winter. Chayote, a tropical squash sometimes covered with prickly spines, contains a single seed that is often edible.

Drain. Toss with butter and season with salt and pepper.

To sauté, heat 3 or 4 tablespoons of butter in a skillet, add the cut-up squash and cook over low heat, tossing often, until squash is crisp-tender, 8 to 10 minutes. Season with salt and pepper and sprinkle with chopped basil, parsley, chives, or summer savory. Zucchini and yellow summer squash are a pleasant combination cooked and served together.

Winter Squash
The most common varieties of winter squashes are the ribbed acorn; the pale butternut; the green and gold banana; the green and blue Hubbard; and the buttercup, or turban. Spaghetti squash is an interesting new arrival in the family. Chayote (also known as christophene or chocho in the West Indies) is

tropical, not native to the United States. It is not strictly a winter *or* summer squash, but like winter squash, it may be stored for some time.

Selection: Look for hard, clean squash, heavy for its size, without soft or decaying spots.

Peak Season: October to January; acorn and butternut squashes are available throughout the year.

Methods of Preparation: Always cooked, they can be steamed, boiled, baked, puréed, used in soups, pies, and croquettes.

To Cook: Wash, cut in half lengthwise, and remove seeds. Cook in a covered saucepan in enough boiling water to cover for about 30 minutes, or until tender. Drain well. Scrape pulp from rind, and mash. Add butter and season with salt and pepper. Two pounds of squash yields about 4 cups of cooked squash.

Baked Acorn Squash

2 acorn squash
2 tablespoons butter
4 tablespoons brown sugar

Wash the squash, cut in half lengthwise, and remove seeds and stringy pulp. Place the squash cut side down in a shallow baking dish with ½ inch of hot water on the bottom of the dish. Bake in a 375-degree oven for 30 minutes. Take a look from time to time to make sure that the water has not evaporated; add a bit more if necessary. Remove the pan from the oven, pour out any water remaining in the pan, and turn the squash cut side up. Brush the cavities with butter and sprinkle with brown sugar and return to the oven for another 20 to 30 minutes. or until the squash are soft and tender.

Yield: 4 servings.

Variations: Sprinkle the cavities with salt and pepper, brush with butter, and sprinkle with browned sesame seeds or toasted slivered Brazil nuts; or fill with cooked green peas.

Baked Butternut Squash

2 small butternut squash
Butter
Sugar
Salt and freshly ground pepper
Cinnamon or powdered ginger

Wash two small butternut squash. Split them in half lengthwise and remove the seeds and stringy pulp. Coat the surfaces of the squash thickly with butter and sprinkle with sugar, salt, pepper, and cinnamon or powdered ginger. Arrange squash cut side up in a shallow baking dish in 1 inch of water. Bake in a 350-degree oven for about 1 hour, or until the squash are very tender. Serve in the shell.

Baked Squash Creole

2 pounds butternut or Hubbard
   squash
2 tablespoons butter
1 medium onion, finely chopped
1 clove garlic, finely minced
½ green pepper, chopped
2 tablespoons flour
1 1-pound can tomatoes
Pinch of sugar
½ teaspoon each dried basil,
   thyme, and marjoram
Salt and freshly ground pepper

Peel the squash and cut it in half. Remove the seeds and stringy portion. Cut into ¾-inch-thick slices and set aside.

In a good-sized skillet, melt the butter and add the onion, garlic, and green pepper. Cook over moderate heat until tender, stirring frequently. Stir in the flour and mix well. Break up the tomatoes if they are whole and add. Cook, stirring constantly, until thickened. Add the sugar, herbs, salt, and pepper. Add the squash slices and mix well. Taste and correct the seasonings. Transfer to a well-greased 1½-quart casserole. Cover and bake in a 375-degree oven for 55 minutes, or until tender.

Yield: 4 to 6 servings.

Spaghetti Squash

A golden yellow football-shaped squash with pulp that turns into spaghetti-like strands after it is cooked. The rind is very hard and the directions that tell you to cut it in wedges must have been designed for cooks with hacksaws and the strength of an Olympic discus-thrower.

If the squash is not too large, it may be boiled in a large pot of water. A medium-size squash, about 2½ pounds, will take about 35 minutes. Pierce the skin with the tines of a fork in several places. Put it in a large kettle, cover it with water, and bring to a boil. Cover the pot, reduce the heat, and simmer. If the squash is too large for one of your pots, you can bake it in a 350-degree oven for 1 hour.

When cool enough to handle, cut the squash in half lengthwise. With a large metal spoon, scrape out the seeds and stringy centers. Scoop and scrape out the remainder of the pulp, right down to the shell.

Transfer the spaghetti strands to a saucepan. Toss with a generous chunk of butter, salt, pepper, Parmesan cheese, or with a tomato sauce or pesto that you would use on spaghetti.

The shell makes an interesting and attention-getting container for the spaghetti squash for a buffet. Cut the top third off the cooked squash, leaving the deeper part for the shell. Scoop out the spaghetti squash strands and mix with a cup or more of grated Cheddar cheese, a cup or more of grated zucchini, tomato sauce, salt, pepper, fresh or dried basil, and chopped fresh parsley. Toss well and spoon back into the shell. Sprinkle generously with freshly grated Parmesan cheese and bake at 350 degrees for 20 minutes, or until heated through.

It might be noted that spaghetti squash has somewhat the texture of firm cooked spaghetti, but an 8-ounce serving contains only 66 calories, whereas the same amount of spaghetti contains more than five times that number.

Zucchini Parmesan

Zucchini has become fashionable in these parts comparatively recently, although it has been popular in Europe for a long time. In France and England, this slender cucumber-shaped vegetable is known as courgette *and the English identify it also as Italian, or baby, marrow. Its flavor is fresh and delicate and many consider it the aristocrat of the squash family.*

2 pounds zucchini
3 tablespoons butter
Salt and freshly ground pepper
1 teaspoon dried basil
½ teaspoon dried thyme
½ teaspoon dried marjoram
¼ cup chicken broth
½ cup freshly grated Parmesan
cheese

Scrub the zucchini well, cut off and discard a slice at both ends, and slice into ¼-inch-thick rounds. Butter a 10-inch round pie plate or quiche dish that can be used for serving. Arrange the zucchini slices in circles around the plate, one slice overlapping the other, starting with a slice in the middle. Dot with butter. Sprinkle lightly with salt, pepper, basil, thyme, and marjoram. Pour chicken broth over all and sprinkle with Parmesan cheese. Cover with foil and bake in a 350-degree oven for 10 minutes. Uncover and continue to bake until the zucchini slices are crisp-tender, about 10 minutes longer.

Yield: 4 to 6 servings.

Baked Stuffed Zucchini

4 to 6 medium-size zucchini
1 small onion, finely chopped
2 tablespoons butter
1 cup finely minced leftover meat
½ cup cooked rice
1 teaspoon dried basil
Salt and freshly ground pepper
Meat gravy (or tomato sauce)

Scrub zucchini and place in boiling water to barely cover. When the water returns to the boil, cover the pot, reduce the heat, and simmer for 3 minutes. Remove immediately, cool under running water, and drain. Cut off a slice from both ends and split the zucchini lengthwise. Scoop out the pulp, leaving a ¼-inch shell, and chop the pulp coarsely. Cook the chopped onion in butter until it turns golden. Add the zucchini pulp and cook an additional 3 minutes, stirring. Combine with the meat, rice, basil, and salt and pepper to taste. Blend in the meat gravy if you have it, or tomato sauce, just enough to moisten the mixture. Taste and correct the seasonings. Spoon the mixture into the zucchini shells and arrange in a greased, shallow baking dish large enough to hold the zucchini halves in a single layer. Bake at 350 degrees for 30 minutes, or until heated through.

Yield: 4 to 6 servings.

Zucchini and Cherry Tomatoes

6 or 7 firm, slender zucchini (about 1½ pounds)
2 tablespoons butter
2 tablespoons oil
2 garlic cloves, peeled
Salt and freshly ground pepper
24 cherry tomatoes
2 tablespoons chopped fresh parsley

Scrub the zucchini well and trim the ends. Cut into ¼-inch-thick slices. Heat the butter and oil in a large skillet. Add the garlic cloves and zucchini slices and sauté until the zucchini is lightly browned and crisp-tender. Sprinkle with salt and pepper. Add the cherry tomatoes and cook, shaking the pan, until heated through, about 2 minutes. The little tomatoes must not be overcooked or the skins will break and they will become mushy. Discard the garlic cloves. Transfer to a warm serving bowl and sprinkle with parsley.

Yield: 6 servings.

Sweet Potatoes

Sweet potatoes are mainly of two types, which are interchangeable in use. There are those with dry yellow flesh and those with soft, moist yellow or orange-red flesh, erroneously called yams. Yams are a different species altogether, one seldom seen in the United States. The sweet potatoes with moist flesh are generally superior to the dry for baking and glazing.

Selection: Look for firm, well-shaped, bright, clean sweet potatoes, free from blemishes. Preferred are chunky, medium-size potatoes that taper toward the ends. Allow ½ to ⅓ pound per serving.

Peak Season: Fall until early spring, but available all year.

Methods of Preparation: Boil or bake before peeling, and then finish preparation. May be mashed, sliced, and sautéed as a vegetable, or used as pie filling, in muffins, custards, cookies, and cake.

To Cook: To boil, scrub potatoes, cut off any woody or bruised parts, place in boiling salted water, and cook, covered, for 25 to 30 minutes, or until a sharp-pointed knife can pierce the potato easily. To bake, place in 400-degree oven for 40 minutes to 1 hour, or until they feel soft when squeezed. Serve with a pat of butter.

Ginger-Glazed Sweet Potatoes

2 pounds sweet potatoes, boiled
½ cup firmly packed brown sugar
½ cup granulated sugar
2 tablespoons crystallized ginger, slivered
1½ tablespoons butter
¼ cup pineapple juice

Peel the cooked sweet potatoes. If large, slice them in half lengthwise. Combine all the remaining ingredients in a large skillet. Bring to a boil, stirring until the sugar is dissolved. Lower the heat and add the potatoes. Simmer over low heat, basting often and turning potatoes until glazed on all sides, about 15 minutes.

Yield: 4 to 6 servings.

Sweet Potato and Carrot Ring

A delicious vegetable-starch combination that goes well with the holiday bird.

6 or 7 large carrots (about 1¼
  pounds)
3 large sweet potatoes (about 1¼
  pounds)
1 egg
1 cup bread crumbs
1¼ cups milk
Salt and freshly ground pepper
2 tablespoons brown sugar

Scrape the carrots and cut into thin rounds. Cook, covered, in salted water until crisp-tender, 15 to 20 minutes. Drain and mash. Don't overcook; the carrots should be firm enough so that, after they are mashed, there will still be a few firm morsels to add texture to the finished dish.

Boil the sweet potatoes. Drain, peel, and mash. Combine the carrots and sweet potatoes in a large bowl. Add the remaining ingredients and beat until well blended. Pack into a well-greased 4-cup ring mold placed in a large baking pan with an inch or so of hot water in the bottom. Bake, uncovered, in a preheated 350-degree oven for 1 hour. To serve, unmold on a round serving platter and fill the center with a vegetable of a contrasting color.

Yield: 4 to 6 servings.

Swiss Chard

Swiss chard is a type of beet that is grown only for its edible leaves. Its root is inedible. Swiss chard is interchangeable with spinach in many preparations.

Selection: Look for thick, juicy-looking white or reddish stalks with tender, fresh leaves. The color of the leaves varies from a light to a dark green, and there is also a red variety. Allow 1 pound for 2 servings.

Peak Season: From July until frost.

Methods of Preparation: Tender young leaves may be used raw in salads. They may be cooked and served as a vegetable, or, like spinach, used in stuffings and quiches. Cream of chard soup, made like cream of spinach soup, is a fine preparation.

To Cook: Trim off root ends. If the vegetable is large and mature, it is advisable to separate the stalks from the leaves and cook each separately. Wash thoroughly in several changes of water and drain. If the leaves are large, cut them into bite-size pieces. Cook them in the water that clings to the leaves after washing. Cook for about 10 minutes, or until tender. Drain well.

Chop the stems into 1-inch pieces and drop them into boiling, salted water to which a little lemon juice has been added. Cook them for 10 to 15 minutes, or until tender. The leaves and stems may be mixed together or served separately. Season with melted butter, salt, pepper, and a squirt of lemon juice, or top with a hollandaise, cheese, or cream sauce.

Oriental-Style Swiss Chard

2 tablespoons vegetable oil
1 clove garlic, finely chopped
1 small onion, finely chopped
1 pound Swiss chard, trimmed
  and chopped
2 tablespoons soy sauce (Japanese
  preferred)
1 tablespoon honey
¼ cup water
2 teaspoons cornstarch
1 tablespoon cold water
Pinch of salt

Heat the oil in a large skillet. Add the garlic and onion and cook until the onion is limp and transparent. Stir in the chard, soy sauce, honey, and water. Make a paste of the cornstarch and water and stir it into the pan, blending until it thickens. Reduce the heat to low, cover the pan, and simmer until the chard is barely tender, 15 to 20 minutes. Stir from time to time. Taste to see if it needs salt; soy sauces vary in the degree of saltiness. Serve hot.

Yield: 2 to 3 servings.

Tomatoes

Tomatoes are so much a part of our cooking today that it is hard to believe that there was a time when people considered them lethal.

Vine-ripened, deep orange-red, locally grown tomatoes are, of course, the ideal. But it is a fact of life that many tomatoes are grown with an eye toward improving their durability and shipping qualities rather than their texture and flavor. However, we compound the felony and make the mediocre specimens we get even more mediocre when we refrigerate them. The flavor of tomatoes will improve when they are held at room temperature. Refrigerate them when they become very ripe, but try to use them before they reach that point. Tomatoes may be chilled shortly before they are served.

When fresh, sun-ripened tomatoes are not available, it is better to use canned Italian plum tomatoes than the mealy specimens found in the market.

Selection: Look for firm, plump tomatoes with a fruity, characteristic aroma. Avoid overripe, soft tomatoes with blemishes, bruises, soft spots, or growth cracks. Underripe tomatoes may be ripened at home. Place them in a warm location away from direct sunlight. To hasten their ripening, put them in a closed paper bag. Allow 1 tomato or ½ pound per serving.

Peak Season: Spring and summer.

Methods of Preparation: Raw in salads, sandwiches, as garnishes. Cooked, may be stewed, broiled, sautéed, or baked; used in casserole dishes, stews, soups, and all-important tomato sauces. Green (unripe) tomatoes are excellent fried. The flavor of tomatoes depends largely on the ratio of sugar to acid, and acidy tomatoes can often be improved with a pinch of sugar.

To peel tomatoes, dip them in boiling water for about a minute. The heat from the boiling water creates a layer of steam between the pulp and the skin, which can be easily slipped off.

To remove seeds and excess liquid from tomatoes, cut them into halves crosswise. Hold a half in the palm of your hand and squeeze very gently over a bowl. The seeds and juice will run out. Use a teaspoon to scrape out the seeds that remain.

When slicing tomatoes for salads or sandwiches, place the tomato stem side up and cut vertical slices as you'd slice a loaf of bread.

Broiled or Baked Tomatoes

4 large, ripe tomatoes
Salt and freshly ground pepper
½ cup fine bread crumbs
1 clove garlic, finely minced
1 tablespoon finely minced fresh
    parsley
1 teaspoon dried basil
2 tablespoons olive or vegetable
    oil

If the tomatoes are very large, they may be cut in half, crosswise; if they are a suitable size for an individual serving, cut off about ½ inch from the stem end. Season the cut end with salt and pepper. In a small bowl, combine the bread crumbs, garlic, parsley, and basil. Sprinkle the cut sides of the tomatoes with the mixture and dribble a little oil over the top of each. Arrange on a heatproof serving dish and bake in a 375-degree oven for 20 to 25 minutes, or until the tomatoes are soft but firm enough to hold their shape. Or place them under the broiler, 4 or 5 inches below the heat unit, and broil until the tomatoes are heated through and the crumbs browned, about 10 minutes. Be careful that the crumbs do not burn.

Yield: 4 servings

Fried Tomatoes with Sour Cream

6 large firm tomatoes
Salt and freshly ground pepper
½ cup flour
4 tablespoons butter
½ cup light cream
2 teaspoons dried basil
Paprika
⅔ cup sour cream

Cut the tomatoes into 1-inch-thick slices. Sprinkle them with salt and pepper and flour them lightly on both sides, shaking off any excess. Melt the butter in a large skillet until it foams. When the foam subsides, add the tomatoes. They must be cooked quickly or they will disintegrate. Brown the tomatoes on both sides—they need only a minute on each side. Turn them with a broad spatula. When done, remove them to a warm platter.

Add the cream to the juices in the skillet, stirring constantly until it thickens. Add a bit more salt, the basil, and enough paprika to color the sauce slightly. Add a few more grinds of pepper, remove from the heat, and stir in the sour cream. Heat through for a moment but do not boil. Pour the sauce over the tomato slices and serve.

Yield: 6 servings.

Sautéed Cherry Tomatoes

Wash cherry tomatoes and remove stems. Heat 2 tablespoons of oil and 2 tablespoons of butter in a skillet. Add 1 garlic clove, finely minced. Add tomatoes and toss in the hot fat until heated through, about 2 minutes. Sprinkle with salt, pepper, and chopped fresh parsley and serve.

Stuffed Tomatoes

A tomato shell provides a natural container for an endless variety of fillings.

To prepare the tomato shells, slice off about ½ inch from the stem end. Scoop out the seeds and pulp down to the shell. Reserve the pulp for stuffing. Sprinkle the insides with salt and pepper and invert the tomatoes to drain for 20 to 30 minutes.

When stuffed, sprinkle with fine bread crumbs and dot with butter. Bake in a 375-degree oven for 20 to 25 minutes, or until heated through, but still firm enough to hold their shape.

Tomato Stuffings

Following are some suggestions for stuffings. The amount is for 4 to 6 tomatoes, depending on their size. Allow ½ cup for a large tomato.

Curried Rice Stuffing. Using a fork, mash the tomato pulp removed from the tomatoes. Place in a small saucepan and season with salt and pepper. Add 4 tablespoons finely chopped green pepper, 1 small finely minced onion, 1 teaspoon Worcestershire sauce, and 1 teaspoon or more curry powder, according to taste. Cook over low heat for about 5 minutes, or until the vegetables are softened. Stir in 2 cups of cooked rice and taste and correct seasonings. Stuff the tomatoes with this mixture. Sprinkle with buttered bread crumbs and bake.

Eggplant Stuffing. Sauté 1 small finely chopped onion in 2 tablespoons butter. Add the tomato pulp, 1 finely minced garlic clove, 2 to 3 cups cubed eggplant, 1 teaspoon curry powder, and ½ teaspoon thyme. Cook slowly, stirring gently, until the eggplant is softened and sauce thickened. Add a few dashes of Tabasco, and salt and pepper. Taste and correct seasoning. Fill the tomatoes with the eggplant mixture, top with buttered bread crumbs, place tomatoes in a shallow baking dish, and bake until the tomatoes are tender.

Mushroom Stuffing. Sauté ½ pound finely chopped mushrooms, 1 small finely chopped onion, and 1 finely minced garlic clove in 4 tablespoons butter for 5 minutes. Add tomato pulp, 1 cup bread crumbs, salt, freshly ground pepper, a pinch of thyme, a pinch of marjoram, and a few dashes of Tabasco and blend well. Taste and correct seasoning. Fill the tomato shells and proceed as above.

Turnips

The most familiar turnip is the round white tuber with a purple band across the top of the skin. When it is young and fresh, it has a mild flavor, somewhere between a tart apple and a crisp radish. It should not be confused with the rutabaga, commonly called the yellow turnip. They are botanically different, although the taste is similar.

Selection: Look for small to medium-size young turnips, about 2 or 3 inches in diameter, with smooth, unblemished skin. If the tops are present, they should be young, fresh, and green. Allow ½ pound per serving.

Peak Season: Available all year.

Methods of Preparation: Raw, sliced or cut into julienne strips and served with a dip; used with discretion in stews, soups, and casseroles; steamed, boiled, baked, creamed, or puréed as a vegetable.

To Cook: Unless turnips are very young, their skins can be bitter and should be pared. Place whole, sliced, diced, or julienne pieces in a few inches of boiling salted water and cook, covered, until just tender. Do not overcook. Test by piercing with a sharp-pointed knife. Smaller pieces will cook in 5 to 10 minutes; whole turnips may need 20 minutes or more.

Turnip Purée

6 medium turnips
3 onions, very thinly sliced
6 tablespoons butter
2 tablespoons chopped fresh parsley
Salt and freshly ground pepper
2 teaspoons caraway seeds

Peel the turnips, cut them into eighths, and cook in boiling salted water, covered, until tender, 10 to 15 minutes. While they are cooking, sauté the onions in 4 tablespoons of butter until they are limp and transparent. Mix with the chopped parsley and keep warm.

Drain the turnips thoroughly and mash them with a fork, beating in the remaining 2 tablespoons butter. Add salt and pepper to taste. Add the caraway seeds and mix through. Transfer the mashed turnips to a heated serving bowl and heap the sautéed onions over the center. Serve hot.

Yield: 3 or 4 servings.

Braised Turnips

1½ pounds turnips
3 tablespoons butter
¾ cup chicken or beef stock
1 tablespoon lemon juice

Peel the turnips and cut in ½-inch-thick slices. Melt the butter in a large skillet. Add the turnips and cook over low heat until they start to soften.

Add the stock, cover the skillet, and simmer slowly until the turnips are tender, about 15 to 20 minutes. Remove the lid and let some of the liquid cook down, leaving a small amount of sauce. Sprinkle with lemon juice and serve.

Yield: 4 servings.

9
Salads

The tag line that often runs through our minds when we are planning a luncheon or dinner menu for family or guests is, "…and a tossed green salad." It conjures up a delightful image of bright crisp greens made scented and shiny with a sprightly vinaigrette. It is difficult to realize that there was a time within this century when salads were considered strange, exotic, and a kind of sissy food. That was before transportation had progressed to the point where fresh salad greens could be a year-round staple. There was also less widespread public interest in food values and nutrition. Not that salads had passed completely unnoticed. In 1825, Brillat-Savarin, the distinguished French lawyer and economist, published his witty book on dining, *The Physiology of Taste.* The book is still in print and has won enduring fame for its author. In it, Brillat-Savarin gave only restricted space to vegetables, saving his enthusiasm for salad. He observed that salad "freshens without enfeebling and fortifies without irritating." He was surely ahead of his time and it was to take more than a century before the tossed green salad, sophisticated in its simplicity, was to become a way of life for most Americans.

Salads can appear during a meal at any time that it pleases the hosts—as an appetizer, to accompany the main course, or as a separate course following the entrée. They are infinite in their variety, depending on the season and your imagination. In addition to the simple salad of tossed greens, there are salads of both cooked and raw vegetables, and the large category of salads containing fish, meat, poultry, fruits, cheeses, legumes, and similar substantial ingredients known as composed salads. Composed salads generally serve as cold entrées.

Greens for Salad

The lettuce family is a large one, offering a wide variety of taste and textures. You can supplement it with vegetables that perform well as salad greens, such as spinach, white, red, and Savoy cabbages, and sorrel leaves. When combining greens, consider their texture and choose those that are complementary. A delicate Bibb or Boston lettuce would be overpowered by a tough escarole or a hardy romaine but would be enhanced by rings or leaves of Belgian endive.

Arugula. Also known as rocket, arugula is a small, flat-leafed green with a distinctive peppery flavor. A few leaves add a zingy flavor to a green salad, and it can also be used alone. It is usually sold in small bunches with the roots left on, and it requires careful washing.

Belgian Endive. Also known as French endive, its botanical name is witloof chicory. A small cigar-shaped compact plant 6 to 8 inches long, it has creamy leaves with pale yellow tips. Its crisp texture and delicately bitter flavor add interest to a mixed green salad. It is one of the choicest and most expensive of salad greens, but there is no waste and a little goes a long way. The leaves can be used whole, shredded, or cut into julienne strips or rings. The separated leaves also make fine receptacles for various hors d'oeuvre mixtures. Endive and cooked beets are a popular salad combination. Endives can be braised or sautéed and served as a vegetable.

Bibb Lettuce. Bright green, crisp, tender, and mild, Bibb, or limestone lettuce, as it is also known, is considered the choicest of the lettuce family. It requires thorough washing to get rid of the soil that clings to the leaves. The small leaves should be served whole, not broken up.

Boston or Butter Lettuce. This is softer and lighter than iceberg, and not as crisp. Loosely packed, with pale green leaves outside and light yellow leaves inside, this tender, round lettuce takes dressing well. Remove the core, as for iceberg. Boston lettuce is fragile and must be washed and dried gently.

Chicory. Also known as curly endive and chicory endive. With its curly fringed leaves, this is a robust, crisp green with a slightly bitter taste and it is best combined with milder greens. It makes a decorative garnish for composed salads.

Chinese or Celery Cabbage. With a flavor somewhere between romaine and cabbage, this pale green and white vegetable, which forms a long head about the size of a bunch of celery, makes a good addition to the salad bowl. The tough outer leaves should be removed. It can also be used in soups or cooked as a vegetable.

Dandelion Greens. Dandelion greens are now grown commercially. The cultivated leaves are larger, lighter green, and less bitter than those that grow wild. They are excellent in salads, either alone or in combination with other greens.

Escarole. This is a variety of endive also known as Batavian endive. It has a bushy head made up of broad leaves that are rather coarse in texture and slightly bitter. It is best to use only the tender inner leaves for salad; the outer leaves can be consigned to the soup pot.

Iceberg or Crisphead Lettuce. An all-purpose lettuce, this has a large, firm head with crisp, brittle, tightly packed leaves.

Although it does not have as much flavor as some of the other lettuces, it has some sterling virtues. The crisp heart, broken into chunks, adds fine texture to a salad in combination with other greens; cut into shreds, it forms a good bed for salads; the flat leaves perform perfectly in a sandwich; and the curved leaves nicely contain a serving of salad. It keeps longer than other lettuces—two weeks or more in the refrigerator if it was in good condition to begin with.

Lamb's Lettuce. Also known as field salad or corn salad. This has small, smooth, tongue-shaped leaves and it comes in small bunches. It is a rather uncommon green because it does not travel well and is consequently not widely available. It has a tangy flavor and is best combined with milder greens in salad.

Leaf or Garden Lettuce. These lettuces do not form heads; the leaves branch loosely from the stalk. The curly green and the curly red-tipped are the most common, the red-tipped adding interesting color contrast to a green salad. The leaves are tender and delicate and must be tossed gently. They should be used as quickly as possible, as they wilt and do not store well.

Romaine or Cos Lettuce. A popular lettuce, romaine has crisp, long, bright leaves. The leaves seem to be coarse but they are actually tender with good flavor and less bitterness than other leaves. It is a hardy green, excellent for salads that need a lot of tossing.

Spinach. For a raw salad, buy fresh, loose spinach rather than the prewashed variety that comes packaged. If it isn't very young and tender, change your salad plan. Wash the spinach well and discard the heavy stems. It makes a lovely salad with sliced, snow-white mushrooms and crisp pieces of bacon, or mixed with salad greens in a tossed salad in which its deep green provides interesting color contrast.

Watercress. Watercress is a peppery-tasting green that is sold in bunches. Its tangy, pungent flavor is present in the leaves and stems, and both are used. It may be mixed with other greens in a salad or used as a delicious (and edible) garnish for hot or cold dishes. It is good rolled in soft white buttered bread as a sandwich.

Herbs. Herbs can contribute interesting, lively flavors to a tossed salad, but they must be used with restraint—a whisper rather than a shout. Use the fresh in preference to the dried. Figure about 1 tablespoon of fresh herbs (1 scant teaspoon of dried) to ¾ cup of vinaigrette. Among the herbs that are successful in salad are tarragon, chervil, parsley, chives, and Italian or flat parsley. Basil is standard with tomatoes, and dill does nice things for cucumbers or tomatoes.

Storing and Preparing Greens

Lettuces should always be refrigerated clean and dry. When you get them home, wash them well under cold running water. The loose, dark outer leaves contain a good deal of nutrients and should not be discarded if they are undamaged. If they won't do for salad, use them in the stockpot for soup. Dry the greens by letting them drain in a colander, wrap them lightly in a soft absorbent towel until dry, and chill them in the refrigerator until you are ready to use them. A salad spinner does an excellent job of drying greens. If the lettuce is completely dry, it may be stored in a plastic bag in the refrigerator crisper drawer.

Iceberg lettuce and Belgian endive are so constructed that they do not need to be separated to be cleaned. It is usually enough to wipe the outside of the endive with a damp cloth and remove any discolored outer leaves. To prepare iceberg lettuce, grasp the head with the core side down, and give it a brisk whack on the kitchen counter. This will loosen the core and you can then twist it out easily with your fingers.

Making a Tossed Salad

Have your salad greens washed and thoroughly dried. The least bit of moisture will dilute the dressing and it will not coat the leaves. Your salad bowl can be glass, china, glazed pottery, or even hard, dense plastic. Well-seasoned wooden bowls have acquired a kind of mystique that we think is misplaced. If the wooden bowl has a treated surface, it might just as well be china, and if it has an untreated surface, it is very likely to become increasingly rancid with age, in spite of your best efforts. Of course, if someone has given you one of those handsome teak or mahogany bowls, do use it as long as you are comfortable with it, but when replacement time comes, consider the advantages of other materials.

Cut or tear the greens into bite-size pieces. Use a stainless steel knife for cutting, not a carbon steel, which can discolor the edges of the salad greens. The old wives' tale about the calamities that will befall salad greens if you cut them instead of tearing them with your hands is quite without foundation. The greens will stand up to a knife, scissors, or your fingers, so do whatever is easiest. You can prepare the greens up to this point well in advance of serving time and refrigerate them covered.

Allow about 2 cups of loosely packed greens for 1 serving. If other ingredients are used in the salad, you will need less.

Toss the salad with the dressing when you are ready to serve it. Vinegar and salt will release juices and the greens will lose their crispness if you dress the salad in advance. The most popular dressing for tossed salads is vinaigrette, the basic oil and vinegar dressing. One of the delights of tossed salads is the endless variety of flavors that can be brought to it. Not sugar, however. There is no place for sugar in a tossed green salad. Garlic is lovely, unless you are one of the people who can't abide it. To introduce garlic into the salad, split a clove and rub the inside of the salad bowl, or rub a dry crust of bread on all sides with a split clove of garlic. This is called a *chapon*. Place the greens in the bowl with the chapon, add the dressing, and toss the salad lightly. Remove the chapon before serving. Its flavor will subtly permeate the greens. Or you can chop the garlic very fine and add it to the dressing. Use just enough dressing to coat the greens and make them shiny; too much will drown them.

Some salad makers prefer to add the dressing ingredients one after another. Start with the oil to coat the greens well, and then add the vinegar, salt, and pepper. This procedure protects the greens from the acid of the vinegar and helps them to hold their crispness.

A flavorful, fruity olive oil brings its special taste and character to the dressing, or you may use any of the blander vegetable oils such as corn, peanut, and safflower, or a combination of olive oil and vegetable oil. Walnut oil, which has become popular recently, is expensive, but a teaspoon or so adds a distinctive flavor. The quality of the vinegar is also important—whether it is sharp, rich, or mellow. Red and white wine vinegars are the most bland, with white wine vinegar the milder of the two, and either one gives the salad a lovely, light quality. As substitutes, you may fall back on cider vinegar or lemon juice, but they should be considered second choice. It isn't ever necessary to buy herb-flavored vinegars because it is simple enough to add your own tarragon, thyme, or rosemary to the vinegar already on your pantry shelf.

The usual proportion of vinegar to oil is one part vinegar to three or four parts oil, but there really is no rigid formula because so much depends on the heaviness of the oil and the aroma and sharpness of the vinegar. Let your taste be your guide. Be miserly with the vinegar in the beginning and taste and add more as you go along. Dressings taste better when freshly made. It takes only a minute or two to put one together, so mix the dressing just before you intend to use it.

Basic Vinaigrette Dressing

½ teaspoon salt
2 tablespoons wine vinegar, or a mixture of vinegar and lemon juice
Freshly ground pepper
6 tablespoons olive or vegetable oil

Combine the salt, 1½ tablespoons vinegar, and pepper in a bowl. Add the oil in a stream, beating until it is well combined. Taste and add more vinegar if needed. Or you may place all the ingredients in a screw-top jar and shake it vigorously for half a minute until thoroughly blended.

Yield: About ½ cup, or enough for 4 salad servings.

Mustard Vinaigrette. Blend about ½ teaspoon Dijon mustard with the vinegar, salt, and pepper before adding the oil.

Blender or Food Processor Vinaigrette

3 shallots, coarsely cut
2 cloves garlic, peeled and sliced
2 tablespoons wine vinegar
½ teaspoon dry mustard
½ cup olive or vegetable oil
Salt and freshly ground pepper
1 teaspoon dried basil

Place all the ingredients in a blender or food processor and blend until smooth.

Yield: ⅔ cup.

Garlic Vinaigrette. Crush 1 garlic clove and ½ teaspoon salt to a paste. Proceed with basic vinaigrette as above. For a more subtle garlic flavor, use a chapon (see page 391).

Lorenzo Dressing. Combine ½ cup chili sauce, 1 teaspoon salt, and freshly ground pepper in a bowl. Dribble in ¾ cup olive oil, beating until well combined. Stir in 2 tablespoons minced watercress leaves. Serve with cold meat salads, sliced tomatoes, or green salads. Makes about 1⅓ cups.

Ravigote. To 1 cup of vinaigrette, add 1 teaspoon drained, chopped capers, 1 teaspoon finely minced shallots or scallions, 1 tablespoon minced fresh parsley, and 1 tablespoon of one of the following fresh herbs: snipped chives, minced tarragon, or chervil. Or use 1 teaspoon of dried herbs. Serve with boiled beef, chicken, and fish.

Roquefort Vinaigrette. Combine 4 tablespoons wine vinegar, ¼ teaspoon salt, and a few grinds of pepper in a bowl. Dribble in ½ cup olive oil and 2 tablespoons heavy cream, beating until well combined. Stir in ¼ cup crumbled Roquefort cheese and a few drops of lemon juice. Good with tossed green salad. Makes about 1½ cups.

Boiled Dressing

An old-fashioned dressing that is still in fashion for coleslaw and potato salad.

1 to 2 teaspoons dry mustard
1½ tablespoons flour
1 tablespoon sugar
1 egg, lightly beaten
2 tablespoons melted butter
¾ cup milk
¼ cup vinegar
Dash of Tabasco or ground red
 pepper
Salt

Combine the mustard, flour, and sugar in a small, heavy-bottomed saucepan. Add the egg and beat until smooth. Stir in the melted butter and milk. Slowly add the vinegar, stirring constantly. Cook over very low heat, stirring constantly, until thickened and smooth. Add Tabasco or ground red pepper and salt to taste. Cool and refrigerate, covered, until needed.

Yield: 1¼ cups.

Honey Lime Fruit Salad Dressing

6 tablespoons fresh lime juice
3 tablespoons honey
6 tablespoons mayonnaise

Place lime juice, honey, and mayonnaise in a small bowl and blend well with a wire whisk.

Yield: about 1 cup.

Mixed Green Salad

1 head romaine lettuce
1 head iceberg lettuce
1 head Boston lettuce
1 bunch watercress
½ cup sliced scallions
1 14-ounce can artichoke hearts
 (water-packed), drained and
 sliced
4 white radishes, sliced
8 fresh white mushrooms, thinly
 sliced
4 tablespoons fresh lemon juice
¾ cup vegetable or olive oil
Salt and freshly ground pepper
1 clove garlic, finely minced

Wash the salad greens carefully, drain well, and pat dry or whirl in a salad spinner. Break, tear, or cut the greens into bite-size pieces. Place in a large salad bowl. Break off and discard a portion of the watercress stems if they are too long. Add the watercress, scallions, artichoke slices, radishes, and mushrooms. Combine the remaining ingredients in a jar and shake well to blend. Pour over the salad and toss well.

Yield: 8 to 10 servings.

Note: Among the vegetables that are at home in mixed green salads are fresh white mushrooms, scallions, cucumber, avocado, cherry tomatoes, zucchini, celery, red onion, radishes, snow peas, sugar peas, carrots, fennel, red and green bell peppers, Jerusalem artichokes, cooked artichoke hearts or bottoms, and bean and alfalfa sprouts. Cut-up tomatoes are not a particularly good idea in a tossed salad because their juices tend to thin the dressing. Dress them separately and use them to garnish the bowl.

Mixed Salad with Blue Cheese

The dressing performs double duty as a marinade.

⅔ cup salad oil

¼ pound blue cheese, crumbled, about 1 cup

2 tablespoons lemon juice

1 tablespoon wine vinegar

Salt and freshly ground pepper

Sprinkle of paprika

1 large red onion, thinly sliced

1 cup fresh white mushrooms, sliced

½ head crisp iceberg lettuce, cut into bite-size pieces (5 to 6 cups)

½ head romaine, cut into bite-size pieces (4 to 5 cups)

2 cups unpeeled raw zucchini, thinly sliced

5 or 6 radishes, thinly sliced

Combine the oil, blue cheese, lemon juice, wine vinegar, salt, pepper, and paprika in a screw-top jar and shake well. Separate the onion rings and place them in a bowl with the mushrooms. Pour the dressing over them and toss well. Cover tightly and refrigerate for 4 or 5 hours, or overnight. When ready to serve, combine the salad greens, zucchini, and radishes in a salad bowl. Toss with the onion-cheese mixture.

Yield: 6 servings.

Greek Summer Salad

1 large head romaine lettuce, cored and coarsely shredded (4 to 6 cups)

1 cucumber, peeled, cut in half lengthwise, seeded, and sliced

1 bunch scallions, trimmed and chopped

1 small red onion, thinly sliced

2 green peppers, thinly sliced in rings

4 radishes, sliced

16 cherry tomatoes, cut in half

½ teaspoon dried oregano

18 black olives (imported)

⅓ pound feta cheese, crumbled

6 to 8 tablespoons olive oil

2 tablespoons wine vinegar

Salt and freshly ground pepper

Combine the lettuce, cucumber crescents, scallions, onion, green pepper, radishes, tomatoes, oregano, olives, and feta cheese in a large salad bowl. Add the olive oil and toss. Add the wine vinegar, salt, and pepper to taste and toss again.

Yield: 6 or more servings.

Caesar Salad

4 slices firm-textured white bread (for croutons)

¾ cup garlic-flavored olive oil (see note)

2 bunches romaine lettuce

Freshly ground black pepper

½ teaspoon salt

2 eggs, boiled for exactly 1 minute

Juice of 1 lemon

6 fillets of anchovies, diced

1 teaspoon Worcestershire sauce

½ cup freshly grated Parmesan cheese

To make the croutons, trim the crusts from the white bread and cut the slices into ½-inch cubes. Brown the cubes in 4 tablespoons of the garlic-flavored oil. Stir them carefully so that they brown evenly on all sides. Remove from the skillet with a slotted spoon and drain them on paper towels. Reserve.

Wash and dry the lettuce well. Tear the leaves into bite-size pieces and place them in a large salad bowl. Sprinkle with the garlic-flavored oil and toss to coat. Grind a generous amount of black pepper over the salad and add the salt. Break in the coddled eggs, squeeze the lemon juice over the eggs, add the anchovies and Worcestershire and toss again. Add more salt, pepper, and lemon juice, if desired. Sprinkle the grated Parmesan cheese over the salad, and toss again. Add the croutons at the last moment before serving.

Yield: 8 or more servings.

Note: To make garlic-flavored oil, crush 2 large garlic cloves and add to ¾ cup olive oil. Let the mixture stand overnight. Discard the garlic.

Meat Salad with Vinaigrette Sauce

Leftover beef or veal can get a new lease on life in a piquant salad.

4 cups cooked beef or veal cut into 1-inch cubes.

2 celery stalks, cut into 1-inch long julienne strips

1 red onion, cut into paper-thin slices

2 tomatoes, peeled, seeded, and cut into small cubes

6 tiny sour gherkins, cut into fine julienne strips

2 tablespoons finely chopped fresh parsley

2 tablespoons Dijon mustard

2 tablespoons red wine vinegar

2 cloves garlic, finely minced

Salt and freshly ground pepper

⅔ cup vegetable oil

Place the meat cubes in a mixing bowl and add the celery, onion, tomatoes, pickles, and parsley.

In a small bowl, combine the mustard, vinegar, garlic, salt, and pepper. Add the oil slowly, whisking vigorously with a wire whisk until the sauce is well emulsified. Pour the sauce over the meat and toss well. Serve at room temperature.

Yield: 4 to 6 servings.

Mixed Vegetable Salad

2 cups cauliflowerets
2 cups sliced zucchini
2 cups sliced yellow summer
squash
2 cups sliced carrots
2 cups broccoli flowerets

Dressing:
4 tablespoons wine vinegar
2 teaspoons Dijon mustard
4 tablespoons grated onion
¼ teaspoon dried thyme
Salt and freshly ground pepper
1 cup olive or salad oil
¼ cup chopped fresh parsley
Watercress sprigs for garnish

Bring a large pot of salted water to a boil and add the vegetables. Cook for 2 minutes, covered, after the water returns to a boil. Drain immediately and run under cold water to stop the cooking. Drain again, cool, and refrigerate the vegetables.

Combine the vinegar, mustard, onion, thyme, salt, and pepper in a 1-quart bowl. Add the oil slowly, beating with a wire whisk until the dressing is thick. Stir in the parsley. Pour over the vegetables 30 minutes before serving, toss well, and let stand at room temperature.

The assorted colors of the vegetables make a most attractive presentation in a clear glass bowl not lined with lettuce leaves. Garnish the top of the salad with watercress sprigs.

Yield: 8 or more servings.

Variation: Blanched string beans, snow peas, or raw sliced mushrooms may be substituted for any of the vegetables. Choose vegetables with contrasting colors.

Cucumber Salad

2 large cucumbers
½ cup white vinegar
2 tablespoons water
¼ cup sugar
Salt and freshly ground pepper
2 tablespoons chopped fresh
parsley

If the cucumbers are waxed, which is frequently the case with cucumbers we buy in urban markets, peel them. Otherwise leave the skins on. But whether peeled or unpeeled, score the length of the cucumbers with the tines of a fork to scallop the edges. Slice cucumbers very thin.

In a deep bowl, combine the remaining ingredients and mix well. Add the cucumber slices and cover them with a plate and a weight. Cans make fine weights. Refrigerate for 3 hours. Drain the cucumbers to serve. The marinade can be saved and used again.

Yield: 4 servings.

Variation: Add a thinly sliced onion to the above. Or sprinkle the insides of scooped-out tomatoes with salt and pepper and fill with cucumber salad mixed with plain yogurt.

Beet and Endive Salad

This makes a good appetizer course and is also a particularly fine accompaniment for cold meats.

6 to 8 medium beets, or 1 1-pound
   can julienned beets
½ cup chopped scallions
2 Belgian endives
Vinaigrette dressing (see page
   392), *or*

Cream Mustard:
1 teaspoon Dijon mustard
Salt and freshly pepper
Lemon juice
½ cup cream

If you are using fresh beets, bake them according to directions on page 335. If using canned beets, drain them well and discard the juice. When the beets are cooked, peel and cool them and cut into julienne strips. Mix them with the chopped scallions and Belgian endive cut into 1-inch-thick rings. Toss with vinaigrette dressing or a cream mustard. For the latter, mix 1 teaspoon Dijon mustard, a pinch of salt and pepper, and a few drops of lemon juice. Slowly beat in ½ cup cream, little by little, stirring vigorously until well blended.

Yield: 4 servings.

Green Bean Salad

The softened onion makes this preparation a bit special.

1 pound tender young green beans
1 large onion
1 tablespoon salt
2 tomatoes, diced
½ cup finely minced fresh parsley
¼ cup snipped fresh dill
¼ cup salad oil
2 tablespoons cider vinegar
Salt and freshly ground pepper

Cut the beans into 1½-inch lengths. Cook in plenty of boiling salted water, uncovered, just until crisp-tender. Start tasting after 4 or 5 minutes to make sure you do not overcook them. As soon as the beans reach the proper degree of tenderness, drain and rinse in cold water to stop the cooking. Drain and set aside.

Slice the onion into thin rings and place in a shallow bowl. Sprinkle with the tablespoon of salt. With the heel of your hand crush the onion until it becomes limp and the juices run out. Rinse the onion rings in cold water to remove the salt. Drain well and pat dry with paper towels.

Return the onion to the bowl and add the tomatoes, beans, parsley, and dill. Toss with the oil. Add the vinegar and salt and pepper to taste and toss again. Chill until ready to serve.

Yield: 4 or 5 servings.

Celery Root in Mustard Sauce (Céleri-Rave Rémoulade)

This may be served as an appetizer course, as part of an assortment of hors d'oeuvre, or as a side dish with cold poached fish, for which it seems to have a natural affinity.

1 pound celery root (celeriac)
3 tablespoon Dijon mustard
¾ cup mayonnaise
2 teaspoons wine vinegar
Crisp lettuce leaves
2 to 3 tablespoons chopped fresh parsley

Peel the celery root and thinly slice it. Cut the slices into thin strips the size of matchsticks. Celery root tends to be tough. To soften it, cover the strips with boiling salted water, and cook for 1 minute. Drain and rinse with fresh cold water; pat dry. Combine the mustard, mayonnaise, and vinegar in a bowl. Add the celery root and toss. Cover the bowl and refrigerate for a few hours or overnight. Serve on lettuce leaves and sprinkle with chopped fresh parsley.

Yield: 4 to 6 servings.

Spinach, Mushroom, and Bean Sprout Salad

1 pound young fresh spinach
½ cup bean sprouts
¼ pound fresh white mushrooms
⅓ cup olive oil
2 tablespoons red wine vinegar
1 teaspoon soy sauce (Japanese preferred)
Salt and freshly ground pepper

Wash the spinach thoroughly in several changes of water. Remove the stems and heavy veins from the larger leaves. Dry well and refrigerate in a vegetable crisper until needed. Rinse the bean sprouts in cold water. Cover with fresh cold water and refrigerate until ready to use. Slice the mushrooms thin.

Mix the oil, vinegar, soy sauce, salt, and pepper. Break the spinach into bite-size pieces and place in a salad bowl. Drain the bean sprouts well and add them and the mushrooms to the bowl. Pour the dressing over and toss.

Yield: 6 servings.

Note: To make a wilted spinach salad, heat the dressing before pouring over the greens.

Tomato Salad

Save this for the time of year when you are able to get juicy red vine-ripened tomatoes.

¼ cup cider vinegar
4 teaspoons Dijon mustard
4 or 5 shallots, coarsely cut
½ teaspoon dried thyme
Salt and freshly ground pepper
½ cup olive oil

In the container of a blender, combine the vinegar, mustard, shallots, thyme, salt, and pepper. Blend, slowly adding the olive oil, until the mixture thickens and becomes creamy. Pour into a container and stir in the parsley. This is an excellent dressing that can be used with other salads as well. You will have about ¾ cup.

¼ cup finely chopped fresh
    parsley
6 large tomatoes, slightly chilled

Shortly before you are ready to serve, slice the tomatoes and arrange them in overlapping slices on a flat platter. Pour the dressing over the tomatoes and let stand at room temperature for 15 minutes.

Yield: 6 to 8 servings.

Variation: Alternate slices of tomato with thin slices of red onion and thin crescents of avocado. Do not peel and add the avocado until just before serving, as avocado darkens quickly when exposed to the air.

Tomato Aspic

A rich, full-bodied tomato aspic that will complement almost any cold food or salad.

2 tablespoons unflavored gelatin
½ cup cold water
2 cups tomato juice
⅔ cup water
⅔ cup tomato sauce
2 teaspoons Worcestershire sauce
1 tablespoon onion juice
1 tablespoon lemon juice
Salt

Sprinkle the gelatin over ½ cup of cold water to soften it. In a medium-size saucepan, combine the tomato juice, water, and tomato sauce and heat to the boiling point. Add the softened gelatin and stir over very low heat until the gelatin is completely dissolved. Cool the mixture and add the remaining ingredients. Taste and correct the seasonings. Pour into a lightly oiled 4-cup mold or individual molds. Refrigerate until firm.

Yield: 5 or 6 servings.

Waldorf Salad

A pleasant fruit-and-nut mixture that can serve as a main course for lunch.

Juice of ½ lemon
3 large crisp apples (Granny
    Smith, Red Delicious, or a
    combination), peeled, cored,
    and diced
1 cup chopped celery
½ cup broken walnut meats
⅓ cup raisins
½ cup seedless grapes, cut in half
    (optional)
⅓ to ½ cup mayonnaise

Squeeze the lemon juice over the apple cubes to keep them from darkening. Add the celery, nuts, raisins, and grapes and mix with enough mayonnaise to moisten. Serve well chilled on crisp greens.

Yield: 2 servings.

Coleslaw

Coleslaw is a perennial favorite and the varied recipes for it would fill a telephone directory. This is a creamy, savory version.

1 small head cabbage
1 large carrot
3 tablespoons finely minced sweet onion or scallion
1 cup mayonnaise
2 teaspoons Dijon mustard
4 tablespoons cider vinegar
½ teaspoon sugar
2 teaspoons dillweed (optional)
½ teaspoon celery seeds
Few dashes of Tabasco sauce
Salt and freshly ground pepper

Cut the cabbage into quarters, remove the core, and shred very fine with a stainless steel knife. Discard any coarse pieces. You should have about 5 cups. Scrape the carrot and shred coarsely on the largest holes of a four-sided vegetable grater. Place the shredded cabbage, carrot, and minced onion in a bowl. In a small bowl combine the mayonnaise, mustard, vinegar, sugar, dillweed, celery seeds, Tabasco, salt, and pepper and mix well. Stir into the cabbage mixture and blend thoroughly. Cover and chill for 3 or 4 hours.

Yield: 4 to 6 servings.

Eggplant Salad

4 tablespoons olive or vegetable oil
2 tablespoons sesame seeds
1 large eggplant
2 cloves garlic, finely minced
3 tablespoons chopped fresh dill
Salt and freshly ground pepper
2 tablespoons lemon juice
Dash of Tabasco sauce
Chopped fresh parsley

Preheat the oven to 400 degrees.

Heat 1 tablespoon of oil in a small skillet and sauté the sesame seeds until they are lightly browned. Watch them carefully as they color quickly. Set aside. Place the eggplant on a baking sheet and bake until completely tender, about 45 minutes. Cool the eggplant under running water and remove the skin carefully. Place the eggplant in a colander and allow to drain. Mash or chop the eggplant or, better still, place it in a blender or food processor. Blend until smooth but not liquefied. Transfer to a bowl and add the garlic, dill, salt, pepper, lemon juice, Tabasco, and the remaining 3 tablespoons of oil. Blend well, taste, and correct the seasonings. Serve in lettuce cups on individual plates and sprinkle each portion with parsley and sesame seeds.

Yield: 4 servings.

Note: This may also be served as an hors d'oeuvre. Heap the eggplant salad in a bowl and surround with an assortment of breads and crackers.

Salade Niçoise

Probably the most famous of all composed salads is this salad of tuna fish and vegetables. It is a perfect luncheon dish, or it may be served in small portions as a first course.

½ pound green beans

3 medium potatoes

4 ripe tomatoes, *or* 16 to 18 cherry tomatoes

1 green pepper

½ cup pitted black olives, preferably the small brine-cured Mediterranean type

2 2-ounce cans anchovy fillets

2 7-ounce cans tuna fish

4 hard-boiled eggs

1 large red onion

2 cups coarsely shredded lettuce

Crisp romaine or Boston lettuce leaves

⅓ cup minced fresh parsley

⅔ cup vinaigrette dressing (see page 392)

Break the green beans into 1-inch lengths and cook just until crisp-tender. Drain and run under cold water to stop the cooking. Boil the potatoes. When done, peel and cut into ⅜-inch-thick slices. Peel the tomatoes and cut them into wedges (if you use cherry tomatoes, leave them whole). Cut the green pepper into thin rings. Drain the olives. If you are using the pitted ones, cut them into eighths. Rinse the anchovy fillets in cold water and drain. Drain the tuna fish. Cut the hard-boiled eggs into quarters and thinly slice the onion.

To assemble, place the shredded lettuce on the bottom of a large bowl and line the sides of the bowl with the romaine or Boston lettuce. Place the tuna in the center and arrange in mounds around it the green beens, potato slices, tomatoes, and hard-boiled egg segments. Scatter the onion slices, olives, anchovies, and green pepper rings over the top and sprinkle with parsley. Toss with dressing at the table just before serving.

Yield: 4 to 6 main-course servings.

Orange and Onion Salad

2 heads Bibb lettuce

2 navel oranges, peeled and sliced

1 large Bermuda onion, very thinly sliced

1 ripe avocado, peeled and cut into cubes

½ cup salad oil

3 tablespoons lemon juice

2 tablespoons whiskey

Pinch of sugar

Salt and freshly ground pepper

Wash and dry the lettuce well and arrange on 4 plates. Place slices of orange and onion on each and sprinkle avocado cubes on top. Combine the remaining ingredients in a screw-top jar and shake well. Pour over the salads.

Yield: 4 servings.

Mushrooms, Zucchini, and Carrots

An eye-pleasing tricolor salad presentation.

½ pound fresh white mushrooms, thinly sliced

Lemon juice

4 large carrots, cut into 3-inch julienne strips

4 medium zucchini, cut into 3-inch julienne strips

Mustard vinaigrette dressing (see page 392)

Plunge sliced mushrooms for ½ minute into boiling water to which a little lemon juice has been added. Drain well. Blanch the julienned carrots in boiling salted water for 2 minutes. Drain well and run under cold water to refresh and stop the cooking. Drain again. Arrange separate mounds of zucchini, mushrooms, and carrots on a lettuce-lined platter and pour dressing over.

Yield: 6 servings.

German Potato Salad

This is a fine salad for a picnic or for party days when the refrigerator is crammed full, because it does not need to be refrigerated.

3 pounds small new potatoes

½ cup (or more) oil

½ cup (or more) vinegar

1 onion, chopped fine

Salt and freshly ground pepper

¼ teaspoon sweet paprika

¼ cup chopped fresh parsley

Garnishes: Parsley sprigs or watercress, green pepper rings, and pimiento strips

The essential in this preparation is warm vinegar on warm potatoes. Scrub the potatoes, cover with boiling salted water, cover the pot, and cook until done, 20 minutes or so. Don't overcook. The potatoes should be tender but still firm. Drain at once. While the potatoes are still warm (protect your hand with a clean pot holder or kitchen mitt), peel and slice them. Place the slices in a bowl and toss with enough oil to coat the potatoes and make them shiny. Heat the vinegar to the boiling point and add slowly, using as much as you need to moisten the mixture. Add the onion, salt, pepper, paprika, and chopped parsley. Toss well, taste, and correct seasoning. Mound on a platter and garnish with parsley sprigs or watercress, green pepper rings, and pimiento strips. Serve at room temperature.

Yield: 6 to 8 servings.

Chicken in Tarragon Mayonnaise

4 chicken breasts
2 tablespoons dried tarragon
½ cup sour cream
⅔ cup mayonnaise
Salt and freshly ground pepper
Leaf lettuce and cherry tomatoes

Poach the chicken breasts according to the recipe on page 163. Reserve the liquid.

In a large bowl, combine the tarragon with ¼ cup of the hot poaching liquid and let stand for 5 minutes to soften and develop full flavor.

Cut the chicken breasts into strips about 1 inch long and ½ inch wide. Stir the sour cream and mayonnaise into the tarragon mixture and blend well. Add the cut-up chicken while still warm and mix well. Add salt and pepper to taste. Chill and serve on a lettuce-lined platter garnished with cherry tomatoes.

Yield: 4 to 6 servings.

Variation: Combine the chicken with avocado strips. Toss with vinaigrette dressing and minced fresh parsley. Sprinkle with crisp, cooked bacon, coarsely chopped. Serve on a bed of curly endive. Or serve the chicken salad in scooped out avocado shells. You will need 2 cups cooked chicken and 2 avocados for 4 servings.

Hot Chicken Salad

The poultry takes on a whole new and beguiling personality in this hot salad preparation. Rich in flavor and a variety of textures, it's a perfect fork-food buffet item. Turkey may be substituted for the chicken.

3 cups cubed cooked chicken
1 tablespoon butter
½ cup slivered almonds
2 cups sliced celery
1 cup mayonnaise
2 tablespoons lemon juice
1 tablespoon grated onion
Salt and freshly ground pepper
½ cup thinly sliced water
  chestnuts
6 tablespoons grated sharp
  Cheddar cheese
½ cup lightly crushed cornflakes
  or potato chips

Preheat the oven to 350 degrees.

Place the cubed chicken in a good-size bowl. Melt the butter in a small skillet and brown the almonds over low heat. Shake the pan frequently. The nuts brown quickly, so keep an eye on them and remove them from the heat as soon as they begin to color.

Combine the chicken with the almonds, celery, mayonnaise, lemon juice, onion, salt, pepper, and water chestnuts and toss well. Transfer to a lightly greased shallow baking dish that can be used for serving. Sprinkle the top with the grated cheese and the cornflakes or potato chips, either of which will give a nice crisp coating. Bake for 20 to 30 minutes, or until heated through.

Yield: 4 servings.

Hot Potato and Egg Salad

A hearty family supper dish for occasions when the larder is low.

4 medium potatoes
3 tablespoons butter
3 tablespoons minced onion
2 tablespoons flour
1 cup milk
1 tablespoon Worcestershire sauce
Salt and freshly ground pepper
8 hard-boiled eggs, chopped
1 cup thinly sliced celery
¼ cup diced green pepper
¼ cup sliced stuffed olives
¼ cup mayonnaise
Chopped fresh parsley

Boil the potatoes until tender. Drain, peel, and dice. Return to the pot and keep warm.

Melt the butter in a small saucepan. Add the onion and sauté for 3 minutes. Stir in the flour and cook and stir until bubbly. Remove from the heat and whisk in the milk. Return to the heat and whisk vigorously until smooth and thickened. Add the Worcestershire and salt and pepper to taste. Pour the sauce over the potatoes and toss gently. Add the chopped eggs, celery, green pepper, and olives. Blend in the mayonnaise. Transfer to a heated bowl and sprinkle with chopped fresh parsley.

Yield: 4 to 6 servings.

Rice Salad

A tasty, crunchy accompaniment to add substance to a cold main course.

1 cup uncooked rice
4 tablespoons vegetable or olive
   oil
2 tablespoons wine vinegar
½ teaspoon curry powder
   (optional)
1 teaspoon Dijon mustard
⅓ cup finely diced pimiento
1 8-ounce can water chestnuts,
   thinly sliced
¼ cup finely chopped scallions
6 radishes, trimmed and thinly
   sliced
½ cup finely chopped green
   pepper
1 tablespoon mayonnaise
Salt and freshly ground
   pepper

Cook the rice in salted water according to the package directions. Add the oil to the warm rice and toss lightly. Use a fork for tossing so that you do not bruise the rice. Combine the vinegar with the curry powder and mustard and toss with the rice. Add the pimiento, water chestnuts, scallions, radishes, green pepper, and mayonnaise and toss again. Taste and adjust the seasonings. You may want some salt and pepper or another splash of vinegar or oil. The curry powder adds a subtle flavor without intruding itself, but if you are very fond of curry flavor, you could increase the amount.

Yield: 6 servings.

White Bean and Tuna Salad

3 cups cooked white beans (see page 301), or canned white beans (cannellini)

⅓ cup olive oil

¼ cup red wine vinegar

Salt and freshly ground pepper

1 small Bermuda onion, finely chopped

1 7-ounce can Italian tuna (packed in oil), drained and flaked

¼ teaspoon dried basil

¼ pound black olives (Greek or French)

2 tablespoons chopped fresh parsley

If you are using the canned beans, drain them and rinse them well in a colander or wire strainer under cold running water to wash off the gummy liquid from the can. Shake them to get rid of the excess moisture. Place the beans in a serving bowl and toss gently with the oil and vinegar, being careful not to mash the beans. Add the remaining ingredients, except the parsley, and toss again lightly to distribute the ingredients. Taste for seasonings and add more oil or vinegar, if needed. Sprinkle with chopped parsley and serve at room temperature.

Yield: 4 servings.

Lentil Salad

This salad may be served cold or warm as the starch at dinner.

1 cup lentils

1 onion stuck with 3 cloves

½ bay leaf

4 cups water

1 teaspoon salt

3 tablespoons olive or vegetable oil

1½ tablespoons red wine vinegar

½ cup finely chopped red onion

¼ cup diced pimiento

2 tablespoons minced fresh parsley

Freshly ground pepper

Place the lentils, onion, bay leaf, water, and salt in a medium-size saucepan and bring to a boil, covered. Reduce the heat and simmer, covered, for 30 to 40 minutes, or until the lentils are tender but not mushy. Drain well and discard the onion and bay leaf. Transfer the lentils to a bowl and, while still warm, toss with the oil, coating the lentils well. Add the vinegar slowly and toss. Add the red onion, pimiento, parsley, and pepper and toss again. Taste and correct the seasonings.

Yield: 6 servings.

Tabbouleh (Bulgur Salad)

A delicious summer salad that goes well with cold poached chicken and green beens vinaigrette.

1 cup bulgur (cracked wheat)
1 cup finely chopped fresh parsley
¼ cup finely chopped fresh mint leaves
2 bunches scallions, white and green parts, finely chopped
3 medium tomatoes, peeled, seeded, and chopped, *or* 1 cup cherry tomatoes, halved
½ cup lemon juice
½ cup olive oil
Salt and freshly ground pepper

Place the bulgur in a bowl and cover with boiling water to the depth of 1 inch above the top of the wheat. Let soak for 1 hour. Line a sieve with a few layers of cheesecloth and drain the cracked wheat. Twist the cheesecloth into a bag and squeeze to extract the excess moisture. Spread the bulgur on a dry towel in a thin layer and let dry. Scrape the bulgur into a mixing bowl and add the remaining ingredients, mixing with a wooden spoon. Taste and correct the seasonings. Chill for 1 to 2 hours before serving. Serve in a lettuce-lined bowl.

Yield: 6 servings.

Variation: Any finely chopped cooked meat or poultry can be added to provide a satisfactory hot weather luncheon dish. Lamb has a particular affinity for bulgur.

Fish Salad

1½ pounds white-fleshed fish (halibut, haddock, flounder, etc.)
2 cups cooked, chilled green peas
½ cup chopped scallions
2 cups cooked, chilled diced beets
½ cup finely chopped dill pickle
½ cup mayonnaise
½ cup sour cream
1 tablespoon Dijon mustard
Salt and freshly ground pepper
Parsley or watercress sprigs for garnish

Poach the fish (see page 197) and flake when cool. When completely cool, place in a bowl with green peas, scallions, beets, and pickles. Combine the remaining ingredients and toss with the fish mixture. Taste and adjust the seasonings. Arrange on a bed of salad greens and garnish with parsley or watercress.

Yield: 4 to 6 servings.

10
Fruits

Fruits are a boon and a comfort to menu planners, particularly at the times of year when the fruit markets smell and look like flower shops, their bins spilling over with a profusion of melons, berries, grapes, apples, pears, and other splendid fruits, all as nutritious as they are good tasting. As an added bonus, fruits are one of the least caloric snacks we can eat, for few fruits contain more than a hundred calories.

Modern methods of growing and storing fruit, improved refrigeration, and fast transportation have made a huge variety of fresh fruits available every month of the year. Unhappily, many of these are picked unripe, held in cold storage, and offered for sale before they have achieved their true taste and texture. As consumers, we must learn to be selective and discriminating. Fruits, like vegetables, are seasonal. They are highest in quality and lowest in price when they are at the peak of their season, and it makes good sense to concentrate on those products that are the freshest and offer the best value each month of the year.

There is no end to ways we can enjoy fruits, alone or in combination. Most of us start our day with fruit in one form or another at breakfast. Fruits can appear in a fruit cup, a fruit compote, a fruit salad, a savory side dish with meat or poultry, or as an ingredient in pastry or cake that can range from simple to dazzling. A platter or a basket of fresh fruits in season or a fine apple or pear served with cheese is a lovely dessert. A simple custard or ice cream topped with fruit takes on a party look. And even fruits that are not quite as good as they ought to be can be rescued by a sauce or a syrup or a sprinkle of lemon or lime juice. Fruits can be baked, poached, or cooked in many other ways that add variety and interest to meals.

Composition

Fruits contain from 75 to 90 percent water, which explains their juiciness. Their next most important constituent is carbohydrate. All fruits contain some vitamin C. Those richest in vitamin C include oranges, grapefruit, cantaloupe, papaya, and strawberries, with lesser amounts in apricots, bananas, blackberries, blueberries, honeydew melons, pineapples, red raspberries, tangerines, and watermelons. Yellow fruits such as cantaloupes, peaches, and apricots are rich in carotene, which the body converts into vitamin A. Most fruits are low in fats. Most are also low in the B vitamins and contain relatively little protein. They have just enough protein to maintain their own life processes but not enough to make a significant contribution to the daily needs of humans. But of great importance is the cellulose they contain, which adds bulk to the diet for the good functioning of the gastrointestinal tract.

When fruits such as apples and bananas are immature, they contain a fair amount of starch and little sugar. As most fruits ripen, that starch converts to sugar. The sweetness of fully ripened melons, oranges, peaches, and strawberries, for example, is due to their high level of sugar.

Buying Fruit

If possible, try to buy fruits that are not prepackaged in snug plastic coverings to protect them from the prying eyes, probing fingers, and inquisitive noses of customers. How can you judge that nice fruity smell when the fruit is encased in a sniff-proof package?

Don't choose your fruit only on the basis of size and appearance. In too many instances, food cultivators have striven for a beautiful fruit that stores well and have overlooked flavor. Fruit with minor skin blemishes or poor color may have good eating quality, and large, beautifully colored fruit may be mealy and tasteless. Experience gives the food shopper a sixth sense about what tastes good as opposed to what looks good. In general, buy fruits that are in season, and buy from local orchards whenever you can.

Storing Fruit

Ripe fruits should be refrigerated or stored in a cool place and used as soon as possible. Except for berries and cherries, wash all fruit thoroughly before refrigerating. Sort out berries, discard any moldy or spoiled ones before they infect their neighbors, and refrigerate them in a dry container. Cold storage adds to the life span of fruits because even after fruits are harvested, their cells do not die. They continue to take in oxygen and give off carbon dioxide, a process called *respiration*. A low storage temperature slows down this process, making it possible for the cells to live longer.

Some varieties of fruit can be bought when they are still hard and ripened at room temperature. But for this to happen, they must be ripe enough to have developed their full potential of sugar. Most fruits ripened at home will never be as succulent as those that were allowed to ripen on the tree, but they may have an acceptable flavor and texture. To ripen fruits at home, keep them at room temperature away from the sun. You can speed up the ripening process by placing them loosely in a closed bag. Look at them daily and refrigerate them as soon as they are ripe. Pears, bananas, and honeydew melons are the exceptions to the observation about the superiority of tree-ripened fruits, for they will develop sweetness, flavor, and texture when they are allowed to ripen off the tree. Actually,

bananas are good only if they are picked green and pears do best when ripened at room temperature. Honeydews are the only melons that become noticeably sweeter after they are picked.

Frozen and Canned Fruit

Frozen and canned fruits are convenient to have on hand for emergency situations or when fresh fruits are not available. A baked fruit compote made of a variety of canned fruits is easily assembled and makes a refreshing addition to a meat or poultry course or as a dessert. Frozen berries are useful for dessert sauces for ice cream, puddings, or crêpes. Frozen raspberries are a particular cause for thanksgiving because they will often fit into a budget when the price of the fresh is zooming up into the stratosphere.

Preparing Fruit

Because of the presence of an enzyme, apples, bananas, peaches, and pears discolor rapidly when they are cut and exposed to air. Immersing the cut or peeled fruit in a solution of lemon or other citrus fruit juices and water will prevent browning, and cooking the fruit in a sugar syrup destroys the enzyme and stops the browning process. A concentrated sugar solution without heat also depresses enzyme activity and sugared sliced peaches do not brown as quickly as unsugared. The sugar or sugar syrup also acts to keep the oxygen in the atmosphere away from the surface of the fruit.

To peel apples and pears, use a swivel-bladed vegetable peeler. It will remove the peel smoothly and evenly, taking the least possible amount of pulp with it. To remove the skins of apricots, nectarines, and peaches, drop them in boiling water for about 30 seconds and the skins can be lifted off easily.

To sweeten fruits, add the sugar just before serving, unless you want a lot of syrup. Sugar, like salt, draws out the water from the cells of the fruit.

Cooking Fruit

Even though cooking diminishes food values, there is no question that some fruits are greatly enhanced when cooked in interesting ways. In addition, some people have difficulty digesting raw fruit. A fine poached pear, glistening and translucent, served with a delicate custard sauce or bathed in a purée of raspberries is impressive enough to provide a fitting crescendo to the most formal dinner.

Fruits may be baked, braised, broiled, poached, puréed, or sautéed, and, for a moment of drama, they can be brought to the table flaming. To test for doneness, pierce the fruit with a thin knitting needle, which will not mark the fruit. When it goes through the fruit without encountering resistance, the fruit is cooked.

Baking

Apples, bananas, peaches, and plums may be baked, peeled or not, as you wish. Cut the fruit into halves, core, and arrange in a shallow buttered baking dish. Dot the fruit with butter, either brown or white sugar, and spices, if you like. Add liquid to the pan—fruit juice, red or white wine, brandy, rum, a liqueur, or water—and baste the fruit with it from time to time. Bake uncovered in a 350-degree oven until the fruit is tender. We call this baking, but it is really braising because we use liquid.

Broiling

Apple or pineapple slices, bananas, peaches, nectarines, and grapefruit may be broiled to serve as a quick, light dessert, or, except for the grapefruit, as a side dish with meat or poultry. Cut grapefruit or oranges in half, loosen sections and remove seeds; peel bananas and split lengthwise; slice pineapple and remove rind; core apples and cut into rings; peel peaches and nectarines, cut in half and remove pits. Arrange the fruit on a lightly oiled baking sheet, cavity side up for peaches and nectarines, dot with butter and brown sugar, and place in a preheated broiler about 3 inches below the heat unit. Broil for 4 or 5 minutes, or until the fruit softens a little and the sugar and butter become brown and bubbly.

Grapefruit can also be topped with maple syrup, honey, or ½ teaspoon orange liqueur per half. Oranges go well with a sprinkling of brown sugar and a dot of butter; try adding some shredded coconut at the last minute.

Deep-Frying

Deep-fried fruits, or fruit fritters, are an all-time favorite. Succulent fruit encased in a crisp, golden batter may be served as a side dish, or, dusted with confectioners' sugar, as a dessert.

Fruit for fritters should be ripe but firm. Cut the fruit in pieces not more than ½ inch thick. You may use peeled, cored apples cut crosswise in circles, canned or fresh pineapple slices, orange segments, halves of canned or poached apricots or pears, or bananas cut in three or four diagonal chunks. It is essential that the fruits be completely dry before being immersed in the batter, or the batter will not adhere. For extra flavor, you may marinate the fruit for about an hour in wine, kirsch, rum, or brandy and use the marinade in place of the milk in the batter. If you marinate the fruit, dry it well and dust it with confectioners' sugar or cookie crumbs before putting it in the batter.

Batter that is heavy with egg yolk will protect the fruit from absorbing fat during cooking. Always cover and refrigerate batter for at least two hours or overnight before using. The resting period adds to the tenderness of the batter. If you do not have time for the resting period, mix the batter with as few strokes as possible so as not to build up the gluten.

Fritter Batter

2 eggs
⅔ cup milk or fruit marinade
1 tablespoon melted butter or vegetable oil
1 cup all-purpose flour
¼ teaspoon salt
2 teaspoons sugar
Vegetable oil for frying
Confectioners' sugar

Separate the eggs and reserve the whites. In a medium-size bowl, mix together lightly the egg yolks, milk or marinade, and melted butter or oil. In another bowl, combine the flour, salt, and sugar and add to the egg yolk mixture. Stir lightly until blended and smooth. Cover the batter and refrigerate for 2 hours or longer. Just before using, beat the egg whites until stiff but not dry and fold them gently into the batter.

Heat about 3 inches of oil in a deep fryer to 375 degrees. Dry the fruit, dust with confectioners' sugar or cookie crumbs. With long-handled kitchen tongs or a slotted spoon, dip the fruit into the batter and drop it gently into the hot fat. Fry only a few pieces at a time so that the fat remains hot. Fry until golden brown on all sides, 4 or 5 minutes. Remove from the fat and drain well on paper towels. Keep warm in a 250-degree oven until all are done. Serve hot dusted with confectioners' sugar.

Yield: Enough batter for 2 cups fruit, or 6 to 8 servings.

Poaching

Fruits poached in a light sugar syrup or wine make delicious desserts and they keep well in the refrigerator. Firm fruits such as apricots, peaches, pears, and pineapple can be successfully poached. Fruits such as apples, gooseberries, and plums may also be poached but they contain less cellulose and they must be watched carefully or they will fall apart. A small amount of sugar in the poaching water helps the fruit to hold its shape, but a large amount will shrink and toughen the skin and slow down the tenderizing process. If you are using fruit that is extremely firm, start the cooking in plain water, and add the sugar toward the end of the cooking when the fruit is partly tenderized. On the other hand, if you have delicate fruit that you want to retain its shape, such as strawberries, use a heavy syrup with a high concentration of sugar.

For a light syrup for fruits such as apples or grapes, use about ⅓ cup sugar to 1 cup water; for a medium syrup for fruits such as apricots, cherries, and pears, use ½ cup sugar to 1 cup water; for a heavy syrup for soft, juicy fruits such as berries, figs, peaches, and plums, use 1 cup sugar to 1 cup water.

To poach fruits, mix sugar and wine, or sugar and water with an acid such as lemon juice or a pinch of cream of tartar. Bring to a boil, and boil slowly for 5 minutes. Add the peeled fruit (it can also be sliced) to the boiling syrup and reduce the heat so that the liquid simmers gently. The cooking time will vary depending on the ripeness of the fruit and the variety. The best way to test is by piercing the fruit with a thin knitting needle. If it goes through the fruit easily without encountering resistance, the fruit is done. Remove it at once from the hot syrup so that it will not lose its shape.

For a particularly nice poaching syrup for apples, use ⅔ cup of sugar, 1 cup water, and the juice and rind of 1 lemon. After the fruit is poached, dissolve ½ cup currant jelly in the thickened syrup and pour over the apples.

Sautéeing

Firm fruits such as sliced bananas, apple rings, quartered pears and peaches, and fingers or slices of fresh pineapple may be sautéed in butter and served as a side dish with meats and poultry or as a dessert. Peel and core or pit fruits and cut them up. Sprinkle them with sugar as they cook to give them a shiny, glazed finish, and toss them during cooking so that they brown evenly. Cook them until they are slightly tender and glazed. They lose all their style if they get too soft and break up, so remove the pan from the heat before that happens. Ice cream topped with thin slices of sautéed bananas is a lovely dessert.

Puréeing

Any fruit, canned, frozen, or fresh, may be puréed. Fresh fruit is first peeled and cut up for quick cooking. Use as little water as possible and sweeten it after cooking. Purée the fruit by forcing it through a food mill or whirling it in a food processor or blender.

Fruit purées are used in soufflés and sauces. They may also be served hot or cold, sprinkled with orange or lemon rind, or topped with cream, crème fraîche, or whipped cream to which you have added cake crumbs browned in butter, coarsely chopped nuts, or crumbled macaroons. Fruit purées make pleasant light desserts combined with stiffly beaten egg whites that have been lightly sweetened.

Dried Fruit

Dried fruits are naturally tougher than fresh fruits because most of the moisture has been removed. To replace their water content and restore their softness, they must be cooked in hot water. Dried fruits are high in both calories and nutritive values. One cup of fresh prune plums, for example, contains 124 calories; the same amount of uncooked dried prunes contains 344 calories. However, dried fruits expand when they are cooked and a mixed compote of just a few prunes, apricots, and peaches cooked to juicy plumpness makes an adequate portion. Cooked dried fruits make a splendid breakfast fruit, or, laced with sherry, an equally lovely dessert. They are also good in cobblers, coffee cakes, puddings, and fruit salads.

Apples, apricots, peaches, plums, pears, dates, figs, currants, and raisins are the most popular dried fruits. They can be bought both loose and packaged. Some have been processed so that they have a high percentage of moisture and are tender enough to eat without further cooking. They provide a very nice garnish on a cheese tray.

Do not wash or soak dried fruit unless called for on the package. Most dried fruits do not require any additional sugar. To cook, cover them with cold water, bring slowly to a boil with a few slices of lemon for additional flavor, reduce the heat, and simmer uncovered for 6 or 7 minutes. Transfer the fruit and the hot liquid to a jar or bowl and cover it tightly. The fruit will continue to soften and plump up in the liquid. Refrigerate when cool.

If you insist upon sweetening, simmer the fruit to tenderize it first and add sugar to taste after the fruit is cooked. Hold it overnight to give the sugar time to diffuse into the fruits.

Store unopened packages of dried fruits on a cool, dry shelf. Don't keep them longer than a few months as they deteriorate with age. Packages of dates and figs should be covered with foil and refrigerated. Once packages of raisins or currants have been opened, the contents should be transferred to jars with tight lids, or the boxes can be covered with plastic wrap to make them airtight. It is often necessary to plump up raisins and currants, particularly for quick-cooking recipes. Rinse them quickly, drain them well, and spread them out on a cookie tin. Cover them tightly with aluminum foil and place them in a 350-degree oven until they puff up and look less wrinkled. They may also be soaked in sherry or other liquid, or they may be heated in a double boiler over boiling water.

Macédoine of Fresh Fruits

A medley of fresh fruits is a perfect way to finish a dinner. Whatever is best and freshest can go into it. Allow about 1 cup of fruit per serving.

Start with a juicy base for the fruits, which could be fresh, sectioned oranges or grapefruit or, if that is not convenient, a 10-ounce package of frozen mixed fruits, which, when thawed, will supply enough liquid.

To Section Oranges and Grapefruit: Chill the fruits before preparing. Cut a slice from the top, then cut peel in strips from top to bottom, cutting deep enough to remove any white membrane. Then cut a slice from the bottom. Hold the fruit firmly in the palm of one hand over a bowl in order not to waste a drop of the juice. With a sharp knife, cut alongside each dividing membrane from the outside to the middle of the core, and peel out the section. Continue until all the sections are removed. Your technique and speed will improve with practice and you will be able to cut segments that are appetizingly firm and whole.

Just about any fruit can be added to a fruit medley. Use at least four. Wash, peel, core, and cut the fruit into 1-inch pieces. Sprinkle with lemon juice to prevent discoloration, and sweeten to taste. For flavoring, add a liqueur such as kirsch, Cointreau, or Grand Marnier. Refrigerate at least 4 hours and stir occasionally so that the flavors blend; top with lemon ice if desired.

You can also layer a selection of fresh fruits with plain yogurt sweetened with brown sugar. Use 1 cup sugar to 2 cups yogurt. Adding chopped, preserved ginger to the fruits gives them a piquant taste.

Curried Baked Fruit

This baked fruit compote can provide a lively counterpoint for a simple poultry or beef main course.

1 large can pear halves
1 large can peach or apricot
  halves, or both
1 large can pineapple chunks
¾ cup dark brown sugar
2 teaspoons curry powder, or more
4 tablespoons butter

Drain the fruits in a colander 1 hour or longer, if you can. Excess liquid remaining on the fruits will make the sauce thin and soupy. Don't worry about dryness; the fruits will still give out a lot of juice. Discard the drained juice, or save it for another purpose.

Preheat the oven to 350 degrees.

Mix together the brown sugar and curry powder. You have to know your own strength with curry. The 2 teaspoons will give it flavor, but you may like it more highly spiced. Grease a 2-quart casserole that can be brought to the table. Arrange a layer of fruit on the bottom, sprinkle with part of the brown sugar mixture, dot with butter, and continue with the layers until all are used. Finish with a sprinkle of brown sugar mixture and butter. Bake for 50 minutes to 1 hour, uncovered, or until the sauce is bubbly. Serve the fruit hot with the main course.

Yield: 6 to 8 servings.

Hot Fruit Compote. This is a dessert version of Curried Baked Fruit.

Allow a 1-pound can of fruit for 2 servings and use a combination of three or four (or all) of the following, according to the number of servings you need: peach halves, pear halves, pineapple chunks, whole apricots, and black cherries. Drain fruits well. Lightly grease a shallow baking dish that can be used for serving and that is large enough to hold the fruit in a single layer.

Distribute the fruits nicely in the casserole and sprinkle them with crumbs made from 8 or 10 coconut macaroons. Dribble 2 or 3 tablespoons of Grand Marnier or some other fruit liqueur over the fruits. Mix together ½ cup or so of brown sugar and 2 tablespoons of melted butter and sprinkle over the fruits. Bake for 1 hour at 350 degrees. Serve hot.

Fruits in Yogurt

1 pint fresh stawberries, washed, hulled, and cut in half

2 cups fresh or canned pineapple cubes

2 bananas, sliced

2 tablespoons lemon juice

3 tablespoons ginger preserved in syrup, chopped

2 cups plain yogurt

1 cup firmly packed brown sugar

Combine the strawberries, pineapple cubes, bananas, lemon juice, and chopped ginger in a bowl, tossing to distribute. In another small bowl, mix together the yogurt and brown sugar. In individual serving bowls, alternate layers of fruit and yogurt, ending with yogurt. Chill in the refrigerator for an hour. Just before serving, sprinkle a little brown sugar on top with a few tiny dice of the preserved ginger.

Yield: 6 servings.

Variation: Use any fruits that look fresh and tempting at your greengrocer's–seedless grapes, orange sections, kiwi, mangoes, papayas, blueberries.

Apples

Selection: Look for apples that have good color for their variety and are firm to the touch. Skins should be smooth and reasonably free of bruises. Tart apples such as greenings and Granny Smiths are excellent for cooking. The most widely available eating apples the year round are McIntosh and Golden and Red Delicious, but there are many juicy, good-tasting varieties that are regional. For baking, use apples that will hold their shape, such as Rome Beauties, York, or Cortland. The Delicious apples hold their shape when baked but are uninteresting in flavor.

Peak Season: Available all year but are at their best from September through November when they are newly harvested.

Methods of Preparation: Apples are splendid fruits eaten out of hand. They may be stewed, baked, sautéed, deep-fried, broiled, and poached. They may be used raw, sliced or diced, in fruit cocktails and fruit salads. They can be candied, spiced, preserved, and made into jellies. They are wonderful in tarts, pies, cakes, and cookies; as fruit stuffings for poultry; and as a side dish with meat, poultry, and game. An unpeeled red apple, cored and cut into eighths, and arranged spokelike around a few slices of good cheese makes an excellent dessert or light luncheon dish.

Braised Apples

6 firm baking apples
½ teaspoon cinnamon
¾ cup sugar
1 thin-skinned, unpeeled orange,
    cut into thin slices
4 thin lemon slices, unpeeled
⅔ cup water

Wash and core the apples. Peel them about a third of the way down.

Mix the cinnamon and sugar together and place in a layer in the bottom of a heavy braising pot or a large sauté pan that has a tightly-fitting cover. The pot must be big enough to contain the apples in a single layer. Cut the orange and lemon slices into eighths and arrange them over the sugar. Place the apples, peeled side down, on the sugar and fruit pieces. Pour the water over the apples. Cover the pot tightly and cook gently over low heat for 15 minutes.

Remove the cover and carefully turn the apples peeled side up, using kitchen tongs or two long-handled spoons. Replace the cover and continue to cook over low heat until the apples are fork-tender. This may take 15 minutes or longer, but watch them carefully and don't overcook or they can fall apart.

When the apples have reached the proper degree of doneness— soft enough to let a spoon pierce them easily, yet firm enough to maintain their shape—remove the apples to a serving dish. Continue to cook the syrup and fruit pieces for an additional 6 or 7 minutes, or until the syrup has thickened. Stuff the cores of the apples with the fruit slices and glaze the tops with a spoonful or two of the syrup. Serve lukewarm or at room temperature.

If you wish to candy the tops of the apples and make them crisp, brown, and bubbly, transfer the apples as soon as they are done to a baking sheet. Stuff the cores with the fruit slices and sprinkle the tops generously with sugar. Place them under the broiler for about 10 minutes, basting them often with the syrup and adding more sugar as needed.

Yield: 6 servings.

Applesauce

Tart apples like greenings, pippins, or Granny Smiths make very nice applesauce. A few McIntosh apples will add additional flavor. You may peel and core the apples before cooking, or cook them with skins and cores and purée them through a food mill. Apples contain an adequate amount of liquid, so add only enough water to create the steam necessary to soften them.

3 pounds apples (9 or 10)
⅓ to ½ cup water
Sugar
½ teaspoon ground cinnamon or
   freshly grated nutmeg

Peel and core the apples (unless you are going to put them through a food mill) and cut them into large chunks. As you cut them, to prevent their turning brown, drop them into a bowl of cold water to which you have added a tablespoon of lemon juice. Place the apples in a saucepan, add water, cover, and cook slowly until they are almost soft, about 15 minutes. Purée them in a food mill, if you wish, to remove the skins and cores. Taste and add a little sugar. The amount of sugar needed is variable since apples have different degrees of tartness. When the apples are sweetened to your taste, simmer uncovered for a few minutes to thicken the sauce and give the sugar time to melt. If you want the applesauce spiced, add the cinnamon or nutmeg at the time you add the sugar.

Yield: 5 to 6 servings.

Chunky Applesauce

For a different version of applesauce, peel, core, and thinly slice 2 pounds of tart apples. Place them in a 12-inch skillet, covered, over very low heat and let them steam and sweat for 2 or 3 minutes. Increase heat to high and add ½ cup firmly packed dark brown sugar, ½ cup apple juice, 2 tablespoons butter, 2 table-spoons fresh lemon juice, and ½ teaspoon cinnamon. Bring to a full boil, reduce heat, and stir apples gently. Cover the pan and simmer until the apples have softened but are still slightly firm and have not lost their shape. Taste and correct seasoning. Serve at room temperature or chilled.

Yield: 4 servings.

Apple Crisp

An old favorite that has never lost its appeal. Tart apples are the important ingredient. If you can't get tart apples, use peaches.

1 cup flour
¾ cup sugar
Pinch of salt
1 teaspoon baking powder
1 egg
5 to 6 cups peeled, cored, and sliced tart apples (about 1½ pounds)
2 tablespoons brown sugar
⅓ cup butter, melted
1 teaspoon cinnamon-sugar

Preheat the oven to 350 degrees.

Combine the flour, sugar, salt, baking powder, and unbeaten egg in a small bowl. Use a fork and a kind of chopping motion to form coarse crumbs. Don't beat or you will end up with one big lump instead of a lot of little ones.

Butter a 1½-quart baking dish or an 8-inch-square pan and spread the apple slices in it. Sprinkle with brown sugar. Spread the flour mixture evenly over the apples. Dribble the melted butter over the topping and sprinkle with the cinnamon-sugar.

Bake for 30 to 40 minutes, or until the topping is lightly browned and the apples are tender. Serve warm or at room temperature. It will still be delicious the next day.

Yield: 6 servings.

Apple Blueberry Crisp. When fresh blueberries are in season, substitute 2 cups of blueberries for 2 cups of the apples and proceed as above.

Easy Apple Pie

It looks like apple pie and tastes like apple pie, but it is a cinch to make. Use either Granny Smiths or greenings.

6 cups peeled, cored, and sliced tart apples (1½ to 2 pounds)
⅓ cup sugar
¼ teaspoon ground cinnamon
2 tablespoons butter
½ cup sugar
1 teaspoon vanilla extract
1 egg, lightly beaten
½ cup flour
½ teaspoon baking powder

Preheat the oven to 400 degrees. Generously butter a 9-inch pie plate and spread the apple slices in it evenly. Combine the ⅓ cup sugar and cinnamon and sprinkle over the apples. Cover tightly with aluminum foil and bake on the center rack of the oven for 20 minutes.

While the apples are baking, cream together in a small bowl the butter and ½ cup sugar. Add the vanilla extract and egg and beat well. Mix together the flour and baking powder and add to the sugar mixture, stirring until smooth. After the apples have baked for 20 minutes, remove the pie plate, discard the aluminum foil, and with a spatula, spread the batter evenly over the apples. Return to the oven and continue to bake until the crust is lightly browned, about 20 minutes. Let stand for at least ½ hour, so that it will firm up and you can cut it into wedges. Serve warm or at room temperature, with whipped cream or ice cream, if you like.

Yield: 8 servings.

Apple Chutney

A spicy, flavorful accompaniment for cold meats, cheeses, and curries.

8 cups unpeeled, diced, tart apples (about 3 pounds)
1 pound brown sugar
⅓ cup cider vinegar
1 large onion, chopped
1 clove garlic, minced
1 bell pepper, red or green, chopped
2 cups raisins
1 teaspoon salt
1 tablespoon mustard seed, *or* 1 teaspoon dry mustard
1 teaspoon powdered ginger
Pinch ground red pepper or Tabasco sauce

In a large, heavy-bottomed pan, combine the apples, sugar, vinegar, onion, garlic, and chopped pepper. Bring slowly to a boil, reduce the heat, and simmer slowly until the mixture becomes fairly thick, 35 to 40 minutes. Add the raisins, salt, mustard, ginger, and ground red pepper or a few shakes of Tabasco and cook for 30 minutes longer. When cool, place in containers, cover, and refrigerate. It will keep indefinitely in the refrigerator.

Yield: 4 pints.

Apricots

Fresh apricots are delicate and they ship poorly, making them a luxury in many areas of the country. During the short season when fresh, tree-ripened apricots are available, they should be eaten and savored in their natural state with no additional adornment. Apricots contain significant amounts of potassium and iron.

Selection: Look for apricots that have a uniform rich yellow or orange color, are firm and plump but yield slightly to pressure. Stay away from those that are heavily tinged with green, have bruise marks, or look wilted and shriveled.

Peak Season: June and July. Imported apricots may be available in December and January.

Methods of Preparation: Raw, eaten out of hand, in fruit salads, or sliced and served with sugar and heavy cream. Cooked, may be poached, baked, puréed, used in jams, pies, puddings, and fritters.

Dried and canned apricots are easily available and are a good substitute for the fresh. Dried, cooked apricots are used in many dishes with meat and fowl.

To peel apricots, plunge them into boiling water for less than a minute. Remove and drop into cold water. The skins should slip off easily.

To stew dried apricots, simmer them in water to cover until soft, about 10 minutes. They generally do not need to be sweetened. You may add a few thin slices of lemon, if you wish.

To purée apricots, cook them in water to cover until very soft and mushy. Purée in a food mill, blender, or food processor. Add sugar to taste.

To poach fresh apricots, peel and leave them whole or cut them in half and remove the pit. Make a syrup of ½ cup sugar to 1 cup water. Add a few drops of lemon juice or a pinch of cream of tartar to the water. Boil the syrup for 5 minutes. Reduce the heat so that the water simmers, add the apricots, and cook gently for 7 to 10 minutes, or until the fruit is tender. Remove the apricots with a slotted spoon and boil the liquid until it reduces to a syrup. Serve the apricots, chilled, with a little of the syrup and top with whipped cream or crème fraîche.

Apricot Cream

1 11-ounce package dried apricots (2 cups)

1 cup water

1 cup orange juice

½ cup sugar

1 tablespoon lemon juice (kirsch, brandy, or an orange liqueur may be substituted)

1 cup heavy cream

½ cup blanched, slivered almonds, lightly toasted

Wash the apricots, drain, and place in a saucepan with the water and orange juice. Bring slowly to a boil, reduce the heat, and cook gently, uncovered, until the apricots are soft, about 20 minutes. Stir in the sugar and cook, stirring, until the sugar is dissolved. Remove from the heat and purée in a blender, food processor, or food mill. Stir in the lemon juice or liqueur and cool.

Whip the cream until stiff peaks form and fold it into the apricot purée. Transfer to a pretty serving bowl, preferably a glass one, and chill well in the refrigerator. Sprinkle with nuts and serve in individual bowls.

Yield: 6 servings.

Apricot Charlotte

8 slices white bread, crusts trimmed
6 tablespoons butter, melted
3 McIntosh apples
1 1-pound can apricots
2 tablespoons butter
2 tablespoons lemon juice
Apricot sauce (see page 465)

Preheat the oven to 400 degrees.

Dip both sides of the bread slices into melted butter and use them to line the bottom and sides of a 1½-quart ovenproof bowl—the Pyrex round-bottomed does nicely. Overlap the slices to provide a firm support for the filling. Cut two or three of the slices into triangles to fill in the spaces.

Peel, core, and slice the apples. Drain the apricots and discard the juice. Heat 2 tablespoons of butter in a saucepan and add the apple slices and drained apricots. Cook over low heat, stirring from time to time, until the mixture is soft and most of the moisture has evaporated, about 10 minutes. Add the lemon juice and mix. Fill the bread-lined dish with the fruit. Place the dish on a baking sheet in the hot oven and bake for 40 to 45 minutes, or until the crust is golden brown. To serve, invert the bowl on a round serving platter. Serve with apricot sauce.

Yield: 4 servings.

Bananas

Besides their pleasant taste and texture, bananas are high in potassium, an important mineral not present in large quantities in most foods.

Selection: Look for firm, yellow bananas free of bruises. They will ripen quickly and easily at room temperature. Tipped with green, they are partly ripe and may be cooked. An all-yellow banana is ready to eat or cook and can be used as an ingredient in baking. Flecked with brown, the banana is fully ripe, at its best and most digestible for eating and baking.

Peak Season: All year.

Methods of Preparation: Raw, for eating out of hand, in fruit salads, mashed for cakes, soufflés, cookies, muffins, breads, and milk shakes; sliced with breakfast cereal or ice cream desserts. May be baked, broiled, or sautéed.

In spite of the once-popular jingle about the cataclysmic results of putting bananas in the refrigerator, that is exactly where they should go once they become very ripe. It is true that the refrigerator stay will turn the banana skin brown, but it does not affect the fruit inside except to slow down further ripening. The life of the banana will be prolonged for about three days before the fruit itself begins to discolor.

Baked Bananas. These make a nice side dish with ham, pork, or poultry. Brush peeled bananas with melted butter and sprinkle lightly with salt; bake in a 375-degree oven until lightly browned and tender, about 15 minutes. For dessert, sprinkle them with lemon juice, brown sugar, and ground cinnamon in addition to the butter. Serve with sweetened whipped cream, vanilla yogurt, or ice cream. They can also be flamed. Warm ¼ cup brandy or rum, ignite, and pour the flaming liquor over the sweetened bananas before serving.

Plantains

A cooking banana, the plantain is longer, starchier, and less sweet than its yellow cousin. It is a staple of the Caribbean diet and is served as a vegetable, much like a starchy potato. Plantains may be combined with onions, pepper, and spices as a kind of vegetable stew.

They are never eaten raw, but they must not be overcooked or they can become bitter. To boil, peel them and simmer in rapidly boiling water for 30 minutes. Season and serve with melted butter. If very ripe, they can be sliced and fried in deep fat.

Glazed Sautéed Bananas

Serve as a vegetable with poultry, or as a dessert.

4 firm bananas
4 tablespoons butter
2 tablespoons lemon juice
4 tablespoons sugar

Peel bananas and cut crosswise into slices ¾ to 1 inch thick. Heat the butter in a large skillet. Brush the banana slices with lemon juice and roll in sugar, and place in the pan in the hot butter. Cook until tender and brown, turning them to brown evenly. Serve hot.

Yield: 4 servings.

Blackberries

Selection: Look for bright, clean berries with good uniform purplish black color. If they are in a cardboard container, take a look at the bottom to make sure it is unstained from mushy or moldy berries.
Peak Season: Summer months.

Methods of Preparation: Fresh as a dessert with cream and sugar; in fruit cups and fruit salads; cooked in pies, puddings, pancakes; preserved in jams, jellies, wine.
Blackberry Pancakes: Substitute for blueberries in pancakes, page 276.

Sour Cream Blackberry Pie

1 unbaked 10-inch pie shell (see page 501)
2 pints blackberries
1 cup sour cream
⅔ cup brown sugar
1 tablespoon flour

Preheat the oven to 450 degrees.

Wash, pick over, and drain the berries thoroughly. Combine the sour cream, brown sugar, and flour in a small bowl and blend well with a wire whisk. Heap the berries into the pie crust and cover them with the sour cream mixture.

Bake for 10 minutes, or until the crust is set. Reduce the heat to 325 degrees and bake for 25 to 35 minutes, or until the berries are soft, juicy, and bubbling.

Yield: 6 to 8 servings.

Blueberries

The cultivated blueberries we find in our markets are dark blue with a typical silvery bloom. The wild varieties are paler in color and they have a more distinctive flavor. People frequently confuse wild blueberries with their relatives, huckleberries, which are darker, more tart and have harder seeds than blueberries. The two are botanically distinct from each other. Blueberries are easy to handle; they involve no peeling, no puttering, no pitting, and no waste.

Selection: Look for berries that are plump, firm, and uniform in size. Avoid stained or leaking containers.

Peak Season: From May through September, according to area. Wild blueberries are at their peak in July.

Methods of Preparation: As a dessert, served with sugar and cream, in fruit salads and fruit cups; cooked as a sauce for ice cream; in pies, puddings, cakes, muffins, pancakes; or preserved in jellies and jams.

To wash blueberries, place them in a bowl of water to float off bits of stems and leaves. Lift the berries out of the water, replace in fresh water and repeat a few times until no more foreign particles appear. Washing the berries in water and draining the water will not get rid of the extraneous little bits and pieces.

Blueberry Buckle

This hearty cake can start the day as a breakfast treat or give it a fine finish as a dessert. It may be served warm with cream, if you like.

4 tablespoons butter
¾ cup sugar
1 egg
½ cup milk
2 cups all-purpose flour
2 teaspoons baking powder
½ teaspoon salt
2 cups fresh blueberries, picked over and washed
Topping:
⅓ cup flour
½ cup sugar
½ teaspoon ground cinnamon
¼ teaspoon freshly grated nutmeg
4 tablespoons butter, softened

Preheat the oven to 375 degrees. Grease and lightly flour a 9-inch-square pan and tap and invert the pan to remove the excess flour.

Cream together the butter and sugar until fluffy. Beat in the egg. Add the milk and mix well. Reserve a few tablespoons of the flour; mix together the remainder of the sifted flour, baking powder, and salt and add to the batter, stirring until smooth. Toss the berries in the reserved flour; this will keep them from sinking to the bottom of the batter during the baking. Gently fold the berries into the batter. Spread the batter in the prepared pan.

Combine the flour, sugar, cinnamon, and nutmeg in a small bowl. Cut the butter into the mixture and, with your fingertips, mix together until crumbly. Sprinkle evenly over the batter.

Bake for 45 to 50 minutes, or until a cake tester comes out dry. When slightly cooled, cut into squares.

Yield: 6 to 8 servings.

Cherries

Selection: Look for cherries that are bright, glossy and plump; they should be firm and juicy. Don't guess at the quality of cherries when buying them; sample one. Bing cherries and Lamberts are the most popular varieties. Bings are round, with a deep mahogany color; Lamberts are similar in flavor and texture but lighter red and somewhat heart-shaped. Sour cherries are smaller, lighter in color, tart in flavor, and are for cooking only.

Peak Season: May through July.

Methods of Preparation: As with other fruits, cherries are sprayed with insecticides and they require thorough washing before use. Don't let them soak; they can become waterlogged. Raw, they are eaten out of hand, or pitted and stemmed and combined with other fruits in salads. A bowl heaped with ripe, juicy cherries is a lovely dessert. Cooked, they are used in pies and tarts, poached, and preserved in jams and jellies. Sour cherries are used in pies and for jams, jellies, and preserves.

Large sweet cherries may be poached pitted or unpitted, as you wish. Boil from ½ to ¾ cup of sugar per cup of water with a few drops of lemon juice for 5 minutes. Add the cherries and poach gently for about 5 minutes, until the cherries are slightly softened but have not lost their shape.

Coconuts

The coconut is not really a nut, although its rich white meat has the taste and texture of one. It belongs to a class of fruit called *drupes,* and the part of the coconut we eat is the drupe's seed.

Selection: Look for a heavy coconut filled with milk that sloshes when you shake it. A coconut without milk is spoiled. Avoid cracked nuts, and those with wet or moldy "eyes," (the three soft, small circles at the top).

Peak Season: October to December, but available all year.

Methods of Preparation: Fresh coconut meat can be eaten out of hand or grated or chopped in the blender, for pies, cakes, cookies, and other baking. It is used as a garnish for fruits. Fresh coconut is more flavorful, less sweet, and less expensive than the packaged. To toast fresh flaked or grated coconut, toss it in an iron skillet over medium heat for 3 to 5 minutes until it browns. The coconut liquid is used with

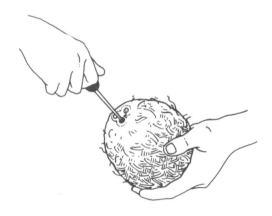

1 *At one end of the coconut, you will see three "eyes." Use a pick, a skewer, or even an awl from the workshop to pierce the eyes. Drain and strain the milk.*

other ingredients in alcoholic drinks or milk shakes. It is very perishable and must be refrigerated and used within 24 hours. The coconut cream that is used in cooking is made by steeping the milk with grated coconut meat.

To open a coconut, pierce the three eyes with a sharp icepick or a skewer. Strain the milk into a glass through a strainer lined with cheesecloth. Tap the coconut all over with a hammer and break it open. It will be easier to crack the coconut if you first heat it in a 325-degree oven for 15 minutes, but no longer. Overheating will destroy the flavor. Slide a knife or a screwdriver between the shell and the meat to dislodge it. The dark skin that coats the white meat can be scraped off with a vegetable peeler or left on to protect your fingers if you are hand grating it. Store the coconut meat tightly covered and refrigerated. Fresh coconut meat may be covered with coconut milk and frozen.

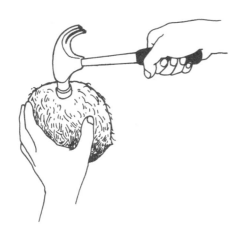

2 *Tap the coconut all over until it cracks open.*

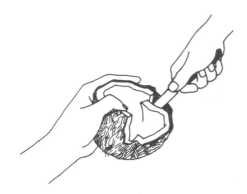

3 *Separate the meat from the fibrous shell using a knife or screwdriver.*

4 *If you plan to grate the coconut meat with a hand grater, leave the dark skin on. If you wish to remove the skin, peel it off with a swivel-bladed vegetable peeler.*

Cranberries

While fresh cranberries are in the markets only part of the year, they freeze very well and will keep firm and fresh for months. Just place the cranberries in the freezer in their original container, unopened, and they will be ready to use without thawing whenever you wish.

Selection: Look for glossy, firm, plump red berries with a lustrous red color.

Peak Season: September through January.

Methods of Preparation: Raw, chopped in a relish with fruits and spices or in breads; cooked, in sauces, jams, jellies, pies, sherbets, ice cream. Cranberry juice is bottled commercially.

To Cook: Cranberries are extremely tart and are usually cooked with sugar. Cook only until they pop open. Their flavor can become bitter if overcooked.

Whole Cranberry Sauce

2 cups sugar
2 cups water
1 pound cranberries, washed and picked over
2 teaspoons grated orange rind

In a medium-size skillet, dissolve the sugar in the water and boil for 5 minutes. Add the cranberries and simmer gently for another 5 minutes, or until the cranberries pop. Add the orange rind. Pour the mixture into a 1½-quart oiled mold and chill until firm. Unmold to serve.

Yield: 8 to 10 servings.

Cranberry Apple Muffins

Fruity, spicy muffins for breakfast or snacking.

2 cups all-purpose flour
1 tablespoon baking powder
½ cup sugar
½ teaspoon each salt, cinnamon, and nutmeg
1 egg, beaten
1 cup milk
4 tablespoons melted butter or vegetable oil
1 cup whole cranberries
1 apple, finely chopped
Ground cinnamon and sugar

Preheat the oven to 400 degrees.

Butter the muffin tins. Sift together flour, baking powder, sugar, salt, cinnamon, and nutmeg into a mixing bowl. Make a well in the center of the dry ingredients and add the egg, milk, and melted butter or oil. Mix very lightly, just until the dry ingredients are moistened. Do not overbeat or try to achieve a silken batter. Stir in the cranberries and half of the chopped apple. Fill the buttered tins about two-thirds full. Distribute the remainder of the apple pieces over the tops of the muffins and sprinkle lightly with sugar and cinnamon. Bake for 20 minutes, or until nicely browned and puffy. Remove immediately from the tins.

Yield: 10 to 12 muffins.

Variation: Substitute chopped dates for the cranberries.

Dates

Dates have been called "the candy that grows on trees."

Selection: Look for fresh shiny fruits with smooth skins. Dates are also sold in a pressed mass; they have been dried in the sun and contain no extra sugar or preservatives. They are available in specialty stores. Dried dates are usually sold in cardboard or plastic containers.

Peak Season: November, but available all year. They are most abundant during the fall and winter.

Methods of Preparation: Delicious cut up with cereal or in fresh fruit salad. May be stuffed with nuts and rolled in sugar as a sweetmeat; chopped in cake and cookie batters and in puddings.

Date Nut Pudding

1 8-ounce package pitted dates
1 cup boiling water
3 tablespoons butter, melted
1¼ cups firmly packed brown sugar
1 egg
1 cup all-purpose flour, sifted
¾ teaspoon baking soda
½ cup walnuts, coarsely chopped
Whipped cream

Preheat the oven to 375 degrees. Oil the blades of kitchen scissors and cut the dates into small pieces. Place dates in a bowl, and pour the boiling water over them. Let cool.

In a medium-size bowl, mix together the melted butter and sugar and beat well. Beat in the egg until well blended. In another bowl, blend together the sifted flour, baking soda, and walnuts. Add the dates and water to the sugar and egg; then mix in the flour and nuts. Transfer to a well-greased 8-inch-square pan. Bake for 40 to 45 minutes, or until the top springs back when pressed lightly in the center. Serve hot or warm topped with whipped cream.

Yield: 6 to 8 servings.

Date Gems

Simple and delicious little confections.

1 8-ounce package pitted dates
3 eggs
1 cup coarsely chopped walnuts
1 teaspoon grated orange rind

Preheat the oven to 350 degrees. Oil the blades of kitchen scissors and cut the dates into tiny pieces. With an electric beater, beat the eggs until thick and light and doubled in volume. The more you beat them, the better the result. Combine the beaten eggs, the dates, walnuts, and orange rind and mix well. Spoon the mixture into small fluted paper baking cups, about 2 inches in diameter. They make an attractive presentation and leave you with no muffin tins to wash. Bake for 20 minutes.

Yield: About 40.

Figs

Fresh figs are delicious, but they are also perishable and quite a luxury in northern markets. Dried figs are an excellent product but they bear little resemblance to a fig in its succulent, tender, fresh state.

Selection: Look for fresh figs that are plump and soft to the touch but not mushy. Figs come in a wide variety of shapes, sizes, and colors, from yellowish green to dark brown to purple or black, and all are equally good.

Peak Season: Fresh, July through October; dried, available all year.

Methods of Preparation: Raw as a finger fruit or a fruit salad ingredient or garnish. They may be peeled or not, according to the toughness of the skin. Fresh figs make a wonderful appetizer with thin slices of prosciutto; or a dessert with cream, crème fraîche, or cheese. Serve figs at room temperature or only slightly chilled so that their natural sweetness is not masked by the cold.

To Stew Dried Figs: These make a fine breakfast fruit. Cover figs with cold water and simmer slowly until tender, about 15 minutes. Refrigerate when cool. Serve with their juice. If serving as a dessert, top with cream, sour cream, or crème fraîche.

Baked Fresh Figs

A special dessert for a special occasion.

12 firm fresh figs
3 tablespoons sugar
½ cup orange juice
½ teaspoon ground cloves
¼ cup orange liqueur (Grand Marnier, Cointreau, curaçao)
Sweetened whipped cream flavored with liqueur

Heat the oven to 300 degrees. Wash the figs and pierce them in a few places with the tines of a fork. Place them in a buttered baking dish that can be brought to the table. Sprinkle the figs with sugar and orange juice. Place in the oven and bake for about 20 minutes, until tender and heated through. Baste from time to time.

When tender, remove from the oven and sprinkle lightly with ground cloves. Warm the liqueur. ignite it, and pour over the figs. Serve blazing. Pass the whipped cream, sweetened to taste and flavored with liqueur.

Yield: 4 servings.

Grapefruit

There was a time when grapefruit was thought to be too sour for eating, but skillful cultivation has improved its flavor and quality to the point where it is high on the list of breakfast favorites. It has a refreshing tang softened with sweetness and is low in calories, high in vitamins.

Selection: Look for fruit that is firm, compact, well shaped, heavy for its size, and thin skinned. Superficial skin defects—scars, discolored patches, or scratches—do not affect the quality of the fruit.

Peak Season: January through April or May, but available all year from California and Arizona.

Methods of Preparation: Raw, cut in half, with segments loosened from peel, served as a breakfast fruit, an appetizer, or a dessert. May be segmented, peeled and eaten like an orange; in fruit salads and combined with greens in vegetable salads. Used in marmalade. Halves may also be broiled or baked.

Use a grapefruit knife to cut all around each section, separating it from the membrane and skin. The curved, flexible blade and serrated edges of the knife help to cut around, not through, the pulp.

Barbados Grapefruit Whip

2 envelopes unflavored gelatin
3½ cups unsweetened grapefruit juice
4 tablespoons sugar
2 egg whites
2 cups grapefruit sections (2 medium grapefruit)
2 tablespoons white rum (optional)
Fresh mint

Sprinkle the gelatin over 1 cup of cold grapefruit juice to soften. Heat the remaining grapefruit juice with 3 tablespoons of sugar until it comes to a boil and the sugar is dissolved. Reduce heat and stir in the gelatin until it is dissolved. Cool and refrigerate until it reaches the consistency of unbeaten egg white.

Beat the egg whites until soft peaks begin to form. Slowly beat in 1 tablespoon sugar. Continue to beat until firm but not dry. Add the grapefruit sections to the thickened gelatin mixture and fold in the beaten egg white and the rum, if you wish. Blend well and taste to see if it is sweet enough. Return to the refrigerator to chill.

Stir and spoon into bowls. This is not meant to be molded. Garnish with sprigs of fresh mint.

Yield: 6 servings.

Grapes

Grapes are unsurpassed for their appealing flavor and sweet taste. Unlike some fruits, they will not improve in flavor or ripen after leaving the vine.

Selection: Look for grapes that are plump, have distinct color typical of their variety, and are firmly attached to the stem in well-formed, good-looking bunches. Don't guess at how they taste; sample one. Avoid grapes already packaged unless you plan to use them for cooking or for salads.

Peak Season: Available all year with different varieties maturing at different times.

Methods of Preparation: Raw, eaten out of hand or combined with other fruit in fruit salads. If not seedless, halve and remove pits before combining with other fruits. Serve with cheese for a first-rate dessert. Cooked, in sauces for chicken and fish (called *Véronique*); in jams, jellies, and preserves. Also used for raisins, wine, and juice.

Fresh Grape Medley

A variety of grapes served in sherbet glasses or goblets makes an attractive dessert.

Use about one pound of sweet seedless grapes and one pound of large black (Ribier) or dark red grapes (Cardinal, Tokay, Emperor), whatever is in season, for 4 to 6 servings. Rinse the grapes in cold water and drain well. Remove seeds by cutting grapes in half, either horizontally or vertically, whichever works best for you, and scooping out the seeds with a sharp-pointed knife. Add as much orange juice as is needed to almost cover the grapes. Add about 3 tablespoons superfine sugar and the grated rind of a lemon. Chill in the refrigerator. Top with whipped cream, crème fraîche, or yogurt, if you wish.

Kiwi Fruit

The kiwi is an unprepossessing little brown fruit with a bright green interior that is completely delicious. Actually, it is a Chinese gooseberry that is cultivated commercially in New Zealand. Like papaya, it is effective as a meat tenderizer.

Selection: The kiwi should yield to light pressure, indicating ripeness.

Peak Season: June to March.

Methods of Preparation: Peel and eat out of hand or use in fruit salads, tarts, or mousses. Its bright color and interesting formation are most attractive in a mélange of fruits.

Kumquats

Shaped like large unshelled pecans, kumquats are the babies of the citrus family, with a flavor distinctly their own.

Selection: Look for plump, firm, golden fruit without blemishes. Stems and leaves are often attached.

Peak Season: November through February.

Methods of Preparation: Raw, unpeeled, sliced thin, and pits removed, used in fruit salads or eaten out of hand. They are most decorative in a bowl of fresh fruit. Cooked, in preserves and jellies, or candied.

Lemons

The lemon is one of our most useful fruits, notable for its tangy flavor, although it is seldom consumed for its own sake. It can sharpen sweets, perk up bland dishes, and add zest to the dull ones. The lemon is an indispensable part of the flavoring of a meal, from tomato juice to dessert soufflé and tea.

Besides the bright sparkle lemon brings to the taste of foods, its vitamin C (ascorbic acid) content keeps fruits and some vegetables from darkening. This same acid has the effect of "cooking" fish and turning it opaque. It acts as a tenderizer for meats, helping to break down the tough fibers.

When using lemon rind use only the yellow part *(zest);* the white underneath is bitter. You will increase the amount of juice you get from citrus fruits if you roll the whole fruit on a table top gently but firmly, pressing it with the palm of your hand, before juicing it. A good-size lemon will generally yield about 3 tablespoons of juice.

Selection: Look for thin-skinned fruits, heavy for their size, as they are the juiciest. Avoid lemons tinged with green, as they will be very acid.

Peak Season: May through August but available all year.

Methods of Preparation: Lemon juice, lemon rind, both grated and slivered, and sometimes whole lemon segments are used as a flavoring ingredient in everything from soups to fruits and baked goods. No self-respecting seafood platter would be served without a garnish of lemon. Also used in beverages and cooked in marmalades and fruit preserves.

Limes

Limes are small fruits that look like green lemons. Their skins are thinner and their acid taste is subtly different from that of the lemon, but they are sometimes used interchangeably.

Selection: Look for limes with a glossy shine and good weight for their size.

Peak Season: June through September, but available all year.

Methods of Preparation: Fresh lime juice is used for beverages, marinades for some fish dishes, sherbets, ice box cakes, and pies. Slices and wedges are used for garnishes for various beverages, melons, salads, and poultry and fish dishes.

Mangoes

Until rather recently, mangoes were familiar only to travelers who journeyed to tropical islands. But now these large, fragrant, oval fruits are being grown in Florida, and they are also imported in quantity into the United States. A mango must be eaten ripe; when it is immature, its juicy orange flesh is acid and bitter.

Selection: Look for mangoes that are firm and let them ripen at room temperature until they are just soft to the touch. The skin color varies according to the species, but in general a ripe mango has more red and yellow areas than green ones.

Peak Season: June, although in some areas mangoes are available from January through August.

Methods of Preparation: Raw, peeled, and eaten as a dessert fruit either alone or in combination with other fruits in fruit salad. May be used as a purée, in ice cream, and in baked goods. The oil in the mango rind is irritating to some people's skin and produces a rash, so it is prudent to avoid touching the skin of the mango with your mouth. Peel the mango with a sharp knife and cut it into sections around the pit, to which the flesh is firmly attached. When mangoes are just mature, but not quite soft, they can be used in chutney, sauces, and for pickling.

Melons

Melons are divided into two main categories: the muskmelon or squash variety, which includes cantaloupe, casaba, cranshaw (or crenshaw), honeydew, honeyball, Persian, Santa Claus, and Spanish melons, among others; and the cucumber variety, whose most impressive member, at least in size, is the watermelon.

Selection: Choosing a perfect melon each time is probably an impossible dream, but there are a few identifiable characteristics of a good melon that may raise your batting average. You will need to feel them, look at them, sniff them, and perhaps sometimes listen to them.

Cantaloupes should have well-defined net tracery on their skins with no suggestion of a greenish cast on the background skin color. A ripe one should have a pleasant, distinctive aroma and should yield slightly to finger pressure at the blossom end. Don't bother to shake it to see if the seeds rattle. The rattling could be a sign of maturity, but the loose seeds could also denote the last stage of maturity and the melon could be slightly sour. They are most plentiful June through August but available all year.

Casabas should have a golden yellow color with a slight softening at the blossom end. It won't do you any good to sniff; casabas have no aroma. Best in September and October.

Cranshaws should be bright yellow and the blossom end should yield to pressure. They have the quintessential melon aroma. Best in August, but available from July through October.

Honeydew should be creamy white or pale yellow with a distinct and pleasing fragrance. The larger it is, the better. As the honeydew ripens, the sugar in it moves outward toward the skin, giving it a dull sheen and making it slightly sticky to the touch. To ripen, keep it away from sunlight and in a warm room for a few days. It is the only melon that becomes noticeably sweeter after it is picked. A properly chosen melon will improve on standing at room temperature. Avoid a honeydew with a greenish white exterior; it was picked too soon and it will never ripen or become sweeter. Honeydews are most plentiful June through October, but they are available all year. Honeyballs are smaller, rounder versions of honeydews.

Persian melons resemble cantaloupes and are about the size of honeydews. Look for the same characteristics as in choosing cantaloupes. Most plentiful June through October.

Santa Claus or Christmas melons are oval in shape and their flesh is pale green. Their peak season is around Christmas.

Spanish melons are similar in taste to cranshaws. They have a dark green, corrugated rind. Use the same testing standards as you do for a cranshaw. Most plentiful June through October.

Watermelons are the mammoths of the melon world. There is no consensus about whether or not thumping a melon will tell you all you need to know about what is going on inside it. What you *can* do when choosing a whole melon is to look for a symmetrical shape, a dull rather than a shiny skin, and a yellow underside. A less chancy procedure is to buy a portion of a cut melon. Look for firm, juicy flesh with good red color and black, evenly distributed seeds. The flesh should be wet and shiny, not mealy looking.

Most plentiful June through August but available from March through October, watermelon is a fine thirst quencher, nibble, or dessert. It is too sweet for an appetizer. If you are using it in a fruit salad or fruit cup, add it at the last minute because it loses its crispness quickly and makes the fruit mixture watery. The rind is delicious pickled.

Peak Season: The peak season for various melons differs. You will find some melons in the markets year round, many imported.

Methods of Preparation: Melons should be served slightly chilled, but not so cold that their fine flavor is masked. Before serving, cut them open and scoop out the pulpy mass of seeds. Melons can be halved, quartered, or sliced, depending on their size. Slices or wedges of melon make lovely appetizer courses for any meal, beginning with breakfast, and are equally fine desserts. (Strips of prosciutto and melon wedges are a classic appetizer combination.) Half a cantaloupe filled with ice cream or a combination of different kinds of melon balls is always a successful dessert. Or top melon balls with scoops of lemon ice.

Nectarines

Contrary to popular belief, the smooth-skinned nectarine is not a fuzzless variety of peach or a cross between the peach and the plum. It is nothing more nor less than a nectarine, and it was cultivated before the beginning of the Christian era. However, the new and better varieties have been crossbred with peaches to improve their size and texture.

Selection: Look for bright, plump nectarines with orange-yellow between the red areas. They are ripe when they yield to gentle pressure.

Peak Season: July and August, but available June through September.

Methods of Preparation: Wash well, dry, and eat them out of hand. Fresh nectarines do not need to be peeled. You can do anything with a nectarine that you do with a peach. Nectarines are used raw in fruit salads and compotes. They are baked in pies, cakes, and cobblers. They may be used to flavor ice cream and puddings. They are also pickled, brandied, and spiced.

Oranges

Oranges are always ripe when picked and need no further ripening. Skin color is no indication of quality. The Valencia, for example, which is the most important variety, has a tendency late in the season to turn from bright orange to greenish, particularly around the stem end. But because consumers expect oranges to be orange, some producers treat their fruits with ethylene gas, which decomposes the chlorophyll in the skin of the green fruit, giving it an orange pigment. They may also tint the orange with a harmless vegetable dye.

Selection: Look for firm, heavy oranges with bright-looking skin. Lightweight oranges are apt to lack flesh and juice. Those that peel easily, such as navels and Florida Temples, are best for eating in sections; the thinner-skinned varieties, such as the common Valencia, are best for juice and for slicing. The color of an orange is no indication of its quality. Oranges that have been tinted artificially must specify "color added." If you plan to candy the orange peel or grate it into batters or sauces, select oranges that have not been color treated.

Peak Season: December until March, but available all year. Different varieties appear on the market at different times. Summer is the poorest season. Valencias are shipped from Florida from February through June and from California mainly from late April until November.

Methods of Preparation: Fresh, peeled and separated into segments, or cut up in salads and fruit cups; cooked with chicken and duck; cooked or raw to flavor many desserts. The peel may be grated or candied to add variety to baked goods. Juice flavors sauces, chutneys, relishes, mousses, gelatins, sherbets and ices, cake frostings and fillings.

Glazed Orange Slices

5 or 6 large navel oranges
1 cup water
1½ cups sugar
4 tablespoons Grand Marnier, curaçao, or other orange liqueur

With a sharp knife or a zester, remove only the colored part of the peel of 2 of the oranges. Avoid the white pith underneath. Cut into thin julienne strips about 1 inch long and simmer in boiling water for 5 minutes. Drain and set aside.

Peel all of the oranges, removing every bit of the white pith and membrane. Cut crosswise into thin slices and place in a glass serving bowl.

In a saucepan, combine the cup of water and sugar. Heat slowly to the boiling point and boil for 5 minutes. Reduce heat, add the orange peel, and simmer for 5 minutes longer, or until the syrup is slightly thickened. Remove from the heat and stir in the liqueur. Spoon the sauce and julienne strips over the orange slices and let cool. Refrigerate when cooled. Let stand at room temperature for an hour or so before serving so that the fruit will not be icy cold.

Yield: 5 or 6 servings.

Poached Oranges with Strawberry Sauce

1 cup strawberry preserves
1 tablespoon cornstarch
1 cup orange juice
½ teaspoon ground cinnamon
6 navel oranges
6 tablespoons sour cream or
  crème fraîche

In a shallow pan large enough to hold the oranges in a single layer, heat the strawberry preserves. Make a smooth paste of the cornstarch and orange juice. Add to the preserves with the cinnamon. Stir until it comes to a boil, lower the heat, and simmer, stirring the sauce until it thickens and becomes clear, 2 or 3 minutes.

Peel the oranges, removing all of the white pith and membrane. Cut them crosswise into three slices and reassemble them, securing the slices with toothpicks to hold them in place. Simmer them in the sauce for 3 or 4 minutes, basting a few times.

Arrange in a serving dish and spoon the sauce over them. The oranges may be served warm, at room temperature, or chilled. To serve, top each orange with a tablespoon of sour cream or crème fraîche.

Yield: 6 servings.

Note: This sauce may be used with other fruits or as an ice cream topping.

Papayas

A sweet, pear-shaped fruit with a melonlike taste and texture.

Selection: Look for fruits that are more than half yellow and are soft enough to yield to pressure between the palms. Avoid any with soft spots or obvious signs of decay. Green papayas will ripen at room temperature. Refrigerate when they turn yellow and soften, and use within a few days.

Peak Season: Late winter and early spring, but available all year.

Methods of Preparation: Cut in half lengthwise, remove the seeds, and serve in the shell with a wedge of lemon or lime. Use raw in fruit salads or puréed for sherbets, ice cream, mousses, and drinks. Green papayas can be cooked as a vegetable.

Peaches

In spite of the more than 2,000 varieties grown throughout the world, peaches fall mainly into two classifications—freestone and clingstone. As their names suggest, freestone types have a pit that separates easily from the flesh and are first choice for eating raw. The clingstones, in which the pit adheres tightly to the flesh, hold their shape well during cooking and are used for freezing and canning, in addition to eating.

Selection: Look for peaches that are firm but yield slightly to pressure. The skin between the red areas should be yellow or at least creamy, but never green. Avoid peaches with bruises or tan spots, which portend the beginning of decay.

When possible, try to buy locally grown peaches in season. The closer you live to a peach orchard, the better your chances of bringing home some beautifully flavored fruit.

Peak Season: July and August, but available from May through October.

Methods of Preparation: Raw, eaten out of hand, or sliced and served in fruit salads or with cream. May be poached, broiled, baked, pickled, brandied, spiced; made into ice cream, pies, shortcakes, mousses, jams, jellies, and preserves.

To peel peaches, drop them into boiling water for one minute, then plunge them into cold water. The skins should slip off readily. If they are to be peeled and held for any length of time before using, sprinkle them with lemon juice to prevent darkening.

To slice peaches, hold the peeled peach over a bowl to catch the juice and cut lengthwise slices.

To poach peaches, make a syrup of 1½ cups water, 1½ cups sugar, and a slice or two of lemon. Boil the syrup for 5 minutes. Drop 6 peeled peaches into the syrup, reduce the heat, and poach gently, basting with the hot liquid and turning the peaches from time to time during the cooking. They may take 15 to 20 minutes or longer, depending on their firmness. When tender but not mushy, remove the peaches with a slotted spoon, and spoon a few tablespoons of syrup over each. Serve with custard sauce or cream.

To broil peaches, peel and cut them in half. Place cut side up on a foil-lined baking tin. Sprinkle lightly with brown sugar and dot with butter. Place the baking tin 4 or 5 inches from the heat and broil until sugar and butter are bubbly. Remove from the oven, put a spoonful of apricot or raspberry preserves in the cavity, and return to the broiler for a minute or two. You may also used canned peach halves, but omit the brown sugar. The syrup in which they are canned makes them sweet enough. Use only butter and a dollop of preserves or maple sugar, if you like.

Peaches in Raspberry Sauce

Some foods have a special affinity for each other, such as peaches and raspberries.

6 large fresh peaches, poached
1 10-ounce package frozen raspberries
1 tablespoon sugar
1 teaspoon cornstarch
2 tablespoons cold water
3 tablespoons kirsch (optional)
¼ cup blanched slivered almonds

Poach the peaches according to the preceding directions. Let stand at room temperature after being poached; do not refrigerate them.

Combine the raspberries and sugar in a small saucepan. Mix the cornstarch with the water and add to the raspberries. Simmer and stir until the sauce comes to a boil and is thickened and clear, about 3 minutes. Remove from the heat and mash through a strainer to remove the seeds. Return to the saucepan and heat just to warm through. Add the kirsch, if desired, and mix. Spoon the warm sauce over the peaches and sprinkle with almonds.

Yield: 6 servings.

Pears

Pears are one of the few fruits that do not have to be tree-ripened to be good. Most of the pears that we buy are picked and shipped when they are full grown but still green. The majority of pear producers feel that pears develop a finer flavor when they are ripened off the tree; the starch converts to sugar and they become sweeter.

Selection: Look for firm, unblemished fruit, although a slight scar or minor surface blemish will not affect the quality. Avoid pears that have a soft spot near the stem. Bear in mind that some pears are green and extremely firm even when ripe. Pears will ripen at room temperature. You can speed up the ripening process by putting the pears in a paper bag in the company of a ripe apple. Look at them daily and refrigerate when ripe.

Peak Season: Pears are available all year, with different varieties harvested at different times. Bartlett, the most popular all-purpose pear, is at peak season from July through December. Peak season for most pears starts in late summer or early fall and they are in good supply all winter.

Methods of Preparation: Raw, eaten out of hand, in fruit salads, and with cheese for dessert. May be poached, baked, broiled, puréed, used in pies, fruit tarts, puddings, and cakes. If peeled, sprinkle with lemon juice to prevent darkening.

Baked Pears

4 large firm pears
½ cup brown sugar
1 cup water
2 tablespoons apricot preserves
3 tablespoons lemon juice

Preheat the oven to 325 degrees.

Wash the pears and cut in half lengthwise. Do not peel. Remove the cores and seeds with a melon ball scoop, which does a tidy job. In a medium-size saucepan, simmer the sugar, water, apricot preserves, and lemon juice for 5 minutes. Arrange the pear halves, cut side down, in a well-buttered shallow baking dish. Pour the boiling syrup over the pears and bake for 1 hour, or until the pears are tender, basting them with the syrup from time to time. Remove from the oven and let the pears cool in the syrup. Serve them warmed or chilled, with a bit of the syrup poured over them.

Yield: 4 servings.

Poached Pears with Custard Sauce

6 large firm pears (Anjou, Bartlett, or Bosc)
3 tablespoons lemon juice
1 cup sugar
2 cups water
1 teaspoon vanilla extract
4 strips lemon peel
Boiled custard (see page 273)

Leave the pears whole with the stem intact and peel them with a swivel-bladed vegetable peeler. They don't need to be cored; just remove the eye at the bottom of the core with a sharp-pointed knife. Trim the bottoms of the pears so that they will sit firmly on their bases. Place each pear as it is peeled in a bowl of cold water to cover, to which you have added the lemon juice.

Combine the sugar, 2 cups water, vanilla, and lemon peel in a pot large enough to hold all the pears without crowding. Bring the syrup to a boil and simmer for 5 minutes. Drain the pears and add them to the syrup. Simmer slowly until the pears can be pierced easily with a knitting needle or a slim skewer and offer no resistance in the center. Cooking time will vary according to the ripeness and variety of the pears. It could be 20 to 25 minutes or longer, but watch them carefully and don't allow them to overcook. Mushy pears defeat your purpose.

When the pears are done, remove them carefully with a slotted spoon or two long-handled spoons and place them in a flat, shallow serving dish. Boil the remaining syrup rapidly until reduced to 1 cup. Discard the lemon peel. Pour a little syrup over each pear and let cool. They may be refrigerated, but let them come to room temperature before serving. Serve pears garnished with the custard sauce.

Yield: 6 servings.

Pears Cardinal. Add 1 10-ounce package of thawed frozen raspberries to the syrup after it is reduced to 1 cup. Boil rapidly for 7 to 8 minutes, or until the sauce thickens. Strain and pour over the pears. Chill. Serve with softly whipped sweetened cream.

Pears in Wine. Peel and prepare the pears as for Poached Pears. Combine 2 cups port wine, 1 cup water, 1 cup sugar, a 2-inch stick of cinnamon, 4 strips lemon peel, and 2 whole cloves. Bring to a boil, simmer for 5 minutes, and add the pears. Poach until they are tender, using the knitting needle test. When tender, remove the pears from the syrup. Reduce the syrup by boiling over high heat. Spoon the syrup over the pears.

Pears Hélène. Serve poached pears with vanilla ice cream and top with Chocolate Sauce (see page 468).

Persimmons

With its brilliant orange color and interesting shape, the satiny-skinned persimmon brings a wonderful burst of color to the fall fruit scene. Persimmons have an unusual sweet, spicy flavor and smooth texture when they are soft and ripe. The astringent, puckery quality that has besmirched their reputation is present only when they are unripe.

Selection: Look for plump, glossy, deep-colored fruit with the green cap attached. Buy soft ones for immediate use; firm ones will ripen at room temperature.

Peak Season: October to January.

Methods of Preparation: Persimmons are ready to be eaten with a spoon when they are washed and split. They don't need to be peeled, but if you prefer them without the skins, plunge them into boiling water for a minute, and then into cold. The skins should peel off easily. Persimmons may be served with cream or used as an ingredient in a variety of puddings, cookies, cakes, or conserves, or in ice cream, sherbet, or custard.

Pineapple

Pineapples are like the little girl in the jingle who was sensational when she was good and awful when she was bad. The pineapple that was ripened on the plant until the flesh brims with sweetness and juice is a delight, but if it is picked too soon, it is a woody, tasteless nothing. Pineapples must be picked at the peak of their ripeness and flavor, for they will never get sweeter or riper after being harvested; they will merely soften and decay. Unlike bananas and pears, pineapples have no starch reserve, and consequently they have no material to convert to sugar.

Selection: Look for pineapples that are plump and fresh looking. Ripe pineapples may have an orange or yellowish skin (although the Sugar Loaf variety remains green even when ripe) and will yield slightly to finger pressure. Fresh, deep green crown leaves are a good sign, but the ease with which they can be plucked out is not a guarantee of ripeness. The aroma is an important clue. Sniff it; a pleasant, fruity fragrance indicates a ripe fruit, as does the slight separation of the little spikes that protrude out of the

eyes of the pineapple skin. Avoid fruit that looks old and dry with brown leaves, or those with dark soft spots at the base. Large pineapples have more edible flesh and are a better buy than the small ones.

Peak Season: April through June, but available all year.

Methods of Preparation: Raw, in slices, fingers, wedges, or cubes. Can be broiled, sautéed, deep-fried, and used in cakes and pies, or as a meat or poultry garnish.

Do not add uncooked fresh pineapple to gelatin desserts—it contains an enzyme that prevents jelling. Canned or cooked pineapple, on the other hand, presents no problem. Canned pineapple, particularly those brands packed in pineapple juice, is among the most successful of canned fruits.

To serve pineapple, cut off the crown and stem ends with a sharp knife. Cut the pineapple into horizontal slices a generous ½ inch thick. Cut off the skin and eyes in the flesh of each slice. Remove the tough core with a sharp-pointed knife. If the pineapple is as sweet as a proper pineapple should be, it won't need anything beyond a knife and fork to eat it with. Otherwise, sprinkle it with a bit of sugar or a tablespoon or two of Grand Marnier or Cointreau and let it rest in the refrigerator—covered, or its aroma will permeate the other foods—for a couple of hours before serving.

To Cook: Pineapples that are disappointing in taste and texture do not have to be a total loss. You can rescue them with any of the following techniques: poach slices in a sugar syrup; sprinkle slices or wedges with brown sugar, dot with butter, and broil 4 to 6 inches below the heat for about 5 minutes, or until browned and bubbling; sauté pineapple cubes in butter with a light sprinkling of sugar to caramelize them.

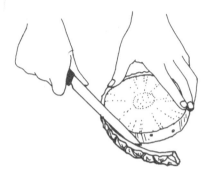

2 *Cut the thorny skin off each slice. Remove the eyes with the point of a knife.*

Pineapple Slices

1 *Using a strong, sharp knife, cut off both ends and then cut thick crosswise slices.*

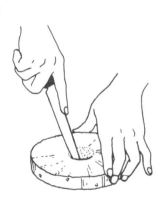

3 *Use a small pastry cutter or knife to cut out the core, if it is tough.*

Pineapple in the Shell. Divide the pineapple lengthwise into quarters, cutting through the leaves so that each quarter will have its own plume. Trim away the core sections. With a sharp, thin-bladed knife, separate the pineapple flesh from the shell in one piece. Slice into wedges ½ inch thick, leaving them in place on the shell. Sugar lightly, if necessary. Place a washed, unhulled strawberry on each wedge and secure with a toothpick. You can use the quarters as part of a fresh fruit arrangement, surrounded by segments of melons and bunches of grapes, cherries, and other fresh fruits, or the pineapple quarters may be served individually as dessert.

Pineapple Basket. Cut the pineapple in half lengthwise. Carve out the pineapple meat, discarding the core, and cut into 1-inch cubes. Mix with other fruits such as orange sections, grapes, strawberries, peaches, and the like, sugar lightly, add lemon juice, and replace in the pineapple shell. The pineapple shell may also be used standing upright with the top removed and then replaced after the shell has been hollowed out and filled with the pineapple cubes and other fruits.

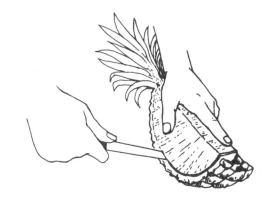

2 *Free the fruit from its shell by running a sharp knife along the length of each quarter, close to the skin. Leave the fruit resting in its shell.*

Pineapple in the Shell

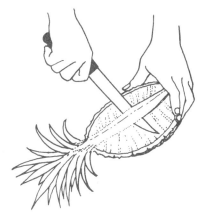

1 *Leaving the crown on, use a strong knife to cut the pineapple into quarters, cutting from top to bottom. Remove the core with a sharp knife.*

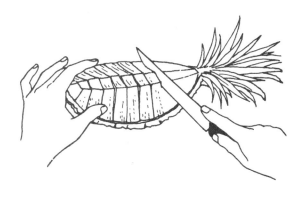

3 *Make crosswise cuts about ½ inch apart. If you wish, you can push slices to alternate sides, so that they are staggered.*

Plums and Fresh Prunes

Plums are a delicious fruit with a refreshing tart sweetness that can be enjoyed when they are eaten out of hand or in a wide variety of cooked preparations. There are thousands of varieties of plums in a wide range of shades and sizes, but mainly they come in three colors: blue or purple, red, or green on the outside and pink, yellow, or green on the inside.

Although all prunes are plums, not all plums are prunes. Fresh prunes are the small blue or purple plums that can be dried. They are particularly sweet and have a freestone pit. Plums and prunes are available fresh in season. Canned plums and dried prunes are available all year round.

Selection: Look for firm plums that have good color for the variety and are at the firm-to-slightly-soft stage of ripeness, yielding to slight pressure. Plums that were picked before they should have been will not ripen after picking.

Peak Season: July and August, but a number of varieties are available from late May until September. Fresh prunes are in season from August through October.

Methods of Preparation: Eaten out of hand, or combined with other fruits in salads and compotes. May be stewed, poached, or baked; used in tarts, cakes, puddings and pies, preserves and jellies.

Nutted Prune Whip

1 cup dried prunes
Water to cover
¼ cup sugar
1 teaspoon vanilla extract
½ cup coarsely chopped walnuts
    or pecans
5 egg whites
Pinch of salt
⅛ teaspoon cream of tartar, *or* 1
    teaspoon lemon juice

Cover the prunes with water and bring slowly to a boil. Simmer until tender. Drain. When cool enough to handle, remove the pits and chop the prunes fine. Combine with the sugar, vanilla, and chopped nuts. Taste and add more sugar, if needed.

Preheat the oven to 375 degrees. Place the rack in the lowest third of the oven.

In a large bowl, beat the egg whites until foamy and add salt. Continue beating, add cream of tartar or lemon juice, and beat until stiff but not dry. Fold carefully into the prune mixture, trying not to deflate the beaten egg whites. Spoon into a greased 2-quart baking dish and bake for 25 to 30 minutes, or until firm and golden brown on top. Serve warm. Top with whipped cream, if you wish.

Yield: 4 to 6 servings.

Fresh Prune Compote

1 pound fresh prunes
¼ cup brown sugar
6 tablespoons orange juice, or more

Preheat the oven to 400 degrees. Wash the prunes and drain well. Cut in half, following the dividing line etched by nature on each one, and remove the pits. Place prunes in a 1-quart baking dish.

Grated rind of 1 orange
½ teaspoon ground cinnamon
1 to 2 tablespoons lemon juice
Heavy cream or crème fraîche
(optional)

Add brown sugar, orange juice, orange rind, cinnamon, and 1 tablespoon lemon juice and mix well. Cover the casserole tightly and bake for 20 minutes. After the first 10 minutes of baking, stir the prunes and taste to see if they need more lemon juice or sugar. If the liquid seems to be low, add 1 or 2 tablespoons of orange juice, and replace the cover. The prunes should reach the proper degree of tenderness in 20 minutes, but taste to make sure.

When done, remove from the oven and cool. Refrigerate when cool. Serve with heavy cream or crème fraîche, if you wish.

Yield: 8 servings.

Pomegranates

The word *pomegranate* literally means "apple with many seeds," a graphic description of this colorful autumn fruit.

Selection: Look for fresh-looking fruit, heavy for its size, with an unbroken rind and no sign of decay. The large ones are better, for they will have juicier and better developed kernels.

Peak Season: October, but available September to early December.

Methods of Preparation: Raw as a dessert or a private nibble. A few shiny crimson seeds added to a French dressing or sprinkled over a salad or rolled in small cream cheese balls add eye appeal and texture. The juice is delicious and can be frozen and used as desired. Squeeze the juice out with a juicer.

No one has yet developed an elegant method of eating a pomegranate. Whether you cut the pomegranate in half and pry out the seeds with a spoon, or cut it into wedges and dig into the seeds with your teeth, you still face the problem of what to do with the seeds after you suck the pulp around them. It should be noted that both the pulp and the seeds are edible, but most people prefer to enjoy the juicy pulp and spit out the seeds. Don't eat the white membrane, which is bitter. Have a sufficient supply of paper napkins.

Quinces

Quince is an autumn fruit that cannot be eaten raw but is delicious when cooked or made into jellies and preserves.

Selection: Look for large, firm quinces with bright yellow color. They are hard even when ripe. Avoid small, knobby ones, which are wasteful.

Peak Season: Fall.

Methods of Preparation: Quinces have a good deal of pectin and are used in marmalade, jel-lies, and preserves; poached and baked.

To Cook: Pare the quinces, cut into sections, and remove the cores. Quinces require a large quantity of sugar to sweeten them, from ¾ to 1 cup of sugar per pound of quinces, boiled into a syrup with enough water to cover. Poach them in the syrup for 30 to 45 minutes. Or bake them in a casserole, covered with the syrup, in a 325-degree oven for about 2 hours, or until tender. Serve cold.

Raspberries

Raspberries are as perishable and delicate as they are expensive and must be handled most gently.

Selection: Look for berries that are plump and fresh looking in dry, unstained containers.

Peak Season: June and July, but available in limited quantities from mid-April through November.

Methods of Preparation: Raspberries are delicious with cream or dusted lightly with confectioners' sugar; in fruit salads and compotes; in jams, jellies, and preserves; interchangeable with strawberries in any preparation; in ice cream, mousses, sherbets, tarts, pies, puddings, soufflés, cakes, sauces, and syrups. The dry-pack frozen raspberries or those frozen in syrup may be substituted in any recipe that calls for raspberry purée.

Rhubarb

In contrast to the plants such as tomatoes and eggplant that are botanically fruits but are eaten as vegetables, rhubarb is botanically a vegetable but is eaten as a fruit. It was known as "pie plant" for reasons that anyone who has ever eaten a tart, juicy rhubarb pie can figure out. Rhubarb is a member of the same family as sorrel.

Selection: Look for crisp, long stalks that may vary in color from light pink (hothouse variety) to cherry red. Avoid stalks that are wilted or flabby; they will not be flavorful. The younger stems with immature leaves are usually the most tender and have the most delicate flavor.

Peak Season: February through June.

Methods of Preparation: May be stewed, baked, steamed, puréed, made into pies. The tender hothouse variety needs little preparation other than cutting off root ends and leaves, but the older rhubarb is somewhat coarser and the tough strings must be peeled off. Only the rhubarb stalk is suitable for eating. The leaves must be discarded because they contain oxalic acid, a toxic substance. Rhubarb needs very little cooking but a considerable amount of sweetening. It combines well with strawberries and apples, and flavors such as grated orange or lemon rind, ginger, mace, and cinnamon.

Stewed Rhubarb

1½ pounds rhubarb
¾ cup sugar
½ cup water
1 teaspoon grated lemon peel

Wash the rhubarb and trim off root and leaf ends. Peel it if it has coarse strings. Cut stalks into 2-inch pieces. In a saucepan, combine sugar, water, and grated lemon peel. Add the rhubarb, cover, and cook gently over low heat for 6 or 7 minutes after it has come to a boil, stirring once or twice. Taste and add sugar if necessary. Serve warm or chilled.

Yield: 4 to 5 servings.

Rhubarb Cream

6 cups sliced rhubarb (about 1½ pounds)
1 to 1½ cups sugar
2 cups heavy cream
1 cup sliced strawberries

Place the rhubarb and 1 cup sugar in a heavy-bottomed saucepan and cook slowly, covered, until the rhubarb is just tender but not falling apart, about 10 minutes. Stir it from time to time. Taste it; rhubarb varies in tartness and you may need the extra half cup of sugar or even more than that to make it sweet enough. Since the chilled temperature at which it will be served and the whipped cream will diminish the sweetness, you can't afford to be too frugal with the sugar. When the rhubarb is tender, remove the saucepan from the heat and let the rhubarb cool to room temperature.

Whip 2 cups of heavy cream until it is stiff. Stir the rhubarb mixture into it and blend well. Pile it into a bowl and allow it to chill in the refrigerator, covered, for at least 4 or 5 hours. Top with sliced strawberries.

Yield: 5 to 6 servings.

Strawberries

Selection: Look for berries with full red color and firm flesh, with the green stem cap attached. Avoid berries with uncolored areas and patches of mold. Watch out for containers stained with juice, a sign that the contents may be overripe or crushed. In the world of strawberries, big is not necessarily better; smaller ones are often juicier and more flavorful.

Peak Season: Generally between mid-April and mid-July, but available all year, with lowest supplies in October and November.

Methods of Preparation: Fresh, sweetened and served with liqueurs, sour cream, sweet cream, crème fraîche, or yogurt; combined with other fruits in salads; in tarts, pies, mousses, ice cream, sauces, purées, jams, jellies, and preserves.

When you bring the berries home, transfer them to a bowl and discard any that are bruised or mildewy. Cover and refrigerate them, unhulled and unwashed.

When strawberries are at their peak—sweet, red, and perfect, filled with flavor and juice— serve them unadorned, hulls in place, heaped in a crystal bowl. Pass the strawberries, accompanied by a bowl of confectioners' sugar, and let your guests ladle out their own servings of berries and sugar, at which point they will do their own dipping. Simple, unpretentious, and relaxed.

To Wash Strawberries: Strawberries are often sandy and they must be washed carefully. Remove the hulls after they are washed, not before, or they will absorb some of the water. Plunge the berries into a bowl of tepid water. Lift them from the bowl with your hands and repeat with cold water until no traces of sand remain in the bowl. Pouring off the water from the berries will not get rid of the sand. Spread the berries out on paper towels to dry. Wash and sugar berries not more than an hour before use or they will soften excessively.

Strawberries Grand Marnier

3 pints strawberries
2 tablespoons sugar
Juice and grated rind of 1 orange
2 tablespoons lemon juice
1 tablespoon brandy
3 tablespoons Grand Marnier

Wash, hull, and drain the berries. Cut up and mash a few in the bottom of a crystal bowl, to add some color to the sauce. Add the remaining berries and the sugar, and mix. Add the remaining ingredients and toss, being careful not to bruise the berries. Spoon out a bit of the sauce and taste it. You may decide it needs a little more sugar or lemon juice, or an extra splash of Grand Marnier. Chill for 1 hour. Serve in dessert bowls or goblets with the sauce.

Yield: 6 servings.

Variation: In blueberry season, add a cup or so of blueberries to the strawberries.

Fresh Strawberry Dessert

2 large seedless oranges
2 pints strawberries
2 teaspoons sugar
1 10-ounce package frozen
  raspberries, thawed
½ cup currant jelly
5 tablespoons orange liqueur
  (Grand Marnier, Cointreau, etc.)
Toasted coconut

Peel the oranges, removing every bit of the white, and slice thinly. Cut each slice in half and arrange over the sides and bottom of a glass serving bowl. Wash the strawberries well and remove the hulls. Toss lightly with the sugar and transfer the strawberries to the bowl. Cover them with the thawed raspberries and juice. In a small saucepan, melt the currant jelly and combine with the orange liqueur. Pour over the berries. Cover and refrigerate for 8 hours, or even the day before it is to be served. Before serving, toast some shredded coconut in a 350-degree oven until lightly browned and scatter it over the top of the fruit.

Yield: 6 to 8 servings.

11
Sauces

Not even today's calorie-conscious climate has diminished the importance of sauces in a cooking repertoire. And with good reason. A few tablespoons of a well-seasoned sauce can spark a simple preparation, rescue some pallid leftovers, or elevate a fine dish to mouth-watering perfection. The world of sauces has been enriched by contributions from many cuisines—hearty pasta sauces from Italy, subtle sweet-sour sauces from the Orient, pungent curry sauces from India, and the all-important classic French sauces such as béchamel, velouté, béarnaise, hollandaise—names that have become part of the culinary language of the world. They are all based on simple techniques that are within the capabilities of anyone who cares to learn.

In the beginning, sauces were probably produced to camouflage the unpleasant side-effects of lack of refrigeration. But even after this disguise became unnecessary, the sauces endured, adding flavor, color, and moisture to foods. It is interesting to note that, while the names of the originators of many essential lifesaving devices have been lost in the mists of time, the name of a gentleman who died in 1703, and whose sole contribution to the better-ment of life was the invention of a simple cream sauce, lives on. Louis de Béchamel (or Béchameil) was steward to Louis XIV, during whose reign the glory of the French kitchen began, when Béchamel concocted his white sauce. It has earned him a place in virtually every cookbook that has appeared since. So much for the power of a sauce.

It goes without saying that in the interest of balanced menu-planning, sauces should be used in moderation—never more than one to a meal, with the possible exclusion of dessert sauces.

There are hundreds, perhaps even thousands, of different sauces, most of which fall into six tidy categories: white sauces; brown sauces; tomato sauces; the hollandaise family of egg yolk and butter sauces; and two uncooked sauces—mayonnaise, made with egg yolk and oil, and the vinaigrettes, also called French dressings, made with oil and vinegar. In addition, there are butter sauces, dessert sauces, and the simplest sauces of all—gravies made from pan juices.

In addition to the sauce recipes in this chapter, there are others scattered throughout the book, which you will find listed in the index.

Thickening Agents

There is nothing mysterious about making a good sauce. The object is to enrich, thicken, or, to use the culinary term, bind a light stock or liquid to make a thickened sauce that will bathe the food it accompanies. Sauces are bound or thickened with a starch such as arrowroot, cornstarch, flour, or potato flour. They may also be thickened with a *roux*, which is a mixture of flour and fat cooked together, or with a *beurre manié*, which is an uncooked mixture of flour and butter; with a protein such as egg yolk; by cooking down, called *reduction*; with cream; with butter; and with puréed vegetables.

Flour-thickened sauces have recently come under assault from the new wave of chefs who represent the *nouvelle cuisine*. They base their sauces on reductions of stock, vegetable purées, crème fraîche, and often outlandish amounts of egg yolks and cream. It is difficult to understand the advantages of using egg yolks (60 calories per yolk) over flour (18 calories per tablespoon), particularly when a properly made and imaginatively seasoned flour-thickened sauce can be absolutely delicious and infinite in its variations.

Flour is effective as a thickener because its starch granules swell when mixed with liquid and heated. Cake flour contains the most starch and consequently gives the most thickening. Pastry flours are next, and all-purpose flours provide the least thickening. Bread flours should never be used for sauces because they contain a significant amount of protein-forming gluten and tend to make sauces stringy and gummy. The slight difference between cake, pastry, and all-purpose flour in their thickening power is of no consequence, and, since all-purpose flour is most widely available, it is the one most generally used. Flour must always be cooked long enough (5 minutes or so) to get rid of its pasty, harsh flavor. Flour mixtures will liquefy or thin out excessively in the presence of a strong acid such as wine or tomatoes. Such a sauce requires a larger quantity of starch than would ordinarily be needed to get the desired consistency. Browning the flour also causes it to lose some of its thickening power. Flour is used to thicken opaque sauces such as béchamel, velouté, and meat gravies.

Cornstarch is a purified floury meal ground from white corn. It does not require long cooking and it makes a smooth, shiny sauce that is familiar to anyone who frequents Chinese restaurants. It is the only thickener used in Chinese cooking. It has twice the thickening power of flour and, consequently, is used in half the quantity: 1 tablespoon of cornstarch equals 2 tablespoons of flour. It is first dissolved in a small amount of cold liquid, preferably the same liquid used to make the sauce—milk, stock, wine, or water—and added toward the end of the cooking. Cornstarch should not be used as a thickener when high temperature and extended cooking time are called for in a recipe because it will thin out. The shiny, translucent quality that cornstarch

gives to sauces makes it more appropriate for use in fruit sauces than in those sauces where you want a smooth, velvety look.

Arrowroot is made from the dried ground rootstalks of the plant of the same name. It is used primarily when you want a clear, transparent sauce. It is more delicate than cornstarch, and it is the choice of many cooks for last-minute thickening because it does not leave a floury aftertaste. It is mixed with liquid before being added to the sauce and then cooked with a minimum of stirring until the sauce is clear. A rounded teaspoon of arrowroot has the thickening power of a tablespoon of flour. It should never be cooked to the boiling point because excessive heating causes thinning. Arrowroot is a lovely thickener for fruit tarts and fruit sauces.

Potato flour, or potato starch, is made, as you might guess, from potatoes. Like cornstarch, 1 tablespoon of potato flour equals 2 tablespoons of flour in thickening power. It cooks clear quickly, has no floury or raw taste, and imparts a somewhat shiny finish to a sauce. It is frequently used to thicken a sauce that has thinned out or that shows signs of separating after cooking. It should not be heated too long or it may liquefy.

Techniques for Thickening Sauces

Roux. The heart of a smooth, rich white or brown sauce is the roux, a cooked mixture of fat and flour. Use a thick, heavy-bottomed saucepan, preferably stainless steel, copper, enameled cast iron—not aluminum, which can discolor the sauce. A thin-bottomed pan is a poor conductor of heat and, if the fat is too hot, the starch granules will shrink instead of swelling, impeding the maximum thickening of the sauce.

To make the roux, heat the butter until the foam subsides and add the flour, stirring well to produce a smooth mixture. Keep over medium-low heat, stirring occasionally, until the butter and flour foam together and are frothy with little bubbles. It is important to cook the flour and fat long enough to get rid of the raw taste of flour and initiate the swelling of the starch granules. Allow 2 to 3 minutes for each 2 tablespoons of butter and flour. In this time, the mixture resembles a honeycomb and turns a pale, strawlike color. Remove from the heat and, when the roux has stopped bubbling, add the liquid all at once, whisking it in quickly and thoroughly to blend the roux and liquid.

Slurry. A slurry is a watery mixture of a starch and cold liquid and is an easy way to thicken a sauce. You can produce a smooth mixture by shaking the starch and liquid together in a tightly capped jar, about 1 tablespoon of flour to each 2 tablespoons of liquid. Add the slurry to the hot mixture and, stirring gently and continuously over medium-low heat, bring the sauce to a boil. Use a wooden spoon for stirring.

Beurre Manié. Also called kneaded butter, this is an uncooked roux, and it can be a kitchen lifesaver, rescuing sauces that have failed to thicken properly. Knead together equal parts of butter and flour until they form a thick paste that can be formed into a ball. Break off small pieces of the paste, a few at a time, and stir them into the simmering liquid. The heat quickly dilates the starch granules and the thickening takes place very quickly. Stop the cooking as soon as the sauce is thick and smooth. This must be done just before serving. Use 1½ to 2 tablespoons of *beurre manié* to 1 cup of liquid for a medium-thick sauce. *Beurre manié* can be stored in a tightly covered jar in your refrigerator for two or three weeks with no damage.

Reduction. You can thicken a liquid by cooking it, uncovered, over high heat until the desired consistency is reached. This is called reduction. Unless you have a trained eye, it is safest to pour the liquid into a measuring cup, note the amount, and return the liquid to the pan and cook until you think it has reduced sufficiently. Then remeasure the liquid. If you have reduced it too much, add water to dilute. Since reduction concentrates and intensifies flavor, do not season the liquid until the desired consistency has been reached. Then taste and correct.

White Sauces

White sauce, also known as cream sauce, béchamel, or velouté, is the basic fabric from which all manner of sauces can be fashioned. The ingredients and trimmings may vary a bit, but the cooking methods are the same. The techniques required for making a perfect béchamel, which is composed of butter, flour, and milk, are exactly the same as those used in making a velouté, which is butter, flour, and broth, or a combination of broth and wine. The broth can be chicken, beef, or fish, depending on the food it is to accompany.

The white sauces are truly valuable kitchen tools. They can be used as a base for sauces for vegetables, eggs, poultry, meat, creamed or gratinéed dishes, seafood, or crêpes, as a binding agent for croquettes, and as a base for mousses. The proportions of flour and butter to liquid will vary, according to the thickness of the sauce that you wish. The following recipes yield 1 cup of sauce.

Thin White Sauce (for soups)	Medium-Thick White Sauce (all-purpose)	Thick White Sauce (for soufflé bases)
1 tablespoon butter	2 tablespoons butter	3 tablespoons butter
1 tablespoon flour	2 tablespoons flour	3 to 4 tablespoons flour
1 cup milk, broth, or vegetable juices	1 cup milk, broth, or vegetable juices	1 cup milk, broth, or vegetable juices
Salt and freshly ground pepper	Salt and freshly ground pepper	Salt and freshly ground pepper

Melt the butter over medium-low heat in a heavy-bottomed nonaluminum saucepan. Blend in the flour, stirring with a wooden spoon. Continue to stir and cook for 2 or 3 minutes, until the flour and butter foam and bubble. Don't let it color more than a pale, buttery yellow.

Remove from the heat and, when the roux has stopped bubbling, add the liquid all at once and beat it vigorously with a wire whisk to blend smoothly. Many recipes tell you to heat the liquid before adding it, which lessens the danger of a lumpy sauce. But it is not necessary if you whisk the liquid in vigorously and quickly, a maneuver that takes care of the lumps and saves you from washing an extra pot. The liquid can be at room temperature if you like, but this, too, is unnecessary.

When the roux has all been absorbed into the liquid, place the saucepan over moderately high heat and bring it to a slow boil. Reduce the heat and keep whisking until the sauce is thickened, 4 or 5 minutes longer. If you have made a white sauce with milk, add from ¼ to ½ teaspoon of salt and a few grinds of pepper and the sauce is done. If you have used seasoned stock, you might want to simmer the sauce longer to increase the flavor. Taste it to see if it needs additional salt and pepper.

You can vary the flavor by using one or more of the following: a grating of fresh nutmeg; a teaspoon of lemon juice; ½ teaspoon Worcestershire sauce; a teaspoon of dry sherry; a teaspoon of onion juice; 2 tablespoons of chopped parsley or chopped chives. Add to the sauce a minute before it is done.

If you are going to put the sauce aside for later use, place a piece of buttered wax paper, buttered side down, on the surface of the sauce, or a light filming of milk over the surface, to keep a skin from forming.

Enrichments for White Sauces

While a good, well-seasoned white sauce is quite suitable for serving just as it is, you may add butter, cream, or egg yolk to further enrich it.

Butter. This is the simplest of all enrichments. One-half to one tablespoon of firm plain or flavored butter is sufficient for one cup of sauce. Whisk it into the hot sauce just before serving. The butter emulsifies, making the sauce shiny and velvety and a bit thicker. Serve the sauce immediately because there is danger of the butter liquefying and thinning out the sauce, or of having the emulsion break, in which case the butter will float to the top of the sauce.

Wine. Add 1 or 2 tablespoons of Madeira, port, or dry sherry per cup of sauce just before serving.

Cream. The basic sauce must be thick enough to withstand the thinning-out effect of the additional cream that is added. Reduce the sauce until very thick, bring it to a simmer, and beat in the cream by spoonfuls until the sauce reaches the desired consistency. Continue stirring even after the cream has been added, until the sauce coats the spoon.

Egg Yolk and Cream. This makes a very rich and velvety sauce, probably not ideal for waistline watchers. Use 2 egg yolks and ½ cup of heavy cream to 1½ cups white sauce. Whisk egg yolks and cream in a bowl. Add half the hot white sauce, bit by bit, to heat the yolks. Return the egg yolk mixture to the rest of the hot sauce, whisking it in slowly. Reheat until one or two bubbles form and remove the sauce from the heat. Because the egg yolks are supported by a flour-based sauce, they will not curdle when heated.

To the Rescue

Chances are if you follow directions carefully, you will have a smooth sauce of the proper consistency—one that is silky and thick enough to flow from the spoon. But just in case the unexpected occurs, here are some emergency repairs:

If the sauce is lumpy, force it through a fine strainer or whirl it in an electric blender and simmer for 4 or 5 minutes.

If the sauce is too thick, bring it to a simmer and beat in some cream, milk, or stock, one tablespoon at a time.

If the sauce is too thin, reduce it over medium-high heat, stirring constantly with a

wooden spoon, until it cooks down to the desired consistency. Or make a *beurre manié* with 1 tablespoon each of butter and flour. Beat the paste into the sauce, bit by bit, until smooth and thickened. Add it slowly. The amount you need will vary according to how thin the sauce was.

Sauces Derived from Béchamel and Velouté

Aurore. Add 3 tablespoons tomato purée to 2 cups velouté sauce. Simmer for a few minutes and swirl in 1 tablespoon butter. Serve with fish.

Caper Sauce. Add 2½ tablespoons drained, chopped capers to 1½ cups velouté or béchamel sauce just before serving and heat through. Caper sauce is good with poached or broiled fish and mutton.

Cheese Sauce. Stir ½ cup shredded sharp Cheddar or Gruyère and a pinch of dry mustard into 1 cup béchamel sauce during the last 2 minutes of cooking, just enough time to melt the cheese. Overheating makes cheese tough and stringy. This is a nice sauce with vegetables, particularly cauliflower and broccoli.

Curried Cream Sauce. This is not to be confused with a genuine curry sauce. It is a cream sauce mildly flavored with curry, pleasant with poultry or egg dishes. Prepare 1 cup medium béchamel sauce, but add from 1 to 2 teaspoons curry powder and ½ teaspoon ground ginger to the flour when you make the roux.

Egg Cream Sauce. Add 2 chopped hard-boiled eggs, 1 teaspoon drained capers, and a couple of dashes of Worcestershire sauce to 1 cup of velouté made with chicken stock and milk. For poached fish.

Horseradish Sauce. Add 1 to 2 tablespoons prepared horseradish (depending on how hot it is), ½ teaspoon dry mustard, 1 teaspoon vinegar, and a pinch of sugar to 1 cup béchamel sauce. This is traditional with boiled beef and is also good with corned beef.

Mornay Sauce. Add 3 tablespoons grated Parmesan cheese and 3 tablespoons grated Gruyère to 1 cup béchamel during the last 2 minutes of cooking and stir until melted. In a small bowl, mix 1 egg yolk with 2 tablespoons cream. Just before serving, beat a few tablespoons of the hot sauce into the yolk-cream mixture and return the mixture to the sauce, beating it in slowly. Stir in 1 tablespoon butter and stir for an additional minute. If you are using this in a dish to be gratinéed (browned under the broiler), sprinkle it lightly with grated Parmesan cheese before browning. Serve with fish, vegetables, and egg dishes.

Mustard Sauce. Stir 1 tablespoon Dijon mustard and a squirt of lemon juice into 1 cup béchamel sauce and heat through. You may

want an additional pinch of salt and a grind or two of pepper. Serve with poached or broiled fish.

Paprika Sauce. Sauté 3 or 4 finely chopped shallots in 1 tablespoon butter until soft but not brown. Add 2 tablespoons sweet Hungarian paprika and stir for a minute or two. Stir constantly while slowly adding 1 cup light cream and ⅓ cup velouté sauce. Taste and correct seasoning. Serve with poultry, veal, or fish.

Parsley or Dill Sauce. Stir 4 tablespoons finely chopped parsley or 2 tablespoons snipped fresh dill and a few drops of Worcestershire sauce into 1 cup béchamel sauce. Serve with poached fish or chicken.

Supreme Sauce. This is a velouté sauce made with chicken stock and enriched with egg yolks and heavy cream. To 1 cup of velouté, add 2 egg yolks lightly beaten with 2 table-spoons heavy cream, warming the egg yolks first with a few tablespoons of hot velouté and then stirring into the sauce. Stir in 1 tablespoon lemon juice. This is a lovely, delicate sauce for fish, poultry, and eggs.

Brown Sauces

Hours of simmering and skimming can go into the making of the classic French brown sauce. But few of us these days have the time for such lengthy preparations, however good the results, and we are all the more likely to be attracted to shortcuts that yield satisfactory results, as outlined here. If you have rich, homemade brown stock in your freezer, you will naturally want to use it for the sauce. If not, canned beef broth (not consommé, which tends to be sweet) will

do. Both of the following sauces keep well in the refrigerator for two to three weeks, or they may be frozen.

A well-flavored brown sauce is the base for many interesting and elegant sauces. By itself, it can turn an open-face meat sandwich into a substantial luncheon dish and make a satisfying main course of leftover meat cubes resting on a bed of hot, freshly cooked noodles.

Basic Brown Sauce

3 tablespoons butter
1 small onion, chopped
1 cup dry red wine
1½ cups beef broth
¼ teaspoon dried thyme
½ bay leaf
3 sprigs parsley
3 tablespoons butter
3 tablespoons flour
Salt and freshly ground pepper

Melt the butter in a heavy saucepan and add the chopped onion. Cook until the onion is golden brown. Add the wine and broth and bring to a boil. Add the thyme, bay leaf, and parsley and cook uncovered over high heat, until the liquid is reduced by about one-third. Knead together the butter and flour (*beurre manié*). Break off small pieces and add them, a few at a time, to the boiling liquid. Stir constantly with a wooden spoon until the sauce has reached the desired thickness—somewhere between that of light and heavy cream. Add salt and pepper to taste. Strain the sauce and discard the bay leaf, parsley and onion bits.

Yield: About 1½ cups.

Brown Sauce II

This version has a slightly different flavor because of the presence of white wine and tomato paste.

2 tablespoons butter
2 carrots, chopped
1 onion, peeled and chopped
3 sprigs parsley
½ teaspoon dried thyme
1 bay leaf
2 tablespoons flour
1 cup dry white wine
1½ cups beef broth
1½ tablespoons tomato paste
Salt and freshly ground pepper

Melt the butter in a heavy saucepan and add the carrots, onion, parsley, thyme, and bay leaf. Cook over low heat, stirring constantly, until the vegetables are golden brown. Stir in the flour and cook until lightly colored. Add the wine, broth, and tomato paste. Cook uncovered until the liquid is reduced by one-third, stirring from time to time to prevent sticking. When sufficiently reduced, cover the pan and simmer gently for another 10 to 15 minutes. Add salt and pepper to taste. Strain and refrigerate until needed.

Yield: 1½ to 2 cups.

Pan Gravy

Pan gravies are another kind of brown sauce, made by deglazing the roasting or sauté pan in which you have cooked meat or poultry. You can produce these sauces with nonchalance and careless abandon, for there is no need to measure and they will taste of the foods whence they came, extending and highlighting the flavor.

After you have finished cooking the meat or poultry, remove it from the pan. Skim off all but a spoonful or two of the fat, add some chopped onion, scallion, or shallot—whatever is at hand—and let it cook for a minute on top of the stove. Then stir in a bit of wine, stock, or even water, scraping up all the little brown bits and pieces of the coagulated juices that have caramelized on the bottom of the pan. Add more stock and wine and boil rapidly until it is reduced to the syrupy stage. Taste it to see if it needs any salt and pepper. If you like, you can swirl in a little butter. It is a delicious kind of sauce and all you need is a spoonful per serving.

You can convert this into a cream gravy by using half a cup of cream instead of the broth or wine and cooking it down.

Sauces Derived from Brown Sauce

Bordelaise (Red Wine Sauce). Cook 1 small chopped onion or 3 or 4 chopped shallots or scallions together with ½ teaspoon dried thyme and 1 cup dry red wine over high heat until reduced by half. Add 1 cup brown sauce and 1 teaspoon lemon juice and simmer for 5 minutes. Strain and stir in 1 tablespoon finely chopped fresh parsley. Serve with grilled steaks, chops, roast beef, or sweetbreads. Makes 1½ cups.

Sauce Diable (Spicy Brown Sauce). Cook 2 finely chopped shallots or scallions in 1 tablespoon butter until limp. Add ½ teaspoon dried tarragon and ¾ cup dry white wine and cook until reduced by half. Combine with 1½ cups brown sauce, 1 teaspoon Worcestershire sauce, and ½ teaspoon dry mustard. Simmer for 3 or 4 minutes. Season with enough freshly ground pepper to give it a spicy taste. Strain and stir in 2 tablespoons finely minced fresh parsley. Serve with broiled meat and poultry. Makes about 1¾ cups.

Madeira Sauce. Combine ¼ cup Madeira wine with 1 cup brown sauce, bring to a boil, and boil until the sauce is reduced by one-third. Taste for seasoning and add an additional tablespoon or two of wine if you think it is needed, but simmer to evaporate the alcohol. This sauce is good with game, fillet of beef, chicken livers, ham, or veal. Makes about 1 cup.

Mushroom Sauce. Sauté ¼ pound sliced mushrooms in 2 tablespoons butter for 2 or 3 minutes. Add 1 cup brown sauce, mix well, and heat through. Add a few squirts of lemon juice and a tablespoon of minced fresh parsley. Serve with roast meat, chicken, and meat loaf. Makes about 1½ cups.

Sauce Piquante (Brown Sauce with Capers and Pickles). Heat 1 tablespoon butter with 2 tablespoons minced onion, and cook until onion is golden. Combine with 1½ cups brown sauce, 2 tablespoons lemon juice, 1 tablespoon drained capers, and a few dashes of Tabasco and heat through. Just before serving, mix in 1 tablespoon chopped pickles and 1 tablespoon chopped fresh parsley. Taste and correct seasoning. Serve with pork, boiled beef, leftover meats, and smoked meats. Makes about 1⅔ cups.

Sauce Robert (Brown Mustard Sauce).

Heat 2 tablespoons butter and add 2 tablespoons finely minced onion or shallots; cook until soft and lightly browned. Add ⅔ cup dry white wine and boil until it has reduced by half. Add 1½ cups brown sauce and 3 table-spoons tomato paste and simmer for 5 minutes. Remove from the heat and stir in 1 tablespoon Dijon mustard, a pinch of sugar, and 1 tablespoon finely chopped dill pickle. Taste and correct seasoning. Add 1 to 2 tablespoons minced fresh parsley and serve. This is a robust, hearty sauce that is good with pork, boiled beef, broiled chicken, hamburgers, or hot meat leftovers. Makes about 1¾ cups.

Tomato Sauces

It is a sad fact of life that, in most parts of the country, we can savor the lovely flavor and rich color of naturally vine-ripened tomatoes only in the summer. The rest of the time we are offered tomatoes that modern-day technology has rushed to maturity with discernible loss in flavor, juiciness, and aroma.

But we can take full advantage of the locally grown tomatoes when they are in season by using them in sauces that can be available all year in the freezer. The long narrow plum tomatoes seem to be more in evidence these days, and they cook up to a good sauce. And when ripe, fresh tomatoes are not available in any form, we can always rely on the canned imported Italian plum tomatoes, which give an excellent account of themselves in a sauce.

Tomato Sauce I

Vine-ripened fresh tomatoes are first choice, but if they are not available, use canned Italian plum tomatoes. If you have more sauce than you need, freeze the excess in 2-cup containers. This is sufficient for 1 pound of pasta.

4 tablespoons olive oil
1 large onion, finely minced
1 celery stalk, finely minced
1 small carrot, scraped and coarsely grated
¼ cup finely minced fresh parsley
2 cloves garlic, finely minced
2 tablespoons chopped fresh basil, *or* 1 teaspoon dried
½ teaspoon dried marjoram
3 pounds fresh ripe plum tomatoes, cut into chunks, *or* 4 cups canned, peeled tomatoes and their juice
2 tablespoons tomato paste
Salt and freshly ground pepper

Heat the oil in a large, nonaluminum pot or skillet, and add the onion, celery, carrot, parsley, garlic, basil, and marjoram. Cook over low heat, stirring often, until the vegetables are soft and tender, but not browned. Add the tomatoes, tomato paste, salt, and pepper. Partly cover and simmer for 1 to 1½ hours, or until the sauce is thick. Stir frequently to make sure the sauce is not scorching.

Purée through a food mill to remove the seeds and skins. Taste and correct the seasonings. The carrot should be sufficient to counteract the acidity of the tomatoes, but if not, add a pinch of sugar. Heat through 2 minutes longer.

Yield: About 5 cups, or enough for 4 to 6 servings.

Tomato Sauce II

This slightly richer sauce with a more intense flavor goes well with fish, shrimp, and pasta.

3 tablespoons olive oil

6 to 8 scallions, *or* 1 onion, chopped

1 1-pound, 13-ounce can Italian plum tomatoes, chopped, with juice

2 or 3 cloves garlic, finely chopped

1 teaspoon dried basil

1 teaspoon dried marjoram

½ teaspoon salt

Freshly ground pepper

1 6-ounce can tomato paste

¾ cup dry white wine

In a large, heavy-bottomed, nonaluminum pot, heat the oil and sauté the scallions or onion until soft and tender, not browned. Add the tomatoes, garlic, basil, marjoram, salt, and pepper and simmer over low heat for 50 minutes, uncovered. Stir from time to time with a wooden spoon and break up the tomatoes. Add the tomato paste and wine, and cook 20 minutes longer. Taste for seasoning and correct.

Yield: About 3 cups.

Mayonnaise

Neither historians nor cooks seem to be able to agree on the identity of the first person who discovered that trickling oil into egg yolks while whisking them produced a smooth, thick, unctuous sauce that could then be deliciously flavored with vinegar and lemon juice. But whoever he (or she?) was deserves our eternal thanks.

Mayonnaise is another close relative of hollandaise, the difference being that hollandaise is an emulsion of egg yolk and butter and is served warm, while mayonnaise is an emulsion of egg yolk and oil and is served cold. Mayonnaise is simpler to make than hollandaise because the egg yolks do not have to be warmed. It can be beaten by hand or made in a blender or food processor, and the pleasure of seeing the glossy, creamy mixture emerge from such pedestrian ingredients as oil and egg yolks should be reason enough for making it. But more important, the end product is infi-

nitely superior to the commercially prepared.

There are a few general rules to bear in mind when making mayonnaise by hand. All ingredients should be at room temperature, for cold oil can cause a broken mayonnaise. If the eggs are right out of the refrigerator, warm them in a bowl of hot water to take the chill off. The egg yolks should be beaten for a minute or two before you add anything to them. This prepares them to absorb the oil more readily. One large egg yolk can absorb 6 ounces, or ¾ cup, of oil. If more oil is used, the sauce could thin out and curdle. When you make mayonnaise by hand, use only the egg yolk; use the whole egg in the blender or food processor method.

The choice of oil is a matter of taste. Olive oil makes itself known by its distinctive taste. If you want a more neutral flavor, use one of the vegetable oils, such as corn or peanut oil. Lemon juice or vinegar is a must; the inclusion of mustard or Tabasco is optional.

Mayonnaise

2 egg yolks from large or extra large eggs
½ teaspoon salt
1 teaspoon Dijon mustard
1 tablespoon fresh lemon juice or vinegar
1½ cups oil (vegetable oil, olive oil, or a combination)
1 tablespoon boiling water

Put the egg yolks, salt, mustard, and lemon juice or vinegar in a bowl and beat with a wire whisk or an electric beater until the yolks become thick and sticky.

Add the oil drop by drop, beating vigorously after each addition. As the sauce begins to thicken (which means that it has emulsi-fied), you can beat in the remaining oil more quickly. Taste it to see if it needs more salt, lemon juice, or vinegar. If the sauce becomes too thick, you can thin it out with a few additional drops of lemon juice. Whisk a tablespoon of boiling water into the finished mayonnaise, which stabilizes it and acts as anti-curdling insurance.

Refrigerate the mayonnaise in a covered jar or bowl. It will keep for a week.

Yield: 1¾ cups.

To the Rescue

Mayonnaise may start to curdle if you have added the oil too fast. But all is not lost. Beat 1 egg yolk in a clean bowl and beat in a few drops of oil. Little by little, beat in the curdled mixture until it becomes smooth and thickens. This also works with a mayonnaise that has not thickened properly.

Aioli (Garlic Mayonnaise)

If you don't love garlic, this sauce may not make your pulse race. However, if it is one of your favorite things, you will find this a wonderful sauce with all kinds of hot and cold fish, with boiled potatoes and vegetables, or as a dip for shrimp and both raw and cooked vegetables.

3 egg yolks
4 to 6 garlic cloves, finely chopped
2 tablespoons lemon juice
¼ teaspoon salt
Freshly ground pepper
1 cup olive oil, or a combination of olive and vegetable oil
2 to 3 tablespoons boiling water, if necessary
1 tablespoon finely chopped parsley

Put egg yolks, garlic (a lot or a little, according to your taste), lemon juice, salt, and pepper in the blender container and blend until just mixed. Dribble in the oil slowly, in a thin steady stream, as for mayonnaise. The sauce will be very thick and you may need to thin it out with 2 or 3 tablespoons boiling water, blending it in. Transfer the sauce to a bowl and stir in the chopped parsley. Cover and refrigerate before serving.

Yield: About 1¾ cups.

Blender Mayonnaise

Making mayonnaise in a blender is a joyfully simple procedure.

1 whole egg
1 teaspoon Dijon mustard
1½ teaspoons vinegar
⅓ teaspoon salt
1 cup oil
1 to 2 tablespoons lemon juice
1 tablespoon boiling water

Place the egg, mustard, vinegar, salt, and ¼ cup of the oil in the container of the electric blender. Blend on medium speed until frothy. Add the remainder of the oil in a slow, steady stream, adding it more quickly as the sauce emulsifies and thickens. Add lemon juice to taste and then the water. Blend only until thick and smooth. Refrigerate in a covered bowl.

Yield: About 1¼ cups.

Mayonnaise Variations

The varieties of sauces based on mayonnaise are as numerous as jelly beans at Easter time. Here are a few:

Avocado Mayonnaise. To 1 cup of mayonnaise, add the grated rind of 1 lime, ½ cup chopped ripe avocado, and 1 or more tablespoons lime juice. Blend in an electric blender until smooth. Chill before serving. Serve with cold fish or fish and egg salads.

Green Mayonnaise. In a saucepan with 1 cup of water boil the following for 2 minutes: 8 or 10 spinach leaves, 3 chopped shallots or 5 or 6 scallions, ¼ cup watercress sprigs, 2 tablespoons parsley, and 1 tablespoon fresh tarragon or 1 teaspoon dried. Drain, plunge into cold water immediately, and pat dry with paper towels. Purée in a blender or food processor and stir into 1½ cups mayonnaise. Serve with cold shellfish or cold poached fish.

Green Goddess Dressing. To 1 cup of mayonnaise, add 1 minced garlic clove, 3 well-drained minced anchovy fillets, 3 tablespoons finely minced chives or scallions, ¼ cup minced parsley, 1 tablespoon lemon juice, 1 tablespoon wine vinegar, ½ teaspoon dried tar-ragon, ⅓ teaspoon salt, freshly ground black pepper, and ½ cup sour cream. Blend well. Serve with fish or shellfish.

Fruit Salad Mayonnaise. To 1 cup of mayonnaise, add ½ cup pineapple juice, 1 teaspoon grated orange rind, and 1 tablespoon Grand Marnier or another orange liqueur. Mix well.

Mustard Mayonnaise. To 1 cup of mayonnaise, add 1 tablespoon Dijon mustard. Serve with cold shrimp, cold meats, and celeriac salad.

Rémoulade Sauce. To 1½ cups of mayonnaise, add 2 tablespoons drained, chopped capers, 1 teaspoon Dijon mustard, 1 tablespoon finely chopped fresh parsley, 1 finely chopped hard-boiled egg, a pinch of dried tarragon, and ½ teaspoon anchovy paste. Serve with cold meat, poultry, and shellfish.

Russian Dressing. To 1 cup of mayonnaise, add 2 teaspoons prepared horseradish, 1 teaspoon Worcestershire sauce, 1 tablespoon finely chopped onion, 2 tablespoons chili sauce or ketchup, and 2 tablespoons red or black caviar. This last ingredient adds a note of authenticity; needlesss to say, it does not have to be Beluga caviar. Russian dressing can be used on composed salads, eggs, shellfish, or for cold chicken and turkey sandwiches in place of the usual butter or plain mayonnaise.

Tartar Sauce. To 1 cup of mayonnaise, add 1 teaspoon mustard, 1 teaspoon finely minced shallots, 1 tablespoon chopped, drained, sweet pickle, 1 tablespoon chopped green olives, 1 teaspoon lemon juice, and 1 tablespoon drained chopped capers. This is a popular accompaniment for fried or broiled fish and shellfish.

Sour Cream Mayonnaise. Blend together equal quantities of sour cream and mayonnaise. Serve with poultry salads or coleslaw. Yogurt may be substituted for the sour cream in the same proportion.

Sauce for Smoked Fish. For a quick sauce to complement the flavor of smoked fish, combine 4 tablespoons mayonnaise, 2 teaspoons (or more) horseradish, and 2 tablespoons sour cream. Makes about ½ cup.

Gribiche Sauce. To 1¼ cups mayonnaise, add 2 tablespoons finely chopped dill or sour pickles, 2 tablespoons minced capers, 1 tablespoon chopped parsley, 1 tablespoon chopped chives, 1 tablespoon chopped fresh tarragon or 1 teaspoon dried. Blend well. Good with poached fish.

The Hollandaise Family

If sauces were royalty, hollandaise would probably be the queen. It is often feared by inexperienced cooks, but is not difficult to make. Hollandaise is simply warm egg yolks flavored with lemon juice into which butter is gradually beaten to make a rich, creamy sauce. The eggs absorb and hold the fat in a thick emulsion. And if the unthinkable occurs, and the sauce curdles or separates, you can repair it. Béarnaise sauce is closely related to hollandaise, but it is more flamboyant and spicier, more intense in flavor. However, basic ingredients, proportions, and preparation are exactly the same for the two sauces.

Interest in the hollandaise family has extended far beyond the kitchen into scientific laboratories. A most prestigious scientific publication recently featured a lengthy, highly technical article about a broken béarnaise sauce. The article was bristling with terms like "colloidal suspension," "electrically charged aggregates," and "geometric arrangements of the molecules." It was written by a physicist who obviously had spent many hours in his laboratory surrounded by test tubes, egg yolks, lemon juice, and butter, in a noble attempt to unravel the mystery of the failed sauce. The only conclusion that he and other similarly dedicated scientists arrived at was that more research was needed.

There are many different recipes for hollandaise. They vary in the proportions of butter to egg yolk, but these general rules apply to all handmade hollandaise sauces:

The egg yolks and lemon juice or vinegar must be heated slowly and gently over very low heat. Too much heat will make them curdle, and curdled yolks cannot retain the emulsified butter.

The butter must be added slowly so that the eggs have a chance to absorb the butter, holding it in suspension. Once the sauce has started to thicken, the butter may be added more quickly.

The amount of butter must not exceed the amount the yolks can absorb—a large, properly heated egg yolk can absorb 3 ounces (6 tablespoons) of butter. Hollandaise is never really hot; it is served tepid (in a warm bowl, not a hot one), over hot vegetables or other hot food.

Leftover hollandaise may be stored in the refrigerator for two or three days. To reheat it, place a tablespoon of sauce in a pan over hot water, adding sauce by the tablespoon, beating well after each addition.

Basic Hollandaise

Hollandaise is traditionally whisked by hand, but you may use a hand-held electric mixer if you prefer. A heavy-bottomed, nonaluminum pot, about 1-quart capacity, is a must. If you do not have a heavy pan, use an asbestos pad or some kind of flame control device under the pan. You can also make the sauce using a stainless steel bowl placed 2 inches above a pot of hot—not boiling— water, or in a glass double boiler, so that you can see that the water does not come to the boil, which will ruin the sauce. But if hollandaise is made in a double boiler, it takes about 10 minutes of unremitting beating for the eggs to reach the proper consistency. Making the sauce over direct, low heat is infinitely quicker.

3 egg yolks
1 tablespoon lemon juice
Dash of Tabasco or pinch of
  cayenne pepper
¼ teaspoon salt
¼ pound (1 stick) unsalted butter,
  melted

Put the egg yolks, lemon juice, Tabasco, and salt in a 1-quart heavy saucepan over very low heat or in the top of a double boiler over, but not touching, hot water. Beat with a wire whisk until the egg yolks have thickened to the consistency of heavy cream. You will begin to see the bottom of the pan between strokes when they are the proper consistency. If the egg yolks are not beaten to this stage, they will not be able to absorb and hold the butter as they should, and the sauce will not thicken properly.

Slowly whisk in the warm, not hot, melted butter by the quarter-teaspoonful until the sauce begins to thicken into a very heavy cream. You can then whisk in the butter a little more rapidly, beating constantly until all the butter has been added.

If the sauce seems to be thickening too fast, add a teaspoon of hot water at intervals to slow the process. If it is too thin, you are adding the butter too quickly, not giving it a chance to be absorbed. When the sauce is thick enough to coat the whisk, it is done.

If you have to keep the sauce for a short time, cover the pan with plastic wrap and let it stand over warm water. Don't let the sauce stand for too long without being refrigerated, because it provides a comfortable environment for bacteria to multiply.

Yield: About ¾ cup.

To the Rescue

If the sauce is not thickening properly (because you beat in the butter too fast), stop everything. Combine 1 teaspoon lemon juice with 1 tablespoon of the sauce in a small bowl warmed in hot water and thoroughly dried, and beat them until the sauce begins to thicken. Then beat in the rest of the sauce, a tablespoonful at a time, whisking before adding the next spoonful. Return to low heat and finish making the sauce.

If the finished sauce breaks or curdles (because you kept it too warm or you exceeded your butter proportion) whisk in a tablespoon of cold water to restore the emulsion. If this doesn't work, in a fresh bowl beat 1 egg yolk with ¼ teaspoon dry mustard until thick. Gradually add the curdled sauce in small amounts, whisking until the sauce becomes smooth.

Beat in more salt, pepper, or lemon juice if you think them necessary. If the sauce is too thick you can beat in droplets of hot water or stock just before serving.

Blender Hollandaise

This is virtually a no-fail method if the butter is hot and added slowly in a thin stream.

3 egg yolks
2 tablespoons fresh lemon juice
¼ teaspoon salt
Dash of Tabasco or cayenne
    pepper
½ cup (1 stick) unsalted butter,
    melted and hot

Combine the egg yolks, lemon juice, salt, and Tabasco or cayenne pepper in a blender, and blend just until the eggs are foamy, about 5 seconds. Heat the butter until it sizzles, but do not let it brown. Remove the insert from the cover of the blender (leave the cover on to prevent spattering) and, with the machine running, pour in the bubbling hot butter in a thin steady stream. It will thicken very quickly, in a matter of seconds rather than minutes. If the sauce is too thick, stir in 1 to 2 tablespoons hot water. Taste and correct the seasonings.

Yield: About ¾ cup.

Béarnaise Sauce

While hollandaise is flavored simply with lemon juice, béarnaise is fashioned with a more complex combination of vinegar, wine, tarragon, and shallots reduced to an aromatic essence. Otherwise, the methods of preparation are identical. The robust character of béarnaise provides perfect balance for grilled steaks, fried or grilled fish, broiled chicken, and many egg and vegetable dishes.

Like hollandaise, béarnaise can be made with a whisk, an electric beater, or a blender.

Blender Béarnaise Sauce

¼ cup wine vinegar
¼ cup dry white vermouth
1 tablespoon shallots, finely chopped
1 teaspoon dried tarragon
Salt and freshly ground pepper
3 large egg yolks at room temperature
¼ pound (1 stick) unsalted butter, heated to bubbling

Place the vinegar, vermouth, shallots, and tarragon in the blender container. Blend until smooth and scrape into a small saucepan. Bring to a boil and reduce to 1 tablespoon of liquid.

Transfer the mixture to the blender and add salt, pepper, and yolks. Blend just until the eggs are foamy. Heat the butter until it sizzles, but do not let it brown. Remove insert from blender lid and, with the machine running, add the hot butter slowly in a thin, steady stream. The sauce will thicken very quickly. If the sauce is prepared in advance, you may cover the blender with a towel to keep it warm. But even cold, a dollop of this sauce does wonders for an ordinary hamburger or a simple vegetable dish.

Yield: About ¾ cup.

Variations on Hollandaise and Béarnaise Sauces

Anchovy Hollandaise. Add 3 finely minced and well-drained anchovy fillets and 1 teaspoon drained capers to the hollandaise, or 1 tablespoon anchovy paste or to taste. Serve with poached fish.

Choron Sauce (Tomato-flavored Béarnaise). Add 1 or 2 tablespoons tomato paste and 3 tablespoons heavy cream to the béarnaise. Serve with steaks, fish, chicken, or poached eggs.

Horseradish Béarnaise. Add to the béarnaise sauce 1 teaspoon prepared horseradish, or more, according to taste. Serve with poached chicken or boiled meats.

Mousseline Sauce. For each cup of hollandaise, fold in ¼ cup softly whipped cream and 1 stiffly beaten egg white. Serve with poached eggs, fish, asparagus, broccoli, or cauliflower.

Mustard Hollandaise. For each cup of hollandaise, blend in 1 tablespoon or more, according to taste, of Dijon mustard. Serve with fish, grilled or poached chicken, or poached eggs.

Butter Sauces

Melted butter or butter emulsified in a small amount of liquid, such as wine or vinegar or a pan gravy made from meat, poultry, or fish, makes fine, quickly prepared sauces.

Noisette Butter. Heat butter slowly in a small skillet until it becomes golden brown. You may use regular butter, but clarified butter is a better choice because it will not burn as readily. Serve with fish or meat.

Maitre d'Hôtel Butter. Add lemon juice to taste and finely chopped parsley, salt, and pepper to noisette butter. Good with pan-fried meats and fish.

Classic Butter Sauce. Combine 2 tablespoons lemon juice, ⅓ cup water, and a pinch of salt and pepper in a small saucepan and cook over high heat until reduced to about 2 tablespoons. Fluff in 1 stick (¼ pound) butter, a tablespoon at a time. Remove from the heat and fold in 4 or 5 tablespoons unsweetened whipped cream. Serve with poached fish or vegetables.

Black Butter. Heat butter slowly until dark brown, but not burned. Add wine vinegar or lemon juice to taste and blend well. Serve with broiled fish or sautéed calves' brains.

Caper Butter. Combine 2 tablespoons capers—the small ones are preferable—with 2 tablespoons of the caper liquid and a dash of salt and pepper. Heat through and blend in 6 tablespoons of butter, a tablespoon at a time. Remove from the heat and fold in 2 tablespoons unsweetened whipped cream. Serve with poached fish.

Mustard Butter. Combine ½ cup dry white wine, 2 tablespoons minced onion or shallots, ¼ cup minced parsley, a pinch of thyme, salt, and pepper and cook over high heat until reduced to about 3 tablespoons. Blend in 1 tablespoon prepared Dijon mustard and 1½ sticks butter, tablespoon by tablespoon. Strain the sauce and add 2 tablespoons whipped cream. Serve with poached or broiled fish or chicken.

Herb Butter. Cream 1 stick of butter and blend in 1 tablespoon each of finely minced parsley, chives, chervil, and tarragon. If you are using dried chervil and tarragon, use 1 teaspoon each. Mix well and form into a roll one inch in diameter. Wrap in wax paper or aluminum foil and refrigerate. Cut into slices and serve as a topping for broiled meats or fish.

Dessert Sauces

Sweet dessert sauces are served warm or cold over baked or steamed puddings, with stewed or baked fruits, soufflés, and with ice cream. Consider the balance of flavors when choosing a sauce; a very sweet dessert might be best served with a tart accompaniment such as crème fraîche or a fruit sauce, while a bland dessert would be helped with a sprightly liqueur-flavored sauce.

Fruit sauces are simply purées of fruit that can be as thick or thin as you like. They can be thinned out with the liquid in which the fruit was cooked, or thickened with the addition of 1 teaspoon cornstarch dissolved in 1 tablespoon cold water for each cup of sauce.

Apricot Sauce

½ pound dried apricots
Water
Sugar
2 tablespoons liqueur (kirsch, brandy, or an orange liqueur), optional

Soak the apricots in water to cover for several hours and simmer them in the same water until they are soft. Do not drain. Blend in a blender or purée them in a food mill. Return to the saucepan and add sugar to taste; you may need ½ cup, more or less. Stir the purée over the heat for a few minutes until the sugar is dissolved. Flavor with a liqueur, if you wish. Refrigerate in a covered jar. This sauce will keep very well, particularly if you pour a bit of brandy or rum over it.

Yield: About 1½ cups.

Fruit Sauce

Any fruit juice that you wish to convert into a sauce may be used.

1 cup unsweetened fruit juice
1 teaspoon cornstarch
4 tablespoons sugar
2 tablespoons fresh lemon juice

In a small saucepan, combine the fruit juice and cornstarch and stir to dissolve. Add the sugar and lemon juice and bring slowly to a boil, stirring. Cook until the sauce becomes thickened and clear. Taste to see if it needs additional sugar and add, if necessary. Serve hot or cold.

Yield: 1 cup.

Blueberry Sauce

This is a delicious sauce in which the blueberries keep their shape. It may be served over ice cream or puddings, and it makes a particularly impressive dessert when poured over ice cream-filled crêpes.

1 tablespoon cornstarch
½ cup port wine
½ cup orange juice
⅓ cup sugar
3 thin lemon slices
1 cup blueberries, washed and drained

In a small saucepan, combine the cornstarch, wine, and orange juice and stir until smooth. Add the sugar and lemon slices and bring to a boil, stirring. Reduce the heat to a simmer and continue stirring until the sauce is clear and thickened, about 3 minutes. Remove from the heat and discard the lemon slices. Add the blueberries and stir gently. This may be served hot or cold. If you wish to serve it hot, add the berries to the hot syrup just before serving. Prolonged cooking will cause the berries to soften.

Yield: About 2 cups.

Brandied Cherry Sauce

May be flamed with additional brandy and served over ice cream.

1 17-ounce can pitted dark sweet cherries
1 teaspoon grated orange peel
1 teaspoon arrowroot
2 tablespoons Cognac

Drain the cherries and reserve the juice. In a small saucepan, combine the juice, orange peel, and arrowroot. Heat to the boiling point, stirring constantly, until the mixture becomes clear. Stir in the cherries and the Cognac. Cool and chill.

Yield: About 2 cups.

Lemon Sauce

½ cup sugar
1 tablespoon cornstarch
1 cup cold water
3 tablespoons butter
Grated rind of 1 lemon
3 tablespoons lemon juice
Pinch of salt

In a small saucepan, mix the sugar with the cornstarch. Add water, stir well, and cook over low heat, stirring constantly, for 5 minutes, or until the sauce is thickened and clear. Stir in the butter, lemon rind, lemon juice, and salt. Taste to see if it needs more lemon juice or sugar. Serve hot or cold with cakes or puddings.

Yield: About 1 cup.

Orange Sauce. Substitute orange juice for the water.

Melba Sauce

A simple sauce that transforms a peach and a scoop of vanilla ice cream into Peach Melba.

½ cup currant jelly
1 cup fresh or frozen raspberries, puréed and strained
Sugar
1 teaspoon cornstarch, dissolved in 1 tablespoon cold water

Combine the jelly and the puréed and strained raspberries in a small saucepan and cook over low heat until the jelly is melted. Add sugar to taste. You will need ¼ cup or more, but taste as you go; you don't want it too sweet. Simmer for 2 minutes and stir in the dissolved cornstarch. Cook, stirring constantly, until the sauce is thickened and clear. Refrigerate in a covered container when cool.

Yield: 1½ cups.

Strawberry Sauce

1 pint strawberries, *or* 1 10-ounce package frozen unsweetened strawberries
½ cup sugar
½ cup water
Kirsch or an orange liqueur (optional)

Wash and hull the berries and rub them through a strainer or a food mill. In a small saucepan, gently boil the sugar and water for 5 minutes. Combine the purée with the syrup and mix well. Flavor with the liqueur, if desired.

Yield: About 2 cups.

Butterscotch Sauce

1 cup light brown sugar
½ cup corn syrup
Pinch of salt
2 tablespoons butter
½ cup cream

Mix together the sugar, syrup, salt, and butter in a small heavy-bottomed saucepan and bring to the boiling point. Reduce the heat and simmer, stirring from time to time, until it reaches the consistency of a heavy syrup. Remove from the heat and, when cooled, stir in the cream. Serve hot or cold. The sauce may be reheated in the top of a double boiler.

Yield: About 2 cups.

Chocolate Sauce

Silky and smooth.

½ cup milk
¼ cup sugar
5 squares semisweet chocolate
1 tablespoon butter
1 teaspoon vanilla extract
1 tablespoon rum, kirsch, or any
other liqueur (optional)

In a small, heavy-bottomed saucepan, combine the milk and sugar. Cook over low heat, stirring constantly, until the sugar dissolves. Add the chocolate broken into small pieces and cook gently, stirring constantly, for 4 or 5 minutes, or until chocolate is melted and sauce is smooth. Remove from the heat, add the butter, and stir until melted. Stir in vanilla extract and liqueur, if desired. Serve warm over ice cream or cream puffs.

Yield: 1¼ cups.

Creamy Fudge Sauce

A rich, creamy chocolate sauce that will keep in the refrigerator for two weeks.

8 tablespoons butter
4 squares unsweetened chocolate
½ cup cocoa
½ cup sugar
1 cup light cream
1½ teaspoons vanilla extract, *or*
1 tablespoon Grand Marnier

In a heavy-bottomed saucepan over low heat, melt the butter and chocolate together. Mix the cocoa with ¼ cup of sugar and stir in. Add the cream and blend in the remaining sugar. Bring to a boil, stirring constantly to prevent scorching. Remove from the heat and stir in the vanilla. Serve warm.

Yield: 2 to 2½ cups.

Note: To store, cover when cool and refrigerate. To reheat the sauce, place the bowl in a pan of hot water over low heat until the sauce reaches pouring consistency. Add additional cream or hot water if the sauce is too thick.

Sour Cream Sauce

Use over fruits or puddings in place of whipped cream.

2 cups sour cream
1 tablespoon sugar
1 teaspoon vanilla extract

Mix all the ingredients until well blended.

Yield: 2 cups.

12
Baking

There was a time when baking was a hazardous undertaking, filled with uncertainties that spilled over into results that could be wonderful or disastrous. Ingredients were unpredictable, stove heat was erratic, and there were no standard measurements—a handful of flour depended on the size of the hand that was involved. But today we have calibrated ovens, improved flours and leavening agents, splendid baking equipment, electrical gadgets that mix and whip and knead, and tested recipes. With all of this, a beginner's first cake or loaf of bread can be a complete success.

However, baking demands accuracy and care. Unlike other kinds of cooking—soups or stews, for instance—you cannot improvise, substitute ingredients, and depend on your instinct and creativity. The magic that transforms such simple ingredients as flour, fat, eggs, and sugar into tender confections or hearty breads is purely a matter of chemistry. Ingredients must be in correct balance with each other, combined properly, baked in the proper size pan, and exposed to the correct degree of heat for the correct amount of time. There is a practical reason for everything.

Despite the necessary precision, baking can be a joyful, gratifying experience, with end results superior to anything that comes from a commercial bakery. Skill and confidence come with practice and you can serve an endless variety of fresh, wholesome, and delicious breads, cakes, and pastries that will be a source of satisfaction for you and provide much pleasure for your family and friends.

Yeast Baking

Can you think of a cozier place than a kitchen fragrant with the tantalizing aroma of home-made bread browning in the oven, or a more satisfying morsel than that first warm crust lavished with butter? Judging by the ever-growing number of people who have discovered the joys of bread baking, this is a feeling shared by many. A recent survey conducted by one of the leading flour manufacturers indicated that about one-third of all flour used in home baking went into yeast products. Obviously, fewer and fewer people are intimidated by that mysterious one-celled living fungus with the wondrous power to turn a mixture of flour and water into a crusty, flavorful loaf of bread.

Ingredients

Flour
All-purpose flour, preferably the unbleached, is the most easily available and the most commonly used for bread baking. It is a blend of hard and soft wheat flours and is rich in a protein called *gluten,* which is a gummy, elastic material that develops when flour is manipulated either by hand or a mixer after water or some other liquid is added. Gluten is capable of great expansion, forming a structural network that holds the gas liberated by the yeast during the baking, and it gives the bread its semirigid form after baking.

Flours such as buckwheat, rye, barley, corn, graham, and oatmeal are also excellent in yeast breads, but they must be used in combination with wheat or whole wheat flour because, alone, they do not provide the necessary gluten. Whole wheat flour has become increasingly popular over the last few years. It is made from the entire wheat kernel—bran, germ, and endosperm. It tends to turn rancid rather quickly, so buy it in quantities that will be used within a month, or else store it in the refrigerator or freezer.

Flour made from hard wheat has a relatively high gluten content and the gluten is strong. This is the bread flour used by commercial bakeries and there appears to be movement in the direction of making this type of bread flour available to the retail market. Until that time, however, the all-purpose flour is satisfactory. Cake and pastry flour, on the other hand, are made of soft wheat and their delicate, less expansive gluten bakes to a crumblier texture, making them unsuitable for yeast baking. It takes a strong gluten to withstand the pressure generated by the carbon dioxide gas that is released from the fermenting yeast.

All-purpose flours are not uniform. They differ in their ability to absorb liquid, which is the reason that most bread recipes give a range for the amount of flour to be used. Weather, too, affects flour, which will absorb moisture on a humid day. Most recipes will call for enough flour to make a soft dough, meaning a dough that pulls away from the sides of the bowl to form a central mass. Always use the lesser amount first, adding more if needed. With experience, you will know by the feel of the dough when you have added enough flour. Good dough is firm, elastic, and smooth. Too much flour will produce a stiff, lifeless dough.

Yeast

Yeast is the key ingredient—the culinary dynamite—in making bread. A touchy one it is, too. It is a tiny living organism that flourishes in the presence of sweetness, warmth, and moisture. In return, it will multiply and produce alcohol and great gassy bubbles of carbon dioxide, causing the batter or the dough to expand. But if the yeast plants are too cold, they will just sit there, alive and well, but doing nothing. If they are heated to too high a temperature, they will die and no more carbon dioxide will be produced. Yeast cells like it best when their warm bath is between 105 and 115 degrees, at which

temperature liquid feels neither hot nor cold when a drop is placed on the inside of your wrist.

Yeast comes in two forms: active dry yeast, packaged in small granules that usually come in quarter-ounce packets that measure about one tablespoon, and cake yeast. Dry yeast will stay fresh in a cool, dry place until the expiration date printed on each package. Cake yeast must be kept refrigerated and used within two weeks. One package of dry yeast dissolved in warm water is equal to about two-thirds of an ounce of compressed yeast. The recipes in this book all call for dry yeast.

There is no hard and fast rule about the amount of yeast needed. As a general guideline, 1 envelope of yeast will leaven 3 cups of flour in a lean dough, that is, one with flour, water, and a little fat; but only 2 to 2½ cups of flour in a rich dough, one with eggs, sugar, and a large amount of fat.

Proofing Yeast. If you are concerned about your dry yeast being past its prime, you can proof it. Dissolve it in about ½ cup of warm water and add a small amount of sugar, molasses, or honey. Stir and let stand. If it bubbles and foams, you will know it is alive and is now ready for your dough. (Reduce the amount of liquid in the recipe by the amount used to proof the yeast. The small amount of sweetening used will not appreciably alter the flavor of the finished loaf.) Cake yeast tells you all you need to know by its appearance; if it is firm, unblemished, and smells fresh, you can be sure it is active.

Liquid

All batters and doughs must contain some liquid, which converts to steam during baking. The steam exerts force that expands the starch cells, affecting the texture of the baked product. Generally, three parts of flour to one of liquid are used to make the soft dough for yeast breads. The liquid must be warm to dissolve the salt and sugar and to disperse the yeast cells throughout the flour.

Water may be used as the liquid in yeast dough, although milk (which is 87 percent water) is more generally used. Milk increases food value and gives a more tender crust; it also keeps the bread fresher longer. Water will give you a crisp crust and a wheaty flavor. Potato water (water in which you have boiled potatoes) makes yeast bread moist and gives it a slightly greater volume but a coarser texture. It also adds to the keeping quality of the bread.

Eggs, too, are considered a liquid; a whole egg is about 75 percent water.

Sugar

In addition to adding flavor to the bread, sugar is the food on which the yeast feeds and grows as it produces the gas bubbles that make the bread light. In breads to which no sugar is added, the sugar is provided through the action of enzymes in the flour that converts the wheat starch into sugar. When combined in small amounts with yeast, sugar hastens its working, but too much sugar will inhibit yeast activity. Sugar in bread, rolls, and muffins will also yield a golden brown crust.

However, sugar, should always be used with discretion in bread, and many fine breads are made without it. You have only to consider the highly prized and greatly admired French bread, that crusty, simple loaf made only with flour, salt, water, and yeast.

Salt

Salt has a more important function in yeast dough than merely improving the taste of the baked product. Yeast produces carbon dioxide very rapidly in dough that contains no salt. The salt acts as a stabilizer, preventing the yeast from producing the gas too rapidly. Yeast dough without salt is sticky and hard to handle. People who must be on salt-free diets have no choice, but breads made without salt are inferior in grain and texture.

Fat

Fat is an optional ingredient in bread and a perfectly good product can be made without it. However, it does produce a more tender loaf, with a richer taste and better keeping qualities.

Butter, margarine, vegetable shortening, lard, and oil can be used, but sweet butter is first choice for the flavor it gives. Vegetable shortenings give unsweetened breads a crisp texture.

Yeast Dough Methods

There are a number of different methods for preparing yeast dough. The results will be different, according to the method used.

The straight dough method requires kneading. The flour is stirred into the dissolved yeast and the dough is kneaded before it is allowed to rise.

The sponge method requires the yeast to be dissolved in the full amount of the liquid to which a portion of the flour is added. This batter is allowed to ferment, which makes it foamy and spongy. The sponge is then added to the rest of the ingredients. This methods speeds up the first rising. Sponge doughs make a lighter-textured, coarser-grained loaf or roll.

Batter breads are the simplest of all breads. They do not require kneading or a second rising. After the yeast is dissolved, the remaining ingredients are added and beaten well with an electric mixer. The batter is then allowed to rise. Since batter breads are not kneaded and the gluten not fully developed, their texture is coarser and more porous than the breads made with the straight dough method.

Mixing

All the ingredients must be mixed thoroughly so that there will be even distribution of the yeast. That lovely thin, even grain will elude you if this is not done.

To mix a kneaded bread, start stirring the flour into the dissolved yeast mixture with a wooden spoon or an electric mixer. Gradually mix in about half the required flour and beat about a minute. Once the dough becomes stiff, you will find it more convenient to use your hands or the spoon to complete the mixing. Reserve the last cup of flour until you see how much you need. When the dough begins to leave the sides of the bowl, turn it out onto a lightly floured board or counter top. The dough should be as soft as possible without being too sticky to handle. Let the dough rest for 5 minutes and it will lose some of its stickiness, for it takes time for the particles of flour to become hydrated. Form the dough into a fairly

The dough is sufficiently mixed when it no longer clings to the sides of the bowl. It should be soft but not too sticky. After turning it out onto a board, let it rest a few minutes.

flat ball and sprinkle it lightly with flour to keep it from sticking to the work surface.

Now we come to the kneading, which is the mechanical action required to develop the gluten that is essential for a high-quality bread. Bread dough can be kneaded in an electric mixer equipped with a dough hook or in a food processor. Machine kneading is quick and efficient—if you can bear to let a machine do a job that is uniquely satisfying when performed by hand.

Dip your hands in flour before you begin. Knead the dough by pushing it away from you with the heel of your hand. Do this twice. Gently pull the far end of the dough toward you and fold it over. Rotate the dough a little and repeat. Much stretching and folding are required, but done so gently and in such a way that the strands of gluten already formed are not broken. Use firm, rhythmic movements with time in between for the dough to relax. The dough will become increasingly smooth and elastic and will stick less and less to your hands and the counter top. After 10 minutes of kneading, the dough should be satiny and elastic and spring back when you depress it with your fingers. It is theoretically possible to overwork yeast dough to the point where the gluten loses its cohesiveness, but more frequently the breadmaker tires before the gluten is fully developed. When this happens, the loaf will not have an even grain. With practice, you will develop a sense of when the dough is exactly the way it should be. When you have a ball of well-kneaded dough, you are ready for the next step—the rising or fermentation period.

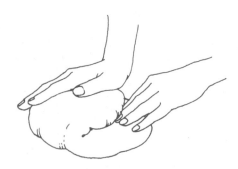

Kneading involves pushing the dough away from you and pulling it toward you. First, push it away with the heel of your hand.

Lift the dough at the far end and pull it toward you so that it folds over on itself. Rotating the dough each time, repeat the pushing and pulling movements, which give the dough elasticity.

Yeast Dough Rises

Place the dough in a well oiled or buttered bowl and turn it to coat the entire surface. This will prevent a dry skin from forming on the dough. Cover the bowl with wax paper and a light towel or cloth and let the dough rise in a warm place free from drafts. An ideal temperature would be about 80 degrees. A cool temperature won't do any real damage to the yeast organisms; it will merely slow them down, and the rising will take longer. If something comes up during the rising process that takes you away from the kitchen for a few hours, just place the covered bowl in the refrigerator; the dough will continue to rise, but more slowly. An unlit gas oven faintly heated by the pilot light provides a friendly environment for the rising process, as does a draft-free spot near a hot range or radiator, but don't set your dough on top of them. The time required is variable, depending on the type of dough and the climate; it can be anywhere from 45 minutes to 2 hours for the first rising, 45 minutes or longer for the second rising (if there is to be one), and 1 hour or less for the final rising after shaping.

During the rising or fermentation period, the yeast cells feed on the sugar, or sucrose, from the flour starch and sugar, and belch bubbles of carbon dioxide. The gas trapped within the network of gluten that was formed during the kneading lightens the dough and makes it expand. Let the fermentation continue until the dough has about doubled in bulk. Very sweet doughs rise more slowly than lean ones. To determine when the dough has risen enough, press the tips of two fingers lightly into the top of the dough about half an inch deep. If the indentations disappear, the dough needs more rising time. But if the dents remain, the dough has risen enough and is ready for the next step—the punching down process.

Punching down the dough helps to redistribute the yeast and to subdivide and increase the number of gas cells, which will give a uniform texture to the finished loaf. Turn the dough out onto a lightly floured surface and hit it with your fist right in the center. The trapped gas will escape and hiss its way out and the dough will deflate. Knead the dough gently for a minute or two and then slap it vigorously on the counter top a few times. All this manhandling reinforces the strength of the gluten frame. Allow the dough to rest about 10 minutes before shaping the loaves.

Some recipes call for a second rising, which results in a finer-textured bread and heightened flavor, but most require only one rising in the bowl and the final rising after the dough has been shaped and placed in the loaf pan or on the baking sheet. The final rising is complete when the dough has approximately doubled in bulk. Don't let the second rising go too far. Dough that is overfermented can turn unpleas-

antly sour when baked and the loaves can burst and fall because the gluten structure has overstretched.

Bread Pans

Bread pans come in assorted sizes; the most commonly used are the large standard size (9¾ by 5¾ by 3 inches) and the medium size (8½ by 4½ by 2¾ inches). A small family might find 3 medium-size loaves more convenient than two large ones.

Bread pans designed for the long loaves of French and Italian breads are easily available, but you can improvise by folding a strip of heavy-duty aluminum foil into a long open tube shape to hold the dough while baking.

Cookie sheets can be used for free-form breads—round, oval, square, or long loaves. Let them rise on the greased sheet you will use for baking.

Muffin tins are useful for rolls, and there is also a large assortment of special pans for special breads, such as brioche.

If glass baking dishes are used, the oven temperature should be lowered 25 degrees, since glass retains heat longer than metal.

Shaping the Loaves

Roll the dough between your hands into one smooth ball and break it apart with your fingers into equal portions according to the number of loaves you plan to make. Have well-greased bread tins ready and shape the loaves one at a time. Stretch each portion of dough into an oblong approximately the same length as the bread pan. Pat the dough into a smooth shape and ease it into the greased pan, with the ends of the dough touching the sides of the pan. The pans should be from one-half to two-thirds full,

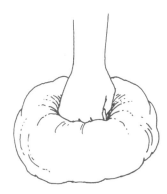

When the dough has doubled in volume, turn it out onto a board again and give it a punch to allow the gases to escape. Knead it again briefly and slap it down on the board a few times.

keeping in mind that the dough will rise again before being baked and then again in the oven. Pat the dough with your hands to smooth and even it, if necessary. Cover and place again in a warm, draft-free spot. As the shaped dough stands, the yeast is producing more carbon dioxide, which again distends the gluten walls and brings the bread close to its final shape and size.

Another way to shape dough is to roll it into an oblong about 9 by 7 inches. Starting at the narrow end, fold the oblong into thirds, overlapping them in the center. Use both hands to press the dough down firmly to shape the loaf evenly. Pinch the dough together along the center fold and at the ends. Place the loaf, sealed side down, in a greased pan.

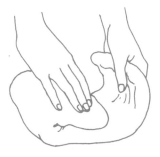

You may prefer to roll the dough into an oblong and then fold it in three, as you would fold a letter.

Allow the dough to rest for 10 minutes, then shape it and put it into a greased loaf pan. It should touch the sides of the pan but not reach any higher than two-thirds of the depth of the pan.

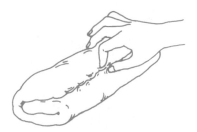

If you have folded the dough, pinch it together at the ends and at the seam before easing it into a greased loaf pan, seam side down.

Glazes

To give breads a brown crust, brush them with a glaze before baking. The shiny brown look is the result of the proteins in the glazing material coagulating and darkening when exposed to the heat of the oven. The yolk of an egg beaten lightly with 2 or 3 tablespoons of milk or cream gives color and finish to breads. Egg white lightly beaten with 3 tablespoons of water gives somewhat the same result. Brush it on before baking and twice while baking. For a crisp crust, spray the dough lightly with cold water before baking, and frequently during the baking period.

Before baking French bread, make several shallow diagonal slashes with a sharp knife or razor blade.

Baking

Always bake bread in a preheated oven. The heat accelerates the production of carbon dioxide by the yeast and the gas within the cells expands, increasing the volume of the loaf by about one-third. If your oven has a glass window, you can observe this phenomenon, called "oven spring," after about 5 minutes of baking. A lovely sight it is, matched by the equally lovely aroma that fills the air. The aroma is caused by the evaporation of the alcohol produced during fermentation. The yeast cells will continue their fermentation process until the interior of the dough reaches 140 degrees, at which point they are killed.

Professional bakers use steam in their ovens to keep breads moist during baking. You can duplicate this in your kitchen with a brick, an oblong baking pan, and boiling water. Heat the brick on top of the stove. When the oven is heated to the proper temperature for baking, pour boiling water into the baking pan and place the hot brick in the center of the pan. Place the pan on the bottom floor of the oven. Steam will be generated that will last throughout the baking period.

Lean bread doughs bake best at 425 degrees, and rich yeast doughs at 375 degrees. When you think the bread is done, test by taking out a loaf (protect your hands with potholders or ovenproof mitts) and turn the loaf over. The bottom should be brown and sound hollow when tapped. If it needs more baking, reduce the oven heat by 50 degrees and replace the bread in the oven without the tin to get a crisper bottom crust. Check every five minutes.

When done, remove bread or rolls from their baking pans immediately and cool on racks to allow the steam to evaporate. If you want a soft crust, cover with a light towel while cooling.

Storing

Bread freezes extremely well. Since homemade breads stale and mold rapidly because they lack the chemical preservatives that are used by most commercial bakeries, the best way to have fresh bread available is to freeze it. Wrap it tightly in a plastic wrap or, better still, heavy-duty aluminum foil. To defrost, heat in the foil in a 350-degree oven for 20 to 25 minutes, or let it defrost at room temperature and reheat it briefly before serving. Properly wrapped, bread can remain frozen from three to four months without any loss in quality or flavor. You can also wrap it in foil and refrigerate it for a brief period.

Basic White Bread

Finely textured, deliciously flavored, and just what good white bread should be. It's as easy to bake four loaves as two; freeze the extra.

2 cups of warm water
2 packages dry yeast
8 tablespoons butter, melted
3 tablespoons sugar
½ cup nonfat dry milk
2 teaspoons salt
2 eggs
7 to 7½ cups all-purpose, unbleached flour

In a large bowl, mix the warm water and yeast and let stand until dissolved, about 5 minutes. Add the melted butter, sugar, dry milk, salt, and eggs and mix well. Add 4 cups of flour and beat until well blended. Mix in another 2½ cups of flour to make a firm dough. Let the dough rest for about 5 minutes.

Sprinkle some of the remaining flour on a board or counter top and turn the dough out onto the floured work surface. Knead for about 10 minutes, kneading in additional flour, until the dough is no longer sticky and becomes smooth and plump. You will probably use a total of 7 cups flour or a bit more.

Grease a large bowl and turn the dough in the bowl to grease all surfaces. Cover the bowl and let rise in a warm spot until doubled in bulk, 1 to 1½ hours. When doubled, turn out onto floured board and punch down briskly several times. Return to the greased bowl, cover, and let rise to double again, about 45 minutes.

Again punch down the dough and break into four even pieces. Shape into loaves and place in four greased 8-inch loaf pans. Cover and let rise until double in bulk and the tops of loaves are rounded, about 30 minutes.

Preheat the oven to 375 degrees. Bake 40 to 50 minutes, or until the tops are brown and the loaves sound hollow when tapped on the bottom. Remove from the pans and cool on a wire rack.

Yield: 4 loaves.

Batter Bread

A coarse-textured but delicious light loaf that requires no kneading.

1 package dry yeast
1¼ cups warm water
2 tablespoons sugar
⅓ cup nonfat dry milk
1 teaspoon salt
4 tablespoons butter, melted
2 eggs, lightly beaten
4 cups all-purpose flour (see note)

In a large mixing bowl, dissolve the yeast in warm water and sugar. Let stand for 5 minutes. Add the dry milk, salt, butter, and eggs. Stir to mix well. Add half the flour and beat well with a wooden spoon. Add the remaining flour and beat well to make a soft dough. Cover the bowl and let rise in a warm spot until doubled in bulk, 1 to 1½ hours.

Uncover and stir the dough for a minute. Spoon into two well-greased 1½-quart loaf pans. Use your fingers to pat dough evenly into the pans. (Oil your fingers if the dough is sticky.) Cover lightly and let rise until doubled in bulk, 45 to 60 minutes. Preheat the oven to 400 degrees.

Bake the loaves for 40 to 45 minutes, or until lightly browned. Turn out of pans and cool on a wire rack.

Yield: 2 loaves.

Note: You can use 2 cups whole wheat flour and 2 cups all-purpose flour. Add ½ cup more water.

French Bread

A fine, homemade American version of French bread.

1 package dry yeast
2 cups warm water
1½ teaspoons sugar
1½ teaspoons salt
6 cups all-purpose unbleached
  flour (see note)
White cornmeal
1 egg white beaten with 2
  tablespoons water

Stir the yeast into the warm water in a large bowl and let it dissolve, about 5 minutes. Stir in the sugar and salt. Add 3 cups of the flour and beat thoroughly. Add 2 more cups of the flour and stir well.

Scrape the dough out onto a lightly floured surface and knead for about 10 minutes, until the dough is smooth and elastic. Knead in additional flour if needed, since the dough may be quite sticky.

Place the dough in an oiled bowl, turning to coat all surfaces. Cover and let rise in a warm spot until doubled in bulk, 1 to 1½ hours. Punch down and knead in the bowl several times to collapse the air bubbles.

Break the dough into two equal pieces. With the palms of your hands, roll each piece back and forth into two cylindrical loaves about 16 inches long. Place the loaves on a lightly greased cookie sheet that has been sprinkled with cornmeal, or use the specially shaped French bread pans, also greased and lightly sprinkled with cornmeal. Make 5 or 6 shallow diagonal slashes in the top of each loaf with a sharp knife or a razor blade. Cover and let rise until doubled in bulk, about 1 hour.

Preheat the oven to 400 degrees. Bake for 15 minutes and lower the heat to 375 degrees. Brush the tops of the loaves with the egg white and return to the oven. Bake an additional 20 to 30 minutes, or until golden. Brush with glaze several times.

Remove from the oven and cool on a rack.

Yield: 2 long loaves.

Note: If bread flour is available, use it in this recipe, using only 4 cups. It will make two 1-pound loaves of delicious bread. Bread flour makes rounder loaves with firmer crusts than all-purpose flour and does not need a bread pan or mold.

You can also use 1 cup of cake flour and 4½ to 5 cups all-purpose flour, which makes a tender soft loaf, very much like the genuine French bread.

To improvise a French bread pan, tear off a 36-inch length of heavy-duty aluminum foil, 18 inches wide. Fold the long side into thirds, then in half. This will give you an oblong 6 inches wide and 18 inches long. Bend the long sides up into a U-shape. Grease it well and arrange the cylindrical loaf in it. Pinch the end of the foil slightly. It will hold the loaf securely as it bakes and may be wiped off and reused.

Whole Wheat Honey Batter Bread

1½ cups whole wheat flour
1½ cups all-purpose flour
1 teaspoon salt
1 envelope dry yeast
1¼ cups warm water
2 tablespoons honey
2 tablespoons butter at room
  temperature

Combine the two flours and salt and blend well. In a large bowl, dissolve the yeast in the water and let it stand for 5 minutes. Add the honey, butter, and half the flour mixture and beat for 2 minutes in an electric beater at medium speed. Add the remaining flour and beat a minute longer, or until smooth. Cover and let rise in a warm, draft-free place until doubled, about 45 minutes.

Stir the batter down using a wooden spoon and beat for a half a minute. Transfer to a well-greased 9 by 5-inch loaf pan. Cover and let rise for about 45 minutes, or until the batter comes to within an inch of the top of the pan.

Preheat the oven to 375 degrees. Bake until the bread is well browned, 40 to 50 minutes. Brush the top with butter while still hot if you like a soft crust. Remove from the pan and let cool on a rack.

Yield: 1 loaf.

Toasted Oat Bread

An all-time favorite, delicious plain or toasted with butter and jam.

2 cups old-fashioned oats
5 to 5½ cups all-purpose flour
¼ cup packed light brown sugar
3 packages dry yeast
2 teaspoons salt
1¾ cup milk
4 tablespoons butter
¼ cup honey
2 eggs, lightly beaten
1 cup dark or light raisins
1½ cups chopped walnuts
1 egg yolk mixed with 1
  tablespoon water or milk

Toast the oats in a heavy skillet until lightly colored and fragrant, stirring constantly, for 7 to 8 minutes. Pour into a large mixing bowl and add 2 cups flour, brown sugar, yeast, and salt. Mix well.

Heat the milk, butter, and honey in a small saucepan until warm, 120 to 130 degrees. Add to the dry ingredients along with the eggs, raisins, and nuts. Stir to mix well.

With a heavy-duty electric mixer or a wooden spoon, gradually add 3 to 3¼ cups flour and beat until the batter is stiff. Turn out onto a lightly floured surface and knead in the remaining flour. Knead until the dough is soft, smooth, and just slightly tacky to the touch.

Place in a greased bowl and turn in the bowl to grease all sides. Cover and let rise in a warm place until doubled in bulk, 1 to 1½ hours.

Punch down and divide into two equal pieces. Form into loaves or rounds and place each in a well-greased 1½-quart round or loaf pan. With a razor blade, cut a shallow cross in the top of the round loaf, or 3 diagonal slashes in the long loaf. Cover and allow to rise for 1 hour, or until doubled in bulk.

Preheat the oven to 350 degrees. Bake for 40 minutes. After 20 minutes, paint the tops of the loaves with the egg yolk.

Remove from the pans and cool on a rack.

Yield: 2 2-pound loaves.

Whole Wheat Bread

2½ cups warm water

2 envelopes dry yeast

2 tablespoons honey

½ cup dry milk

½ cup melted butter

2 eggs, lightly beaten

1 teaspoon salt

3½ to 4 cups whole wheat flour

3½ to 4 cups cake flour (not self-rising)

1 egg beaten with 2 tablespoons milk or water

Put the water in a large mixing bowl. Sprinkle the yeast over the water, and stir to dissolve. Let stand for 10 minutes.

Add the honey, dry milk, butter, eggs, and salt and mix well.

Stir in the flours alternately, a cup at a time, and beat after each addition. Add enough flour to make a soft, workable dough. Turn out onto a lightly floured board. Knead vigorously, adding up to 1 cup additional flour if necessary. (Use a little of each flour.) Knead for 10 minutes, or until the dough becomes satiny and elastic.

Place the dough in a large greased bowl and turn to grease all surfaces. Cover and let rise in a warm place until doubled in bulk, 1 to 1½ hours. Punch down, let it rest for 2 or 3 minutes, and knead it for a few more minutes. Place the dough back in the bowl, cover, and let rise again until doubled, approximately 30 minutes.

When the dough has doubled in bulk, turn it out onto the floured surface again and punch it down. Let it rest for a couple of minutes. Form the dough into a large ball and divide it in two. Roll or pat each piece into a rectangle the length of the bread pan. Roll up tightly lengthwise, pinching the sides and bottom. Place seam side down in greased 9 by 5-inch bread pans. Be certain that the dough touches the ends of the pan. Cover and let rise in a warm place until the dough has doubled, 45 minutes to 1 hour.

Preheat the oven to 400 degrees. Bake for 15 minutes and lower the heat to 325 degrees. Brush the tops of the loaves with egg glaze and bake for 30 to 40 minutes longer, or until the loaves sound hollow when tapped on the bottom. Remove from the pans and cool on a wire rack.

Yield: 2 loaves.

Russian Pumpernickel

A dense, hearty bread with rich dark color and robust flavor, delicious in a sandwich, with cheeses, or simply buttered.

3 packages dry yeast
1 cup lukewarm water
2 cups rye or whole wheat flour
6 to 7 cups white flour
¼ cup molasses
¼ cup sugar
2 tablespoons salt
3 tablespoons oil
2 teaspoons instant coffee
   dissolved in 2 cups warm water
¼ cup vinegar
¼ cup cocoa
2 tablespoons caraway seeds
2 teaspoons grated onion
1 egg white mixed with 3
   tablespoons water

Stir the yeast into the cup of water and let stand for 5 minutes to dissolve.

In a large mixing bowl, combine the 2 cups of rye flour, 2 cups of white flour, molasses, sugar, salt, oil, coffee-flavored water, vinegar, cocoa, caraway seeds, grated onion, and yeast mixture. Beat with an electric beater for 3 minutes, scraping the sides of the bowl frequently with a rubber spatula.

Add 2 cups more of the white flour and work it into the mixture with a wooden spoon, mixing well. Gradually add another 2 cups—more, if needed—to make a dough that you can handle, working it in with your hands. Turn out on a lightly floured surface and knead until smooth and elastic, about 10 minutes. Add remaining flour if necessary.

Place the dough in a greased bowl, turning it to coat all surfaces. Cover with a damp towel and let rise in a warm place until almost doubled in bulk, about 1½ hours. Punch down and knead lightly to release air bubbles.

Divide the dough into three parts and shape into oblong loaves. Place in well-greased loaf pans and make 3 shallow diagonal slashes on the top of each loaf with a sharp knife. Cover with a towel and let rise again in a warm place until doubled in bulk and the tops of the loaves are rounded.

Preheat the oven to 375 degrees. Bake for 45 minutes, or until bread is nicely browned and the bottom sounds hollow when tapped. Brush the tops with the egg white once or twice during the baking. When done, remove from the pans and cool on racks.

Yield: 3 loaves.

Cinnamon Buns

Featherlight buns for breakfast or snacks. The sponge method gives an airy and light texture.

1 package dry yeast
2 tablespoons warm water
Pinch sugar
1 cup warm milk
½ cup (1 stick) butter, melted
½ cup sugar
1 teaspoon salt
3 eggs, well beaten
4 to 4½ cups all-purpose flour

Filling:
½ cup (1 stick) butter, cut into
  small bits
1 cup sugar
1 teaspoon ground cinnamon
½ cup coarsely chopped walnuts
⅓ cup raisins, plumped in hot
  water to cover for 5 minutes
  and drained

Icing:
1 cup confectioners' sugar
1 tablespoon melted butter
1 teaspoon vanilla extract
1 to 1½ tablespoons milk or cream

Dissolve the yeast in warm water and sugar. Set aside until bubbly, 5 to 10 minutes.

In a large bowl, combine the milk, melted butter, sugar, salt, eggs, and yeast mixture and mix well. Add about 2½ cups flour and beat until smooth. Cover the bowl and let rise in a warm place for about 1½ hours.

Stir down and add enough additional flour to make a soft dough. Turn out on a lightly floured board and knead until smooth and elastic, about 10 minutes.

Wash out the bowl and butter it well. Add the dough and turn it to coat all surfaces. Cover and let rise in a warm place until doubled in bulk, about 1 to 1½ hours.

Put the dough on a lightly floured board and punch down. Roll or pat it into a 14 by 18-inch rectangle. For the filling, spread the dough evenly with bits of butter. Sprinkle with sugar mixed with cinnamon, nuts, and well-dried raisins. Starting with the long side, roll up tightly like a jelly roll. Pinch the bottom seam closed. Cut into 18 equal-size pieces and arrange, touching, in two greased 9 by 9-inch baking dishes. Cover and let rise until doubled in bulk, about 1 hour.

Preheat the oven to 375 degrees.

Bake for 25 to 30 minutes, or until golden and puffed. Cool for 5 to 7 minutes in the pan, then turn out on a rack.

Combine the confectioners' sugar, butter, and vanilla. Add enough cream or milk so that the icing is soft. Drizzle it over the buns while they are still warm.

Yield: 18 buns.

Variation: For featherlight rolls, follow the above directions through punching down the dough. Shape the dough into balls, twists, or any shape desired. Arrange in well-buttered muffin tins. Allow to rise until doubled in bulk. Bake at 425 degrees for 12 to 15 minutes.

Brioche

A simplified version of the classic French breakfast bread.

1 package dry yeast
1½ tablespoons sugar
½ teaspoon salt
3 cups all-purpose flour
¼ cup warm water
3 eggs
¾ cup (1½ sticks) butter
1 egg yolk mixed with 1
   tablespoon water

In a large bowl, mix the yeast, sugar, salt, and ½ cup of flour. Add the water and beat on medium speed. Beat in 1 egg and 1 cup of flour. Add another egg, and beat in the butter, 1 tablespoon at a time, then another egg and a cup of flour. Beat for about 1 minute, or until the dough breaks into shreds on the beaters. Scrape out onto a floured surface and knead in the remaining ½ cup of flour until smooth and elastic. Roll into a ball and place in a greased bowl. Turn to coat the dough. Cover and allow to rise in a warm spot until doubled in volume, about 1½ hours. Turn out onto floured surface, punch down, and knead for 2 or 3 minutes. Return to the greased bowl, turn to coat the dough, cover the bowl with plastic wrap, and refrigerate overnight.

Turn the dough out onto a floured surface and knead for 2 or 3 minutes. Grease 12 brioche molds or muffin tins and set on a cookie sheet. Pull off and shape 12 balls of a size that will fill two-thirds of each mold, and another 12 smaller pieces shaped like cones with rounded tops and pointed ends. With a floured knife, cut a slash in the top of each large ball and fit one of the small pieces, pointed end down, into each opening. Push the edges together to hold the cap firmly.

Cover and let rise in a warm spot for 1 hour, or until doubled in bulk.

Preheat the oven to 350 degrees. Bake for 10 minutes and brush carefully with egg yolk glaze. Continue baking for another 10 to 12 minutes, brushing with glaze once or twice during that time. Do not let the glaze drip into the brioche molds because it bakes very fast and could form a seal around the brioches, keeping the dough from rising. The tops should be brown and shiny when done. Remove from the tins and cool on a rack.

Yield: 1 dozen brioches.

Nutted Coffee Cake

3 to 4 cups all-purpose flour
¼ cup sugar
1 teaspoon salt
1 package dry yeast
½ cup milk
½ cup water
4 tablespoons butter
1 egg, lightly beaten
Nut filling (recipe follows)
Confectioners' sugar icing (recipe follows)

In a large bowl mix 1 cup flour, sugar, salt, and yeast.

Heat the milk, water, and butter in a saucepan to about 120 degrees. Add gradually to the dry ingredients. Beat for 2 minutes at medium speed with an electric mixer. Add the egg and ½ cup flour. Beat at high speed for 2 minutes. Slowly add enough additional flour to make a soft dough. Turn out onto a lightly floured surface and knead until smooth, about 10 minutes.

Place in a greased bowl, cover lightly, and allow to rise in a warm place until doubled in volume. Turn out onto a lightly floured board and punch down. Knead a few times. Roll or press out to a 20 by 15-inch rectangle. Spread with the nut filling and roll up tightly, starting from the long side, like a jelly roll.

Pinch the edges to seal and gently roll back and forth to lengthen the roll to about 25 inches. Coil the roll into a firm round, pinching the edges to seal. Arrange on a greased baking sheet, cover lightly, and let rise in a warm place until doubled in bulk.

Preheat the oven to 325 degrees. Bake for 40 to 45 minutes. Dribble the top with Confectioners' Sugar Icing while still warm.

Yield: 10 to 12 servings.

Nut Filling

4 tablespoons butter, softened
¼ cup firmly packed brown sugar
1 egg, lightly beaten
2 tablespoons milk
1 teaspoon orange extract
2 cups finely chopped pecans or walnuts

Mix together the butter, brown sugar, and egg in a small bowl. Stir in the milk, orange extract, and nuts. Mix well.

Confectioners' Sugar Icing

1 teaspoon vanilla extract
1½ tablespoons water or orange juice
1¼ to 1½ cups confectioners' sugar

Combine the vanilla extract and water or orange juice in a small bowl. Slowly beat in the sugar until very thick. Beat until creamy and light.

Puccio's Pizza

This is a thick, Sicilian-style pizza made with a light batter bread dough. Prepare the sauce while the dough is rising or chilling so that it can cool to room temperature; hot sauce will make pizza dough soggy.

1 package dry yeast
1½ cups warm water
1 tablespoon sugar
1 tablespoon salt
⅓ cup olive oil
3½ cups all-purpose unbleached flour
Topping (recipe follows)

In a large bowl, dissolve the yeast in warm water. Add the sugar, salt, and olive oil and stir to mix well. Let stand for 5 minutes. Using a wooden spoon or a heavy-duty electric mixer, stir in the flour and mix until it forms a doughy batter that pulls away from the sides of the bowl. Push down into the bowl, cover, and let rise in a warm place until it doubles in bulk, 1 to 1½ hours. Push down with a spoon and chill for 30 to 60 minutes. This is a sticky dough, but chilling it will make it easier to handle.

When ready to complete, press the chilled pizza dough into an oiled lasagna pan, about 9 by 14 inches. You may find it easier to handle the dough if you oil your hands lightly. Press the dough to the shape of the pan, making a small raised ridge around the outside edge to hold the sauce. Be sure the dough touches the pan on all sides. Preheat the oven to 400 degrees.

Pizza Topping

1 1-pound, 12-ounce can Italian plum tomatoes
¼ cup olive oil
1 medium onion, coarsely chopped
1 clove garlic, minced (optional)
Pinch of sugar
½ teaspoon salt
Freshly ground pepper
½ pound mozzarella cheese, cut into small cubes or shredded
3 tablespoons grated Parmesan cheese
2 tablespoons dry bread crumbs
½ teaspoon dried oregano
½ teaspoon dried basil

Drain the tomatoes (saving the juice for another use) and chop them coarsely. Heat the oil in a saucepan and cook the onion until soft and lightly colored. Add the garlic, drained tomatoes, sugar, salt, and pepper. Cook briskly for 7 to 10 minutes, stirring constantly until thick. Set aside to cool.

Spoon the sauce evenly over the pizza dough and sprinkle the top with the cheeses, bread crumbs, oregano, and basil. Bake in the 400-degree oven for 10 minutes, reduce the heat to 350 degrees, and bake for 20 to 25 minutes longer, or until the outer crust is golden brown and crisp. Remove pizza from the oven and allow to stand for 5 minutes before cutting.

Yield: 6 to 8 servings.

Note: You may add anchovies, pepperoni, sautéed mushrooms, or cooked sausage to the topping.

Quick Breads

Quick breads are breads or muffins that do not require kneading. They are put together quickly and depend for their leavening on baking powder or baking soda or a combination of both. The fruit and nut breads more nearly resemble cake than bread. They have a soft crumb and are sweet. They will slice better if given a few hours to firm up after baking.

Muffins

The simplest of all hot breads to prepare.

2 cups all-purpose flour
2½ tablespoons sugar
½ teaspoon salt
1 tablespoon baking powder
1 egg, slightly beaten
1 cup milk
¼ cup melted butter or vegetable oil

Preheat the oven to 400 degrees. Butter 12 3-inch muffin tins or 16 2½-inch muffin tins.

Mix together the flour, sugar, salt, and baking powder. In a small bowl, combine the lightly beaten egg, milk, and melted butter. Stir into the flour mixture just enough to moisten all the flour. If you overbeat the batter, the muffins will have pointed heads and an uneven grain. Spoon the batter into the greased tins, filling them two-thirds full. Bake for 25 minutes, or until nicely browned. Let stand a minute or two before removing from the pan. Serve while warm.

Yield: 12 to 16 muffins.

Whole Wheat Muffins. Use 1 cup white flour and ¾ cup whole wheat flour. Add ¼ cup chopped dates or raisins to the dry ingredients. Sprinkle the tops with chopped nuts, if desired.

Cheese Muffins. Omit the sugar and add ½ to 1 cup shredded sharp Cheddar or Swiss cheese and a few drops of Tabasco to the batter.

Buttermilk Biscuits

Hot biscuits are a lovely treat. Don't save them for weekend breakfasts only.

2 cups all-purpose flour
1 teaspoon salt
2 teaspoons baking power
½ teaspoon baking soda
4 tablespoons butter
1 egg, lightly beaten
¾ cup buttermilk
Melted butter or milk (optional)

Place the flour, salt, baking powder, and baking soda in a mixing bowl. Add the butter and combine with a pastry blender or your fingertips until the mixture is like coarse meal.

Combine the egg and buttermilk. Pour all but 1 or 2 tablespoons into the flour mixture. Combine quickly with a fork until the mixture leaves the side of the bowl. Add the remaining egg-milk mixture if it seems too dry.

Turn out on a lightly floured surface and press lightly. Pat or roll out to a ½-inch thickness. Cut into rounds or squares about 2 to 3 inches across. Gather and press together the remaining bits and continue until all the dough is used.

Preheat the oven to 425 degrees.

Arrange the biscuits on a greased baking sheet 1 inch apart (for crusty biscuits) or touching (for softer biscuits). Brush the tops with melted butter or milk if a browner top is desired. Bake for 12 minutes, or until puffed and lightly browned. Serve immediately.

Yield: 14 to 16 biscuits.

Variations:

Herb Biscuit Topping (for pot pies). Add ¼ cup finely chopped parsley and chives, mixed, to the dry ingredients. Pat into a round to cover a meat or poultry pie. Be certain to press the dough against the rim of the casserole so that it will not pull away from the sides.

Shortcake. Add 2 tablespoons sugar to the dry ingredients. Pat to a 1-inch thickness and cut into 3-inch rounds or one large round. Bake for 10 to 20 minutes, depending on size. Split the biscuits, and fill while still warm with fresh strawberries, raspberries, or blueberries. Top with sweetened whipped cream.

Whole Wheat Biscuits. Substitute whole wheat flour for white. Brush the tops with melted butter before baking.

Popovers

Crusty outside, soft and warm within, a perfect receptacle for jam or scrambled eggs.

2 eggs
1 cup milk
1 cup all-purpose flour
¼ teaspoon salt
4 tablespoons butter, melted

Preheat the oven to 425 degrees.

Grease custard cups or muffin tins and set aside.

Combine the eggs and milk in a blender. Add flour and salt and blend only until smooth. Stir in the butter. If you are using custard cups, arrange them on a baking sheet. Fill each cup or muffin tin half full.

Bake the popovers for 25 to 30 minutes, or until puffed and brown. Pierce them with a knife to dry them out and serve immediately.

Yield: 10 to 14 popovers.

Yorkshire Pudding. Remove roast ribs of beef from the roasting pan and cover lightly to keep warm. Pour off the fat from the pan and use 4 tablespoons in place of butter in recipe above. Stir the fat into the batter and pour into a 9-inch pie plate. Bake in a preheated 425-degree oven for 30 to 40 minutes.

Mary Mac's Corn Bread

Rich and moist. Serve at breakfast with butter and syrup and at dinner with fried chicken.

¾ cup cornmeal
1½ cups all-purpose flour
4 teaspoons baking powder
¾ teaspoon salt
⅓ cup sugar
¼ teaspoon allspice
4 tablespoons butter
2 eggs, lightly beaten
1 cup light cream or half-and-half
1 tablespoon brown sugar

Preheat the oven to 400 degrees.

Combine the cornmeal, flour, baking powder, salt, sugar, and allspice in a bowl. Melt the butter in an 8 by 8-inch baking dish in the oven. Mix together the eggs, cream and brown sugar. Add to the dry ingredients and combine with just a few strokes. Do not overmix; the batter will be lumpy and dry in spots.

Spoon into the hot baking dish and bake for 25 to 30 minutes. Cut into squares and serve warm.

Yield: 16 2-inch squares.

Banana Bread

½ cup (1 stick) butter at room
   temperature
¾ cup sugar
2 eggs
1 teaspoon vanilla extract
¼ cup buttermilk
3 medium bananas, puréed or
   mashed, about 1 cup
½ teaspoon salt
1 teaspoon baking soda
¾ cup chopped walnuts or pecans
1⅔ cups all-purpose flour

Preheat the oven to 350 degrees.

Cream the butter and sugar in a large bowl until very fluffy and light in color. Add the eggs and vanilla and beat until thick.

Put the buttermilk in a 2-cup measuring cup. Add enough mashed bananas to make 1¼ cups. Scrape into the egg and butter mixture. Add salt, soda, and walnuts. Stir to mix well. The batter will look curdled at this point because of the interaction of the soda and buttermilk. Sprinkle flour over the batter and fold lightly, just until flour is absorbed. Do not overmix.

Pour into a greased 8½-inch springform pan, or a 9 by 5-inch loaf pan. Bake for 45 to 60 minutes, or until a cake tester or skewer inserted in the center comes out dry. Remove from the pan and cool on a rack.

Yield: 1 loaf.

Orange Bread

1½ cups all-purpose flour
1 cup whole wheat flour
1 cup sugar
3½ teaspoons baking powder
1 teaspoon salt
1 egg
4 teaspoons grated orange rind
¾ cup fresh orange juice
¾ cup milk
4 tablespoons butter, melted
1 teaspoon orange extract

Preheat the oven to 350 degrees.

Combine the flours, sugar, baking powder, and salt in a large bowl. Beat the egg with the remaining ingredients and add to the dry ingredients. Stir just until moistened.

Spoon the batter into a greased 9 by 5-inch loaf pan and bake for 1 to 1¼ hours. Cool in the pan for 7 to 10 minutes on a rack; turn out of pan and cool completely.

Yield: 1 loaf.

Applesauce Raisin Bread

1 egg, lightly beaten
1 cup applesauce
4 tablespoons butter, melted
½ cup sugar
2½ cups all-purpose flour
2 teaspoons baking powder
½ teaspoon baking soda
½ teaspoon salt
¾ teaspoon cinnamon
¼ teaspoon freshly grated nutmeg
1 cup seedless raisins
¾ cup coarsely chopped pecans
  or walnuts

Preheat the oven to 350 degrees. Butter a 9 by 5-inch loaf pan.

In a large bowl, mix together the egg, applesauce, and melted butter, blending well. Stir in the sugar and mix thoroughly. In another bowl, blend together the flour, baking powder, baking soda, salt, cinnamon, and nutmeg, reserving a couple of tablespoons of the flour for dredging the raisins. Add the flour mixture gradually to the egg and sugar mixture, stirring only enough to blend well. Dredge the raisins lightly in the reserved flour. Add them to the batter with the nuts. Turn the batter into the pan and bake for 1 hour, or until a cake tester comes out dry. Cool on a rack.

Yield: 1 loaf.

Pies and Pastries

There are no great secrets to making perfect pastry, even though it is viewed with a degree of alarm by many cooks who are not the least bit put off by other cooking procedures. It is a skill worth acquiring; a flaky, delicious shell will enhance any filling from a simple vegetable quiche to an extravagant confection of custard and fruits and, on the more practical side, it can stretch a modest amount of meat, fish, vegetables, or fruit into a noteworthy course.

There are many variations of pastry. In its simplest form, it consists of flour, shortening, and water, which gives us the American pie crust. The French version, *pâte brisée,* is made with butter and may or may not contain sugar, depending on how it is to be used. The word *brisé* in French means "broken to pieces"; *pâte* is "dough"; thus a flaky dough. The basic *pâte brisée* is an all-purpose pastry that can be used for quiches, dessert pies, and tarts. The difference between a pie and a tart is that a pie may have one or two crusts and be filled with anything from fruits or custard to meats or poultry, whereas a tart is always sweet and its

filling is exposed. Another type of pastry is the multilayered, flaky puff pastry, used for meat pies and dessert confections. There is also the *pâte à choux,* or cream puff pastry, a simple preparation that results in a featherlight crust surrounding a cavity that can be filled with ice cream, whipped cream, or custard.

Success in pastry making depends on combining the basic ingredients in the right quantities and using the proper techniques. A tender *pâte brisée* demands a delicate balance of fat and flour, and not too much liquid. Use standard measuring cups and spoons, and measure accurately. Make the dough as quickly and with as little handling as possible. The aim is to develop just enough gluten in the flour to obtain a manageable dough that will remain flaky after baking. If the dough has been worked too much, the excess of gluten will make the pastry tough and elastic; if too little, the dough will tear and crumble and be difficult to roll out.

Basic Ingredients Used in Pastry Making

Flour

Use all-purpose flour, bleached or unbleached. (We prefer the latter.) Unless the recipe directs you to sift flour, measure it by spooning the flour lightly into a dry measuring cup placed on a square of wax paper. Don't shake the cup or the flour will pack down. When the cup is completely full, level the flour with a knife or spatula and transfer the flour to a mixing bowl. Repeat with as much flour as needed. When all the flour is in the bowl, add the salt and distribute it well with a fork or your fingers.

To measure flour, use a "dry" measuring cup, which measures right to the upper rim. Spoon the flour into the cup without packing it, and use a knife or spatula to level off the excess.

Fat

Fat contributes tenderness, or shortness, to pastry through its action of waterproofing flour, which limits the development of gluten. It also adds to the flakiness by separating the dough into layers. The colder and harder the fat used, the flakier the crust will be, which is why you are directed to chill or freeze the butter before using. The characteristics of the pastry will depend in part on the particular fat used. Soft fats such as oil or melted butter will give you a tender, crumbly pastry, but not a flaky one. Use the fat of your choice, keeping in mind how each works.

Lard is 100 percent fat. Because of its particular crystalline structure, lard creates a flakier texture in pastry dough than most other fats. It is often used in combination with vegetable shortening.

Vegetable shortening, like lard, is 100 percent fat and creates a flaky crust with good texture but one that is bland and lacking in flavor.

Butter gives fine taste and color to a crust and is first choice of many pastry bakers. Use unsalted butter in baking. It is often used in combination with vegetable shortening.

Margarine produces a crust similar to that of butter but without the butter flavor. Use only the stick margarine and place it in the freezer for 15 or 20 minutes before using.

Oil tends to coat each particle of flour and, as a result, little gluten is developed. It makes a tender crust but with a texture that might be described as mealy.

Salt

Salt has no function except to season the flour and omitting it makes no difference in pastry except for taste.

Liquid Ingredients

The amount of water used in pastry is critical and must be carefully controlled. You need enough to develop the gluten and hold the flour particles together, but too much will create excessive gluten, causing the crust to become tough. Chilled water is desirable because it slows down the formation of gluten strands. Lemon or orange juice, as well as vinegar, sour cream, or soured milk, which are called for in some recipes, help to soften the gluten strands.

Eggs used in a pastry crust are considered part of the liquid ingredients. The coagulation of their proteins yields a firmer crust that can be useful if there is a great deal of moisture in the filling.

Proportion of Ingredients

Since the cook's skill and the absorbing powers of flour vary, there must be flexibility in the exact amounts of ingredients called for. In general, the ratio of flour to shortening—by volume, not by weight—is 3 parts flour to 1 part shortening. If you use more than that amount of shortening, you will have a tender crust, but one that could be greasy and crumbly and unnecessarily high in calories.

Use approximately half as much water as shortening. For example, if you are making a pastry with 8 tablespoons of shortening (½ cup or ¼ pound), you will not use more than 4 tablespoons of liquid. This amount is generally enough to hold the dough together without making it sticky and tough. If the day is humid, there will be more moisture in the flour and you will need less water.

Greater evaporation at higher altitudes may mean that you need a trifle more liquid when baking.

General Rules for Pastry Dough

Handle the dough lightly in order to incorporate as much air as possible and to inhibit the development of gluten. Use your fingertips and not the whole hand to work the ingredients together. The palms of the hands retain more heat than the fingertips and this heat can make the shortening too soft to give you a flaky crust.

Have all the ingredients cold. Chilled water will slow down the formation of gluten strands.

Chill the dough after it is prepared and before rolling it out. It can be chilled anywhere from 30 minutes to 2 days, but remove it from the refrigerator about an hour before shaping it. The chilling tenderizes the dough, makes it easier to handle, and helps to minimize shrinking during baking.

Chill the bottom crust in the baking pan before filling. This will help to keep the baked bottom crust from becoming soggy.

Work the flour and fat together with your fingertips or a pastry blender to obtain particles resembling small peas or coarse meal. Do not use the whole hand, which gives off too much heat.

Watch out for the finishes of your baking pans. Dark, nonshiny metal pans will give you a brown crust, but they can also brown pies too quickly and you may have to shorten the baking time. Glass or ceramic pie plates work well, but both these materials retain heat and should be baked in oven heat about 25 degrees less than the recipe calls for, unless it specifies these materials.

Always start the baking in a preheated oven. This causes the fat in the dough to begin to melt, the gluten to set, and the starch to gelatinize. As the liquid ingredients become heated, steam develops. It is these pockets of steam that separate the leaves of the baking dough, which makes the pastry porous and flaky.

Pie and Tart Pans

You can use a 9- or 10-inch aluminum or glass pie plate 1¼ inches deep, a fluted porcelain pie plate, a quiche or tart pan with a removable bottom, a springform pan, or a flan ring. A flan ring is a bottomless metal ring that is set on a heavy aluminum buttered cookie sheet. It is lovely for open-faced tarts because, after baking, the tart can be slipped off onto the serving plate and the mold lifted off, leaving the attractively shaped tart. Flan rings come in a variety of shapes and sizes of tin, stainless steel, or other metals. Use a baking sheet that is rimless on one side so that the baked tart can be easily pushed from the sheet to the serving dish.

Rolling Out the Pastry

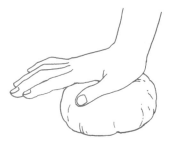

Shape the dough for one crust into a ball and use the heel of your hand to flatten it into a thick disk.

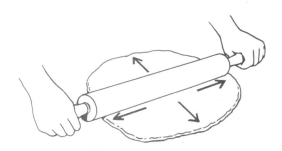

On a cool, floured surface, roll the dough, always from the center out, in all directions. Rotate the dough from time to time so it does not stick to the surface.

If you are making a two-crust pie, divide the dough into two portions, one slightly larger than the other. The larger one is for the bottom. Shape it into a ball and flatten it slightly. Flour the work surface and rolling pin lightly. Work as quickly as you can on a cool surface. A marble slab is perfect, but a Formica counter top will do almost as well, as long as it is in a cool part of the kitchen. The fat melts if the dough gets too warm and becomes difficult to work with. Roll the dough from the center out. Do not push the roller back and forth, which will stretch the dough. Use short, smooth strokes, rolling lightly outward in all directions. Lift and rotate the dough to make sure it is not sticking. Roll out the pastry until it is about ⅛ inch thick and at least 2 inches wider than the inverted pie plate. Lightly dust the surface of the dough with flour and fold it into quarters. Lift it gently into the pie plate with the point of the wedge in the center. Unfold the dough and ease it into the pan loosely, being careful not to stretch the pastry, which will cause it to shrink while baking. Pat it into place so that no air spaces are left between the crust and the pan. Trim the dough hanging over the edge with a sharp knife or scissors, leaving a little extra for a rim around the outside edge.

If the pastry should break while you are lining the mold or pan, you can repair it easily by pressing the broken edges together with your fingertips. Holes in the pastry can be filled in with some of the trimmings from the dough.

Pour in the filling. Roll out the top crust as you did the bottom one, making it about an inch larger than the circumference of the pie plate. Brush the edge of the bottom crust with water; lift the top crust carefully on the rolling pin and place it in position over the filling.

Seal the edge by tucking the top crust over the bottom to make a high, stand-up rim. Flute it by pressing the outer edge between thumb and forefinger at half-inch intervals. You can

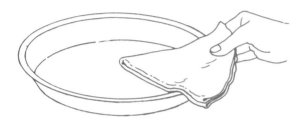

When the dough is ⅛ inch thick and large enough to fit the pie plate with some overhang, flour it lightly and fold it in four. Ease it into the pie plate and unfold it gently.

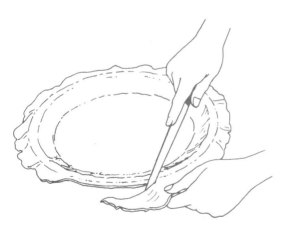

When the dough has been fitted and gently pressed into the plate, use a knife or scissors to remove the excess, leaving just enough overhang to form a rim.

also press the edges together with the tines of a fork or use the imprint of your thumb to make a scalloped pattern.

Prick the top crust with a fork in several places or cut vents so that steam can escape while the pie is baking.

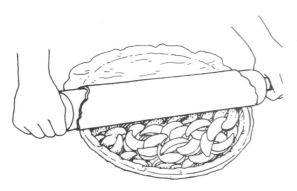

Fill the pie and roll out the top crust. Then roll the upper crust loosely onto the rolling pin and unroll it over the pie.

To flute the rim, pinch the dough between thumb and forefinger on the outside, while pressing it outward with the forefinger of the other hand. Repeat every half inch, all around the circumference.

Cut the top crust as you have cut the bottom one, and fold the overhang of the top crust under the edge of the bottom one. This will seal and give thickness to the rim.

Lattice Crust

Roll pastry into an oblong ¼ inch thick and 10 inches long. Cut nine strips of dough about ½ inch wide. Place four strips over the pie filling. Place the remaining five strips diagonally over the bottom four to fashion a lattice effect. Fold the edge of the bottom crust up over the ends of the strips and press firmly. Flute or crimp the outside edge.

Glazing

Glazing a pie before baking gives it a finished look. Brush savory pies with beaten whole egg or egg yolk thinned with a little water or milk. Sweet pies may be glazed by brushing with milk or egg white and, just before they are done, sprinkling with granulated sugar. You may also mix ½ cup confectioners' sugar with 1 tablespoon water and brush it over the top the moment the pie comes out of the oven, while it is still very hot.

Baking

Filled pie shells are generally baked at 425 degrees for the first 10 minutes and then at 350 degrees until done. The higher baking time at the beginning helps to produce a crisp crust. However, baking times can vary. If the tops and edges begin to brown too quickly, cover with a piece of aluminum foil or adjust the oven heat. Place juicy fruit pies on a baking sheet or a large piece of foil to catch the drippings. For a crisp bottom crust, bake the pies on the lowest rack of the oven. Pie crusts don't actually need a buttered pan, but buttering helps to brown the bottom and is recommended.

Single-Crust Pie Shell

Baking an empty crust that is later filled with a precooked filling or fresh fruit is called baking "blind." Remove the ball of dough from the refrigerator and let it warm up for about an hour. Roll it out and ease it gently into the pie plate or tart form without stretching. Leave a 1-inch overhang along the outside rim. Turn the edge under to make a double thickness. Flute it

or press it with the tines of a fork. If using a pan with a fluted edge, be sure that the dough is pressed well—without stretching—into the fluting. Prick the dough generously all over, sides and bottom, with a fork. If the pastry shell has become a bit soft after the rolling and fitting, refrigerate it or freeze it for about 10 minutes, until it becomes firm. The chilling helps to prevent shrinkage. To keep the bottom of the shell from lifting during baking, line the shell with foil or wax paper, and weight it with 4 or 5 cups of dried beans or raw rice, which can be stored in a jar and used repeatedly. You might find it more convenient to fill two or three "baking bags" with the beans or rice to serve as weights. They can be lifted out easily and used over and over. Another method of keeping the crust from puffing is simply to watch it carefully as it bakes. As soon as you see any puffing of the crust, prick it with a fork to let the air escape; then press down with the back of a spoon or fork.

To bake, preheat the oven to 400 degrees. Cut a long piece of foil and cover the fluted edge, pressing it gently so that it adheres. Bake in the center of the oven for 10 minutes, remove the foil, beans, and foil collar, and continue to bake for 5 to 8 minutes longer, or until the shell is golden. When the shell is almost done, brush the bottom with an egg white mixed with 2 tablespoons of water. This will help to keep the bottom from becoming soggy when the filling is added.

Fill the shell when cooled.

Another way to treat the rim is to press it down all around with the tines of a fork.

When an empty pie shell is baking, the bottom may puff up and rise if not weighted down. Place foil or wax paper inside the shell and fill with beans or rice.

Storing and Freezing

Unbaked pie dough will keep in the refrigerator, tightly wrapped in plastic wrap or foil, for at least four days. Let it soften at room temperature for about an hour before you attempt to roll it out. Unbaked pie dough can be frozen for three months or more.

When you are preparing a pie ahead of time, roll the dough out, line the pan with it, wrap it well, and refrigerate.

Unfilled pie shells may be frozen either baked or unbaked, but unbaked is better. A baked pie shell should not be frozen longer than six weeks. After that, it loses its crispness. An unbaked pie shell, well wrapped, can be frozen for at least three months. It can be baked while still frozen in a 450-degree oven for 15 to 20 minutes, or until lightly browned. You always have to add a few minutes to the usual baking time for frozen dough.

Fruit pies will freeze successfully but pies with cream or custard fillings cannot be frozen, as anyone who has ever attempted to freeze a quiche can tell you. The custard weeps and the crust becomes soggy. On the whole, unbaked pies stand up better after freezing than the baked ones, so if you find you have prepared more than you need, freeze them unbaked. You can unwrap them and bake them directly from the freezer. Allow about 20 minutes longer baking time than required for an unfrozen pie.

Basic Pie Pastry

2 cups all-purpose flour
½ teaspoon salt
1½ sticks butter (¾ cup), chilled,
   or ⅓ cup butter and ½ cup
   vegetable shortening, *or* ⅔ cup
   vegetable shortening
4 to 5 tablespoons ice water,
   approximately

Measure the flour and place in a bowl. Add salt and stir well with a fork. Cut the chilled, firm fat into ¼-inch cubes and rub them into the flour, using the tips of your fingers or a pastry blender, until the particles are the size of small peas and look like coarse meal. Gradually add the cold water, 1 tablespoon at a time, sprinkling it evenly over the flour-fat mixture and tossing it lightly with a fork. Add only enough water so that the dough can be gathered into a ball. As soon as you can gather it into a ball, stop handling it. Wrap it in wax paper, foil, or plastic wrap and refrigerate it for at least 30 minutes before rolling.

Yield: Enough for a 2-crust pie or 12 4-inch tarts.

Tart Pastry I (Pâte Brisée)

One of the most useful of all pastry doughs for pies, tarts, and quiches. It produces a flaky crust.

8 tablespoons (1 stick) unsalted
   butter
1½ cups all-purpose flour
½ teaspoon salt
1 tablespoon sugar (for dessert
   pastry only)
3 to 4 tablespoons ice water

Cut the butter into ¼-inch bits and refrigerate. It must be well chilled. Mix the flour, salt, and sugar (if using) in a large mixing bowl. Add the cold butter and mix with your fingertips until the mixture resembles coarse meal. Add 3 to 4 tablespoons ice water and mix with your fingers just until the mixture adheres and forms a ball. Don't overblend it—pieces of butter should be visible. It is the butter solids that help to make the dough flaky. Wrap in wax paper or plastic and refrigerate for 30 to 40 minutes, or until firm.

Let the dough come to room temperature and roll on a lightly floured surface until it measures about 12 inches in diameter and is ⅛ inch thick. Ease the dough into a buttered 10-inch pie plate or tart tin and press it gently into sides and bottom of the pan. Trim off excess pastry. Refrigerate for 30 minutes before baking.

Yield: Enough for a single-crust tart or quiche.

Tart Pastry II

This is an almost cookielike crust that works well for pies, quiches, and tarts. It has a crumbly rather than a flaky texture. The egg yolks give it extra firmness so that it provides a strong shell that will hold any filling.

1½ cups all-purpose flour

½ teaspoon salt

1 tablespoon sugar (for dessert pastry only)

8 tablespoons sweet butter, chilled, cut into ¼-inch bits

2 egg yolks, slightly beaten

2 to 3 tablespoons ice water, or a combination of lemon juice and water

Combine the flour, salt, and sugar (if using) in a bowl. Add the cold butter and mix with your fingertips until the mixture resembles coarse meal. Add the egg yolks and water and/or lemon juice and mix with your fingers just until the mixture adheres and forms a ball. Proceed as in the directions for Tart Pastry I.

Yield: Enough for a single-crust tart or quiche.

Cream Cheese Pastry

This is also known as kipfel *dough or Viennese pastry. It is rich, flaky, and delicate and does beautifully with either sweet filling or fillings for appetizers. It is often used for tarts, tiny hors d'oeuvre shells, and bite-size turnovers filled with meats, fowl, fish, or fruit preserves.*

2 cups all-purpose flour

½ teaspoon salt

½ pound butter (2 sticks), cut into bits

½ pound cream cheese, cut into bits

Combine the flour and salt in a mixing bowl. Cut in the butter and cream cheese and mix together with your fingertips or a pastry blender to form a soft dough. Chill in the refrigerator if it seems too soft to roll. Roll out to about ⅛-inch thickness on a lightly floured surface and fit into a pie pan or tart tin, patting it into place. Prick dough generously. Chill well before baking. Bake in a preheated 400-degree oven until golden. The baking time will depend on the thickness of the dough, generally 8 to 10 minutes.

Yield: Enough for 2 baking shells or 12 4-inch tarts.

Note: If you are making small tarts, refrigerate half the dough while you are working with the other half because it becomes soft quickly in a warm kitchen.

Variation: Use 1 cup of finely sieved farmer cheese or cottage cheese in place of the cream cheese. The pastry will be less rich, but it is tender and excellent for appetizers with chopped chicken livers, deviled ham, hot cheese, and shellfish.

Sour Cream Pastry

A wonderfully flaky and light pastry for fruit tarts and cookies, resembling the incomparable puff paste in texture, but a breeze to make. Sour cream pastries are best when fresh; if they are not to be served within a day or two, they should be frozen

1½ cups all-purpose flour
½ pound (2 sticks) butter
½ cup sour cream

Place the flour in a bowl and cut in the butter. Mix together with your fingertips or a pastry blender until the mixture looks like coarse crumbs. Stir in the sour cream and blend well. Place on the counter top and knead it only until it forms a soft dough. Form it into a disk and wrap it tightly in wax paper or plastic. Refrigerate for two or three hours or overnight. You may also freeze it if you wish.

Yield: Enough for a single-crust tart.

Crumb Crust

Crumb crusts are not really a pastry; they are a shortcut to pie making and they make perfect shells for fluffy, chiffon-type fillings, ice cream pies, cheese cakes, and the like. They need not be baked, but they must be thoroughly chilled or the filling will cause the crumbs to fall apart. They may be used to line a pie plate or a springform pan and will yield a substantial crust.

1½ cups fine crumbs (graham crackers or vanilla or chocolate wafers)
⅓ cup butter
4 tablespoons brown or white sugar
Ground nuts, cocoa, unsweetened or sweetened chocolate (optional)

Prepare the crumbs by rolling the crackers or wafers between sheets of wax paper. Or, better yet, whir them in a blender or food processor until they are fine. The essential consideration is that they be uniformly fine.

Melt the butter over low heat, remove from the heat, and add the crumbs and sugar and mix well. If using nuts (about 2 tablespoons, finely ground), or cocoa (1 tablespoon), add with the sugar. If you wish to use the chocolate, add 1 square (1 ounce) to the butter after it is melted and stir over very low heat until the chocolate is melted. Watch it carefully, making sure it doesn't scorch. Add to the crumbs and blend.

Preheat the oven to 350 degrees.

Transfer the crumb mixture to an 8- or 9-inch oiled springform or pie pan and pat evenly and firmly over the sides and bottom. Bake for 8 to 10 minutes, or until the crust looks firm. You can also freeze the crust—15 to 20 minutes in the freezer will do it—but baking gives a firmer crust that will support even a moist filling. Cool before filling.

Yield: Enough for a single-crust pie

Meringue Shell

A light, crisp dessert shell.

4 egg whites
⅛ teaspoon cream of tartar
Pinch of salt
1 cup superfine sugar (see note)

Line a 9-inch pie plate with foil. Oil the foil generously. Preheat the oven to 250 degrees.

Beat the egg whites in a large bowl until foamy. Add the cream of tartar and salt and continue beating until soft peaks form. Add the sugar gradually, a tablespoon at a time, and continue beating until glossy, stiff peaks form.

Spread the meringue over the bottom and up the sides of the prepared pie plate so that the bottom is about ⅜ inch thick and the sides 1 inch thick. Bake for 1 hour. Turn off the heat and leave in the oven until cool and dry—overnight, if convenient.

When ready to fill, peel the foil from the meringue shell and return the shell to the pie plate. Fill the shell just before serving with sweetened whipped cream or ice cream topped with strawberries, blueberries, Chocolate Sauce (see page 468), or with Lemon Cream (see page 516).

Yield: Enough for a single pie shell.

Note: You can prepare your own superfine sugar by pulverizing granulated sugar in the blender for 2 or 3 minutes.

Apple Pie

1 recipe Basic Pie Pastry (see page 501)
5 or 6 firm, tart apples (Granny Smith, greening, McIntosh, or a combination)
¾ cup sugar
1½ tablespoons flour
1 teaspoon freshly grated cinnamon
½ teaspoon freshly grated nutmeg
Pinch salt
1 teaspoon grated lemon rind

Cut the pastry in two, using the larger part for the bottom crust. Set the other portion of the dough aside. Roll out the larger part on a lightly floured surface and line a 9-inch pie pan with the dough. Refrigerate while you prepare the filling.

Preheat the oven to 450 degrees.

Peel the apples and cut them into quarters. Remove the core and cut the quarters lengthwise into slices about ⅛ inch thick. You should have 6 or 7 cups. Combine the sugar, flour, cinnamon, nutmeg, salt, and lemon rind in a large bowl. Add the apples and toss to coat evenly. Arrange the apples in the pie plate, piling

2 tablespoons lemon juice
2 tablespoons butter
1 egg yolk beaten with 1
tablespoon milk

them higher in the center. Sprinkle with lemon juice and dot with butter. Roll out the remaining pastry. Moisten the rim of the bottom crust with a little water. Place the second crust over the apples and press the edges together. Trim pastry rim and flute the edge.

Cut 5 small slits in the top of the pie to allow the steam to escape. Place the pie on a cookie sheet or a square of foil to catch the drippings as it bakes. Bake for 10 minutes. Reduce the oven heat to 400 degrees and continue baking 40 to 50 minutes longer. Brush with egg glaze about 15 minutes before it is done.

Cool on a rack. Serve warm or at room temperature.

Yield: 6 to 8 servings.

Apple Tart

This may be prepared in a 10-inch tart pan or baked free-form on a cookie sheet.

1 recipe Tart Pastry I (see page 501)
4 to 5 apples, peeled, cored, and thinly sliced (Granny Smith, greening, McIntosh, or Cortland)
½ cup sugar
3 tablespoons butter, cut into small pieces

Lemon Apricot Glaze (optional):
¼ cup apricot preserves
1 tablespoon fresh lemon juice
1 tablespoon water
1 teaspoon grated lemon rind

Preheat the oven to 400 degrees.

Line a 10-inch tart shell with the pastry dough rolled ⅛ inch thick, or roll the dough into a rectangle and arrange on a large cookie sheet.

Arrange the apple slices over the dough in one layer, overlapping each other like roof shingles, in concentric circles if using a round tart pan and in straight rows if the shape is rectangular. Be generous with the apple slices; they shrink a bit during baking. If you are doing a free-form shape, leave a 1½-inch border of dough free of apples to serve as a frame for the tart. Turn the edges of the dough over the apples to enclose them.

Sprinkle the sugar over the apples and the pastry border, and dot the apples evenly with the butter. Bake for 65 to 70 minutes or until the pastry is crisp and golden and the apples lightly browned. If you wish to glaze the tart, combine the apricot preserves, lemon juice, water, and lemon rind in a small sauce-pan and simmer for 2 or 3 minutes, until well blended. Press through a strainer and brush the top of the tart while still hot.

Serve the tart warm or at room temperature.

Yield: 6 to 8 servings.

Sour Cherry Tart

1 recipe Tart Pastry II (see page 502)

3 1-pound cans red sour pitted cherries (water-packed)

1 cup sugar

3 tablespoons kirsch or Maraschino

5 teaspoons cornstarch or arrowroot

¼ teaspoon almond extract

Sweetened whipped cream

Roll out the pastry and fit into a 10-inch tart pan, preferably one with a removable bottom. Chill while you prepare the filling.

Drain the cherries and place them in a bowl. Sprinkle with sugar and the liqueur. Stir gently or shake the bowl to mix so that you do not break the cherries. Let them macerate for one hour. Stir or gently shake several times.

Preheat the oven to 375 degrees.

Drain the cherries thoroughly, reserving the liquid. Measure the liquid; add enough water to make 1 cup. Place the liquid in a small saucepan with the cornstarch or arrowroot, mix well, and bring to a boil, stirring constantly until it becomes thickened and clear. Remove from the heat and combine with the cherries. Stir in the almond extract. Pour into the unbaked tart shell. Bake for 45 to 50 minutes, or until the crust is golden. Serve warm or at room temperature with a dollop of whipped cream.

Yield: 6 to 8 servings.

Fruit Tart

Use the fruit of your choice—grapes, strawberries, blueberries, raspberries, or cooked or canned peaches, plums, pears, or apricots.

1 baked cream cheese pastry shell (see page 502)

1 egg white mixed with 1 tablespoon water

1 recipe pastry cream (see page 516)

2½ to 3 cups fresh or cooked fruits, or 1½ quarts berries, washed, hulled, and dried

1 cup red currant, raspberry, or apple jelly

1 to 2 tablespoons kirsch or other liqueur (optional)

Prepare and bake the cream cheese pastry shell. Brush with the egg white mixture just before removing from the oven. This will prevent the crust from becoming soggy when filled. Let cool.

Prepare the pastry cream and refrigerate until cold.

Spread the cooled pastry cream evenly over the baked pastry shell. Arrange the fruits attractively over the pastry cream. Melt the jelly and push through a wire strainer. Thin out with the liqueur, if desired. Spoon the jelly glaze over the tops of the fruits.

Yield: 6 to 8 servings.

Lemon Tart

1 baked and cooled 9-inch tart
shell, made with Tart Pastry I
(see page 501)

1½ cups water

2½ tablespoons cornstarch

1 envelope unflavored gelatin

⅔ cup strained, freshly squeezed
lemon juice (4 to 5 lemons)

⅓ cup sugar

7 egg yolks, well beaten

2 tablespoons butter

1 cup heavy cream

½ cup heavy cream, whipped and
sweetened (optional)

4 thin slices of lemon, cut in half
(optional)

Prepare and cool the tart shell.

Combine ¼ cup cold water with the cornstarch and set aside.
Soften the gelatin in ¼ cup cold water in a heatproof cup. Place
in a pan of hot water and stir until clear and completely
dissolved.

Combine the remaining 1 cup water, lemon juice, and sugar and
bring to a boil. Reduce heat and stir until the sugar has
dissolved. Stir in the cornstarch and gelatin. Mix well and bring
just to a boil. Add several spoonfuls of the hot liquid to the
beaten egg yolks. Stir well and combine the egg yolks with the
hot mixture, stirring constantly. Over low heat, stir and bring just
to the boil. Remove from the heat.

Stir in the butter. Pour into a large mixing bowl and cover with
plastic wrap placed directly on the surface of the filling. Chill in
the refrigerator or set the bowl in a larger bowl of ice water to
cool.

Whip the 1 cup cream until stiff. Stir several spoonfuls into the
lemon filling and fold in the remaining cream with a rubber
spatula. Spoon the filling into the cooled pastry shell.

Just before serving, pipe or spoon sweetened whipped cream on
top and garnish with lemon slices, if desired.

Yield: 6 to 8 servings.

Lime Chiffon Pie

A light, airy dessert to end a substantial dinner.

1 baked 9-inch crumb crust (see recipe page 503)
1 envelope unflavored gelatin
¼ cup cold water
1 cup sugar
Pinch of salt
4 eggs, separated
½ cup lime juice
1½ teaspoons grated lime rind
½ cup heavy cream, whipped and sweetened, *or* some grated lime rind

Prepare the crust and let it cool.

Combine the gelatin, water, ½ cup of sugar, and salt in a saucepan. Beat together the egg yolks and lime juice and stir into the gelatin mixture. Place over low heat and simmer, stirring, until the mixture thickens and coats a spoon. Remove from the heat and stir in the grated rind. Chill until the filling is the consistency of unbeaten egg whites.

In a large bowl, beat the egg whites until soft peaks form. Gradually add the remaining ½ cup of sugar and continue to beat until the mixture holds stiff peaks. Fold the beaten egg whites into the lime mixture and blend well. No white streaks should be present. Pile the filling into the crumb crust and chill in the refrigerator for 4 or 5 hours, or until firm. Or cover lightly with plastic wrap and refrigerate overnight.

Decorate with sweetneed whipped cream before serving, or, in the interest of saving calories, some grated lime rind.

Yield: 8 servings.

Old-Fashioned Pecan Pie

A Southern specialty that is popular everywhere.

1 recipe Tart Pastry I (see page 501)
3 eggs
1 cup white corn syrup
1 cup dark brown sugar
½ teaspoon salt
4 tablespoons melted butter
1 teaspoon vanilla extract
1 heaping cup pecan halves
Sweetened whipped cream (optional)

Roll out the pastry and fit it into a 9-inch pie pan. Place in the freezer while you prepare the filling. Preheat the oven to 375 degrees.

In a large bowl, beat the eggs lightly. Stir in the corn syrup, sugar, salt, butter, and vanilla and mix well. Add the pecans and mix. Pour into the unbaked pie shell and bake for 30 to 40 minutes, or until the filling is firm. Remove from the oven and cool on a rack. Serve with sweetened whipped cream, if desired.

Yield: 6 to 8 servings.

Pumpkin Cream Pie

Rich, creamy, and fragrant with ginger and nutmeg.

1 recipe Tart Pastry I (see page 501)
1½ cups pumpkin purée
¾ cup sugar
½ teaspoon salt
½ teaspoon freshly grated ginger
½ teaspoon freshly grated nutmeg
3 eggs, beaten
1 cup milk or half-and-half
¼ cup dark rum
¾ cup heavy cream

Roll out the pastry and fit into a 9-inch pie plate. Refrigerate while you are preparing the filling.

Preheat the oven to 425 degrees.

Combine the pumpkin purée with the remaining ingredients in a large bowl. Stir until well blended. Pour into the pie shell.

Bake for 15 minutes. Reduce the heat to 350 degrees and bake for 30 to 40 minutes longer, or until set. The center will still be a little soft, but it will continue to cook and become firm as it stands. Cool on a rack.

Yield: 6 to 8 servings.

Puff Pastry

Puff pastry is a marvel of buttery flakiness that literally melts in your mouth and can add luster to the reputation of any cook. Of French origin, it has now become very much a part of the American cooking scene, used for tarts, patty shells, pastries and pastry crusts, cookies, and wrappings for meat and poultry.

Puff pastry consists of a simple dough and a mass of softened butter. The butter is spread over the dough, the dough folded to encase it, and then the two are rolled out together, folded and rerolled four, five, or six times, creating hundreds of very thin layers of dough sandwiched between hundreds of layers of butter. When placed in a hot oven, the butter melts and is absorbed by the starches. As steam is created, each layer swells individually and the pastry puffs up to five or six times its original height.

It is not difficult to make puff pastry, but it is time-consuming, because the dough needs considerable time in between the rollings and foldings for chilling and resting. But it is well

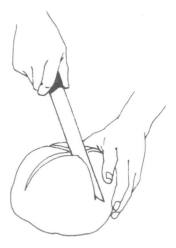

When the dough has been mixed and lightly kneaded, form it into a slightly flattened ball. Make a ¾-inch-deep cut in the dough in the form of a cross, and chill the dough.

worth making in quantity; the unbaked dough will keep for many months in the freezer.

You will need 4 cups unbleached all-purpose flour, 1 teaspoon salt, 2 cups (1 pound) butter, chilled, 1¼ to 1⅓ cups ice water, and 1 teaspoon lemon juice. Measure the flour and salt into a large bowl. Add 8 tablespoons of butter cut into small pieces, 1 cup of ice water, and the lemon juice. Work all the ingredients together with your fingertips and add as much additional ice water as you need to form a ball of dough. The dough should be a good workable consistency—pliable and medium firm, not hard. Turn the dough out onto a floured surface and knead it very slightly, 1 or 2 minutes, or until smooth. Overkneading will develop gluten, which is undesirable in this dough, making it difficult to roll out. Shape the dough into a thick round, sprinkle lightly with flour, and cut a cross in the center top about

Place the block of chilled butter on the dough, and bring the corners in to form an envelope of dough around the butter. Seal the edges and chill the package you have formed.

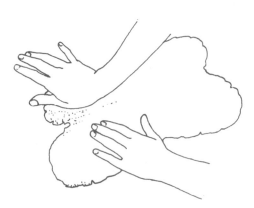

On a floured board, pat the dough into a square. Then, with the heel of the hand, push out the four corners, so that the dough is shaped like a cloverleaf.

After rolling the chilled dough package into a 16 by 8-inch rectangle, fold it in three, as you would fold a letter. Seal the edges lightly to keep the butter in.

¾ inch deep. Chill in the refrigerator, uncovered, for 30 minutes.

Meanwhile, on a piece of wax paper, work the remaining ¾ pound of butter with your hands into one piece about 7 inches square. Pat it lightly with flour, wrap it in wax paper, and refrigerate for about 20 minutes.

When the dough is chilled, place it on a lightly floured surface and pat it into a 9-inch square. Push out the four corners of the dough with the heel of your hand. Center the butter on the dough and encase it by folding the four corners to meet in the center without overlapping, like the back of an envelope. Press the edges gently together. Refrigerate about 20 minutes.

Place the dough package, seam side down, on a lightly floured surface. With a lightly floured rolling pin, roll the dough into a rectangle 16 by 8 inches. (Use a ruler or cut a piece of wax paper to this size.) Roll gently but firmly. Do not bear down on the dough; the aim is to flatten the butter between the two layers of dough and keep it in one unbroken sheet. Fold the dough into thirds by lifting one end toward the center and bringing the other over it, making three layers. Pinch the edges together to prevent the butter from leaking. This rolling is known as a "turn." Always check to make sure that the dough is not sticking to the work surface. If the dough splits and butter starts to ooze—which can happen—dust the split area heavily with flour to seal it.

Turn the dough so that the narrow side is toward you and roll and fold into thirds as before. You have now completed two turns. To keep track of the number, make two indentations in the dough with your fingers, or mark the number on a slip of paper. Wrap the dough in wax paper, slip it into a plastic bag, and refrigerate it for 45 minutes to an hour. The vegetable crisper is a perfect place. Don't let it get too cold.

For turn three, place the dough lengthwise on the work surface with the open ends at the top and bottom. Roll into a 16 by 8-inch rectangle and fold into thirds. If you find the dough too hard and cold to roll after chilling, tap it gently and evenly with the rolling pin to soften it a little. For turn four, again rotate dough, roll and fold. The dough can be used at this point, after being refrigerated for 2 hours, for meat pies, but for fancy tarts or pastries or whenever you want the maximum of puffy lightness, give the dough one more pair of turns—five and six—done exactly as the others, with chilling in between.

Wrap the dough and chill it for an hour before rolling out. It will keep very well in the refrigerator for 2 or 3 days. Frozen puff pastry should be defrosted in the refrigerator in the original freezer wrappings. It will take from 6 to 8 hours to thaw.

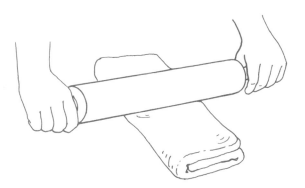

For the next turn, place the dough with one narrow end facing you and roll again into a rectangle. Fold in three again and chill. Be sure to keep count of the number of turns.

Napoleons

A flaky, crisp confection, aptly described by its French name, mille feuilles *("a thousand leaves").*

1 recipe puff pastry (see page 509)
1 recipe Pastry Cream (see page 516)

Vanilla Glaze:
2 cups confectioners' sugar
¼ teaspoon vanilla extract
2 to 3 tablespoons boiling water

Chocolate Icing:
1 ounce unsweetened chocolate
1 teaspoon butter
3 tablespoons confectioners' sugar
4 teaspoons boiling water, approximately

Cut the puff pastry in two and refrigerate one half. Preheat the oven to 425 degrees. Butter a large cookie sheet and sprinkle it with water. Shake off the excess. This will prevent the pastry from overbrowning on the bottom.

On a lightly floured surface, roll out the pastry approximately ⅛ inch thick into a 9 by 10-inch rectangle. Carefully lift the dough to the moist baking sheet and prick it all over at half-inch intervals with a fork. Bake it for 20 to 25 minutes, or until golden and well risen. Cool the pastry on a wire rack. Roll and bake the other half of the dough in the same way. Carefully cut the 2 rectangles in two lengthwise, giving you 4 strips, each 5 by 9 inches. Cover two of the strips with the pastry cream and cover each with one of the remaining strips.

For the vanilla glaze, combine the confectioners' sugar and vanilla in a bowl. Stir in 2 to 3 tablespoons of boiling water, until the mixture is of spreading consistency. Spread over the top of each strip.

For the chocolate icing, melt together the chocolate and butter in a heavy saucepan over low heat. Cool. Stir in the confectioners' sugar and mix until smooth. Add enough boiling water to make the icing soft enough to drizzle over the top of each strip. Cut each strip into four portions.

Yield: 8 napoleons.

Palmiers

½ recipe puff pastry (see page 509), *or* 1 recipe sour cream pastry (see page 503)
1 cup sugar, approximately

Sprinkle the work surface generously with granulated sugar. Roll the pastry into a rectangle about 10 inches wide and ⅛ inch thick. The length will depend on how much dough you are working with. Sprinkle more sugar on the surface as you are working—the dough should be well sugared. Trim the edges so that the rectangle is neat and tidy (you can reroll the scraps and use them for little cutouts). Fold the long edges of the dough toward the center and fold again to almost meet in the center. Then close it like a book, making a compact roll between 2 and 2½ inches wide. Wrap securely and chill for an hour or so. It is easier to slice the dough when it is firm.

Preheat the oven to 400 degrees. Line a cookie sheet with a large piece of aluminum foil. Cut the pastry into ½-inch slices. Dip both cut sides of the slices in sugar and place on the baking sheet about 2 inches apart. The cookies spread as they bake. Bake on the middle rack of the oven for 10 minutes, or until the sugar has melted and turned golden brown; turn the cookies and continue to bake until the sugar is caramelized on the second side. Remove from the oven and slip the foil off the cookie sheet. When the cookies can be easily removed from the foil, continue cooling on a wire rack. Repeat with the remaining dough.

The cookies can be stored in an airtight container for 2 or 3 days, but they should be frozen if they are to be kept longer.

Yield: About 30 cookies.

Cream Puff Pastry (Pâte à Choux)

Cream puff pastry can be fashioned into airy puffs that make fine hors d'oeuvre when filled with a cheese mixture, or chopped chicken or shellfish in a mustardy mayonnaise. It makes equally impressive desserts—cream puffs, chocolate éclairs, or profiteroles filled with ice cream and served with a mantle of chocolate sauce.

You simply cannot fail with puff shells. The magic of the golden crust surrounding a cavity lies in the steam produced by the evaporation of the water in the egg white during baking. The steam presses against the protein walls formed by the flour and eggs and pushes them out, forming a hole in the center of the puff.

The puffs freeze beautifully, stored in a plastic freezer bag. Thaw them when you're ready to use them and crisp them on a cookie sheet in a 325-degree oven for 5 minutes. Cool on a rack and fill.

1 cup all-purpose flour
Large pinch of salt
1 teaspoon sugar (for dessert puffs only)
1 cup water
½ cup (1 stick) butter
4 large eggs, beaten

Sift the flour onto a square of wax paper. In a large, heavy-bottomed saucepan, combine the salt, sugar (if making dessert puffs), water, and butter cut into small pieces. Cook over high heat, stirring with a wooden spoon or spatula, until it boils vigorously. Remove from the heat and add the flour all at once. Return to low heat and beat the mixture until the dough is smooth and leaves the sides of the pan, forming a ball. Remove from the heat.

Beat in the beaten eggs, the equivalent of 1 egg at a time, incorporating each addition well before adding the next. Beat for an additional minute after the last of the egg is added, or until the paste is smooth and shiny. If you are not going to use the pastry at once, rub lightly with butter and cover with wax paper to prevent a skin from forming.

Cream Puffs

A pastry bag makes neat puffs, but you can do a perfectly good job dropping the pastry on the baking sheet, using 2 spoons. If using a pastry bag, use a ½-inch round tube for small puffs and ¾-inch round tube for the 3-inch puffs.

1 recipe Cream Puff Pastry (see page 513)
2 cups heavy cream
½ cup confectioners' sugar
1 teaspoon vanilla extract

Preheat the oven to 400 degrees. Butter a heavy baking sheet. Drop the dough by rounded tablespoonfuls into 10 or 12 mounds. Shape them high and place them 2 to 3 inches apart. They need plenty of room as they will triple in size. If there are any sharp peaks, flatten them gently with a wet fingertip. Bake for 15 minutes. Reduce the heat to 350 degrees and bake 30 to 35 minutes longer, or until they are firm and light brown. Don't open the oven door for the first half hour of baking. It is essential not to underbake the puffs or they will collapse and have a moist inside. Remove the finished puffs from the oven, cut one or two slits in the tops and sides of each to let steam escape, and cool on a rack.

To fill, cut the top third off each puff. Remove any soft dough from the insides and discard. Whip 2 cups of heavy cream with about ½ cup of confectioners' sugar and 1 teaspoon of vanilla extract. Spoon the whipped cream into the bottom halves of the puffs, mounding it, and cover with the top portion. Let a bit of cream peek out at the joining. Sprinkle with confectioners' sugar, or cover tops with Cream Puff Chocolate Glaze or Mocha Icing and refrigerate. Serve with Chocolate Sauce (see page 468), if desired.

Yield: 10 to 12 cream puffs.

Chocolate Éclairs

Follow the same procedure as for Cream Puffs but shape the dough on the buttered cookie sheet into 3-inch lengths, 1 inch wide. Leave 2 inches between each. Bake in a preheated 400-degree oven for 15 minutes, reduce the heat to 350 degrees, and bake for an additional 15 to 20 minutes, or until light brown and dry. Cool on a rack. When cool, cut éclairs in half lengthwise. Fill with pastry cream (see page 516) or sweetened whipped cream and top with Chocolate Glaze or Mocha Icing. Refrigerate until serving time.

Yield: 10 to 12 éclairs.

Cream Puff Chocolate Glaze

4 ounces semisweet chocolate

½ cup heavy cream

1 tablespoon butter

3 tablespoons confectioners' sugar

2 tablespoons dark rum or Grand Marnier

Melt the chocolate with the cream over very low heat, stirring. Remove from the heat when the chocolate is melted and beat in the butter and sugar with a wooden spoon. Stir in the liqueur. Dribble over the tops of cream puffs or éclairs.

Mocha Icing

3 ounces sweet chocolate

2 tablespoons butter

¼ cup water

1 teaspoon instant coffee

1 cup confectioners' sugar

Melt the chocolate and butter over very low heat. When melted, add the water and coffee and remove from the heat. Blend in sugar and stir until smooth and creamy.

With a spatula, spread the icing over the tops of cream puffs or éclairs.

Cocktail Puffs or Profiteroles

For cocktail-size puffs, drop mounds of batter ½ inch in diameter on a buttered cookie sheet, about 2 inches apart. For dessert profiteroles, to be filled with pastry cream, whipped cream, or ice cream, shape the dough into mounds 1 inch in diameter and ¾ inch high. Bake in a preheated 400-degree oven for 12 minutes. Reduce the temperature to 350 degrees and bake for 20 minutes longer, or until the puffs are crisp and brown. Pierce the side of each to let steam escape, and cool on a rack.

Yield: 60 cocktail-size puffs or 30 profiteroles.

Curried Chicken Filling

3 tablespoons mayonnaise

½ teaspoon curry powder

¼ teaspoon dry mustard

1 tablespoon chopped fresh parsley

Squirt of lemon juice

1 cup finely minced cooked chicken

Combine the mayonnaise, curry powder, mustard, parsley, and lemon juice. Blend well with the minced chicken. Taste for seasoning. Cut cooked puffs open on one side near the top and fill with the chicken mixture. Close the tops. Just before serving, heat in a 350-degree oven for 5 or 6 minutes.

Variation: Substitute 1 cup crab meat, chopped shrimp, or tuna fish for the chicken.

Cheese Filling

1 cup grated sharp Cheddar or Swiss cheese

2 tablespoons minced parsley

2 tablespoons chopped walnuts

Combine the cheese, parsley, and walnuts. Cut the puffs open on one side near the top and fill with 1 teaspoon of the cheese mixture. Close the tops. Heat in a 350-degree oven for 5 or 6 minutes before serving.

Pastry Cream

4 tablespoons cornstarch
2 cups milk
3 egg yolks
¼ cup sugar
¼ teaspoon salt
4 tablespoons butter
1 teaspoon vanilla extract

Dissolve the cornstarch in 4 tablespoons of milk. Add the egg yolks and mix well.

In a small saucepan, heat the remaining milk along with the sugar, salt, and butter. As soon as the mixture begins to boil, add several spoonfuls to the egg yolk mixture. Lower the heat and slowly pour the egg yolks back into the saucepan. Stir constantly with a whisk over medium heat until thick and smooth, about 1 minute.

Remove from the heat, cool slightly, and add the vanilla. When cool, cover and chill. Use to fill puffs and éclairs. If mixture is too thick, thin it out with a few drops of milk or rum.

Chocolate Cream. Mix 2 tablespoons cocoa and 1 tablespoon additional sugar with the cornstarch.

Mocha Cream. Mix 1 tablespoon cocoa, 1 tablespoon instant coffee, and 1 tablespoon additional sugar with the cornstarch.

Coffee Cream. Add instant coffee to taste to the milk before combining with the egg yolks.

Lemon or Orange Flavoring. Add 2 tablespoons freshly grated rind to the hot milk.

Liqueur Flavoring. Substitute about 1 ounce of liqueur of your choice for the vanilla.

Whipped Cream. Whip 1 cup heavy cream and fold into the pastry cream.

Cake Baking

There have always been the born bakers—people who are gifted with a mysterious and innate sense of the balance of ingredients. Given some flour, fat, eggs, and sugar, they can do no wrong. However, cookbooks were not written for the likes of them and most of us are well advised to approach a cake recipe with a degree of reverence. This does not mean that there is no room for variation. If this were so, there would only be one formula and never a new one. Some recipes are more "tolerant" than others and will withstand some deviations, but you will avoid failures if you follow recipes scrupulously and not skip over what may appear to be an unnecessary step.

With the growing public interest in fresh,

wholesome foods and the avoidance whenever possible of chemical preservatives and artificial flavorings, the cake mix vogue seems to be on the wane. Starting a cake from scratch is not much more involved than dealing with a packaged mix to which you must still add ingredients, and it is an infinitely more rewarding undertaking.

There are two basic kinds of cake: those made with fat, and the sponge and angel food types made without fat. Although the fat or shortening may be butter, margarine, oil, or vegetable shortening, the cakes are generically called "butter" cakes and they include the ever-popular chocolate, white, and gold layer cakes, cakes rich with spices and studded with raisins and nuts, gingerbread, and pound cakes. Baking powder or baking soda are used as leavening. Angel and sponge cakes are sometimes called "foam" cakes because they depend for their leavening exclusively on the air bubbles trapped in their egg-rich dough.

Measuring

All baking recipes these days are based on level measurements. Terms like "heaping" and "scant" were dropped from baking language a long time ago. For accurate measurements, you need both dry and liquid measuring cups. It is impossible to be accurate if you pour liquid into a dry measure where it can spill over the top, or put flour and sugar, which need to be leveled off, into a glass measuring cup with a lip.

Many recipes today do not call for sifted flour because in present-day manufacturing procedures, flour is sifted many times during its processing. To measure flour without sifting, place a dry measuring cup on a square of wax paper and spoon the flour lightly into the measuring cup until full to overflowing. Level the

flour by running a knife or spatula across the top of the cup. Never try to level the flour by shaking the cup, as this will repack the flour, and too much flour will give you a heavy, compact cake. Mix the salt and baking powder into the flour and blend them well with a fork. Good distribution of the baking powder is essential if the cake is to have small cells and a fine grain.

Flour should be sifted for delicate cakes like sponge or angel food because the lightened flour is easier to fold into the beaten egg white. Always sift flour before measuring. To ensure even distribution of salt and baking powder, sift them together with the flour.

To measure brown sugar, pack it firmly into a dry measuring cup. If brown sugar or confectioners' sugar is lumpy, push it through a sieve, using the back of a spoon. It is generally not necessary to sift granulated sugar, unless it is inordinately lumpy. Spoon it lightly into a dry measuring cup, as you do the flour, and level it off.

To measure bulk fats that are not packaged in quarter-pound sticks with graduated markings, use the water displacement method. Since a solid displaces its own weight in water, you would measure ⅓ cup of fat by filling a glass measuring cup with ⅓ cup water and adding fat until the water level rises to ⅔ cup. Drain off the water, and the amount of fat remaining in the cup will equal ⅓ cup.

Measuring spoons come in graduated sizes from ¼ teaspoon to 1 tablespoon. Fill the proper size and level the top with a knife or spatula.

Ingredients

Flour

Aside from the type of cake known as a torte, in which ground nuts or crumbs may be used, flour is the ingredient in cake batter that holds the gas bubbles and that gives the baked cake its form. Flour can vary enormously in its ability to absorb moisture and, to keep it as dry as possible, it should be stored in airtight, screw-top jars.

Most cakes are made from all-purpose flour, bleached or unbleached, which is a blend of hard and soft wheat flours. Cake flour is made of soft wheat, and its delicate, less expansive gluten yields a crumblier texture. If your recipe calls for cake flour, which you happen not to have, you can substitute 1 cup less 2 tablespoons (⅞ cup) of all-purpose flour for each cup of cake flour. In reverse, if you need to substitute cake flour for all-purpose, use 2 tablespoons more per cup of cake flour for each cup of all-purpose.

Self-rising flour is all-purpose flour to which baking powder and salt have been added in the proportions of 1½ teaspoons baking powder and ½ teaspoon salt to each cup of flour. Use it only when called for in a recipe. It is not recommended for making breads and it is not interchangeable with all-purpose flour in the recipes in this book.

Although all-purpose flour has been sifted in processing, there are so-called presifted flours, which are very finely ground and give a different texture to baking. Although manufacturers may suggest that they can be used in place of cake flour, some of these presifted flours have a higher percentage of hard wheat and their greater gluten content may toughen cakes.

Eggs

Nowhere is the magic of the wondrous egg more evident than in cake baking. Eggs expand when beaten and trap the air beaten into them into the cake mixture, thus giving the cake lightness. Eggs are the main leavening agent for old-fashioned sponge cake and pound cake. It is air instead of the carbon dioxide formed from baking powder that causes the cake to rise. Even when its main function is not as a leavening, the egg acts as a toughening agent, binding the mixture. In addition, it gives the batter color, richness, and taste.

Eggs are considered part of the liquid ingredients and the size of the egg will make a difference in the cake. The recipes in this book are based on large eggs. For substitutions, see page 576.

The entire egg may be beaten into the creamed butter and sugar in a butter cake, but the cake will be lighter if only the beaten egg yolk is added to the creamed mixture and the beaten egg white folded in as the final step.

Sugar

Sugar performs a few extra functions in cake making besides the obvious one of adding sweetness. Sugar crystals have sharp edges that help to pull bubbles of air into the fat during the creaming process. In large quantities, sugar contributes to tenderness and it gives color to the cake as it bakes and browns in the oven.

Granulated sugar is the most commonly used sweetener.

Superfine sugar is finely pulverized granulated sugar. It dissolves quickly and is often used to sweeten berries, in making meringues, and in angel cakes, where its fast dissolving properties are advantageous. You can buy it or you can create your own by giving ordinary granulated sugar a few whirls in the electric blender. It may be substituted cup for cup with granulated sugar in recipes.

Confectioners' sugar is a powdery sugar that has a small amount of cornstarch added to prevent caking. Press it through a strainer with the back of a spoon if it lumps. It is used for uncooked icings and for sweetening whipped cream. Do not substitute it for granulated sugar in baking.

Brown sugar is a less refined and moister beet or cane sugar that is available light and dark. The dark is more strongly flavored. They both lump and harden easily and must be kept in tightly closed containers. If the sugar becomes very lumpy, sprinkle with a few drops of water and heat in a low oven for a few minutes. Brown sugar in this book refers to the light form. The dark brown is specified where a stronger flavor is desired.

Fat

Fat has an important function in shortened cakes in that it serves as a means of incorporating air into the batter. The process of creaming the butter or other shortening, in which it is worked with a spoon, your fingers, or an electric beater until it is light and fluffy, introduces air bubbles into the batter. These bubbles act as a leavening agent. All fats do not cream equally well. Regular lard, for example, because of its chemical structure, will not hold as many tiny bubbles of trapped air as vegetable shortening or butter.

Butter, margarine, vegetable shortening, salad oil, or a combination of hard fats are used in cake baking. Liquid oil is not interchangeable with hard fats unless the balance of the other ingredients is adjusted. Unsalted butter is the first choice of many cooks because of its distinctive flavor, but vegetable shortening or stick margarine will produce a tender cake with good texture. Some people find a combination of butter for flavor and vegetable shortening for its creaming and emulsifying properties a successful combination.

Chiffon cakes, in which egg yolks and stiffly beaten egg whites are added separately, are made with oil.

Fats also act as a tenderizing agent in cakes, as they do in pastry dough.

Leavenings

Double-acting baking powder is the most commonly used leavening and it is the one called for in all standard recipes. It is called double-acting because it starts its work in the cold dough and finishes it when the dough comes in contact with the heat from the hot oven. All baking powders contain an acid and an alkaline material. They react with one another in the presence of the liquid ingredients in the batter, generating carbon dioxide, which takes the form of tiny bubbles in the dough. The bubbles dilate in the heat of the oven, expanding the batter, which is then set by the heat to form the light-textured crumb that comes out of the oven as cake.

Should you have any doubts about whether your baking powder is still effective, you can test it by mixing 1 teaspoon baking powder with ⅓ cup hot water. If it bubbles vigorously, it is in good shape.

If you have run out of baking powder, you can produce your own acid-alkali mixture. Mix together ¼ teaspoon baking soda and ½ teaspoon cream of tartar for each teaspoon of baking powder the recipe calls for. This must be freshly mixed as it will not store well.

Baking soda is used as a leavening in recipes that contain some acid ingredient like sour milk, buttermilk, molasses, honey, or spice. It neutralizes the acid ingredient and produces a tender crumb. Some recipes call for both baking soda and baking powder.

Baking soda, as it is made today, is fine enough to be added with the other dry ingredients instead of having to be dissolved in liquid, as was formerly necessary. By adding it dry, all of the carbon dioxide gas it forms is retained within the batter instead of being lost to the atmosphere.

In sponge cakes, angel food cakes, and pound cakes, the leavening is the air beaten into the eggs or creamed into the butter, and the steam that results from the action of the heat of the oven on the liquid in the batter.

Cake mixtures can hold only a certain amount of gas and, if too much leavening is used, the cake can become overinflated during baking and then collapse, resulting in a heavy, dense texture.

Salt

Salt has no function in cake batter except as a flavor.

Chocolate

For many people, the thought of chocolate conjures up all kinds of eating delights. It is available unsweetened, semisweet, and sweet, and the recipe will specify which type is needed. The unsweetened is used most often in cooking. It is generally packaged in 1-ounce squares.

Chocolate scorches easily and it must be melted slowly. You can melt it over direct heat if you use a heavy-bottomed pan, very low heat, and watch it carefully. A flame control device gives you added protection against burning. Remove the pan from the heat before the chocolate is completely melted and stir it until it is entirely melted and smooth. It may also be melted in the top of a double boiler over hot water or in a shallow, heatproof bowl in a low oven, about 175 degrees. When melting chocolate by itself, be sure that the container is totally dry. The smallest amount of moisture can sometimes cause the chocolate to "tighten," or become stiff. If this should happen, stir in 1 teaspoon solid vegetable shortening to each ounce of chocolate and it will smooth out again.

Chocolate stores well at room temperature. It should not be refrigerated. The grayish pallor that may appear on chocolate when it has been stored at a high temperature is harmless, although esthetically unpleasing; it is merely the fat content coming to the surface. The chocolate is perfectly edible and usable.

To substitute cocoa for chocolate, use 3 tablespoons cocoa and 1 tablespoon butter for each ounce of chocolate. This substitution works more successfully in sauces than in baking. If you need to substitute semisweet chocolate for unsweetened, make the adjustment in the recipe using less sugar, more chocolate, and a dash of vanilla.

Dried Fruits

Dredge dried fruits lightly in flour before adding them to cake batter to keep them from falling to the bottom. Baking will not soften raisins or other dried fruits that have become hard. Plump them by soaking in water or, if they are very hard, boil them for 10 minutes. Drain and dry them well before adding.

Baking at High Altitudes

At altitudes of 3,000 feet above sea level, carbon dioxide gas expands more rapidly, since there is less air pressure to be overcome as the cake rises. For this reason, the amount of baking powder must be decreased. A higher proportion of egg can be used at high altitudes without making the cake tough, and the amount of liquid in cake batter may need to be increased because water vaporizes at a lower temperature. It may also be necessary to reduce the amount of sugar.

Preparing Cake Pans

Have the proper size pans out and prepared before you start mixing the batter. If the pan is too big, the cake may not rise properly and may brown unevenly. If too small, the texture may be coarse and the batter could overflow before it sets. Cake pans may be filled from one-half to not more than two-thirds full. Loaf and tube pans may be filled higher.

Greasing and flouring will prevent the cake from sticking. Apply soft butter or vegetable shortening evenly around the bottom and sides of the pan, using a wad of crumpled wax paper, your fingers, or a pastry brush. Sprinkle a little flour into each pan and shake it to coat the pan evenly. Then invert it and tap out the excess.

As an added precaution against sticking and for ease of turning out, use a liner of wax paper or cooking parchment. Set the pan on the sheet of paper and trace around it. If you need liners for more than one pan, cut as many as you need at one time. Place the liner over the bottom of the greased pan and grease the wax paper. Cooking parchment does not need to be greased. The paper will peel off easily when the cake is turned out to cool. Pans with a nonstick coating do not need greasing, but a paper liner helps to keep too solid a crust from forming, particularly if the baking period is long.

Pans for angel or sponge cakes are never greased. The cake will rise more easily if it doesn't have to deal with a slippery pan. The pans should be completely clean and free of grease.

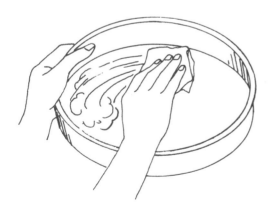

Before a cake pan is filled with batter, it must be greased and floured. Spread butter or shortening with wax paper (the wrapper from a stick of butter is useful), a pastry brush, or your fingers.

Drop a handful of flour into the pan and shake, tap, and turn the pan until a film of flour coats the bottom and sides, then invert and tap to remove excess flour. Line the bottom with wax paper.

Bright, shiny pans will give you a thin, evenly browned crust. Their shiny surfaces deflect some of the radiant energy in the oven and slow down the baking rate, while dark pans absorb heat and bake your cakes more quickly. If you must use dark pans, insulate them with greased wax paper to keep the crusts from getting too browned and heavy. Glass pans are practical and, being transparent, allow you to oversee the degree of browning. When baking in glass, lower the oven temperature about 25 degrees below that recommended for metal pans. The springform pan, engineered so that the rim can be separated from the bottom when a clamp is released, is a practical solution to the problem of removing delicate cakes like tortes and cheesecakes from the pan without breaking them. Many bundt pans, the round cake pans with fluting on the top and a central tube, designed especially for the German coffee cake of the same name, are now lined with nonstick surfaces, making the removal of the cake easier.

Mixing Cake Batters

Assemble all your ingredients and measure them before you begin. It is best if they are at room temperature, particularly the fat and the eggs. If you are going to separate eggs, bear in mind that eggs separate more easily when cold, but both whites and yolks will whip to greater volume when they are at room temperature. You can separate them while they are still chilled from the refrigerator and let them warm up on the kitchen counter. Start heating the oven 10 minutes or so before you plan to have the batter ready for baking. A preheated oven is recommended because it allows for more rapid heat penetration.

The same general principles pertain whether you are mixing by hand or using an electric mixer. For a cake made with shortening, the butter is first creamed or beaten until it is soft enough to mix with the other ingredients. If it is at room temperature, you won't have any difficulty working with it. Don't heat or melt it or you won't be able to incorporate the air bubbles into it. Add the sugar gradually, beating it in well, until the mixture is light and fluffy. Don't cut corners on the creaming. It takes time to incorporate air for a light texture: 8 to 10 minutes on medium speed of an electric mixer and more than 10 minutes with a portable mixer.

The eggs or egg yolks are added next with the flavorings. With an electric mixer you can add the eggs all at once, but if you are beating by hand, add them one at a time, beating well after each addition. If you are beating by hand, the sifted dry ingredients and any other liquids are added in three or more alternating steps, beginning and ending with the dry ingredients. With an electric mixer, it may be done at one time. Adding the flour in small amounts incorporates it quickly, avoiding the danger of overbeating, which will stretch the gluten. The mixture is stirred, rather than beaten. Two minutes in an electric mixer at medium speed will do it. It is important that batters not be overmixed once the dry ingredients have been added. If your recipe calls for beaten egg whites, beat them just before adding them to the batter and then fold them in gently so as not to diminish the air you have just pumped into them.

Angel cakes and sponge cakes are fragile and the procedures for preparing them differ from butter cakes, as you will see in the recipes that follow.

A cake batter with shortening can stand covered in the baking pan for a few hours without too much damage, if for some reason you are unable to bake it at the time. But do not allow it to stand in the mixing bowl and then transfer it, because air bubbles will be lost.

Baking Cakes

Place pans in the preheated oven so that there is even heat circulation around them. The pans should not touch each other, nor should they touch the sides of the oven. Place them on the center rack. If you are baking more than two layers, or if your oven is small, you may have to use two racks. Place the racks in the middle third of the oven but be sure you allow enough room for the cake on the lower rack to rise. Position the pans so one is not directly over the other. If the cakes do not appear to be baking evenly, turn the pans a few times during the baking.

Bake cakes at the exact temperature and time called for in the recipe. Start testing 5 minutes before the time is up. If a range of time is given, test when the cake has baked the shorter time suggested. Touch the top of the cake lightly with your finger; most cakes, unless they are very rich, will spring back, leaving no imprint. If an imprint remains, the cake needs more baking. You can also use a cake tester or a toothpick. Stick it gently into the center of the cake. If it comes out with crumbs or batter clinging to it, the cake needs to bake longer; if it comes out clean and dry, the cake is done.

Cooling Cakes

Cakes should be cooled in the baking pan set on a wire rack for about 5 minutes, unless otherwise directed in the recipe. Loosen the edges of the cake with a spatula. Cover with a cake rack and invert. Remove the pan. Peel off the wax paper, if present. Place a second rack over the bottom of the cake and invert cake and rack again so that the bottom of the cake is resting on the rack. Let the cake cool completely in this position.

Angel and sponge cakes need longer cooling in the pan in an upside-down position. Follow the recipe directions.

Always frost cakes after they are cooled.

Let the cake cool in its pan on a wire rack for 5 minutes or so. Run a spatula or knife around the sides of the cake to release it from the pan.

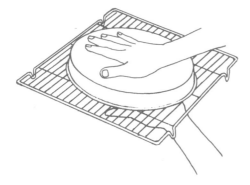

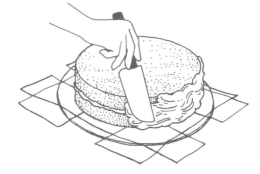

With the cake still in its pan, place a wire rack on top. Supporting the bottom of the cake pan with your hand, turn the two upside-down, so the cake is facing down on the wire rack. Lift off the pan.

Cut a 12-inch square of wax paper into 4 strips and slip these under the cooled cake before icing it. This will keep the cake plate clean. Ice the sides of the cake before frosting the top.

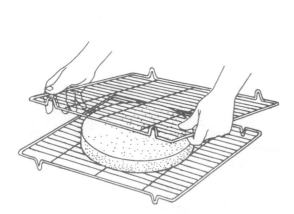

Remove wax paper from the bottom of the cake, which is now face down on a rack. Put another rack above the cake to form a sandwich. Invert the racks with the cake in between, and lift off the top rack.

For a decorative touch, swirl up peaks with the back of a spoon. You can also make rows of wavy lines with a fork, or form a spiral with the tip of a spatula. Remove wax paper before serving.

Frostings

Frostings offer eye appeal as well as flavor and they also serve as a protective coating for cakes, keeping them moist.

To frost a two-layer cake, brush away any loose crumbs from the sides. Place the first layer top side down on a flat cake plate so that the flat surfaces of the two layers meet. If the cake is uneven in any way, you can trim it before frosting and no one will be the wiser.

To keep the cake plate clean while frosting, divide a 12-inch square of wax paper into four 3-inch strips. Place the strips under the edges of the cake. After the frosting has set, you can slip the strips out, leaving a neat, tidy cake plate.

Spread the filling or about one-third of the icing over the top of the bottom layer. Cover with the top layer. With a wide knife or spatula, spread the frosting over the sides and then the top. You can use the back of a teaspoon to form swirls and peaks over the sides and top.

Storing Cakes

As with most foods, fresh is always better, but if you are planning to keep a cake for several days, wrap it in plastic or foil, store it in a cake box, protect it with a dome, or refrigerate it. Cakes with custard fillings or cream must be refrigerated.

All cakes can be frozen. Protect them well by wrapping in moistureproof freezer wrap, snugly sealed. Let the cake thaw for an hour or two at room temperature before removing the wrapping. Moisture condenses while the cake is thawing and, if wrapped, the moisture collects on the outside of the wrapping instead of on the cake.

It is best to freeze a cake without the frosting, but you can place the frosted cake on some foil resting on a plate and put it in the freezer. After it is frozen, which doesn't take very long, remove the plate, close up the foil to make an airtight package, and return it to the freezer.

Basic 2-Egg Layer Cake

½ cup (1 stick) butter
1 cup sugar
2 eggs
1 teaspoon vanilla extract
2 cups all-purpose flour
½ teaspoon salt
2 teaspoons baking powder
¾ cup milk

Preheat the oven to 350 degrees. Butter two 8- or 9-inch round cake pans, line with wax paper, and butter the paper. With an electric mixer at medium speed, cream the butter and sugar until light and fluffy. Add the eggs and vanilla and beat until fluffy. (If beating by hand, add 1 egg at a time). Thoroughly stir together the flour, salt, and baking powder and add to the egg mixture alternately with the milk, beginning and ending with the flour. Scrape the sides and bottom of the bowl while mixing. Turn into prepared cake pans and bake for 25 to 30 minutes, or until a cake tester inserted in the middle comes out dry. Cool in pans for 10 minutes; remove the paper and cool on wire racks. Cool completely before frosting.

Yield: 8 to 10 servings.

Chocolate Chip Orange Cake. Add 1 tablespoon grated orange rind to the butter when creaming. Fold ½ cup semisweet chocolate bits into the batter. Put the layers together with a filling of Orange Butter Cream (see page 544) and cover the top layer with Chocolate Glaze (see page 543).

Peppermint Candy Cake. Decrease the sugar to ¾ cup. Stir in ⅓ cup finely crushed peppermint stick candy. Frost the cake with chocolate frosting.

Buttermilk Cake. Use ½ teaspoon baking soda and 1 teaspoon baking powder instead of the 2 teaspoons baking powder. Use 1 cup buttermilk instead of the milk.

Cupcakes

Almost any cake batter can be baked in cupcake form. For ease in handling, bake then in fluted paper cups set in muffin tins. They can be frosted or garnished with nuts or diced dried fruits, or dusted with confectioners' sugar. Fill the cups about half full and bake in a 375-degree oven for 15 to 20 minutes.

Lemon Coconut Cupcakes. Add the grated peel of 1 lemon to the above recipe, beating it in with the eggs. Mix together ½ cup flaked coconut and ¼ cup chopped walnuts or pecans. Cover each cupcake with about a teaspoon of the mixture, pressing it in lightly, and bake as directed.

Chocolate Fudge Cake

Cocoa for dusting pans
3 squares unsweetened chocolate
2¼ cups cake flour
2 teaspoons baking soda
½ teaspoon salt
½ cup (1 stick) sweet butter
2¼ cups light brown sugar, packed
3 eggs
1½ teaspoons vanilla extract
1 cup sour cream
1 cup boiling water
Whipped Cream Filling (recipe follows)
Chocolate Icing (recipe follows)

Preheat the oven to 350 degrees. Grease two 9-inch round cake pans and sprinkle with cocoa, coating the bottom and sides. Tap out any excess.

Melt the chocolate in a small bowl over hot water or in a heavy-bottomed pan over very low heat. Use a flame control device to make sure the chocolate does not scorch. Remove from the heat before it is thoroughly melted and stir until smooth. Set aside. Combine the flour, baking soda, and salt in a bowl and set aside.

Cream the butter until fluffy and light. Add the sugar and eggs and continue to beat until fluffy and very thick, about 5 minutes. Beat in the vanilla and melted chocolate.

Stir in the dry ingredients alternately with the sour cream, beating well after each addition until batter is smooth. Stir in the boiling water. Pour into the prepared pans.

Bake for 30 to 35 minutes, or until the centers spring back when lightly touched with the fingertips.

Cool on a rack for 7 to 10 minutes. Turn out of pans onto a rack and cool completely.

Place one layer on a serving plate and cover with half the whipped cream filling. Top with the second layer. Cover the top and sides with the chocolate icing. Decorate the top with remaining whipped cream filling. Chill until serving time.

Yield: 8 to 10 servings.

Whipped Cream Filling

¾ teaspoon unflavored gelatin
1 tablespoon cold water
1½ cups heavy cream

Soften the gelatin in 1 tablespoon water in a heatproof cup. Put the cup in hot water and stir the gelatin until it is clear and completely dissolved. Beat the heavy cream until it thickens and slowly beat in the dissolved gelatin. Continue to beat until thick. Refrigerate for 10 to 15 minutes before spreading on cake.

Chocolate Icing

3 squares unsweetened chocolate
3 tablespoons butter
1½ cups confectioners' sugar
½ cup milk or water, heated to the boiling point

Melt the chocolate and butter in a small saucepan over low heat. Remove from the heat and stir in the confectioners' sugar and the warmed milk or water and beat until smooth. Spread while still warm on the cooled cake.

Chocolate Loaf Cake

A quickly made, moist, not-too-sweet chocolate cake with good texture. It is unusual in that two of the standard cake ingredients, the egg and fat, are introduced in the form of mayonnaise.

2 cups all-purpose flour
1¼ cups sugar
Pinch salt
1¾ teaspoons baking soda
⅓ cup cocoa
1 cup cold water
1 teaspoon vanilla extract
¾ cup mayonnaise

Preheat the oven to 350 degrees. Butter a 9 by 5-inch loaf pan. Line the bottom with wax paper and butter the wax paper. You may also use two 8-inch round cake pans, lined with buttered wax paper.

In a large bowl, combine the flour, sugar, salt, baking soda, and cocoa and mix well. Add the water and vanilla and beat until smooth. Add the mayonnaise and beat until the batter is completely smooth and free of lumps. Transfer the batter to the pan and bake for 50 minutes for the loaf, 30 to 35 minutes for the layers, or until a cake tester comes out dry. Cool for at least 20 minutes on a rack before removing from the pan. Remove from the pan and peel off the wax paper. The cake has such a rich, fudgy taste that a little confectioners' sugar sprinkled over the top to give it a finished look is all that it needs. The layers can be frosted with Fluffy White Frosting (see page 542).

Yield: 8 to 10 servings.

Pound Cake

The classic pound cake, tender and moist. The name is derived from the quantity of its ingredients—a pound each of butter, sugar, eggs, and flour. It contains no baking powder.

1 pound sweet butter
1 pound confectioners' sugar
8 large eggs
1½ teaspoons vanilla
4 cups sifted cake flour

Preheat the oven to 325 degrees. Butter and lightly flour a 10-inch bundt or tube pan and set aside. This may also be baked in two 9 by 5-inch loaf pans, greased and lined with greased wax paper. Have all the ingredients at room temperature.

In the large bowl of an electric mixer, beat the butter until fluffy. Slowly add the sugar and continue beating until light, thick, and almost white, 10 to 12 minutes. Since this cake has no leavening, its texture and lightness depend on the air bubbles that are beaten into it.

Add eggs one at a time, beating well after each addition. Add vanilla. Add flour and stir only enough to incorporate. Do not overmix.

Transfer the batter to the prepared pan and bake for 1¼ to 1½ hours, or until a cake tester comes out clean and dry. The loaf pans will need from 1 to 1¼ hours. The cake will also begin to shrink from the edges of the pan a bit. Cool in the pan for 5 to 7 minutes. Turn out on a wire rack and cool completely. Peel off wax paper, if used.

Yield: 1 10-inch cake or 2 9 by 5-inch loaves.

Meringue Cake with Sour Cream Custard

Light and lovely with a crisp meringue top and bottom and a luscious sour cream filling.

½ cup (1 stick) butter
1 cup superfine sugar
4 egg yolks, well beaten
3 tablespoons milk
1 teaspoon vanilla extract
1 cup sifted cake flour
1 teaspoon baking powder

Meringue:
5 egg whites
¾ cup superfine sugar
1 cup finely chopped nuts

Custard Filling:
1 egg yolk
4 tablespoons sugar
1½ tablespoons cornstarch
1½ cups sour cream
1 tablespoon butter
1 teaspoon vanilla extract

Preheat the oven to 350 degrees. Butter two 9-inch round layer cake pans, line with wax paper, and butter the paper. Set aside.

Cream the butter and sugar until light and fluffy. Stir in the well-beaten egg yolks. Stir in the milk and vanilla and add the sifted flour mixed with the baking powder. Beat only until smooth. Divide the batter into the prepared pans, smoothing the tops with a rubber spatula.

In a large bowl, beat the egg whites until frothy. Slowly add the sugar, a little at a time, and continue beating until stiff peaks form. Divide the meringue between the two cakes, smoothing it evenly over the batter. Sprinkle the tops with the chopped nuts, gently patting them into place. Bake for 30 to 35 minutes, or until a cake tester comes out dry. The meringue will puff up and then settle back.

While the layers are baking, prepare the custard. In a small bowl, beat the egg yolk and add the sugar mixed with cornstarch. Stir in the sour cream. Transfer to the top of a double boiler over boiling water or to a heavy-bottomed saucepan over very low heat. Add the butter and cook, stirring, until the sauce thickens. Taste to see if more sugar is needed and add if necessary. Cook, stirring, until the custard coats the spoon. Stir in the vanilla and remove from the heat. Allow to cool.

When the cake layers are done, remove from the oven and let stand for 10 minutes. Remove one layer and place on a round serving plate with the meringue side down. Remove the other layer from the pan and place on rack to cool, meringue side up. When the layers are completely cool, spread the custard over the bottom layer and cover with the top layer, meringue side up. Refrigerate until serving time.

Yield: 8 to 10 servings.

Bavarian Apple Cake

A thin layer of cake crowned with browned apple slices and nuts.

8 tablespoons (1 stick) sweet butter

¾ cup granulated sugar

Pinch of salt

2 eggs

2 tablespoons water

1 cup flour

1 teaspoon baking powder

3 large firm, tart apples (Granny Smith or greening), peeled, cored, and thinly sliced

½ cup brown sugar

1½ teaspoons cinnamon

½ cup coarsely chopped walnuts or pecans

Preheat the oven to 350 degrees. Butter and lightly flour a 9-inch springform pan.

Cream 4 tablespoons of butter and ¼ cup of granulated sugar until light and fluffy. Add salt, eggs, water, flour, and baking powder and beat until smooth. Scrape into the springform pan and spread the batter evenly over the bottom with a spatula.

In a large bowl, combine the apple slices with the remaining ½ cup of sugar, the brown sugar, cinnamon, and nuts. Mix well and heap evenly over the batter. Dot the top with the remaining 4 tablespoons of butter cut into small pieces.

Bake about 1 hour, or until a cake tester inserted deep in the center of the cake comes out dry. Remove from the oven and allow to cool on a wire rack for 20 to 30 minutes before removing the sides of the springform. Serve warm or at room temperature with sweetened whipped cream or ice cream, if desired.

Yield: 6 to 8 servings.

Pumpkin Spice Cake

Outstandingly good—tender, moist and fragrant with spices.

2 cups all-purpose flour
2 teaspoons baking powder
1 teaspoon baking soda
½ teaspoon salt
1½ teaspoon ground cinnamon
½ teaspoon ground cloves
¼ teaspoon ground allspice
¼ teaspoon ground ginger
2 cups sugar
4 eggs
1 1-pound can pumpkin, *or* 2 cups cooked, puréed pumpkin
1 cup vegetable oil
1 cup 40 percent bran breakfast cereal
1½ ounces bourbon (optional)
1 cup coarsely chopped nuts or light or dark raisins

Preheat the oven to 350 degrees. Grease a 10-inch bundt pan.

In a medium-size bowl, blend together the flour, baking powder, soda, salt, cinnamon, cloves, allspice, ginger, and sugar. (Reserve a few tablespoons of flour to flour the nuts or raisins before adding them to the batter so that they won't sink to the bottom.)

In a large bowl, beat the eggs until foamy. Add the pumpkin, oil, and bran cereal and mix well.

Fold the dry ingredients, bourbon (if using), and nuts or raisins into the egg mixture, mixing only until combined. Do not overmix.

Transfer the batter to the baking pan and bake for 1 hour and 10 minutes, or until a cake tester comes out dry. Cool for 15 minutes, remove from the pan, and cool completely on a wire rack.

Yield: 12 or more servings.

Carrot Cake

2 cups all-purpose flour
1 teaspoon baking powder
2 teaspoons baking soda
½ teaspoon salt
2 teaspoons cinnamon
4 eggs
1½ cups sugar
1½ cups vegetable oil
3 cups grated raw carrots (about 1 pound)
1½ cups coarsely chopped pecans or walnuts
1 teaspoon vanilla extract

Preheat the oven to 325 degrees. Grease a 10-inch tube or Bundt pan and set aside. If using loaf pans, line with a sheet of wax paper and butter it.

Combine the flour, baking powder, soda, salt, and cinnamon. In a large bowl, beat the eggs by hand or with an electric mixer. Add the sugar and oil and beat until well mixed. Stir in the carrots, flour mixture, nuts, and vanilla. Blend well.

Pour the batter into the prepared pan. Bake for 1 to 1¼ hours for the tube pan, 45 to 55 minutes for loaves, or until a cake tester comes out dry. Remove to a wire rack. Allow to stand for 5 to 7 minutes; turn the cake out onto a rack. Serve warm, plain or with Cream Cheese Frosting (page 544).

Yield: 1 10-inch cake or 2 loaves.

Variation: Substitute 1 8-ounce can drained crushed pineapple for 1 cup of grated carrots.

Apricot Baba Ring

½ cup milk
4 tablespoons (½ stick) butter
5 egg yolks
1 cup sugar
1 cup sifted all-purpose flour
1 teaspoon baking powder
Pinch salt
1 teaspoon grated orange or
  lemon rind
½ teaspoon vanilla extract
1 1-pound, 13-ounce can apricots
2 ounces white rum
1 cup shredded coconut
1 quart vanilla ice cream

Preheat the oven to 350 degrees. Butter the bottom of a 6-cup ring mold.

In a small saucepan, combine the milk and the butter and heat until the butter is melted. In a medium-size bowl, beat the egg yolks with an electric beater until they are foamy. Slowly add the sugar and continue beating until the mixture becomes thick and lemon-colored, and falls from the beaters in a ribbon. Mix together the sifted flour, baking powder, salt, and grated rind. Add the milk mixture to the egg yolks alternately with the flour and mix only until smooth. Stir in the vanilla. Pour the batter into the ring mold and bake for 30 to 35 minutes, or until a cake tester comes out dry. Cool for 10 minutes and turn out on a rack.

Drain the apricots, reserving the syrup. Remove the pits from the apricots and purée the apricots through a food mill. Transfer the cake to a round serving dish and, while it is still warm, pour ½ cup of the apricot syrup mixed with the rum over it. If you wish, you can also flavor the apricot purée with a bit of rum. Spread the apricot purée over the cake and sprinkle with coconut. When ready to serve, fill the center with ice cream balls.

Yield: 8 servings.

Gingerbread Ring with Butterscotch Sauce

½ cup (1 stick) butter
½ cup brown sugar
1 egg, well beaten
1½ cups all-purpose flour
1 teaspoon ground ginger
1 teaspoon cinnamon
½ teaspoon ground cloves
1 teaspoon baking soda
Pinch salt
½ cup molasses
½ cup boiling water
Butterscotch Sauce (see page 467)

Preheat the oven to 375 degrees. Butter and flour a 4-cup ring mold or a 9 by 5-inch loaf pan. In a large bowl, cream the butter and sugar until light and fluffy. Beat in the egg. In another bowl, combine the flour, ginger, cinnamon, cloves, baking soda, and salt and mix well. Combine the molasses and water in a measuring cup and mix well.

Add the flour mixture alternately with the molasses mixture to the creamed sugar and butter, ending with the flour, and beat well between additions. Transfer the batter to the baking pan and bake for 30 minutes, or until a cake tester comes out dry.

Cool in the pan for 15 minutes on a wire rack. Remove from the pan and cool on the rack. The center of the ring mold can be filled with whipped cream or ice cream balls. Serve with Butterscotch Sauce (see page 467).

Yield: 8 servings.

Zucchini Cake

Cocoa for dusting the pan
2 cups all-purpose flour
1 teaspoon baking powder
1 teaspoon baking soda
1 teaspoon cinnamon
½ teaspoon nutmeg
½ teaspoon salt
¼ teaspoon cocoa
3 eggs
2 cups sugar
½ cup vegetable oil
¾ cup buttermilk or yogurt
2 cups firmly packed, unpeeled, shredded zucchini (3 to 4 medium)
1 teaspoon vanilla extract
1 cup coarsely chopped nuts (pecans, walnuts, or Brazil nuts)

Preheat the oven to 350 degrees. Grease a 10-inch bundt or tube pan and dust with cocoa. Or use two small buttered loaf pans (8½ by 4½ by 2½ inches), lined with wax paper and buttered.

Combine the flour, baking powder, soda, cinnamon, nutmeg, salt, and cocoa and mix well. Set aside.

In a large bowl, beat the eggs until light. Add the sugar slowly and continue to beat until thick and lemon-colored. Slowly beat in the oil. Stir in the buttermilk or yogurt, zucchini, and vanilla and blend well. Add the flour mixture and mix only until incorporated. Stir in the nuts. Transfer to baking pan or pans. Bake for 40 to 45 minutes for loaves; 1 to 1¼ hours for the tube pan. Cool in the pan for 5 minutes before turning out on a rack to finish cooling. Dribble with Uncooked Confectioners' Glaze (page 542) or Cream Cheese Frosting (page 544) while still warm.

Yield: 1 10-inch cake or 2 loaves.

Chiffon Spice Cake

2¼ cups cake flour, sifted
1 teaspoon baking powder
¾ teaspoon baking soda
1 teaspoon salt
¾ teaspoon freshly grated nutmeg
¾ teaspoon ground cloves
¾ teaspoon cinnamon
1 cup brown sugar, packed
⅓ cup oil
1 cup buttermilk
2 eggs, separated
½ cup sugar

Preheat the oven to 350 degrees. Grease and flour two 8- or 9-inch round layer cake tins or one oblong pan, 13 by 9½ inches.

Sift the flour into a large mixing bowl with the baking powder, baking soda, salt, nutmeg, cloves, cinnamon, and brown sugar and mix well. Add the oil and ⅔ cup of buttermilk. Beat for a minute with the electric beater at medium speed. Scrape the sides and bottom of the bowl frequently. Add the remaining buttermilk and egg yolks. Beat an additional minute, continuing to scrape the sides and bottom of the bowl.

In another bowl, beat the egg whites until frothy with a dry, clean beater. Gradually beat in the sugar and continue beating until stiff and glossy but not dry. Gently fold the egg whites into the batter. Pour into prepared pans. Bake layers for 30 to 35 minutes, oblong 40 to 45 minutes, or until a cake tester comes out dry. Cool cake in the pan for about 5 minutes and turn out on racks. When completely cooled, spread Raisin Cream Filling (page 545) between layers and frost with Fluffy White Icing (page 542).

Yield: 2 layers or 1 loaf.

Sponge Cake

The true sponge cake is made without baking powder or fat, its light texture dependent entirely on the air beaten into the eggs.

6 eggs, separated, at room temperature
1 cup superfine sugar
2 tablespoons cold water
Grated rind of 1 lemon
1 tablespoon lemon juice
Pinch salt
¼ teaspoon cream of tartar
1 cup sifted cake flour

Preheat the oven to 325 degrees. Line the bottom of a 10-inch tube pan or two 8-inch round cake pans with wax paper. Place the egg yolks in a large mixing bowl and beat until thick and lemon-colored. Gradually add ½ cup sugar, 1 tablespoon at a time, and beat thoroughly until creamy. Combine the water, lemon rind, and lemon juice and slowly stir into the egg yolks. In a large bowl and with clean dry beaters, beat the egg whites until foamy. Add the salt and cream of tartar and beat until soft peaks form. Beat in the remaining ½ cup of sugar, a tablespoon at a time, and continue beating until the meringue is stiff but not dry. Stir one-quarter of the whites into the yolk mixture and sift the flour on top. Gently fold the flour into the egg yolks with a rubber spatula. Spoon the remaining egg whites over the top and fold gently until well blended. Spoon into the prepared pan. With a spatula, carefully cut through the batter 5 or 6 times to break up large air bubbles. Bake for 50 to 60 minutes in the tube pan, or until the top springs back when touched lightly with the finger. The layers will need 25 to 35 minutes. Invert the tube pan on a funnel or bottle; put the layers on a wire rack and cool completely. Remove cake from the pan and peel off the wax paper. Dust with confectioners' sugar, or frost with any frosting of your choice.

Yield 1 10-inch cake, or 2 layers.

Orange Sponge Cake

4 eggs, separated, at room temperature
1 cup sugar
½ cup orange juice
2 teaspoons grated orange rind (optional)
Pinch salt
1 cup cake flour
1 teaspoon baking powder

Preheat the oven to 325 degrees. Line the bottom of an 8-inch tube pan or two 8-inch round cake pans with wax paper cut to fit. Beat the egg yolks until light and lemon-colored. Add ¾ cup of sugar and continue to beat well until creamy. Add orange juice and rind, if using, and beat an additional 2 or 3 minutes, or until well mixed. Sift together the salt, flour, and baking powder and beat in until well blended, another 2 minutes.

Beat the egg whites until soft peaks form. Gradually add the remaining ¼ cup of sugar, a tablespoon at a time, and continue beating until stiff and glossy, but not dry. Gently stir one-quarter of the whites into the batter. Carefully fold the remaining whites into the batter, until no specks of white are to be seen. Spoon the batter into the ungreased tube pan or cake tins. The tube pan will need 40 to 50 minutes; the layers about 25 minutes. It is done when the top springs back when touched lightly with the finger.

Invert the tube pan on a funnel or bottle; put the layers on a wire rack. Cool completely before removing from the pan. Cut around the sides and tube with a thin spatula and rap the pan sharply on a table edge to loosen the cake.

Yield: 1 8-inch cake or 2 layers.

Angel Food Cake

A worthy use for the egg whites you have been saving in your freezer.

1 cup sifted cake flour
1¼ cups superfine granulated
    sugar
1¼ cups egg whites (about 12) at
    room temperature
1¼ teaspoons cream of tartar
¼ teaspoon salt
1 teaspoon vanilla extract
1 teaspoon almond extract

Preheat the oven to 325 degrees. Sift the flour with ½ cup of sugar and set aside.

In a large bowl, beat the egg whites until foamy. Add the cream of tartar and salt and beat until soft peaks form. Add the vanilla and almond extract and beat in the remaining ¾ cup of sugar, 2 tablespoons at a time, and continue beating until stiff and glossy. Sift the flour and sugar over the egg whites and fold it in while sifting, cutting down through the center of the mixture with a wide rubber spatula, lifting a small amount, and turning it over. Move the bowl a quarter of a turn with each stroke to incorporate evenly. Cut and fold only until the flour disappears.

Bake in an ungreased tube pan for 55 to 60 minutes, or until the top springs back when lightly touched, or a cake tester comes out dry. Invert the pan on a bottle and let it hang until completely cooled. To remove the cake from the pan, loosen around the sides and tube with a spatula. Turn the pan over and hit the edge sharply to loosen.

Frost or leave plain as you prefer. Angel food cake does not freeze well; having no fat, it becomes tough. But slices of the cake are delicious toasted.

Yield: 1 10-inch cake.

Pineapple Upside-Down Cake

Upside-down cakes come out of the pan all finished and ready to be served warm or cool.

½ cup (1 stick) butter
¾ cup light brown sugar
7 slices canned pineapple, drained
½ cup pecan halves
3 eggs
1⅓ cups granulated sugar
½ cup water
1 teaspoon vanilla extract
Pinch salt
1½ cups all-purpose flour
1½ teaspoons baking powder
7 candied or Maraschino cherries

Preheat the oven to 325 degrees.

Melt the butter and brown sugar in a 10-inch cast-iron skillet. Tilt the pan so that the butter coats the sides. Arrange the pineapple slices over the bottom. Tuck the pecan halves around in the empty spaces. Remove from the stove and let cool.

In a large bowl, beat the eggs well with an electric beater; add the granulated sugar and beat for 5 minutes. Add the water and beat 5 minutes longer. Stir in the vanilla. In a separate bowl, combine the salt, flour, and baking powder and mix well. Fold the flour mixture into the egg mixture. Pour the batter gently over the pineapple slices. Bake for about 30 minutes, or until the cake begins to draw away from the sides of the pan and the top is light brown.

Cool on a wire rack for 5 minutes. Run a spatula around the outside edge of the cake to loosen it, if necessary. Cover the pan with a round platter and carefully invert it. Lift off the skillet. Fill the holes in the pineapple slices with the cherries. Serve warm with whipped cream or ice cream, if desired.

Yield: 8 to 10 servings.

Variation: Use canned apricots in place of the pineapple slices.

Chocolate Roll

A rich and delicate dessert, made without flour.

Cocoa for dusting the pan and the cooked cake
6 ounces semisweet chocolate
2 ounces double-strength coffee
2 ounces dark rum, or a chocolate- or coffee-flavored liqueur

Butter a 12 by 18-inch jelly roll pan. Line with foil and butter the foil well. Line with wax paper and butter heavily. Dust with cocoa. Shake out excess.

Heat the chocolate and coffee over hot water or a flame control device until melted and smooth. Stir often to prevent scorching. Remove from heat and add the rum or liqueur. Let cool.

6 eggs, separated
¾ cup sugar
Pinch of salt
1½ cups heavy cream
1 tablespoon confectioners' sugar
1 to 2 tablespoons rum or liqueur
   (optional)

Beat the egg yolks with an electric mixer until creamy. Add the sugar gradually and continue to beat until very thick and pale in color, about 10 minutes.

Mix the chocolate and yolk mixtures together. Beat the egg whites until foamy. Add the salt and continue to beat until stiff but not dry. Stir one-quarter of the whites into the chocolate mixture and fold in remaining whites until well mixed.

Preheat the oven to 350 degrees.

Spoon the mixture into the prepared pan. Spread evenly to all edges. Bake for 15 to 17 minutes, or just until cake begins to shrink from the edges and a cake tester comes out dry. Remove from the oven and place on a rack. Cover with a damp towel and let stand for 15 to 20 minutes.

Remove the towel and dust the cake with cocoa. Use a small strainer and sift the cocoa through it directly onto the cake. Arrange a large, dry towel over the cake. Invert the cake onto the towel. Carefully peel off the wax paper and cut off any crisp edges from the cake.

Whip the cream until soft mounds form. Add the confectioners' sugar and rum or liqueur, if desired, and continue to whip until stiff. Spread the whipped cream evenly over the cake.

Starting from the long side, lift the towel to help start the cake rolling. There may be a few cracks but they can be disguised.

Use a long stiff piece of cardboard or two large spatulas to transfer the cake roll, seam side down, to a serving dish. Sprinkle additional cocoa or confectioners' sugar on the cake. Pipe additional whipped cream on it to camouflage any cracks that occur. Slice and serve.

Yield: 8 servings.

Lemon Sponge Roll

¾ cup cake flour

1 teaspoon baking powder

4 eggs, separated, at room temperature

¾ cup superfine sugar

Pinch salt

⅛ teaspoon cream of tartar

Confectioners' sugar

Lemon filling (see page 545)

Preheat the oven to 400 degrees. Grease a 15 by 10 by 1-inch jelly roll pan. Line with wax paper and grease and lightly flour the paper. Sift together the flour and baking powder and set aside.

In a large mixing bowl, beat the egg yolks until thick and lemon-colored. Gradually add ½ cup of sugar and beat thoroughly until creamy. In a large bowl and with clean, dry beaters, beat the egg whites until foamy. Add the salt and cream of tartar and beat until soft peaks form. Beat in the remaining ¼ cup of sugar, 1 tablespoon at a time, and continue beating until stiff, glossy peaks form. Stir one-quarter of the whites into the yolk mixture and sprinkle the sifted flour and baking powder on top. Gently fold the flour into the egg yolks with a rubber spatula. Spoon the remaining egg whites over the top and fold in gently until well blended.

Spoon the batter into the pan and smooth the top. Bake for 10 to 12 minutes, or until delicately browned and the top springs back when touched lightly.

Spread a clean kitchen towel on a flat surface and sprinkle the towel with confectioners' sugar. Loosen the edges of the cake with a spatula and immediately invert on the towel. You will need to work quickly, for these cakes must be rolled while they are still warm and pliable. Lift off the pan and peel off the wax paper. Cut off the crisp edges of the cake with a sharp knife. Starting at the long side, carefully roll up both the cake and towel. Cool the roll on a rack, seam side down. The towel prevents the cake from sticking to itself.

Carefully unroll the cake when it is completely cool and remove the towel. Spread the filling over the cake to within ½ inch of all the edges. Reroll the cake and place it on a serving platter. It can be sprinkled with confectioners' sugar or garnished with a few rosettes of whipped cream.

Yield: 8 to 10 servings.

Variations: The sponge roll may be filled with sweetened whipped cream, with jam, or with whipped cream combined with a few fresh blueberries, raspberries, or tiny cantaloupe balls.

Amaretti Torte

Tortes are cakes in which crumbs or ground nuts are used in place of flour. Amaretti cookies are crisp, Italian macaroons that are delicious by themselves and a great cooking ingredient, as you will see in this moist, rich cake. It improves on standing, so make it a day in advance of serving.

⅔ cup amaretti crumbs

1 cup butter

1 cup sugar

5 eggs, separated, at room temperature

⅓ cup all-purpose flour

4 ounces semisweet chocolate, grated or chopped

1 tablespoon Amaretto liqueur (optional)

Confectioners' sugar

Butter a 10-inch springform pan. Sprinkle the bottom and sides with cocoa and tap out excess. Process enough amaretti cookies in a food processor or blender to give you ⅔ cup of crumbs. Set aside.

Cream the butter and ¾ cup of sugar until very light and fluffy. Beat in the egg yolks, one at a time. After the last yolk is added, beat for 10 to 12 minutes. Stir in the crumbs and the flour and beat until well blended. Add the chocolate and liqueur and beat again.

Preheat the oven to 350 degrees.

Beat the whites until soft peaks form. Add the remaining ¼ cup sugar slowly and continue to beat until stiff, glossy peaks form. Stir one-third of the whites into the batter and fold in the remaining whites gently, incorporating them well.

Spoon the batter into the pan and bake for 45 to 60 minutes. The outer border should be firm and the center soft. Remove from the oven and immediately run a knife around the edge of the torte. The cake will sink slightly. Cool the cake for 30 minutes on a wire rack. Remove the rim of the springform. Sprinkle confectioners' sugar over the top of the cake.

Yield: 8 to 10 servings.

Nut Torte

This looks like a three-layer cake when cut, with the torte base, apricot jam, and cream topping.

4 eggs, separated
1¼ cups sugar
3 tablespoons dark rum
2 cups ground walnuts (about 8 ounces)
¾ teaspoon gelatin
1 tablespoon cold water
1½ cups heavy cream
½ cup apricot jam

Preheat the oven to 325 degrees.

Beat the egg yolks with an electric mixer, adding ¾ cup of sugar and the rum gradually. Beat until very thick and the mixture falls from the beater into a ribbon.

Beat the egg whites until soft peaks form. Gradually add the remaining ½ cup of sugar and beat until stiff, glossy peaks form.

Stir one-quarter of the whites and all of the nuts into the egg yolk mixture. Fold the remaining egg whites into the mixture using a large rubber spatula or your hands. Pour into a 10-inch spring-form pan with only the bottom buttered. Bake for 50 to 60 minutes, or until golden brown and a cake tester comes out dry.

Remove from the oven and immediately run a spatula or knife around the edge of the cake. Allow to cool for 20 to 30 minutes on a wire rack; remove the sides of the pan. Cool completely.

Combine the gelatin and cold water in a heatproof cup. Place the cup in a pan of hot water and stir until the gelatin is clear and completely dissolved. Beat the cream until it thickens and slowly add the dissolved gelatin. Continue beating until thick.

Carefully spread the jam on top of the cake, which will have cracks, but the jam and the cream topping will hide them. Pipe or smooth the cream on top of the cake. Refrigerate until cream is set.

Yield: 8 to 10 servings.

New York-Style Cheesecake

There are as many versions of cheesecake as there are bakers, but this is a creamy, rich, and delicious one.

1 pound cream cheese, at room temperature
1 pound ricotta cheese
1½ cups sugar
4 eggs
3 tablespoons cornstarch
3 tablespoons flour
Juice of one lemon
1 teaspoon vanilla extract
½ cup (1 stick) butter, melted
1 pint sour cream

Preheat the oven to 250 degrees. Grease a 9- to 10-inch spring-form pan and set aside.

With an electric mixer, beat the cream cheese and ricotta together until smooth and well mixed. Gradually add the sugar, eggs, cornstarch, flour, lemon juice, and vanilla. Blend well. Add the butter and sour cream. Beat until well mixed and smooth.

Pour into the prepared pan and bake for 1 hour. Turn oven off and let the cake stand undisturbed 8 hours or overnight in the turned-off oven. Remove and run a knife around the sides of the cheesecake. Remove the sides and refrigerate the cake until well chilled.

Yield: 12 to 16 servings.

Note: If you wish, you may serve fresh strawberries, blueberries, or raspberries with this cake. We prefer it unadorned.

Chocolate Cheesecake

1½ pounds cream cheese, at room temperature
1 cup granulated sugar
4 eggs
1½ tablespoons flour
1½ tablespoons cornstarch
8 ounces semisweet chocolate, melted
1 cup sour cream
½ cup strong coffee, *or* ¼ cup coffee and ¼ cup rum or coffee- or chocolate-flavored liqueur
1 teaspoon vanilla extract
Confectioners' sugar (optional)

Preheat the oven to 250 degrees. Grease a 10-inch springform pan.

In a large bowl, beat the cream cheese with an electric mixer until smooth. Gradually add the sugar, eggs, flour, and cornstarch and beat until blended. Add the melted chocolate, sour cream, coffee, and vanilla and beat until smooth.

Pour the batter into the pan and bake for 1 hour. Turn oven off and let the cake remain undisturbed 8 hours or overnight. Remove from the oven and run a knife or spatula around the sides of the cake. Remove the sides of the pan. Refrigerate the cake until very cold. Sprinkle with confectioners' sugar, if desired, before serving.

Yield: 10 to 12 servings.

Uncooked Confectioners' Glaze

Sift 1¼ cups confectioners' sugar. Mix with 1 to 2 tablespoons water, liqueur, or lemon or orange juice. Beat until smooth. Brush on pastries or cakes.

Fluffy White Frosting I

1½ cups sugar
¼ cup water
2 egg whites
2 tablespoons light corn syrup
½ teaspoon salt
1 teaspoon vanilla extract

Combine all the ingredients except the vanilla in a heatproof bowl. Place over simmering water and beat with an electric mixer or a wire whisk until it triples in volume and holds stiff peaks. Remove from the heat and beat in the vanilla. Spread on cake while the frosting is still a bit warm. This will fill and frost an 8- or 9-inch 2-layer cake.

Fluffy White Frosting II

½ cup boiling water
1 cup sugar
1 egg white
¼ teaspoon cream of tartar
1 teaspoon vanilla extract

Combine all the ingredients except the vanilla in the small bowl of an electric beater. Beat at high speed for 10 minutes, or until it holds stiff peaks. Beat in the vanilla. This will frost the top and sides of an 8- or 9-inch 2-layer cake.

Uncooked Chocolate Fudge Frosting

4 squares unsweetened chocolate
½ cup (1 stick) butter
1 pound (3½ cups) confectioners' sugar
½ cup milk or light cream
2 teaspoons vanilla extract

Melt the chocolate and butter over very low heat, or in a small bowl over simmering water. Remove from the heat when it is almost melted and stir until smooth. Cool to lukewarm. Combine the sugar, milk, and vanilla. Add chocolate mixture to sugar and beat with a wooden spoon until thick and spreadable. This will fill and frost an 8- or 9-inch 2-layer cake.

Chocolate Sour Cream Frosting

1 12-ounce package semisweet chocolate bits
½ teaspoon salt
1 cup sour cream

Melt the chocolate over very low heat or in a bowl over simmering water. Remove from the heat when it is almost melted and stir until smooth. Cool to lukewarm. Stir in the salt and sour cream. Ice cake at once. This will frost an 8- or 9-inch 2-layer cake.

Chocolate Cream Cheese Frosting

1 12-ounce package semisweet chocolate
1 8-ounce package cream cheese, softened
1 teaspoon vanilla extract
½ teaspoon salt
2 tablespoons milk or cream
1 pound (3½ cups) confectioners' sugar

Melt the chocolate over very low heat or in a bowl over simmering water. Remove from the heat when it is almost melted and stir until smooth. Cool. In a large mixing bowl, combine the chocolate, cream cheese, vanilla, and salt and beat well. Add the milk and gradually beat in the sugar until smooth. This is enough to fill and frost an 8- or 9-inch 2-layer cake.

Fluffy Mocha Frosting

1½ cups sugar
⅓ cup cold water
2 egg whites, unbeaten
2 teaspoons instant coffee
¼ teaspoon cream of tartar
Pinch salt
1 teaspoon vanilla extract
2 ounces unsweetened chocolate, melted and cooled

In a heatproof bowl, combine the sugar, water, egg whites, instant coffee, cream of tartar, and salt. Beat with an electric beater just until blended. Place over a pot of simmering water (not touching) and cook and beat until stiff peaks form, about 7 minutes. Add vanilla and the cooled melted chocolate, and beat until well blended and of spreading consistency. This is enough to fill and frost an 8- or 9-inch 2-layer cake.

Chocolate Glaze

½ cup semisweet chocolate bits
2 tablespoons butter
1 tablespoon light corn syrup

Combine all ingredients in a heavy-bottomed saucepan and stir over very low heat until the chocolate is melted and the mixture is smooth. Spread over cake at once. This is enough to cover the top of an 8- or 9-inch cake.

Cream Cheese Frosting

1½ cups confectioners' sugar
3 ounces cream cheese, softened
1 tablespoon milk
1 teaspoon vanilla extract

Beat together the confectioners' sugar and cream cheese until blended. Stir in the milk and vanilla and beat until creamy. If you wish a thinner glaze, add more milk, a few drops at a time, until the proper consistency is reached. This will frost a 10-inch cake.

Caramel Frosting

⅔ cup butter
1¼ cups firmly packed brown sugar
Pinch salt
⅓ cup milk
2 cups confectioners' sugar

Melt the butter over low heat and add the brown sugar and salt. Cook until smooth, stirring constantly, 2 or 3 minutes. Add the milk and continue to heat and stir until the mixture comes to a boil. Remove from the heat and cool to room temperature. Add the confectioners' sugar gradually, beating until well blended with an electric beater. If the frosting seems too thin, beat in 1 tablespoon of confectioners' sugar at a time until the proper consistency is reached. This will fill and frost an 8-inch 2-layer cake.

Butter Cream Frosting

½ cup soft butter
3 cups confectioners' sugar
1 egg yolk
3 to 4 tablespoons milk or light cream
1 teaspoon vanilla extract

Cream the butter and add half the sugar gradually. Cream well. Add the egg yolk and beat until the mixture is fluffy. Add the remaining sugar alternately with the milk or cream. Use only enough liquid to give the frosting the proper consistency for spreading. Beat in the vanilla extract. This will fill and frost an 8- or 9-inch 2-layer cake, or a 9 by 12-inch rectangle, or a 10-inch tube cake.

Chocolate Butter Cream. Blend 2 ounces melted unsweetened chocolate into the creamed butter and proceed as above.

Almond Butter Cream. Substitute ½ teaspoon almond extract for vanilla.

Mocha Butter Cream. Blend in ¼ cup unsweetened cocoa and 1 teaspoon instant coffee with the creamed butter.

Lemon or Orange Butter Cream. Use lemon juice or orange juice in place of milk and omit vanilla. Beat in the grated rind of 1 lemon or 1 orange.

Lemon Filling

1 cup sugar
2½ tablespoons flour
¼ cup lemon juice
1 egg
1 tablespoon butter

Combine all the ingredients in a small, **heavy-bottomed** saucepan and cook over low heat, stirring constantly until **thick and smooth.**

Cool completely, then chill before spreading on sponge roll or using as a layer cake filling.

Raisin Cream Filling

⅔ cup sugar
2 egg yolks
⅔ cup light cream
1 cup seedless raisins
¼ teaspoon vanilla
½ cup coarsely chopped pecans
   or walnuts

In a small bowl, beat sugar and egg yolks until creamy, thick, and light-colored. Transfer to a heavy-bottomed 1-quart saucepan. Add the cream and raisins and cook over very low heat, stirring constantly, until slightly thickened, 6 or 7 minutes. Remove from the heat and stir in vanilla and nuts. When cool, spread between cake layers.

Orange Custard Filling

½ cup sugar
3 tablespoons cornstarch
Pinch salt
1 teaspoon grated orange peel
⅔ cup orange juice
2 egg yolks, lightly beaten
1 tablespoon butter

In a small saucepan, combine the sugar, cornstarch, and salt. Stir in the orange peel and orange juice. Cook and stir over medium heat until the mixture comes to a boil and is thickened and smooth. Slowly stir about ½ cup of the mixture into the lightly beaten egg yolks and return the egg yolks slowly to the saucepan. Cook and stir over low heat 1 or 2 minutes longer, until very thick. Remove from the heat and stir the butter into the custard. Cover the surface with plastic wrap or wax paper and cool. Refrigerate when cooled. Spread the custard between cooked cake layers.

Pecan Filling

1 teaspoon cornstarch
⅓ cup sugar
2 tablespoons butter
3 egg yolks, well beaten
⅔ cup milk
Pinch salt
½ teaspoon vanilla extract
1 cup pecans, coarsely chopped

Combine the cornstarch and sugar; cream with the butter. Add the beaten egg yolks and milk and beat well. Pour into a heavy-bottomed pan and, over low heat, cook and stir until the mixture thickens and coats the spoon. Do not allow it to come to a boil. Add the salt and vanilla and cool. Chill when cooled. Stir in the nuts and spread filling between two cake layers.

Cookies

There is a great deal of satisfaction in baking cookies. A fresh homemade batch can provide a family treat with little effort, and there is a great variety to choose from. There are bar cookies, for which the batter is spread in a pan, baked, and cut into squares or rectangles; molded or shaped cookies, which are made with a stiff dough shaped into balls or crescents; refrigerator cookies, made from dough shaped into a roll, chilled thoroughly, and sliced thin; pressed cookies, which are pushed through a cookie press into interesting forms; and rolled cookies, cut out of rolled dough with a cookie cutter. And then there are the ubiquitous drop cookies, pushed from a spoon or through a pastry tube onto cookie sheets. Among the most popular of this last category are the Toll House cookies, and you can't do better than the recipe printed on the packages of semisweet chocolate morsels. Except for bar cookies, all the other types may be made from the basic butter cookie recipe that follows.

Equipment

Use sturdy baking sheets, preferably of shiny, heavy aluminum with low sides that will not deflect the heat. Most cookies will not bake properly in pans with high sides. Bar cookies, such as brownies, are baked in greased pans 1½ to 2 inches deep. Large baking sheets are a convenience because they hold a lot of cookies, but make sure that there are at least 2 inches of space between the cookie tins and the sides of the oven so that the heat can circulate freely.

Ingredients

All-purpose flour and granulated sugar are suitable for almost all cookies. Superfine sugar is recommended for meringues, however, because it dissolves easily. You can fashion your own by whirling granulated sugar through the blender for a minute or two. Many cookie recipes call for soft shortening, which means a solid shortening that has been allowed to stand at room temperature until it will cream easily by hand or with an electric mixer. If you are mixing by hand, use a long-handled wooden spoon; it will make thorough mixing easier.

Baking

A rich cookie dough, like a rich pie dough, doesn't need a greased pan, but a light greasing offers insurance against the possibility of sticking, and it won't do any harm. Solid vegetable shortening, if you happen to have it on hand, is even better than butter for greasing cookie sheets, because it does not brown as readily.

Ideally, it is best to bake cookies one sheet at a time on the center rack, unless the oven is big enough to accommodate two tins, side by side. However, you can bake two tins at a time on separate racks by placing the first sheet of cookies on the lower rack and, when they are almost done, moving them to the upper rack and sliding another sheet onto the lower rack. As a time-saver for one-sheet baking, place the second batch of unbaked cookies on a sheet of cooking parchment or lightly greased aluminum foil (shiny side up) cut to the size of the baking sheet. The paper can be transferred to the cookie sheet immediately after the first batch is baked.

Be a clock watcher or set your kitchen timer when cookies are in the oven, They bake so quickly it's easy to forget them. Baking times can vary; if you like cookies soft and chewy, keep them in the oven for less time than called for and if you like them crisp, let them bake a bit longer.

Cool cookies on wire racks in a single layer. They can stick together if they are stacked before they are completely cool.

Frosted Chocolate Cookies

2 squares unsweetened chocolate
½ cup butter
1½ cups light brown sugar
1 egg, well beaten
½ cup buttermilk or yogurt
1½ cups all-purpose flour
¼ teaspoon baking powder
½ teaspoon baking soda
½ teaspoon salt

Preheat the oven to 375 degrees. Grease the cookie sheets.

Melt the chocolate over boiling water or very low heat, stirring to prevent scorching. When melted, remove from the heat and set aside.

Cream the butter, add the sugar, and cream until fluffy. Mix in the well-beaten egg and buttermilk or yogurt. Blend in the melted chocolate. In a separate bowl, mix together the flour, baking powder, baking soda, and salt. Stir into the creamed mixture until smooth.

Drop by teaspoonfuls onto the cookie sheet, leaving generous space between each. Bake for 10 to 12 minutes. Cool on wire racks. Frost when cool.

Yield: About 70 cookies.

Frosting

1 egg, well beaten
1 teaspoon heavy cream
1¾ cups confectioners' sugar
1 square unsweetened chocolate, melted

Combine all the ingredients and beat well until smooth.

Basic Butter Cookies

This is an all-purpose recipe that may be used for drop, pressed, shaped, or refrigerator cookies. Have all ingredients at room temperature.

½ cup (1 stick) butter
½ cup sugar
2 egg yolks
1 teaspoon vanilla extract
1 cup all-purpose flour

Preheat the oven to 350 degrees. Grease the baking sheet. Cream the butter and sugar until light and fluffy, by hand or in the large bowl of an electric mixer. Add the egg yolks and vanilla and beat well. Add the flour and beat only until mixed through. Overbeating will develop the gluten, which will give you a tough instead of a tender cookie.

Shape cookies according to your choice (see instructions below), arrange on the baking sheet, and bake in the center rack of a preheated oven. Bake for 8 to 10 minutes, or until the edges are lightly brown and the centers just firm to the touch. Remove and cool on wire racks.

Yield: About 30 cookies.

Drop Cookies. Use one teaspoon to hold the dough and another to scrape the dough from the spoon onto the baking sheet. Drop by spoonfuls onto the baking sheet, leaving at least 2 inches between mounds.

Rolled Cookies. The dough must be well chilled. After preparing it, flatten it into a ½-inch-thick rectangle and wrap it in wax paper, plastic, or aluminum foil. Refrigerate for 1 hour, or until firm. Roll out between two sheets of wax paper to slightly less than ¼ inch thick. Leave the paper in place and chill in the refrigerator for another 30 minutes. With a cookie cutter or a small glass, cut as many shapes as possible. Place them on buttered baking sheets, leaving an inch between cookies. Refrigerate for 30 minutes longer. While this is chilling, gather up the scraps, reroll, refrigerate, and repeat as above until all is used.

Piped Cookies. The dough must be well chilled. Wrap it in plastic wrap and refrigerate it for an hour. Fill a cookie press or a pastry bag fitted with a star-shaped tube with the cookie dough. Pipe the cookies onto the prepared sheet, leaving about an inch between cookies. Chill for 30 minutes before baking. If at any time the dough becomes too soft to hold its shape, chill it in the refrigerator.

Refrigerator Cookies. Shape the dough into a long cylinder, 1½ to 2 inches in diameter. Wrap in wax paper, plastic, or foil and chill it overnight, or about 12 hours. Cut slices a scant ¼ inch thick with a sharp knife and bake on a buttered cookie sheet, leaving space between cookies. For added visual interest, roll the cylinder in finely chopped nuts mixed with cinnamon or cocoa before slicing. The dough can be kept in the refrigerator for a week and you can cut and bake as needed.

Decorating. Cookies may be glazed before they are baked with a brushing of milk, cream, or lightly beaten egg white and sprinkled with a mixture of cinnamon and sugar (2 tablespoons sugar to ½ teaspoon cinnamon) or with finely chopped nuts. For a shiny finish, brush the cookies after baking with warm corn syrup.

Old-Fashioned Molasses Cookies

Chewy, dark, country-style cookies.

1 cup brown sugar
1 cup vegetable shortening or butter
1 egg
½ teaspoon salt
¼ cup dark molasses
¼ cup maple syrup
½ cup warm water
1 teaspoon baking soda
1 teaspoon cinnamon
1 teaspoon freshly grated nutmeg
2¼ to 2½ cups all-purpose flour

Preheat the oven to 350 degrees. Grease cookie sheets.

In the large bowl of an electric mixer, beat the brown sugar and shortening at low speed until creamy. Add, one after another and beating in between, the egg, salt, molasses, maple syrup, water, baking soda, cinnamon, and nutmeg. Beat in enough flour to give you the consistency for drop cookies. Blend at medium speed until smooth.

Drop by teaspoonfuls onto the cookie sheet, leaving at least 2 inches between. Bake for about 10 minutes and remove while they are still a little soft, unless you prefer them very crisp. Cool on wire racks. Store in an airtight tin to keep them from drying out.

Yield: About 60 cookies.

Raisin-Nut Chocolate Chip Cookies

½ pound (2 sticks) butter
¾ cup firmly packed brown sugar
¾ cup granulated sugar
1 teaspoon vanilla extract
2 eggs
2½ cups flour
1 teaspoon baking soda
½ teaspoon salt
2 cups dark raisins
1 cup coarsely chopped Brazil nuts, pecans, or walnuts
1 12-ounce package semisweet chocolate bits

Preheat the oven to 375 degrees. Grease a large baking sheet.

Cream the butter and sugars together until very creamy and fluffy. Stir in the remaining ingredients and mix well. Drop by spoonfuls onto a baking sheet, 1 to 1½ inches apart (the cookies will spread as they bake). Bake for 6 to 8 minutes, or until browned. Remove and cool on a rack.

Yield: About 7 dozen.

Chocolate Macaroons

Cocoa for dusting cookie sheet
1 6-ounce package semisweet chocolate bits
1 can (or 6-ounce package) coconut
2 teaspoons vanilla extract
6 egg whites
Pinch of salt
½ cup superfine sugar

Preheat the oven to 350 degrees. Grease a cookie sheet and dust with cocoa.

Melt the chocolate over hot water, or use a flame control device. Remove from the heat and stir in the coconut and vanilla. Set aside.

Beat the egg whites until foamy. Add salt and continue to beat until soft peaks form. Add the sugar gradually and beat until glossy stiff peaks form.

Fold the whites into the chocolate mixture. Drop by spoonfuls onto the baking sheet, leaving space between. Bake for 10 to 12 minutes. Remove from the pan and cool on a rack.

Yield: About 2 dozen.

Pine Nut Cookies

¼ pound (1 stick) butter
½ cup granulated sugar
1 egg yolk
1 teaspoon vanilla extract
1 cup all-purpose flour
½ cup pine nuts

Preheat the oven to 350 degrees. Grease and flour a baking sheet.

Cream the butter and sugar until light and fluffy. Beat in the remaining ingredients.

Drop by teaspoonfuls onto the baking sheet. Bake for 20 to 25 minutes, or until golden. Remove and cool on a rack.

Yield: About 3 dozen.

Meringue Kisses

These delicate cookies are universal favorites. They require long, slow cooking if they are to be properly crisp.

3 egg whites, at room temperature
¼ teaspoon cream of tartar
Pinch salt
1 cup superfine sugar
1 teaspoon vanilla extract

Line cookie sheets with parchment paper or aluminum foil, or grease and flour the sheets. Preheat the oven (see below).

With an electric beater, beat the egg whites at low speed until just foamy. Add the cream of tartar and salt and increase the speed to moderate. Beat until soft peaks form. Continue to beat and add the sugar slowly, a tablespoon at a time. When half the sugar has been added, add the vanilla, and continue adding the sugar as before until the meringue is very stiff and glossy. Using a pastry bag or two spoons, drop the meringues on the baking sheet, allowing an inch between each. Do not allow the meringue to stand; shape the cookies and bake them immediately. Meringues may be baked in a preheated 225-degree oven for 1 hour and then left in the turned-off oven for another 3 or 4 hours, or until completely cooled. Or place them in an oven preheated to 400 degrees, immediately turn off the heat, and leave the cookies undisturbed in the oven overnight. Do not open the oven door until you are ready to remove the meringues. The cookies can fall if they are exposed to a blast of cold air.

Yield: 2 dozen small meringues.

Chocolate Nut Meringues. Lightly fold into the stiffly beaten whites a 6-ounce package of semisweet chocolate bits and 1 cup coarsely chopped nuts.

Date Nut Kisses. Lightly fold into the stiffly beaten whites 1 cup dates cut into small pieces and 1 cup broken pecans.

Almond Crescents

½ pound (2 sticks) butter at room temperature
5 tablespoons sugar
2 cups all-purpose flour
1 cup finely ground almonds
1 cup vanilla-flavored confectioners' sugar (see note)

Preheat the oven to 325 degrees. Lightly butter a cookie sheet.

Combine the butter, sugar, flour, and ground almonds in a mixing bowl. Mix with your fingertips until all the ingredients are blended together and form a dough. Take a small handful of the dough and roll it into a long, thin roll about the thickness of a cocktail frankfurter. Break off pieces about 2 inches long and shape them into neat little crescents with tapered ends. Place them on the cookie sheet, leaving an inch of space between. Bake for 20 to 25 minutes. Don't let them brown; they are done when you can see a faint golden tinge near the bottom. Remove from the oven and, with a wide metal spatula, transfer them to a rack to cool. Place a mound of confectioners' sugar on a large piece of wax paper on the counter and roll the crescents in the sugar while still slightly warm.

Store the cookies in an airtight container. They will stay fresh for a week or more.

Yield: About 5 dozen.

Note: Vanilla-flavored confectioners' sugar is a convenient thing to have on hand as a topping for a variety of cakes and cookies. Cut a vanilla bean into ½-inch pieces and scatter them through a closed jar of confectioners' sugar. In a few days, the sugar will absorb the subtle vanilla flavor.

Ginger Cookies

2 cups all-purpose flour, sifted
1 tablespoon ground ginger
2 teaspoons baking soda
1 teaspoon cinnamon
½ teaspoon salt
¾ cup (1½ sticks) butter
1 cup sugar
1 egg
¼ cup molasses
Granulated sugar for dipping

Preheat the oven to 350 degrees. Sift flour and sift again with ginger, baking soda, cinnamon, and salt. Return to the sifter and set aside. With an electric beater, cream the butter; add the sugar gradually and beat until light and fluffy. Beat in the egg and molasses. Sift one-third of the flour mixture over the molasses mixture and stir to blend well. Repeat until all the flour is incorporated. Roll the dough into small balls about the size of a walnut between the palms of the hands. Roll the balls in the granulated sugar and place on ungreased baking sheets a good 2 inches apart. Bake for 12 minutes, or until tops are slightly rounded and crackly. Remove with a broad spatula and let cool on wire racks. Store in an airtight tin when completely cooled.

Yield: About 4 dozen.

Butter Rings

1 cup butter
½ cup confectioners' sugar
1 hard-boiled egg yolk, sieved
1 raw egg yolk
1 teaspoon vanilla extract
2¼ cups all-purpose flour
1 egg white, lightly beaten
Granulated sugar

Cream the butter until softened, add the sugar, and cream until light and fluffy. Add the sieved egg yolk, the raw egg yolk, and vanilla and blend well. Stir in the flour and mix until smooth. Flatten the dough into a disk and wrap in wax paper or aluminum foil. Chill for a few hours until firm.

Preheat the oven to 350 degrees. Lightly grease a cookie sheet. Work with a small amount of dough at a time, keeping the rest chilled. Break off pieces of dough about the size of a walnut and roll out to a length of 6 inches. Shape in a circle with the two ends overlapping each other about an inch from the ends. Place on cookie sheet, leaving about 1½ inches between each. Brush lightly with egg white and sprinkle with sugar. Bake for about 12 minutes, or until lightly golden on the bottom. Cool on wire racks.

Yield: About 3 dozen.

Peanut Butter Cookies

1 cup butter
1 cup peanut butter
1½ cups granulated sugar
½ cup brown sugar
2 eggs, well beaten
3 cups flour
¾ teaspoon baking soda
¾ teaspoon baking powder
1 teaspoon freshly grated nutmeg
¼ teaspoon salt
Superfine sugar for dusting

Cream the butter and peanut butter until well blended and fluffy. Gradually add the two sugars, creaming until light. Mix in the well-beaten eggs. In a separate bowl, mix together the flour, baking soda, baking powder, nutmeg, and salt. Add the flour mixture to the creamed mixture and stir until incorporated and smooth. Divide the dough in half and roll each half into a 2-inch cylinder. Wrap and chill in the refrigerator for at least 2 hours.

Preheat the oven to 375 degrees. Grease cookie sheets. Slice off thin cookies from the roll and place them on the cookie sheet, leaving 1 to 1½ inches between each. Sprinkle with the superfine sugar and bake on the center rack for 10 to 12 minutes. Cool on a wire rack.

Yield: About 7 dozen.

Brownies

You may cut this recipe in half, but the brownies are so fudgy and delicious (and freeze so well), you'll be glad you didn't.

4 squares unsweetened chocolate
½ pound (2 sticks) butter
2 cups sugar
1 teaspoon vanilla extract
4 eggs, lightly beaten
1½ cups all-purpose flour
Pinch salt
1½ cups coarsely broken walnuts

Grease a 9 by 13-inch baking pan, 2 inches high. Preheat the oven to 350 degrees.

Melt the chocolate in a double boiler over simmering water or in a heavy-bottomed saucepan over very low heat. Watch carefully to make sure it does not scorch. Cool.

Cream the butter and sugar until light and fluffy. Stir in the cooled chocolate and vanilla. Add the lightly beaten eggs and stir until smooth and blended. Fold in the flour and salt until well blended. Stir in the walnuts.

Spread the batter evenly in the baking pan, smoothing it out with a spatula. (For half the recipe, use an 8 by 8-inch pan.) Bake for 30 to 35 minutes, or until shiny and firm on top. Do not overbake. Cool pan on wire rack. Cut into squares or oblongs when cool.

Yield: About 48 brownies.

Oatmeal Fruit Squares

4 tablespoons (½ stick) butter
1 cup brown sugar, firmly packed
1 egg
1 teaspoon vanilla extract
¼ cup all-purpose flour
1 teaspoon baking powder
¼ teaspoon salt
¾ cup rolled oats
¾ cup dried currants or raisins
½ cup coarsely chopped walnuts
Confectioners' sugar

Preheat the oven to 350 degrees. Grease an 8-inch-square baking pan.

In a small saucepan over low heat, melt the butter with the brown sugar and stir until the sugar is dissolved. Cool slightly. In a medium-size bowl, beat the egg lightly and stir in the butter-sugar mixture. Stir in the vanilla. Blend together the flour, baking powder, and salt and stir into the egg mixture with the oats, currants or raisins, and walnuts. Transfer to the baking pan and bake for 25 minutes, or until golden brown and a cake tester comes out dry. Cool on wire rack. Sprinkle lightly with confectioners' sugar. Cut into 16 squares while still slightly warm.

Yield: 16 squares.

13
Refrigerator Desserts

Unlike most of the preceding chapters, in which heat plays a major role in the preparation of food, the star performer in this section is cold—chilling and freezing temperatures that perform the final "cooking" of an infinite number of refreshing, taste-pleasing dishes. They range from light airy mousses, Bavarian creams, and fruit jellies to ice cream, sherbets, and ices. Refrigerator preparations make first-rate company fare because they must be made well in advance and generally require no attention until the moment of serving.

Mousses

Cold mousses come in endless variety. Common to all is their airy, velvety texture. Sometimes gelatin is added for firmness, or whipped cream or beaten egg white for lightness. (For more about gelatin, see following section.)

Sweet mousses, either chilled or frozen, make lovely desserts for dinner parties. Chocolate, mocha, lemon, orange, or other fruit-based mousses are light enough to follow even the most substantial dinner. Many mousses are firm enough to be unmolded. If possible, use molds made of metal for these. Glass and ceramic molds will work, but metal is preferable because it is a good conductor and chills quickly. To make unmolding easier, brush the inside lightly with vegetable oil before filling it. Don't use butter, which will harden when cold and look unattractive. The vegetable spray-on coatings that keep foods from sticking are also effective. Wetting the mold with water before filling it is also helpful in unmolding.

A cold dessert soufflé, or soufflé glacé, is merely a mousse in disguise. It has nothing to do with an oven-baked soufflé, although it looks as if it had risen like one. This illusion is achieved by chilling or freezing the mousse in a soufflé dish prepared with a collar that extends above the rim. The dish is filled with the mousse to the very top of the collar. After the dessert is frozen and the collar removed, the effect is of a towering soufflé. Soufflés glacés are either chilled or frozen; the frozen ones do not contain gelatin.

To prepare a collar, use a piece of aluminum foil or waxed paper long enough to wrap around the soufflé dish and overlap a few inches. Fold it in half lengthwise. Brush the top half of one side with tasteless vegetable oil, to make it easy to remove the collar before serving. Wrap the collar around the soufflé dish so that it extends 3 or 4 inches above the rim, oiled side up and facing in. Tie securely around the dish with string or fasten with straight pins.

Cut a collar longer than the circumference of the soufflé dish and wide enough so that, doubled, it reaches 3 inches above the rim. Fold lengthwise, oil the inside upper surface, and tie around the dish.

Whipping Cream. For success in whipping cream, the cream, bowl, and beaters should be very cold so that the butterfat remains firm. Chill the bowl and beaters in the refrigerator or freezer before using. For all frozen desserts, the cream should be whipped only until it barely mounds; it will stiffen further when added to the base. If cream is overbeaten in frozen desserts, the finished product will have an unpleasantly buttery taste. On the other hand, cream that is used to decorate cakes or to top a dessert should be whipped until stiff.

Gelatin and Its Uses

Gelatin is a tasteless organic substance, basically a protein derived from collagenous connective tissue, that can solidify or set liquids. It must be used in correct proportions because too much in a preparation will give you a rubbery, overly firm result and too little won't set your mold. One envelope of gelatin contains 1 tablespoon, which will set 2 cups of liquid mixed with 2 cups of solid ingredients. If you are using gelatin to line a mold and you want a firm coating, use 1 envelope of gelatin for each 1½ cups of liquid.

The unflavored gelatin must be softened first in cold liquid and then dissolved in hot. If this is not done, the gelatin will solidify in rubbery strands and lumps instead of forming a smooth, even jelly. To soften, sprinkle the gelatin over cold water or other cold liquid in the proportion of 1 envelope to ¼ cup liquid. It will soften in three or four minutes. Then stir it over moderate heat until the granules dissolve completely. If you want to add the gelatin to liquid that is already hot, you may do so, but only *after* it has softened in cold liquid.

If gelatin mixture is to be beaten, it must first be cooled until it reaches the consistency of thick egg white. When whipped at this stage, it will double in volume. Whipped cream should be added only after the gelatin has reached the thick egg white consistency or the gelatin will not be able to support the air bubbles in the cream, and the mixture will separate.

If fruits are to be combined with gelatin, the mixture should be cooled and allowed to stand until it is the thickness of thick egg white. The gelatin will be thick enough at this stage to keep the fruit from floating. Uncooked fruit is especially likely to float because of the pockets of air in the fruit cells. Gelatin will not set a mixture with raw pineapple because of an enzyme in the pineapple. However, cooked or canned pineapple will not interfere with the setting action because the enzyme has been destroyed in the cooking or processing.

Unmolding

The unmolding process will be easier if the mold was lightly oiled with salad oil or rinsed with cold water before being filled.

To unmold, fill a bowl that is larger than the mold with warm water. Dip the mold into the water just to the rim and hold it for a few seconds. Remove it from the water and run a thin knife carefully around the edge. This breaks the air seal that is holding the gelatin to the mold. By loosening it, you allow the air to come between the gelatin and the container. Place a large, flat plate over the top of the mold; hold the plate firmly and invert them. Shake gently, holding the serving dish tightly to the mold. The mold should lift off easily. If it doesn't, cover the mold with a hot, damp towel and let it sit for a few minutes.

1 *After dipping the mold in water for a few seconds, run the tip of a knife around the edge to break the seal.*

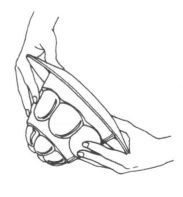

2 *Put a plate over the mold and, holding the plate and mold tightly together, turn them over, shaking slightly to loosen the jelly. Set them down with the plate on the bottom, and lift off the mold.*

Chocolate Mousse

The lightest and airiest of all mousses.

6 ounces sweet chocolate

2 ounces unsweetened chocolate

6 large eggs, separated, at room temperature

3 tablespoons water

4 tablespoons orange liqueur, such as Grand Marnier or Curaçao

2 cups whipping cream

7 tablespoons superfine sugar

Additional whipped cream and grated chocolate for garnish

Break the sweet and unsweetened chocolate into small chunks and melt carefully over hot water or very low heat. Watch it carefully to make sure it doesn't scorch. Set aside to cool.

Put the egg yolks in a heavy-bottomed saucepan and add the water. With the pan over very low heat or a flame control pad, beat continuously and vigorously with a wire whisk. When the yolks start to thicken, add the liqueur, and continue beating. The mixture must not be allowed to get too hot or the eggs will curdle. When the mixture becomes thick and creamy, remove it from the heat. Fold in the melted chocolate and transfer the sauce to a mixing bowl.

Beat the cream until it mounds softly, gradually adding 3 table-spoons of sugar. Fold the whipped cream into the chocolate mixture.

Using clean, dry beaters, beat the egg whites until soft peaks begin to form. Slowly add the remaining ¼ cup sugar and beat until stiff. Gently fold the beaten egg whites into the chocolate cream mixture until evenly blended.

Use a very large serving spoon to transfer the mixture to an attractive serving bowl, preferably a glass one—you will lose less air this way than by pouring it in. Chill until ready to serve.

At serving time, garnish with additional whipped cream and sprinkle the top with grated chocolate, if desired.

Yield: 10 to 12 servings.

Quick Mocha Mousse

Quick and easy, this is also a great idea for calorie-conscious people who are afflicted with chocolatomania. Chilled in tiny Chinese tea cups or little pots au chocolat, *it can be stretched to 6 satisfying servings.*

1 6-ounce package chocolate bits
2 large eggs
1 tablespoon instant coffee
2 tablespoons Grand Marnier or other orange liqueur
¾ cup skim or whole milk
1 teaspoon vanilla extract

In a blender or food processor, blend the chocolate bits, eggs, coffee, and liqueur until liquefied. Heat the milk almost to the boiling point and add to the mixture in the blender or food processor. Blend until more than doubled in volume, 4 or 5 minutes in a blender. Add the vanilla.

Pour into 6 small cups and chill for at least 6 hours, or overnight.

Yield: 6 servings.

White Chocolate Mousse

White chocolate is not "legally" chocolate because it does not contain chocolate liquor, the liquid that results when cocoa beans are ground. The best quality white chocolate is made with cocoa butter. Avoid those that contain vegetable fats because they taste somewhat like pure vegetable shortening.

6 ounces white chocolate
⅓ cup milk
1 to 2 tablespoons light rum
3 egg whites
Strawberry sauce (recipe follows), or dark chocolate shavings, optional

Combine the chocolate and milk in the top of a double boiler set over hot water, or use a flame control device set over low heat. Stir until chocolate is melted and the mixture is smooth. Remove from the heat, add rum, and cool to room temperature.

Beat the egg whites until stiff; stir one or two spoonfuls into the chocolate; gently, but thoroughly, fold in the remaining whites. Pour into individual glasses or a 1-quart bowl. Cover and chill for 2 hours.

Serve with strawberry sauce or chocolate shavings, if desired.

Yield: 6 to 8 servings.

2 pints strawberries, washed and hulled, *or* 1 16-ounce container frozen berries
2 tablespoons light rum
Sugar to taste

Strawberry Sauce
Puréc berries in a blender or food processor. Add the rum and sugar. Serve over the mousse.

Lemon Mousse

3 lemons
4 eggs, separated
1½ cups sugar
1 package unflavored gelatin
¼ cup cold water
1 teaspoon cornstarch
¼ cup Grand Marnier or Cointreau
1½ cups heavy cream
3 tablespoons confectioners' sugar

Squeeze the juice from the lemons and set aside. Beat the egg yolks until thick. Gradually add the sugar and continue to beat until very thick and the mixture falls back on itself in a ribbon when the beaters are lifted.

Sprinkle the gelatin over the cold water in a small heatproof cup. Place in a pan of hot water and stir until the gelatin is completely dissolved and the liquid is clear.

In a large bowl, dissolve the cornstarch in several spoonfuls of lemon juice. Add the remaining juice and gelatin. Stir well and add to the egg yolk mixture. Place over simmering water in the top of a double boiler, or over a flame control device. Cook, stirring, until it thickens. Remove from the heat, stir in 2 tablespoons liqueur, and chill.

Whip the cream with remaining liqueur and confectioners' sugar. Beat the egg whites until stiff but not dry. Stir a few spoonfuls of the cream and a few spoonfuls of egg whites into the cooled gelatin mixture. Fold in the remaining cream and egg whites gently, but thoroughly.

Pour into a serving bowl or individual goblets and chill for 1 to 2 hours before serving. Garnish with a dollop of whipped cream before serving, if desired.

Yield: 8 servings.

Frozen Lime Soufflé

⅔ cup pastry cream (recipe follows)
⅔ cup egg whites (about 6), at room temperature
¾ cup superfine sugar
Juice and grated peel of 4 limes (about ½ cup juice)
2 cups heavy cream, whipped
Lime slices for garnish

Prepare the pastry cream so that it will be well chilled.

In a large bowl, beat the egg whites until soft peaks form. Gradually add the sugar and continue beating until stiff, glossy peaks form. Combine the pastry cream with the lime juice and grated peel. Stir one-fourth of the meringue and whipped cream into the pastry cream mixture. Fold in the remainder of the meringue and cream and incorporate well. Spoon into a lightly oiled 6-cup soufflé dish fitted with a collar (see page 556). Freeze 6 hours, or overnight. Remove the collar before serving and garnish with lime slices, if desired.

Yield: 6 to 8 servings.

Pastry Cream

2 egg yolks
¼ cup sugar
3 tablespoons flour
1 cup milk, heated
¼ teaspoon vanilla extract
1 tablespoon Grand Marnier

In a small bowl, beat the egg yolks and sugar until thick and pale lemon-colored. Beat in the flour. Heat the milk until small bubbles appear around the edges. Very slowly, beat the hot milk into the egg mixture. Transfer to a small, heavy-bottomed saucepan and cook over low heat, stirring constantly, until smooth and thick. Do not allow to come to a boil. Remove from the heat and stir in the vanilla and Grand Marnier. Cool, cover, and chill.

Lemon Snow Pudding

1 envelope unflavored gelatin
¼ cup cold water
1 cup boiling water
½ cup sugar
¼ cup lemon juice
1 teaspoon grated lemon peel
2 egg whites
2 tablespoons sugar
2 cups thinly sliced fresh or canned peaches or pears

Sprinkle the gelatin over the cold water to soften. Add the boiling water and sugar and stir until the gelatin and sugar are dissolved. Stir in the lemon juice and grated lemon peel and refrigerate until it reaches the consistency of unbeaten egg white.

Beat the egg whites until soft peaks form. Slowly add the 2 tablespoons of sugar and continue beating until the peaks are stiff and glossy. Fold the beaten egg whites into the thickened gelatin mixture. Pour into a lightly oiled 3½- to 4-cup mold and chill until firm. Unmold and garnish with fruit slices.

Yield: 4 servings.

Variation: Serve with Custard Sauce (page 273) or Blueberry Sauce (page 466).

Fruit Juice Whip

Light, fluffy whips are a cinch to prepare, refreshing to eat, and do very nicely as dessert for family dinners. Nutritionally, they are ever so much more desirable than the artificially flavored prepared gelatin mixes, which are very high in sodium and often overly sweet. You have a choice of fruit juices—pineapple, orange, apricot, cranberry, apple, or tangerine.

1 envelope unflavored gelatin
⅓ cup sugar
1¾ cups fruit juice
½ teaspoon grated lemon rind

Mix the gelatin and sugar together in a small saucepan. Add ½ cup of the fruit juice (see note) and let the gelatin soften for 3 or 4 minutes. Place over low heat and stir constantly until the gelatin is dissolved. Remove from the heat and stir in remaining fruit juice and lemon rind. Chill in the refrigerator until the mixture becomes slightly thicker than the consistency of un-beaten egg white. Beat with a rotary beater or electric mixer until it doubles in volume and is a mass of light fluffiness. Spoon into dessert dishes and chill until firm.

Yield: 4 servings.

Note: If you are using fresh or frozen pineapple juice, boil it for 2 minutes before combining it with the gelatin.

Variation: Substitute 1⅔ cups cold strong coffee for the fruit juice. Omit lemon rind and add 1 teaspoon vanilla extract.

Bavarian Cream

The classic Bavarian cream is a time-consuming and rather elaborate preparation involving a cooked custard made with many egg yolks. This is a streamlined version with a creamy, velvety quality. It can be molded and served with a garnish of strawberries, or any other fresh fruit.

1 tablespoon unflavored gelatin
¼ cup cold water
½ cup sugar
⅛ teaspoon salt
2 eggs, separated
1¼ cups milk
1 teaspoon vanilla extract
1 cup heavy cream

Sprinkle the gelatin over ¼ cup cold water and let it soften for 3 or 4 minutes. Combine ¼ cup of the sugar and salt in the top of a double boiler or a heavy-bottomed saucepan. In a separate bowl, beat the egg yolks and milk together and add to the sugar. Stir in the softened gelatin and stir constantly over low heat until slightly thickened. Do not overcook or boil or the egg yolks will curdle. Remove from the heat and stir in the vanilla. Refrigerate until cool, about 15 minutes.

Beat the egg whites until stiff but not dry, beating in the remaining ¼ cup sugar. Fold them into the custard. Beat the cream until it softly mounds and fold into the custard. Spoon the mixture into a lightly oiled 6-cup mold, cover, and chill until firm. Unmold on a serving platter and garnish as desired.

Yield: 6 servings.

Trifle (Zuppa Inglese)

An extravagant mélange of mouth-watering flavors.

9 -inch sponge cake, 1¼ inches thick, *or* 3 packages not-too-fresh ladyfingers
¾ cup dark rum or Marsala
2 cups raspberries, strawberries, sliced peaches or any fruit combination, sweetened to taste
Custard sauce (see page 562)
1 cup heavy cream
2 egg whites
1 tablespoon sugar
Sliced nuts (optional)

Slice the sponge cake horizontally into three thin layers. Line the bottom of a glass serving bowl with a layer of sponge cake, or use 1 package of ladyfingers.

Sprinkle the cake with ¼ cup rum or Marsala. Cover with about one-third of the fruit and one-third of the custard. Repeat with the cake or ladyfingers, rum or wine, fruit, and custard sauce for two additional layers.

Beat the heavy cream until stiff, and set aside. Beat the egg whites until soft peaks form. Slowly add the sugar and continue to beat until stiff, glossy peaks form. Fold the whipped cream into the egg whites and spoon over the top of the trifle. Garnish with sliced, toasted almonds, pine nuts, or pistachio nuts, if desired. Chill for 2 to 4 hours before serving.

Yield: 6 to 8 servings.

Ice Cream

The last few generations that have grown up in a period of unlimited ice and mechanical refrigeration can have little appreciation for a past era when ice cream was an event to be anticipated, then savored and cherished. The excitement started with the delivery of a large block of ice to the back door, and it mounted steadily until the magical moment when the dasher, dripping with melting sweetness, became available for that first delicious lick. Familiarity has not dimmed the brilliance of the rich, creamy stuff and ice cream is still the number one favorite among desserts. However good the commercial products, homemade ice creams, sherbets and water ices are quite special, different in taste and texture from most store-bought varieties.

There are several kinds of homemade ice cream. Some people consider the variety known as "French" the finest. It is made with a custard base, using egg yolks as a thickening agent. Others think that nothing can hold a candle to the "Philadelphia" ice cream. This uses only light or heavy cream and sugar and is simply thickened by the freezing process.

Ice cream can be made in a hand-operated or electric freezer, or in your freezer trays. Points would have to be given to the crank-type freezer product, but you can achieve a creditable result with ice cream made in a refrigerator tray if you settle for less than the ultimate in a velvety ice cream. In churned ice cream, the mixture is constantly agitated while it is beginning to freeze. This keeps the ice crystals small and it is the small crystals that give the ice cream its smoothness. The fat that is supplied by milk and cream also helps to keep the ice crystals small, which explains why milk sherbets have a finer texture than ices made with a water base.

Refrigerator Freezer Method

You may freeze in a refrigerator freezer any ice creams that contain a thickening agent such as gelatin, egg yolk, flour, or cornstarch. Prepare the mixture according to the recipe and freeze as quickly as possible for about an hour, or until the edges harden but the center is still mushy. This can be done in ice cube trays with dividers removed or in a metal cake pan. Transfer the mixture to a chilled bowl and beat quickly with a fork or chilled beater until just smooth. Work rapidly before it melts. Return to the trays, cover, and place in the freezing compartment. Repeat the beating at half-hour intervals, one or two more times. The more beatings the ice cream gets, the smoother it will be. After the last beating, leave undisturbed until it has become completely firm, 2 to 3 hours. Allow the ice cream to soften slightly before serving for best flavor.

Ice Cream Freezer Method

When using an electric or hand-operated ice cream freezer, follow the manufacturer's directions for the amount of ice needed. An excess of salt will shorten the freezing time, but it results in a coarse texture. Rock salt or coarse salt may be used (fine salt tends to cake) in the proportion of 1 cup of salt to 6 cups of crushed ice, or whatever is recommended by the manufacturer. In the freezing process, the salt lowers the freezing point of the water and thus produces a brine that is colder than ice. It is the

1 *Pour the chilled cream mixture into the freezer can. Leave enough room in the can to allow for expansion as air is incorporated into the mixture by the churning action.*

3 *Both ice and salt are needed to freeze the cream mixture. Pack layers of crushed ice and coarse salt or rock salt between the walls of the bucket and the can.*

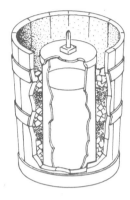

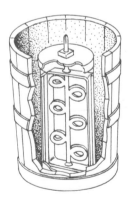

2 *As seen in this cutaway view, the freezer can (containing the cream mixture) has been seated inside the bucket, and the dasher fitted inside the can. Then place the lid on the container.*

4 *After attaching the crank to the dasher, leave the freezer for a few minutes before you begin cranking. Crank slowly at first, gradually increasing speed as the mixture freezes.*

brine that withdraws heat from the ice cream mix through the walls of the metal container.

Chill the cream mixture (this reduces the freezing time) and fill the freezer can less than three-quarters full. You need room for the increase in volume that is produced by the air that is beaten in while the ice cream is being agitated. Fit the can into the freezer. Adjust the dasher and cover securely with the lid. Pack the freezer with alternate layers of crushed ice and salt until they reach slightly above the mixture in the can. Connect the dasher to the crank mechanism, wait for a couple of minutes, and start cranking. If you are cranking by hand, start slowly. Too rapid agitation during the early cooling period could cause the fat droplets to unite and the ice cream could have a greasy texture. Turn the crank slowly until you feel a slight pull, then go full steam ahead until the ice cream is frozen. You will know when this has happened, for you will scarcely be able to move the crank. Don't stop until then, or the ice cream will not be smooth. An electric freezer has its own built-in signal and will slow down and stop.

When the ice cream is frozen, remove the can from the tub, wipe off the lid to make sure that no salt or water gets into the cream container, and remove the lid. Remove the dasher and press down the ice cream firmly with a spoon. Cover the container with wax paper or foil and replace the lid, first plugging the dasher hole with a piece of aluminum foil. Drain the water from the freezer tub, replace the can, repack with more salt and ice, and let the ice cream rest and mellow for a few hours. Most ice cream benefits from a period of "ripening." The ice cream will keep this way for up to four hours, or it may be stored in the freezer, if there is space. For extra protection, you can insulate the ice cream with layers of newspaper.

5 *Once the mixture is frozen, the freezer is dismantled. With the lid wiped clean and removed, take out the dasher and scrape off the ice cream clinging to it. Pack the cream down firmly.*

6 *Before placing the container back in the bucket (with fresh ice and salt) or in the freezer for the ice cream to mellow a few hours, cover the can first with foil or wax paper, then with its lid.*

Ices and Sherbets

Ices are made of water and sugar or a sugar syrup and are most often flavored with fruit juices. They have a somewhat granular texture and are served classically in the middle of elaborate banquets to freshen the palate and restore the appetite. Sherbets contain whipped egg white, gelatin, milk, or cream to give them a smooth, frothy texture.

The proportion of sugar in ices and sherbets is much greater than in ice cream and iced milks. Be careful not to use more than 1 part of sugar to every 4 parts of liquid, as sugar prevents freezing. Except in a few cases, ices and sherbets benefit from the relentless beating of a churn freezer. If you hope to achieve the tiny crystals and smooth texture in the refrigerator tray, you will have to beat the sherbet well and often during the freezing process; first, after about an hour when the mixture is set around

the sides but still mushy in the center, and, ideally, every half hour after that until the mixture is frozen solid.

You can freeze the mixture in ice cube trays with the dividers removed. A standard ice cube tray holds one pint. Loaf pans, stainless steel bowls, or any metal mold or container would also be suitable.

Take the sherbet out of the freezer and let it soften a bit in the refrigerator before serving it. The freezing time for sherbets and ices varies, depending on how cold your freezer is and how often you have taken them out to beat them. Fast freezing is advantageous, not only in time-saving but also in texture, so set your freezer at the lowest temperature possible. Don't forget to return it to the normal setting when the freezing is complete.

Basic Vanilla Ice Cream

This is the simplest of all ice creams, identified as "Philadelphia" ice cream.

4 cups light or heavy cream *or* 2 cups heavy cream and 2 cups light cream
¾ cup granulated sugar
Pinch of salt
2 teaspoons vanilla extract, *or* a 2-inch piece of vanilla bean, finely grated

Stir the cream and sugar together until the sugar is dissolved, 5 or 6 minutes. Add the pinch of salt and vanilla and freeze in an electric or hand-operated ice cream freezer.

Yield: About 1½ quarts.

French Vanilla Ice Cream

4 egg yolks
½ cup sugar
Pinch salt
2 cups milk
2 cups heavy cream
1 tablespoon vanilla extract, *or* a
2-inch piece of vanilla bean,
finely grated

Combine the egg yolks, sugar, and salt in a heavy-bottomed large saucepan, or the top of a double boiler. Beat together with a wire whisk or electric beater until pale and creamy. In another pot, heat the milk until little bubbles appear around the edges of the pan, a process called scalding. Pour the milk very slowly into the egg mixture, stirring constantly. Add the grated vanilla bean, if you are using it. Cook over medium heat or in the double boiler over hot water, until the mixture thickens and coats the back of a wooden spoon, about 5 minutes. Remove from the heat and cool. Stir in the heavy cream and the vanilla extract if the bean was not used. Chill. Freeze in an electric or hand-operated ice cream freezer.

Yield: About 1½ quarts.

Variations for either Basic Vanilla or French Ice Creams:

Coffee Ice Cream. Reduce the vanilla to 1 teaspoon. Add 2 tablespoons instant coffee when adding the vanilla.

Chocolate Chip Mint Ice Cream. Substitute 1 teaspoon oil of peppermint for the vanilla. Color lightly with green vegetable coloring. Add 1 cup miniature chocolate bits before freezing.

Toasted Almond Ice Cream. Just before freezing, add 1 cup finely chopped blanched almonds that have been toasted until golden.

Ginger Ice Cream. Reduce the vanilla to 1 teaspoon. Add ⅔ cup finely chopped preserved stem ginger and 3 tablespoons of the syrup in which the ginger is preserved when adding the vanilla.

Maple Walnut Ice Cream. Substitute ½ cup of maple syrup for the sugar. Add 1 cup coarsely chopped walnuts before freezing.

Fresh Peach Ice Cream. Add 2 cups of fresh, crushed, sugared peaches (or 1 10-ounce package of sliced frozen, thawed, and crushed peaches) with 1 tablespoon of lemon juice to the ice cream when half-frozen. Mix well and continue freezing. Ice cream is half-frozen after about 15 minutes in a hand-cranked freezer; 10 minutes in an electric one.

Blueberry Parfait

A purist might insist that a parfait is a particular kind of frozen dessert that begins with a sugar syrup and, like a mousse, is not stirred as it freezes. However, popular usage has broadened the meaning of the word, and ice creams layered with a variety of sauces and served in tall, slender parfait glasses are considered proper "parfaits." This one is an interesting combination of fruit flavors and colors that add tangy flavor to the cold, refreshing ice cream.

1 10-ounce package frozen raspberries, thawed

¼ cup sugar

1 tablespoon cornstarch

2 cups fresh blueberries, *or* 1 10-ounce package unsweetened blueberries, thawed and drained

2 teaspoons lemon juice

1 quart vanilla ice cream

2 tablespoons frozen orange juice concentrate, thawed

1 teaspoon ground cinnamon

Push the raspberries and syrup through a strainer. Discard the seeds. Add water to the purée to make 1 cup. Combine the sugar and cornstarch in a small saucepan, add the raspberry purée, and cook, stirring, until the mixture thickens and comes to a boil. Remove from the heat and let cool a bit. Stir in the blueberries and lemon juice, cover, and chill.

Place the ice cream in a bowl and stir to soften. Mix in the orange juice concentrate and cinnamon, cover, and replace in the freezer until firm, 2 or 3 hours.

At serving time, spoon layers of ice cream and the fruit mixture into 6 parfait glasses, beginning and ending with ice cream. Serve immediately.

Yield: 6 servings.

Strawberry or Raspberry Ice Cream

A quick, delicious dessert (not a true ice cream). Serve with additional crushed berries as a sauce.

2 16-ounce containers frozen berries (defrosted adequately to break apart)

2 tablespoons Grand Marnier

2 cups heavy whipping cream

Place the berries in the container of a food processor or blender and add the liqueur. Blend just enough to break up the berries. They should not be puréed.

Whip the cream until stiff and fold in the berries. Pour into a bowl, cover, and place in the freezer. This may be served immediately, but it develops a more delicious flavor if allowed to stand in the freezer. If it freezes solidly allow to soften slightly before serving.

Yield: 1½ quarts.

Orange Lemon Ice

Scoops of this ice topping a bowl of cut-up fresh fruits make a refreshing hot-weather dessert.

Grated rind of an orange
Grated rind of a lemon
1¾ cups sugar
4 cups water
2 cups orange juice
4 tablespoons fresh lemon juice

In a saucepan, combine the orange rind, lemon rind, and sugar. Stir in the water, bring to a boil, and boil for 5 minutes. Chill well. When cold, add the orange juice and lemon juice. Pour into two ice cube trays and cover with plastic wrap, foil, or wax paper. Place in the freezer. When mixture is frozen to a mushy state, remove it to a chilled bowl and quickly beat with an electric or rotary beater until smooth. Return the mixture to trays, cover, and freeze again. Repeat every half hour until the mixture is completely frozen.

Yield: 1 quart.

Fruit Sherbet

A relatively low calorie treat with a lovely texture.

3 cups puréed fruit (strawberries, raspberries, cantaloupe, peaches, grapefruit, watermelon, mango, etc.)
½ to 1 cup sugar, depending on the sweetness of the fruit
2 tablespoons lime or lemon juice
2 tablespoons rum, Grand Marnier or other appropriate liqueur (optional)
2 egg whites

Combine the fruit, half the sugar, lime juice, and liqueur in a blender or food processor and process until well mixed. Pour into a metal pan, cover tightly with foil, and freeze.

Stir with a wooden spoon every 20 to 30 minutes. Remove from the freezer when mushy. Beat the egg whites until foamy, gradually add the remaining sugar, and continue beating until soft peaks form. Stir into partly frozen fruit mixture and return to the freezer.

When solid, allow to soften a bit and break up into pieces. Whip or process until smooth. Spoon into an airtight container and freeze. Allow to soften a bit before serving.

Yield: About 1 quart.

Frozen Fruit Yogurt

½ cup sugar (or more to taste)

½ cup orange or lemon juice

Grated peel of an orange or lemon

2 cups cut-up fruit (bananas, berries, peaches)

1 cup plain or fruit yogurt

2 egg whites, beaten with 2 tablespoons sugar until soft peaks form

Combine the sugar, juice, grated peel, and fruit in a blender or food processor. Blend until puréed. Stir in the yogurt. Taste and add more sugar, if desired.

Pour into a metal cake pan, cover with foil, and freeze. This will take 2 to 2½ hours. Stir often with a wooden spoon, pushing the frozen edges to the center.

When quite firm but not solid, break up in pieces and mix in a blender or food processor until smooth. Stir in softly beaten egg whites to blend, and spoon the mixture into an airtight container until ready to serve.

For maximum flavor, remove from the freezer and place in the refrigerator 1 hour before serving.

Yield: 1 quart.

Table of Equivalent Amounts
(Approximate)

Item	Weights or Units	Cups and Spoons
Almonds	4 ounces 1 pound in shell	¾ cup lightly packed ⅔ cup ground
Apples	1 pound (3 medium)	2½ cups pared and sliced; 1¼ cups applesauce
Bacon	2 ounces, diced raw	⅓ cup
Bananas	1 pound (3 or 4)	2 cups sliced; 1½ cups mashed

Butter	½ ounce (⅛ stick)
	1 ounce (¼ stick)
	2 ounces (½ stick)
	4 ounces (1 stick),
	  ¼ pound
	8 ounces (2 sticks),
	  ½ pound
	16 ounces (4 sticks),
	  1 pound
		1 tablespoon
		2 tablespoons
		4 tablespoons, ¼ cup
		
		8 tablespoons, ½ cup
		
		16 tablespoons, 1 cup
		
		2 cups

Beans, dry	1 pound, raw	2½ cups raw; 5 to 7 cups cooked
Beets	1 pound (4 medium)	2 cups diced and cooked
Berries	1 quart	3½ cups
Bread crumbs	3 to 4 slices oven-dried bread 1 slice fresh bread	 1 cup fine dry crumbs ½ cup fresh crumbs
Cabbage	½ pound	3 cups shredded
Carrots	1 pound (6 or 7)	3 cups shredded; 3½ cups grated; 2½ cups diced; 1⅓ cups puréed
Celery	1 large stalk	½ cup diced or sliced

Cheese, cottage
      cream
      hard cheese,
      grated
	8 ounces (½ pound)
	3 ounces
	2 ounces
	4 ounces
		1 cup
		6 tablespoons
		½ cup
		1 cup

Cherries	1 pound	2½ cups pitted

Item	Weights or Units	Cups and Spoons
Chestnuts	1½ pounds in shell; 1 pound, shelled	2½ cups peeled
Chicken	3½ pounds raw, cleaned 1 large raw chicken breast	3 cups cooked 2 cups cooked and diced
Coconut, flaked	3½ ounces	1⅓ cups
Cornmeal	1 cup uncooked	4 cups cooked
Cracker crumbs	28 soda crackers 15 graham crackers 19 chocolate wafers 22 vanilla wafers	1 cup fine crumbs 1 cup fine crumbs 1 cup fine crumbs 1 cup fine crumbs
Cranberries	1 pound	4 cups; 3 to 3½ cups sauce
Dates, pitted	8-ounce package	1¼ cups chopped
Eggplant	1½ pounds	2½ cups diced and cooked
Eggs	5 large 1 egg white 1 egg yolk 8 large egg whites 12 large egg yolks	1 cup 1 to 1½ tablespoons 1 tablespoon 1 cup 1 cup
Flour	¼ ounce 1¼ ounces 5 ounces 1 pound (16 ounces)	1 tablespoon ¼ cup; 4 tablespoons 1 cup 3½ cups unsifted
Garlic, 1 medium clove	1/16 ounce	⅛ teaspoon
Greens for salad	1 serving	2 cups loosely packed
Herbs, fresh, leaves only	½ ounce	¼ cup pressed down or 2 tablespoons chopped (1 tablespoon fresh = ⅓ to ½ teaspoon dried)
Lemon	1 medium	2 to 3 tablespoons juice; 1 tablespoon grated peel
Lime	1 medium	1½ to 2 tablespoons juice

Item	Weights or Units	Cups and Spoons
Macaroni, spaghetti, noodles	½ pound	4 cups cooked
Mushrooms	1 pound	4 to 5 cups sliced uncooked
Nut meats	8 ounces (½ pound)	2 cups
Onion	1 pound (4 or 5 medium yellow) 1 large	2½ to 3½ cups sliced or diced ½ cup chopped (about)
Orange	1 medium peel of 1 medium	1 cup sectioned; ⅓ to ½ cup juice 2 to 3 tablespoons grated peel
Peas (green)	1 pound	1 cup shelled
Peppers (bell)	1 pound (3 to 6)	4 cups chopped
Potatoes	1 pound (4 medium)	1½ to 2 cups mashed; 3 to 3½ cups sliced or diced
Pumpkin	1 pound	1 cup and a bit more
Raisins, small seedless, and currants	4 ounces	¾ cup
Rhubarb	1 pound	2 cups cut and cooked
Rice	8 ounces raw	1 cup raw; 3 cups cooked
Shallot	½ ounce (1 large)	1 tablespoon minced
Spinach, raw cooked	1 pound 1 pound	4 cups 1½ cups
Sugar, granulated brown confectioners'	1 pound 6½ ounces 2 ounces 1 pound 1 pound	2¼ to 2½ cups 1 cup ⅓ cup 2⅛ to 2¼ cups firmly packed 4 cups unsifted or 4½ to 5 cups sifted
Tomatoes, fresh canned	1 pound (3 medium) 35-ounce can	1½ cups peeled, seeded and juiced. 1¾ cups strained pulp
Zucchini	1 pound	3½ cups sliced; 2 cups grated and squeezed

Emergency Substitutions

When you are caught short of a staple item, a substitution can be a life saver. Here are some useful ones.

Ingredient	Amount	Equivalent
Arrowroot	1 tablespoon	2 tablespoons flour, or 1 tablespoon cornstarch or potato flour
Baking powder	1 teaspoon	¼ teaspoon baking soda and ½ teaspoon cream of tartar mixed freshly
Broth, chicken or beef	1 cup	1 bouillon cube or envelope instant broth powder mixed with 1 cup of boiling water, or 1 teaspoon beef extract dissolved in 1 cup boiling water
Chocolate	1 ounce (1 square) unsweetened	3 tablespoons cocoa plus 1 tablespoon butter
Cornstarch	1 tablespoon	2 tablespoons flour
Light corn syrup	1 cup	1¼ cups sugar plus ⅓ cup liquid boiled together until syrupy
Light cream	1 cup	⅞ cup milk plus 3 tablespoons butter (for cooking only)
Egg	1 medium	2 egg yolks plus 1 tablespoon water if used in baking recipes with flour; for custards and puddings, 2 egg yolks; 3 tablespoons mixed broken yolk and white
Flour	2 tablespoons	1 tablespoon cornstarch, arrowroot, or potato flour for thickening

Ingredient	Amount	Equivalent
Cake flour	1 cup (sifted)	1 cup sifted all-purpose flour less 2 tablespoons
All-purpose flour	1 cup (sifted)	1 cup plus 2 tablespoons sifted cake flour
Self-rising flour	1 cup	1 cup sifted all-purpose flour plus 1¼ teaspoons baking powder and a pinch of salt
Milk, whole fresh	1 cup	½ cup evaporated milk plus ½ cup water, or 1 cup reconstituted nonfat dry milk plus 2 tablespoons butter
Sour milk	1 cup	1 cup sweet milk less 1 tablespoon plus 1 tablespoon lemon juice or white vinegar; or 1¼ teaspoons cream of tartar to 1 cup of milk. Let stand 5 to 10 minutes before using
Liquid hot pepper seasoning	Few drops	Pinch ground red pepper (cayenne)
Potato flour (or starch)	1 tablespoon	2 tablespoons flour or 1 tablespoon cornstarch or arrowroot
Raisins or dried currants (for baking)	1 cup	1 cup finely chopped soft prunes or dates
Sugar, confectioners'	1 cup	⅞ cup granulated sugar whirred quickly through the blender with 1 tablespoon cornstarch

Table of Weights and Measures

A pinch equals the amount that can be picked up and held between thumb and forefinger, about ⅛ teaspoon.

60 drops	= 1 teaspoon		2 cups	= 1 pint (16 ounces)
3 teaspoons	= 1 tablespoon		4 cups	= 32 ounces
2 tablespoons	= 1 ounce or ⅛ cup			= 1 quart
4 tablespoons	= ¼ cup		4 quarts	= 1 gallon
8 tablespoons	= ½ cup		8 quarts (dry)	= 1 peck
16 tablespoons	= 1 cup		4 pecks (dry)	= 1 bushel
	= ½ pint			
	= 8 ounces			

The Metric System

The United States is the only major country that has not yet converted to the metric system, but it is possible that this may one day change. In the metric system, weight is expressed in grams (g) and kilograms (kg); liquid volume in liters (l), deciliters (dl), centiliters (cl), and milliliters (ml); and length in meters (m) and centimeters (cm). Instead of Fahrenheit, temperature is measured in Celsius, a name that has replaced Centigrade. Calories may be expressed in kilojoules. One calorie equals approximately 4.2 kilojoules.

Metric cup and spoon measures can in most cases be used interchangeably with the customary cup and spoon measures commonly used in American house-holds. To give you a general idea of approximate equivalents, a pound is about 450 grams and an ounce is about 30 grams. A liter is roughly the same as the American quart, a deciliter is 1/10 of a liter, a centiliter 1/100 of a liter, and a milliliter 1/1000 of a liter. To convert a Celsius temperature to Fahrenheit, multiply the Celsius temperature by 2 to obtain, quite closely, the corresponding Fahrenheit temperature. This method of conversion is accurate within 9 degrees for Fahrenheit temperatures within the 240 to 400 degree range.

The conversion tables that follow give approximate equivalents, rounded off to the nearest whole number, in order to avoid a string of decimals that would be confusing. The conversions are precise enough for cooking.

Conversion Tables for Metric Measurements

Liquid Measures

(1 liter = 10 deciliters (dl) = 100 centiliters (cl) = 1,000 milliliters (ml))

Spoons, cups, pints, and quarts	Liquid ounces	Metric equivalent
1 tsp	¹⁄₁₆ oz	½ cl; 5 ml
1 Tb	½ oz	15 ml
¼ c; 4 Tb	2 oz	½ dl; 59 ml
⅓ c; 5 Tb	2⅔ oz	¾ dl; 79 ml
½ c	4 oz	1 dl; 119 ml
1 c	8 oz	¼ l; 237 ml
1¼ c	10 oz	3 dl; 296 ml
2 c; 1 pt	16 oz	½ l; 473 ml
2½ c	20 oz	592 ml
3 c	24 oz	710 ml; ¾ l
4 c; 1 qt	32 oz	1 l; 946 ml
4 qt; 1 gal	128 oz	3¾ l; 3,785 ml
5 qt		4¾ l
6 qt		5¾ l
8 qt		7½ l

Conversion formula: To convert liters to quarts, multiply the liters by .95; quarts to liters, multiply the quarts by 1.057.

Weight

American ounces	American pounds	Grams	Kilograms
⅓ oz		10 g	
½ oz		15 g	
1 oz		30 g	
3½ oz		100 g	
4 oz	¼ lb	114 g	
5 oz		140 g	
8 oz	½ lb	227 g	
9 oz		250 g	¼ kg
16 oz	1 lb	450 g	
18 oz	1⅛ lb	500 g	½ kg
32 oz	2 lb	900 g	
36 oz	2¼ lb	1000 g	1 kg
	3 lb	1350 g	1⅓ kg
	4 lb	2800 g	1¾ kg

Conversion formula: To convert ounces into grams, multiply the ounces by 28.35; grams into ounces, multiply the grams by .035.

Temperatures

Fahrenheit	Celsius
32°F*	0°C
60°F	16°C
75°F	24°C
80°F	27°C
95°F	37°C
150°F	65°C
175°F	79°C
212°F**	100°C
250°F	121°C
300°F	149°C
350°F	177°C
400°F	205°C
450°F	232°C
500°F	260°C

* water freezes
** water boils

Conversion formula: To convert Fahrenheit into Celsius, subtract 32, multiply by 5, divide by 9. To convert Celsius to Fahrenheit, multiply by 9, divide by 5, add 32.

Index